FINANCIAL ACCOUNTING

A User Perspective

FIRST CANADIAN EDITION

FINANCIAL ACCOUNTING
A User Perspective

FIRST CANADIAN EDITION

Robert E. Hoskin
University of Connecticut

Ronald A. Davidson
Simon Fraser University

Maureen R. Fizzell
Simon Fraser University

John Wiley & Sons Canada, Ltd
Toronto/ New York/ Chichester/ Weinheim/ Brisbane/ Singapore

This textbook was created entirely by electronic means using the Macintosh platform — QuarkXpress, Illustrator, and Photoshop. Film was produced using disk-to-film technology.

Canadian Cataloguing in Publication Data

Hoskin, Robert E., 1949-
    Financial accounting : a user perspective

1st Canadian ed.
Includes bibliographical references and index.
ISBN 0-471-64142-1

1. Accounting. I. Davidson, Ronald Allen. II. Fizzell, Maureen. III. Title.

HF5635.H85 1997   657   C96-931795-6

Production Credits

Acquisitions Editor: John Horne
Publishing Services Director: Karen Bryan
Developmental Editors: Leah Johnson/Michael Schellenberg
Cover Illustration: Anson Liaw
Cover and Interior Design: Christine Rae
Graphic Artist: Christine Rae
Typesetter: Compeer Typographical Services Ltd.
Printing and Binding: Tri-Graphic Printing Limited

Printed and Bound in Canada

10 9 8 7 6 5 4 3

To our families, especially our spouses Lynne and Charles, who put up with the many hours of work involved in preparing this Canadian edition, and to our children Sharon, Susan, Andrew, Carrie, and Scott.

◖◗ ABOUT THE AUTHORS

Robert E. Hoskin, B.Sc., M.Sc., M.A., Ph.D.
Associate Dean and Professor, University of Connecticut

Robert E. Hoskin has been an associate professor in the School of Business Administration at the University of Connecticut since 1986. In 1996, he became Associate Dean. In 1990, he spent six months with Price Waterhouse in Hartford as a faculty intern. This lead to the development of a course in property and liability insurance, now published by Price Waterhouse under the name *Crash: An Introduction to Property and Liability Insurance*. Prior to the University of Connecticut, he was an assistant professor at Fuqua School of Business. In 1979 and 1980, he was an accounting lecturer at Cornell University and Duke University. Robert Hoskin is the author of 12 papers and publications and the co-author of two financial accounting books. Robert Hoskin received a Ph.D. and M.A. from Cornell University, an M.Sc. in Chemistry from Bowling Green State University, and a B.Sc. in Education from Ohio State University.

Ronald A. Davidson, B.Comm., M.B.A., Ph.D., CA
Associate Professor, Simon Fraser University

Ronald Davidson is an associate professor of Accounting at Simon Fraser University and is a Chartered Accountant. He has also taught at the University of Calgary, the University of Bahrain, the University of Saskatchewan, the University of Alberta, and the University of Arizona. As well, he was a practising chartered accountant for 16 years, culminating in his own practice in LaRonge, Saskatchewan from 1978-1983. He has 25 research publications, which have appeared in the following accounting and management journals: *Journal of Accounting Research*, *Contemporary Accounting Research*, *Auditing: A Journal of Theory and Practice*, and *Accounting Horizons*. He received a Ph.D. in Accounting and Auditing from the University of Arizona, an M.B.A. from York University in Toronto, Ontario, and a B. Comm. from the University of Manitoba. His main research interests are in the behavioural aspects of auditing. He is a member of the Canadian Institute of Chartered Accountants and was elected Member of the Governing Council of the Institute of Chartered Accountants of British Columbia.

Maureen Fizzell, B.Ed., B.Comm., M.Sc., CMA
Lecturer and Director of the Undergraduate Program, Simon Fraser University

Maureen Fizzell has been teaching at the university level for 12 years, nine years at the University of Saskatchewan and three years at Simon Fraser University. In September 1995, she was appointed as the Director of the Undergraduate Program in the Faculty of Business Administration at Simon Fraser University. Over her university teaching career she has taught financial accounting from the introductory to the advanced level. Maureen Fizzell is an active CMA member, participating on committees, critiquing exams, and acting as a liaison between university students and the Society. During her 12 years, she has received two teaching awards. She received the Most Effective Professor in the Classroom Award at the University of Saskatchewan in 1990. In 1996, she was one of the recipients of the Canada Trust Distinguished Teaching Award at Simon Fraser University.

PREFACE

Background

Recently, organizations like the Accounting Education Change Commission (AECC) have recommended a change in emphasis at the introductory level of accounting. In the past, many schools have emphasized the "how to" of accounting, showing students how financial items are measured, recorded, and reported. This type of knowledge is important for students who intend to become accountants but many students in introductory accounting have other career goals in mind. Accounting information is at the backbone of many decisions made in organizations. As a result, the AECC and other organizations advocate a shift to an emphasis on accounting information and how it effects decision making in organizations. For most students, how the information can be used is more important than how it was prepared.

Financial Accounting: A User's Perspective sets out to address that shift by complementing the fundamental procedural aspects of accounting with information about who uses accounting information and what decisions they make from it. We have designed this text to achieve a balance between the preparation and use of accounting information. Throughout the book, we focus on users and introduce ratio analysis (a way of organizing the accounting data so that conclusions can be made). As well, excerpts from real companies' financial statements are included as examples and problems so that students have the opportunity to see the variety of ways accounting information is reported.

User Perspective

Virtually all introductory accounting students, both graduate and undergraduate, will become users of accounting information, while only a few will become preparers. Therefore, this text emphasizes a user's perspective and focuses on understanding and using corporate financial statements as a primary source for accounting information. In our experience, this approach is the most effective way of preparing students to work with accounting information. As well, it provides a solid foundation for students who continue on in accounting.

Integral to this approach is the extensive use of real financial statement data. Throughout the text you will find excerpts from the annual reports of actual corporations, reprinted exactly as they originally appeared. The Big Rock Brewery Limited annual report is presented in its entirety, along with excerpts from over 50 Canadian and international corporations. Each chapter provides a unique set of problems in the "Reading and Interpreting Published Financial Statements" section, which requires students to analyze and interpret corporate financial statement disclosures.

Organization

In order to focus on the understanding and use of financial statements and to emphasize the importance of topics such as cash flows, ratio analysis, and consolidations, this text is organized in a unique manner.

Chapter 1 lays the conceptual groundwork for the mechanics of the accounting system, and guides students through the Big Rock annual report. Students learn basic accounting terminology and are introduced to the three major accounting statements: income statement, balance sheet, and statement of changes in financial position. This chapter also presents background material on the standard setting process and the conceptual framework underlying accounting.

Chapter 2 builds on the basics from Chapter 1, presenting the traditional presentation of the accounting system using the basic accounting equation and ending with a full description of the double entry accounting system and the accounting cycle. The early introduction of the SCFP enables students to appreciate the differences between the income statement and SCFP which are crucial to understanding accrual basis financial statements.

Chapter 3 introduces accounting in a manufacturing environment and expands on the complexities of accrual basis accounting. Many companies in Canada still manufacture products. The financial information that they produce is different in some respects from retail companies. It is important that students understand the distinction between the two types of companies. The chapter also demonstrates presentation and format issues on the income statement and balance sheet. The accounting for a manufacturing entity has been included in the appendix to the chapter. This treatment allows instructors the option of concentrating on either the user perspective or the preparer side.

Chapter 4 caps the discussion of the income statement with revenue recognition criteria and methods. This topic is often not emphasized in introductory texts. However, the authors recognize that the revenue recognition policies established by a corporation can have a major impact on its operating results. It is, therefore, important for students to have some understanding of these policies early in the course.

Chapter 5 reflects the importance of the cash flow statement in at least two ways: it is unique in covering the interpretation as well as the construction of the statement and secondly, the coverage occurs earlier than in other introductory texts. Because this topic is a difficult one for many students, the chapter explains the linkage of the cash flow statement to the operating policies of the corporation (accounts receivable, inventory, and accounts payable policies) helping students to interpret the information in the operating section of the cash flow statement. By the end of Chapter 5 students will have a basic understanding of the three major financial statements.

Chapters 6 through 11 discuss the major asset, liability, and equity accounts that students will see in published financial statements. In each of these chapters, students are alerted to the important aspects of these items so that they can better interpret financial accounting information.

Financial statement analysis issues are discussed in all chapters and are summarized and extended in Chapter 12 after students have learned about the major asset, liability and equity accounts. Financial ratios associated with the topics under discussion are introduced in each chapter. From their first exposure to accounting, students are given tools that they can use to analyze financial statements. By the time they reach Chapter 12 where all the ratios are summarized and extended, they have worked with all the ratios. Chapter 12 gives them an opportunity to pull the analysis together and work with the total corporate entity. In some cases, this takes the coverage slightly beyond what is usual in introductory texts.

Because real corporations are complex, and generally prepare consolidated financial statements, Chapter 13 covers long-term investments in other corporations and the consolidation process. Recognizing that consolidation procedures are complicated and beyond the scope of an introductory text book, we have kept this discussion very simple. In keeping with the user orientation, the financial statement impacts of the consolidation policies are considered.

FEATURES OF THIS BOOK

The text's user orientation supports the goals set out by the Bedford Report and the AECC. In addition to the content and organization, the following pedagogical features support the approach:

An International Perspective: Reports from Other Countries

International issues are integrated into the text in several ways. Where appropriate, international differences are discussed in the main body of the text. Additional international material is set off from the main body in boxed-in areas. Actual foreign financial statements are included in some of the boxed-in areas and are included in some of the problems at the end of the chapters.

Ethics in Accounting

Ethical issues are raised in most chapters by special boxed-in sections. These exhibits are designed to raise the reader's consciousness on ethical issues, and to provide a source of in-class discussion topics.

Critical Thinking

While many of the problems in the "Reading and Interpreting Published Financial Statements" sections are challenging problems, special critical thinking problems and case questions have been included at the end of most chapters. These problems require students to critically analyze issues. They can be used as the basis for term papers, class discussion, debates, etc. Some suggestions for how to use these problems are included in the Instructor's Manual.

Communication

The critical thinking assignments and case problems provide many opportunities for students to polish written and oral communications skills. Suggestions for writing and speaking exercises as well as grading guidelines are included in the Instructor's Manual that supports this text.

◢◣ Writing

The critical thinking problems and case problems at the end of most chapters allow a reasonable opportunity to assign writing projects to students.

◢◣ In-Text Student Aids

Each chapter includes the following sections: text, summary problem, synonyms & abbreviations, glossary, and problems:

SUMMARY PROBLEM The summary problem at the end of each chapter is designed to illustrate the main points in the chapter. Many of these problems elaborate on topics discussed in the chapter and provide an example for students to aid them when tackling the end of chapter problems.

SYNONYMS & ABBREVIATIONS This section contains terms used in the chapter and their common synonyms as well as any common abbreviations that are used in the chapter.

GLOSSARY There is a glossary at the end of each chapter which defines the key terms introduced in the chapter. Key words are boldfaced the first time they are used in a chapter.

PROBLEMS The problem section of each chapter is divided into five parts: Assessing Your Recall, Applying Your Knowledge, Reading and Interpreting Published Financial Statements, Case, and Critical Thinking Problem.
- The *Assessing Your Recall* section is designed to assess the understanding of basic terms and concepts introduced in the chapter.
- The *Applying Your Knowledge* section is designed to apply the concepts and procedures discussed in the chapter in a hypothetical situation. These problems are most like those found in a traditional text and will often re-enforce the technical side of accounting.
- The *Reading and Interpreting Published Financial Statements* section is unique to this book and contains problems that make use of corporate financial statement disclosures. The problems typically involve some type of analysis and interpretation of financial statement data.
- The *Case* is a hypothetical scenario in which students are asked to identify problems, evaluate situations and make recommendations. The required part of the case often asks for a written report.
- The *Critical Thinking Question* often takes students beyond the structured data in the chapter by asking them to consider controversial areas associated with one or more of the chapter's topics.

◢◣ For the Student

■ ■ Study Guide

This volume provides in-depth explanations of the text material and offers numerous demonstration problems. In addition to guiding students through chapter content, it gives them additional opportunities to test their knowledge and skills. The Study Guide includes true/false statements, multiple choice questions, exercises, and problems with solutions.

For the Instructor

Solutions Manual

This volume contains the solutions to all end of chapter materials except the critical thinking questions. It also contains suggestions for how to use the critical thinking questions.

Instructor's Manual

This volume contains suggested course outlines and guidance on how to present the material contained in each chapter. It also includes suggested solutions to the critical thinking questions.

Computerized Test Bank

This volume provides approximately 1,000 test items consisting of true/false statements, multiple choice questions, short answer, analytical exercises, and essays. Suggested solutions are included. The Test Bank is available in an electronic format to facilitate test preparation on an IBM PC or compatible.

Transparency Masters

Two types of transparency masters are available for classroom use. The Teaching Transparency Masters highlight key concepts and principles as well as graphs and diagrams included in the text material. Approximately 60 transparency masters are available in the Instructor's Manual. The Solutions Manual contains transparency masters for over 150 selected end of chapter exercises and problems.

Acknowledgments

We would like to thank Robert Hoskin who developed the original concept for this book and who put so much time and energy into its first edition.

We would also like to thank the many reviewers who provided very valuable comments during several stages of the book's development. Their insights and suggestions have helped us improve the quality of this first Canadian edition. They are:

G. Baxter, University of Saskatchewan
Kevin Berry, University of New Brunswick
Ann Clarke-Okah, Carleton University
Joan E. D. Conrod, Dalhousie University
Brock Dykeman, University College of the Cariboo
Leo Gallant, St. Francis Xavier University

Darrell Herauf, Carleton University
Charlotte Heywood, Wilfrid Laurier University
Al Hunter, University of Lethbridge
Philippe Levy, McGill University
L. Lindsay, University of Saskatchewan
Terry Litovitz, University of Toronto
Don Lockwood, University of British Columbia
Robert Schenk, Bishop's University
Jan Thatcher, Lakehead University
Shu-Lun Wong, Memorial University

We are very grateful to everyone at John Wiley and Sons Canada, Limited: John Horne, Diane Wood, Carolyn Wells, Karen Bryan, Michael Schellenberg, and all the sales representatives. We would also like to thank Leah Johnson for her editorial contributions.

◤◣ Canadian Organizations

We would like to express our deep gratitude to the following Canadian companies who gave us permission to use their financial statements in the text. Without their permission, *Financial Accounting: A User's Perspective* would not have been able to achieve the wide breadth of examples that it contains:

Algoma Central Corporation
Alliance Central Communications Corporation
AT Plastics Incorporated
BCE Incorporated
Bema Gold Corporation
Big Rock Brewery Incorporated
Camdev Corporation
Cara Operations Limited
CHC Helicopters Corporation
Comac Food Group Incorporated
Cominco Limited
Doman Industries Limited
Enerflex Systems Limited
Fletcher Challenge Canada Limited
Fundy Cable Limited
Haley Industries Limited
Imperial Metals Corporation
Imperial Parking Limited
H. Jager Developments Incorporated
Mackenzie Financial Corporation
Meridian Techologies Incorporated
Mosaid Technologies Incorporated
Petromet Resources Limited
Purcell Energy Limited
Queenstake Resources Limited

Redaurum Limited
Semi-Tech Corporation
SofQuad International Incorporated
Telepanel Systems Incorporated
Tritech Precision Incorporated
Western Star Trucks Holdings Limited

◤◥ Concluding Remarks

We hope that both students and instructors will find the materials contained in this book useful as they attempt to cope with the extremely complicated world of corporate financial reporting. We have tried to be extremely careful in editing the book and the associated Solutions Manual and Instructor's Manual so that there are a minimal number of errors. The remaining errors are, of course, ours and we look forward to hearing from you concerning any that you find so that we might improve upon the product.

Ron Davidson
    Simon Fraser University, October, 1996

Maureen Fizzell
    Simon Fraser University, October, 1996

BRIEF TABLE OF CONTENTS

◖◗ TABLE OF CONTENTS

CHAPTER

Overview of

Corporate Financial Reporting

Financial statements are reports from the management of corporations to their shareholders that summarize how the corporation performed during the previous year. Financial statements are included in a larger **annual report** that is the main method management uses to report the results of the corporation's activities during the year. The annual report is sent to all shareholders, but it is also used by many other parties that have an interest in the corporation such as bankers, lenders, analysts, and credit-rating agencies.

The primary goal of this book is to help you become an intelligent reader of corporate financial statements. You may become a manager, accountant, banker, or financial analyst. Even if you don't, you probably will become an investor in the shares or bonds of a corporation at some time in your career. In your various business roles, you will make decisions about corporations, such as whether or not to invest in their shares or to lend them money. In making these decisions, you must be able to understand the information that is presented in corporate financial statements. You must know not only what each piece of information tells you about the corporation, but also what it doesn't tell you. You should also recognize that some important information is not contained in the financial statements, yet is useful in certain decision-making contexts.

We have written this book for a broad readership, understanding that many of you will play multiple roles as shareholders (owners), creditors, and managers of corporations. We have assumed that you know little or nothing about accounting. We have not assumed that you are training to be an accountant, although that may be your objective. Therefore, this book does not emphasize accounting procedures. Instead, the underlying concepts of accounting and the analysis of financial statements are emphasized. However, a complete understanding of the end result of the accounting process is probably not possible without an overall view of how the accounting system works. For this reason, the first few chapters present the mechanics of the accounting system. Subsequent chapters are devoted to accounting issues and concepts, and to analyzing financial statements.

Throughout the book, information from real corporations is used to illustrate the topic at hand. In addition to numerous examples of financial statement information from a variety of corporations, the complete annual report of Big Rock Brewery Ltd. for 1995 is included in Appendix A of this chapter. Occasional references will be made to the Big Rock report throughout the text. Page numbers from this annual report will be preceded by "BR-;" that is, page 10 from the annual report will be referred to as "BR-10." Because different corporations use slightly different

---

AN INTERNATIONAL PERSPECTIVE
REPORTS FROM OTHER COUNTRIES

Another goal of the book is to expose you to accounting requirements in countries other than Canada. Integrated into the discussion of most chapters are examples in which the accounting guidelines in other countries differ from those in Canada. These sections are set off from the main text, as is this paragraph, so that you can easily identify discussions relating to international standards rather than to Canadian standards.

terminology to refer to items in their financial statements, it is sometimes confusing to read their statements. To assist you in interpreting these financial statements, lists of abbreviations and synonyms are provided at the end of most chapters. A glossary that briefly defines or explains the terms used is also provided at the end of each chapter.

FORMS OF ORGANIZATION

Business is conducted by many different types or forms of organizations in Canada. Although the accounting issues discussed in this book apply to some degree to all these forms of organization, attention is directed primarily toward the accounting issues facing *corporations*. Almost every large business in Canada is a corporation. Other forms of business include *sole proprietorships*, *partnerships*, *limited partnerships*, *joint ventures*, and *Crown Corporations*. These forms of organization are discussed in more detail in Chapter 11.

A corporation is a legal entity that is separate from its owners. Individuals become owners of corporations by investing in (purchasing) shares of a corporation. Except for some small corporations, shareholders typically do not become involved in the day-to-day operation of the business. The shareholders (via their elected representatives on the Board of Directors) hire individuals known as senior management to manage the day-to-day operations. These senior managers, along with the managers they hire, are collectively referred to as **management**. To keep shareholders informed of the performance of their investment in the corporation, management reports periodically to shareholders. This periodic report typically is sent to shareholders on a quarterly basis in a *quarterly report*. The fourth-quarter report is combined with the prior three quarters to produce a financial statement that covers the entire fiscal year.

USERS OF FINANCIAL STATEMENTS

Accounting is primarily concerned with the communication of financial information to users. Accountants must first identify what information should be recorded, then must ensure that the corporation's accounting system will accurately collect and record this information. Because businesses are involved in many thousands of transactions each year, accountants must summarize this information in a format understandable, and therefore useful, to users. Accountants are very concerned that the information they provide is both reliable and relevant to users.

Although annual reports and corporate financial statements are prepared by managers primarily for shareholders, they are also analyzed by other users of financial data who are both external and internal to the corporation. Exhibit 1-1 lists some of these users.

EXHIBIT 1-1

Users of Financial Statement Information

Internal users:
- Management
- Board of Directors

External users:
- Shareholders
- Potential investors
- Creditors (for example, bankers and suppliers)
- Regulators
- Taxing authorities
- Other corporations, including competitors
- Security analysts
- Credit-rating agencies
- Labour unions

Internal Users

Management and the Board of Directors

Management and the Board of Directors, as primary internal users, make use of accounting data to make many types of decisions such as pricing products and deciding whether to buy or lease equipment. Because of their position in the corporation, managers have access to many sources of financial information beyond what is included in the financial statements. Their uses of accounting data are important, but are generally covered in courses and books devoted to **managerial accounting** or **cost accounting**. Our primary focus will therefore be on the value of accounting data to external users. **Financial accounting** courses are oriented primarily to the study of the accounting data provided to these outside users. In most academic programs, both a financial and a managerial accounting course are required to expose students to both types of accounting information.

External Users

The information disclosed in financial statements is sensitive to external users' needs because **management**, which prepares the statements, wishes to communicate information to shareholders, creditors, and others about the financial status of the corporation. Management can, therefore, disclose almost any information it considers important for an understanding of the corporation, subject to some limitations set by various regulatory bodies.

■ ■ Shareholders and Potential Investors

Shareholders and **potential investors** need information that will enable them to assess how well management has been running the corporation. They want to make decisions about buying more shares or selling some or all of the shares they already own. They want to decide if the people currently sitting on the **Board of Directors** are adequately overseeing the management team they have selected. Information in the financial statements will contribute to those decisions. Other sources of information for these users include press releases, business newspapers and magazines, and experts like stock brokers and financial advisors.

■ ■ Creditors

Creditors usually come from three major groups. The first group includes those who sell goods or services to the corporation and are willing to wait a short period of time for payment. These users are very interested in the short-term cash level in the corporation because they want to be paid. The second group are financial institutions, such as banks, who have loaned money to the corporation. They are also interested in the cash level of the corporation, but they need to assess the cash flow further into the future. They want not only the principal of the debt repaid, but also an interest charge. The third group are investors who have purchased long-term debt instruments such as corporate bonds from the corporation. Similar to banks, these users have both a long-term and a short-term interest in the cash level. These creditor groups use the financial statements as a source of information that enables them to assess the future cash flows of the corporation. They will make their lending or investing decisions based on their assessment of the riskiness of non-collection.

■ ■ Regulators

The **regulators** who are interested in the financial statements are numerous. For example, the government establishes regulations for how a business becomes incorporated and for its conduct after incorporation. It is, therefore, interested in ensuring that the corporation follows those regulations. Environmental groups monitor the activities of corporations to ensure that environmental standards are being met.

■ ■ Taxing Authorities

The federal taxing authority in Canada, **Revenue Canada**, uses financial statements extensively in its assessment of the amount of tax to be paid by businesses. Revenue Canada establishes its rules for how taxable income should be measured. These rules often follow the same guidelines that are used for accounting income, but there are several areas in which they deviate. Later in this text we will describe some of those deviations and explain their impact on the financial statements.

■ ■ Other Users

Additional users of financial statement information include other corporations, security analysts, credit-rating agencies and labour unions. Other corporations may want information about the performance of another corporation if they enter into cooperative agreements or contracts with that corporation. Security analysts and credit-rating agencies provide information about the strengths and weaknesses of corporations to users who want to invest. Labour unions need to understand the financial health of the corporation in order to negotiate labour issues with management.

All of these users, with their various needs, use the same set of financial statements. It is therefore important that the financial statements provide information to as wide a group of users as possible. As you would guess, however, there are many pieces of information particular users may want but cannot find in the financial statements. They, therefore, must develop alternate sources of information.

CONCEPTUAL FRAMEWORK

In Canada, the *Accounting Standards Board (AcSB)* of the *Canadian Institute of Chartered Accountants* sets accounting guidelines, which are published in the *CICA Handbook*. These accounting guidelines have the force of law as they are recognized in both federal and provincial statutes that regulate business corporations. In the United States, the *Financial Accounting Standards Board (FASB)* sets accounting standards for American corporations.

The set of accounting guidelines that corporations use is referred to as **Generally Accepted Accounting Principles**, or **GAAP** (usually pronounced as "gap"). Many different methods of deriving these principles have been used over time. *Deductive methods* have been used that start with some generally accepted definitions (of assets, liabilities, and income, for instance) and concepts, and then logically derive accounting methods and other accounting principles from them. These methods are similar to the process mathematicians use in the development of mathe-

AN INTERNATIONAL PERSPECTIVE
REPORTS FROM OTHER COUNTRIES

In general, every country has developed its own set of accounting standards, which reflect the political, social, and economic environments of the country. With the development of world markets for both products and capital, there has been an increasing need for better understanding among countries with regard to financial reporting. Over the years, numerous organizations have attempted to set international accounting standards. There are currently several groups involved in the process of trying to develop international accounting standards; predominant among them is the *International Accounting Standards Committee (IASC)*. The IASC is an independent, private-sector body that is funded by donations from accounting organizations around the world and the *International Federation of Accountants (IFAC)*. By mid-1996, IASC had issued 32 *International Accounting Standards (IASs)*. The IASC has developed relationships with the primary standard-setting bodies in numerous countries, including the **Canadian Institute of Chartered Accountants (CICA)** in order to promote the development of international accounting standards.

matical theory. The problem with this approach has been the difficulty in achieving a consensus on the underlying definitions and concepts.

Inductive approaches have also been used. These approaches generally take into consideration the methods in current practice and attempt to develop (induce) general principles from these methods. Current standard-setting under the CICA combines an inductive approach and a deductive approach. On the deductive side, the CICA has developed a set of underlying objectives and concepts called financial statement concepts, or the **conceptual framework**. This framework has then been used deductively to justify new accounting standards. On the inductive side, the conceptual framework and the new accounting standards have all been established by a political process of reaching consensus among the various users of financial information.

The purpose of the conceptual framework is to describe the concepts that underlie financial accounting. This framework is used to develop accounting guidelines from which financial statements are prepared so that external users can find information on which they can base decisions about the entity. The financial statements should describe what the entity owns, to whom it has obligations and what is left over after the obligations are satisfied. They should also show the changes that have occurred in the aforementioned items. The final purpose of financial statements should be to describe the results of the operations of the entity.

◣◥ Qualitative Characteristics of Accounting Information

Accounting data should possess four essential characteristics. Exhibit 1-2 provides a hierarchy of these characteristics.

EXHIBIT 1-2

Qualitative Characteristics of Accounting Information

Understandability
Relevance
    Predictive value and feedback value
    Timeliness
Reliability
    Representational faithfulness
    Verifiability
    Neutrality
    Conservatism
Comparability

Understandability, the first qualitative characteristic, is related to the user of accounting information. The information must be *understandable* to the user. The underlying assumption is that the user is reasonably well informed about accounting terminology and procedures.

Relevance refers to whether the information is capable of making a difference in a decision. Information may have three kinds of value: predictive value, feedback value, and timeliness. **Predictive value** means that the information is useful in predicting future results and, therefore, should be useful to users who make decisions that depend on accurate predictions of future events. Predictive value is based on an underlying assumption that the past is a good predictor of the future. **Feedback value** is information that allows users to assess the outcomes of previous decisions, providing them with feedback on decisions made in the past. This can be helpful as users learn from their past successes and failures. Finally, **timeliness** is important because old information loses its relevance to users. If the information is not timely, it may lose its ability to make a difference in a decision. With the rapid changes that are evident around us, timeliness will become even more important in decision-making.

Reliability of information rests on four fundamental characteristics: representational faithfulness, verifiability, neutrality, and conservatism. **Representational faithfulness** means that the information faithfully represents the attribute, characteristic, or economic event that it purports to represent. For example, suppose the accounting system produces a dollar total for sales that is supposed to represent all sales made during a single year. This amount should include all sales made in that year and exclude all sales made in any other year.

Verifiability means that independent measurers using the same measurement methods should agree on the appropriate value. Determining the cost of an item based on evidence such as invoices and cancelled cheques possesses a high degree of verifiability. Determining the market value of a piece of real estate possesses a much lower degree of verifiability because it is based solely on opinions.

Neutrality means that the information is not calculated or presented in a way that would bias users towards making certain desired decisions and not making other, undesired decisions. For example, an inflated estimate of an asset's value is biased and not neutral.

Conservatism means that, if estimates must be made in financial statements, they should err on the side of understating rather than overstating net assets and net income. Note that Conservatism may conflict with Neutrality. If conflict occurs, Conservatism overrides Neutrality.

Comparability generally refers to the ability of information produced by different corporations, particularly within a given industry, to be compared. A high degree of comparability allows for better comparisons across corporations and potentially better decisions. Within Canadian GAAP, however, there are no guidelines that require all corporations in an industry to use the same accounting methods. Because different methods will produce different financial statement amounts, it is important for users to understand what methods are available to corporations and how the various methods will impact on the accounting numbers. Comparability is enhanced with the consistent application of accounting methods by a given corporation over time. Much of the predictive value of accounting information depends on the trends of the data over time. If different methods are used to produce that information over time, the predictive value of the information is diminished.

Finally, there are two overriding **constraints** on information provided by management: the cost/benefit constraint, and the materiality criterion. The **cost/benefit constraint** states simply that the value of benefits received from information should exceed the cost of producing it. The value of benefits received from information, however, is very difficult to measure. This can lead to problems because the corporation bears the cost of producing the information, yet the benefits are perceived mainly by outside users.

Materiality is a pervasive concept that affects many aspects of the production of information. It is generally thought of as the minimum size of a transaction that can significantly affect decisions. For example, when a corporation purchases a building, there is a major cost over a period of years that may affect an investor's decision to buy shares. On the other hand, if the corporation purchases a pencil sharpener, the cost is so small that it will not affect an investor's decision. Both materiality and the cost/benefit constraint are kept in mind as the CICA adopts and implements new accounting guidelines and as accountants implement those guidelines.

These qualitative characteristics and constraints help form the underlying basis on which accounting guidelines are established. As we discuss these guidelines in the book, referring back to these characteristics and constraints should help you understand and remember the guidelines being used.

BUSINESS ACTIVITIES

To understand the information in financial statements, it is useful to think about the fundamental types of activities that all businesses engage in and report on. The basic activities of businesses are **financing**, **investing**, and **operating activities**.

Financing Activities

Financing refers to the activity of obtaining **funds** (cash) that can be used to buy major assets such as the buildings and equipment used by virtually every business. This activity is necessary, of course, to start the business, but it is also a continuing activity as the business grows and expands its operations. Funds are obtained from two primary sources outside the corporation: **creditors** and **investors**. Creditors expect to be repaid on a timely basis and very often charge the business in the form of interest for the use of their money, goods, or services. The amount to be repaid is generally a fixed amount. Investors, on the other hand, invest in the corporation in the hope that their investment will generate a profit. They earn profits either by receiving **dividends** (withdrawals of funds from the corporation) or by selling their shares to another investor. Of course, investors may experience either a gain or a loss on the sale of their shares.

A primary internal source of new funds to the corporation is the profit generated by the business that is not paid out to shareholders in the form of dividends. These profits are called **retained earnings**. If the corporation is unprofitable, or if all profits are distributed to shareholders in the form of dividends, the only way the corporation can expand is to either get more funds from investors (existing shareholders or new investors), or borrow more from creditors. How much to borrow from creditors and how much to obtain from investors are important decisions that the management of the corporation must make. Those decisions can determine whether a corporation grows, goes bankrupt or is bought by some other corporation. Examples of financing activities follow.

 TYPICAL FINANCING ACTIVITIES:
Borrowing money
Repaying loans
Issuing shares
Repurchasing shares
Paying dividends on shares

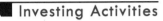 Investing Activities

Once the corporation obtains funds, it must invest those funds to accomplish its purposes. Most corporations make both long-term and short-term investments. Most short-term investments are considered operating activities, such as the purchase of raw materials and inventories. Some short-term investments, such as the investment in the shares of other corporations (called marketable securities) and most long-term investments are considered investment activities. Long-term investment in property, plant, and equipment to produce goods and services for sale is one such investing activity. Long-term investments in the shares of other corporations would also be considered an investing activity. Examples of investing activities follow.

 TYPICAL INVESTING ACTIVITIES:
Purchase of property, plant, and equipment
Sale of property, plant, and equipment
Investments in the shares of other corporations
Sale of investments in shares of other corporations

Operating Activities

Operating activities are those associated with developing, producing, marketing, and selling the products and/or services of the corporation. While financing and investing activities are necessary to conduct operations, they tend to occur on a more sporadic basis than the activities thought of as operating activities. The day-to-day continuing activities are generally classified as operations. Examples of operating activities follow.

 TYPICAL OPERATING ACTIVITIES:

Sales to customers	Payments on accounts payable
Collections on accounts receivable	Payment of operating expenses
Purchase of inventory	Payment of tax expense

Financial statements provide information about the operating, financing, and investing activities of a corporation. By the end of this book, you should be able to interpret financial statements as they relate to these activities. To start you on the journey to becoming a successful user of financial statement information, we have included for you the annual report of a Canadian corporation, Big Rock Brewery Ltd.

◖◗ BIG ROCK BREWERY LTD. ANNUAL REPORT

The 1995 annual report for Big Rock constitutes Appendix A at the end of this chapter. As mentioned earlier, references to its page numbers are prefixed by "BR-." The Big Rock annual report will probably appear very complex, particularly if you have never before been exposed to accounting. The fact is, however, that Big Rock is a fairly simple company. We selected it because it is a good example of annual reporting, it illustrates finally, almost all the reporting issues discussed in this book in spite of its simplicity, and, because Big Rock offers a challenge to you, the reader, to understand a modern company. The "pain" in trying to understand Big Rock will be rewarded by the "gain" in your understanding of real, complex business organizations.

A survey of the various types of information contained in the Big Rock Annual Report follows.

◣◢ Corporate Profile

The report starts with a short section describing the business activities and history of the company. Big Rock produces and markets specialty draught and bottled beer across the four western provinces and into some centres in the United States. Its headquarters are in Calgary, Alberta.

◣◢ Report to the Shareholders

The report to the shareholders appears on pages BR-2 through BR-3. The report is written by the president. The president has the opportunity to give a global view of where the corporation has been, what it accomplished last year and where it is going in the future.

Immediately following the report to shareholders is a short comment from Big Rock's resident artist. The company is not required to include this section in its report.

◣◢ Management's Discussion and Analysis

Many corporations use this report (page BR-5) to make more extensive detailed comments on the company and its operating results. This report provides an opportunity for senior management to discuss with shareholders the performance of the corporation. Often the information is presented from the perspective of the various divisions of the corporation. It also is one of the few places in the annual report where you will find *prospective* (i.e., forward-looking) information. As you will discover shortly, most of the information presented in the annual report is *retrospective* (i.e., based on past events). If your interest is in the future of the company, the report to the shareholders is a good place to get management's opinion about the future directions and prospects of the corporation. The report should be read skeptically, however, since much of what is said reflects top management's opinion. In such a report, there is an inherent bias toward presenting results to the shareholders in the best possible light.

Board of Directors and Management

Somewhere in every annual report there is a list of the **Board of Directors** of the company. Sometimes the report also includes their pictures. These directors are elected by shareholders to serve as their representatives, and as such they provide advice and counsel to the management of the corporation. They also have broad powers to vote on issues relevant to shareholders, and to hire and fire management. A listing of the senior management of the corporation is also included somewhere in the report; for Big Rock, this list can be found on page BR-21.

Financial Section

The remainder of the annual report contains all the financial information about the performance and status of the corporation (BR-1 and BR-6 through BR-20). In general, this section contains the following major components:

C **OMPONENTS OF THE FINANCIAL SECTION:**
Summary of financial highlights for past 5 to 10 years
Independent Auditors' Report
Financial Statements
    Income Statement
    Balance Sheet
    Statement of Retained Earnings
    Statement of Changes in Financial Position
    Notes to Financial Statements
Supporting schedules

Each of these components is discussed at some length in the sections that follow. Virtually all the disclosure contained in this section is in compliance with either the guidelines in the *CICA Handbook* or the Alberta Securities Commission (ASC), although management would surely disclose most of this information voluntarily to shareholders in the absence of requirements by the CICA or the ASC.

■ ■ Financial Statements

There are three major statements that appear in all sets of financial statements. They are the **income statement**, the **balance sheet**, and the **statement of changes in financial position**. In addition to these, a corporation will sometimes include a **statement of retained earnings**. In this chapter, only the income statement, balance sheet, and statement of changes in financial position will be discussed.

INCOME STATEMENT The **income statement** (BR-8) is also known as the **statement of earnings**. This statement describes the result of the operating activities of the current period. The results of those activities add up to the net income amount or *bottom line*. In corporations, net income is defined as **revenues** (money or resources flowing into the corporation as a result of sale transactions) less **expenses** (money or resources flowing out of the corporation related to sale transactions). This is different from the concept of income used in preparing individual income tax returns. Income to individuals, for tax purposes, is generally the gross amount of money earned by the individual (salary) with very few deductions allowed. Individuals cannot, for example, deduct the cost of groceries or clothing. In a business, the rules are such that almost all expenditures qualify as expenses in the determination of earnings. There may be a delay in recognizing some expenditures as expenses, such as **amortization**. Amortization is the deduction of a portion of the cost of a piece of machinery each period over the life of the machinery; eventually, the entire expenditure is treated as an expense in the determination of net income.

Refer to the Statement of Income and Retained Earnings for Big Rock (BR-8). Note that this statement combines the income and the retained earnings statements. It covers a period of time as indicated at the top of the statement where it reads, "Years ended March 31." The revenues and expenses are the amounts recognized during each of the years ended March 31, 1995 and 1994. The activities reported in this statement are primarily the operating activities of the corporation. The statement is a report of the operating performance of the corporation during the year and measures the inflow of revenues and the outflow of expenses from the shareholders' point of view. For this reason, it is sometimes called a **flow statement**. Another way of putting it is that the earnings statement captures the net change in the shareholders' wealth, as measured in the accounting records, across a designated time period. In this case, that time period is one year.

As you will note in the statement, there is one revenue category called Sales which represents the inflow of resources from the sale of inventory, namely, beer. Depending on the operating activities of a corporation, you might also find revenue from performing services or earning interest. The level of detail provided in a corporation's statement depends on the usefulness of the disclosure. Since Big Rock is involved only in the brewery business, the statement can be quite simple.

Another related reason for the breakdown into different types of revenues is that shareholders (and other users of financial statements) want to forecast the future performance of the corporation. The amounts that are reported in the financial statements are largely historical in nature. For example, the values reported for the assets of the corporation are generally based on what the corporation historically paid for them, not on what they are currently worth on the market. These historical numbers may be useful to forecast the future. Because of the differences in the nature of various aspects of a corporation, the growth rates of the different types of revenues and expenses may differ greatly. If the reader of the financial statements is not provided with any detail about the breakdown in revenues and expenses, it will be very difficult to forecast them accurately.

Costs and expenses are also listed under various categories, including cost of sales (the expenditures for goods sold during the period) and operating expenses. These cost and expense categories are also provided to explain to the shareholders, in more detail, the performance of the corporation. The expense category of Government Commissions and Taxes on Big Rock's income statement is more common in a corporation such as this one because the government imposes special taxes on the alcoholic beverage industry. Big Rock's statement has another interesting item, Gain (Loss) on Disposal of Capital Assets. This represents the sale of assets normally used by the corporation in its operating activities, in this case, likely the sale of equipment. The last expense, Income Taxes (provision for income taxes), is listed as a separate expense because it depends on both the revenues and expenses reported.

At the bottom of the income statement is an **earnings per share** disclosure. Earnings per share is the net income of the corporation divided by the average number of common shares that are outstanding during the year. Shareholders find this calculation useful since it puts the performance of their investment in the corporation into proper perspective. In other words, a shareholder who holds 1,000 shares of Big Rock can determine his or her share of the earnings during the period. In 1995, Big Rock earned $0.40 per share. Therefore, that investor's share of the earnings for 1995 would be $400. Big Rock also has a fully diluted earnings per share amount which indicates that the corporation has either debt or share options that can be converted into common shares. If they are converted, the earnings per share would drop by one cent to $0.39.

Big Rock is a simple company with all of its operations run out of one business entity. As businesses expand they will often establish other corporations, or buy shares in other corporations. This enables them to expand operations and diversify the risk.

Reviewing the income statement for Big Rock, you can see that the earnings (net income) for 1995 were $1,742,332. Corporations will often round amounts to the nearest $100, $1,000 or, in the case of very large corporations, $1,000,000. The units in which the numbers are expressed must be stated somewhere on the statement. Usually, they can be found in parentheses at the top of the statement. This brings up an issue that was discussed earlier in the conceptual framework section: materiality. If an auditor were to find a $2,000 mistake when trying to verify how fairly the statements presented the earnings of a company, how much difference would it make if the corporation rounded its amounts to the nearest $1,000? The answer is, it would not make much difference in the overall analysis of the financial status of the corporation. On the other hand, a $2,000 mistake in the tax reporting of an individual's earnings would certainly get the attention of Revenue Canada. How material an item is depends, in part, on the size of the entity being considered.

On page 16 is a list of some of the more common items you can expect to see on an income statement.

COMMON INCOME STATEMENT ITEMS:

Sales Revenues The total amount of sales for the period.

Other Income Various types of revenues or income to the corporation other than sales revenues.

Cost of Goods Sold The cost of the units of inventory that were sold during the period.

Selling, General, and Administrative Expense The total amount of other expenses of the corporation during the period that do not fit into any other category.

Amortization Expense The allocation of part of the original cost of long-lived items like equipment.

Interest Expense The amount of interest incurred on the debt of the corporation during the period.

Tax Expense (Provision for Taxes) The taxes levied on the profits of the corporation during the period.

BALANCE SHEET The balance sheet (BR-7) is also known as the **Statement of Financial Position**. Financial *position* suggests that this statement represents the financial status of the corporation at a particular point in time. In fact, at the top of the statement, the words "March 31" appear. The amounts in the statement are those that exist on March 31 in 1995 and 1994, respectively. These dates may also be thought of as the beginning and end points of the current accounting period. In the transition from one accounting period to the next, the ending balances of one accounting period become the beginning balances of the next accounting period. This statement has been described by various authors as a snapshot of the financial position of the corporation at a particular point in time.

So what makes up the financial position of the corporation? Individuals, if asked about their own financial positions, would probably start by listing what they own-such as a car or a house, and then listing what they owe to other people, such as bank loans and credit card balances. The net of what is owned less what is owed would be a measure of their net worth (wealth or equity) at a particular point in time. A corporation lists exactly the same types of things in its balance sheet. In Big Rock's statement, there are two major categories: **assets**, and **liabilities and shareholders' equity**.

Assets When asked for a simple definition of an **asset**, many people reply that it is something of value that the corporation either owns or has the right to use. In fact, the accounting definition of an asset is very similar. In this book, assets will be those things that meet the following criteria: (1) the corporation owns or has the right to use them; (2) they have *probable future value*; and (3) the event that gave the corporation the ownership of or right to them has already happened. The word *future* has been added to *value* since the corporation would not want to list things that had value in the past but do not have value in the future. *Probable* is also added because businesses exist in an uncertain world and the value of an asset is subject to change. One of the risks of ownership of an asset, in fact, is that its value may change over time.

CHARACTERISTICS OF AN ASSET:

1. Something that has probable future value.

2. The corporation owns or has the right to use the probable future value.

3. The event that gave the corporation the ownership or right has already happened.

The assets that Big Rock lists in its balance sheet include cash, accounts receivable, inventories, prepaid expenses, capital assets, and other assets. A full discussion of how each of these meets the criteria of ownership and probable future value is left to later chapters. As an example, however, ownership of inventory by the corporation is evidenced either by possession or by legal documentation. It has future value because the corporation can later sell the inventory and receive cash in the amount of the selling price. The presence of the inventory or the documents indicates that the event that gave ownership to the corporation has already happened. The cash, in turn, has value because the corporation can use it to obtain other goods and services. The total assets of Big Rock as at March 31, 1995, are $13,888,295. Following is a list of assets normally found in a balance sheet.

COMMON BALANCE SHEET ASSETS:

Cash The amount of currency that the corporation has, including amounts in chequing and savings accounts.

Temporary Investments Short-term investments in securities of other corporations, such as treasury bills, shares and bonds

Accounts Receivable Amounts owed to the corporation that result from credit sales to customers.

Inventory Goods held for resale to customers.

Prepaid Expenses Expenses that have been paid for but have not yet been used. An example is prepaid insurance.

Capital Assets Investments in land, buildings, equipment, and intangibles that the corporation uses over the long term. Intangibles are investments in assets such as patents, trademarks and goodwill.

Big Rock prepares a **classified balance sheet**. A classified balance sheet is one in which the assets and liabilities are classified as **current** and **noncurrent**. For assets, current means that the asset will be turned into cash or consumed in the next year or operating cycle. The *operating cycle* of a corporation refers to the time period between the initial investment of cash in products or services and the return of cash from the sale of the product or service. Assets such as cash, accounts receivables and inventories are classified as current, and assets such as capital assets are classified as noncurrent.

Assets and liabilities are listed on the balance sheet in *liquidity order*. Liquidity refers to how quickly the corporation can turn the asset into cash. Noncurrent assets are the least liquid because they will be used over a long period of time and will not quickly be turned into cash. Accounts receivable, on the other hand, are amounts owed to the corporation by its customers who bought goods on credit. The corporation hopes that these will be collected quickly (many corporations have collection policies that give customers 30 days to pay). Therefore, accounts receivable are fairly liquid. Inventories are less liquid than receivables since they must be sold first, which normally results in an account receivable. Cash is then received when the account receivable is collected.

An **unclassified balance sheet** is, then, a balance sheet in which current assets or liabilities are not distinguished from noncurrent assets or liabilities. Even in an unclassified balance sheet, however, assets and liabilities are still listed primarily in the order of their liquidity. For instance, the cash, receivables (current receivables), inventories, and capital assets will have the same order as in the Big Rock report even if they are not specifically identified as current or noncurrent.

Liabilities A simple definition of **liabilities** might be "amounts that the corporation owes to others." The accounting definition of liabilities encompasses this concept and, consistent with the earlier definition of assets, will be used to refer to items that require *a probable future sacrifice of resources*. In most cases, the resource is cash, but recognize that a corporation could satisfy a liability with services or goods. For example, a warranty liability could be satisfied with a new part or with the services of a repair person.

Big Rock, in its classified balance sheet, lists among its liabilities bank indebtedness, accounts payable, income taxes payable, current portion of long-term debt, long-term debt, deferred income taxes and commitments. Note that Big Rock classifies liabilities as current or noncurrent in its balance sheet. **Current liabilities** are those that will require the use of current assets or will be replaced by another current liability in the next year or operating cycle. The following list includes some of the more common liabilities found in financial statements.

C OMMON BALANCE SHEET LIABILITIES:

Bank Indebtedness Amounts owed to the bank on short term-credit.

Accounts Payable Amounts owed to suppliers from the purchase of goods on credit.

Notes Payable Amounts owed to a creditor (bank or supplier) that are represented by a formal agreement called a note (sometimes called a promissory note).

Dividends Payable Amounts owed to shareholders for dividends that are declared by the Board of Directors.

Accrued Liabilities Amounts owed to others based on expenses that have been incurred by the corporation but are not yet due, such as interest expense and warranty expense.

Taxes Payable Amounts owed to taxing authorities.

Long-term Debt Amounts owed to creditors over periods longer than one year.

Deferred Income Taxes Amounts representing probable future taxes the corporation will have to pay to Revenue Canada.

Shareholders' Equity The last major category in the balance sheet is the section called equity. It is frequently referred to as **shareholders' equity**. In Big Rock's section on shareholders' equity, note the listings for share capital and retained earnings. This section captures the value of the shareholders' interest in the corporation as measured by the accounting guidelines. Note that the total assets equal the total liabilities and equity. Both are listed as $13,888,295 by Big Rock on March 31, 1995. This relationship is described by the **basic accounting equation**:

> **Basic Accounting Equation**
>
> Assets = Liabilities + Shareholders' Equity

This equation gives meaning to the description of this statement as the balance sheet. If the equation is rearranged, it can be seen that shareholders' equity is equal to assets minus liabilities:

> **Basic Accounting Equation (rearranged)**
>
> Shareholders' Equity = Assets − Liabilities
> (Net Assets)

To state this relationship another way, shareholders' equity is the difference between what the investors own and what the corporation owes to others, as measured in the **accounting books**. Because of this relationship, shareholders' equity is sometimes referred to as the *net assets* of the corporation (net refers to the net of the assets less the liabilities) or the *net book value* of the corporation. It is the equivalent of an individual's personal net wealth. The shareholders' wealth as measured by the accounting statements is a residual concept. The shareholders can claim the residual of the assets that are left over after paying all of the liabilities. You should note that the market value of the shares of a corporation is another measure of the shareholders' wealth in the corporation. This value could be very different from the book value of shareholders' equity because accounting records are not necessarily based on market values.

Shareholders' equity is generally made up of two accounts: **share capital** and **retained earnings**. The first, share capital, is used to record the amount that the investors originally paid (invested) for the shares that the corporation issued. The retained earnings account is used to keep track of the earnings of the corporation less any amounts that are paid from the corporation to the shareholders in the form of **dividends**. Dividends will be paid to shareholders only when approved by a vote of the Board of Directors. The change in the retained earnings of a corporation during a given period can be explained by the net income less the dividends declared as follows:

> **Change in Retained Earnings:**
>
> Change in Retained Earnings = Net Income − Dividends

Other accounts can appear in this section. During the early part of this book, these other accounts will be ignored in order to concentrate on common share capital and retained earnings. The other accounts will be discussed in later sections of the book. Following is a list of some of the more common account titles that appear in the shareholders' equity section.

C OMMON BALANCE SHEET SHAREHOLDERS' EQUITY ACCOUNTS:

Share Capital Represents the shares that have been issued by the company and is usually stated at an amount equal to what was originally paid by investors for the shares. Shares can be of different types, with different rights and privileges attached to each.

Retained Earnings The earnings of the corporation that have been kept (retained) and not paid out in the form of dividends.

STATEMENT OF CHANGES IN FINANCIAL POSITION The **statement of changes in financial position**, sometimes called the **Cash Flows Statement** (BR-9), is a flow statement that is, in some ways, similar to the income statement. It measures inflows and outflows of cash during a specific period of time. Note how the words at the top of the statement indicate that the statement is for "Years ended March 31," which is the same terminology used on the income statement. The difference is that instead of measuring the increase and decrease in shareholders' wealth, this statement measures the increase and decrease in cash and highly liquid assets and liabilities called **cash equivalents**. Remember that a liquid item is one that can be converted very quickly to cash. Since cash is very important to the operation of the corporation, this statement is vital to any user's evaluation of a corporation.

Today the cash flow statement has three sections that report the sources and uses of cash and cash equivalents for the three business activities described earlier: **operating**, **financing** and **investing**. Note that, in the statement of changes in financial position in Exhibit 1-3, there is no similar breakdown into these three categories. Only the funds flow from operating activities are separated from the other working capital flows.

S UBSECTIONS OF THE STATEMENT OF CHANGES IN FINANCIAL POSITION:

Cash from operating activities

Cash from financing activities

Cash from investing activities

In order to evaluate the liquidity position of a corporation, users need to evaluate where cash is coming from and where it is being spent. Big Rock generated a positive cash flow of $1,777,726 from its operating activities in 1995. **Operating activities** include all inflows and outflows of cash related to the sale of goods and services of the corporation. The starting point in this section is net income, which is a summary of the income from operating activities from the income statement. There are adjustments to this number, because the recognition of revenues and expenses (as will be seen in the next chapter) does not necessarily coincide with the receipt and payment of cash. For instance, sales could be either cash sales or sales on account (i.e., the customer can pay at a later date, resulting in an account receivable rather than cash). Expenses may also be paid later if the corporation is given credit by its suppliers (this would result in an account payable). Because the operating activities are the backbone of the corporation, a positive cash flow from operations is essential to corporate health.

EXHIBIT 1-3

CRISTALERIAS DE CHILE S.A. AND SUBSIDIARY
CONSOLIDATED STATEMENT OF CHANGES IN FINANCIAL POSITION
(Restated for general price-level changes and expressed in thousands of constant
Chilean pesos as of December 31, 1994 and thousands of U.S. dollars)

	Years ended December 31			
	1992	1993	1994	1994
	ThCh$	ThCh$	ThCh$	ThUS$
SOURCES OF FUNDS				
Funds From Operations				
Net income	11,762,294	7,501,101	10,748,665	26,677
Depreciation (Note 6)	1,543,220	1,804,358	2,422,961	6,013
Amortization	(20,392)	15,825	930,010	2,308
(Gain) loss or sale of property, plant and equipment	(127,429)	(4,020)	1,812	4
Gain on sale of permanent investments	(1,849,021)	—	—	—
Equity in net income of related companies	(1,021,055)	(1,014,642)	(981,595)	(2,436)
Net price-level restatement of non-current assets and liabilities	(160,582)	198,411	(926,498)	(2,299)
Other funds from operations	(845,507)	608,934	570,553	1,416
Total funds from operations	9,281,528	9,109,967	12,765,908	31,683
Funds from Other Sources				
Proceeds from issuance of shares	—	—	42,977,354	106,665
Proceeds from sale of property, plant and equipment	4,891,286	34,064	57,964	144
Proceeds from sale of permanent investments in related companies	2,421,874	—	—	—
Dividends received	479,356	386,114	121,113	301
Increase in long-term liabilities	—	2,527,185	4,449,059	11,042
Other non-operating funds	1,361,345	5,583,637	512,703	1,272
Total funds from other sources	9,153,861	8,531,000	48,118,193	119,424
Total source of funds	18,435,389	7,640,967	60,884,101	151,107
Application of Funds				
Additions to property, plant and equipment	2,215,160	11,542,054	3,481,277	8,640
Permanent investments in related companies	606,038	547,739	21,211,663	52,545
Decrease in long-term liabilities	41,464	62,453	—	—
Dividends paid	3,310,544	4,029,657	2,605,326	5,466
Investment in Government securities	4,644,096	—	—	—
Transfer of liabilities from long-term, to short-term	2,087,661	1,962,237	1,970,450	4,890

EXHIBIT 1-3 (continued)

CRISTALERIAS DE CHILE S.A. AND SUBSIDIARY
CONSOLIDATED STATEMENT OF CHANGES IN FINANCIAL POSITION
(Restated for general price-level changes and expressed in thousands of constant
Chilean pesos as of December 31, 1994 and thousands of U.S. dollars)

	Years ended December 31			
	1992	1993	1994	1994
	ThCh$	ThCh$	ThCh$	ThUS$
Other applications of funds	177,842	587,532	2,934,011	7,282
Total application of funds	13,082,805	18,731,672	32,202,737	79,923
Increase (decrease) in working capital	5,352,584	(1,090,705)	28,681,364	71,184

CHANGES IN WORKING CAPITAL:

Increase (Decrease) in Current Assets:

Cash and time deposits	(2,652,460)	2,716,515	29,311,835	72,748
Marketable securities	(158,015)	6,550,076	(7,624,432)	(18,923)
Accounts receivable	(203,472)	(649,403)	1,348,844	3,348
Accounts receivable from related companies	176,764	(6,659)	(16,474)	(41)
Inventories	277,606	380,398	(330,775)	(821)
Other current assets	9,273,011	(9,732,393)	6,625,079	16,443
Net changes in current assets	6,713,434	(741,466)	29,314,077	72,754

(Increase) Decrease in Current Liabilities:

Current portion of long-term bank liabilities	133,486	(53,070)	(152,229)	(378)
Current portion of bonds payable	(267,531)	14,720	27,069	67
Dividends payable	(161,414)	(44,191)	114,383	284
Royalties and accounts payable	210,172	(148,790)	(146,829)	(364)
Accounts payable to related companies	(722,010)	222,191	603,895	1,499
Provisions and witholdings	(301,696)	(242,998)	(799,805)	(1,985)
Other current liabilities	(251,857)	(97,101)	(279,197)	(693)
Net changes in current liabilities	(1,360,859)	(349,239)	(632,713)	(1,570)
Increase (decrease) in working capital	5,352,584	(1,090,705)	28,681,364	71,184

The positive cash flow of $1,047,574 from financial activities indicates that Big Rock used outside sources for more cash; the bank borrowings were greater than the bank repayments and it raised $40,000 by issuing more shares. **Financing activities**, as you will recall, are those transactions that either provide new funds from investors, or return funds to investors. Investors can be either shareholders or lenders, and the typical activities in this category are the issuance and repurchase of shares and the issuance and repayment of debt.

Investing activities generally involve the purchase and sale of long-term assets such as property, plant, and equipment, and investment in other corporations. These typical activities can be seen from the disclosure by Big Rock. The negative cash flow (of $3,503,014) from investing activities indicates that Big Rock purchased more cap-

AN INTERNATIONAL PERSPECTIVE
REPORTS FROM OTHER COUNTRIES

In some countries, the working capital format (current assets minus current liabilities) is still used. Exhibit 1-3 shows the statement of changes in financial position for Cristalerias De Chile S.A. and Subsidiary, a Chilean company. This is a statement of changes in financial position using working capital as a definition for funds. The currency units expressed in the statement are in thousands of Chilean Peso (Th Ch). Note the line item called "Total funds from operations," which is the total flow of working capital from operations. Its counterpart in the cash flow statement is the "cash from operations" line. At the bottom of the statement of changes in financial position in Exhibit 1-3, there is also a section called "Increase in working capital," which itemizes how the components of working capital changed during the period. This statement is very similar to the ones that were prepared in Canada prior to 1989.

ital assets during the year. Those capital assets were used by the corporation for operating activities to generate a positive cash flow. These amounts in 1995 indicate that Big Rock is doing quite well with respect to cash flow. Examine the amounts for Big Rock for 1994 and see if you can draw the same conclusion.

The preparation and interpretation of the statement of changes in financial position are discussed in detail in Chapter 5.

SUMMARY OF FINANCIAL STATEMENTS
INCOME STATEMENT
• Measures the operating performance of a corporation over a period of time.
BALANCE SHEET
• Measures the resources controlled by a corporation (assets) and the claims to those resources (liability and equity holders) at a given point in time.
STATEMENT OF CHANGES IN FINANCIAL POSITION
• Measures the sources and uses of cash through operating, financing and investing activities over a period of time.

Notes to the Financial Statements

You may have noticed that various items on the financial statements direct the reader to specific notes. In such notes to the financial statements (BR-10 to BR-19), management has a chance to provide more detail about the referenced items. For example, on Big Rock's income statement the income taxes item includes a reference to *Note 8*. Note 8 goes into greater detail about taxes owed, deferred taxes, and tax rates. Financial statements are thus kept simple and uncluttered by including additional explanations in notes rather than on the financial statements themselves.

A full discussion of notes will be left to succeeding chapters, but some attention should be paid to the first note in any statement. The first note is usually a summary of the significant accounting policies of the corporation. Within GAAP there are choices and judgements to be made by management. The first note describes the choices that were made by management. The auditors, of course, review these choices for conformity with GAAP. As you progress through the book, the choices made by management will have important implications for the interpretation of the statements they present. As an example, note how, on page BR-10, Big Rock's inventories are valued primarily using the first-in first-out, or FIFO, method. This method will produce a different balance in the inventory account on the balance sheet from that produced by a similar company using an alternative method, such as the last-in first-out, or LIFO, method. Comparing the two corporations using these two different methods would be difficult. To aid users in comparing various corporations, they must disclose their major accounting policies in this note.

Summary of Industry Segments

Information about various segments of the corporation is provided as a part of management's discussion (BR-16). This is a requirement for any corporation that has more than one significant segment. A segment represents a business activity. Big Rock tells you that it has only one business activity, the production and marketing of specialty draught and bottled beer. It tells you as well the percentage of sales that are made outside Canada. This information is important to the reader because it helps to explain the kinds of risks an investor takes when buying Big Rock shares. Segments can differ significantly with regard to risk and are affected in different ways by economic factors such as commodity prices, inflation, exchange rates and interest rates. It is important to know the relative amounts invested in these segments if an overall assessment of the risk of this corporation is to be made.

Selected Financial Data (5- to 10-Year Summaries)

Another part of the management discussion provides key financial figures for a period of time more extensive than that provided in the main financial statements. For many corporations, a five-year summary is provided, but it is not uncommon to see ten-year summaries. This type of information is useful to the reader to spot trends in the data that would not be evident in the two years' worth of income data, cash flow data or balance sheet data that are presented in the main financial statements. Big Rock provides a seven-year summary at the beginning of the report (BR-1).

ETHICS IN ACCOUNTING

The management of a corporation has both a moral and a legal obligation to safeguard the investment shareholders have entrusted to them. To ensure that management fulfills this stewardship function with regard to the resources of the corporation, shareholders typically provide some incentives for and controls over management. Management compensation arrangements are often tied to the financial statement performance of the corporation to provide incentives for management to make decisions that are in the best interests of the shareholders. Auditors are also hired to review the financial statements to ensure they adequately reflect the transactions of the company. There are also legal responsibilities placed on the behaviour of management.

Independent Auditor's Report

The financial statements are prepared by the management of the company. *Independent auditors* are hired by shareholders to provide an opinion about the fairness of the presentation and the conformity to accounting guidelines. Auditors add credibility to the financial statements by expressing their professional opinion as to whether the financial statements fairly present the results of the corporation.

Corporations such as Big Rock are not audited by one person alone, but by a firm of auditors. Auditors apply a set of procedures to test the financial statements to determine if they comply with generally accepted accounting principles and to assess the fairness of the presentation. Audit reports are often expressed in a standard format of three paragraphs. The first paragraph states what financial statements have been audited, that the financial statements are the responsibility of management, and that the auditors' responsibility is to express an opinion about the financial statements. The second paragraph explains how they conducted the audit using accepted auditing standards. The third paragraph is the auditors' opinion about the financial statements. The audit report of Big Rock (BR-6) follows this format. A standard format like this is called an **unqualified opinion**. It means that the financial statements present fairly, in all material respects, the financial position, results of operations, and cash flows of the entity in conformity with Generally Accepted Accounting Principles.

In Canada the unqualified or "**clean" opinion** is the most commonly seen opinion. Corporations prefer to have a clean opinion attached to their financial statements. If an opinion other than an unqualified one is being contemplated by the auditors, management is informed about the reason(s) for the opinion prior to the issuance of the financial statements. Management then has an opportunity to change the financial statements to resolve the problem(s) the auditors have detected. If the issue is controversial, there may be some negotiation between management and the auditors as to how best to resolve the problem. If no resolution is reached and management decides to issue the statements as originally prepared, a **qualified** or adverse opinion will be included with the statements. This rarely happens in practice because the problems are resolved prior to statement issuance.

In any set of financial statements, the auditors' report should be read because it can alert the reader to major problems the corporation may be experiencing. In other words, it can provide a "red flag." Readers must then investigate further to make their own assessments of the extent of the problems the company is facing. Also, recognize that there may be significant problems that the auditors did not identify with their tests or that are beyond the responsibility of the auditors.

Most large corporations are audited by large accounting firms because of the size and expertise needed on the audit team. Until the late 1980s, the eight largest accounting firms were known as the Big Eight. The Big Eight audited virtually all the large corporations in Canada and, as international firms themselves, many corporations in other parts of the world. In the late 1980s, two mergers among the Big Eight resulted in what are now known as the Big Six. The Big Six, in alphabetical order, are: Arthur Andersen & Co., Coopers & Lybrand, Deloitte & Touche, Ernst & Young, KPMG Peat Marwick, and Price Waterhouse.

In Canada there are three professional accounting organizations that establish the professional standards of accountants. The members of the **Canadian Institute of Chartered Accountants** are called **Chartered Accountants (CAs)**. The organization of the **Certified Management Accountants (CMAs)** is the **Society of Management Accountants of Canada**. The **Certified General Accountants' Association of Canada** establishes the standards for the **Certified General Accountants (CGAs)**. These professional accountants perform audits, supervise and perform accounting functions inside organizations and provide decision-making functions inside and outside organizations.

ETHICS IN ACCOUNTING

Auditors are hired by the shareholders to review the financial statements presented to the shareholders by the management of the corporation. The auditors, as they conduct their review, must maintain their independence from the management. In order to ensure their independence and encourage ethical behaviour, the professional accounting organizations have developed codes of professional conduct. The codes state the responsibilities of auditors to the public, clients, and colleagues. For example, accountants normally cannot audit corporations in which they own shares. In addition, the codes describe the scope and nature of the services provided by auditors.

SUMMARY

In this chapter we discussed the various users of financial accounting information and provided an overview of the types of information that they would need. A brief introduction to the accounting framework underlying accounting guidelines was followed by a detailed explanation of the various components of the annual report of Big Rock Brewery Ltd. In the annual report, you discovered the information components of three major financial statements: the income statement, balance sheet, and statement of changes in financial position. Subsequent chapters will build on this framework. In Chapters 2 through 5, the mechanics of preparing these statements and more information about their decision-making capabilities are discussed. Details of each individual asset, liability, and shareholders' equity account are discussed in Chapters 6 through 11. Chapter 12 considers financial statement analysis to provide some tools to interpret and link the major financial statements. Finally, Chapter 13 discusses complex business organizations and the major accounting issues related to mergers, acquisitions, and consolidated financial statements.

SUMMARY PROBLEM

The major financial statements of Meridian Technologies Inc. from its 1995 annual report are included in Exhibit 1-4.

EXHIBIT 1-4

MERIDIAN TECHNOLOGIES INC.
Consolidated Balance Sheets
As at March 31

	1995	1994
	($000)	($000)
Assets		
Cash	3,979	4,591
Accounts receivable	44,555	27,181
Inventory (note 2)	25,896	16,799
Prepaid expenses	8,804	8,158
Total current assets	83,234	56,729
Investments and loans (note 3)	220	1,322
Land, buildings and equipment (note 4)	143,708	92,956
Goodwill	3,022	3,302
	230,184	154,309
Liabilities and Shareholders' Equity		
Accounts payable and accrued liabilities	45,319	25,505
Current portion of long-term debt (note 5)	3,914	2,006
Total current liabilities	49,233	27,511
Long-term debt (note 5)	44,163	18,394
	93,396	45,905
Deferred income taxes		1,630
Common shares (note 6)	133,079	95,489
Retained earnings	2,544	10,287
Cumulative translation adjustment	1,165	998
Total shareholders' equity	136,788	106,774
	230,184	154,309

See accompanying notes

On behalf of the Board:

Director

Director

EXHIBIT 1-4 (continued)

MERIDIAN TECHNOLOGIES INC.
Consolidated Statements of Operations
Years ended March 31

	1995	1994
	($000)	($000)
Revenues	**199,372**	147,539
Expenses:		
Cost of sales	**185,756**	126,810
Selling and general	**12,739**	9,002
Depreciation and amortization	**8,319**	5,027
	206,814	140,839
Operating (loss) earnings before interest and taxes	**(7,442)**	6,700
Interest expense (note 5)	**(2,620)**	(1,199)
(Loss) earnings before income taxes	**(10,062)**	5,501
Income tax recovery (expense) (note 7)	**2,319**	(2,195)
Net (loss) earnings	**(7,743)**	3,306
(Loss) earnings per share	**$ (0.33)**	$ 0.19
Weighted average number of shares	**23,190,634**	17,579,387

Consolidated Statements of Retained Earnings
Years ended March 31

	1995	1994
	($000)	($000)
Retained earnings, beginning of year	**10,287**	6,981
Net (loss) earnings	**(7,743)**	3,306
Retained earnings, end of year	**2,544**	10,287

See accompanying notes

1. Find the following amounts in the statements:
   a. Revenues in 1995
   b. Operating costs in 1995
   c. Financing expenses in 1995
   d. Income tax expense in 1995
   e. Net income (earnings) in 1995
   f. Inventories at the end of 1995
   g. Accounts payable at the beginning of 1995
   h. Retained earnings at the end of 1995
   i. Long-term borrowings (debt) at the beginning of 1995
   j. Cash provided from operating activities in 1995

EXHIBIT 1-4 (continued)

MERIDIAN TECHNOLOGIES INC.
Consolidated Statements of Changes in Financial Position
Years ended March 31

	1995	1994
	($000)	($000)
Operations:		
Net (loss) earnings	(7,743)	3,306
Depreciation and amortization	8,319	5,027
Deferred income taxes	(1,630)	(350)
Other	259	(33)
	(795)	7,950
Investment in working capital	(5,782)	(4,151)
	(6,577)	3,799
Financing:		
Common shares issued	37,590	40,547
Increase in long-term debt	53,455	22,144
Repayment of long-term debt	(25,778)	(26,743)
Debenture converted		(1,500)
	65,267	34,448
Investments:		
Purchase of buildings and equipment	(59,050)	(54,458)
Investments and loans	1,202	1,987
Pre-production working capital	(1,621)	(668)
Translation adjustment	167	998
	(59,302)	(52,141)
Decrease in cash	(612)	(13,894)
Cash, beginning of year	4,591	18,485
Cash, end of year	3,979	4,591

Cash includes short-term deposits and is net of bank indebtedness

See accompanying notes

    k. Cash payments to acquire capital assets in 1995
    l. Dividends paid in 1995
    m. Cash proceeds from new borrowings in 1995
    n. Cash provided from investing activities in 1995

2. Does Meridian Technologies Inc. finance its business primarily with debt or with shareholders' equity? Support your answer with appropriate data.

3. List the two largest sources of cash and the two largest uses of cash in 1995. (Consider operations to be a single source or use of cash.)

4. Explain the change in retained earnings from December 31, 1994, to December 31, 1995.

SUGGESTED SOLUTION TO SUMMARY PROBLEM

All answers are in thousands of dollars unless otherwise stated.

1. The following answers are found on the statement of operations, Exhibit 1-4:
   a. Revenues in 1995 = $199,372
   b. Operating costs in 1995 = $206,814
   c. Financing expenses in 1995 = $2,620
   d. Income tax expense in 1995 = Recovery of $2,319
   e. Net income in 1995 = Loss of ($7,743)

   The following answers are found on the balance sheet, Exhibit 1-4:
   f. Inventories at the end of 1995 = $25,896
   g. Accounts payable at the beginning of 1995 = $25,505 (The end of 1994 is the same as the beginning of 1995.)
   h. Retained earnings at the end of 1995 = $2,544
   i. Long-term borrowings at the beginning of 1995 = $18,394

   The following answers are found on the statement of changes in financial position, Exhibit 1-4:
   j. Cash produced from operating activities in 1995 = ($6,577)
   k. Cash payments to acquire capital assets in 1995 = $59,050 (Purchase of buildings and equipment under the investing activities)
   l. Dividends paid in 1995 = $0 (If dividends had been paid in 1995, the amounts would have been disclosed under financing activities and on the statement of retained earnings.)
   m. Cash proceeds from new borrowings in 1995 = $53,455 (From increase in long-term debt.)
   n. Cash provided from investing activities in 1995 = ($59,302)

2. Meridian Technologies Inc. uses more shareholders' equity to finance its business than debt. This can be seen by comparing the total liabilities to the total shareholders' equity (balance sheet) as shown below:

   Total liabilities (12/31/95) $93,396
   Total shareholders' equity (12/31/95) $136,788
   Total liabilities and shareholders' equity $230,184
   Total liabilities are, therefore, 41% ($93,396/$230,184) of the total sources of financing for Meridian Technologies Inc.

3. The two largest sources of cash are proceeds from the issuance of shares ($37,590) and proceeds from the issuance of long-term debt ($53,455). The two largest uses are the capital expenditures ($59,050) and the repayment of long-term debt ($25,778).

4. The retained earnings change from the end of 1994 to the end of 1995 of $7,743 ($10,287 − $2,544) can be explained by the net loss for the period ($7,743). This change is shown on the consolidated statements of operations, Exhibit 1-4.

ABBREVIATIONS USED

AcSB	Accounting Standards Board
ASC	Alberta Securities Commission
CA	Chartered Accountant

CGA   Certified General Accountant
CICA   Canadian Institute of Chartered Accountants
CMA   Certified Management Accountant
FASB   Financial Accounting Standards Board
GAAP   Generally Accepted Accounting Principles
IAS   International Accounting Standards
IASC   International Accounting Standards Committee
IFAC   International Federation of Accountants

SYNONYMS

Accounts Receivable/Current Receivables

Balance sheet equation/Accounting equation

Capital Assets/Property, Plant, and Equipment/Plant Assets/Fixed Assets

Common Shares/Share Capital/Capital Stock

Earnings Statement/Statement of Earnings/Income Statement/Net Income
    Statement/Consolidated Statement of Earnings/Profit and Loss Statement

Equity/Owners' Equity/Shareholders' Equity

Financial reporting books/Reporting books/Books/Accounting records

Liabilities/Debt

Managerial accounting/Cost accounting

Net income/Profit/Earnings

Retained Earnings/Earnings Retained in the Business/Earnings Reinvested in the Business

Statement of Changes in Financial Position/Cash Flow/Statement of Cash
    Flow/Consolidated Statement of Cash Flow

Statement of Financial Position/Balance Sheet/Consolidated Balance Sheet

GLOSSARY

Accounting Standards Board (AcSB) The CICA committee in Canada that sets accounting standards.

Assets Elements of the balance sheet that have probable future value, are owned or controlled by the corporation and are the result of a past transaction.

Auditor A professionally trained accountant who examines the accounting records and statements of the corporation to determine whether they fairly present the financial position and operating results of the corporation in accordance with GAAP.

Balance sheet A financial statement showing the asset, liability, and shareholders' equity account balances of the corporation.

Basic accounting equation The equation that describes the relationship between assets, liabilities, and shareholders' equity. It is as follows:

Assets = Liabilities + Shareholders' Equity

Board of Directors The governing body of a corporation elected by the shareholders to represent their ownership interest.

Books The accounting records of the corporation. Usually this term refers to the records reported to shareholders rather than to any other body, such as the tax authority.

Capital stock Synonym for Share Capital.

Cash flow statement Synonym for the statement of changes in financial position.

Classified balance sheet A balance sheet in which the assets and liabilities are listed in liquidity order and are categorized into current and noncurrent sections.

Clean opinion Synonym for unqualified opinion.

Common shares The shares issued by a corporation to its owners. Shares represent the ownership interest in the corporation.

Comparability A quality of accounting information that improves the ability of financial statement readers to compare different sets of financial statements.

Conceptual framework The framework set out in Section 1000 of the *CICA Handbook* to guide the AcSB as they set new accounting standards.

Consistency A quality of accounting information that requires consistent application of accounting principles over time.

Consolidated financial statements Financial statements that represent the combined financial results of a parent company and its subsidiaries.

Cost accounting A branch of accounting that studies how cost information is used internally within the corporation.

Cost/benefit constraint A constraint that states that the cost of implementing a new accounting standard should be less than the benefits that will be derived.

Creditors Individuals or entities that are owed something by the corporation.

Current asset/liability For assets, current means that the asset will be turned into cash or used within the next year or operating cycle of the corporation. For liabilities, current means that the liability will require the payment of cash or the rendering of service or will be replaced by another current liability within the next year or operating cycle of the corporation.

Dividends Payments made to shareholders from earnings that represent a return on their investment in the corporation. Dividends are paid only after they are declared by the Board of Directors.

Earnings The profits generated by a corporation during a specified time period. Earnings are determined by subtracting expenses from the revenues of the corporation.

Earnings per share A ratio calculated by dividing the earnings for the period by the average number of shares outstanding during the period.

Entity The business reported by the financial statements, usually a corporation.

Equity A term sometimes used to describe the sum of liabilities and shareholders' equity; sometimes also used to refer simply to the shareholders' equity section, which can lead to some confusion in the use of this term.

Expenses The costs associated with the production of revenues by the corporation; represent decreases in shareholders' wealth.

FASB Financial Accounting Standards Board, the regulatory body that currently sets accounting standards in the United States.

Feedback value A quality of accounting information that gives it relevance to decision-makers. The information provides feedback on previous decisions.

Financial accounting The study of the accounting concepts and principles used to prepare financial statements for external users.

Financial reporting books The accounting records that are summarized and reported to shareholders and other users via the financial statements.

Financing activities Activities of the corporation in which funds are raised to support the other activities of the corporation. The two major ways to raise funds are to issue shares or borrow money.

Flow statement A statement that describes certain types of inflows and outflows of the corporation. The cash flows statement and the income statement are both examples of flow statements.

GAAP Generally Accepted Accounting Principles.

Investing activities The activities of the corporation involved with long-term investments, primarily investments in property, plant, and equipment and in shares of other corporations.

Liability An element of the balance sheet characterized by a probable future sacrifice of resources of the corporation.

Liquidity The length of time required to turn assets into cash.

Management The individuals responsible for running or managing the corporation.

Managerial accounting The study of the preparation and uses of accounting information by the management of the corporation.

Materiality A concept used to indicate items that will affect decision-making. In auditing it means those items that are large enough to have a significant effect in the evaluation of the presentation of the financial results of a company.

Minority shareholders Synonym for minority interest or noncontrolling interest.

Net income Synonym for earnings.

Neutrality A quality of accounting information indicating that the methods or principles applied should not depend on the self-interest of the corporation being measured but be neutral with regard to the potential outcomes of the corporation.

Noncurrent asset/liability Assets or liabilities, which do not fit the definition of current assets and liabilities.

Operating activities The activities of the corporation that involve the sales of goods and services to customers.

Operating cycle The time period between the initial investment of cash in products or services and the return of cash from the sale of the product or service.

Owners Synonym for shareholders.

Owners' equity Synonym for owners' equity.

Predictive value A quality of accounting information that makes the information relevant to decision makers. Its relevance stems from its ability to predict the future.

Privately held company A company whose shares are held by a few individuals and do not trade in an active stock market.

Publicly traded company A company whose shares are traded in a public stock market.

Qualified opinion An audit opinion that finds some exception to the fair presentation of the financial results.

Relevance A quality of accounting information indicating that the information should be relevant to the decisions of the user.

Reliability A quality of accounting information indicating that the information should be reliable to be of use to decision makers.

Reporting books Synonym of financial reporting books.

Representational faithfulness A quality of accounting information indicating that the information should accurately represent the attribute or characteristic that it purports to represent.

Retained earnings Earnings that are retained within the corporation and not paid out to shareholders in the form of dividends.

Revenues Inflows of resources to the corporation that result from the sales of goods and/or services.

Share capital The investment in a corporation by the shareholders.

Shareholders The individuals or entities that own shares in a corporation.

Shareholders' equity The section of the balance sheet that represents the shareholders' wealth; equivalent to the assets less the liabilities.

Statement of cash flows Synonym for the statement of changes in financial position.

Statement of changes in financial position A financial statement that shows the cash flows of the corporation during the accounting period categorized into operating, investing and financing activities.

Statement of financial position Synonym for balance sheet.

Tax books The accounting records the corporation keeps to report to the taxing authority.

Taxing authority An agency that assesses and collects taxes from the corporation.

Timeliness A quality of accounting information indicating that information must be timely in order to be relevant to decision makers.

Unclassified balance sheet A balance sheet that does not classify assets and liabilities into current and noncurrent categories.

Unqualified opinion An audit opinion that states that the financial statements present fairly the financial position and operating results of the corporation in conformity with GAAP.

Verifiability The capability of accounting information to be verified by an independent measurer.

Working capital The difference between the current assets and the current liabilities.

ASSIGNMENT MATERIAL

Assessing Your Recall

1. Describe and illustrate the three major types of activities in which all corporations engage.

2. Describe and illustrate the three major categories of items that appear in a typical balance sheet.

3. Describe the purpose of the three main financial statements that are contained in all annual reports.

4. Discuss the meaning of Generally Accepted Accounting Principles, and describe the organizations that establish these principles.

5. What is the purpose of an auditor's opinion, and what types of opinions can they render?

6. Identify at least three major users of corporate financial statements, and briefly state how they might use the information from the statements.

7. List three types of information that users should be able to learn from financial statements.

8. List and briefly describe the major qualitative characteristics that accounting information should possess, according to the CICA conceptual framework.

9. Explain the meaning of the term "books" as it is used in accounting.

◣◥ Applying Your Knowledge

10. Compare and contrast the statement of income and the statement of changes in financial position with regard to their purpose.

11. Use the following abbreviations to respond to this question.

CA	Current Assets
NCA	Noncurrent Assets
CL	Current Liabilities
NCL	Noncurrent Liabilities
SC	Share Capital
RE	Retained Earnings
NI	Income statement item
SCFP	Statement of Changes in Financial Position item

Classify the following items according to where the item would appear in the financial statements:

a. Inventory
b. Taxes payable
c. Interest expense
d. Dividends
e. Sales to customers
f. Manufacturing equipment
g. New issuance of common shares
h. Cash
i. Bonds payable (debt due in 10 years)
j. Employee wages

12. Use the following abbreviations to respond to this question.

OA	Operating Activities item
FA	Financing Activities item
IA	Investing Activities item

Classify each of the following transactions according to whether they are operating, financing, or investing activities:

a. Cash collected from customers
b. Repayment of debt
c. Payment of dividends
d. Purchase of a truck (by a manufacturing company)
e. Purchase of a truck for resale (by a truck dealer)
f. Purchase of shares of another company
g. Sale of a building
h. Utility expenses incurred

13. Compute the missing balance sheet amounts in each of the following independent situations:

	A	B	C	D
Current Assets	?	$650,000	$230,000	$40,000
Noncurrent Assets	250,000	?	400,000	?
Total Assets	?	1,050,000	?	190,000
Current Liabilities	50,000	500,000	300,000	25,000
Noncurrent Liabilities	?	90,000	?	10,000
Shareholders' Equity	225,000	?	80,000	?
Total Liabilities and Shareholders' Equity	350,000	?	?	?

14. Compute the missing amounts in the reconciliation of retained earnings in each of the following independent situations:

	A	B	C	D
Retained Earnings Dec. 31, Year 1	$20,000	$100,000	?	$40,000
Net Income	15,000	?	400,000	22,000
Dividends Declared and Paid	6,000	35,000	250,000	?
Retained Earnings Dec. 31, Year 2	?	115,000	300,000	52,000

15. For each of the following corporations, list at least two types of assets and one type of liability that you would expect to find on its balance sheet (try to include at least one item for each company that is unique to its business):

a. Transwest Energy Inc. This company is involved in oil and gas exploration and production.
b. MacMillan Bloedel This company is primarily in the forest products business, selling both paper and wood products.
c. Sask Tel (Saskatchewan Telephone Company) This telecommunications company provides phone service and equipment in Saskatchewan.
d. Sun Life This is a multiline (property/casualty, life, health, etc.) insurance company.
e. Philip Morris Companies Inc. Primarily in the tobacco business, this company has diversified into foods, beer, financial services and real estate.
f. Royal Bank of Canada This is a major commercial bank.
g. Canadian Airlines International This is a major airline.

16. For each of the corporations listed in Problem 15, list at least two line items that you would expect to find on its income statement (try to include at least one item for each company that is unique to its business).

17. For each of the corporations listed in Problem 15, list at least two line items that you would expect to find on its statement of changes in financial position (try to include at least one item for each company that is unique to its business).

◤◣ Reading and Interpreting Published Financial Statements

Base your answers to problems 18-26 on the financial statements for AT Plastics Inc. in Exhibit 1-5.

18. Determine the amount of dividends that AT Plastics Inc. declared in 1994. The only events that affected retained earnings were dividends and earnings.

19. Verify that total assets equal total liabilities and shareholders' equity for AT Plastics Inc. in 1994.

20. AT Plastics Inc. prepared a classified balance sheet. Calculate the amount of working capital that AT Plastics Inc. had at the end of 1994. State explicitly what assets and liabilities you have included as current for the purpose of your calculation.

21. Find the following amounts in the statements of AT Plastics Inc.:
    a. Revenues from sale of goods in 1994
    b. Cost of services sold in 1994
    c. Interest expense in 1994
    d. Income tax expense (Provision for income taxes) in 1993
    e. Net income in 1993
    f. Inventories at the end of 1994
    g. Accounts payable at the beginning of 1994
    h. Retained earnings at the end of 1994
    i. Long-term borrowings at the beginning of 1994
    j. Cash produced from operating activities in 1994
    k. Cash payments to acquire property, plant, and equipment (fixed assets) in 1994
    l. Cash proceeds from new borrowings in 1994
    m. Cash produced or used for investing activities in 1994

22. Did AT Plastics Inc. finance the corporation mainly from creditors (total liabilities) or from shareholders (shareholders' equity) in 1994? Support your answer with appropriate data.

23. List the three largest sources of cash and the three largest uses of cash in 1994. (Consider operations to be a single source or use of cash.)

24. Suggest some reasons why net income was $15,035,000 in 1994 yet cash flow from operations was a $21,056,000.

25. In note 9 (Exhibit 1-6), AT Plastics Inc. describes an acquisition that it made during the year. Many acquisitions result in the creation of an asset called goodwill. What do you think goodwill is, and where would you expect to find it in the financial statements of AT Plastics? If you wanted to know how much goodwill there was, where would you look?

EXHIBIT 1-5

AT PLASTICS INC.
Consolidated Balance Sheets
As at December 31

(thousands of dollars)	1994	1993
ASSETS		
CURRENT		
Cash	$ 1,357	$ –
Accounts receivable	25,968	19,756
Inventory (note 2)	26,227	23,987
Prepaids	961	435
Investment tax credits recoverable	577	439
	55,090	44,617
FIXED (note 3)	151,201	152,762
OTHER (note 4)	11,355	9,552
	$217,646	$206,931
LIABILITIES		
CURRENT		
Bank overdraft	$ –	$ 15,355
Accounts payable	24,159	18,619
Current portion of long-term debt (note 5)	5,554	158,107
Obligation under capital leases (note 6)	175	326
	29,888	192,407
LONG-TERM DEBT (note 5)	99,217	17,443
OBLIGATION UNDER CAPITAL LEASES (note 6)	496	87
OTHER LIABILITIES (note 7)	2,414	–
	102,127	17,530
	132,015	209,937
SHAREHOLDERS' EQUITY		
CAPITAL STOCK (note 8)	100,667	25,355
DEFICIT	(15,036)	(28,361)
	85,631	(3,006)
	$217,646	$206,931

See accompanying notes to consolidated financial statements.

Approved by the Board

EGERTON W. KING
Director

JOHN N. ABELL
Director

EXHIBIT 1-5 (continued)

AT PLASTICS INC.
Consolidated Statements of Operations and Deficit
For the years ended December 31

(thousands of dollars, except per share amounts)	1994	1993
SALES	$ 184,558	$ 157,494
COST OF SALES AND OTHER EXPENSES	148,086	126,821
INCOME BEFORE THE UNDERNOTED ITEMS	36,472	30,673
LESS		
Interest on long-term debt	11,617	22,724
Depreciation and amortization	10,433	13,578
Other interest	587	1,079
Other (income) expense (note 10)	(2,345)	509
	20,292	37,890
INCOME (LOSS) BEFORE INCOME TAXES	16,180	(7,217)
INCOME TAXES	1,145	502
NET INCOME (LOSS) FOR THE YEAR	15,035	(7,719)
DEFICIT AT BEGINNING OF YEAR	(28,361)	(20,642)
DIVIDENDS	(1,710)	–
DEFICIT AT END OF YEAR	$ (15,036)	$ (28,361)
NET INCOME (LOSS) PER SHARE (note 12)	$ 1.29	$ (1.97)

See accompanying notes to consolidated financial statements.

26. AT Plastics Inc. indicates that the prices of its common shares in the fourth quarter of 1994 ranged from $12.125 to $10.25 per share. Note 8 (Exhibit 1-7) shows that there were 12,668,416 common shares outstanding at the end of 1994. Compute the average total market value of the common shares of AT Plastics Inc. in the fourth quarter of 1994. Compare this with the value of shareholders' equity at the end of 1994 as represented in the balance sheet. If these numbers are different, offer an explanation for this discrepancy.

Base your answers to Problems 27-33 on the 1995 financial statements of Mosaid Technologies Incorporated, which are in Exhibit 1-8. Mosaid Technologies, an Ontario corporation, designs memory chips and supplies engineering test systems around the world.

27. Find the following amounts in the statements of Mosaid Technologies Inc.:
    a. Revenues from operations in 1995
    b. Cost of products sold (labour and materials) in 1995
    c. Interest revenue in 1995
    d. Income tax expense in 1995
    e. Net Income in 1994
    f. Inventories at the end of 1995

EXHIBIT 1-5 (continued)

AT PLASTICS INC.
Consolidated Statements of Changes in Financial Position
For the years ended December 31

(thousands of dollars)	1994	1993
CASH FROM (USED IN)		
OPERATIONS		
Net income (loss) for the year	$ 15,035	$ (7,719)
Add items charged to income not affecting cash		
Depreciation and amortization	10,433	13,578
Amortization of exchange on long-term debt	352	–
Gain on settlement of debt	(2,697)	–
Cash flow before change in working capital	23,123	5,859
Change in operating working capital	(2,067)	930
	21,056	6,789
FINANCING ACTIVITIES		
Senior secured notes issued	97,731	–
Common Shares issued	72,312	–
Preferred Shares issued	3,000	–
Long-term debt repaid	(165,047)	(11,124)
Change in capital leases	233	(431)
Interest accrued on long-term debt	–	10,383
	8,229	(1,172)
DIVIDENDS PAID	(1,710)	–
INVESTING ACTIVITIES		
Purchase of fixed assets	(9,018)	(5,857)
Change in other assets	(1,845)	(1,698)
	(10,863)	(7,555)
INCREASE (DECREASE) IN CASH DURING YEAR	16,712	(1,938)
BANK OVERDRAFT AT BEGINNING OF YEAR	(15,355)	(13,417)
CASH (BANK OVERDRAFT) AT END OF YEAR	$ 1,357	$ (15,355)

See accompanying notes to consolidated financial statements.

    g. Accounts Payable at the beginning of 1995
    h. Retained earnings at the end of 1995
    i. Obligations under capital leases at the beginning of 1995
    j. Cash produced from operating activities in 1995
    k. Cash payments to acquire property, plant, and equipment (exclude leased assets) in 1995
    l. Dividends paid in 1995
    m. Cash proceeds from new share issuances in 1995
    n. Cash produced or used for investing activities in 1995

EXHIBIT 1-6

AT PLASTICS INC.
Excerpted from Notes to the Statements

9. Acquisition

During 1994, the Company acquired the remaining 50% of the issued and outstanding shares of Alberta Ag-Industries Ltd. The purchase method has been used to account for this transaction and the results of operations are included from the effective date of the acquisition. The excess of the purchase price over the assigned values of the assets acquired has been recorded as goodwill in the amount of $1,109,000. Prior to the date of acquisition:

I) the investment was accounted for using the equity basis.

II) the Company made sales in the normal course of business to Alberta Ag-Industries Ltd. in the amount of $5,770,000 (1993 - $5,443,000).

EXHIBIT 1-7

AT PLASTICS INC.
Excerpted from Notes to the Statements

8. Capital Stock

Issued and fully paid

(thousands of dollars, except numbers of shares)	1994 NUMBER OF SHARES	1994 AMOUNT	1993 NUMBER OF SHARES	1993 AMOUNT
Common shares	12,668,416	$ 97,667	–	$ –
Series 2 Class 11 Preferred Shares	3,000	3,000	–	–
Series 1 Class 11 Preferred Shares	–	–	500,000	3,500
Series 1 Class A shares	–	–	1,556,598	19,968
Series 2 Class A shares	–	–	89,846	872
Series 6 Class A shares	–	–	1,545	15
Series 1 Class B shares	–	–	57,635	835
Series 2 Class B shares	–	–	11,365	165
Series 1 Class C shares	–	–	266,975	–
Series 2 Class C shares	–	–	64,025	–
	12,671,416	$ 100,667	2,547,989	$ 25,355

During 1994:

A. Prior to an initial public offering of Common Shares in February 1994 (Note B):

I) all issued Class A, B and C and Class II Preferred Shares were converted on a one for one basis to Common Shares.

II) the Common Shares were split on a 1.5416 for one basis.

AT PLASTICS INC.
Excerpted from Notes to the Statements

III) the articles of the Company were amended and restated to provide for an authorized capital comprising an unlimited number of Class I and Class II Preferred Shares and an unlimited number of Common Shares. The series 2 Class II Preferred Shares are non-voting, convertible and are redeemable and retractable after June 14, 1999.

IV) the Company issued 72,006 Common Shares (post-share split) to certain institutional shareholders for no consideration.

B. Pursuant to an initial public offering the Company issued 8,627,205 Common Shares, for net proceeds of $71,997,000 and 3,000 series 2 Class II Preferred Shares, for net proceeds of $3,000,000.

C. 41,200 Common Shares were issued under a share purchase plan, for net proceeds of $315,000.

The authorized capital at December 31, 1993 consisted of Class I and II Preferred Shares, Class A, B and C shares, Common Shares and non-voting equity shares. During 1994 the authorized capital was amended and restated as noted in 8A(iii).

As of December 31, 1994, options to purchase 220,551 Common Shares at an exercise price of $9.00 were outstanding. These options are exercisable over time and expire at the latest June 1999.

28. Does Mosaid Technologies Inc. finance its business primarily from creditors (total liabilities) or from shareholders (shareholders' equity) in 1995? Support your answer with appropriate data.

29. When is Mosaid Technologies Inc.'s fiscal year-end?

30. List the three largest sources of cash and the three largest uses of cash in 1995. (Consider operations to be a single source or use of cash.)

31. Suggest some reasons why net income in 1995 is up substantially from that in 1994.

32. List the three assets and the three liabilities that experienced the largest dollar changes from the end of 1994 to the end of 1995.

EXHIBIT 1-8

MOSAID TECHNOLOGIES INCORPORATED
Consolidated Statement of Earnings and Retained Earnings
Years ended April 30, 1995 and 1994
(in thousands, except per share amounts)

	1995	1994
Revenues		
Operations	$ 23,202	$ 14,348
Interest	1,084	369
	$ 24,286	$ 14,717
Expenses		
Labour and materials	5,275	3,979
Research and development (Note 8)	4,741	3,228
Selling and marketing	4,576	2,573
General and administration (Note 8)	2,578	1,618
Foreign exchange loss (gain)	147	(222)
Bad debt (recovery) expense	(19)	74
	17,298	11,250
Earnings before income taxes	6,988	3,467
Income tax expense (Note 3)	2,504	542
Net earnings	4,484	2,925
Retained earnings, beginning of year	4,560	1,635
Retained earnings, end of year	$ 9,044	$ 4,560
Earnings per share (Note 11)		
Basic	$ .66	$ .59
Fully diluted	$ .60	$ .51

See accompanying Notes to the Consolidated Financial Statements.

EXHIBIT 1-8 (continued)

MOSAID TECHNOLOGIES INCORPORATED
Consolidated Balance Sheets
Years ended April 30, 1995 and 1994

(in thousands)	1995	1994
Current Assets		
Cash and short-term marketable securities	**$ 19,364**	$ 18,579
Accounts receivable	**7,738**	3,550
Revenues recognized in excess of amounts billed	**965**	628
Income taxes receivable	**-**	476
Inventories (Note 2)	**1,966**	889
Prepaid expenses	**135**	145
	30,168	24,267
Investment Tax Credits (Note 3)	**700**	285
Capital Assets (Note 4)	**2,808**	1,043
Other Assets	**-**	50
	$ 33,676	$ 25,645
Current Liabilities		
Accounts payable and accrued liabilities	**$ 3,691**	$ 2,121
Income taxes payable	**32**	-
Deferred income taxes	**249**	-
Deferred revenue	**749**	189
Obligations under capital leases – current portion	**22**	61
	4,743	2,371
Obligations Under Capital Leases	**50**	9
Deferred Income Taxes	**756**	-
	$ 5,549	$ 2,380
Shareholders' Equity		
Share capital (Note 7)	**19,083**	18,705
Retained earnings	**9,044**	4,560
	28,127	23,265
	$ 33,676	$ 25,645

See accompanying Notes to the Consolidated Financial Statements.

Thomas I. Csathy
Director

Robert F. Harland
Director

EXHIBIT 1-8 (continued)

MOSAID TECHNOLOGIES INCORPORATED
Consolidated Statement of Changes in Financial Position
Years ended April 30, 1995 and 1994

(in thousands)	1995	1994
Operating		
Net earnings	$ 4,484	$ 2,925
Items not affecting cash		
Amortization	912	485
Loss (gain) on disposal of capital assets	7	(24)
Investment tax credits	(415)	-
Deferred income taxes	1,005	-
	5,993	3,386
Change in non-cash working capital items	(2,954)	(461)
	3,039	2,925
Investing		
Acquisition of capital assets – net	(2,618)	(789)
Proceeds from disposal of capital assets	2	42
Acquisition of capital assets under capital leases	(68)	-
Other assets	50	(50)
	(2,634)	(797)
Financing		
Increase in obligations under capital leases	68	-
Repayment of obligations under capital leases	(66)	(73)
Issue of common shares (net of costs of $29; 1994 – $1,345)	378	16,438
	380	16,365
Net cash inflow	785	18,493
Cash position, beginning of year	18,579	86
Cash position, end of year	$ 19,364	$ 18,579
Cash comprises the following:		
Cash	$ 3,879	$ 735
Marketable securities	15,485	17,844
	$ 19,364	$ 18,579

See accompanying Notes to the Consolidated Financial Statements.

33. Total assets of Mosaid Technologies Inc. at April 30, 1994, and April 30, 1995, were $25,645 thousand and $33,676 thousand, respectively. Total shareholders' equity at these same two dates was $23,265 thousand and $28,127 thousand, respectively. Compute the ratio of debt to total assets for each of the years 1994 and 1995. How has Mosaid Technologies Inc. been financing its business?

EXHIBIT 1-9

FUNDY CABLE LTD./LTEE
Consolidated Statements of Income
For the years ended August 31, 1994 and 1993

(in thousands of dollars, except per share amounts)	1994	1993
Revenue	$43,221	$34,680
Expenses		
Operating	16,723	13,043
Administrative and selling	11,069	10,194
Programming	1,104	830
	28,896	24,067
Operating Income Before the Following	14,325	10,613
Interest on long-term debt	6,202	4,838
Other interest	122	96
Amortization of bond discount	(1,071)	(775)
Depreciation	4,360	3,597
Amortization	1,788	1,192
Gain on disposal of fixed assets	(88)	-
	11,313	8,948
Income Before Income Taxes and Share of Losses of an Affiliated Company	3,012	1,665
Provision for (Recovery of) Income Taxes (Note 8)	789	(82)
	2,223	1,747
Share of Losses of an Affiliated Company	(2,446)	(2,286)
Loss for the Year	($223)	($539)
Loss applicable to Multiple Voting Shares and Subordinate Voting Shares	($523)	($882)
Basic Earnings (Loss) per Share (Note 9)	($0.13)	($0.30)
Weighted Average Number of Outstanding Shares	3,926,000	2,929,000

See accompanying Notes to Consolidated Financial Statements

FUNDY CABLE LTD./LTÉE
CONSOLIDATED STATEMENTS OF DEFICIT
FOR THE YEARS ENDED AUGUST 31, 1994 AND 1993

(in thousands of dollars)	1994	1993
Balance - Beginning of Year	($7,701)	($6,819)
Adjustments on amalgamation - February 1, 1994	36	-
Loss for the year	(223)	(539)
Dividends - Preferred	(300)	(343)
	(487)	(882)
Balance - End of Year	($8,188)	($7,701)

See accompanying Notes to Consolidated Financial Statements

EXHIBIT 1-9 (continued)

FUNDY CABLE LTD./LTEE
Consolidated Balance Sheets
As at August 31, 1994 and 1993

(in thousands of dollars)	1994	1993
Assets (Note 6)		
Current Assets		
Accounts receivable	$2,891	$2,464
Due from affiliated companies	66	188
Inventory	415	487
Prepaid expenses	390	263
	3,762	3,402
Investment in an Affiliated Company (Note 3)	10,167	9,513
Fixed Assets (Note 4)	31,392	23,197
Other Assets (Note 5)	55,599	17,573
	$100,920	$53,685
Liabilities and Shareholders' Equity		
Current Liabilities		
Bank advances (Note 6)	$5,090	$1,353
Accounts payable and accrued liabilities	6,419	4,433
Income taxes payable	358	55
Prepaid subscriber balances	1,579	764
Current portion of long-term debt	1,170	3,069
	14,616	9,674
Long-Term Debt (Note 6)	70,069	49,613
Deferred Income Taxes	517	1,129
	85,202	60,416
Shareholders' Equity		
Capital Stock (Notes 6 and 7)	23,906	970
Deficit	(8,188)	(7,701)
	15,718	(6,731)
	$100,920	$53,685

See accompanying Notes to Consolidated Financial Statements

On Behalf of the Board

Director   Director

EXHIBIT 1-9 (continued)

FUNDY CABLE LTD./LTEE
Consolidated Statements of Changes in Financial Position
For the years ended August 31, 1994 and 1993

(in thousands of dollars, except per share amounts)	1994	1993
Operating Activities		
Net income before share of losses of an affiliated company	$2,223	$1,747
Items not affecting cash -		
Depreciation	4,360	3,597
Amortization	1,788	1,192
Amortization of bond discount	(1,071)	(775)
(Gain) loss on disposal of fixed assets	(88)	72
Deferred income taxes	377	(175)
Cash flow from operations before the following	7,589	5,658
Change in non-cash working capital balances	2,643	595
	10,232	6,253
Investing Activities		
Net fixed asset additions	(8,407)	(4,337)
Fixed assets acquired on purchase of CSL	(4,060)	-
Net increase in other assets	(38,814)	(83)
Deposit on aquisitions	(1,000)	(2,000)
Increase in deferred tax liability	210	-
Increase in investment in an affiliated company	(2,029)	(1,108)
	(54,100)	(7,528)
Financing Activities		
Increase in long-term debt - net	18,557	856
Issue of capital stock - net	21,874	-
Redemption of shares	-	(358)
Dividends - Preferred	(300)	(343)
	40,131	155
Increase in Bank Advances	(3,737)	(1,120)
Bank Advances - Beginning of Year	(1,353)	(233)
Bank Advances - End of Year	($5,090)	($1,353)
Cash Flow from Operations, net of Dividends on Preferred Shares	$7,289	$5,315
Cash Flow per Share (Note 9)	$1.86	$1.81

See accompanying Notes to Consolidated Financial Statements

Base your answers to problems 34-39 on the financial statements of Fundy Cable Ltd. which are included in Exhibit 1-9. Fundy Cable, a New Brunswick corporation, is a Canadian communication company primarily involved in cable television distribution.

34. Find the following amounts in the statements of Fundy Cable Ltd.:
    a. Revenue in 1994
    b. Cost of products sold (operating expense) in 1994
    c. Interest expense in 1993
    d. Income tax expense in 1994
    e. Net income (loss) in 1994
    f. Inventory at the beginning of 1994
    g. Prepaid subscriber balances in 1994
    h. Retained earnings at the end of 1994
    i. Long-term borrowings at the beginning of 1994
    j. Cash produced from operating activities in 1994
    k. Cash payments to acquire property, plant, and equipment (fixed assets) in 1994 (net)
    l. Dividends paid in 1994
    m. Cash produced or used for investing activities in 1994

35. Does Fundy Cable Ltd. finance its business primarily from creditors (total liabilities) or from shareholders (shareholders' equity) in 1994? Support your answer with appropriate data.

36. When is Fundy Cable Ltd.'s fiscal year-end?

37. List the three largest sources of cash and the three largest uses of cash in 1994. (Consider operations to be a single source or use of cash.)

38. Explain the change in retained earnings from the end of 1993 to the end of 1994.

39. Net income from continuing operations has increased during the year, yet the cash balance (i.e., bank advances — Fundy Cable Ltd. has no cash but rather a line of credit with the bank) has significantly declined over the same period. From the major categories presented on the statement of changes in financial position, can you suggest reasons why Fundy Cable Ltd. has experienced this decrease in cash?

Base your answers to Problems 40-44 on the financial statements of Nokia Corporation and Subsidiaries presented in Exhibit 1-10.

40. Find the following amounts in the statements of Nokia Corporation (express your answers in both Finnish Markka and U.S. dollars, if possible):
    a. Net sales in 1994
    b. Cost of products sold in 1994
    c. Interest expense in 1994
    d. Income tax expense in 1994
    e. Net income in 1994
    f. Inventories at the beginning of 1994
    g. Accounts payable and accrued liabilities at the beginning of 1994
    h. Retained earnings at the end of 1994
    i. Share capital at the beginning of 1994

EXHIBIT 1-10

NOKIA CORPORATION AND SUBSIDIARIES
Consolidated Profit and Loss Statement
(in millions, except for per share amounts)

	Year ended December 31,			
	1992	1993	1994	1994
Net sales	FIM 18,168	FIM 23,697	FIM 30,177	USD 7,052
Cost of goods sold	(13,354)	(17,216)	(20,808)	(4,863)
Research and development expenses	(1,113)	(1,472)	(1,937)	(453)
Selling, general and administrative expenses	(3,413)	(3,544)	(3,836)	(896)
Operating profit	288	1,465	3,596	840
Share of results of associated companies, net of tax	(5)	28	22	5
Financial income and expenses	(441)	(347)	384	90
Profit (loss) before tax, minority interests and extraordinary items	(158)	1,146	4,002	935
Tax	(167)	(229)	(932)	(218)
Minority interests	(88)	(80)	(75)	(17)
Profit (loss) before extraordinary items	(413)	767	2,995	700
Extraordinary items	(310)	(1,917)	944	221
Net profit (loss)	FIM (723)	FIM (1,150)	FIM 3,939	USD 921
Earnings (loss) per share	FIM (1.71)	FIM 3.07	FIM 10.97	USD 2.56

  j. Cash produced from operating activities in 1994
  k. Cash payments to acquire property, plant and equipment (capital expenditures) in 1994
  l. Dividends paid in 1994
  m. Cash proceeds from new borrowings in 1994
  n. Cash proceeds from the issuance of common shares in 1994

41. Did Nokia Corporation finance its business primarily from creditors (total liabilities) or from shareholders (shareholders' equity) in 1994? Support your answer with appropriate data.

42. When is Nokia Corporations' fiscal year-end?

43. In 1994 net income was FIM 3,939 yet the net cash flow was FIM 2,260. From the major categories presented on the cash flow statement, suggest reasons why this might be the case for Nokia Corporation.

44. Describe any major differences you see between the information presented in the Nokia Corporation and AT Plastics Ltd. statements (Exhibit 1-5).

EXHIBIT 1-10 (continued)

NOKIA CORPORATION AND SUBSIDIARIES
Consolidated Balance Sheet
(in millions)

	December 31,		
	1993	1994	1994
ASSETS			
Current assets			
Cash and cash equivalents	FIM 3,297	FIM 5,268	USD 1,231
Accounts receivable, less allowance for doubtful accounts (1993 MFIM 159, 1994 MFIM 197)	6,227	7,935	1,831
Inventories	5,129	6,803	1,590
	14,653	20,006	4,652
Property, plant and equipment, net	4,770	5,097	1,191
Investments	2,092	1,810	423
Goodwill and other intangible assets	590	541	126
Long-term loan receivables	278	222	52
Other non-current assets	264	273	64
	7,994	7,943	1,856
Total assets	FIM 22,647	FIM 27,949	USD 6,508
LIABILITIES AND SHAREHOLDERS' EQUITY			
Current Liabilities			
Short-term borrowings	FIM 3,435	FIM 2,453	USD 573
Current portion of long-term debt	139	278	65
Accounts payable and accrued liabilities	5,976	8,086	1,890
Advance payments	534	502	117
Restructuring provision	1,436	-	
	11,520	11,319	2,645
Long-term liabilities			
Long-term debt	3,397	3,071	718
Other long-term liabilities	683	486	113
	4,080	3,557	831
Minority interest	536	555	130
Shareholders' equity			
Share capital	1,378	1,498	350
Other restricted equity	3,329	5,594	1,284
Treasury shares	(348)	(437)	(102)
Untaxed reserves	1,717	1,727	404
Retained earnings	435	4,136	966
	6,511	12,518	2,902
Total liabilities and shareholder's equity	FIM 22,647	FIM 27,949	USD 6,508

EXHIBIT 1-10 (continued)

NOKIA CORPORATION AND SUBSIDIARIES
Consolidated Cash Flow Statement
(in millions)

	Year ended December 31,			
	1992	1993	1994	1994
Cash flow from operating activities				
Profit (loss) before tax, minority interests and extraordinary items	FIM (158)	FIM 1,146	FIM 4,002	USD 935
Adjustments for:				
Depreciation	950	996	1,009	236
Equity hedging	—	—	259	61
Unrealized foreign exchange gains and losses	216	79	(171)	(40)
Share of result of associated companies	31	3	(22)	(5)
Other operating income and expenses	(56)	(41)	(222)	(52)
Dividend income	(98)	(152)	(142)	(33)
Interest income	(550)	(524)	(405)	(95)
Interest expense	928	858	580	135
Operating profit before change in net working capital	1,263	2,365	4,888	1,142
Short-term trade receivables, (increase)	(461)	(697)	(1,312)	(306)
Inventories, (increase) decrease	271	(1,182)	(2,262)	(529)
Interest-free short-term liabilities, increase	574	815	2,124	496
Cash generated from operations	1,647	1,301	3,438	803
Interest received	635	531	349	(82)
Interest paid	(941)	(908)	(568)	(133)
Income taxes paid	168	(133)	(326)	(76)
Cash flow before extraordinary items	1,173	791	2,893	676
Extraordinary expenses paid	(263)	(86)	(350)	(82)
Net cash from operating activities	910	705	2,543	594
Cash flow from investing activities				
Acquisition of Group companies, net of acquired cash	(155)	(471)	(80)	(19)
Treasury shares acquired	(345)	—	(78)	(18)
Investments in other shares	(44)	(100)	(351)	(82)
Capital expenditures	(838)	(1,186)	(1,967)	(460)
Proceeds from disposal of shares in Group companies, net of disposed cash	3	191	45	11

EXHIBIT 1-10 (continued)

NOKIA CORPORATION AND SUBSIDIARIES
Consolidated Cash Flow Statement
(in millions)

| | Year ended December 31, | | | |
	1992	1993	1994	1994
Proceeds from sale of other shares	14	864	634	148
Proceeds from sale of fixed assets	144	177	24	6
Dividends received	98	152	142	33
Net cash used in investing activities	(1,123)	(373)	(1,631)	(381)
Cash flow from financing activities				
Proceeds from issuance of share capital	—	918	2,490	582
Capital investment by minority shareholders	19	5	23	5
Proceeds from (payments of) long-term liabilities	(1,098)	479	(267)	(62)
Proceeds from (payments of) short-term borrowings	476	(1,582)	(571)	(134)
Proceeds from (payments of) short-term receivables	243	(24)	29	7
Dividends paid	(158)	(173)	(211)	(49)
Net cash provdied by (used in) financing activities	(594)	(261)	1,348	315
Net increase (decrease) in cash and cash equivalents	(807)	71	2,260	528
Cash and cash equivalents at beginning of period	3,925	3,226	3,008	703
Cash and cash equivalents at end of period	FIM 3,118	FIM 3,297	FIM 5,268	USD 1,231

◤◣ Critical Thinking Question

Donna Bovolaneas and Pankaj Puri (*CA Magazine*, October 1995) argue that the accounting guidelines for life insurance companies, banks, trust companies, and securities dealers should be similar.

1. Briefly discuss the differences in the business activities undertaken by corporations in these industries compared to the business activities of most other corporations.

2. Briefly discuss why the accounting guidelines for these industries might be different from those of other industries.

3. Briefly discuss why accounting guidelines should be identical for all industries.

4. Briefly discuss why accounting guidelines should not be identical for all industries.

APPENDIX A

CONTENTS

CORPORATE PROFILE

BIG ROCK BREWERY LTD. is a regional producer and marketer of specialty draught and bottled beer located in Calgary, Alberta, Canada. Founded in 1985 by Ed McNally, the Company is dedicated to the brewing of premium beers using only malted barley, hops, water and yeast. The Company's products are currently marketed in the four Western Canadian provinces of Alberta, British Columbia, Saskatchewan and Manitoba and also through independent distributors in the United States. Big Rock Brewery has enjoyed consistent growth through careful marketing, utilization of innovative brewing technology and unfailing attention to quality control.

Cover illustration by
Big Rock Artist, Dirk Van Wyk

NOTICE OF ANNUAL
MEETING OF SHAREHOLDERS

July 31, 1995
11:00 A.M.
Auditorium
3rd Floor, Bow Valley Square II
205 - 5th Avenue S.W.
Calgary, Alberta

FINANCIAL HIGHLIGHTS

| | March 31 | | | | September 30 | | |
	1995	1994	1993	(Six Months) 1992	1991	1990	1989
Net Sales	$13,689,792	$9,568,287	$7,035,849	$2,901,668	$5,451,167	$3,842,121	$2,752,985
Income before Income Tax	2,802,332	2,099,721	1,427,237	465,007	936,010	385,107	162,338
Net Income	1,742,332	1,307,721	924,737	297,007	887,710	354,696	135,680
Earnings per share	0.40	0.30	0.22	0.08	0.25	0.10	0.04
Shareholders' Equity	10,198,202	8,415,870	7,108,149	3,901,329	3,156,722	2,269,012	1,794,316
Average Shares Outstanding	4,408,700	4,406,200	4,406,200	3,706,200	3,508,200	3,508,200	3,408,200

(in thousands)
12,000
11,000
10,000
9,000
8,000
7,000
6,000
5,000
4,000
3,000
2,000

1989 1990 1991 1992 (six months) 1993 1994 1995

$162 $385 $936 $465 $1,427 $2,099 $2,802

Pre-Tax Income

Sales

REPORT TO SHAREHOLDERS

A LOOK BACK

We have been so busy building and brewing at Big Rock that it is hard to believe that we are about to celebrate our tenth anniversary in the beer business. Ten years ago, we were accumulating new and used brewing equipment in a small warehouse in South East Calgary. Our objective was an ambitious one - to produce a premium, unpasteurized product with no additives or preservatives, using local two row malted barley and traditional brewing methods.

Our brewmaster, Bernd Pieper, brought invaluable experience from breweries in Europe and Africa. Although he was somewhat taken aback by our very frugal and modest beginnings, he instilled in us the confidence that we could achieve our lofty ambitions.

In a market dominated by light, pasteurized lagers, unpasteurized, European-style ales were almost unknown. We always believed that if we could consistently produce a premium, pure malt, traditional-style beer with a distinctive character and taste, we would not fail.

Our persistence was rewarded. As sales climbed, the challenges of servicing our growing markets were met. Big Rock has undergone three major capacity expansions, and each time our sales goals were met or exceeded.

The Company's growth hinged on two major factors. Strict adherence to the principles of quality and customer service have been the mainstays of our operation. Investment in state-of-the-art brewing technology has made Big Rock a leader in the industry. We were most fortunate, during our first ten years, in acquiring new technology designed to improve the quality and stability of unpasteurized beers. We purchased a new multi-micro, sterile filtration system, the first of its kind in North America. Subsequently, we purchased a double-evacuation Krones filler and an automated kegging system. From our modest beginnings we have

succeeded beyond the most optimistic expectations. Today, Big Rock is one of the leading craft brewers in North America.

As of fiscal year end, production exceeded 120,000 HL. The brewery has taken advantage of advances in brewing technology to enhance the stability and shelf life of its unpasteurized products. Utilization of cold, multi-microfiltration and oxygen exclusion in the bottling process has enabled the Company to extend its markets geographically. Big Rock products can now be found from Southern California to the Northwest Territories and from Winnipeg to Vancouver.

We have brewed a selection of beers which have won international recognition and our sales continue to grow in all areas. Introduction of innovative product lines has also contributed to the Company's expansion. Big Rock introduced Canada's first wheat ale (Grasshopper Wheat Ale) and rye ale (Magpie Rye Ale) which have boosted Company sales figures.

YEAR TO DATE

The possibility of contract brewing in Eastern Canada and the U.S. was examined extensively in 1995. Because of problems encountered in brewing the same beer with different water and in different facilities, these experiments were abandoned.

To accommodate projected growth, a decision was made to build our own completely new 300,000 HL brewery here in Calgary. Here we have the right water, the right malt and we have been able to consistently produce identical results, brew after brew. Land has been purchased for the new brewery with room to accommodate future expansion. The plans for the new structure are almost finalized and contracts for the new equipment are being studied. On completion of the new brewery, the present brewing facility will be closed. Most of the existing facility will be transferred to the new site bringing production capacity to a total of 450,000 HL.

2

A LOOK AHEAD

Another period of exciting growth has begun. All of us at Big Rock are confident that the craft brewing industry is still in its infancy and will continue double digit growth for the next five years. (This view is shared by financial analysts in the U.S. and Canada).

All of our original brewers and technicians are still with us and are eager to start on this next period of growth. We now have a second brewmaster who brings a wealth of skills to the brewery. In addition, Big Rock has established an apprenticeship program for our young brewers. In conjunction with this program, the Company will send a trainee to the Master Brewer's program at Heriot-Watt University.

Big Rock is well positioned to meet the next phase of growth. A strong team spirit, well engineered facilities and a tremendously loyal customer base give us a solid foundation upon which to grow. The enthusiasm and talent of Big Rock's employees will ensure our continued success.

Thanks to our directors who have assisted me in steering this course of steady growth. We have accomplished much together despite many challenges. We have always been unswerving in our commitment to the highest quality in brewing. The first sign we posted in the brewery is still there - "To brew a masterpiece, no compromise can be tolerated".

Special thanks to Bill Lupien who has stepped down from the Board for business reasons. He has been, and continues to be, a great friend and advisor.

The first ten years have seen tremendous changes at Big Rock. We look forward to another decade of accomplishments as we prepare for an exciting new phase of growth.

E.E. McNally, President

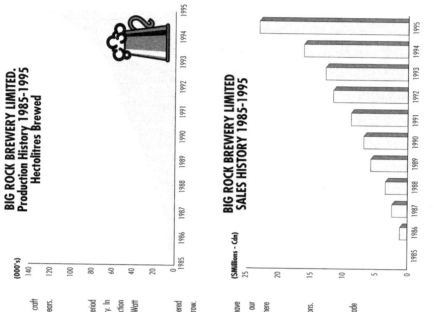

BIG ROCK BREWERY LIMITED.
Production History 1985-1995
Hectolitres Brewed

BIG ROCK BREWERY LIMITED
SALES HISTORY 1985-1995

3

BIG ROCK BREWERY LTD.

Although nothing exists in isolation, it is of some interest and appropriate brevity that we look at the transit of Jupiter in the coming months.

The jovial nature of value, expansiveness and generosity may be difficult during the retrograde motion of the planet. It's movement turns again in August.

At the end of September, the transiting Jupiter comes onto the natal Uranus position. A time for idealism with surprises and sudden opportunities. According to some house system calculations, Jupiter will enter the second house in October which would emphasize material and financial gains as value increases.

At the end of November, a conjunction is reached with natal Mars. This is a time of high energy, hard work and an emphasis on mind-body co-ordination. Caution for physical accidents is advised. At the year-end, Jupiter transits Neptune. A very idealistic time of working toward a good cause. This is not an ego trip but a good time to relate to major social causes.

The old-fashioned view of Jupiter's return to its original (natal) position was one of exceptional luck and good fortune. More contemporary interpretations of this transit are viewed as a renewal on a deeper level. A change of octave. A time to find "new" meaning. Yes, even astrological information is subject to "trendy" interpretation. After all, we can only function in this here and now (and how).

On the mundane level, all this adds up to very exciting if not to say frantic time ahead. It is in the nature (natal chart) of this brewery to be generous, expansive, and growing, but that does not have to mean the old "bigger is better". There are tendencies now to increase value within a new context.

Big Rock brewery is in the process of creating these tendencies - giving them form. We don't know what they look like or feel like but the ideology is to make them happen.

Dirk Van Wyk - Artist-in-Residence
And Occasional Astrologer

*Inspirational reading - "The Holographic Universe" - Talbot

MANAGEMENT'S DISCUSSION AND ANALYSIS

GROSS REVENUES

The Company had sales of $23.1 million representing a 43 per cent increase from the previous year.

Production volumes increased 40 per cent from 85,000 HL to 120,000 HL in 1995.

Two products accounted for a significant increase in sales volume during the year. Grasshopper Wheat Ale, which was launched in April, 1994, exceeded the company's expectations both in Canada and the United States and is currently our second biggest seller in Alberta. Warthog Ale, introduced in August, 1993, continued its growth both in Canada and the United States. Other Big Rock brands enjoyed gains during the year.

GOVERNMENT COMMISSIONS AND TAXES

Government commissions and taxes increased 43 per cent to $9.4 million consistent with the Company's sales growth. This amount reflects the Alberta Liquor Control Board Commission, Federal Sales and Excise Tax.

COST OF GOODS SOLD

During the year, the Company's cost of goods sold as a percentage of net sales decreased to 44.2 per cent from 45.6 per cent in the previous year. This improvement is attributable to increased plant efficiency, lower labour rates per unit and reduced malt cost. This success was achieved in spite of cost increases for glass, paper and energy.

SELLING, GENERAL AND ADMINISTRATIVE

Selling and administration costs for 1995 were $3.9 million in 1995 compared with $2.8 million in 1994. As a percentage of net sales, these costs were 29 per cent for both 1994 and 1995.

During the year, the Company recorded higher delivery and storage costs reflecting the increase in the number of retail liquor stores since privatization of the Alberta Liquor Control Board's retail operations.

Salaries and commissions for out-of-province operations significantly increased primarily as a result of dramatic growth both in British Columbia and Manitoba markets. The Company provides a commission to distributors on product sold and remmittance paid to the Company by Provincial liquor boards.

CAPITAL EXPENDITURES

The Company had $3.6 million in capital expenditures in 1995. Included in this amount are 16,000 Sankey kegs, an automated keg filler and sanitizing machine, six fermenters and a 22 ounce bottle filler.

LOSS ON DISPOSAL OF CAPITAL ASSETS

During the year, the Company replaced its kegs and kegging equipment to conform with current industry beer dispensing standards resulting in a $0.4 million loss. In addition, the Company wrote down a used filtration system to its current estimated value.

BANK FINANCING AND REPAYMENT

On March 31, 1995, the Company had $1.5 million in bank debt outstanding. Of this amount $1.2 million was a term loan for capital expenditures and $0.3 million was a revolving operating line. Both rates are at a floating interest rate of prime plus 1/2 and prime plus 1/8 respectively.

AUDITORS' REPORT

To the Shareholders of
Big Rock Brewery Ltd.

We have audited the balance sheet of Big Rock Brewery Ltd. as at March 31, 1995 and 1994 and the statements of income and retained earnings and changes in financial position for the year then ended. These financial statements are the responsibility of the Company's management. Our responsibility is to express an opinion on these financial statements based on our audit.

We conducted our audit in accordance with generally accepted auditing standards in Canada. Those standards require that we plan and perform an audit to obtain reasonable assurance whether the financial statements are free of material misstatement. An audit includes examining, on a test basis, evidence supporting the amounts and disclosures in the financial statements. An audit also includes assessing the accounting principles used and significant estimates made by management, as well as evaluating the overall financial statement presentation.

In our opinion, these financial statements present fairly, in all material respects, the financial position of the Company as at March 31, 1995 and 1994 and the results of its operations and the changes in its financial position for the years then ended in accordance with generally accepted accounting principles in Canada.

Calgary, Canada
May 12, 1995

Horwath, Schroeder & Tobin
**HORWATH, SCHROEDER & TOBIN
CHARTERED ACCOUNTANTS**

6

STATEMENT 1

BIG ROCK BREWERY LTD.

BALANCE SHEET
MARCH 31, 1995 AND 1994
(Denominated in Canadian Dollars)

ASSETS

	1995	1994
CURRENT ASSETS		
Cash	$ 42,317	$ 311,960
Accounts receivable	1,481,068	1,177,089
Inventories (Note 2)	1,653,042	943,033
Prepaid expenses and other	85,865	67,138
Total current assets	3,262,292	2,499,220
CAPITAL ASSETS (Note 3)	10,596,468	7,959,570
OTHER	29,535	10,000
	$ 13,888,295	$ 10,468,790

LIABILITIES

	1995	1994
CURRENT LIABILITIES		
Bank indebtedness (Note 4)	$ 408,071	$
Accounts payable	462,739	609,357
Income taxes payable	238,809	392,663
Current portion of long-term debt (Note 5)	220,476	80,400
Total current liabilities	1,330,095	1,082,420
LONG-TERM DEBT (Note 5)	956,498	89,000
DEFERRED INCOME TAXES	1,403,500	881,500
COMMITMENTS (Note 11)		
Total liabilities	3,690,093	2,052,920

SHAREHOLDERS' EQUITY

	1995	1994
SHARE CAPITAL (Note 6)	5,402,784	5,362,784
RETAINED EARNINGS (Statement 2)	4,795,418	3,053,086
Total shareholders' equity	10,198,202	8,415,870
	$ 13,888,295	$ 10,468,790

Approved by the Board:

E.E. McNally, Director

J.A. McKee, Director

7

BIG ROCK BREWERY LTD.

STATEMENT 2

STATEMENT OF INCOME AND RETAINED EARNINGS
YEARS ENDED MARCH 31, 1995 AND 1994
(Denominated in Canadian Dollars)

	1995	1994
SALES	$ 23,078,655	$ 16,140,745
GOVERNMENT COMMISSIONS AND TAXES	9,388,863	6,572,458
COST OF SALES	6,054,940	4,363,698
GROSS PROFIT	7,634,852	5,204,589
EXPENSES		
Amortization	405,451	414,946
Selling, general and administrative (Schedule)	3,942,690	2,756,846
Interest on long-term debt	43,249	12,891
Total expenses	4,391,390	3,184,683
INCOME BEFORE THE FOLLOWING	3,243,462	2,019,906
GAIN (LOSS) ON DISPOSAL OF CAPITAL ASSETS (Note 7)	(441,130)	79,815
INCOME BEFORE INCOME TAXES	2,802,332	2,099,721
INCOME TAXES (Note 8)	1,060,000	792,000
NET INCOME FOR YEAR	1,742,332	1,307,721
RETAINED EARNINGS BEGINNING OF YEAR	3,053,086	1,745,365
RETAINED EARNINGS END OF YEAR	$ 4,795,418	$ 3,053,086
EARNINGS PER SHARE (Note 9)		
Basic	40¢	30¢
Fully diluted	39¢	29¢

8

STATEMENT 3

BIG ROCK BREWERY LTD.

STATEMENT OF CHANGES IN FINANCIAL POSITION
YEARS ENDED MARCH 31, 1995 AND 1994
(Denominated in Canadian Dollars)

	1995	1994
CASH PROVIDED BY (USED FOR): OPERATING ACTIVITIES		
Net income for year (Statement 2)	$ 1,742,332	$ 1,307,721
Items not affecting cash		
Amortization	405,451	414,946
(Gain) loss on disposal of capital assets	441,130	(79,815)
Deferred income taxes	522,000	316,000
Changes in other working capital elements	(1,333,187)	(102,913)
	1,777,726	1,855,939
FINANCING ACTIVITIES		
Bank loan repayments	(292,426)	(80,400)
Bank loan borrowings	1,300,000	90,000
Share capital issued	40,000	
	1,047,574	9,600
INVESTING ACTIVITIES		
Purchase of capital assets	(3,559,438)	(1,209,930)
Deposits on capital assets	(122,498)	(263,718)
Increase in other assets	(19,535)	
Proceeds on disposal of capital assets	198,457	165,348
Share purchase loans collected		462,344
	(3,503,014)	(845,956)
NET INCREASE (DECREASE) IN CASH	(677,714)	1,019,583
CASH (DEFICIENCY) BEGINNING OF YEAR	311,960	(707,623)
CASH (DEFICIENCY) END OF YEAR	$ (365,754)	$ 311,960
CASH (DEFICIENCY) COMPRISED OF:		
Cash	42,317	311,960
Excess of cheques written over funds on deposit	(69,071)	
Demand bank loans	(339,000)	
	$ (365,754)	$ 311,960

9

BIG ROCK BREWERY LTD.

NOTES TO FINANCIAL STATEMENT

MARCH 31, 1995 AND 1994

1. SIGNIFICANT ACCOUNTING POLICIES

The company has adopted the following significant accounting policies:

a. Principles of accounting

The company follows accounting policies generally accepted in Canada. Differences from United States accounting principles are described in Note 13 to these financial statements.

All figures are reported in Canadian dollars. Exchange rates between the U.S. and Canadian dollars for each of the years reported in these financial statements, with bracketed figures reflecting the average exchange rate for the year, are:

	Canadian Equivalent of $1 U.S.
March 31, 1995	1.3837 (1.3125)
March 31, 1994	1.2469 (1.2297)

b. Inventories

Inventories of raw materials and supplies are valued at the lower of cost (first-in, first-out method) and replacement cost. Inventories of brews in process and finished product are valued at the lower of cost (including direct materials, labour and overhead costs) and net realizable value.

Returnable glass containers are initially recorded at cost. In order to charge operations for wear and disappearance the cost of bottles are charged to operations over their estimated useful life.

c. Capital assets

Capital assets are stated at cost less accumulated amortization and government assistance received. Amortization is recorded on the straight-line basis over the estimated useful lives of the assets to their estimated salvage or residual values. No amortization is recorded on assets in the year of acquisition. Amortization rates are as follows:

Buildings	40 years	2.5%
Production equipment	6 1/2 to 30 years	3.3% to 15%
Vehicles	4 years	25%
Furniture and fixtures	6 1/2 years	15%

10

1. SIGNIFICANT ACCOUNTING POLICIES (Cont'd)

d. Government assistance and investment tax credits

Government assistance in the form of grants and investment tax credits are accrued when earned. Such assistance is applied to reduce the related expenses or asset costs.

e. Revenue recognition

Revenue is recognized at the time of shipment at the gross sales price charged to the purchaser. Invoices for sales to Canadian customers are submitted to the respective provincial Liquor Control Boards who pay the company after deducting Liquor Control Board commissions. Excise taxes are assessed on production. Commissions and taxes are comprised as follows:

	1995	1994
Liquor Control Board commissions	$ 7,023,449	$ 5,135,099
Excise and sales taxes	2,365,414	1,437,359
	$ 9,388,863	$ 6,572,458

Product, which is returned due to expired shelf life and for which the customer is given credit, is netted against gross sales. Product returns totalled $81,226 in 1995 and $185,491 in 1994.

f. Deferred income taxes

The company follows the tax allocation method of accounting for the tax effect of the timing differences between taxable income and accounting income. Timing differences result principally from claiming capital cost allowance for income tax purposes in excess of amortization on capital assets.

g. Foreign Exchange

Transactions in foreign currencies are recorded in Canadian dollars at the exchange rates in effect at the date of the transaction. Monetary assets and liabilities in foreign currencies have been converted to Canadian dollars at exchange rates in effect at the balance sheet date. Foreign exchange gains and losses included in earnings for the year are not material.

h. Earnings per share

Earnings per share are calculated using the weighted average number of shares outstanding during the period.

11

2. INVENTORIES

	1995	1994
Raw materials and returnable glass	$ 1,027,743	$ 562,084
Brews in progress	196,737	165,668
Finished product	333,509	131,162
Dispensing units	38,142	42,124
Promotional goods	56,911	41,995
	$ 1,653,042	$ 943,033

3. CAPITAL ASSETS

	1995			1994
	Cost	Accumulated Amortization	Net Book Value	Net Book Value
Land	$ 328,200	$	$ 328,200	$ 328,200
Buildings	2,340,840	298,185	2,042,655	2,034,972
Production equipment	8,480,033	925,797	7,554,236	5,024,530
Vehicles	130,451	90,622	39,829	46,004
Furniture and fixtures	199,974	69,030	130,944	98,593
Surplus equipment	114,388		114,388	163,553
Equipment deposits (Note 11)	386,216		386,216	263,718
	$11,980,102	$1,383,634	$10,596,468	$ 7,959,570

The cost of building and equipment includes capitalized interest and labour totalling $702,438 for the year ended March 31, 1995 (1994 - $477,898). $40,000 interest was capitalized in the year (1994 - $NIL).

Surplus equipment, for which the company is seeking purchasers, consists of brewing and bottling equipment.

12

4. BANK INDEBTEDNESS

	1995	1994
Excess of cheques written over funds on deposit	$ 69,071	
Revolving demand loan	339,000	
	$ 408,071	

The company has a revolving line of credit to a maximum limit of $750,000 and which bears interest at Royal Bank prime plus 1/8% per annum (effective rate at March 31, 1995 - 9.875%; March 31, 1994 - 6.5%).

A general security agreement and a general assignment of book debts has been provided as security.

5. LONG-TERM DEBT

	1995	1994
Royal Bank demand term loan bearing interest at prime plus 1/2% per annum with monthly blended interest and principal payments of $26,700. A fixed and floating charge debenture on the land, buildings and equipment and an assignment of fire and life insurance has been provided as security.	$1,176,974	
Royal Bank demand term loan repaid in the year		$ 169,400
Less current portion	(220,476)	(80,400)
	$ 956,498	$ 89,000

Estimated principal repayments required for subsequent years are as follows:

Year ending March 31,		
1996	$	220,476
1997		241,918
1998		265,446
1999		291,263
2000		157,871
		$ 1,176,974

13

6. SHARE CAPITAL

Authorized

Twenty million (20,000,000) common shares.

One million (1,000,000) preferred shares which may be issued in one or more series with rights, privileges, restrictions and conditions as fixed by the directors prior to the issue of each series.

Common Shares Outstanding

	1995		1994	
	Shares	Amount	Shares	Amount
Beginning of year	4,406,200	$ 5,362,784	4,406,200	$ 5,362,784
Stock options exercised in the year	10,000	40,000		
End of year	4,416,200	$ 5,402,784	4,406,200	$ 5,362,784

As of March 31, 1995, 310,000 (1994 - 120,000) common shares were reserved for the exercising of stock options by staff, two of the directors and a consultant to the company. These options are exercisable as follows:

Expiry Date	# of Shares	Exercise Value
October 31, 1997	110,000	$ 4.00
December 15, 1999	200,000	$14.65

7. LOSS ON DISPOSAL OF CAPITAL ASSETS

During the year, the company replaced its kegs and kegging equipment to conform with the most current industry beer dispensing standards. A loss of $379,130 resulted on the disposal. In addition, the company wrote down certain other surplus equipment to its estimated salvage value by $62,000.

14

8. INCOME TAXES

The company is classified as a public company for Canadian income tax purposes engaged in manufacturing and processing activities. Statutory tax rates in effect on March 31, 1995 were 37.4% (1994 - 38.4%) on taxable income. The company's effective tax expense is summarized as follows:

	1995	1994
Income before income tax expense	$ 2,802,332	$ 2,099,721
Income tax expense at statutory rate	1,046,400	806,000
Effect on taxes of		
Non-deductible expenses	19,800	4,300
Deductible share issuance costs	(16,400)	(16,800)
Other (net)	10,200	(1,500)
Income tax expense (effective rate: 37.8%, 1994 - 37.7%)	$ 1,060,000	$ 792,000
Current income tax expense	538,000	476,000
Deferred income tax expense	522,000	316,000
	$ 1,060,000	$ 792,000

9. EARNINGS PER SHARE

	1995	1994
Basic	40¢	30¢
Average common shares outstanding	4,408,700	4,406,200
Fully diluted	39¢	29¢
Average common shares	4,584,533	4,526,200

To determine fully diluted earnings per share, net income consists of net income per financial statements plus an assumed rate of return, after income taxes, on the proceeds which would have been received on the exercise of options. The options are treated, for calculation of average common shares, as if exercised at the beginning of the year or on the day the options were granted, if later.

15

10. REMUNERATION OF DIRECTORS AND OFFICERS

Direct remuneration to Directors and Officers of the company (2 individuals) totalled $255,240 for the year ended March 31, 1995 (March 31, 1994 - $216,000).

11. COMMITMENTS

The company leases warehouse premises in Edmonton and Calgary on which the leases expire in August, 1997 and 1999 respectively. Annual lease payments, including estimated utilities and property taxes, are as follows:

1996	$ 117,000
1997	101,000
1998	91,000
1999 (five months)	38,000

The company has committed to purchase kegs and fermentation tanks for a total cost of $1,200,000 of which $386,216 had been paid as a deposit at year end and is included in capital assets.

12. INDUSTRY SEGMENT

The company's principal business activity is the production and marketing of specialty draught and bottled beer. The company's beers are primarily marketed in Alberta, Canada and in accordance with provincial laws, all beer sold in the Province must be sold through the Alberta Liquor Control Board (ALCB) or establishments licensed by the ALCB. Sales through independent distributors in the Western United States comprise approximately 23.5% of net sales for the year ended March 31, 1995 and 24% for the year ended March 31, 1994.

13. DIFFERENCES BETWEEN CANADIAN AND UNITED STATES GENERALLY ACCEPTED ACCOUNTING PRINCIPLES

Generally accepted accounting principles ("G.A.A.P.") used in the United States of America differ in certain respects from G.A.A.P. used in Canada. Differences which materially affect these financial statements are:

a. Demand Loans

In accordance with Canadian banking practices all of the company's bank loans are payable on demand but provide for monthly repayment instalments over an assumed term and accordingly are classified as long-term debt for amounts due in the following fiscal period. United States G.A.A.P. classify all demand loans as current liabilities and not as long-term debt.

16

13. DIFFERENCES BETWEEN CANADIAN AND UNITED STATES GENERALLY ACCEPTED ACCOUNTING PRINCIPLES

b. Earnings Per Share

United States G.A.A.P. calculation

Net income per share based upon the weighted average numbers of shares outstanding during each year plus common stock equivalents, such as common share purchase options unless they are antidilutive. Primary income per share would be computed as if common share purchase options were exercised at the beginning of the year, and as if funds obtained thereby were used to purchase common shares of the company for cancellation at the average market price during the year. Fully diluted net income per share would be calculated as if the proceeds from the exercise of common share purchase options were used to purchase the company's common shares at its average market price during the year or its market value at the end of the year whichever is higher.

Had the financial statements been prepared in accordance with United States G.A.A.P. as previously described, the following changes would have been made:

	1995	1994
LIABILITIES		
Total current liabilities		
Canadian G.A.A.P.	$ 1,372,235	$ 1,082,420
Long-term debt repayable on demand for which repayment provisions have been agreed to	956,498	89,000
United States G.A.A.P.	$ 2,328,833	$ 1,171,420
Long-term debt		
Canadian G.A.A.P.	$ 956,498	$ 89,000
Transferred to current liabilities	(956,498)	(89,000)
United States G.A.A.P.		

17

13. DIFFERENCES BETWEEN CANADIAN AND UNITED STATES GENERALLY ACCEPTED ACCOUNTING PRINCIPLES (Cont'd)

STATEMENT OF CHANGES IN FINANCIAL POSITION

Under United States G.A.A.P. the statement of changes in financial position is called the statement of cash flow. The application of United States G.A.A.P. as noted above would necessitate the following presentation changes:

	1995	1994
Financing Activities		
Canadian G.A.A.P.		$ 9,600
Share purchase loans repaid		462,344
United States G.A.A.P.		$ 471,944
Investing Activities		
Canadian G.A.A.P.		$ (845,956)
Share purchase loans repaid		
Transferred to financing activities		(462,344)
United States G.A.A.P.		$(1,308,300)
EARNINGS PER SHARE		
Primary earnings per share		
United States G.A.A.P.	38¢	30¢
Weighted average number of shares outstanding		
United States G.A.A.P.	**$ 4,626,700**	$ 4,406,200
Fully diluted earnings per share		
United States G.A.A.P.	38¢	29¢
Weighted average number of shares outstanding		
United States G.A.A.P.	**$ 4,626,700**	$ 4,526,200

18

14. SUBSEQUENT EVENTS

Subsequent to the year-end date the company's offer to purchase a 14.4 acre site for potential future plant expansion for $1,669,240 was accepted by the vendor. A deposit of $166,924 has been paid and $389,489 is payable on closing, September 5, 1995, and $556,413 plus accrued interest at bank prime plus 1% per annum is payable on each of September 6, 1996 and 1997.

A statement of claim has been issued seeking damages in the amount of $150,000 and seeking to restrain the use of one of the company's marks. In the opinion of the company's counsel, the claim is without merit.

15. PRIOR YEAR'S FIGURES

Certain of prior year's figures have been reclassified to conform with the presentation format adopted in the current year.

19

BIG ROCK BREWERY LTD.

SCHEDULE

SCHEDULE OF SELLING, GENERAL AND ADMINISTRATIVE EXPENSES

YEARS ENDED MARCH 31, 1995 AND 1994

(Denominated in Canadian Dollars)

	1995	1994
Advertising, promotion and market development	$ 969,404	$ 850,076
Bad debt expense	40,000	(17,881)
Bank charges and foreign exchange	5,768	72,824
Business and property taxes	72,977	567,153
Delivery and storage	891,631	47,845
Insurance, licences and fees	61,413	143,484
Office	203,186	100,097
Professional fees	151,162	31,401
Repairs and maintenance	35,319	159,096
Salaries and commissions - out of province	553,728	763,435
Salaries, benefits and subcontractors	958,102	39,316
Stock exchange listing fees		
	$ 3,942,690	$2,756,846

20

CORPORATE INFORMATION

DIRECTORS

Mr. Edward E. McNally
Chairman, C.E.O.
Big Rock Brewery Ltd.
Calgary, Alberta

Mr. Richard G. Burge
President
Burge Development Corp.
Oakland, California

Mr. Robert H. Hartley
Rancher
High River, Alberta

Mr. Richard W. Jones
Consultant
PaineWebber Inc.
Los Angeles, California

Mr Otto L. Leverkus
Big Coulee Ranch
Nanton, Alberta

Mr. J Angus McKee
President, C.E.O.
Gulfstream Resources Canada Limited
Calgary, Alberta

Mr. William E. McNally
Barrister and Solicitor
Calgary, Alberta

Mr. Mac H. Van Wielingen
President, Managing Director
PowerWest Financial Ltd.
Calgary, Alberta

OFFICERS AND SENIOR PERSONNEL

Edward E. McNally
President

Mitchell E. Westnedge
Treasurer

Bernd Pieper
Brewmaster

HEAD OFFICE

6403 - 35th Street S.E.
Calgary, Alberta T2C 1N2
Telephone (403) 279-2917
Fax (403) 236-7523

AUDITORS

Horwath, Schroeder & Tobin
Chartered Accountants
Calgary, Alberta

TRANSFER AGENTS

R-M Trust Company
600, 333 - 7th Avenue S.W.
Calgary, Alberta T2P 2Z3

The Company's Common stock is traded on the Alberta Stock Exchange under the symbol BR and on the NASDAQ System under the symbol BEER-F.

21

CHAPTER

2

Accounting Systems

The accounting system measures, records and aggregates the effects on the corporation of numerous economic events. To interpret the information in the financial statements, you must be able to understand the process by which accounting information is obtained, and the guidelines by which it is classified and aggregated for financial statements. Only then can you use accounting information effectively to make decisions. Chapter 1 provided an overview of the types of information that are presented in financial statements. This chapter is devoted to explaining how accountants collect, classify, and aggregate that information. It is a chapter that is necessarily technical in nature.

There are several possible approaches to understanding the accounting systems that corporations use. The approach taken in this chapter is to use the basic accounting equation discussed in Chapter 1 to illustrate how data can be collected from a typical set of **transactions**. We then move from transactions to the three major financial statements, and conclude by describing a typical manual accounting system.

BASIC ACCOUNTING EQUATION

The basis of all accounting systems is the basic accounting equation. This equation was stated in Chapter 1 as:

> Basic Accounting Equation:
>
> Assets = Liabilities + Shareholders' Equity

When transactions are recorded in the accounting system, the equality of this equation must always be maintained. The balance sheet provides readers with information about this equality at the beginning and at the end of the current accounting period by showing amounts from the previous year in the outside column, and amounts from the current year in the inside column. A statement with the amounts for two years is called a **comparative statement** (see Big Rock Brewery Ltd's balance sheet in Appendix A of Chapter 1). The users of financial information typically want to know more than just the balance sheet amounts. They usually want to know something more about how the corporation's financial position changed from the beginning to the end of the year. An income statement and a statement of changes in financial position are both useful for this purpose. The balance sheet equation will be used to record a set of typical transactions for a hypothetical company, and an income statement and statement of changes in financial position will be constructed from this information.

TRANSACTIONS ANALYSIS AND ACCOUNTING ENTRIES

The basic accounting equation can be used to illustrate the functioning of the accounting system and the preparation of financial statements. We will use the typical transactions of a retail sales company to demonstrate the analysis and recording of transactions in the accounting system.

Assume that the Demo Retail Corporation is formed as a corporation in December of 19x0[1] with the issuance of common shares for $7,500[2]. Before the end of December, Demo uses $4,500 of the cash received from that issuance to buy equipment. It also buys $2,500 of inventory on account. ("On account" means that Demo has been extended credit by its suppliers and will be required to pay for the inventory at some later date. Typical terms for this type of credit include payment within 30 days.) On December 31, 19x0, Demo would like to prepare financial statements. Because Demo has not yet begun its normal operation of selling goods to customers, it has not yet earned any income. Therefore, it has no need for an income statement. It could, however, prepare a statement of changes in financial position and a balance sheet. The statement of changes in financial position for December would simply show the cash inflow from the issuance of shares ($7,500) and the outflow to buy equipment ($4,500). To prepare the balance sheet, we would use the basic accounting equation developed earlier.

Balance sheet preparation begins with an analysis of the transactions. In December 19x0, there were three transactions to record. They are as follows[3]:

A. Issuance of common shares for $7,500.
B. Purchase of equipment for $4,500.
C. Purchase of inventory for $2,500, on account.

Each of these transactions is analyzed in the following subsections and recorded in the balance sheet equation that appears in Exhibit 2-1. Note that the beginning balances in all the accounts are zero because this is a new corporation.

◣◥ Transaction A

Demo issued common shares for $7,500.

◼◼ Analysis

The shareholders of the corporation have contributed $7,500 to the corporation in exchange for ownership rights. The cash received by the corporation increases its cash asset, and the ownership interest is represented by an increase in common shares. Look again at exhibit 2-1. The entry can be summarized as follows:

---

[1] The problems and examples in the text that do not use data from real companies are given artificial dates so as not to confuse them with real companies. Therefore, a year designation of "19x0" represents year 0, "19x1" represents year one, and so on.

[2] The numbers used in this and most other made-up examples are stated in small round numbers for ease of presentation. If you want to think of them in more realistic terms, you might multiply all numbers by one thousand or one million.

[3] We will designate these transactions with letters to distinguish them from the numbered transactions in January, which are discussed later in the chapter.

EFFECTS OF TRANSACTION A:

Assets (Cash) increase by $7,500

Shareholders' Equity (Common Shares) increases by $7,500

See Exhibit 2-1 for the recording of this transaction. The transaction can be summarized as follows:

Effects of Transaction A on the Balance Sheet (Exhibit 2-1):

				Assets	=	Liabilities	+	Shareholders' Equity	
Cash	+	Inventory	+	Equipment	=	Accounts Payable	+	Common Shares	+ Retained Earnings
+7,500					=			+7,500	

EXHIBIT 2-1

DEMO RETAIL CORPORATION

Basic Accounting Equation (Amounts in Dollars)

	Cash	+	Inventory	+	Assets	=	Liabilities	+	Shareholders' Equity		
					Equipment	=	Accounts Payable	+	Common Shares	+	Retained Earnings
Balances	0	+	0	+	0	=	0	+	0	+	0
Transaction #											
A	+7,500					=			+7,500		
B	−4,500				+4,500	=					
C			+2,500			=	+2,500				
Ending balances	3,000	+	2,500	+	4,500	=	2,500	+	7,500	+	0
Totals					10,000	=	10,000				

Transaction B

Demo purchased equipment for $4,500.

Analysis

Because the purchase of equipment requires an outflow of cash, cash decreases. The equipment purchased is generally regarded as a long-term asset because it will be used by the corporation over several future periods. The asset will be used up or consumed over those future periods, and the annual amount that is consumed or used will be shown as an **amortization** expense. The expensing of part of this amount is shown later in the transactions for January. The entry can be summarized as follows:

EFFECTS OF TRANSACTION B:

Assets (Cash) decrease by $4,500

Assets (Equipment) increase by $4,500

See Exhibit 2-1 for the recording of this transaction. The transaction can be summarized as follows:

			Effects of Transaction B on the Balance Sheet (Exhibit 2-1):				
			Assets	=	Liabilities	+	Shareholders' Equity
Cash	+	Inventory	+	Equipment	=	Accounts Payable + Common Shares + Retained Earnings	
−4,500				+4,500	=		

◤◣ Transaction C

Demo purchased $2,500 of inventory on account.

■ ■ Analysis

The substance of this transaction is that Demo has received an asset (inventory) from its supplier and in exchange has given the supplier a promise to pay. The promise to pay represents an obligation of the corporation and is therefore recorded as a liability. This liability is usually referred to as an **account payable**. The inventory is usually recorded at the amount the corporation will have to pay to acquire it (its cost). The entry can be summarized as follows:

EFFECTS OF TRANSACTION C:

Assets (Inventory) increase by $2,500

Liabilities (Accounts Payable) increase by $2,500

See Exhibit 2-1 for the recording of this transaction. The transaction can be summarized as follows:

			Effects of Transaction C on the Balance Sheet (Exhibit 2-1):				
			Assets	=	Liabilities	+	Shareholders' Equity
Cash	+	Inventory	+	Equipment	=	Accounts Payable + Common Shares + Retained Earnings	
		+2,500			=	+2,500	

At the bottom of Exhibit 2-1, you can see the net result of transactions A, B, and C. These figures represent the balance sheet at the end of December 19x0. The balance sheet could be formally represented as follows:

DEMO RETAIL CORPORATION
Balance Sheet
As of December 31, 19x0

Assets		**Liabilities**	
Cash	$ 3,000	Accounts payable	$ 2,500
Inventory	2,500		

(continued)

DEMO RETAIL CORPORATION (continued)
Balance Sheet
As of December 31, 19x0

Assets		Liabilities	
Equipment	4,500	Shareholders' equity	
		Common shares	7,500
		Retained Earnings	0
		Total liabilities and	
Total assets	$10,000	shareholders' equity	$10,000

Note that the total assets of Demo equal the sum of the liabilities and shareholders' equity, as they should, to satisfy the basic accounting equation.

To continue with the example, assume that during January the following events occurred that affect the account balances of Demo:

1. Demo sold units of inventory to customers, on account[4], for $2,500.[5] The units sold were from the inventory purchased in December.

2. The cost of the units removed from inventory for sales in January totalled $1,800.

3. The new inventory Demo bought to replace the units sold in January totalled $2,100. All of these purchases were made on account.

4. During the month, Demo received $2,200 from customers as payments on their accounts.

5. Demo made payments of $2,700 on its accounts payable.

6. Demo's accountant determined that the equipment should be amortized $150 for January.

7. On the last day of January, Demo purchased land for $15,000 as a site for a future retail outlet. In order to pay for the land, Demo raised money by borrowing $10,000 from the bank and issuing new shares for $5,000.

8. Dividends in the amount of $250 were declared and paid in January.

◖ BALANCE SHEET ANALYSIS

For each of the events or transactions that affect the corporation, the accountant must analyze the economic substance of the transaction. The accountant must decide what accounts are affected and by how much. We call this **transaction analysis**. We have already done this for transactions A, B, and C which occurred in December. It is at this stage of the accounting process that the accountant's training and knowledge are most needed. Not only must the economic substance of the transaction be analyzed, but the accountant must know which accounting guidelines apply to the transaction.

---

[4] The term "on account" in a sales transaction means that the corporation is granting the customer credit. The customer will then pay for the goods at some later date based on the agreement with the seller about the terms.

[5] The dollar amounts here are aggregate totals for all units that were sold during the month. Information about individual units would likely be recorded daily and would be of use to the sales or marketing manager, but we are interested in the aggregate effects of sales in this example.

EXHIBIT 2-2

DEMO RETAIL CORPORATION
Basic Accounting Equation
(Amounts in Dollars)

	Cash	+	Accounts Receivable	+	Inventory	+	Land	+	Equipment	=	Accounts Payable	+	Bank Loan	+	Common Shares	+	Retained Earnings
Balances	3,000	+	0	+	2,500	+	0	+	4,500	=	2,500	+	0	+	7,500	+	0
Transaction #																	
1			+2,500							=							+2,500
2					−1,800					=							−1,800
3					+2,100					=	+2,100						
4	+2,200		−2,200							=							
5	−2,700									=	−2,700						
6									−150	=							−150
7a	+5,000									=					+5,000		
7b	+10,000									=			+10,000				
7c	−15,000						+15,000			=							
8	−250									=							−250
Ending balances	2,250	+	300	+	2,800	+	15,000	+	4,350	=	1,900	+	10,000	+	12,500	+	300
Totals									24,700	=	24,700						

For each of the preceding transactions the substance will be analyzed and an appropriate entry proposed. Generally accepted accounting principles (GAAP) for the transaction will then be discussed. The transaction will be entered into the "accounting system" (the basic accounting equation). The recording of the transactions appears in Exhibit 2-2, but you may want to try to construct your own exhibit as you work through the transactions.

Transaction 1

Demo sold units of inventory to customers, on account, for $2,500. The units sold were from the inventory purchased in December.

Analysis

The substance of a sale transaction is that the corporation has exchanged an asset that it possesses for an asset that the customer possesses. The asset given up by the corporation may be an item of inventory if the corporation is a retailer or a manufacturer, or it may be some type of expertise or service if the corporation is a service provider. In this case, Demo is a retailer and the asset given up is inventory. The asset received in exchange from the customer is generally cash, but other possibilities exist. For example, when a new car is purchased, the buyer's old car is often traded in as part of the deal. Also, the customer may exchange a promise to pay later. This is typically called a **sale on account**, and it results in the corporation receiving a promise to pay, that is, an **account receivable**, in exchange for the inventory. This transaction is a sale on account.

Because this is an exchange, there are two parts of the transaction to consider: the outflow of the asset given up and the inflow of the asset received in the exchange. The outflow decreases assets (inventory) owned by the corporation and decreases the wealth of the shareholders (retained earnings). The inflow, on the other hand, increases the wealth of the shareholders and increases assets (accounts receivable). If the inflow is worth more than the outflow in the exchange, the corporation has generated a **profit** from the sale transaction. If the inflow is less than the outflow, a loss results. The increases and decreases in shareholders' wealth in this transaction are typically called the **sales revenue** (inflow) and **cost of goods sold** (outflow), respectively. Because the analysis shown in Exhibit 2-2 focuses only on the balance sheet, the effects of both the sales revenue and the cost of goods sold will be shown as affecting the retained earnings portion of the shareholders' equity.

The remaining question in the analysis is how to value the inflow and the outflow. Based on the information in Transaction 1, the total selling price of the goods sold was $2,500. Therefore, sales revenue (retained earnings) and accounts receivable both increase by $2,500. There is no information given in Transaction 1 regarding the cost of goods sold. This is covered in Transaction 2. It may seem odd to analyze and record these two simultaneous events separately. Nonetheless, this is typical of how the events are recorded in most corporations. For example, in a department store, when a clerk rings up a sale, a record is made of the sales revenue amount and the increase in cash (or accounts receivable in the case of a sale on account). The clerk does not know the cost of the goods sold at the time of sale. The cost is determined at the end of the period as described under Transaction 2. To summarize:

> ### EFFECTS OF TRANSACTION 1:
>
> Assets (Accounts Receivable) increase by $2,500
> Shareholders' Equity (Retained Earnings) increases by $2,500

■ ■GAAP

The timing of the recognition of revenues and expenses is an important decision that management must make in preparing financial statements. There is an underlying conflict between reporting income information in a timely manner and being assured that the transaction is a *bona fide* sale. To take two extreme positions, it might be argued, at one extreme, that a corporation should recognize a sale when a customer signs a contract for the future delivery of the product. At the other extreme, it might be argued that the corporation should wait until cash is collected before recognizing the transaction as a sale. In the first case, the corporation is counting on delivering the product and ultimately collecting the cash from the sale. These are both uncertain events and, if they do not materialize, shareholders may be misled by the income statement into thinking the corporation is doing better than it really is. In the second case, by delaying recognition of the sale until cash is collected, it is clear that by that time the transaction is a *bona fide* sale, but it may not be providing shareholders with a very good measure of the corporation's performance (on the income statement) during the period prior to collection of the cash. Sales that had been made but were in the process of collection would not appear on the income statement.

The two extremes just discussed are represented in two bases on which accountants generally prepare financial statements: the **accrual basis** and the **cash basis**. The accrual basis attempts to measure performance (i.e., **revenues** and **expenses**) in the period in which the performance takes place rather than when the cash is collected. When the accrual basis is used, criteria are set to avoid recognizing revenues in cases where it is highly unlikely that the corporation will ever receive the cash or where the amount of cash the corporation will receive is difficult to estimate. These criteria are called **revenue recognition criteria** and are discussed in detail in Chapter 4. In brief, the criteria are set to provide shareholders with assurance that the amounts stated as revenues and expenses are reasonable and that there is a high probability that the revenues and expenses recorded will ultimately result in similar cash flows. The accrual basis is used by most businesses and will be used throughout this book.

When the cash basis is used, events are recorded only when their cash effects occur. For example, sales revenue is recorded only when cash is received from the customer, and the cost of goods sold is recorded only when the cash is paid out for inventory. You can see that on this basis you could be recording expenses for inventory earlier than you recorded the revenue for selling it. The mistiming of recording activities such as this would make it difficult for managers to make decisions about pricing and inventory acquisition. Because of the potentially misleading information produced by the cash basis, it is not used very often. It is, however, still used by some farmers, lawyers, and professional service corporations to account for their businesses. In the past, most **not-for-profit organizations** used the cash basis, but today many of them are switching to the accrual basis.

In a business such as Demo, the revenue recognition criteria are generally met when the product is exchanged with the customer. Therefore, in the preceding analysis, the result of Transaction 1 is to recognize revenues (increase retained earnings). Demo should not wait until the cash is collected (see Transaction 4). On a cash basis, of course, Demo would not recognize revenue as a result of Transaction 1.

Another aspect of accrual basis accounting is the **matching concept**. This concept requires that all costs associated with generating sales revenue should be matched with the revenue earned on the income statement. That is, the cost of goods sold related to this revenue should be recognized in the same period as the sales revenue. See the analysis of Transaction 2 for the recording of the cost of goods sold.

Refer to Exhibit 2-2 and the following summary for the proper recording of Transaction 1 in the basic accounting equation. Note that the equation is balanced after the entry is made. The effects on the basic accounting equation can be summarized as follows:

				Assets	= Liabilities	+	Shareholders' Equity	
	Accounts				Accounts	Bank	Common	Retained
Cash +	Receivable +	Inventory +	Land	+ Equipment =	Payable +	Loan +	Shares +	Earnings
	+2,500			=				+2,500

Effects of Transaction 1 on the Basic Accounting Equation (Exhibit 2-2):

Note that this transaction has no effect on cash. The cash effects of the sale of goods will be felt by the corporation only in the period in which the receivable is collected. This will lead to a difference between the cash received from operations and the **net income** for the period.

◤◣ Transaction 2

The cost of units removed from inventory for sales in January totalled $1,800.

■ ■ Analysis

As explained in the analysis of Transaction 1, there are two parts to the sale transaction. Transaction 1 included information about the revenue side of the transaction. Here in Transaction 2, the costs that are to be matched with the revenue are given. The effect of the outflow of the inventory is to decrease the inventory asset and to decrease the shareholders' wealth because the corporation no longer holds title to the inventory. The decrease in shareholders' wealth (that is, retained earnings) by the cost of goods sold is one of the many expenses that the corporation shows on its income statement. To summarize:

> **EFFECTS OF TRANSACTION 2:**
> Assets (inventory) decrease by $1,800
> Shareholders' Equity (retained earnings) decreases by $1,800

■ ■ GAAP

As explained earlier in the analysis of Transaction 1, when the revenues from the sale are recognized, the matching concept requires that the costs associated with that revenue be recognized as well. For a retailer such as Demo, the cost of the inventory is simply the wholesale price that Demo paid to acquire the inventory. Under accrual basis accounting the cost of the inventory is held in the inventory account until it is sold. Typically, the cost of goods sold is determined at the end of the period by physically counting the number of units still available in inventory and then attaching unit costs to those units. By knowing the cost of the inventory that are still unsold at the end of the period (ending inventory) and the cost of the inventory with which the period began (beginning inventory), as well as the purchases during the period, the corporation's accountant can calculate the cost of those units that were sold as follows:

Cost of Goods Sold calculation:

	Beginning Inventory
+	Purchases
=	Cost of Goods Available for Sale
−	Ending inventory
=	Cost of Goods Sold

The determination of the cost of the units of inventory that are sold is discussed in greater depth in Chapter 7.

Refer to Exhibit 2-2 for the recording of this transaction. The entry is summarized as follows:

Effects of Transaction 2 on the Basic Accounting Equation (Exhibit 2-2):									
				Assets	=	Liabilities	+	Shareholders' Equity	
	Accounts					Accounts	Bank	Common	Retained
Cash +	Receivable +	Inventory +	Land	+ Equipment =		Payable +	Loan +	Shares +	Earnings
		−1,800			=				−1,800

Note that this transaction has no effect on cash. The cash flow effects of inventory occur at the time payment for the inventory is made. This leads to a difference between the cash from operations and the net income for the period.

◤◣ Transaction 3

Purchases of new inventory to replace the units sold in January totalled $2,100. All these purchases were made on account.

■■ Analysis

The purchase of inventory has the effect of increasing the inventory asset. Because the inventory is bought on account, Demo has given the seller a promise to pay at some time in the future. Demo should record an increase in accounts payable to indicate its liability to the seller. Note that, on the seller's books, this transaction results in a corresponding account receivable. To summarize:

> **EFFECTS OF TRANSACTION 3:**
> Assets (Inventory) increase by $2,100
> Liabilities (Accounts Payable) increase by $2,100

■■ GAAP

With the accrual basis of accounting, inventory is considered an asset until the revenue recognition criteria are met. The valuation principle for inventory under GAAP is that it be recorded at its acquisition cost (i.e., the price paid to obtain it). When inventory is purchased on account, the inventory is valued at the amount of the liability incurred in the transaction, that is, the value of the accounts payable. Accounts payable are liabilities that are generally settled in a short amount of time (30 to 60 days) and are valued at the gross amount owed. There is generally no recognition[6] of interest on accounts payable even though it is a "loan" from the seller. Occasionally, inventory is purchased on longer-term credit, which results in a formal loan document called a **note payable**. In the case of a note payable, interest is usually explicitly recognized. The interest would be recorded as an expense and as either an outflow of cash, or as a new liability on its own.

---

[6] The term "recognition" means an item in the accounting system.

See Exhibit 2-2 for the recording of this transaction in the accounting system. The entry is summarized as follows:

					Assets	=	Liabilities	+		Shareholders' Equity	
	Accounts						Accounts	Bank		Common	Retained
Cash	+ Receivable	+ Inventory	+ Land	+ Equipment	=		Payable +	Loan	+ Shares	+ Earnings	
		+2,100				=	+2,100				

Effects of Transaction 3 on the Basic Accounting Equation (Exhibit 2-2):

Note that this transaction had no effect on cash. The cash effects of purchasing inventory will be shown when the account payable is paid. Also, note that it had no effect on shareholders' wealth (retained earnings). Income will be affected when the inventory is sold.

Transaction 4

During the month, Demo received $2,200 from customers as payments on their accounts.

Analysis

The receipt of cash from customers means that cash increases. Because the customer no longer owes this amount to the corporation, the value of the customer's account receivable decreases by the amount of the payment. The entry can be summarized as follows:

EFFECTS OF TRANSACTION 4:
Assets (Cash) increase by $2,200
Assets (Accounts Receivable) decrease by $2,200

GAAP

Accounts receivable generally are short-term loans from the seller to the buyer and do not typically result in the recognition of interest. The amount of the receivable is stated at the selling price to the buyer. If this were a note receivable that explicitly included interest, the cash received would be larger than the selling price, and the excess amount above the selling price would represent **interest revenue**. See Exhibit 2-2 for the recording of this transaction. The transaction can be summarized as follows:

Effects of Transaction 4 on the Basic Accounting Equation (Exhibit 2-2):

					Assets	=	Liabilities	+		Shareholders' Equity	
	Accounts						Accounts	Bank		Common	Retained
Cash	+ Receivable	+ Inventory	+ Land	+ Equipment	=		Payable +	Loan	+ Shares	+ Earnings	
+2,200	−2,200					=					

Note that this transaction does affect cash but not shareholders' wealth (retained earnings). The income effect related to accounts receivable was recorded earlier when the original sale occurred.

▶◣ Transaction 5

Demo made payments of $2,700 on its accounts payable.

■ ■ Analysis

Cash payments result in a decrease in cash. In this case, because the payment is on an account payable, there is a corresponding decrease in the accounts payable account. To summarize:

EFFECTS OF TRANSACTION 5:
Assets (Cash) decrease by $2,700
Liabilities (Accounts Payable) decrease by $2,700

■ ■ GAAP

Note that no part of the payment is interest. When longer-term loans are involved, the payment would have to be divided between the amount that represents interest and the amount that represents repayment of the original amount of the loan. See Exhibit 2-2 for the recording of the transaction. The transaction can be summarized as follows:

Effects of Transaction 5 on the Basic Accounting Equation (Exhibit 2-2):

					Assets =	Liabilities	+	Shareholders' Equity	
	Accounts					Accounts	Bank	Common	Retained
Cash +	Receivable +	Inventory +	Land	+ Equipment =	Payable +	Loan +	Shares +	Earnings
−2,700					=	−2,700			

Note that cash is affected by this transaction but shareholders' equity (retained earnings) is not. The income effects of inventory are shown in the period in which the inventory is sold. The period of sale could be either prior to or after the payment of cash.

▶◣ Transaction 6

Demo's accountant determined that the equipment should be amortized $150 for January.

■ ■ Analysis

Whenever an expenditure is made by a corporation to acquire an asset, there are three general questions to ask regarding the nature of the transaction:

1. Has an asset been created?
2. If so, what is the value of the asset?
3. How does the asset get used up over time, and when does it cease to exist?

To address the first question, the criteria for an asset must be evaluated. Does the item have probable future value, and does the corporation own it or have the rights to use it? If the answer to both of these questions is yes, an asset exists and should be recorded. When Demo originally purchased its equipment, the answers to both recognition criteria questions were yes. Demo owned the equipment (because it held title to the equipment), and the equipment had future value (because it was to be used to sell products and thus generate revenues). The equipment, therefore, qualified as an asset.

The answer to the second question, under GAAP, is to value the equipment at its acquisition cost (sometimes called *historical cost*). In the example, assume that the $4,500 value of the equipment at December 31, 19x0, represents its historical cost.

The third question is a little more difficult to answer. For an asset such as inventory, the answer is relatively simple: The asset ceases to exist when it is sold and the corporation gives up title to the asset. The inventory stays on the books until it is sold, and then the cost appears as an expense (cost of goods sold) on the income statement. For equipment, the answer is more complicated. The equipment is used up as time passes, and the equipment is used to generate revenues from the sale of the company's products. Equipment has an estimated useful life. For example, it may last for only five years, at which time it is sold, discarded or traded in for a new piece of equipment.

Because the asset is used up over time, some of the cost of the asset should be shown as an expense in each period in which it is used. Another reason to show some of the cost as an expense is that the expense of using the equipment should be matched (the matching concept) with the revenues generated from the use of the equipment. How much should be shown as an expense in any period is a function of how much of the asset gets used up during that period of time. The amount shown as an expense in any period is called the **amortization** of the asset. There are numerous ways to calculate how much amortization should be taken in a given period. These methods are discussed in detail in Chapter 8. The most common method used is **straight-line amortization**, which assumes that an asset is used evenly throughout its life and that the same amount of amortization should be taken in every time period. The formula for calculating straight-line amortization is:

$$\text{Straight-line Amortization} = \frac{\text{Original Cost} - \text{Estimated Residual Value}}{\text{Estimated Useful Life}}$$

Two estimates are required to perform the calculation. The **useful life** of the asset must be estimated. This could be expressed in years or months, depending on the length of the accounting period. In the example, this would be months. The second estimate is **residual value**. This is an estimate of what the asset will be worth at the end of its useful life. The quantity in the numerator of the calculation is sometimes called the **amortization value** of the asset because it is the amount that should be amortized over the useful life of the asset.

In the case of Demo Retail Corporation, if it is assumed that the equipment had an original cost of $4,500, an estimated useful life of two years (24 months), and a residual value at the end of two years of $900, the monthly amortization would then be calculated as:

$$\text{Straight-line Amortization} = \frac{\$4,500 - \$900}{24 \text{ months}}$$
$$= \$150/\text{month}$$

At the end of each month, Demo should reduce the value of the equipment by $150 and show a $150 expense on the income statement (amortization expense). To summarize:

EFFECTS OF TRANSACTION 6:
Assets (Equipment) decrease by $150
Shareholders' Equity (Retained Earnings) decreases by $150

GAAP

Several amortization methods are commonly used by corporations and are discussed in Chapter 8. The choice of methods is influenced by the pattern of use of the asset and the most appropriate method to capture that pattern of use.

See Exhibit 2-2 for the recording of this transaction. The transaction can be summarized as follows:

Effects of Transaction 6 on the Basic Accounting Equation (Exhibit 2-2):

Cash	+	Accounts Receivable	+	Inventory	+	Land	+	Equipment	=	Accounts Payable	+	Bank Loan	+	Common Shares	+	Retained Earnings
								−150	=							−150

Assets = Liabilities + Shareholders' Equity

Note that the reduction in the equipment account is taken directly out of this account. In Chapter 3 we will show that, in practice, the reduction in a capital asset due to amortization is kept in a separate account called **accumulated amortization**. For now, however, the number of accounts is being kept to a minimum. Note that this transaction has no effect on cash. The cash outflow due to equipment is shown in the period in which the asset is purchased. There might also be a cash inflow in the period in which the equipment is sold.

Transaction 7

On the last day of January, Demo purchased land for $15,000 as a site for a future retail outlet. In order to pay for the land, Demo raised money by borrowing $10,000 from the bank and issuing new shares for $5,000.

■ ■ Analysis

It is instructive to view Transaction 7 as a combination of three transactions: the issuance of shares, the borrowing of money, and the purchase of land. These three are discussed as if each occurred separately.

Issuance of Shares One way for a corporation to raise money is to issue new shares. New shareholders will provide cash to the corporation in exchange for share certificates that signify ownership in the corporation. In this case, the shares are worth $5,000. The shares could be directly exchanged for the land, or they could have been issued to obtain cash and then the cash paid to the landowner. We will assume the latter. In either case, the appropriate way to value the shares is at their **fair market value** at the date of the transaction. The effect of the transaction is that cash increases by $5,000 and shareholders' equity increases by $5,000. The new shareholders have made a contribution to the corporation.

In Canada, shares generally are recorded at the amount that the shareholders paid for them. To summarize (this part of the transaction is referred to as Transaction 7a):

EFFECTS OF TRANSACTION 7A:
Assets (Cash) increase by $5,000
Shareholders' Equity (Common Shares) increases by $5,000

Borrowing Money A second method for raising money is to borrow it. In this case, Demo has borrowed $10,000 from the bank. The effect of this transaction is that cash increases and a new obligation is created to show the amount owed to the bank. The amount of the loan is called the *principal* of the loan. The principal does not include interest. Interest will be added to the amount owed to the bank as time passes. For example, if the interest rate on this loan is 8% per year (interest rates are generally stated on an annual basis), the interest added in the first year of the loan will be 8% of the principal of $10,000, or $800. The terminology is that *interest accrues* on the loan at 8%. The accrued interest at the end of the first year will be $800. At the point of acquiring the loan, the accountant records only the principal of the loan because no time has passed since the loan was taken out. To summarize (Transaction 7b):

EFFECTS OF TRANSACTION 7B:
Assets (Cash) increase by $10,000
Liabilities (Bank Loans) increase by $10,000

Purchase of Land The purchase of land for cash means that cash decreases by the amount of the purchase price and that land increases by the same amount. GAAP requires that land be recorded at its acquisition cost. Land is an asset because it has probable future value and the company holds title to it. The probable future value can be viewed as either its future sales price or its future use (in this case, its use as a site for a retail outlet). Land is not amortized because it is not consumed the way other capital assets, like equipment, are. To summarize (Transaction 7c):

EFFECTS OF TRANSACTION 7C:

Assets (Cash) decrease by $15,000
Assets (Land) increase by $15,000

■ ■ GAAP

Cash transactions are usually easy to value under GAAP because there is an objective measure of the value given up. In exchange transactions, where cash is not involved, the "cost" is not as easily determined. If, for example, in this transaction the loan had been made by the original owner of the land and the shares had been issued to the original owner of the land, and no cash had changed hands, it might be difficult to assign values to the shares and the loan. These types of transactions are called **nonmonetary exchanges**. Under GAAP, the general rule is that these transactions should be valued at the fair market value of the consideration given up in the transaction. In this example, that would be the fair market value of the shares and the loan. In our example, it is assumed that the share issuance and bank borrowing are separate from the purchase of the land. The transaction is, therefore, a monetary exchange, even though there is no net effect on cash. See Exhibit 2-2 for the recording of the net effects of this transaction in the basic accounting equation. Remember that the transaction has been split up into separate transactions labelled 7a, 7b, and 7c. The transaction can be summarized as follows:

Effects of Transaction 7 on the Basic Accounting Equation (Exhibit 2-2):

	Cash +	Accounts Receivable +	Inventory +	Land	+ Equipment =	Assets = Accounts Payable +	Liabilities Bank Loan	+	Shareholders' Equity Common Shares +	Retained Earnings
7a	+5,000				=				+5,000	
7b	+10,000				=		+10,000			
7c	−15,000			+15,000	=					

Note that these transactions do not affect income (retained earnings) but do affect cash although, in this case, the effects on cash are offsetting.

▲ ■ Transaction 8

Dividends in the amount of $250 were declared and paid in January.

■ ■ Analysis

Dividends are payments to the shareholders of the corporation as authorized by the corporation's board of directors. They are a return to the shareholders of part of the accumulated earnings of the corporation. They are not expenses of doing business because they are not incurred for the purpose of generating revenues. The effect of Transaction 8 is to reduce the shareholders' equity (retained earnings) and either to increase liabilities (dividends payable) if they have not been paid, or to decrease assets (cash) if they have been paid.

EFFECTS OF TRANSACTION 8:

Assets (Cash) decrease by $250

Shareholders' Equity (Retained Earnings) decreases by $250

■ ■GAAP

Dividends are **declared** by a vote of the board of directors of a corporation. At the date of declaration, they become a legal liability of the corporation. As just illustrated, the accounting records should show a decrease in retained earnings (usually through an account called the **dividends declared account**) and an increase in the **dividends payable account**. The dividends declared account affects retained earnings. The change in this account explains part of the change in the retained earnings account from the beginning of the period to the end of the period. It is very important, however, to note that dividends are not an expense and do not appear on the income statement. They will appear on a statement of changes in financial position when they are paid, and many corporations prepare a statement of retained earnings, which shows the dividends declared during the period.

There is generally a delay between the date the dividends are declared and the date they are paid, and therefore the cash effects are not recognized until the payment date. In the case of Demo, dividends are declared and paid in the same accounting period, so that the dividends payable account is ignored.

See Exhibit 2-2 for the recording of the effects of this transaction in the balance sheet equation. The transaction can be summarized as follows:

Effects of Transaction 6 on the Basic Accounting Equation (Exhibit 2-2):															
						Assets	=	Liabilities	+			Shareholders' Equity			
		Accounts						Accounts		Bank		Common		Retained	
Cash	+	Receivable	+	Inventory	+	Land	+ Equipment =	Payable	+	Loan	+	Shares	+	Earnings	
−250							=							−250	

This completes the analysis of the eight transactions of the Demo Retail Corporation.

Note that the Demo balance sheet that follows is a **classified balance sheet** in which current assets and liabilities are distinguished from noncurrent. Because the accounting period involved is one month, the balances for both the beginning of the month[7] and the end of the month are shown.

---

[7] Note that the beginning balances in January are the same as the ending balances from December.

DEMO RETAIL CORPORATION
Balance Sheet

	January 31, 19x1	December 31, 19x0
Cash	$ 2,250	$ 3,000
Accounts receivable	300	0
Inventory	2,800	2,500
Total current assets	$ 5,350	$ 5,500
Land	15,000	0
Equipment	4,350	4,500
Total assets	$24,700	$10,000
Accounts payable	$ 1,900	$ 2,500
Total current liabilities	$ 1,900	$ 2,500
Bank loan	10,000	0
Total liabilities	$11,900	$ 2,500
Common shares	$12,500	$ 7,500
Retained earnings	300	0
Total shareholders' equity	$12,800	$ 7,500
Total liabilities and shareholders' equity	$24,700	$10,000

◖◗ INCOME STATEMENT

The income statement can be constructed from the information on the transactions recorded in the retained earnings account in Exhibit 2-2 (refer back to chapter 1 for a description of the income statement). Note that the dividend amount does not belong on the income statement because it is not an expense used to derive net income. Rather, it is a payment of earnings to the shareholders. The income statement would be constructed as follows:

DEMO RETAIL CORPORATION
Income Statement
For the month ended January 31, 19x1

Sales revenues	$2,500
Cost of goods sold	(1,800)
Gross profit	700
Amortization expense	(150)
Net income	$ 550

Demo operated profitably during the month of January, earning a net income of $550.

By itself, a net income of $550 tells users very little about a corporation other than that it has a positive income flow. To understand the profitability of a corporation more fully, users will often use ratio analysis, a technique you will see used frequently throughout this text. A ratio divides one financial statement amount by another financial statement amount. This allows users to understand how some amounts are related to other amounts. As you have seen from the financial statements illustrated so far, there are many numbers from which meaningful relationships can be derived. Ratios allow users to compare different corporations that are of different sizes, or to compare the same corporation over time. Ratio analysis can be used to assess profitability, the effectiveness of management, and the ability of the corporation to meet debt obligations. As we introduce new topics to you, we will be showing you ratios that can help users understand and evaluate a set of financial statements. A complete discussion of these ratios can be found in Chapter 12.

We are going to start by examining profitability ratios. Profitability ratios are usually constructed by comparing some measure of the profit (net income) of the corporation to the amount invested or by comparing it to the revenues of the corporation. We will calculate three such measures.

▶▲ Profitability Ratios

The **profit margin ratio** is calculated by dividing the profit generated by the corporation by the revenues that produced that profit. For Demo, this ratio is 22% (net income/revenues = $550/$2,500). This indicates that Demo earned, as profit, 22% of the revenue amount.

The **return on assets** invested is another measure of profitability. It is calculated by dividing the profit of the corporation by the average total assets invested in the corporation. The average assets can be calculated using the information in the balance sheet. For Demo, the average is $17,350 [($10,000 + $24,700)/2]. In January of 19X1, the return on asset was 3.2% (net income/average total assets = $550/$17,350). This means that for each $100.00 of assets, Demo earned $3.20 of profit.

The third measure of performance considered is the **return on equity**. This measure compares the profit (income) with the amount invested by the shareholders (average total shareholders' equity). The measure is 5.4% (net income/average shareholders' equity = $550/$10,150) for Demo. The $10,150 is the average of the sum of the shareholders' equity accounts (common shares and retained earnings). The average is calculated as [($7,500 + $12,800)/2]. This measure means that the shareholders have earned a 5.4% return on their investment in one month.

The interpretation of these ratios must be made either within the context of the past performance of the corporation or in comparison with other corporations in the same industry. More will be said about these ratios and their interpretation in Chapter 12.

◖◗ STATEMENT OF CHANGES IN FINANCIAL POSITION

A statement of changes in financial position can now be constructed from the information in the cash column in Exhibit 2-2. The statement of changes in financial position explains the changes in cash flow by detailing the changes in operating, financing, and investing activities (refer back to Chapter 1). The operating section of Demo's statement of changes in financial position appears somewhat different from that of Big Rock, shown in Chapter 1. The reason is that GAAP allows for this section to be prepared using a direct or an indirect method. The direct method has been used here, whereas Big Rock used the indirect method. The explanation for this difference is presented in Chapter 5.

DEMO RETAIL CORPORATION
Statement of Changes in Financial Position

	Month Ended January 31, 19x1	
Operating activities:		
Cash receipts from customers	$ 2,200	
Cash disbursement to suppliers	(2,700)	
Cash flow used in operations		$ (500)
Investing activities:		
Purchase of land		(15,000)
Financing activities:		
Proceeds from issuance of common shares	5,000	
Proceeds from bank loan	10,000	
Dividends paid	(250)	
Cash flow from financing		14,750
Decrease in cash		($750)

The important part of the cash flow analysis is interpreting what the statement of changes in financial position shows about the health of the corporation. Subsequent chapters discuss many of the detailed analyses that can be done with the data in the statement of changes in financial position. For now, there are two basic questions that can serve as a start for the analysis of this statement. The first is: Is the cash from operations sufficient to sustain, in the long run, the other activities of the corporation? A corporation can be healthy in the long run only when it produces a reasonable amount of cash from operations. Cash can be obtained from financing activities (issuance of new debt or shares) and from investment activities (the sale of investments or capital assets), but these sources cannot sustain the corporation forever because there are limits to the corporation's access to them.

The second question relates to the first: Of the sources and uses of cash, which are continuing items from period to period, and which are simply sporadic or non-continuing? A large source or use of cash in one period may not have long-run implications if it does not continue in the future. To address this question, the historical trend in the statement of changes in financial position data must be considered. The statement of changes in financial position for Doman Industries Limited is shown in Exhibit 2-3. Note that cash from operations generated a positive amount in each of the two years presented and that the amount increased over those two years.

To assess whether the cash from operations is adequate to meet Doman's needs, look at the major uses of cash. In 1994, the three largest uses of cash were as follows (in thousands):

Additions to property, plant and equipment	$ 68,639
Reduction of long-term debt	63,555
Debt issue expenses	13,121
	$145,315

EXHIBIT 2-3

DOMAN INDUSTRIES LIMITED

Consolidated Condensed Statements of Changes in Financial Position

	Years Ended December 31,	
	1994	1993
	($000's)	
Operating Activities		
Net earnings..........	$ 55,794	$ 40,199
Add (deduct) items not involving cash:		
Amortization of property, plant and equipment	52,129	46,194
Amortization of deferred charges.............	11,047	13,341
Deferred income taxes	37,311	25,730
Other items	(217)	1,088
Working capital provided by operations ("cash flow") (per share — $4.37 in 1994 and $4.15 in 1993) (Note 13(a))..........	156,064	126,552
Net (increase) in non-cash working capital items (Note 16(d))	(26,405)	(6,068)
Funds provided by operating activities	129,659	120,484
Financing Activities		
Reduction of long-term debt	(63,555)	(2,445)
Debt issue expenses...........	(13,121)	—
Issue of shares for cash, net of issue expenses............	52,785	39,971
Shares to be issued	—	52,500
Share subscription receivable	—	(52,500)
Redemption of preferred shares..........	(177)	—
Cash dividends on		
Preferred shares..........	(5,299)	(7,007)
Common and non-voting shares...........	(7,138)	(3,192)
Other...........	1,630	—
Funds (used in) provided by financing activities............	(34,875)	27,327
Investing Activities		
Acquisition of Eacom Timber Sales Ltd. (including bank indebtedness assumed of $13,802,000) (Note 2)	—	(13,994)
Additions to property, plant and equipment	(68,639)	(30,070)
Additions to investments...........	(4)	(5,566)
Disposals of property, plant and equipment	1,606	1,957
Disposals of investments............	—	10,988
Funds (used in) investing activities............	(67,037)	(36,685)
Increase in cash............	27,747	111,126
Cash, beginning of year	8,826	(102,300)
Cash, end of year	$ 36,573	$ 8,826

CASH is defined to comprise cash balances net of current bank indebtedness

The total of these uses was more than the cash produced from operations of $129,659. To make up for the shortfall from operations, Doman issued shares and raised $52,785. In trying to forecast whether *future* operations will be sufficient to cover these major uses, the corporation must assess whether these uses are likely to continue at the same level. If they continue at the same level, Doman will have to make up for the shortfall from operations with other sources of cash. This would not be good because it would require further borrowings or issuances of shares.

Of the three major uses, the acquisition of property, plant and equipment seems to be consistent over the two years but greatly increased in the current year. Replacing capital assets is typical of most corporations, since there is a continuing need to replace them if the corporation wants to continue its current activities or to grow. Doman also seems to borrow and repay long-term debt as well as issue shares as a way to supplement its cash flow. If the net cash provided by (used in) financing activities is considered, it is obvious that, over the last two years, Doman has been borrowing and repaying its loans and raising more cash by issuing shares. If the increase in cash flows from operations continues as it has over the last two years, Doman will likely be able to decrease its reliance on outside sources of cash.[8]

Returning to the analysis of Demo Retail Corporation, even though the company was profitable, based on the income statement ($550), the analysis of cash flow indicates a negative cash flow from operations of $500 and an overall decrease in cash of $750. Further, considering the starting balance in cash of $3,000, it is clear that Demo could operate for a few more months at this rate and still have some cash remaining. It cannot, however, continue to operate indefinitely with a negative cash flow (i.e., net cash outflow). The corporation would run out of cash in a little over three months. This should raise questions about why Demo has this cash drain, even though it appears to be profitable. When we look at the three types of activities, the biggest concern is the negative cash flow from operations. Analyzing why Demo is having difficulty generating cash from operations is beyond the scope of this chapter, but Demo's problem represents an important issue that will be addressed in various sections of this book, most thoroughly in Chapter 5. In fact, problems related to cash flows are key reasons why new businesses fail in their first year. For now, it is important to understand that, while the income statement provides important information about the changes in the shareholders' wealth, it does not reveal everything that is important to know about the corporation. The statement of changes in financial position can provide additional useful information about the corporation's operations that is not adequately captured by the income statement. With only one month's worth of data for Demo, it is impossible to comment on the continuing nature of the items on Demo's statement of changes in financial position.

DOUBLE ENTRY ACCOUNTING SYSTEMS

The recording of transactions in the basic accounting equation is sufficient if the corporation has only a few transactions to record. However, the plus and minus system used here becomes confusing and somewhat cumbersome when large numbers of accounts and transactions are considered. To overcome this confusion, accountants have developed an alternative system to record transactions. This alternative system is known as a **double entry accounting system**. We will demonstrate the system by using a device known as a **T-account**. To translate from the equation system to the T-account system, imagine replacing the equality sign in the balance sheet equation with a big "T" as follows:

> Replace the basic accounting equation:
> Assets = Liabilities + Shareholders' Equity
>
> With a T-account:
>
> | Assets | Liabilities + Shareholders' Equity |
> |--------|-----------------------------------|

---

[8] One caveat should be stated here: A complete analysis of Doman's cash situation is not possible without a review of all the financial statements and related footnotes.

Note that assets appear on the left side of the T-account and liabilities and shareholders' equity appear on the right side. The equality expressed in the basic accounting equation must still be maintained in the T-account system. Translated, this means that the totals from the left side of the T-accounts must equal the totals from the right side of the T-accounts. The left side of the account is known as the **debit** side, and the right side as the **credit** side. The words *debit* and *credit* have no meaning in accounting other than "left" and "right." Do not try to attach any other meaning to these terms as it will surely lead you astray in your thinking about the accounts of the corporation. The abbreviations for *debit* and *credit* are **Dr**. and **Cr**., respectively. The balance in the accounting system can now be expressed in terms of debits and credits rather than in terms of the left and right side of the basic accounting equation. The balance sheet equality requires that debits equal credits.

The T-account concept also carries over into the accounting for specific asset and liability accounts. Each asset and liability has its own T-account; these accounts, added together, result in the big T-account. See Exhibit 2-4.

In Exhibit 2-4, note that there are letters preceding the account names. These letters will be used throughout this book to designate the type of account. At this point, there are only three designations to worry about: **A** represents an asset account, **L** a liability account, and **SE** a shareholders' equity account. We will periodically add other designations as we proceed through the book. These letters will be a helpful reminder of the nature of the account with which you are dealing.

Because assets are listed on the debit side of the large T-account by convention, they normally have balances on the debit side of the individual T-accounts. Likewise, liabilities and shareholders' equity accounts have credit balances. In Exhibit 2-5, the beginning balances for Demo Retail Corporation are entered into a set of T-accounts. Beside each balance, you will see a check mark (✓), which is used to designate a balance in the account rather than a new entry. Also, note that the sum of the debit balances ($10,000) equals the sum of the credit balances ($10,000), which means that the system is balanced.

Because assets have debit balances, increases in asset accounts should be entered on the debit side of the account. Decreases in assets should be entered on the credit side. For liabilities and shareholders' equity, the reverse is true. Increases are entered on the credit side of the account, and decreases are entered on the debit side. Exhibit 2-6 lists the appropriate entries for asset, liability, and shareholders' equity accounts.

EXHIBIT 2-4

Individual T-Accounts

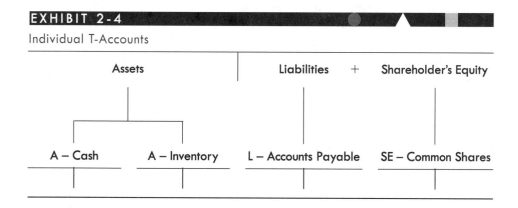

EXHIBIT 2-5

DEMO RETAIL CORPORATION

T-Accounts

A – Cash			L – Accounts Payable	
✓ 3,000			2,500	✓

A – Accounts Receivable			SE – Common Shares	
✓ 0			7,500	✓

A – Inventory			SE – Retained Earnings	
✓ 2,500			0	✓

A – Equipment	
✓ 4,500	

EXHIBIT 2-6

Entries to T-Accounts

Assets	
✓ Beginning balance Increases	Decreases
✓ Ending balance	

Liabilities	
Decreases	Beginning balance ✓ Increases
	Ending balance ✓

Shareholders' Equity	
Decreases	Beginning balance ✓ Increases
	Ending balance ✓

The accounts shown in Exhibits 2-5 and 2-6 are all balance sheet accounts. They have balances that carry over from one period to the next. These accounts are sometimes called **permanent accounts**. One of the permanent accounts is the retained earnings account. The change in the retained earnings account during a given period is the net of the revenues and expenses for the period and the decrease due to dividends declared. In order to keep track of the individual revenue and expense amounts, as well as the dividends declared during the period, the retained earnings account can be subdivided into several separate accounts. These separate accounts are called **temporary accounts** because they are used temporarily, during the accounting period, to keep track of revenues, expenses, and dividends. The balances in these accounts ultimately have to affect the retained earnings account. Exhibit 2-7 shows the subdivision of the retained earnings account into the temporary revenue, expense, and dividends declared accounts.

EXHIBIT 2-7

Retained Earnings: Income Statement Accounts

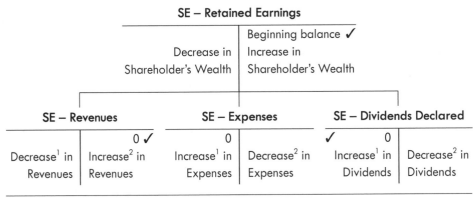

¹ Decrease in Shareholders' Wealth
² Increase in Shareholder's Wealth

Several things should be noted concerning the revenue, expense, and dividends declared accounts. First, notice that the beginning balance in these accounts is zero. Because these accounts are used to keep track of revenues, expenses, and dividends declared during the period, their beginning balances must be zero so that the last period's data are not combined with that of the current period. At the end of the period, the balance in each of the temporary accounts will be used to help prepare the income statement, but then must be transferred into the permanent retained earnings account to produce the final ending balance in the retained earnings account. In this way, the retained earnings account keeps track of the cumulative amounts of revenues and expenses less dividends, and the temporary accounts keep track of only the current year amounts.

Note further that while revenues, expenses, and dividends declared are all shareholders' equity accounts, increases and decreases correspond to different entries. For revenues, credits represent increases and debits represent decreases. For expenses and dividends declared, the opposite is true: debits represent increases, and credits represent decreases. Therefore, by the end of a given accounting period (prior to transferring the balances to the retained earnings account), revenues have credit balances, expenses have debit balances, and dividends declared has a debit balance. The debit balances in the expense and dividends declared accounts are probably best understood if we remember that they both represent **decreases** in the shareholders' equity. Because shareholders' equity is represented by a credit balance, the decreases in shareholders' equity must be represented by debit balances. Further, because these are temporary accounts and their balances will be transferred to retained earnings, the debit balances will not persist in the permanent accounts. They will be offset by the credit balance revenue accounts. It is possible to have a debit balance in the retained earnings account if expenses have exceeded revenues (i.e., the corporation has suffered losses). If you look at the balance sheet of AT Plastics Inc. in Exhibit 2-8, you will see that its retained earnings in 1994 is a deficit (a debit balance). After a net income of $24,284 and dividend of $2,280 in 1995, that deficit in retained earnings has disappeared. Most corporations do not have a deficit position in their retained earnings.

EXHIBIT 2-8

AT PLASTICS INC.
Balance Sheet
As at December 31

(thousands of dollars)	1995	1994
ASSETS		
CURRENT		
Cash and short-term investments	$ 7,861	$ 1,357
Accounts receivable	24,617	25,968
Inventory (note 2)	35,348	26,227
Prepaids	1,133	961
	68,959	54,513
FIXED (note 3)	151,835	151,201
OTHER (note 4)	10,879	11,932
	$231,673	$ 217,646
LIABILITIES		
CURRENT		
Accounts payable	$ 21,918	$ 24,159
Current portion of long-term debt (note 5)	6,566	5,554
Obligation under capital leases (note 6)	188	175
	28,672	29,888
LONG-TERM DEBT (note 5)	90,269	99,217
OBLIGATION UNDER CAPITAL LEASES (note 6)	310	496
OTHER LIABILITIES (note 7)	1,190	2,414
DEFERRED INCOME TAXES	3,597	—
	95,366	102,127
	124,038	132,015
SHAREHOLDERS' EQUITY		
CAPITAL STOCK (note 8)	100,667	100,667
RETAINED EARNINGS (DEFICIT)	6,968	(15,036)
	107,635	85,631
	$231,673	$ 217,646

See accompanying note to consolidated financial statements.

Approved by the Board

Egerton W. King
Director

John Abell
Director

Accounting Cycle

Before we demonstrate how T-accounts can be used to capture the transactions of Demo Retail Corporation, we want to step back from these details and look at the whole system in which transactions are measured, recorded, and communicated. This system is called the **accounting cycle**. Envision for a moment a corporation that has just been formed and whose managers need to install an accounting system. What is the first thing they need to decide? One of the first decisions they must make is what information they need to run the business. What information is important for them to make decisions? What information do outside users need to know about the corporation? Accounting systems are information systems, so managers should decide at the start what information they want and need to operate the business. Although corporations may be in the same industry, each corporation will develop its own unique information system.

■■ Chart of Accounts

The types of accounting information to be recorded in the accounting system are generally summarized in a **chart of accounts**. Exhibit 2-9 lists the chart of accounts for the Demo Retail Corporation. The chart of accounts should be viewed as dynamic and not something that can never be changed. As the business changes, there may be a need for a different type of account. For example, suppose that the corporation originally was unwilling to provide credit to its customers. There would be no need for an accounts receivable account because the corporation was strictly a cash business. Later, if the corporation decided to allow customers to buy on credit, it would need to add an accounts receivable account to the chart of accounts. A key point to note is that the design of the chart of accounts can facilitate additional information or be a handicap depending upon how carefully it is conceived.

EXHIBIT 2-9

DEMO RETAIL CORPORATION
Chart of Accounts

Permanent accounts
    Assets
        Cash
        Accounts Receivable
        Inventory
        Equipment
    Liabilities
        Accounts Payable
    Shareholders' Equity
        Common Shares
        Retained Earnings
Temporary accounts
    Income statement accounts
        Sales Revenues
        Cost of Goods Sold
    Dividends Declared

In an actual system, the chart of accounts would typically list account numbers that would be useful in identifying accounts within a computer system. In this book, accounts will be designated by their names and not by account numbers. An account can be given any name that makes sense and is descriptive of its purpose. Commonly used terms for each type of account will be discussed throughout the book. Several of these names, such as accounts receivable, inventory, accounts payable, retained earnings, have already been mentioned.

The chart of accounts is the starting point for the accounting cycle of the corporation. The complete cycle is illustrated in Exhibit 2-10. Each of the steps in the cycle is discussed in the following subsections.

EXHIBIT 2-10

Accounting Cycle

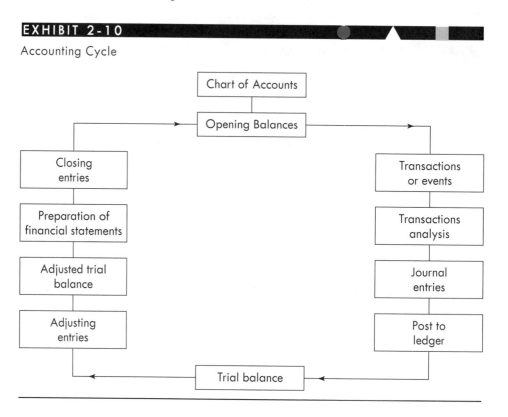

■ ■ Opening Balances

After the chart of accounts has been established and the corporation commences business, the corporation's accountant needs to record in the accounting system the results of the various transactions that affect the corporation. The system could be as simple as a notebook with sheets of paper representing the accounts and entries made by hand, or it could be as sophisticated as an on-line computer system in which entries are made via a terminal. For purposes of this book, a manual system will be used, but the same entries apply to any accounting system, no matter how simple or how sophisticated.

The first step in the cycle is to initialize the accounts by entering zero balances in all the accounts. In subsequent accounting periods, the beginning balances will be the balances carried forward from the end of the last accounting cycle.

■ ■ Transactions or Events

The next step in the cycle is to recognize that some event or transaction has occurred that affects the assets, liabilities, and/or shareholders' equity of the corporation. The transaction or event is usually evidenced by some sort of signal such as a *source document* — a piece of documentation received or created by the corporation. Examples of source documents would be invoices, cheques, cash register tapes, bank deposit slips or order forms. The first transaction that would be signalled for corporations would be the receipt of cash from the shareholders and the issuance of common shares.

Transactions Analysis

After a signal has been received that a transaction or event has occurred, the accountant must analyze the transaction or event to decide what accounts have been affected and by how much. This phase of the process is called **transactions analysis**. Transactions analysis was performed earlier in this chapter when the transactions of the Demo Retail Corporation were analyzed. For routine transactions, such as the purchase and sale of goods, the transaction needs to be analyzed only once. After that, each subsequent transaction is the same and can be entered into the accounting system without further analysis. Unique and unusual transactions require further transactions analysis, and generally require the services of a professional accountant who understands the use of appropriate (GAAP) accounting methods. For routine transactions, an accountant is probably not needed, and an accounting clerk could record the transactions in the accounting system.

Journal Entries

After the accountant has decided how to account for the transaction, an entry must be made to the system. The initial entry is usually made in what is known as the **journal**. The journal is a chronological listing of all the events that are recorded in the accounting system. The entry made to the journal is called a **journal entry**. The journal could be as simple as a piece of paper on which is recorded the running list of the transactions that have occurred. The transactions are dated and assigned a transaction number. The journal entry then consists of the date, the transaction number, the accounts affected (and their account numbers), and a listing of the appropriate debits and credits. Exhibit 2-11 demonstrates what a journal entry might look like for the first two transactions for Demo Retail Corporation in January. For simplicity, assume that all transactions in January took place on January 31. By convention, in a journal entry, the debit entries are listed first and credit entries second. Credit entries are also indented from the debit entries. Note that each complete journal entry maintains the balance in the system, that is, debits equal credits. A proper journal entry must always maintain this balance. An explanation of the transaction is included with each transaction so that the circumstances of the transaction are available for future reference.

Posting to the Ledger

The information needed to run the business would now be recorded in the accounting system (journal). The problem is that the information is not very accessible. If, for example, the manager wanted to know the balance in cash, the accountant would have to take the beginning balance in cash and add or subtract all the journal entries that affected cash. If a corporation has recorded hundreds of journal entries, this

EXHIBIT 2-11

DEMO RETAIL CORPORATION
Journal Entries

Monthly Journal
January, 19x1

Transaction	Date	Account Name	Debit	Credit
	19x1			
1	Jan. 31	A — Accounts receivable	2,500	
		SE — Sales revenue		2,500
		Sold inventory on account.		
2	Jan. 31	SE — Cost of goods sold	1,800	
		A — inventory		1,800
		Recorded cost of inventory sold.		

could take a long time. To make the individual account information more accessible in a logical and deliberate way, the accountant then proceeds to the next step in the accounting cycle. In this step, the journal entries are **posted to the ledger**.

The **ledger** is a system (in a simple case, a set of notebook pages) in which each account is listed separately (a separate page). In a computerized system, each account might be represented by a separate computer file. **Posting** is the process of transferring the information from the journal to the ledger accounts. Each page of the ledger represents a specific T-account. The ledger account would include the name (and number) of the account, its beginning balance, and then a listing of all the postings that affected the account during the period. Each listing would include the transaction number reference, the date, and the appropriate debit or credit. The transaction number reference would allow a user to go backward in the system to determine the source of an amount in an individual account. Note that, if the journal entries are posted properly, the balance in the ledger system is preserved. Exhibit 2-12 shows two ledger accounts and the posting of the first January transaction for the Demo Corporation.

The posting to the ledger can take place on a monthly basis, a weekly basis, a daily basis, or with any frequency desired. The timing of the postings is determined to some extent by the management's (or the shareholders') need for up-to-date information. If managers need to know the balance in a particular account, say inventory, on a daily basis, then the postings should be done at least daily. If management needs to know the amount of inventory on an hourly basis, then the posting has to be done more frequently. Many computer systems account for transactions in what is called "real time," which means that accounts are updated instantaneously. Other computer systems collect journal entries in "batches" and post them all at one time. In general, managers like to have information sooner rather than later and, as the cost of computer technology continues to decrease, there has been a proliferation of "real-time" systems in the corporate world.

At this point it is important to note that a system consisting only of journal entries would make it difficult to determine the balance in any one account. A system of only ledger accounts, without the original journal entries, would make it difficult to understand the sources of amounts in individual accounts. We need both

EXHIBIT 2-12

Posting to the Ledger

DEMO RETAIL CORPORATION
Ledger

A – Accounts Receivable				Sales – Revenue		
Balance	0				0	Balance
Jan. 31 1	2,500			2,500	1	Jan. 31

journal entries and ledger accounts in order to collect information in a way that makes it readily accessible.

■ ■ Trial Balance

While most errors should be detected at the journal entry and posting phases of the accounting cycle, some errors may persist. One device for detecting errors is to produce a **trial balance**. The **trial balance** is a listing of all debit and credit balance accounts in the general ledger. A check can then be made to ensure that the total of the debit balances equals the total of the credit balances. If these are not equal, a mistake has been made at some point during the process and must be corrected. The trial balance assists in detecting balance errors, but it does not, in general, allow detection of errors in which the wrong account was debited or credited. Errors such as these can be detected by examining the accounts and their balances for reasonableness. However, if one minor entry was made to a wrong account, it may not be detected in this phase. Exhibit 2-13 illustrates the appearance of a trial balance using the data from the Demo Retail Corporation problem.

EXHIBIT 2-13

DEMO RETAIL CORPORATION
Trial Balance

Account	Debit	Credit
Cash	$2,250	
Accounts receivable	300	
Inventory	2,800	
Land	15,000	
Equipment	4,350	
Accounts payable		$1,900
Bank loan		10,000
Common shares		12,500
Retained earnings		0
Dividends declared	250	
Sales revenues		2,500
Cost of goods sold	1,800	
Amortization expense	150	
Totals	$26,900	$26,900

■ ■ Adjusting Entries

If an error is detected in the trial balance phase, it must be corrected. An entry to correct an error is one type of **adjusting entry** that is made at the end of the accounting period. A second type of adjusting entry is made for transactions or events that were not recognized and recorded during the period. Examples of this type of event are the amortization of the capital assets, the recognition of interest that is owed on loans, and the recognition that some of the office supplies have been used. Accountants in most businesses have a set of this second type of adjusting entry that they typically make at the end of every period. Care must be taken to ensure that all events and transactions have been accounted for. Adjusting entries are then journalized and posted in the same way as other accounting entries.

ETHICS IN ACCOUNTING

Many adjusting entries require estimates and judgements by management. These estimates and judgements provide an opportunity to manipulate both balance sheet values and income. Suppose that you, as a staff accountant, are asked to postpone the write-off of some old plant and equipment that is currently idle. It is clear to you that the idled equipment will never be used again. The write-off would need to be recognized as a loss and would, therefore, have a significant negative impact on the income statement. Management has asked you to postpone the write-off because the corporation has applied for a large loan and the loss from the write-off could significantly affect the reported performance of the company. What should you do? As you consider your response to this ethical question, it is sometimes helpful to think about who will be affected by your decision (including yourself) and how they will be helped or hurt by your decision. Particularly think of who are the users/potential users of the financial statements. This should help you structure your understanding of the situation and justify your decision in the context of these effects.

■ ■ Adjusted Trial Balance

After all the adjusting entries have been made, an **adjusted trial balance** is computed. This is done to ensure that no errors have occurred in the posting of the adjusting entries.

■ ■ Financial Statement Preparation

After the adjusted trial balance has been computed and any corrections have been made, the financial statements for the period can be prepared. Note that, at this point, the temporary accounts still have balances in them and the retained earnings account has the same balance as it did at the beginning of the period. No entries have been made directly to the retained earnings account. The income statement can, therefore, be prepared from the information in the temporary accounts. Note also that the dividends declared account is *not* a part of the income statement. Dividends are *not* an *expense* of doing business; they are a return to shareholders of part of their accumulated wealth in the company.

The balance sheet can be prepared from the balances in the permanent accounts with the one exception of retained earnings, which does not, at this point, include the effects of revenues, expenses, and dividends. The preparation of the statement of changes in financial position could be done in a simple case from the information in the ledger account for cash. The preparation of the statement of changes in financial position in a more complex case is discussed in greater detail in Chapter 5.

■ ■ Closing Entries

After the income statement is prepared, the balances in the temporary accounts must be transferred to the retained earnings account (a permanent account). This will reset the balance in each temporary account to zero to start the next accounting cycle. The entries that accomplish this are called **closing entries**. Closing entries will be distinguished from other entries in the examples in this book by lettering the entries rather than numbering them. Sometimes companies use a single temporary account to accumulate all the income statement accounts. This account is usually called an **income summary account**. The balances from all the individual revenue and expense accounts are closed to this summary account. The balance in the income summary account is then closed to retained earnings. This will be demonstrated for the Demo Retail Corporation. Again, because the dividends declared account is not an income statement account, it would be closed directly to retained earnings and would not affect the income summary account.

■ ■ Accounting Cycle Frequency

One final issue with regard to the accounting cycle is: how often should the cycle be completed? That is, how often should financial statements be prepared? Another way to put it is: how long should an accounting period be? The answer is that financial statements should be prepared as often as necessary to provide timely information to management and shareholders. Since this preparation is not without cost, a balance must be struck between the benefits from having up-to-date information and the cost of preparing the statements. In some businesses, the need for up-to-date information is great, in which case daily reports may be necessary. In other businesses, a monthly statement is probably sufficient. Regardless of what time period is selected, the procedures just described are appropriate.

For companies whose shares are traded on a public stock exchange, there is a requirement that the companies file financial statements quarterly, as well as on an annual basis. The frequency with which financial statements are prepared is sometimes expressed in terms of how often a company **closes its books**. If it closes its books monthly, the accounting cycle for the corporation is one month long, and the temporary accounts are reset on a monthly basis. Adjusting entries, such as those for amortization, interest, and used office supplies, are then made once a month.

Demo Retail Corporation T-Accounts

Return now to the Demo Retail Corporation, and use the T-account system to record the transactions for January. The beginning balances (the balances that carried over from the end of December, 19x0) have been entered into the T-accounts in Exhibit 2-14. Note that the temporary accounts for revenue, expense, and dividends declared have been segregated from the permanent accounts and have zero balances.

EXHIBIT 2-14

DEMO RETAIL CORPORATION
T-Accounts: Beginning Balances

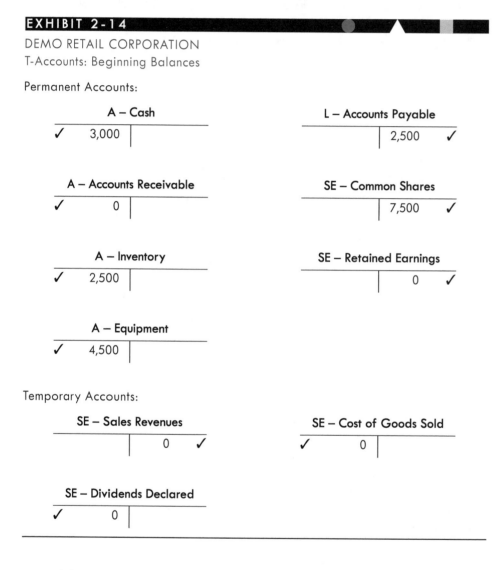

Permanent Accounts:

A – Cash		
✓ 3,000		

A – Accounts Receivable		
✓ 0		

A – Inventory		
✓ 2,500		

A – Equipment		
✓ 4,500		

L – Accounts Payable		
	2,500 ✓	

SE – Common Shares		
	7,500 ✓	

SE – Retained Earnings		
	0 ✓	

Temporary Accounts:

SE – Sales Revenues		
	0 ✓	

SE – Cost of Goods Sold		
✓ 0		

SE – Dividends Declared		
✓ 0		

Exhibit 2-15 shows all eight of the transactions for Demo in January in journal entry form. In Exhibit 2-16, all the journal entries have been posted to the ledger T-accounts. Notice how the transactions have been numbered so that it is easy to determine which entries are associated with one another. The title of Exhibit 2-16 indicates that the accounts are in the adjusted trial balance phase, which means the temporary accounts have not been closed to retained earnings but all adjusting entries have been completed and posted. The balances in all accounts have been

EXHIBIT 2-15

DEMO RETAIL CORPORATION
Journal Entries for Transactions in January 19x1

(1)	A – Accounts receivable	2,500	
	SE – Sales revenues		2,500
	Sold inventory on account.		
(2)	SE – Cost of goods sold	1,800	
	A – Inventory		1,800
	Recorded cost of inventory sold.		
(3)	A – Inventory	2,100	
	L – Accounts payable		2,100
	Bought inventory on account.		
(4)	A – Cash	2,200	
	A – Accounts receivable		2,200
	Collected on accounts receivable.		
(5)	L – Accounts payable	2,700	
	A – Cash		2,700
	Paid on accounts payable.		
(6)	SE - Amortization expense	150	
	A – Equipment		150
	Recorded amortization of equipment.		
(7a)	A – Cash	5,000	
	SE – Common shares		5,000
	Issued common shares.		
(7b)	A – Cash	10,000	
	L – Bank loan		10,000
	Obtained a bank loan.		
(7c)	A – Land	15,000	
	A – Cash		15,000
	Bought land.		
(8)	SE – Dividends declared	250	
	A – Cash		250
	Declared and paid dividends.		

calculated. As a result of the transactions that occurred in January, Demo had to add some new accounts to its chart of accounts. The new accounts are land, bank loan and amortization expense. These accounts have been added; note that their beginning balances were set to zero.

In Exhibit 2-17, the temporary accounts and the retained earnings account from Exhibit 2-16 are shown, as well as the closing entries to transfer the balances from the temporary accounts to the permanent account, retained earnings. Note that these entries have been lettered to distinguish them from the regular entries of the period. An income summary account has also been used to collect all the revenue and expense balances before closing the net amount ($550) to the retained earnings account. The dividends declared account has been closed directly to retained earnings.

EXHIBIT 2-16

DEMO RETAIL CORPORATION
T-Accounts: After Adjusting Entries

Permanent accounts:

	A – Cash		
✓	3,000		
(4)	2,200	2,700	(5)
(7a)	5,000	15,000	(7c)
(7b)	10,000	250	(8)
✓	2,250		

	A – Accounts Receivable		
✓	0		
(1)	2,500	2,200	(4)
✓	300		

	A – Inventory		
✓	2,500		
(3)	2,100	1,800	(2)
✓	2,800		

	A – Land		
✓	0		
(7c)	15,000		
✓	15,000		

	A – Equipment		
✓	4,500	0	
		150	(6)
✓	4,350		

	L – Accounts Payable		
		2,500	✓
(5)	2,700	2,100	(3)
		1,900	✓

	L – Bank Loan		
		0	✓
		10,000	(7b)
		10,000	✓

	SE – Common Shares		
		7,500	✓
		5,000	(7a)
		12,500	✓

	SE – Retained Earnings		
		0	✓

Temporary accounts:

	SE – Sales Revenues		
		0	✓
		2,500	(1)
		2,500	✓

	SE – Cost of Goods Sold	
✓		0	
(2)		1,800	
✓		1,800	

	SE – Dividends Declared	
✓	0		
(8)	250		
✓	250		

	SE – Amortization Expense	
✓		0	
(6)		150	
✓		150	

EXHIBIT 2-17

DEMO RETAIL CORPORATION
T-Accounts: Closing Entries

	SE – Retained Earnings		
		0	✓
(E)	250	550	(D)
		300	✓

	SE – Income Summary		
		0	✓
(B)	1,800	2,500	(A)
(C)	150		
		550	✓
(D)	550		
		0	✓

	SE – Sales Revenues		
		0	✓
		2,500	(1)
		2,500	
(A)	2,500		
		0	✓

	SE – Costs of Goods Sold		
✓	0		
(2)	1,800		
	1,800		
		1,800	(B)
✓	0		

	SE – Dividends Declared		
✓	0		
(8)	250	250	(E)
✓	0		

	SE – Amortization Expense		
✓	0		
(6)	150		
	150		
		150	(C)
✓		0	

EXHIBIT 2-18

Demo Retail Corporation
Statement of Retained Earnings
For the month ended January 31, 19x1

Retained Earnings, Jan. 1	$0
Add:	
Net Income	550
Deduct:	
Dividends Declared	250
Retained Earnings, Jan. 31	$300

The income statement, balance sheet, and statement of changes in financial position for Demo Retail Corporation for this accounting period were shown earlier in the chapter. The preparation of the income statement and balance sheet can be made directly from the balances in Exhibits 2-16 and 2-17. The statement of changes in financial position can be prepared using the transactions identified in the cash account in Exhibit 2-16. Exhibit 2-18 shows one additional statement that many corporations prepare, a statement of retained earnings. Note that dividends are shown on this statement.

The format and order of presentation of the line items on the income statement and balance sheet are addressed in Chapter 3. The format of the statement of changes in financial position is discussed in more detail in Chapter 5.

◖◗ SUMMARY

This chapter has introduced the basic operations of a double entry accounting system by starting with the basic accounting equation. The procedures were further explained by describing the double entry system and walking through the accounting cycle using a series of transactions. A retail corporation served as the example in this explanation, but the same procedures would be used in any profit organization. In the next chapter these basics will be applied again in a manufacturing operation. More details of the accrual basis of accounting, as well as some finer points regarding the balance sheet and income statement presentation, will also be discussed.

SUMMARY PROBLEM

The balance sheet of Wagners Retail Company as of January 1, 19x1 is shown in Exhibit 2-19. The following transactions occurred during 19x1:

1. Goods with an aggregate selling price of $80,000 were sold, all on account.

2. A review of accounts receivable showed that $750 remained uncollected as of December 31, 19x1.

3. Salaries totalling $20,500 were earned by employees. Cash payments for salaries totalled $20,375.

4. Purchases of inventory, all on account, totalled $39,700. (Assume that this is the only item that affects accounts payable.)

5. Payments on accounts payable totalled $37,300.

6. A count of inventory at December 31, 19x1 revealed that $9,700 remained unsold in ending inventory.

7. Rent for each month is prepaid on the last day of the preceding month. Monthly payments during 19x1 were $1,300/month.

8. Interest on the bank loan accrues at 9% and is payable at the end of each month. On December 31, 19x1, $200 of the principal of the loan was repaid.

9. Amortization expense on the equipment totalled $2,000.

10. New equipment was purchased for $4,500.

11. The tax rate is 40% for 19x1. Taxes are computed at the end of each quarter and are paid one month later. Assume that the taxes on income in 19x1 were evenly spread across the four quarters of the year.

12. Dividends of $210 were declared and paid.

Required:

Prepare journal entries to record the effects of the transactions above, post the journal entries to T-accounts, and close the temporary income accounts first to an income summary account, and then to retained earnings. Prepare an income statement and a balance sheet.

EXHIBIT 2-19

WAGNERS RETAIL COMPANY
Balance Sheet
As of January 1, 19x1

Assets	
Cash	$4,500
Accounts receivable	500
Inventory	7,500
Prepaid rent	1,200
Equipment	9,200
Total assets	$22,900

Liabilities	
Accounts payable	$5,400
Accrued salaries payable	400
Income taxes payable	360
Bank loan	800
Total liabilities	$ 6,960

Shareholders' equity	
Common shares	3,600
Retained earnings	12,340
Total shareholders' equity	$15,940
Total liabilities and shareholders' equity	$22,900

SUGGESTED SOLUTION TO SUMMARY PROBLEM

The journal entries are shown in Exhibit 2-20. The posting of the entries to the T-accounts is shown in Exhibit 2-21. The entries are numbered to correspond with the transaction number in the journal entries. Closing entries are lettered to distinguish them from regular entries. Financial statements are shown in Exhibits 2-22 and 2-23. The following detail is provided for selected transactions:

Transaction 2. The ending balance of $750 is provided in the problem. The cash receipts from customers are then determined from the other information in the T-account (beginning balance, debit entries, and ending balance).

Transaction 3. Salaries earned during the period should be shown as expenses. Salaries paid during the period reflect the payment of salaries from the previous period (i.e., the beginning balance in the accrued salaries payable account) as well as the payment of salaries during the current period. The ending balance in the salaries payable account reflects the salaries that were earned during the current period but not paid at year-end.

Transaction 6. The physical count of unsold inventory provides the ending balance in the inventory account. The cost of goods sold is then determined by considering the beginning balance, the purchases of inventory, and the ending balance.

Transaction 7. The beginning balance ($1,200) in prepaid rent is the payment made on December 31 of the prior year that covers rent expense in January of 19x1. This, along with 11 months of payments (11 × $1,300/month = $14,300) during 19x1, constitutes the rent expense for the year of $15,500 ($1,200 + $14,300). The final payment in 19x1 of $1,300 applies to the first month in 19x2 and is, therefore, the ending balance in the prepaid rent account.

Transaction 8. Because the interest expense is paid at the end of each month, there is no accrued liability to be shown at the end of the period. The cash payments for interest, in this case, are the same as the expense. The expense is calculated by multiplying the principal ($800) times the interest rate (9%).

Transaction 11. To determine the tax expense for the period, income before taxes must first be determined. In the T-accounts in Exhibit 2-23, the income before taxes is summarized in the income summary account. The intermediate balance of $4,428 is the income before taxes. The tax expense is then calculated by taking 40% of this number, resulting in $1,771 for the year (40% × $4,428 = $1,771). The beginning balance in the taxes payable account is the tax computed for the last quarter of the previous year that is paid in January of 19x1. The quarterly payments in 19x1 are $443 ($1,771/4), assuming the income is evenly distributed across the quarters. The payment for the beginning balance in the tax payable account and three of the quarterly payments constitute the payments for taxes in 19x1 of $1,689 [$360 + (3 × $443)]. The last quarter's amount of $442 ($1 less than the other three quarterly payments due to rounding error) is still payable at December 31, 19x1 and is, therefore, the ending balance in the taxes payable account.

EXHIBIT 2-20

WAGNER RETAIL COMPANY
General Journal
19x1

Transaction	Account name	Debit	Credit
1	Accounts receivable	80,000	
	Sales revenue		80,000
	Sold goods on account.		
2	Cash	79,750	
	Accounts receivable		79,750
	Collected accounts receivable.		

EXHIBIT 2-20 (continued)

WAGNER RETAIL COMPANY
General Journal
19x1

Transaction	Account name	Debit	Credit
3a	Salaries expense	20,500	
	Accrued salaries		20,500
	Salaries owed to employees.		
3b	Accrued salaries	20,375	
	Cash		20,375
	Paid salaries owed.		
4	Inventory	39,700	
	Accounts payable		39,700
	Purchased inventory on account.		
5	Accounts payable	37,300	
	Cash		37,300
	Payments on accounts payable.		
6	Cost of goods sold	37,500	
	Inventory		37,500
	Cost of inventory sold during the year.		
7a	Prepaid rent	15,600	
	Cash		15,600
	Paid monthly rent of 1,300 in advance.		
7b	Rent expense	15,500	
	Prepaid rent		15,500
	Record rent for January to December.		
8a	Interest expense	72	
	Cash		72
	Paid 9% interest on bank loan.		
8b	Bank loan	200	
	Cash		200
	Reduced principal of the bank loan.		
9	Amortization expense	2,000	
	Equipment		2,000
	Recorded equipment amortization.		
10	Equipment	4,500	
	Cash		4,500
	Purchased equipment.		
11a	Tax expense	1,771	
	Taxes payable		1,771
	Record tax owed on 19x1 income.		
11b	Taxes payable	1,689	
	Cash		1,689
	Tax amount paid to Revenue Canada.		
12	Dividends declared	210	
	Cash		210
	Dividends declared and paid.		

EXHIBIT 2-21

WAGNERS RETAIL COMPANY
T-Accounts

A – Cash

✓	4,500			
(2)	79,750	20,375	(3b)	
		37,300	(5)	
		15,600	(7a)	
		72	(8a)	
		200	(8b)	
		4,500	(10)	
		1,689	(11b)	
		210	(12)	
✓	4,304			

L – Accounts Payable

		5,400		✓
(5)	37,300	39,700		(4)
		7,800		✓

A – Accounts Receivable

✓	500		
(1)	80,000	79,750	(2)
✓	750		

L – Accrued Salaries

		400	✓
(3b)	20,375	20,500	(3a)
		525	✓

A – Inventory

✓	7,500		
(4)	39,700	37,500	(6)
✓	9,700		

L – Taxes Payable

		360	✓
(11b)	1,689	1,771	(11a)
		442	✓

A – Prepaid Rend

✓	1,200		
(7a)	15,600	15,500	(7b)
✓	1,300		

L – Bank Loan

		800	✓
(8b)	200		
		600	✓

A – Equipment

✓	9,200		
(10)	4,500	2,000	(9)
✓	11,700		

SE – Common Shares

	3,600	✓
	3,600	✓

SE – Retained Earnings

		12,340	✓
(H)	210	2,657	(I)
		14,787	✓

EXHIBIT 2-21 (continued)

WAGNERS RETAIL COMPANY

Temporary Accounts

SE – Sales Revenues

	0	✓	
	80,000	(1)	
	80,000		
(A)	80,000		
	0	✓	

SE – Salary Expense

✓	0		
(3a)	20,500		
	20,500		
		20,500	(B)
✓	0		

SE – Cost of Goods Sold

✓	0		
(6)	37,500		
	37,500		
(A)		37,500	(C)
✓	0		

SE – Rent Expense

✓	0		
(7b)	15,500		
	15,500		
		15,500	(D)
✓	0		

SE – Interest Expense

✓	0		
(8a)	72		
		72	
		72	(E)
✓	0		

SE – Amortization Expense

✓	0		
(9)	2,000		
	2,000		
		2,000	(F)
✓	0		

SE – Tax Expense

✓	0		
(11a)	1,771		
	1,771		
		1,771	(G)
✓	0		

SE – Dividends Declared

✓	0		
(12)	210		
	210		
		210	(H)
✓	0		

SE – Income Summary

		0	✓
(B)	20,500	80,000	(A)
(C)	37,500		
(D)	15,500		
(E)	72		
(F)	2,000		
		4,428	
(G)	1,771		
		2,657	
(I)	2,657		
		0	✓

EXHIBIT 2-22

WAGNERS RETAIL COMPANY
Income Statement
For the year ended December 31, 19x1

Revenues		$80,000
Expenses:		
Cost of goods sold	$37,500	
Salary expense	20,500	
Rent expense	15,500	
Amortization expense	2,000	
Interest expense	72	
Total expenses		75,572
Income before taxes		$ 4,428
Tax expense		1,771
Net income		$ 2,657

EXHIBIT 2-23

WAGNERS RETAIL COMPANY
Balance Sheet
As at December 31

	19x1	19x0
Assets		
Cash	$ 4,304	$ 4,500
Accounts receivable	750	500
Inventory	9,700	7,500
Prepaid rent	1,300	1,200
Equipment	11,700	9,200
Total assets	$27,754	$22,900
Liabilities		
Accounts payable	$ 7,800	$ 5,400
Accrued salaries	525	400
Taxes payable	442	360
Bank loan	600	800
Total liabilities	$ 9,367	$ 6,960
Shareholders' equity		
Common shares	3,600	3,600
Retained earnings	14,787	12,340
Total shareholders' equity	$18,387	$15,940
Total liabilities and		
shareholders' equity	$27,754	$22,900

ABBREVIATIONS USED

A	Asset
Cr.	Credit
Dr.	Debit
GAAP	Generally Accepted Accounting Principles
Inv.	Inventory
L	Liability
SE	Shareholders' equity

SYNONYMS

Amortization/depreciation

Permanent accounts/Real accounts

Posting to the ledger/Posting/Post

Profit/Net Income/Return

Temporary accounts/Nominal accounts

GLOSSARY

Accounting cycle The sequence of steps that occur in the recording of transactions and events in the accounting system.

Accounts payable The liabilities that result when the corporation buys inventory or supplies on credit. It represents a future obligation.

Accounts receivable The asset that results when a customer buys goods or services on credit. It represents the right to receive cash from the customer.

Accrual basis The accounting basis used by almost all corporations that recognizes revenues and expenses in the period in which they are earned or incurred and not in the period in which the cash inflow or outflow occurs.

Adjusted trial balance A listing of the account balances after adjusting entries are made but before the closing entries are made.

Adjusting entry An entry made at the end of the period to record an event or transaction that has not been recorded during the current accounting period. Events or transactions that are not signalled in any other way are recorded through adjusting entries.

Amortization The expense taken each period based on the use of a noncurrent asset, such as plant or equipment. Amortization is a process that uses a systematic and rational method, such as the straight-line method, to allocate the cost of a noncurrent asset to each of the years of its useful life. Amortization is sometimes referred to as depreciation.

Amortization value The portion of the cost of a noncurrent asset, such as plant or equipment, that is to be amortized over its useful life. The amortization value is equal to the original cost of the asset less its estimated residual value.

Cash basis The accounting basis used by some entities in which revenues and expenses are recognized when the cash inflow or outflow occurs.

Chart of accounts A listing of the names of the accounts used in the accounting system.

Close the books The process by which the corporation makes closing entries to complete one accounting period and sets the balances in the temporary accounts to zero to start the next period.

Closing entries Entries made at the end of the accounting period to transfer the balances from the temporary income statement and dividend accounts to the retained earnings account.

Cost of goods sold The expense that is recorded for the cost of the goods sold during the period.

Credit An entry made to the right side of an account or a reference to the right side of an account.

Debit An entry made to the left side of an account or a reference to the left side of an account.

Depreciation A synonym for amortization.

Dividends declared A distribution of assets (usually cash) to the shareholders of a corporation. The Board of Directors of the corporation votes to formally declare the distribution, at which point it becomes a legal obligation of the corporation.

Double entry accounting system An accounting system that maintains the equality of the balance sheet equation. Each entry requires that equal amounts of debits and credits be made.

Fair market value The value of an asset or liability based on the price that could be obtained from, or paid to, an independent third party in an arms-length transaction.

GAAP Generally accepted accounting principles.

Income summary account An account used to summarize all the temporary income statement accounts prior to their being closed to retained earnings.

Journal A place where transactions and events are originally recorded in the accounting system.

Journal entry An entry made to the journal to record a transaction or event.

Ledger A place where transactions and events are summarized in account balances. Entries are recorded in the ledger by a process known as posting.

Matching concept A concept in accounting that requires all expenses related to the production of revenues to be recorded during the same time period as the revenues. The expenses are said to be matched with the revenues.

Net income The difference between the revenues and the expenses recognized during the period.

Nonmonetary exchange An exchange of goods or services in which the assets or liabilities exchanged are nonmonetary (i.e., not money or cash).

Note payable A formal loan document representing the amount owed by a corporation. There is usually interest owed on this type of debt.

Permanent accounts Accounts whose balance carries over from one period to the next. All balance sheet accounts are considered permanent accounts.

Posting A synonym for posting to the ledger.

Posting to the ledger The process of transferring the information recorded in a journal entry to the ledger system.

Profit A synonym for net income.

Profit margin ratio A ratio that compares the profit during an accounting period with the related revenues.

Residual value The estimate of the value of an asset at the end of its useful life, made at the time of purchase of the asset.

Return on assets A ratio that compares the net income for the period with the investment in assets.

Return on equity A ratio that compares the net income for the period with the investment shareholders make in the company.

Revenue recognition criteria Criteria established within GAAP that describe when revenues should be recognized in the financial statements.

Sale on account A sale in which the seller receives a promise to pay at a later date from the buyer.

Sales revenue The amount of sales recognized during the accounting period based on the revenue recognition criteria.

Straight-line amortization An amortization method that calculates the amount of amortizationexpense for each period by dividing the amortization value by the estimated number of years of useful life.

T-account A device used to represent a ledger account.

Temporary accounts Accounts used to keep track of information temporarily during an accounting period. Balances in these accounts are eventually transferred to a permanent account at the end of the period using a closing entry.

Transaction An exchange of resources with an outside entity or an internal event that affects the balance in individual asset, liability or shareholders' equity accounts.

Transaction analysis The process by which the accountant decides what accounts are affected and by how much they are affected by an economic transaction or event.

Trial balance A listing of the account balances.

Useful life The estimate of the expected life over which an asset will be used.

ASSIGNMENT MATERIAL

▼◢ Assessing Your Recall

1. In the adjusted trial balance phase of the accounting cycle, the retained earnings account has its beginning of period balance, whereas the rest of the permanent accounts have their proper end of period balance. Explain why this is the case.

2. Discuss why dividends do not appear on the income statement but do appear on the statement of changes in financial position.

3. What advantages and disadvantages are there in using the cash basis of accounting rather than the accrual basis?

4. Identify the three major sections in the statement of changes in financial position and briefly describe the nature of the transactions that appear in each section.

5. Respond to each of the following statements with a true or false answer:
   a. Debits increase liability accounts.
   b. Revenues are credit entries to shareholders' equity.
   c. Cash receipts from customers are debited to accounts receivable.
   d. Dividends declared decrease cash immediately.
   e. The cash basis recognizes expenses when they are incurred.
   f. There is no such thing as a prepaid rent account on the cash basis.
   g. Dividends are an expense of doing business and should appear on the income statement.

6. Indicate whether each of the following accounts normally has a debit or a credit balance:
   a. Accounts Receivable
   b. Accounts Payable
   c. Sales Revenue
   d. Dividends Declared
   e. Dividends Payable
   f. Amortization Expense
   g. Common Shares
   h. Prepaid Rent
   i. Deposits from Customers

7. Draw the accounting cycle, and briefly describe each step.

8. Briefly describe how a company typically calculates the cost of goods sold.

9. "Expense accounts have debit balances, and debit entries increase these accounts." Reconcile this statement with the normal effects of entries on shareholders' equity accounts and the resulting balances.

10. What are revenue recognition criteria, and how does the matching concept relate to these criteria?

▶◣ Applying Your Knowledge

11. Given the following transactions, what income would be reported on the cash basis and on the accrual basis:

    Credit sales to customers totalled $15,000.

    Cash collections on account from customers totalled $13,000.

    Cost of goods sold during the period was $8,000.

    Payments made to suppliers of inventory totalled $7,500.

    Salaries of $4,000 were paid; salaries of $600 remained unpaid at year-end; there were no salaries unpaid at the beginning of the year.

    Insurance premiums on a two-year policy were paid in the amount of $600. At year-end, 18 months of coverage remain.

12. Explain why you agree or disagree with the following statement: "Retained earnings are like money in the bank; you can always use them to pay your bills if you get into trouble."

13. Compare and contrast the income statement and the statement of changes in financial position.

14. For each of the transactions below, indicate which accounts are affected, whether they increase or decrease, and whether they should be debited (Dr.) or credited (Cr.).

    a. Issue common shares for cash.

    b. Buy equipment from a supplier on credit (short-term).

    c. Buy inventory from a supplier partly with cash and partly on account.

    d. Sell a unit of inventory to a customer on account.

    e. Receive a payment from a customer on his or her account.

    f. Borrow money from the bank.

    g. Declare a dividend (to be paid later).

    h. Pay a dividend (that was previously declared).

    i. Recognize wages earned by employees (to be paid at the end of the next pay period).

15. For each of the following transactions, indicate how income and cash flow are affected (increase, decrease, no effect) and by how much:

    a. Issue common shares for $1,000.

    b. Sell, on account, a unit of inventory for $150 that cost $115. The unit is already in inventory.

    c. Purchase equipment for $500 cash.

    d. Amortize plant and equipment by $300.

    e. Purchase a unit of inventory, on account, for $100.

    f. Make a payment on accounts payable for $200.

    g. Receive a payment from a customer for $75 on his or her account.

    h. Declare a dividend for $400.

    i. Pay a dividend for $400.

16. Construct journal entries for each of the following transactions:

    a. Borrow $1,500 from the bank.

    b. Buy land for $20,000 in cash.

   c. Issue common shares for $5,000.

   d. Buy inventory costing $3,000 on account.

   e. Sell inventory costing $2,500 to customers, on account, for $3,500.

   f. Receive a payment from a customer for $500 representing a down payment on a unit of inventory that must be ordered.

   g. Make a payment of $250 to the electric company for power used during the current period.

   h. Declare a dividend of $350.

   i. Amortize equipment by $500.

17. Construct journal entries for each of the following transactions:

   a. Issue common shares for $10,000.

   b. At the time of sale of a piece of inventory, recognize the warranty cost, which is estimated to be $500. Hint: This is a possible future cost to the corporation. If the sale is recognized in the current period, all associated expenses should be matched to that revenue in the same period.

   c. Receive a payment from a customer on his or her account in the amount of $325.

   d. Make a payment to the bank of $850. Of this amount, $750 represents interest and the rest is a repayment of principal.

   e. Return a unit of inventory costing $200 that was damaged in shipment. You have already paid for the unit and request a refund from the supplier.

   f. Dividends of $175 that were previously declared are paid.

   g. Purchase equipment costing $1,800. You pay $600 in cash and give the supplier a note payable for the balance of the purchase price.

   h. Sales on account of $15,000 are reported for the period.

   i. A count of physical inventory at the end of the period indicates an ending balance of $575. The beginning balance was $485, and the purchases for the period were $11,500. Record the cost of goods sold.

18. For each of the following transactions, indicate what, if any, adjusting entries would be needed to account for the effects of the transaction in the future:

   a. Purchase equipment.

   b. Borrow money from the bank.

   c. Purchase inventory on account.

   d. Pay rent in advance for a warehouse.

   e. Pay for an insurance policy on an office building.

   f. Sell inventory for cash to customers.

   g. Sign a warranty agreement with a customer that covers a product that was sold to them. See 17 (b) for more information about this type of transaction.

   h. Buy a patent for a new production process.

19. Indicate the effects of the following transactions on the income statement equations and the statement of changes in financial position. Assume that the fiscal year-end of the corporation is December 31.

   a. Borrow $2,500 from the bank on Jan. 1, 19X1.

   b. Pay interest on the bank loan on Dec. 31, 19X1. The interest rate is 10%.

c. Buy equipment on Jan. 1, 19X1 for $2,000. The equipment has an estimated useful life of five years and an estimated residual value at the end of five years of $500.

d. Record the amortization for the equipment as of Dec. 31, 19X1, assuming the corporation uses the straight-line method.

e. Sales for the period totalled $5,500, of which $3,500 were on account. The cost of the products sold was $3,600.

f. Collections from customers on account totalled $2,800.

g. Purchases of inventory on account during 19X1 totalled $2,700.

h. Payments to suppliers totalled $2,900 during 19X1.

i. Employees earned salaries of $800 during 19X1.

j. All employee salaries were paid by year-end except the salaries for the last week in December, which totalled $50.

k. Dividends were declared and paid in the amount of $100.

20. Indicate the effects of the following transactions on the income statement and the statement of changes in financial position. Assume that the fiscal year-end of the corporation is December 31.

a. Issue common shares for $25,000.

b. Pay an insurance premium of $600 on July 1 that provides coverage for the 12-month period starting July 1.

c. Recognize the amount of insurance expense that has been used from July 1 through December 31, assuming the facts in Transaction b.

d. Sales recorded for the period totalled $60,000, of which $25,000 were cash sales.

e. Cash collections on customer accounts totalled $37,000.

f. Sign a contract to purchase a piece of equipment that costs $1,200, and put a downpayment of $100 on the purchase.

g. Dividends of $1,300 are declared.

h. Dividends of $1,150 are paid.

i. Amortization of $3,300 was taken on the property, plant and equipment.

j. Purchase $1,350 of inventory on account.

k. Inventory costing $795 was sold.

21. The T. George Company started business on Jan. 1, 19X2. Listed below are the transactions that occurred during 19X2.

Required:

a. Set up T-accounts as needed, and enter the transactions in the T-accounts. Make sure that you indicate the type of account and that you designate, appropriately, the beginning and ending balances, as well as the referencing of the transactions.

b. Prepare a balance sheet, an income statement, and statement of changes in financial position for 19X2.

Transactions:

1) On Jan. 1, 19X2, the company issued 10,000 common shares for $175,000.

2) On Jan. 1, 19X2, the company borrowed $125,000 from the bank.

3) On Jan. 2, 19x2, the company purchased (for cash) land and a building costing $200,000. The building was recently appraised at $140,000. Hint: you must record the land and building in separate accounts.

4) Inventory costing $100,000 was purchased on account.

5) An investment was made in Calhoun Company shares in the amount of $75,000.

6) Sales to customers totalled $190,000 in 19x2. Of these, $30,000 were cash sales.

7) Collections on accounts receivable totalled $135,000.

8) Payments to suppliers totalled $92,000 in 19x2.

9) Salaries paid to employees totalled $44,000. There were no unpaid salaries at year-end.

10) A physical count of unsold inventories at year-end revealed inventory costed at $10,000 was still on hand.

11) The building was estimated to have a useful life of 20 years and a residual value of $20,000. The company uses straight-line amortization.

12) The interest on the bank loan is recognized each month and is paid on the first day of the succeeding month; that is, January's interest is recognized in January and paid on February 1. The interest rate is 12%.

13) The investment in Calhoun Company paid dividends of $5,000 in 19x2. All of it had been received by year-end.

14) Dividends of $15,000 were declared on Dec. 15, 19x2 and were scheduled to be paid on Jan. 10, 19x3.

22. The Jones Tool Company started business on October 1, 19x3. Its fiscal year runs through September 30 of the following year. Following are the transactions that occurred during fiscal 19x4 (the year starting Oct. 1, 19x3 and ending Sept. 30, 19x4).

Required:

a. Set up T-accounts as needed, and enter the transactions in the T-accounts. Make sure that you indicate the type of account and that you designate, appropriately, the beginning and ending balances, as well as the referencing of the transactions.

b. Prepare an income statement, balance sheet, and a statement of changes in financial position for fiscal 19x4.

Transactions:

1) On Oct. 1, 19x3 J. Jones contributed $100,000 to start the business. Jones is the only owner. She received 10,000 shares.

2) On Oct. 2, 19x3, Jones borrowed $300,000 from a venture capitalist (a lender who specializes in start-up companies). The interest rate on the loan is 11%.

3) On Oct. 3, 19x3, Jones rented a building. The rental agreement was a two-year contract that called for quarterly rental payments of $20,000, payable in advance on Dec. 31, March 31, June 30 and Sept. 30. The first payment was made on Oct. 3, 19x3 and covers the period from Oct. 3 to Dec. 31.

4) On Oct. 3, 19x3, Jones purchased equipment costing $250,000. The equipment had an estimated useful life of seven years and a residual value of $40,000.

5) On Oct. 3, 19x3, Jones purchased initial inventory with a cash payment of $100,000.

6) Sales during the year totalled $800,000, of which $720,000 were credit sales.

7) Collections from customers on account totalled $640,000.

8) Additional purchases of inventory during the year totalled $550,000, all on account.

9) Payments to suppliers totalled $495,000.

10) Inventory on hand at year-end amounted to $115,000.

11) The corporation declared and paid a dividend of $40,000 to J. Jones.

12) Interest on the loan from the venture capitalist was paid at year-end, Sept. 30, as well as $20,000 of the principal.

13) Other selling and administrative expenses totalled $90,000 for the year. Of these, $20,000 were unpaid as of year-end.

14) The income tax rate is 30%. Assume that Jones made payments during the year equal to three quarters of the ultimate tax bill, and the rest are accrued at year-end. Also, assume that the way net income is calculated for tax purposes does not differ from the method used for reporting purposes.

15) Make all adjusting entries for the year.

23. The A.J. Smith Company started business on Jan. 1, 19x4. Following are the transactions that occurred during 19x4.

Required:

a. Construct journal entries for the following transactions.

b. Set up T-accounts as needed, and post the transactions to the T-accounts. Make sure that you indicate the type of account and that you designate, appropriately, the beginning and ending balances, as well as the referencing of the transactions.

c. Prepare a balance sheet, an income statement, and a statement of changes in financial position for fiscal 19x4.

Transactions:

1) On Jan. 1, 19x4, the company issued 25,000 common shares at $15 per share.

2) On Jan. 1, 19x4, the company purchased land and buildings from another company in exchange for $50,000 in cash and 25,000 common shares. The land's value is approximately one-fifth of the total value of the transaction. Hint: you must record the land and building in separate accounts.

3) Equipment worth $100,000 was purchased on July 1, 19x4, in exchange for $50,000 in cash and a one-year, 10% note, principal amount $50,000. The note pays semi-annual interest, and interest was unpaid on Dec. 31, 19x4.

4) The equipment is amortized using the straight-line method, with an estimated useful life of 10 years and an estimated residual value of $0.

5) The buildings purchased in transaction 2) are amortized using the straight-line method, with an estimated useful life of 30 years and an estimated residual value of $40,000.

6) During the year, inventory costing $200,000 was purchased, all on account.

7) Sales during the year were $215,000, of which credit sales were $175,000.

8) Inventory costing $160,000 was sold during the year.

9) Payments to suppliers totalled $175,000.

10) At the end of the year, accounts receivable had a debit balance of $10,000.

11) On March 31, 19X4, the company rented out a portion of its building to Fantek Corporation. Fantek is required to make quarterly payments of $5,000 each. The payments are due on March 31, June 30, Sept. 30, and Dec. 31 of each year, with the first payment on March 31, 19X4. All scheduled payments were made during 19X4.

12) Selling and distribution expenses amounted to $30,000, all paid in cash.

13) During the year, inventory worth $10,000 was destroyed by fire. The inventory was not insured.

14) The company pays taxes at a rate of 30%. During the year, $3,000 was paid to Revenue Canada.

15) Dividends of $4,000 were declared during the year, and $1,000 remained unpaid at year-end.

24. Following are descriptions of line items that should appear on a statement of changes in financial position for the Lockwood Company. Organize these items in a formal statement of changes in financial position, and comment on the health of the company to the extent that you can.

Cash flow line items:
Cash receipts from customers $5,000
Purchase of equipment $12,000
Proceeds from the issuance of shares $20,000
Investment in General Electric shares $3,000
Cash disbursements to suppliers $3,400
Cash payments to employees (salaries) $1,900
Proceeds from the sale of equipment $6,000
Dividends paid $2,500
Repayment of bank loan $8,000

25. Many transactions take place between two independent entities. How you record a particular transaction depends on whose perspective you take. For each of the following transactions, construct the journal entry you would make to record the transaction from each of the perspectives given:

a. Purchase of inventory from a supplier (buyer's and seller's perspectives).

b. Loan from the bank (borrower's and bank's perspectives).

c. Deposit by customer on the purchase of a unit of inventory to be delivered at a later time (company's and customer's perspectives).

d. Company A invests in shares of Company B and obtains the shares directly from Company B (Company A's and Company B's perspectives).

e. Company A invests in shares of Company B and obtains the shares by buying them on the Toronto Stock Exchange, i.e., they had previously been issued by Company B and now trade in the stock market (Company A's and Company B's perspectives).

f. Prepayment of insurance premiums (company's and insurance company's perspectives).

▲◣ Reading and Interpreting Published Financial Statements

26. Base your answers to the following questions on the financial statements of Enerflex Systems Ltd. that you will find in Exhibit 2-24.

a. Determine the amount of cash dividends declared during fiscal 1994.

b. Determine the amount of dividends paid during fiscal 1994.

c. Assuming that all sales were on account, determine the amount of cash collected from customers in 1994.

d. Assuming that the only transactions that flow through the accounts payable to suppliers and others are purchases of inventory, and assuming that all additions to the inventory account were purchases of inventory, determine the cash payments made to suppliers in 1994.

e. Given the change in income taxes payable, was the tax expense in 1994 greater than or less than the cash paid to Revenue Canada? (Ignore deferred taxes in your answer.)

27. Base your answers to the following questions on the financial statements of Cominco Ltd. in Exhibit 2-25.

a. Determine the amount of dividends declared during fiscal 1994.

b. Determine the amount of dividends paid during fiscal 1994.

c. Assuming that all sales were on account, determine the amount of cash collected from customers in 1994. Should you include both sales of products and services in your answer?

d. Assuming that the only transactions that flow through the accounts payable to suppliers and others are purchases of inventory, and assuming that all additions to the inventory account were purchases of inventory, determine the cash payments made to suppliers in 1994. What effect does the cost of services sold have on your answer, that is, should it be included in your answer?

e. [Optional] In shareholders' equity, there is an account called "Cumulative Translation Adjustment." The account is used to capture the effects of translating the financial statements of foreign subsidiaries from their native currency to Canadian dollars. Given the balance that you see in this account, has this translation been favourable or unfavourable for the shareholders? Second, what does the change in this balance from 1993 to 1994 indicate in terms of shareholders' wealth?

28. Exhibit 2-26 includes two financial statements from AT Plastics Ltd.

a. Refer to the consolidated statement of changes in financial position, and compare the net income in each of the last two years to the cash flow from operations in the last two years.

EXHIBIT 2-24

ENERFLEX SYSTEMS LTD.
Consolidated Statements of Financial Position

(Thousands)

	December 31	
	1994	1993
Assets		
Current Assets		
Accounts receivable	$ 50,171	$ 26,106
Inventory (note 1)	18,925	16,780
Total current assets	69,096	42,886
Rental Equipment (note 2)	18,078	9,515
Property, Plant and Equipment (note 3)	13,770	8,012
Goodwill, net of accumulated amortization	1,561	1,607
	$ 102,505	$ 62,020
Liabilities and Shareholders' Equity		
Current Liabilities		
Bank loans (note 4)	$ 12,002	$ 7,837
Accounts payable and accrued liabilities	37,935	18,850
Income taxes payable	6,094	3,614
Deferred income taxes - current	(1,067)	(664)
Current portion of long-term debt (note 4)	76	70
Total current liabilities	55,040	29,707
Long-term Debt (note 4)	4,716	4,792
Deferred Income Taxes	1,156	1,063
	60,912	35,562
Shareholders' Equity		
Share capital (note 5)	34,158	34,158
Retained earnings (deficit)	7,435	(7,700)
	41,593	26,458
	$ 102,505	$ 62,020

Commitments and Contingencies (note 6)

On behalf of the Board:

Director

Director

EXHIBIT 2-24 (continued)

ENERFLEX SYSTEMS LTD.
Consolidated Statements of Income

(Thousands, except per share amounts)   *Year Ended December 31*

	1994	1993
Sales (note 7)	$ 217,342	$ 119,983
Cost of Goods Sold	166,055	92,149
Gross Margin	51,287	27,834
Expenses (Income)		
Selling, general and administrative (note 8)	20,646	13,570
Interest (note 4)	1,345	1,114
Gain on sale of rental equipment	(872)	(438)
	21,119	14,246
Income before Income Taxes	30,168	13,588
Income Taxes (note 9)	12,389	5,893
Net Income	$ 17,779	$ 7,695
Net Income per Common Share (note 10)	$ 2.35	$ 1.02*

*Pro forma

ENERFLEX SYSTEMS LTD.
Consolidated Statements of Shareholders' Equity

(Thousands)

	Preferred Shares	Common Shares	Retained Earnings (Deficit)	Total Shareholders' Equity
Balance at January 1, 1993	$ 2,800	$ 6,249	$ 14,357	$23,406
Net income			7,695	7,695
Redemption of preferred shares, January 1993	(2,800)			(2,800)
Cash dividends, January 1993				
Preferred shares			(24)	(24)
Common shares			(2,600)	(2,600)
Gross proceeds from the public issue of common shares on September 22, 1993		36,000		36,000
Expenses of issue ($3,094) less income taxes ($1,252)		(1,842)		(1,842)
Distribution to shareholders (note 5)		(6,249)	(27,128)	(33,377)
Balance at December 31, 1993	–	34,158	(7,700)	26,458
Net income			17,779	17,779
Cash dividends			(2,644)	(2,644)
Balance at December 31, 1994	$ –	$ 34,158	$ 7,435	$41,593

EXHIBIT 2-24 (continued)

ENERFLEX SYSTEMS LTD.
Consolidated Statements of Changes in Financial Position

(Thousands)	Year Ended December 31	
	1994	1993
Operating Activities		
Net income	**$ 17,779**	$ 7,695
Depreciation and amortization	**2,326**	2,313
Deferred income taxes	**(310)**	(706)
Gain on sale of rental equipment	**(872)**	(438)
Funds from operations	**18,923**	8,864
Changes in non-cash working capital	**(4,645)**	(7,016)
	14,278	1,848
Investment Activities		
Acquisition of property, plant and equipment	**(7,161)**	(1,561)
Acquisition of rental equipment	**(8,568)**	(2,677)
	(15,729)	(4,238)
Financing Activities		
Net proceeds from public issue of common shares	**–**	34,158
Redemption of preferred shares	**–**	(2,800)
Distribution to shareholders of record prior to public issue	**–**	(33,377)
Dividends paid	**(2,644)**	(2,624)
Mortgage repayments	**(70)**	(64)
	(2,714)	(4,707)
Bank Loans		
Increase in bank loans during year	**4,165**	7,097
Beginning of year	**7,837**	740
End of year	**$ 12,002**	$ 7,837

b. In general, why are there differences between cash flows from operations and net income? Refer specifically to the differences due to sale transactions and depreciation.

c. Comment on AT Plastics' ability to pay for its cash needs over the last two years using its cash from operations. Do you think that AT Plastics Ltd. is in a favourable cash flow position? Support your answer.

EXHIBIT 2-25

COMINCO LTD.
Consolidated Statements of Operations
Years Ended December 31, 1994 and 1993

	1994	1993
		(thousands)
Revenue		
Sales of products and services	$1,097,931	$ 982,504
Gain on sale of exploration properties	25,610	20,997
Income from sale of investments and other	3,267	11,314
Equity in net earnings of associated companies	11,761	10,029
	1,138,569	1,024,844
Costs and Expenses		
Costs of products and distribution	772,016	949,725
Depreciation, depletion and amortization	115,774	127,271
General, administrative and selling	53,792	56,403
Interest (Note 11)	32,469	37,129
Mineral exploration	41,419	30,739
	1,015,470	1,201,267
Earnings (Loss) Before the Following	123,099	(176,423)
Gain on sale of power expansion rights (Note 15[f])	51,356	—
Gain on sale of associated companies (Note 12)	64,716	57,935
Earnings (Loss) Before Taxes and Minority Interest	239,171	(118,488)
Income and resource tax (expense) recovery (Note 13)	(109,519)	6,522
Minority interest	2,424	(1,244)
Net Earnings (Loss)	$ 132,076	$ (113,210)
Net Earnings (Loss) Per Common Share (Note 9[e])	$ 1.62	$ (1.46)

Consolidated Statements of Earnings
Reinvested in the Business
Years Ended December 31, 1994 and 1993

	1994	1993
		(thousands)
Amount at Beginning of Year	$ 393,002	$ 509,451
Net Earnings (Loss)	132,076	(113,210)
	525,078	396,241
Premium on redemption of preferred shares	54	158
Dividends paid		
Preferred – Series A $2.00 per share	276	287
– Series B $2.44 per share	2,715	2,794
	3,045	3,239
Amount at End of Year	$ 522,033	$ 393,002

EXHIBIT 2-25 (continued)

COMINCO LTD.
Consolidated Balance Sheets
At December 31, 1994 and 1993

	1994	1993
		(thousands)
Current Assets		
Cash and short-term investments	$ 46,112	$ 12,327
Accounts receivable	207,723	191,953
Inventories (Note 2)	366,921	293,307
Prepaid expenses	11,580	8,629
	632,336	506,216
Investments		
Associated companies (Note 12)	—	48,100
Other (Note 4)	40,770	33,878
	40,770	81,978
Fixed Assets (Note 5)		
Land, buildings and equipment	1,528,972	1,464,428
Mineral properties and development	191,525	170,521
	1,720,497	1,634,949
Other Assets (Note 6)	52,367	48,077
	$2,445,970	$ 2,271,220
Current Liabilities		
Bank loans and notes payable	$ 3,998	$ 11,669
Accounts payable and accrued liabilities	208,681	169,878
Income and resource taxes	38,513	11,687
Long-term debt due within one year	52,519	31,824
	303,711	225,058
Long-Term Debt (Note 7)	505,496	622,022
Deferred Liabilities (Note 8)	115,212	113,573
Income Tax Provided but not Currently Payable	305,270	240,107
Minority Interests	39,441	33,520
Shareholders' Equity		
Capital (Note 9)	609,017	609,123
Earnings reinvested in the business	522,033	393,002
Cumulative translation adjustment (Note 10)	45,790	34,815
	1,176,840	1,036,940
	$2,445,970	$ 2,271,220

Commitments and Contingencies (Note 15)

Approved by the Board:

N. B. Keevil   Director   D.A. Thompson   Director

EXHIBIT 2-25 (continued)

COMINCO LTD.

Consolidated Statements of Changes in Cash Resources

Years Ended December 31, 1994 and 1993

	1994	1993
		(thousands)
Cash From (Used In) Operations		
Net earnings (Loss)	$ 132,076	$ (113,210)
Add (deduct) items not involving cash		
Depreciation, depletion and amortization	115,774	127,271
Deferred income and resource taxes	70,402	(10,593)
Minority interest	(2,424)	1,244
Earnings from associates net of dividends	(9,977)	(8,012)
Gain on sale of investments	(118,520)	(74,092)
Other items	(48,869)	25,924
	138,462	(51,468)
(Increase) decrease in non-cash working capital items	(3,537)	29,545
	134,925	(21,923)
Cash From (Used In) Financing Activities		
Dividends paid to preferred shareholders	(2,991)	(3,081)
Redemption of preferred shares	(801)	(2,094)
Issue of common shares	641	—
Issue of common shares by Cominco Resources, net of share issue costs	11,603	—
Additions to long-term debt	55,887	148,218
Repayment of long-term debt	(181,137)	(183,062)
	(116,798)	(40,019)
Cash From (Used In) Investing Activities		
Proceeds from disposal of assets and investments (Note 12 and 15[f])	203,315	266,832
Fixed assets additions (Note 15[d])	(171,543)	(189,789)
Investment in other companies	(6,052)	—
Other items	(2,391)	(4,047)
	23,329	72,996
Increase in Cash Resources	41,456	11,054
Net Cash (Borrowings) at Beginning of Year	658	(10,396)
Net Cash at End of Year	$ 42,114	$ 658

Cash comprises cash and short-term investments net of short-term borrowings.

EXHIBIT 2-26

AT PLASTICS LTD.
Consolidated Statements of Operations and Retained Earnings
For the years ended December 31, 1995 and 1994

(thousands of dollars, except per share amounts)	1995	1994
SALES	$204,758	$184,558
COST OF SALES AND OTHER EXPENSES	154,395	148,086
INCOME BEFORE THE UNDERNOTED ITEMS	50,363	36,472
LESS		
Interest on long-term debt	9,945	11,617
Depreciation and amortization	11,477	10,433
Other interest (income)	(389)	587
Other expense (income) (note 10)	357	(2,345)
	21,390	20,292
INCOME BEFORE INCOME TAXES	28,973	16,180
INCOME TAXES		
Current	1,092	1,145
Deferred	3,597	—
	4,689	1,145
NET INCOME FOR THE YEAR	24,284	15,035
DEFICIT AT BEGINNING OF YEAR	(15,036)	(28,361)
DIVIDENDS	(2,280)	(1,710)
RETAINED EARNINGS (DEFICIT) AT END OF YEAR	$ 6,968	$(15,036)
NET INCOME PER SHARE (note 12)	$ 1.92	$ 1.29

29. Base your answers to the following questions on the financial statements of AT Plastics that you will find in the Exhibit for problems 28 and in Exhibit 2-8 included earlier in the chapter.
   a. Determine the amount of dividends declared during 1995.
   b. Determine the amount of dividends paid during fiscal 1995.
   c. Assuming that all sales were on account, determine the amount of cash collected from customers.
   d. Assuming that the only transactions that flow through the accounts payable to suppliers and others are purchases of inventory and assuming that all additions to the inventory account were purchases of inventory, determine the cash payments made to suppliers.

EXHIBIT 2-26 (continued)

AT PLASTICS LTD.
Consolidated Statements of Changes in Financial Position
For the years ended December 31, 1995 and 1994

(thousands of dollars)	1995	1994
CASH FROM (USED IN)		
OPERATIONS		
Net income for the year	$ **24,284**	$ 15,035
Add items charged to income not affecting cash		
Depreciation and amortization	**11,477**	10,433
Deferred income taxes	**3,597**	—
Amortization of exchange on long-term debt	**295**	352
Gain on settlement of debt	**—**	(2,697)
Cash flow before change in working capital and other liabilities	**39,653**	23,123
Change in operating working capital and other liabilities	**(11,407)**	(1,929)
	28,246	21,194
FINANCING ACTIVITIES		
Long-term debt repaid	**(5,330)**	(165,047)
Change in capital leases	**(173)**	233
Senior secured notes issued	**—**	97,731
Common shares issued	**—**	72,312
Preferred shares issued	**—**	3,000
	(5,503)	8,229
DIVIDENDS PAID	**(2,280)**	(1,710)
INVESTING ACTIVITIES		
Purchase of fixed assets	**(12,037)**	(9,018)
Change in other assets	**(1,922)**	(1,983)
	(13,959)	(11,001)
Increase In Cash During Year	**6,504**	16,712
Cash (Bank Overdraft) At Beginning Of Year	**1,357**	(15,355)
Cash And Short-Term Investments At End Of Year	$ **7,861**	$ 1,357

CASE

Saskco Chicken Products

Saskco Chicken Products is a new corporation established by four entrepreneurs from Moose Jaw. They intend to purchase live chickens, process them and sell them as frozen pieces and whole chickens. They initially anticipate hiring three workers to process the chickens. The four owners will work in the business and have the following titles: President (oversees the whole operation including finance and accounting), VP Marketing, VP Operations (in charge of the processing operations), and VP Procurement (in charge of purchasing chickens from farmers). The President of Saskco Chicken Products has hired you for three months to help the corporation set up its accounting system. In anticipation of establishing a computerized accounting package, develop a list of account titles that you think this corporation will need to start operations. For each account title, write a brief one-line explanation for its inclusion in the chart of accounts.

▶▲ Critical Thinking Question

Using the statements of changes in financial position for Camdev Corporation (Exhibit 2-27) and the statement of cash flows of Comac Food Group Inc. (Exhibit 2-28), compare the methods used by the two corporations to finance their activities. What are the future implications of the method(s) of financing used? By referring to the statements, explain why they need outside financing.

EXHIBIT 2-27

CAMDEV CORPORATION
Statement of Changes in Financial Position
Year ended January 31
(in thousands of Canadian dollars)

	1995	1994
OPERATING ACTIVITIES		
Net loss	$ (6,726)	(1,524)
Add:		
Depreciation and amortization	5,445	4,660
Amortization of financing costs	1,725	1,803
CASH FLOW FROM OPERATIONS	444	4,939
Net changes in non-cash balances related to operations:		
Amounts receivable and other	953	(4,384)
Accounts payable and accrued liabilities	1,530	3,285
CASH PROVIDED BY (APPLIED TO) OPERATING ACTIVITIES	2,927	3,840
FINANCING ACTIVITIES		
Debt issued	17,236	11,837
Debt repaid	(18,455)	(17,618)
CASH PROVIDED BY (APPLIED TO) FINANCING ACTIVITIES	(1,219)	(5,781)
INVESTMENT ACTIVITIES		
Expenditures on rental properties	(20,058)	(21,076)
Land held for sale or development	(2,032)	(2,077)
Costs recovered from sale of land	12,809	8,303
Notes receivable	1,700	8,989
Proceeds from investment	–	7,018
Other	(1,204)	2,357
CASH PROVIDED BY (APPLIED TO) INVESTMENT ACTIVITIES	(8,785)	3,514
Increase (decrease) in cash during year	(7,077)	1,573
CASH – beginning of year	14,820	13,247
CASH – end of year	$ 7,743	14,820

Cash comprises cash and short-term deposits.
See accompanying notes to financial statements.

EXHIBIT 2-28

COMAC FOOD GROUP INC.
Statement of Cash Flows
Years ended March 31

	1995 $	1994 $
Cash provided by (used in)		
OPERATING ACTIVITIES		
Net earnings for year	211,000	58,000
Items not requiring cash		
Amortization	99,000	100,000
Gain on sale of assets	—	(7,000)
	310,000	151,000
Net change in non-cash working capital related to		
operating activities	(234,000)	(14,000)
	76,000	137,000
INVESTING ACTIVITIES		
Decrease in notes receivable	113,000	83,000
Additions to capital assets	(52,000)	(17,000)
Additions to deferred charges	(5,000)	(7,000)
Proceeds from disposal of capital assets	6,000	7,000
Acquisition of subsidiary minority interest	(75,000)	—
	(13,000)	66,000
FINANCING ACTIVITIES		
Long term debt	18,000	(187,000)
Capital lease obligations	15,000	11,000
Repayment of capital lease obligations	(11,000)	(3,000)
Repayment of notes payable	(25,000)	(17,000)
Issuance of common shares	131,000	2,000
Dividends accrued	(69,000)	(47,000)
Dividends in arrears	69,000	47,000
	128,000	(194,000)
Increase in cash	191,000	9,000
Cash position, beginning of year	6,000	(3,000)
Cash position, end of year	197,000	6,000
Cash flow from operations per share [note 14]		
Basic	$.026	$.013
Fully diluted	$.023	$.011

Cash position consists of cash and short term deposits net of bank indebtedness.

See accompanying notes

CHAPTER

3

Manufacturing Corporations

Format of the Income
Statement and Balance Sheet

In Chapter 1, we discussed the basic financial statements prepared by many corporations. In Chapter 2, we described the features of a basic accounting system that corporations use to record and accumulate the information presented in financial statements. Those basic features were illustrated with hypothetical retail corporations as examples. In this chapter, manufacturing corporations are discussed to illustrate the differences between their financial statements and those of a retail organization, and the special characteristics that affect their accounting systems. Also in this chapter, the basic format and features of the income statement and balance sheet are discussed.

BASICS OF MANUFACTURING CORPORATIONS

The corporations we have considered so far were involved mainly in retail sales. By retail sales we mean the selling of products such as clothing or food to consumers. Most retail businesses do not produce the items they sell; they buy them ready for sale. They buy at wholesale prices and sell at retail prices. Manufacturing corporations differ from retailers in that they manufacture the products they sell. Therefore, their financial statements are slightly more complex than those of retail corporations because they reflect the additional manufacturing processes undertaken in the manufacture of products. That means the accounting systems used by manufacturers must also be more complex than those of retailers because manufacturers must record and accumulate the additional costs incurred to manufacture their products. The main part of this chapter discusses the format and content of manufacturers' financial statements. Details of the accounting entries used by manufacturing corporations are provided in Appendix B, located at the end of this chapter.

Unlike retailers, whose main cost is the wholesale price they pay for goods, manufacturers incur many types of costs in producing their products. These costs include raw materials, labour, and factory maintenance. Accurate measurement of production costs is necessary for both accounting and decision-making purposes. For accounting purposes, accurate numbers are needed for the income statement to show the costs incurred to produce the goods manufactured and sold. They are also needed for the balance sheet to show the value of inventory assets on hand. For decision-making purposes, managers must know the real cost of producing every unit of their products in order to price the products appropriately—to recover all costs and earn a profit. Management may also use these cost figures to decide if they should continue to produce the products in their own plants, or buy them at a lower cost from other manufacturers, perhaps in a foreign country.

To understand the different items that appear in the financial statements of manufacturing corporations, thought must be given to the types of costs incurred in a manufacturing operation, and to how those costs should be reflected in the financial statements. In the following sections, these different types of manufacturing costs are discussed.

Manufacturing Costs

Exhibit 3-1 shows a list of some of the typical costs incurred in a manufacturing operation. The list is not exhaustive, but it is representative of many common costs.

EXHIBIT 3-1

TYPICAL COSTS INCURRED BY MANUFACTURERS

Raw materials
Labour
Heat, light, and power
Amortization on equipment and buildings
Selling costs
    Advertising
    Commissions
    Rebates/Coupons
    Salespersons' salaries
Administrative staff salaries
President's salary
Maintenance
Warehouse
Transportation
Insurance
Taxes
    Property
    Income
    Sales
Research and development
Distribution
Accounting and computer systems

The calculation and analysis of manufacturing costs can be quite complex. In the simplest possible example, assume that a corporation produces just one product and that every unit of the product is identical. Assume also that they never hold any inventory because every unit produced is sold immediately (we will also assume they hold no inventories of raw materials or work in process). In this case, the total of all costs incurred would also equal the cost of goods sold. Per-unit costs could be calculated simply by dividing the total of all costs incurred by the total number of units produced.

Next, assume that not all goods produced are sold immediately. Then the corporation would have some unsold finished goods on hand at the end of the accounting period. An additional calculation would now be necessary because some of the costs would be for goods produced and sold, while remaining costs would relate to the goods not yet sold. These unsold items would be shown on the balance sheet as the inventory asset. To determine the cost per unit of items manufactured in this scenario, all the costs incurred could be added together and divided by the number of units produced during the period. At the end of the accounting period, the total costs could then be allocated to the cost of goods sold and ending inventory based on the number of units sold, and the number remaining in ending inventory times the unit cost just calculated.

To complicate the situation even further, assume the corporation produces two different products. The calculation of a unit cost is suddenly not so easy. Some costs, such as **raw materials** (the materials that are used to produce the product) and **direct labour** (labour directly used to produce the product), can still be traced to particular products. Material and labour cost records detailing all materials and labour used could be kept for each of the products. These types of costs are sometimes called the **direct costs** of manufacturing. Other costs, such as factory heating, light, and power, or the president's salary, cannot be so directly related to a given product. These are sometimes called **indirect costs**.

Direct costs are relatively easy to allocate to products by using cost records maintained during production. **Indirect costs**, on the other hand, must be allocated in some other way to each product. The president's or the plant manager's salaries, for example, can be allocated based on the amount of time each spends on each product. The president, however, may spend time not only on each product produced but also on developing new products, starting other lines of business, or performing other functions for the corporation. Therefore, the allocation of the president's salary to individual products or product lines will always be arbitrary. In fact, some of the cost of the president's salary should not be allocated to production at all because some time may be spent on developing new ventures unrelated to the production process. On the other hand, 100% of the plant manager's salary, or better yet, the production supervisor's salary, is properly allocated to the production of products because all of these employees' time is normally spent on production. There is still a problem, however, deciding how much of their salaries should go to each product or product line.

Because of the allocation problem for some types of costs, accountants divide costs into two categories: **product costs** and **period costs**. **Product costs** refer to costs that are most closely associated with the production of the product. **Period costs** are those costs that are difficult to associate directly with the production of products and are more easily associated with a period of time. The president's salary would fit into this second category.

■ ■ Product Costs

Product costs include direct production costs such as direct labour and direct materials. Indirect costs such as heat, light, and power, amortization of manufacturing equipment, salaries of plant supervisors, plant maintenance, and plant insurance are also considered product costs. These indirect costs must be allocated among the various products in some systematic fashion. Product costs are also sometimes called **inventoriable costs** because they are the costs that are associated with inventory and end up as cost of goods sold on the income statement when the product is sold.

The indirect costs of manufacturing are also known as **overhead costs**. The three major categories of manufacturing costs are direct materials, direct labour, and overhead. Overhead costs are generally aggregated and then allocated to products on some systematic (but arbitrary) basis. In production processes where direct labour is a major component of the costs of production, the allocation is generally based on the number of direct labour hours (or dollars) used to produce the product, and an overhead rate is determined as the amount of overhead costs per direct labour hour (or dollar). As plants have become more automated, the use of direct labour has diminished and the use of this allocation method makes less sense. Other methods, such as a rate based on machine hours, have been developed to allocate overhead more reasonably.

■ ■ Gross Profit Ratio

When analyzing the financial statements of a corporation that either produces or buys for resale the products it sells, an important indicator that should be calculated is the **gross profit ratio**. This ratio relates the total cost of products sold to the total sales revenue they generate. The **gross profit ratio** actually shows the proportion of the total sales revenue that is left over after the total product costs have been considered. In other words, it tells you what proportion of sales revenue is available to pay for all costs other than product costs. This ratio is calculated as follows:

$$\text{Gross profit ratio} = \frac{\text{Gross profit}}{\text{Net sales}}$$

As an example, the 1994 financial statements of Tritech Precision Inc. (which is headquartered in Toronto, Ontario, and manufactures iron, steel, and aluminum castings for other manufacturing and mining corporations) showed the following information:

	1994	1993
Sales	$99,566,000	$ 71,289,000
Cost of goods sold	79,736,000	58,714,000
Gross profit	19,830,000	12,575,000

Thus the gross profit ratios for 1994 and 1993 are as follows:

$$1994: \quad \frac{19,830,000}{99,566,000} = 19.92\%$$

$$1993: \quad \frac{12,575,000}{71,289,000} = 17.64\%$$

The gross profit ratio increased from 17.64% in 1993 to 19.92% in 1994. Generally, this is a good sign.

The gross profit ratio, as with almost all ratios, does not tell us much on its own. It is most useful for comparing several corporations or for analyzing the operations of one corporation over time. In general, a larger ratio is better than a smaller one. Some stores such as Wal-Mart tend to have relatively low gross profit ratios but make up for the low ratio by achieving larger sales volumes. Specialty stores such as Birks Jewellers tend to have higher gross profit ratios.

■ ■ Period Costs

Period costs are those costs—such as administrative and selling costs—that are most directly associated with a time period rather than with the actual production of goods. The president's salary, as explained earlier, as well as the salaries and expenses of other administrative personnel, fall into this category. Amortization of the administrative facilities or amortization of the portion of a building related to the administrative function are also considered period costs.

Interest on borrowed money is another period cost because it relates to the use of money for a particular time period. Even though most corporations treat interest as a period cost, there is some debate regarding this treatment. Many corporations finance the cost of producing inventory by borrowing money for short periods of time. Sometimes these loans are called **working capital loans**. It can be argued that if borrowing is a necessary cost of producing inventory, the cost of borrowing might properly be included as a cost of inventory. However, almost all corporations treat interest as a period cost. This controversy illustrates how the line between period costs and product costs is not always clearly defined and is not necessarily fixed. The deciding factor should be which method results in the most useful numbers, given the objectives of management and the corporation.

Deciding whether a cost is a product cost or a period cost has implications for the financial statements. Product costs are directly or indirectly associated with the production of products and so affect the per-unit cost of producing each product. Period costs do not affect product costs but their full amount appears as expenses in the income statement. Therefore, some product costs will end up as inventory assets in the balance sheet and their full amount will not affect the corporation's net income until the next accounting period, when the inventory is sold. Thus the decision whether a cost should be treated as a period cost or a product cost has important implications. Classifying a cost as a period cost results in lower per-unit manufacturing costs, but also lower inventory assets and lower net income. Classifying a cost as a product cost results in higher per-unit costs (with resulting higher prices), higher inventory assets, and higher net income.

ETHICS IN ACCOUNTING

The application of overhead to units of production is a systematic but arbitrary process. In addition, the application of overhead costs to units depends on the number of units produced; that is, the more units produced, the less the overhead cost per unit and the lower the total per-unit cost. Inappropriate allocation of overhead costs can lead to misstated values for units produced.

Inadequate specification of overhead costs can lead to unethical behaviours. For example, the government sometimes signs contracts on a "cost plus" basis. Cost plus means the government agrees to pay the contractor's costs, plus some amount for profit. If the method of allocating overhead costs is not clearly specified in the contract, what would stop the contractor from allocating all of the overhead costs to just the items sold to the government under the contract? This is not just a hypothetical example; there have been well-publicized examples of the government paying $400 for a hammer and $600 for a toilet seat under a contract. While we as taxpayers might object to such exorbitant prices, management of the contracting corporations defends such practices by arguing they are acting within the terms of the contract.

◤◣ Inventory Accounts

Manufacturers maintain several types of inventories, both physically and in their records. When manufacturers purchase materials that will be used in the production process to produce goods, they are assets called **raw materials inventory**. An example would be Ford Motors buying steel to be used to produce cars. As raw materials are used in the production of products, the related raw material costs are transferred from the raw materials to the **work-in-process account**. An example would be Ford using the steel in cars on the assembly line. Work-in-process inventory is used to accumulate all the costs of producing the products. Exhibit 3-2 shows how raw materials inventory and related production costs such as direct labour and overhead are combined into the work-in-process inventory.

EXHIBIT 3-2

Manufacturing Cost Flows

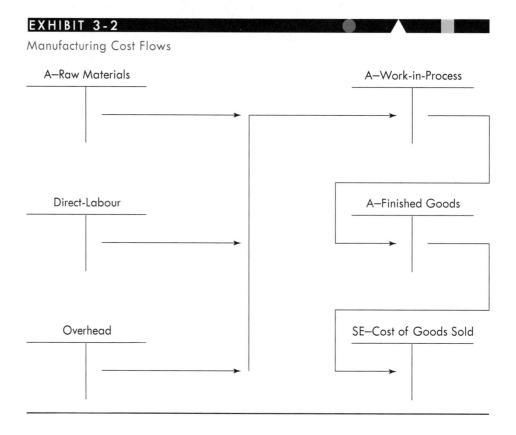

Notice, in this exhibit, that direct labour and overhead are not marked as assets ("A"). The reason for this is that labour and most overhead items are not items that the corporation buys ahead of time and holds as assets until they are used. Labour costs, for example, are incurred as they are used in the production process. Records of these costs are used merely to accumulate these costs.

When products are finished, their costs are then transferred from work-in-process to **finished goods**. For Ford, cars that are ready for delivery to dealers would be included in their finished goods inventory. The product costs remain as finished goods inventory until the products are sold, at which time the costs are transferred to **cost of goods sold**. Refer to Exhibit 3-2 for a summary of this process.

A detailed discussion of the accounting for overhead costs and their allocation and the flow of transactions through direct labour, direct materials, and overhead is beyond the scope of this book. However, you should be aware of the overall flow of these items and their related costs. Manufacturing corporations will almost always start each year with some work-in-process inventory. This will consist of items that are only partly finished. For example, Ford will always have some unfinished cars on their assembly lines except for the short period of time when they shut down the lines to convert to the next year's models. During the year manufacturers add more raw materials and incur more direct labour and overhead costs to produce finished items from this work-in-process. Items that are finished will be transferred to finished goods inventory awaiting sale. As soon as items are sold, they become cost of goods sold.

You can see that manufacturing corporations will thus have three types of inventories: raw materials, work-in-process, and finished goods. Their cost of goods sold would be more fully described as cost of goods *manufactured* and sold. These groupings are important and must be considered whenever you analyze financial statements of manufacturing corporations. Finished goods are available for sale immediately. Work-in-process inventory is not immediately available for sale as it must first be finished. Raw materials must be entered into the manufacturing process and turned into finished goods before they are available for sale. In addition to these timing differences, the corporation will have to incur additional costs before the raw materials and work-in-process inventories are available for sale.

An example of the disclosure of the different types of inventory can be seen in Exhibit 3-3 for Tritech Precision Inc. Note that Tritech Precision discloses the details of its inventory in the notes. The balance sheet shows only the total inventories of $11,864,000 in 1994.

EXHIBIT 3-3

TRITECH PRECISION INC.
Excerpted from Notes to the Statements
Disclosure of Inventory Categories

3. Inventory
The components of inventory are as follows:

(in thousands of dollars)		1994		Proforma 1993		1993
Raw materials and supplies	$	3,214	$	3,234	$	2,425
Work-in-process		1,987		622		–
Customer dies in progress		2,698		3,906		–
Finished goods		3,965		3,370		3,058
	$	11,864	$	11,132	$	5,483

■ ■ Inventory Turnover Ratio

A ratio that is useful when analyzing how well a corporation utilizes its inventory is called the **inventory turnover ratio**. The inventory turnover ratio indicates how fast inventory is sold or, alternatively, how long inventory is held prior to sale. The calculation of the inventory turnover uses a measure of the flow of inventory in the numerator (top number) and a measure of the balance in inventory in the denominator (bottom number). It is calculated as follows:

$$\text{Inventory Turnover} = \frac{\text{Cost of Goods Sold}}{\text{Average Inventory}}$$

Note that the numerator contains the cost of goods sold, not the sales value of goods sold (revenues). Total sales revenue, while it does measure the flow of goods sold to customers, would be inappropriate in the numerator because it is based on the selling price of the inventory while the denominator is measured at cost. Cost of goods sold is measured at cost and so is more appropriate. Use of an average inventory in the denominator is better than using just one inventory figure because averages reduce fluctuations that may occur in any one year.

Tritech Precision Inc.'s cost of goods sold for 1994 was $79,736,000. Its 1994 inventory turnover can thus be calculated as follows:

$$\frac{79,736,000}{\frac{(11,132,000 + 11,864,000)}{2}} = \frac{79,736,000}{11,498,000} = 6.9$$

This ratio of 6.9 means that Tritech "turned over" its inventory 6.9 times during 1994. You can think of the turning over of inventory as the complete sale and replacement of the inventory. Of course this does not happen all at once because manufacturing corporations buy and sell their inventory on a daily basis, so the inventory on hand never goes down to zero at any point in time.

INCOME STATEMENT FORMAT

One of the most fundamental objectives of financial reporting is to ensure that financial statements provide information that is useful to the user. To be useful, information should help current and potential investors, creditors, and other users assess the amount, timing, and certainty of prospective net cash flows to the enterprise.

The purpose of the income statement is to provide information about the performance of the corporation. The basic format of the income statement summarizes all revenues and expenses to show the net income. The information provided is primarily historical. The revenues are the historical amounts received or receivable from the sale of goods and services, and the expenses are based on the amounts actually paid or payable in the future for the goods and services used to produce the revenues. Some of the expenses may represent very old costs, such as the amortization of very old assets such as buildings.

For the income statement to provide information about future cash flows of the corporation, the connection between the amounts presented in the income statement and those future cash flows must be understood. Accrual basis accounting requires that revenues and expenses be recorded at amounts that are ultimately expected to be received or paid in cash. For example, to estimate the actual amount of cash that will be collected from sales, the corporation estimates the amount of sales that will not be collected (**bad debts**) and deducts that amount from sales. On the expense side, estimates are made for some expenses where amounts are not yet paid, such as interest or tax expenses. In both cases, the figures reflect management's estimates about future cash flows. In this sense, the income statement provides information to the reader about management's assessment of the ultimate cash flows from the business of the period. This means that the income statement, on an accrual basis, provides more information about **future** cash flows than an income statement prepared on a cash basis, which only reflects cash flows that have already occurred.

A second aspect of providing information about future cash flows is the forecasting ability of the income statement. If the trends in revenues and expenses over several time periods are examined, the revenues and expenses that will occur in the future may be predicted. An understanding of the relationship of revenues and expenses to future cash flows will allow a reasonable prediction of the amount of cash flows that will result in future periods.

The ability to predict future revenues and expenses depends on the type of item considered, the industry, and the corporation's history. The sales revenue and cost of goods sold figures are reasonably predictable if the business is in a fairly stable product line. New businesses and new products make this type of forecasting more difficult. Other types of items are not as predictable. Sales of plant and equipment, for example, tend to be more sporadic than the normal sales of goods or services. Some items may occur only once and will, therefore, not be repeated. The closing of a plant or the sale of a business unit is an event that has income statement implications in the current period but may not be repeated in the future.

To enable readers of the income statement to make the best estimates of future results, the continuing items should be separated from the noncontinuing items. For this reason, the format of the income statement is designed to highlight these differences.

The result of all this is that the normal income statement format is designed to provide information about **continuing** and **noncontinuing operations**. Exhibit 3-4 provides an overview of the major sections of a typical income statement. Each of these is discussed in the following subsections.

Income From Continuing Operations

This section provides information about the revenues and expenses resulting from the sales of goods and services to customers. The operations reported are those that are expected to continue in the future. A separate section later in the income statement contains the results of those operations that management has decided to discontinue.

Income statements can be either **single-step** or **multistep**. In Exhibit 3-5, the income statement of Mosaid Technologies Incorporated provides an example of a **single-step income statement**. In this type of statement, all the revenues are listed together and all the expenses (except for income tax expense) are listed together. Thus Mosaid shows revenues from operations of $23,202,000 plus interest revenue of $1,084,000, for total revenues of $24,286,000. The six different expenses total $17,298,000, producing income before taxes of $6,988,000.

EXHIBIT 3-4

Income Statement Format

XYZ CORPORATION

Income Statement

For the year ended December 31, 19x0

Income from continuing operations

Operating revenues	$ XXX
Operating expenses	(XXX)
Income from continuing operations	XXX
Income from nonoperating sources	
Gain (loss) on sale of property, plant, and equipment	XXX
Financing revenue	XXX
Financing expense	(XXX)
Other	XXX
Total income from nonoperating sources	XXX
Income from unusual or infrequent events	XXX
Income before taxes	XXX
Provision for income taxes (on all items above)	(XXX)
Net income before discontinued operations and extraordinary items	XXX
Income from discontinued operations (net of tax)	XXX
Income from extraordinary items (net of tax)	XXX
Net income	$XXX

On the other hand, in Exhibit 3-6, the income statement of Semi-Tech Corporation illustrates a **multistep income statement**. In this type of statement, the results of different types of operations are segregated. In the top sections of the statement, the results of the main business of the corporation are reported, resulting in the net line item called "Operating income" of $160,600,000. Below that, other continuing operations are reported, such as equity earnings from Semi-Tech (Global) Company Limited of $12,000,000. Note that the figure of $135,200,000 is a subtotal of all the amounts above it which represent the main business activities of Semi-Tech, those related to Singer operations (which produces sewing machines and other items). The next item, $12,000,000, represents another main business component, Global, which invests in electronics and other industries around the world.

Additional information regarding the performance and profitability of various operating units and operations in different geographical areas can generally be found in the notes to the financial statements if the corporation has different lines of business that are easily separated, or operations in several geographical areas.

Income From Nonoperating Sources

In this section of the income statement, the results of transactions that do not involve the normal sale of goods and services are reported. The typical types of items found here are interest income and expense, the gain or loss on the sale of

EXHIBIT 3-5

MOSAID TECHNOLOGIES INCORPORATED
Consolidated Statement of Earnings
and Retained Earnings
years ended April 30, 1995 and 1994

(in thousands, except per share amounts)

	1995	1994
Revenues		
Operations	$ 23,202	$ 14,348
Interest	1,084	369
	$ 24,286	$ 14,717
Expenses		
Labour and materials	5,275	3,979
Research and development (Note 8)	4,741	3,228
Selling and marketing	4,576	2,573
General and administration (Note 8)	2,578	1,618
Foreign exchange loss (gain)	147	(222)
Bad debt (recovery) expense	(19)	74
	17,298	11,250
Earnings before income taxes	6,988	3,467
Income tax expense (Note 3)	2,504	542
Net earnings	4,484	2,925
Retained earnings, beginning of year	4,560	1,635
Retained earnings, end of year	$ 9,044	$ 4,560
Earnings per share (Note 11)		
Basic	$ .66	$ .59
Fully diluted	$ .60	$ .51

See accompanying Notes to the Consolidated Financial Statements.

plant and equipment, restructuring expenses, and other, mainly one-time, events or transactions. Examples can be seen in the Consolidated Statements of Income and Retained Earnings of Semi-Tech Corporation presented in Exhibit 3-6. The three items in the section "Other income (expenses)" are nonoperating items. They include interest expense of $65,700,000; royalty and license income of $22,400,000; and miscellaneous income items totaling $17,900,000.

◤◣ Income From Unusual or Infrequent Events

Sometimes unusual or infrequent events occur that the corporation would like to segregate from the rest of the results so the reader of the income statement can

EXHIBIT 3-6

SEMI-TECH CORPORATION
Consolidated Statements of Income and Retained Earnings
(In millions of Canadian dollars, except per share data)

	Year Ended March 31, 1995	Period from May 1, 1993 to March 31, 1994
Revenues	$ 1,563.8	$ 582.8
Costs and expenses		
Cost of sales	1,046.8	399.5
Selling and administrative expenses	334.3	107.7
Amortization of goodwill	22.1	7.1
Operating income	160.6	68.5
Other income (expenses):		
Interest, net of related foreign exchange adjustments	(65.7)	(13.1)
Royalties and license income	22.4	10.8
Miscellaneous, net	17.9	3.6
Income related to Singer operations	135.2	69.8
Equity earnings from Semi-Tech (Global) Company Limited	12.0	17.2
Income related to Singer operations and Global equity interest	147.2	87.0
Corporate items:		
Non-cash interest on Senior Secured Discount Notes	(51.3)	(28.7)
Corporate income (expenses), net	(0.5)	(2.1)
Income before income taxes and minority interests	95.4	56.2
Provision for income taxes	23.5	7.4
Income before minority interests	71.9	48.8
Minority interests	66.0	34.1
Net income	5.9	14.7
Retained earnings, beginning of period	170.6	169.2
Dividend paid	(26.6)	(13.3)
Retained earnings, end of period	$ 149.9	$ 170.6
Earnings per share:		
Basic	$ 0.09	$ 0.29
Fully diluted	$ 0.06	$ 0.26

(See accompanying notes to financial statements)

understand the nature of the event and make an assessment of its continuing or non-continuing status. These types of items are reported either with the other nonoperating events or in a section by themselves.

An example of an unusual and infrequent item can be seen in Exhibit 3-7, the Consolidated Statement of Operations (the income statement) of H. Jager Developments Inc. (involved in property development and forest products). Note that the three items shown immediately below the line "Earnings (Loss) Before

EXHIBIT 3-7

H. JAGER DEVELOPMENTS INC.
Consolidated Statement of Operations
Years Ended April 30, 1995 and 1994

	1995	1994
SALES	$ 6,526,506	$ 4,383,373
DIRECT COSTS	5,701,235	4,313,040
	825,271	70,333
EXPENSES		
General and administrative	532,531	845,255
Depreciation and amortization	35,151	41,343
Interest	6,087	28,769
	573,769	915,367
EARNINGS (LOSS) BEFORE UNDERNOTED	251,502	(845,034)
Loss on sale of securities	(904)	—
Gain on sale of fixed and other assets	27,540	—
Write-down of land and housing under development	(99,095)	(260,000)
EARNINGS (LOSS) BEFORE INCOME TAXES	179,043	(1,105,034)
INCOME TAXES (Note 10)	—	—
NET EARNINGS (LOSS)	179,043	(1,105,034)
DEFICIT, beginning of year	(1,210,171)	(105,137)
DEFICIT, end of year	$ (1,031,128)	$ (1,210,171)
EARNINGS (LOSS) PER SHARE	$ 0.01	$ (0.11)

Undernoted" are unusual and infrequent items. The first item of $(904) is a loss on sale of securities, the second of $27,540 is a gain on the sale of assets, and the third of $(99,095) recognizes a reduction in the value of assets under development. These three items are unusual and do not occur frequently and so are shown separately.

Corporate Income Taxes

At the end of the income statement sections that have been discussed so far, there has been a line item for the corporate income tax expense computed on the net of all the items listed above. An example can be seen in the income statement of

Mosaid Technologies Incorporated shown in Exhibit 3-5, with the income tax expense of $2,504,000. Sometimes the term **provision for income taxes** is used instead of income tax expense, as shown in the income statement of Semi-Tech Corporation in Exhibit 3-6, in the amount of $23,500,000. Taxes are computed on the basis of aggregate net income and are not listed separately for each operating and nonoperating item. Semi-Tech Corporation's income statement in Exhibit 3-6 provides a good example of this line item.

Two additional items may appear after the computation of tax expenses: **discontinued operations**, and **extraordinary items** (although extraordinary items are very rarely found). These items appear below the operating and nonoperating items (they are sometimes called "below the line" items) because of their unusual or unique nature. Because they appear after the computation of taxes, the tax effect of these transactions must be reported along with the item itself. They are reported on what is known as a **net of tax** basis. This means that the tax effects of the item have been netted against the before-tax numbers to produce a net, after-tax number. If, for example, discontinued operations result in a loss of $1,000 before taxes and saves $400 in taxes (due to the deductibility of the loss), the net of tax amount would be a $600 loss ($1,000 − $400). The tax effects of these "below the line" items are not included in the line item called tax expense.

Discontinued Operations

Discontinued operations are significant parts of the corporation that management has decided to discontinue. There are criteria for deciding what constitutes a discontinued operation. Once management has decided to discontinue a line of business, there are two types of results that must be reported in the income statement. During the time it takes to dispose of the business segment, which may be quite long, the business may continue to operate. The income from operating these discontinued operations must be reported separately from other income. In addition, if the business is being sold, either in whole or in part, there will be a gain or loss on the disposal of the business. This gain or loss must also be reported separately from the results of the operations up to the time of disposal. The disclosure of both types of results is illustrated in Exhibit 3-8 for Algoma Central Corporation. Note that the details of the income from discontinued operations of $1,493,000, including the applicable tax effects, are reported in a note to the financial statements.

Extraordinary Items

Although extraordinary items are rarely found in income statements, they are interesting. To be classified as extraordinary, items must be **unusual, infrequent**, and **not resulting from management decisions**. A recent example was a corporation that lost money when the armoured car carrying the corporation's cash was robbed and no insurance could be claimed on the loss because of improper procedures being used.

Extraordinary items are shown separately because they are beyond the control of the corporation and are not expected to recur in the future.

EXHIBIT 3-8

ALGOMA CENTRAL CORPORATION
Consolidated Statements of Income and Retained Earnings
Years ended December 31

	1994	1993
REVENUE	$ 163,965,000	$ 130,328,000
EXPENSES		
Operations	113,260,000	89,880,000
Depreciation and amortization	17,976,000	15,549,000
Administrative and general	8,263,000	6,478,000
	139,499,000	111,907,000
INCOME FROM CONTINUING OPERATIONS BEFORE THE UNDERNOTED	24,466,000	18,421,000
INTEREST EXPENSE	(4,500,000)	(5,588,000)
GAIN ON DISPOSAL OF FLORIDA REAL ESTATE	—	3,540,000
INCOME FROM CONTINUING OPERATIONS BEFORE INCOME TAXES	19,966,000	16,373,000
INCOME TAX PROVISION (Note 2)	7,733,000	5,031,000
INCOME FROM CONTINUING OPERATIONS	12,233,000	11,342,000
INCOME (LOSS) FROM DISCONTINUED OPERATIONS (Note 3)	1,493,000	(4,481,000)
NET INCOME	13,726,000	6,861,000
RETAINED EARNINGS, BEGINNING OF YEAR	45,300,000	38,439,000
RETAINED EARNINGS, END OF YEAR	$ 59,026,000	$ 45,300,000
EARNINGS (LOSS) PER SHARE		
Continuing operations	$ 3.15	$ 2.91
Discontinued operations	0.38	(1.15)
	$ 3.53	$ 1.76

Notes to the Consolidated Financial Statements
December 31, 1994 and 1993

3. **Discontinued operations**

On July 28, 1994 the Corporation completed agreements with Wisconsin Central Transportaion Corporation to sell its railway operations. The sale closed on January 31, 1995 upon receiving regulatory approvals. Accordingly, the railway operations have been treated as discontinued operations in the 1994 consolidated financial statements and the comparative balances for 1993 have been restated.

The results of discontinued operations are summarized below:

	1994	1993
Revenue	$ 27,892,000	$ 28,886,000
(Loss) income before income taxes	$ (1,332,000)	$ 2,798,000
Income tax recovery (provision)	745,000	(1,125,000)
	(587,000)	1,673,000

EXHIBIT 3-8 (continued)

ALGOMA CENTRAL CORPORATION
Notes to the Consolidated Financial Statements
December 31, 1994 and 1993

Gain (loss) on discontinued operations, net of income tax provision of $712,000 (1993 recovery of $8,845,000)	2,080,000	(6,154,000)
	$ 1,493,000	$ (4,481,000)

The Corporation has allocated interest expense of $1,914,000 (1993 - $824,000) to discontinued operations.

Cash flow from discontinued operations consists of the following:

	1994	1993
Operating activities	$ 34,000	$ 7,783,000
Investing activities	155,000	(3,408,000)
	$ 189,000	$ 4,375,000

AN INTERNATIONAL PERSPECTIVE
REPORTS FROM OTHER COUNTRIES

The criteria used in other countries to identify extraordinary items are different from those used in Canada. For example, the United States classifies several items as extraordinary that are not considered extraordinary in Canada. Corporations report these differences if they provide a reconciliation of their net income reported under Canadian GAAP with the amount that would be reported under American GAAP. In 1995, Franklin Supply Company Ltd. (a Canadian corporation) provided the reconciliation shown in Exhibit 3.9.

Earnings Per Share

In addition to net income, **earnings per share** is shown, either in the income statement or in a note to the financial statements. Earnings per share relates the net income to the common shares outstanding. In many cases, this is a simple calculation that consists of dividing the net income of the corporation by the average number of common shares outstanding during the year. A weighted average is used if the number of common shares outstanding changed during the year. Note the disclosure of earnings per share in Exhibits 3-5 and 3-6 for Mosaid and Semi-Tech. For Mosaid, the earnings per share is $0.66. For Semi-Tech, the earnings per share figure is $0.09. There are other earnings per share figures that are also disclosed in certain circumstances. These are discussed in more detail in Chapter 12. An example of an additional earnings per share figure can be found in Exhibit 3-8 for Algoma Central where the effects of discontinued operations are broken out in the computation of earnings per share.

BALANCE SHEET FORMAT

The format of the balance sheet is less varied than that of the income statement. There are separate sections for assets, liabilities, and shareholders' equity. The most

EXHIBIT 3-9

FRANKLIN SUPPLY COMPANY LTD.
Excerpted from Notes to the Statements

(b) Extraordinary items

The reduction of income taxes relating to the utilization of previously unrecorded loss carry-forwards in the current year is settled against the provision for income taxes under Canadian GAAP but is an extraordinary item under U.S. GAAP.

The gain on corporate on corporate refinancing is an unusual item under Canadian GAAP but is an extraordinary item under U.S. GAAP.

The reconciliations of the statements of operations from Canadian to U.S. GAAP for periods affected by extraordinary items are as follows:

	Year Ended June 30, 1995 U.S. $	Year Ended June 30, 1995 Cdn. $	Year Ended June 30, 1994 Cdn. $	Nine months Ended June 30, 1993 Cdn. $
Net income for the period under Canadian GAAP	14,722	20,219	1,953,282	4,112,389
Additional provision for income taxes under U.S. GAAP	(96,000)	(131,000)	(972,000)	(321,000)
Unusual item under Canadian GAAP (note 12)	—	—	—	(3,387,491)
Net income (loss) before extraordinary items Under U.S. GAAP	(81,278)	(110,781)	981,282	403,898
Extraordinary gain on utilization of previously unrecorded loss carryforwards under U.S. GAAP	96,000	131,000	972,000	321,000
Extraordinary gain on corporate refinancing under U.S. GAAP	—	—	—	3,387,491
Net income for the period under U.S. GAAP	14,722	20,219	1,953,282	4,112,389

commonly used format presents assets on the left-hand side of the page and liabilities and shareholders' equity on the right-hand side. Alternatively, assets may be at the top of the page and liabilities and shareholders' equity at the bottom.

Within both current asset and liability sections, the individual items are generally listed in the order of their **liquidity**. In the case of assets, liquidity refers to the ability to convert the asset into cash. For liabilities, liquidity refers to how quickly the liability will require the use of cash. Current assets and liabilities are generally listed from most liquid to least liquid.

AN INTERNATIONAL PERSPECTIVE
REPORTS FROM OTHER COUNTRIES

The format and terminology used in Canadian income statements are different from those used in other countries. As an example, refer to the income statement of Jacques Vert Plc (a British corporation that manufactures and retails women's fashion wear) in Exhibit 3-10. The first difference is that the statement is called the "Consolidated Profit and Loss Account," which differs from the usual "Income Statement" or "Statement of Operations" used in Canada. Revenues in the report are referred to as "Turnover." Near the bottom of the report, dividends are subtracted from the "Profit on ordinary activities after taxation" (the equivalent of net income) to produce a line item called "Amount transferred to reserves." This is the amount of profit that increases the retained earnings account.

EXHIBIT 3-10

JACQUES VERT PLC
Consolidated Profit and Loss Account
For the 52 (53) weeks ended
(in £000)

	29 April 1995	30 April 1994
Turnover	49,694	45,140
Cost of sales	(43,974)	(40,448)
Gross profit	5,720	4,692
Net operating expenses	(2,371)	(2,362)
Operating profit for the period	3,349	2,330
Net interest payable	(216)	(237)
Profit on ordinary activities before taxation	3,133	2,093
Taxation	(1,031)	(814)
Profit on ordinary activities after taxation	2,102	1,279
Dividends	(642)	(428)
Amount transferred to reserves	1,460	851
Earnings per share	22.1 pence	13.45 pence

In many corporations, assets and liabilities, in addition to being listed in liquidity order, are classified as **current** and **noncurrent**. **Current** means that the item will produce or require the use of cash in the next year or operating cycle of the corporation, whichever is longer. **Noncurrent** items are all items not classified as current. Balance sheets that classify assets and liabilities in this way are called **classified balance sheets**. In Exhibit 3-11, the classified balance sheet of Imperial Parking Limited serves as an example. Note that in 1995 Imperial has current assets of $11,107,000, and other assets that include fixed assets, management and lease agreements, goodwill, and other assets. Current liabilities total $18,458,000; long-term liabilities total $4,349,000; and shareholders' equity totals $28,427,000.

EXHIBIT 3-11

IMPERIAL PARKING LIMITED
Consolidated Balance Sheets
As at March 31 in 1995 and 1994
(stated in thousands of dollars)

	1995	1994
		(note 2(l))
ASSETS		
Current assets:		
Cash and cash equivalents	$ 3,599	$ 11,352
Accounts receivable	4,169	2,182
Inventory	1,944	1,304
Deposits and prepaid expenses	1,395	938
	11,107	15,776
Other assets (note 4)	3,747	2,148
Fixed assets (note 5)	8,224	5,718
Management and lease agreements (note 6)	17,003	3,577
Goodwill (note 7)	11,153	11,491
	$ 51,234	$ 38,710
LIABILITIES AND SHAREHOLDERS' EQUITY		
Current liabilities:		
Bank indebtedness (note 8)	$ 1,700	$ –
Rents payable	6,687	3,496
Trade accounts payable and other accrued liabilities	7,314	4,512
Deferred revenue	1,662	1,045
Current portion of long-term debt	1,095	6,739
	18,458	15,792
Long-term debt (note 9)	4,349	969
	22,807	16,761
Shareholders' equity:		
Share capital (note 10)	31,114	26,163
Deficit	2,687	4,214
	28,427	21,949
Commitments and contingencies (note 12)		
	$ 51,234	$ 38,710

On behalf of the Board:

Director   *Director*

Some corporations choose not to classify their balance sheets, producing instead an **unclassified balance sheet**. One reason for an unclassified balance sheet is that the corporation may be a combination of very different types of industries, for which the classifications of a current item may be quite different. An example of an unclassified balance sheet is given in Exhibit 3-12 for Mackenzie Financial

EXHIBIT 3-12

MACKENZIE FINANCIAL CORPORATION
Consolidated Balance Sheet
As at March 31
(thousands of dollars)

	1995	1994
Assets		
Cash and short-term investments	$ 144,455	$ 112,473
Accounts and other receivables	52,187	46,599
Income taxes receivable	–	10,854
Mortgage loans	189,932	142,027
Deferred selling commissions and investment		
in related partnerships *(note 3)*	112,757	100,526
Investment in affiliated companies	56,039	55,539
Management contracts	17,534	20,708
Capital assets *(note 4)*	22,705	16,760
Goodwill *(note 5)*	8,293	9,463
Other assets *(note 6)*	14,661	11,865
	$ 618,563	$ 526,814
Liabilities		
Bank loans *(note 7)*	$ 13,012	$ 4,767
Accounts payable and accrued liabilities	34,592	38,159
Income taxes payable	10,257	–
Customer deposits *(note 8)*	213,880	179,345
Notes payable *(notes 3 and 9)*	44,184	50,000
Deferred taxes	48,423	22,718
	$ 364,348	$ 294,989
Commitments and Contingencies *(notes 7 and 13)*		
Shareholders' Equity		
Capital Stock *(note 10)*		
Authorized – Unlimited number of common shares		
Issued and outstanding		
– 59,264,115 (1994 – 59,254,115) common shares	$ 38,813	$ 38,761
Retained earnings	215,402	193,064
	$ 254,215	$ 231,825
	$ 618,563	$ 526,814

(The accompanying notes are an integral part of these consolidated financial statements.)

Signed on behalf of the Board

Alexander Christ
Director

F. Warren Hurst
Director

Corporation. Mackenzie's principal business is the marketing and management of public mutual funds in Canada and the U. S., but it also operates a trust company, a brokerage firm, and a supplier of software services.

AN INTERNATIONAL PERSPECTIVE
REPORTS FROM OTHER COUNTRIES

The format of the balance sheet can appear somewhat different in other countries. For example, in the United Kingdom (U.K.), the classification of assets and liabilities is rearranged so that current liabilities are reported with current assets, and noncurrent assets are listed first. The balance sheet takes the following form:

Fixed assets		XXX
Current assets	XXX	
less:		
Current liabilities	XXX	
Net current assets		XXX
Total assets less current liabilities		XXX
Noncurrent liabilities		XXX
Net assets		XXX
Capital and reserves (shareholders' equity)		XXX

The balance sheet of Jacques Vert Plc, a British clothing business, in Exhibit 3-13 illustrates this type of presentation. Note that there are some differences in terminology: the term "stocks" corresponds to inventories, "debtors" to accounts receivable, "called up share capital" and "share premium account" are equivalent to common shares, and "profit and loss account" is equivalent to the retained earnings account.

SUMMARY

In this chapter, we presented some of the differences you will find in manufacturing corporations compared to corporations engaged mainly in retail sales. We also discussed some of the various statement format issues relating to the income statement and balance sheet. The Appendix to this chapter provides details of the accounting entries for manufacturing corporations. In the next chapter, attention is directed to the cash-to-cash cycle of the corporation, the criteria for revenue recognition, and the various methods of revenue recognition.

EXHIBIT·3-13

JACQUES VERT PLC
Balance Sheets
29 April
(in £000)

	29 April 1995	30 April 1994
Fixed assets	4,463	4,169
Current assets:		
Stocks	8,198	7,336
Debtors:		
amount falling due within one year	7,059	6,955
amount falling due after more than one year	107	71
Cash at bank and in hand	334	502
	15,698	14,864
Creditors:		
amounts falling due within one year	(9,856)	(9,715)
Net current assets	5,842	5,149
Total assets less current liabilities	10,305	9,318
Creditors:		
amounts falling due after more than one year	(81)	(100)
Provisions for liabilities and charges	(423)	(883)
Net assets	9,081	8,335
Capital and reserves		
Called up share capital	952	951
Share premium account	1,098	1,089
Profit and loss account	7,751	6,295
	9,801	8,335

SUMMARY PROBLEM

The income statements of two similar manufacturing corporations, ABC
Manufacturing Corporation and XYZ Manufacturing Corporation for the year ended
December 31, 19X0 are shown below. Analyze these statements and recommend
which would be the better investment.

Summary Income statements

	ABC	XYZ
Net sales	$1,000,000	$1,000,000
Cost of goods sold	(600,000)	(700,000)
Gross profit on sales	$ 400,000	$ 300,000
Administrative expenses	(200,000	(100,000)
Amortization	$ (50,000)	$ (50,000)
Operating income before interest expense	$ 150,000	$ 150,000
Gain on sale of land		25,000
Interest expense	$ (50,000)	$ (75,000)

Income from continuing operations before taxes	$ 100,000	$ 100,000
Income taxes	$ (25,000)	$ (25,000)
Income from continuing operations	$ 75,000	75,000
Income from discontinued operations		25,000
Net income	$ 75,000	$ 100,000
Earnings per share	$0.75	$1.30

Cost of goods manufactured and sold

Raw materials inventory, January 1	$10,000	$10,000
Purchases of raw materials	150,000	150,000
	$ 160,000	$ 160,000
Raw materials inventory, December 31	(15,000)	(15,000)
Raw materials used in processing	$ 145,000	$ 145,000
Labour costs	300,000	300,000
Factory utilities	40,000	40,000
Factory insurance	20,000	20,000
Administrative costs allocated	100,000	200,000
Work-in-process, January 1	75,000	75,000
	$ 680,000	$ 780,000
Work-in-process, December 31	(85,000)	(85,000)
Cost of goods finished during the year	$ 595,000	$ 695,000
Finished goods inventory, January 1	55,000	55,000
	$ 650,000	$ 750,000
Finished goods inventory, December 31	(50,000)	(50,000)
Cost of goods sold	$ 600,000	$ 700,000

SUGGESTED SOLUTION TO SUMMARY PROBLEM

Whenever you compare the income statements of two similar corporations, first look at the net incomes. In this case, the net income of XYZ is larger, $100,000 compared to $75,000 for ABC.

Next, consider the total sales, cost of goods sold, and gross profits. The total sales are the same, $1,000,000, but ABC has a smaller cost of goods sold ($600,000 compared to $700,000) and a larger gross profit on sales ($400,000 compared to $300,000). These figures may show that ABC has either a more efficient manufacturing process, or a better mark-up in their pricing. However, when you examine the manufacturing costs, you see they are almost identical except that XYZ allocated $100,000 more to administrative costs than did ABC ($200,000 compared to $100,000). This suggests that XYZ may have excessive administrative costs. But when you examine the income statements further, you see that ABC has an additional $200,000 in administrative costs while XYZ has an additional $100,000. Thus you can see that the total administrative costs are the same ($300,000) for both corporations. The apparently higher gross profit of ABC results only from a different policy of allocating administrative costs to manufacturing.

An important additional effect of the practice of allocating more overhead costs to production must be considered. Not only will the cost of goods sold be higher, but the ending work-in-process and finished goods inventories will also be higher because of the higher production costs. This has the effect of delaying the recognition of expenses by increasing the inventory values. Thus, if these two corporations were identical in all other aspects, then XYZ would have higher asset values simply because of this policy.

Continuing the analysis of the income statement, you should look for differences between the two corporations, especially in items that may not continue into the future. In this case, you will see two such items. XYZ shows a gain on the sale of land of $25,000 and income from discontinued operations of $25,000. These items will not continue into the future, so $50,000 of XYZ's net income must be considered separately. Only $50,000 of the $100,000 net income should be considered when you try to anticipate the future results.

An additional difference is that XYZ has higher interest expense, $75,000 compared to $50,000 for ABC. This suggests that XYZ is financed more by debt than equity, making it riskier than ABC. Debt can cause bankruptcy if it is not repaid, but equity cannot.

In summary, ABC appears to be the better investment for the future, even though its net income is lower than that of XYZ. There are two reasons for this decision. First, ABC has higher continuing income ($75,000 compared to $50,000), which should mean ABC would be expected to have higher income in the future. Second, XYZ has higher risk because of its higher interest-bearing debt, and the higher debt has not resulted in higher net income. Note that the earnings per share figures do not enter into this analysis. Earnings per share figures are useful mainly to analyze the earnings of the same corporation over time, but they are not very useful in comparing different corporations. (Later we will see that several earnings per share figures are produced to help make more detailed analyses.)

ABBREVIATIONS USED

A	Asset
L	Liability
SE	Shareholders' equity
Plc	Public limited company (U.K.)
U.K.	United Kingdom
£	British pounds

SYNONYMS

Called-up share capital (U.K.)/Common shares

Product costs/Inventoriable costs

Profit & Loss Account (U.K.)/Net Income

Profit for the financial year (U.K.)/Net income

Provision for dividends (Italy)/Dividends declared

Stocks (U.K.)/Inventory

Income tax expense/Provision for income taxes/Income tax provision

Trading profit (U.K.)/Gross margin/Gross profit

Turnover (U.K.)/Sales Revenues

GLOSSARY

Classified balance sheet A balance sheet in which the assets and liabilities are classified into current and noncurrent sections.

Continuing operations The operations of the corporation that are expected to continue into the future.

Contra-asset account (Appendix) An account used to record reductions in a related asset account. An example is accumulated amortization.

Current asset An asset that will be used or turned into cash within the next year or operating cycle of the corporation, whichever is longer.

Current liability A liability that will require the use of cash or will be replaced by another current liability within the next year or operating cycle of the corporation.

Direct costs Costs that are directly associated with the production of inventory units. Examples would be direct material and direct labour costs.

Discontinued operations Operations of the corporation that are being phased out and will, therefore, not continue in the future.

Earnings per share A calculation in which the earnings of the corporation are divided by the average number of common shares outstanding during the period.

Extraordinary item A gain or loss appearing on the income statement that meets three criteria: (1) it is unusual, (2) it is infrequent, and (3) it is primarily caused by a decision made by someone outside the corporation.

Finished goods inventory An inventory account that contains the cost of units that have been completed and are ready for sale.

Indirect costs Costs incurred in the production process that are only indirectly associated with a particular unit. Supervisory and maintenance labour costs are examples.

Inventory turnover ratio The number of times that inventory is replaced during the accounting period. It is calculated as the cost of goods sold divided by the average inventory.

Liquidity A quality of an asset that describes how quickly it can be converted into cash.

Multistep income statement An income statement in which revenues and expenses from different types of operations of the corporation are shown in separate sections of the statement.

Net of tax A term that describes how an income statement item might be reported. The item would be shown on the statement minus the tax effect of the item. This type of presentation is reserved for discontinued operations and extraordinary items.

Noncurrent A term used to refer to an asset or liability that is not classified as current.

Overhead costs Costs incurred in the production of units of inventory that are considered indirect costs.

Period costs Costs that are difficult to associate directly with the production of products and are more easily associated with a period of time.

Product costs Costs incurred by a manufacturing corporation in the production of inventory.

Raw materials inventory An inventory account that contains the costs of the raw materials purchased for use in the production process of the corporation.

Single-step income statement An income statement in which all revenues are listed in one section and all expenses except income taxes in a second section.

Unclassified balance sheet A balance sheet in which assets and liabilities are not classified into current and noncurrent categories.

Work-in-process inventory An inventory account used to accumulate the various costs of producing a unit of inventory while the unit is in the production process. The three major costs included are those for raw materials, labour, and overhead.

ASSIGNMENT MATERIAL

◣◤ Assessing your recall

1. Discuss differences between product costs and period costs.

2. Identify the three basic types of product costs for a typical manufacturer.

3. List at least three costs that would be considered overhead costs.

4. Diagram and describe the flow of manufacturing costs through a manufacturer's accounting system.

5. Identify and briefly describe the major sections of the income statement.

6. What is the standard format of a balance sheet?

7. Explain the meaning of the terms current and noncurrent as they apply to the balance sheet.

8. Explain the meaning of the term "liquidity."

9. What two types of disclosure are made in the income statement with regard to discontinued operations?

◣◤ Applying your knowledge

10. Indicate whether each of the following costs is a product cost or a period expense:
    a. Salary of the factory supervisor
    b. Paint used in finishing the product
    c. Paint used in the renovation of the factory building
    d. Travel allowance for the sales force
    e. Operating cost of the central computer facility
    f. Salaries of the factory line workers
    g. Amortization of the administrative building

11. Indicate whether each of the following costs is a product cost or a period expense:
    a. President's salary
    b. Cleaning supplies used by the factory maintenance staff
    c. Shipping warehouse employees' salaries
    d. Interest on general borrowings of the corporation
    e. Interest on money borrowed to purchase inventory
    f. Materials requisitioned for use in production
    g. Electricity cost
    h. Insurance that covers the loss of inventory

12. Compute the missing data in the following independent situations:

	A	B	C	D
Raw materials January 1	$10,000	$3,500	$25,000	?
Purchases	?	$18,000	$86,000	$2,800
Materials requisitioned	$75,000	?	$92,000	$2,450
Raw materials December 31	$12,000	$2,300	?	$800

13. Compute the missing data in the following independent situations:

	A	B	C	D
Work-in-process January 1	$13,000	$2,600	$38,000	?
Raw materials	?	$8,000	$26,000	$4,900
Direct labour	$43,000	$13,500	$12,000	$9,500
Overhead	$17,500	$5,400	$3,000	$4,750
Cost of goods completed	$95,000	?	$51,000	$22,400
Work-in-process December 31	$16,500	$1,900	?	$1,900

14. Compute the missing data in the following independent situations:

	A	B	C	D
Finished goods January 1	$26,000	$4,300	$54,000	?
Cost of goods manufactured	?	$13,800	$89,000	$46,900
Cost of goods sold	$83,000	?	$95,500	$49,400
Finished goods December 31	$19,500	$6,000	?	$2,500

15. The Turgeon Company reported the following data related to its manufacturing operations during 19X2:

Balances:

	Jan. 1/x2	Dec. 31/x2
Raw materials inventory	$33,500	$37,000
Work-in-process inventory	$56,800	$54,500
Finished goods inventory	$85,000	$92,400

Cost incurred:

Raw materials purchased	$145,000
Factory direct labour	$358,000
Factory maintenance	$ 66,000
Factory amortization	$113,000
President's salary	$125,000
Sales force salaries	$225,000
Sales force expenses	$ 35,000
Heat, light, and power	$ 25,000
(100% applies to manufacturing)	
Insurance	$ 36,000
(50% applies to manufacturing)	

Calculate:

a. The cost of raw materials requisitioned for production during the year.

b. The cost of the units that were completed and transferred to finished goods during the year.

c. The cost of goods sold for the year.

16. The Waybright Company reported the following data related to its manufacturing operations during 19x3 (Waybright has a June 30 fiscal year-end):

Balances:

	July 1/x2	June 30/x3
Raw materials	$ 5,500	$ 7,300
Work-in-process inventory	$23,400	$25,700
Finished goods	$48,500	$41,600
Costs incurred:		
Raw materials purchased		$ 83,000
Factory direct labour		$153,000
Factory supplies		$ 36,000
Factory amortization		$ 93,000
President's salary		$103,000
Sales force salaries		$ 56,000
Sales force expenses		$ 5,200
Heat, light, & power		$ 12,000
(75% applies to manufacturing)		
Insurance		$ 7,000
(60% applies to manufacturing)		

Calculate:

a. The cost of the materials requisitioned for production during the year.

b. The cost of the units that were completed and transferred to finished goods during the year.

c. The cost of goods sold for the year.

17. Prepare an income statement (ignore taxes) in proper form from the following information concerning the results of Biggs & Company Ltd. (a company located in Nova Scotia, where major earthquakes are not common but windstorms are) for the year ended December 31, 19x2:

Sales revenue	$150,000
Cost of goods sold	(115,000)
Interest expense	(15,000)
Gain on the sale of equipment	1,200
Loss on discontinued operations	(33,000)
Earthquake damage	(3,500)
Windstorm damage	(1,300)
Extraordinary gain	5,000
Dividend revenue	500
Dividends declared	(3,500)

18. Prepare a classified balance sheet for the Novasco Manufacturing Corporation as of December 31, 19x3 based on the trial balance at that date:

	Debits	Credits
Cash	$80,000	
Temporary investments	90,000	
Property, plant, and equipment	280,000	
Raw materials	55,000	
Work-in-process	90,000	
Finished goods	160,000	
Accounts receivable	110,000	
Cost of goods sold	450,000	
Interest expense	25,000	
Loss on sale of equipment	1,900	
Selling expenses	150,500	
Dividends declared	35,000	
Sales revenues		$650,000
Interest revenue		10,000
Accounts payable		75,000
Short-term borrowings		125,000
Long-term debt		300,000
Dividends payable		7,000
Accrued salaries payable		28,000
Accumulated amortization		65,000
Common shares		150,000
Retained earnings		117,400
	$1,527,400	$1,527,400

Reading and Interpreting Published Financial Statements

19. Refer to the financial statements of Telepanel Systems Inc., including Notes 3 and 4, for the year ended January 31, 1995 and 1994, shown in Exhibit 3-14, and answer the following questions:
   a. Calculate the cost of the goods completed and transferred to finished goods in 1995.
   b. Calculate the total costs added to the work-in-process account during 1995.
   c. Assuming that the average balance in finished goods inventory represents the cost of one "batch" of product, how many batches did Telepanel have to complete in 1995 to meet its sales demand?
   d. At the end of 1995 what percent of Telepanel's total assets is invested in inventory? What percent is invested in property, plant, and equipment?
   e. Does Telepanel have a classified or an unclassified balance sheet? Explain.
   f. What would the bankers want to know about the inventories and cost of goods sold? Why? Would shareholders have the same interests? Why or why not?

EXHIBIT 3-14

TELEPANEL SYSTEMS INC.
Consolidated Balance Sheet
(in Canadian dollars)

	January 31	
	1995	1994
Assets		
Current assets		
Cash (Note 2)	$ 3,230,364	$ 3,394,243
Short-term deposits	–	2,000,000
Accounts receivable	592,377	170,418
Inventories (Note 3)	2,228,695	903,565
Prepaid expenses	163,443	37,771
	6,214,879	6,505,997
Fixed assets (Note 4)	568,721	505,743
Deferred expense (Note 5)	243,118	296,105
	$ 7,026,718	$ 7,307,845
Liabilities		
Current liabilities		
Bank and other indebtedness (Note 6)	$ 1,555,524	$ 259,703
Accounts payable and accrued liabilities (Note 7)	868,463	499,424
	2,423,987	759,127
Shareholders' Equity		
Capital stock (Note 8)	23,625,480	22,420,348
Deficit	(19,022,749)	(15,871,630)
	4,602,731	6,548,718
	$ 7,026,718	$ 7,307,845

Approved by the Board

_____   _____
Director   Director

See accompanying notes to financial statements.

EXHIBIT 3-14 (continued)

TELEPANEL SYSTEMS INC.
Consolidated Statement of Operations and Deficit
(in Canadian dollars)

| | Year ended January 31 | | |
	1995	1994	1993
Product sales	$ 3,381,131	$ 433,448	$ 353,578
Expenses			
Manufacturing	4,023,591	814,969	404,896
Selling, general and administration	2,041,725	1,847,006	1,206,915
Research and development	476,041	449,885	287,114
Patent enforcement	–	20,125	138,274
Patent licence fees	–	301,795	122,556
Depreciation	125,663	74,972	30,068
Interest	71,869	12,740	11,074
	6,738,889	3,521,492	2,200,897
Loss from operations before the undernoted item, interest earned and other revenue	(3,357,758)	(3,088,044)	(1,847,319)
Interest earned	206,639	237,805	75,162
Other revenue (Note 9)	–	62,500	889,000
	206,639	300,305	964,162
Loss from operations before the undernoted item	(3,151,119)	(2,787,739)	(883,157)
Unusual items related to issuance of shares (Note 10)	–	–	9,052,137
Loss for the year	(3,151,119)	(2,787,739)	(9,935,294)
Deficit, beginning of year	(15,871,630)	(22,136,028)	(12,200,734)
Reduction of deficit on reduction of capital stock (Note 11)	–	9,052,137	–
Deficit, end of year	$ (19,022,749)	$ (15,871,630)	$ (22,136,028)
Loss per common share	$ (0.22)	$ (0.21)	$(1.09)

See accompanying notes to financial statements.

EXHIBIT 3-14 (continued)

TELEPANEL SYSTEMS INC.
Consolidated Statement of Changes in Financial Position
(in Canadian dollars)

	Year ended January 31		
	1995	1994	1993
Cash provided by (used in)			
Operating activities			
Loss for the year	$ (3,151,119)	$ (2,787,739)	$ (9,935,294)
Items not requiring a current outlay of cash			
Deferred expense amortization	52,987	15,585	–
Unusual items	–	–	9,052,137
Depreciation	125,663	74,972	30,068
Changes in noncash working capital (Note 13)	(1,503,722)	(1,024,141)	911,026
	(4,476,191)	(3,721,323)	57,937
Financing activities			
Issuance of common shares and warrants	1,205,132	7,230,675	1,165,515
Bank and other indebtedness	1,295,821	72,292	62,430
Deferred credit	–	–	110,000
	2,500,953	7,302,967	1,337,945
Investing activities			
Purchase of fixed assets, net	(188,641)	(450,235)	(52,544)
Short-term deposits	2,000,000	(2,000,000)	–
Long-term receivables	–	–	68,010
Deferred expense	–	–	(311,690)
	1,811,359	(2,450,235)	(296,224)
Increase (decrease) in cash during the year	(163,879)	1,131,409	1,099,658
Cash, beginning of year	3,394,243	2,262,834	1,163,176
Cash, end of year	$ 3,230,364	$ 3,394,243	$ 2,262,834
Supplemental Information Cash paid during the year for Income taxes	$ –	$ –	$ –
Interest	$ 71,869	$ 12,740	$ 11,074

See accompanying notes to financial statements.

EXHIBIT 3-14 (continued)

TELEPANEL SYSTEMS INC.

3. Inventories

	1995	1994
Raw materials	$890,685	$509,140
Work in progress	297,905	11,984
Finished goods	922,100	316,926
Deposits on purchases	118,005	65,515
	$2,228,695	$903,565

4. Fixed assets

	1995		
	Cost	Accumulated depreciation	Net
Computer equipment	$227,258	$180,173	$47,085
Furniture and equipment			
Manufacturing	836,809	321,796	515,013
Office	38,755	32,132	6,623
	$1,102,822	$534,101	$568,721

	1994		
	Cost	Accumulated depreciation and amortization	Net
Computer equipment	$202,020	$163,214	$38,806
Furniture and equipment			
Manufacturing	673,406	214,748	458,658
Office	38,755	30,476	8,279
	$914,181	$408,438	$505,743

20. In the Consolidated Statement of Earnings and Retained Earnings of Mosaid Technologies Incorporated shown in Exhibit 3-5, there is no mention of amortization expense. In the statement of changes in financial position for Mosaid shown in Exhibit 3-15, there is a line item in the operating activities section indicating that amortization amounted to $912,000 in 1995.

Required:

a. Explain why you do not see this large expense in the income statement.

b. Explain why the amount of the amortization expense would be important to bankers and to shareholders.

EXHIBIT 3-15

MOSAID TECHNOLOGIES INCORPORATED
Consolidated Statement of Changes in Financial Position
(in thousands)

	year ended April 30	
	1995	**1994**
Operating		
Net earnings	**$ 4,484**	$ 2,925
Items not affecting cash		
Amortization	**912**	485
Loss (gain) on disposal of capital assets	**7**	(24)
Investment tax credits	**(415)**	-
Deferred income taxes	**1,005**	-
	5,993	3,386
Change in non-cash working capital items	**(2,954)**	(461)
	3,039	2,925
Investing		
Acquisition of capital assets – net	**(2,618)**	(789)
Proceeds from disposal of capital assets	**2**	42
Acquisition of capital assets under capital leases	**(68)**	-
Other assets	**50**	(50)
	(2,634)	(797)
Financing		
Increase in obligations under capital leases	**68**	-
Repayment of obligations under capital leases	**(66)**	(73)
Issue of common shares (net of costs of $29; 1994 – $1,345)	**378**	16,438
	380	16,365
Net cash inflow	**785**	18,493
Cash position, beginning of year	**18,579**	86
Cash position, end of year	**$ 19,364**	$ 18,579
Cash comprises the following:		
Cash	**$ 3,879**	$ 735
Marketable securities	**15,485**	17,844
	$ 19,364	$ 18,579

See accompanying Notes to the Consolidated Financial Statements.

CASE

ONTA INDUSTRIES LTD.

Onta Industries Ltd. manufactures gift items such as pens, key chains, mini-flashlights, and many other small plastic items. These items are sold both in retail stores and directly to customers who have their corporate names and logos printed on the items for promotional use. To date they have produced all of these items in their Toronto factory, but have recently received an offer from a Chinese company in Shanghai to sell them pens for $0.50 each, landed in Vancouver. These pens would be identical to those currently produced. The printing of any corporate logo would still be done in the Toronto factory. The president of Onta has asked you to recommend if the pens should be purchased from Shanghai or produced in Toronto.

Upon investigating, you find the following information.

Number of pens sold per year	1,000,000
Direct material cost per pen	$0.23
Direct labour cost per pen	$0.18
Factory overhead allocated per pen	$0.18
Cost of printing logos per pen	$0.03
Administrative overhead allocated per pen	$0.05
Cost of shipping from Vancouver per pen	$0.03
Import duties per pen	$0.05
Selling cost per pen	$0.10
Sales price per pen	$0.95

Required:

a. Recommend if the pens should be produced in Toronto or purchased from Shanghai. Justify your recommendation with figures both per pen and in total.

b. If Onta pays corporate income tax at 30%, what would be the differential effect on net income of buying the pens?

c. What other considerations should you point out before this decision is made?

◤◥ Critical Thinking Question

21. Assume you are in charge of a government agency that has agreed to buy a computer system designed and built specifically for your agency. You agreed to pay all direct costs of producing the system, plus 20% for overhead and profit.

Required

a. List which costs you would accept as direct costs and which should be classified as overhead. Justify your choices.

b. Now assume the role of the president of the systems company and answer the same question.

APPENDIX B

MANUFACTURING ACCOUNTING SYSTEMS

In Chapter 2 we explained the accounting systems that are used by many corporations, including those whose primary business is the buying and selling of goods. However, as explained in this chapter, the basic business of manufacturing corporations is different because it involves the actual production, and not just the sale, of products.

Remember that the basic purpose of accounting is to produce information that is useful to users such as shareholders, potential shareholders, bankers, and management. Therefore accounting systems must be designed to suit the types of business operated by corporations. A very basic accounting system was described in Chapter 2 to help you understand how accounting numbers are recorded and accumulated. In Chapter 3 we described how manufacturing corporations were different from corporations that do not manufacture the products they sell. To accumulate the additional costs incurred by manufacturing corporations, their accounting systems must be tailored to their specific needs. In this appendix, we illustrate the details of manufacturing corporations, especially in the areas where they are different from those described in Chapter 2.

■◐ MODEL MANUFACTURING CORPORATION

To illustrate the accounting systems of a manufacturing corporation, a hypothetical corporation, the Model Manufacturing Corporation, will be used as an example. The balance sheet of the Model Manufacturing Corporation as of December 31, 19x0, is given in Exhibit 3-A1. The term *prepaid* refers to costs that have already required the outflow of cash, but have not yet been consumed or used, which means that they appear as assets. A complete examination of these items is found in the following analysis of the transactions of the corporation.

The transactions for Model Manufacturing Corporation in 19x1 are summarized below. Each transaction will be analyzed and entries made in T-account form in Exhibit 3A-2.

Transactions for 19x1:

1. Sales for the year totalled $43,000, of which $30,000 were on account.

2. Collections from customers on account totalled $28,000.

3. Raw materials costing $11,700 were purchased on account.

4. Labour records indicate that labour costs incurred from January 1, 19x1 through December 15, 19x1 amounted to $22,000. Seventy-five percent of the labour cost is associated with the manufacture of inventory and the rest with administrative work. All wages and salaries through December 15, 19x1 have been paid by December 31, 19x1.

5. Labour incurred from December 15, 19x1 through December 31, 19x1 amounted to $2,000 and would be paid in the first week of January 19x2.

EXHIBIT 3A-1

MODEL MANUFACTURING CORPORATION
Balance Sheet
December 31, 19x0

Assets

Cash	$ 1,800
Accounts receivable	3,500
Inventory	
Raw materials	1,500
Work-in-process inventory	3,000
Finished goods	2,500
Prepaid rent	900
Prepaid insurance	300
Total current assets	$13,500
Property, plant, and equipment	15,000
Less: Accumulated amortization	(6,000)
Total Property, plant, and equipment	$ 9,000
Total assets	$22,500

Liabilities

Accounts payable	$ 2,000
Accrued salaries payable	1,500
Short-term debt	3,500
Total current liabilities	$ 7,000
Bank loan (long-term)	4,500
Total liabilities	$11,500
Shareholders' equity	
Common shares	$ 5,000
Retained earnings	6,000
Total shareholders' equity	$11,000
Total liabilities and shareholders' equity	$22,500

6. Rent is for manufacturing equipment. It is paid quarterly, in advance, on March 31, June 30, September 30, and December 31 in equal payments. The total payments in 19x1 were $3,960.

7. Insurance is paid semi-annually on April 1 and October 1. Payments totalled $1,440 in 19x1. 80% of the insurance is on the manufacturing facility, and the rest is administrative.

8. The plant and equipment is amortized straight-line over 12 years, with a residual value of $3,000. 75% of the property, plant, and equipment is manufacturing-related, and the rest is administrative. No property, plant, and equipment was purchased or sold in 19x1.

9. Payments on accounts payable totalled $11,000.

EXHIBIT 3A-2

MODEL MANUFACTURING COMPANY
T-account Entries

	A – Cash		
✓	1,800		
(1)	13,000	23,500	(4b)
(2)	28,000	3,960	(6a)
		1,440	(7a)
		11,000	(9)
		675	(11)
		900	(12)
	1,325		

	A – Prepaid Rent		
✓	900		
(6a)	3,960	3,870	(6b)
✓	990		

	A – Accounts Receivable		
✓	3,500		
(1)	30,000	28,000	(2)
✓	5,500		

	A – Prepaid Insurance		
✓	300		
(7a)	1,440	1,380	(7b)
✓	360		

	A – Raw Materials		
✓	1,500		
(3)	11,700	12,000	(10a)
✓	1,200		

	A – PP&E	
✓	15,000	
✓	15,000	

	A – Work-in-Process		
✓	3,000		
(4a)	16,500	34,524	(10b)
(5)	1,500		
(6b)	3,870		
(7b)	1,104		
(8)	750		
(10a)	12,000		
✓	4,200		

	XA – Accumulated Amortization		
✓		6,000	✓
		1,000	(8)
		7,000	✓

	A – Finished Goods		
✓	2,500		
(10b)	34,524	33,524	(10c)
✓	3,500		

	L – Accounts Payable		
		2,000	✓
(9)	11,000	11,700	(3)
		2,700	✓

	SE – Common Shares		
		5,000	✓
		5,000	✓

EXHIBIT 3A-2 (continued)

MODEL MANUFACTURING COMPANY
T-account Entries

L – Accrued Salaries

		1,500	✓
(4b)	23,500	22,000	(4a)
		2,000	(5)
		2,000	✓

L – Short Term Debt

	3,500	✓
	3,500	✓

SE – Retained Earnings

	6,000	✓
	6,000	✓

L – Bank Loan

	4,500	✓
	4,500	✓

L – Taxes Payable

	0	✓
	413	(13)
	413	✓

SE – Revenues

	0	✓
	43,000	(1)
	43,000	✓

SE – Cost of Goods Sold

✓	0	
(10c)	33,524	
✓	33,524	

SE – Salaries Expense

✓	0	
(4a)	5,500	
(5)	500	
✓	6,000	

SE – Insurance Expense

✓	0	
(7b)	276	
✓	276	

SE – Amortization Expense

✓	0	
(8)	250	
✓	250	

SE – Interest Expense

✓	0	
(11)	675	
✓	675	

SE – Other Administrative Expense

✓	0	
(12)	900	
✓	900	

SE – Tax Expense

✓	0	
(13)	413	
✓	413	

10. Account of the inventories at December 31, 19X1 revealed the following balances:

Raw materials	$1,200
Work-in-process inventory	4,200
Finished goods	3,500

11. Interest rates on the corporation's debt are as follows:

Short-term debt	9%
Bank loan	8%

All interest was paid by year-end and is treated as a period expense.

12. Other administrative and selling expenses totalling $900 were paid in cash.

13. Taxes on income are levied at a rate of 30%. Taxes are accrued at year-end and paid by March 15 of the following year. There were no taxes payable at the beginning of the year because there was no taxable income in 19X0. Assume that the income reported to Revenue Canada is the same as the income reported to shareholders.

The transactions of the Model Manufacturing Corporation are recorded in T-accounts in Exhibit 3A-2. Refer to this exhibit as each of the transactions is discussed in the following subsections.

Transaction 1

Sales for the year totalled $43,000, of which $30,000 were on account.

Analysis

The effect of this transaction is to increase sales revenue by $43,000. The effect on assets is split, with accounts receivable increasing by $30,000 and cash increasing by $13,000 (the difference between total sales and credit sales). Many corporations have both cash sales and credit sales. Think of a typical department store that accepts both cash and store credit cards. Manufacturing corporations generally offer similar types of credit arrangements to their customers, but they also offer incentives to pay cash, such as a price discount for cash sales.

JOURNAL ENTRY FOR TRANSACTION 1:		
A – Cash	13,000	
A – Accounts Receivable	30,000	
SE – Revenues		43,000

Transaction 2

Collections from customers on account totalled $28,000.

Analysis

Collections from customers result in an increase in cash and a decrease in the outstanding accounts receivable. There are other events that affect accounts receivable, such as bad debts and returned goods. The accounting for these events is discussed in Chapters 4 and 6.

> **JOURNAL ENTRY FOR TRANSACTION 2:**
> A – Cash   28,000
>   A – Accounts Receivable   28,000

◢◣ Transaction 3

Raw materials costing $11,700 were purchased on account.

■ ■ Analysis

Raw materials are purchased and placed in a raw materials inventory account until they are needed during production. The effect of the transaction is, therefore, to increase the raw materials inventory by $11,700. Since the purchases are on account, the accounts payable account also increases by the same amount.

> **JOURNAL ENTRY FOR TRANSACTION 3:**
> A – Raw Materials   11,700
>   L – Accounts Payable   11,700

◢◣ Transaction 4

Labour records indicate that labour incurred from January 1, 19X1 through December 15, 19X1 amounted to $22,000. 75% of the labour cost is associated with the manufacture of inventory and the rest with administrative work. All wages and salaries through December 15, 19X1 had been paid by December 31, 19X1.

■ ■ Analysis

Labour is both a product cost and a period cost. It is a product cost in the sense that certain types of labour are required to produce the product. Other types of labour are period expenses because they are not directly associated with the production of inventory. In the case of Model Manufacturing Corporation, 75% of the costs are manufacturing, which means that they are product costs and should be added to work-in-process inventory. The remainder of the labour costs are administrative and are treated as period expenses.

Because most corporations pay **salaries** and **wages** with a delay from when they are incurred, the cash paid out for salaries during a given period may not be the same as the costs incurred for the hours worked during the same period. In accrual basis accounting, wages and salaries expense and the labour cost added to work-in-process inventory must be based on wages and salaries earned during the period and not those paid during the period.

The wages and salaries earned during 19X1 include the $22,000 in wages and salaries earned from January 1, 19X1 through December 15, 19X1 and the wages and salaries earned from December 15, 19x1 through December 31, 19x1, which are discussed in Transaction 5. In this section, discussion is limited to the wages and salaries earned between January 1, 19x1 and December 15, 19x1. The wages and salaries earned during this period must be divided between the work-in process account and the wages and salaries expense account. As 75% of the wages and salaries relate to manufacturing, $16,500 (75% of $22,000) must be added to work-in-process inventory. The remaining wages and salaries of $5,500 ($22,000 minus $16,500) are administrative and are shown in the wages and salaries expense account. See Transaction 4(a) in Exhibit 3A-2.

Cash payments for wages and salaries made during the year by Model Manufacturing Corporation relate both to wages and salaries earned during the year (the majority of the payments) and to the wages and salaries that were accrued at the end of the previous year. Exhibit 3A-3 diagrams the situation of any accrued expense, that is, an expense incurred in one accounting period and paid in a later accounting period. Salaries and wages, for example, may be paid every two weeks. If the last pay date in December is one week from the end of the month, the wages and salaries earned during the last week in December will not be paid until the end of the first week in January. Therefore, wages and salaries earned during the last week of December must be recorded.

The wages and salaries accrued at the end of last year are summarized in the beginning balance of the accrued wages and salaries payable account. For Model Manufacturing Corporation, the $1,500 in the accrued wages and salaries payable account was accrued in 19x0 and is paid in 19x1, along with the $22,000 in wages and salaries earned and paid from January 1, 19x1 through December 15, 19x1. Therefore, the total wages and salaries paid during 19x1 were $23,500. See Transaction 4(b) in Exhibit 3A-2.

EXHIBIT 3A-3

Accrued Expenses

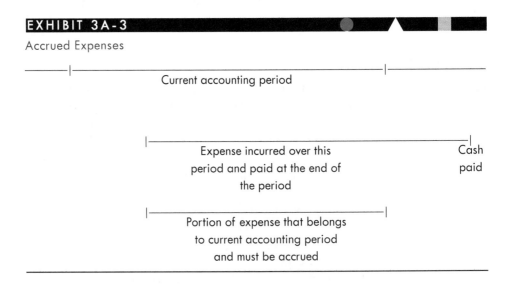

JOURNAL ENTRY FOR TRANSACTION 4:

(4a)

A – Work-in-process inventory	16,500	
SE – Wages and salaries expense	5,500	
L – Accrued wages and salaries payable		22,000

(4b)

L – Accrued wages and salaries payable	23,500	
A – Cash		23,500

Transaction 5

Labour incurred from December 15, 19X1 through December 31, 19X1 amounted to $2,000 and would be paid in the first week of January 19X2.

Analysis

As explained earlier, wages and salaries earned before the end of the accounting period and paid in the next accounting period must be accrued. Therefore, the $2,000 in wages and salaries must be recorded as a payable, and the related expense must be divided between the work-in-process inventory account and the wages and salaries expense account. The split is 75/25, with work-in-process inventory receiving $1,500 of the total and wages and salaries expense receiving $500.

JOURNAL ENTRY FOR TRANSACTION 5:

SE – Wages and salaries expense	500	
A – Work-in-process inventory	1,500	
L – Accrued wages and salaries payable		2,000

Transaction 6

Rent is paid for manufacturing equipment. It is paid quarterly, in advance, on March 31, June 30, September 30, and December 31 in equal payments. The total payments in 19X1 were $3,960.

Analysis

Rent, in this case, is a prepaid item. A prepaid item is one for which the cash flow occurs in one period and the expense related to the item is incurred (or consumed) in the following period. Prepaid items may also be thought of as deferred expenses. Exhibit 3A-4 displays a time line highlighting the effects of a prepaid expense. Part of the cash payment applies to expenses in the period in which the payment occurs. The other portion of the payment applies to the following accounting period.

EXHIBIT 3A-4

Prepaid Expenses

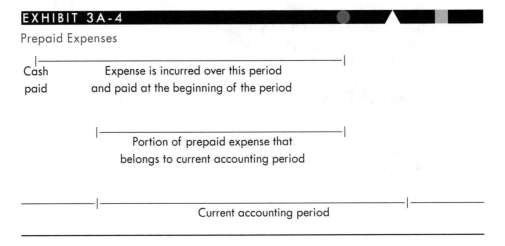

| Cash paid | Expense is incurred over this period and paid at the beginning of the period |

Portion of prepaid expense that belongs to current accounting period

Current accounting period

The beginning balance of $900 in the prepaid rent account of Model Manufacturing Corporation is rent that was paid on December 31, 19x0 and applies to the months of January through March. The payments on March 31, 19x1, June 30, 19x1, and September 30, 19x1 of $990 each ($3,960 divided by 4) apply to the remainder of 19x1. The total expenses incurred in 19x1 would therefore be $3,870 [$900 + ($990 × 3)]. As rent relates to manufacturing equipment, this amount should be added to the work-in-process inventory account in 19x1. The payment of $990 on December 31, 19x1 covers rent expense for January through March of 19x2 and, therefore, should be the balance in the prepaid rent account on December 31, 19x1. See Exhibit 3A-2 to verify the entries that produce this result.

JOURNAL ENTRY FOR TRANSACTION 6:

(6a)

| A — Prepaid Rent | 3,960 | |
| A — Cash | | 3,960 |

(6b)

| A — Work-in-process inventory | 3,870 | |
| A — Prepaid Rent | | 3,870 |

Transaction 7

Insurance is paid semi-annually on April 1 and October 1. Payments totalled $1,440 in 19x1. 80% of the insurance is on the manufacturing facility, and the rest is administrative.

Analysis

Prepaid insurance is similar to prepaid rent. Therefore, the analysis of this account is similar to that of prepaid rent, just discussed. The only difference is that the insurance relates partly to manufacturing and partly to administrative expenses. The expenses incurred during the year must, therefore, be divided between the work-in-process inventory and the insurance expense accounts.

The balance in the prepaid insurance account at December 31, 19x0 ($300) is the amount of the insurance paid on October 1, 19x0 that applies to January through March of 19x1. This, along with the entire payment on April 1, 19x1 ($720) and half the payment on October 1, 19x1 ($360), should be shown as expense in 19x1. The total expense is $1,380 ($300 + $720 + $360) and is split $1,104 (80%) to work-in-process inventory and $276 (20%) to insurance expense. The rest of the October 1, 19x1 payment ($360) remains in the prepaid insurance account as of December 31, 19x1 and applies to January through March of 19x2.

JOURNAL ENTRY FOR TRANSACTION 7:

(7a)

A – Prepaid Insurance	1,440	
A – Cash		1,440

(7b)

SE – Insurance Expense	276	
A – Work-in-Process Inventory	1,104	
A – Prepaid Insurance		1,380

Transaction 8

The property, plant, and equipment are amortized straight-line over 12 years, with a residual value of $3,000. 75% of the property, plant, and equipment is manufacturing-related, and the rest is administrative. No property, plant, and equipment was purchased or sold in 19x1.

Analysis

In Chapter 2, amortization expense was recorded as a debit to the amortization expense account and a credit directly to the asset account. Most corporations, rather than crediting the asset account directly for amortization, maintain a separate account that accumulates the amortization from period to period. This account is called the **accumulated amortization account**. As credits are made to this account, it has a credit balance. The credit reduces the balance in the related asset account, and this type of account is called a **contra-asset account**. Accumulated amortization, a contra-asset account, reduces the debit balance in the property, plant, and equipment account. The balance in the property, plant, and equipment account, therefore, represents the original cost of the property, plant, or equipment. Note the symbol **XA** that appears on the accumulated amortization account. This symbol is used in the book to indicate a contra-asset account.

The calculation of the straight-line amortization expense per period uses the formula described in Chapter 2. The original cost of the property, plant, and equipment (obtained from the beginning balance of the property, plant, and equipment account, $15,000) is reduced by the residual of $3,000 and divided by the useful life of 12 years. This results in amortization expense per year of $1,000. This total is then split 75% to manufacturing and 25% to period expenses. Observe that if a corporation is growing and inventory is growing as well, some expenses of the current period are deferred until later accounting periods.

JOURNAL ENTRY FOR TRANSACTION 8:

A – Work-in-process inventory	750	
SE – Amortization Expense	250	
XA – Accumulated Amortization		$1,000

Transaction 9

Payments on accounts payable totalled $11,000.

Analysis

The payments on accounts payable were discussed in Chapter 2 and result in a decrease in the cash balance and a decrease in the accounts payable balance.

JOURNAL ENTRY FOR TRANSACTION 9:

L – Accounts Payable	11,000	
A – Cash		11,000

Transaction 10

A count of the inventories at December 31, 19X1 revealed the following balances:

Raw Materials	$1,200
Work-in-process	4,200
Finished Goods	3,500

Analysis

In most manufacturing corporations, inventories are counted and priced at year-end to determine the proper amount that should be reported in the ending inventory. This also allows the corporation to determine its cost of goods sold for the year. The cost of goods sold is determined by first using the ending raw materials inventory balance, along with the information about the beginning balance and the debits made to the account for the purchases during the period (Transaction 3), to calculate how much material was transferred out of raw materials inventory and into work-in-process inventory (see entry 10a). The amount transferred can be calculated as follows:

Raw materials inventory

Beginning balance	$1,500
Purchases	11,700
Total	$13,200
Less: Ending balance	(1,200)
Amount transferred to work-in-process inventory	$12,000

JOURNAL ENTRY FOR TRANSACTION 10:

(10a)

A — Work-in-process Inventory	12,000	
A — Raw Materials Inventory		12,000

(10b)

A — Finished Goods Inventory	34,524	
A — Work-in-process Inventory		34,524

(10c)

SE — Cost of Goods Sold	33,524	
A — Finished Goods Inventory		33,524

The cost of the goods completed and transferred to finished goods is then determined by knowing the ending balance in the work-in-process inventory account (entry 10b) and the beginning balance and entries made to the work-in-process inventory account during the period as follows:

Work-in-Process Inventory

Beginning balance	$3,000
Salaries (entry 4a)	16,500
Salary (entry 5)	1,500
Rent (entry 6b)	3,870
Insurance (entry 7b)	1,104
Amortization (entry 8)	750
Raw materials (entry 10a)	12,000
Total	$38,724
Less: Ending balance	(4,200)
Amount transferred to finished goods	$34,524

Finally, the ending balance in finished goods is subtracted from the sum of the beginning balance in finished goods and the debit entry for the goods completed and transferred to finished goods to determine the cost of goods sold (entry 10c) as follows:

Finished Goods Inventory

Beginning balance	$2,500
Purchases	34,524
Total	$37,024
Less: Ending balance	3,500
Amount transferred to cost of goods sold	$33,524

◤◣ Transaction 11

Interest rates on the corporation's debt are as follows:

Short-term debt	9%
Bank loan	8%

All interest was paid by year-end and is treated as a period expense.

■ ■ Analysis

There are two fundamental effects on the accounts that must be calculated for interest. The first is the effect on expenses, that is, how much interest expense was incurred during the period. The second effect is to determine the cash flows that occur as a result of interest. As there was no interest payable account balance at the beginning of the year and as all interest was paid in cash by year-end, there will be no difference between the expense incurred and the cash paid for interest in this example.

Interest expense is calculated by multiplying the **interest rate** times the **principal** amount of the loan, times the **fraction of the year** the loan has been outstanding. As both loans were outstanding from the beginning of the year, the fraction of the year is 100%. The principal of the loan is the amount listed on the balance sheet at the beginning of the year. The calculation of the interest incurred is therefore:

Short-term debt:
$$\text{Interest expense} = \text{Principal} \times \text{Interest Rate} \times \text{Fraction of Year}$$
$$= \$3,500 \times 9\% \times 1$$
$$= \$315$$

Bank loan:
$$\text{Interest expense} = \text{Principal} \times \text{Interest Rate} \times \text{Fraction of Year}$$
$$= \$4,500 \times 8\% \times 1$$
$$= \$360$$

Because all this interest is treated as a period expense, and since all interest is paid in cash by year-end, one entry can be made to show the aggregate effects of this transaction. See entry 11 in Exhibit 3A-2.

JOURNAL ENTRY FOR TRANSACTION 11:

SE – Interest Expense	675	
A – Cash		675

Transaction 12

Other administrative and selling expenses totalling $900 were paid in cash.

Analysis

Administrative and selling expenses are treated as period expenses and, therefore, the effect of this entry is to increase administration expense and decrease cash by $900.

JOURNAL ENTRY FOR TRANSACTION 12:

SE – Other Administrative Expenses	900	
A – Cash		900

Transaction 13

Taxes on income are levied at a rate of 30%. Taxes are accrued at year-end and paid by March 15 of the following year. There were no taxes payable at the beginning of the year because there was no taxable income in 19X0. Assume that the income reported to Revenue Canada is the same as the income reported to shareholders.

Analysis

To calculate the tax expense for the period, the net income before tax must be determined from the revenues and expenses listed in the temporary accounts. The income before taxes is calculated as follows:

Revenues	$43,000
Less: Cost of goods sold	33,524
Salaries expense	6,000
Amortization expense	250
Insurance expense	276
Interest expense	675
Other administrative expenses	900
Total expenses	$41,625
Income before taxes	$ 1,375

The tax expense is then calculated by multiplying the net income before tax by the tax rate, which results in $413 (rounded to the nearest dollar) of tax expense ($1,375 × 30%).

The tax payments during the period would be for any taxes owed at January 1, 19x1 (there were none) and any taxes that came due during 19x1. In the case of Model Manufacturing, taxes were accrued only at year-end and would not be paid until March 15, 19x2. Therefore, all the tax expense just calculated results in a tax payable amount at December 31, 19x1. See Exhibit 3A-2 for the recording of this transaction.

JOURNAL ENTRY FOR TRANSACTION 13:

SE – Tax Expense	413	
L – Taxes Payable		413

The description of the transaction states that the income reported to Revenue Canada is the same as that reported to the shareholders. The reason for this statement, as mentioned earlier in the book, is that the rules governing the reporting of income to Revenue Canada differ from the guidelines under GAAP. Therefore, the amount owed to Revenue Canada could differ from the calculation of tax expense just defined. Any differences may lead to the recording of an amount called deferred taxes. Deferred taxes are discussed in Chapter 9. For now, it will be assumed that the reporting for both Revenue Canada and GAAP purposes is the same so that no deferred tax entry is needed.

■ ■ Conclusion of Example

Make sure that you complete your understanding of the Model Manufacturing Corporation example by reviewing all the accounts in Exhibit 3A-2. The accounts have been left in adjusted trial balance form, and you might want to test your knowledge of the closing process by making the entries on your own. You should end up with a balance in the retained earnings account of $6,962.

APPENDIX SUMMARY PROBLEM

The balance sheet of the Template Manufacturing Corporation as of December 31, 19x7, is given in Exhibit 3A-5, and the transactions for Template in 19x8 are summarized.

Required:

a. Prepare T-accounts for the Template Manufacturing Corporation, and enter the opening balances and the transactions for 19x8. Open new accounts as you need them.

b. Enter the closing entries in the T-accounts. Use an income summary account.

c. Prepare classified balance sheets (beginning and ending of the year) and a single-step income statement for the Template Manufacturing Corporation for 19x8.

Transactions for 19x8:

1. Sales for the year totalled $760,000, all of which were on account.

2. A review of accounts receivable at the end of the year showed a balance of $35,000.

3. Amortization of $19,600 was incurred, 80% of which was due to factory building and equipment and the remainder to office furniture.

EXHIBIT 3A-5

TEMPLATE MANUFACTURING CORPORATION
Balance Sheet
December 31, 19x7

Assets

Cash	$ 55,000
Accounts receivable	39,500
Inventory: Raw materials	18,000
Work-in-process inventory	76,000
Finished goods	73,000
Prepaid rent	15,000
Total current assets	$ 276,500
Property, plant, and equipment	350,000
Less: Accumulated amortization	(100,000)
Total property, plant, and equipment	250,000
Total assets	526,500

Liabilities

Accounts payable	$ 33,000
Accrued salaries payable	9,000
Taxes payable	16,000
Notes payable	8,000
Total current liabilities	$ 66,000
Long-term debt	75,000
Total liabilities	$ 141,000
Common shares	185,000
Retained earnings	200,500
Total shareholders' equity	$ 385,500
Total liabilities and shareholders' equity	$ 526,500

---

4. Purchases of new property, plant, and equipment totalled $40,700, all paid in cash.

5. The corporation sold property, plant, and equipment for $5,000. The book value of the property, plant, and equipment was $5,000, and the original cost was $10,000. (Book value = Original cost − accumulated amortization.)

6. Rent is paid for manufacturing equipment. Payments are made quarterly, in advance, on March 31, June 30, September 30, and December 31. Two payments of $15,000 each were made through the end of June. Rent increased to $16,500 per quarter, starting with the September 30 payment.

7. Employees earned wages of $150,000 during the year. Of these, $125,000 were manufacturing employees and the rest administrative. As of December 31, 19x8, $11,000 was owed to employees.

8. Purchases of raw materials, all on account, amounted to $231,000 (assume that this is the only item that affects accounts payable).

9. The corporation owed suppliers $36,000 as of December 31, 19X8.

10. A count of ending inventories revealed the following amounts in ending inventory:

Raw materials	$21,000
Work-in-process inventory	72,000
Finished goods	77,000

11. The note payable carries a 9% interest rate, and interest is due annually on December 31. On June 30, 19X8, the corporation paid off $6,000 of the principal, plus accrued interest. The rest of the principal is not due until 19X9.

12. Long-term debt at December 31, 19X7 carried an interest rate of 10%, with interest payments due semi-annually on June 30 and December 31. On January 1, 19X8, the corporation paid off $25,000 of the principal of this long-term debt. On September 30, 19X8, the corporation issued $27,000 of additional long-term debt at an interest rate of 12% with interest payment terms identical to the existing borrowings.

13. Other selling and administrative expenses of $45,000 were paid in cash.

14. The corporation's net income is taxed at 30% and, as of December 31, 19X8, $7,442 was owed to Revenue Canada.

15. The corporation declared $40,000 in dividends each quarter during 19X8; dividends were payable on April 15, 19X8, July 15, 19X8, October 15, 19X8, and January 15, 19X9.

SUGGESTED SOLUTION TO APPENDIX SUMMARY PROBLEM

The T-account solution is shown in Exhibit 3A-6.

Explanations of certain transactions are:

Transaction 2. The information given is the ending balance in the accounts receivable account. Cash collections are calculated based on the beginning and ending balances in the account and the debit for sales on account as follows:

Beginning balance	39,500
Sales	760,000
Total	799,500
Less: Ending balance	35,000
Payments received	764,500

Transaction 3. The amortization for the period is split between the work-in-process inventory account (manufacturing component) and the amortization expense account (administrative component).

EXHIBIT 3A-6

TEMPLATE MANUFACTURING CORPORATION
T-accounts Entries

	A – Cash		
✓	55,000		
(2)	764,500	40,700	(4)
(5)	5,000	63,000	(6a)
(12b)	27,000	148,000	(7b)
		228,000	(9)
		450	(11a)
		6,000	(11b)
		25,000	(12a)
		5,810	(12c)
		45,000	(13)
		83,450	(14b)
		120,000	(15b)
✓	86,090		

	A – Prepaid Rent		
✓	15,000		
(6a)	63,000	61,500	(6b)
✓	16,500		

	A – Accounts Receivable		
✓	39,500		
(1)	760,000	764,500	(2)
✓	35,000		

	A – Raw Materials		
✓	18,000		
(8)	231,000	228,000	(10a)
✓	21,000		

	A – PP&E		
✓	350,000		
(4)	40,700	10,000	(5)
✓	380,700		

	A – Work-in-Process		
✓	76,000		
(3)	15,680	434,180	(10b)
(6b)	61,500		
(7a)	125,000		
(10a)	228,000		
✓	72,000		

	XA – Accumulated Amortization		
		100,000	✓
(5)	5,000	19,600	(3)
		114,600	✓

	A – Finished Goods		
✓	73,000		
(10b)	434,180	430,180	(10c)
✓	77,000		

	L – Account Payable		
		33,000	✓
(9)	228,000	231,000	(8)
		36,000	✓

	SE – Common Shares		
		185,000	✓
		185,000	✓

EXHIBIT 3A-6 (continued)

TEMPLATE MANUFACTURING CORPORATION

T-accounts Entries

L – Accrued Salaries

		9,000	✓
(7b)	148,000	150,000	(7a)
		11,000	✓

L – Note Payable

		8,000	✓
(11b)	6,000		
		2,000	✓

SE – Retained Earnings

		200,500	✓

L – Long-term Debt

		75,000	✓
(12a)	25,000	27,000	(12b)
		77,000	✓

L – Taxes Payable

		16,000	✓
(14b)	83,450	74,892	(14a)
		7,442	✓

L – Dividends Payable

		0	✓
(15b)	120,000	160,000	(15a)
		40,000	✓

SE – Revenues

		0	✓
		760,000	(1)
		760,000	✓

SE – Cost of Goods Sold

✓	0	
(10c)	430,180	
✓	430,180	

SE – Salaries Expense

✓	0	
(7a)	25,000	
✓	25,000	

SE – Amortization Expense

✓	0	
(3)	3,920	
✓	3,920	

SE – Interest Expense

✓	0	
(11a)	450	
(12c)	5,810	
✓	6,260	

EXHIBIT 3A-6 (continued)

TEMPLATE MANUFACTURING CORPORATION
T-accounts Entries

SE – Other S&A Expense				SE – Tax Expense	
✓	0		✓	0	
(13)	45,000		(14a)	74,892	
✓	45,000		✓	74,892	

SE – Dividends Declared		
✓	0	
(15a)	160,000	
✓	160,000	

Transaction 5. The entry to record the sale of property, plant, and equipment is shown as follows:

A – Cash	5,000	
XA – Accumulated Amortization	5,000	
A – Property, Plant and Equipment		10,000

Transaction 6. The beginning balance in the prepaid rent account on December 31, 19x7 of $15,000 represents the payment made on December 31, 19x7 that covers rent for the first quarter of 19x8. The first two payments in 19x8 of $30,000 (2 × $15,000) cover the second and third quarter. The third payment of $16,500 on September 30, 19x8 covers the fourth quarter. Therefore, the rent expense added to the work-in-process inventory account during 19x8 (entry 6b) should be the sum of these amounts or $61,500 [(3 × $15,000) + $16,500]. The last payment of $16,500 on December 31, 19x8 applies to the first quarter of 19x9 and should be the ending balance in the prepaid rent account. The total cash payments (entry 6a) during the period total $63,000 [(2 × $15,000) + (2 × $16,500)].

Transaction 7. The wages earned during the period are split between work-in-process inventory and salaries expense (entry 7a). The ending balance in the salaries payable account ($11,000), given in the problem, allows the calculation of the amount paid for wages during 19x8 (entry 7b) as follows:

Beginning balance	9,000
Salaries earned	150,000
Total	159,000
Less: Ending balance	(11,000)
Salary payments	148,000

Transaction 10. The ending balances in the three inventory accounts are used to determine how much is transferred out of raw materials and into work-in-process inventory (entry 10a), out of work-in-process inventory and into finished goods (entry 10b), and out of finished goods and into cost of goods sold (entry 10c).

Transaction 11. The interest incurred during the year is the same as the amount paid as it is due on December 31 each year. It can be calculated according to the following schedule:

$6,000 × 9% × 6/12 =	$270
$2,000 × 9% × 12/12 =	180
Interest expense	$450

Transaction 12. The interest incurred during the year is the same as the amount paid as the second payment coincides with the end of the year (December 31). The interest expense is calculated according to the schedule that follows. Note that, as $25,000 of the debt that existed on December 31, 19x7 is paid off on January 1, 19x8, it does not accumulate interest. Only $50,000 of the long-term debt from 19x7 continues into 19x8.

$50,000 × 10% × 12/12 =	$5,000
$27,000 × 12% × 3/12 =	810
Interest expense	$5,810

Transaction 14. Taxes are computed on the income before taxes, which is $249,640 in 19x8 (see the income summary T-account in Exhibit 3A-6). The tax expense is $74,892 (30% × $249,640). The ending balance in the taxes payable account is then used to calculate how much Template paid in taxes in 19x8 as follows:

Beginning balance	$16,000
Tax expense	74,892
Total	$90,892
Less: Ending balance	7,442
Tax payments	$83,450

Transaction 15. Because the last dividend declared in 19x8 is still payable as of December 31, 19x8, a new account, dividends payable, must be created. The first three dividends are paid in cash.

b. The closing entries for the temporary accounts in Exhibit 3A-6 are shown in Exhibit 3A-7. Only the balances in the temporary accounts are shown in Exhibit 3A-7, along with the closing entries. See Exhibit 3A-6 for the entries made during the year to arrive at these balances.

c. The balance sheets for the Template Manufacturing Corporation are shown in Exhibit 3A-8, and the income statement is shown in Exhibit 3A-9.

EXHIBIT 3A-7

TEMPLATE MANUFACTURING CORPORATION
T-account Closing Entries

SE – Income Summary

		0	✓
		760,000	(A)
(B)	430,180		
(C)	25,000		
(D)	3,920		
(E)	6,260		
(F)	45,000		
		249,640	✓
(G)	74,892		
		174,748	✓
(H)	174,748		
		0	✓

(Income before taxes)

SE – Retained Earnings

		200,500	✓
(I)	160,000	174,748	(H)
		215,248	✓

SE – Revenues

		760,000	✓
(A)	760,000		
		0	✓

SE – Cost of Goods Sold

	430,180		
		430,180	(B)
	0		

SE – Salaries Expense

	25,000		✓
		25,000	(C)
✓	0		✓

SE – Amortization Expense

✓	3,920		
		3,920	(D)
✓	0		

SE – Interest Expense

✓	6,260		
		6,260	(E)
✓	0		

SE – Other S&A Expense

✓	45,000		
		45,000	(F)
✓	0		

SE – Tax Expense

✓	74,892		
		74,892	(G)
✓	0		

L – Dividends Declared

✓	160,000		
		160,000	(I)
✓	0		

EXHIBIT 3A-8

TEMPLATE MANUFACTURING CORPORATION
Balance Sheet
December 31

	19x8	19x7
Assets		
Cash	$ 86,090	$ 55,000
Accounts receivable	35,000	39,500
Inventory		
Raw materials	21,000	18,000
Work-in-process inventory	72,000	76,000
Finished goods	77,000	73,000
Prepaid rent	16,500	15,000
Total current assets	$ 307,590	$ 276,500
Property, plant, and equipment	380,700	350,000
Less: accumulated amortization	(114,600)	(100,000)
Total assets	$ 573,690	$ 526,500
Liabilities		
Accounts payable	$ 36,000	$ 33,000
Accrued salaries payable	11,000	9,000
Taxes payable	7,442	16,000
Notes payable	2,000	8,000
Dividends payable	40,000	0
Total current liabilities	$ 96,442	$ 66,000
Long-term debt	77,000	75,000
Total liabilities	$ 173,442	$ 141,000
Shareholders' Equity		
Common shares	185,000	185,000
Retained earnings	215,248	200,500
Total shareholders' equity	$ 400,248	$ 385,500
Total liabilities and shareholders' equity	$ 573,690	$ 526,500

EXHIBIT 3A-9

TEMPLATE MANUFACTURING CORPORATION
Income Statement
Year Ended December 31, 19x8

Revenues	$760,000
Less:	
Cost of goods sold	430,180
Salaries expense	25,000
Amortization expense	3,920
Interest expense	6,260
Other selling and administrative expenses	45,000
Total expenses	$510,360
Income before taxes	249,640
Provision for income taxes	74,892
Net income	$174,748

◖◗ APPENDIX ASSIGNMENT MATERIAL

◤◣ Applying your knowledge

1. Oakdale Manufacturers showed the following balances on January 1, 19X1:

Raw materials	$25,000
Work-in-process inventory	$86,000
Finished goods	$105,000

Required:
Prepare all journal entries associated with the transactions that occurred during 19X1 for Oakdale Manufacturers.

Transactions, 19X1:
a. Raw materials were purchased on account for $200,000.
b. Raw materials costing $196,000 were requisitioned and used in the production process.
c. Wages earned were as follows:

Factory workers	$225,000
Sales force	$125,000
Administration	$175,000

d. Wages paid during the year totalled $505,000.
e. Amortization was as follows:

Manufacturing	$75,000
Selling	$ 9,000
Administrative	$23,000

f. Other operating costs (all paid in cash) totalled $44,000. Of these, three-quarters related to manufacturing operations and the rest to selling and administrative.
g. Physical inventory counts at year-end revealed the following balances:

Work-in-process inventory	$ 75,000
Finished good	$117,000

2. Fernwood Manufacturers showed the following balances on January 1, 19X1:

Raw materials	$133,000
Work-in-process inventory	$ 65,000
Finished goods	$255,000

Required:
Use T-accounts to record the entries associated with the transactions that occurred during 19X1 for Fernwood Manufacturers.

Transactions, 19X1:
a. Raw materials were purchased on account for $950,000.
b. Raw materials costing $146,000 remained in ending inventory on December 31, 19X1.
c. Wages earned were as follows:

Factory workers	$125,000
Sales force	$300,000
Administration	$135,000

d. Wages paid during the year totalled $575,000.

e. Amortization was as follows:

Manufacturing	$145,000
Selling	88,000
Administrative	$ 15,000

f. Other operating costs (all paid in cash) totalled $63,000. Of these, half related to manufacturing operations and the rest to selling and administrative.

g. Goods completed and transferred to finished goods during the year totalled $1,250,000.

h. A physical inventory count of finished goods inventory at year-end revealed inventory worth $360,000.

3. On January 1, 19X1, SBA Enterprises had the following balances in its accounts:

Assets:		
Cash		$ 84,400
Accounts receivable		72,000
Prepaid rent		10,000
Inventories:		
Raw materials		15,479
Work-in-process		26,670
Finished goods		6,350
Property plant, and equipment		550,000
Accumulated amortization		(220,000)
Total Assets		$ 544,899
Liabilities:		
Accounts payable		$ 59,000
Deposits from customers		6,400
Warranty liability		1,020
Salaries payable		5,624
Interest payable		8,750
Mortgage payable		437,500
Total Liabilities		$ 518,294
Shareholders' equity:		
Common shares		$ 15,000
Retained earnings		11,605
Total shareholders' equity		$ 26,605
Total liabilities and shareholders' equity		$ 544,899

Required:

a. Prepare T-accounts for SBA Enterprises, and enter the opening balances and the transactions for 19X1, which follow. Open new accounts as you need them.

b. Enter the closing entries in the T-accounts.

c. Prepare balance sheets (beginning and ending of the year) and the income statement for SBA Enterprises for 19X1.

Transactions:

1) SBA sells a product known as a gizmo. During 19x1, SBA signed contracts to build 1,250 gizmos for customers. The contract terms call for a 10% down payment at the time of contract signing with the balance due 30 days from delivery of the gizmos. The selling price for all contracts in the last two years has been $800 per gizmo. SBA recognizes revenue at the time of delivery of the gizmo.

2) During 19x1, SBA delivered 1,230 gizmos to customers.

3) A review of outstanding accounts receivable at December 31, 19x1 indicated that $79,200 was still owed to SBA by customers.

4) SBA purchased $284,000 of raw materials on account during 19x1.

5) SBA owed suppliers $64,000 at December 31, 19x1.

6) SBA paid $45,000 to renew a rental agreement for a computer system on May 1, 19x1. The agreement is for a one-year period, and the entire rental amount was paid in advance. The computer system is used to operate the production line.

7) A count and valuation of ending inventories on December 31, 19x1 revealed the following:

Raw materials	$23,000
Work-in-process	32,385
Finished goods	9,525

8) SBA purchased $140,000 worth of property, plant, and equipment during 19x1.

9) SBA took out a mortgage for $25,000 to pay for part of the property, plant, and equipment purchases in item 8. The mortgage was taken out on November 1, 19x1 and carried an interest rate of 9%, with interest payments due every six months. The principal was not due until maturity.

10) The other mortgages of the corporation were outstanding all year and carried an interest rate of 8%, with interest rate payments due on April 1 and October 1. On December 31, 19x1, SBA paid off $75,000 of the principal on these mortgages.

11) SBA sold property, plant, and equipment originally costing $137,000 with a book value of $3,000 and recorded a loss of $1,500. (Book value = original cost − accumulated amortization)

12) Amortization of $137,000 was taken during 19x1. Of this, $125,000 related to manufacturing equipment and the rest to administrative equipment.

13) Salaries of $315,976 were earned by employees during 19x1. Manufacturing employees accounted for 90% of the salaries. SBA pays salaries every two weeks and, at year-end, $6,100 was owed to employees.

14) Utilities (all of which relate to manufacturing) amounted to $32,485 and were paid in full at year-end.

15) Warranty liability is estimated at 1.5% of sales. During 19x1, $14,550 was paid on warranty service.

16) SBA paid $5,000 for advertising expenses during 19x1. All advertising had been run by December 31, 19x1.

17) SBA declared and paid $30,000 of dividends during 19x1.

18) Miscellaneous selling and administrative expenses of $15,000 were paid in cash during 19x1.

4. The Husky Furniture Corporation had the following balances in its accounts as of December 31, 19x5:

	Debit	Credit
Cash	$4,600	
Accounts receivable	12,000	
Inventory		
Raw materials	2,000	
Work-in-process	3,500	
Finished goods	3,000	
Prepaid rent	800	
Notes receivable	3,200	
Property plant, and equipment	110,000	
Accumulated amortization		$ 55,000
Accounts payable		16,380
Dividends payable		6,000
Long-term debt		25,000
Common shares		30,000
Retained earnings		6,720
	$139,100	$139,100

Required:

a. Prepare T-accounts for Husky Furniture Corporation, and enter the opening balances and the transactions for 19x6. Open new accounts as you need them.
b. Enter the closing entries in the T-accounts.
c. Prepare balance sheets (beginning and ending of the year) and the income statement for Husky Furniture Corporation for 19x6.

Transactions 19x6:

1) Sales totalled $500,000, of which $200,000 were cash.
2) Cash collections on accounts receivable from customers totalled $292,000.
3) Idle cash of $50,000 was invested in marketable securities. The intent of the corporation is to sell these securities within a year of their purchase.
4) Raw materials purchases for the period were $205,000, all of which were on account.
5) Payments to suppliers on account totalled $215,000.
6) Factory workers earned $150,000 during the year, and all wages were paid by the end of the year.
7) Cash outlays for heat, light, and power for the plant amounted to $30,000.
8) Some of the machinery used in the plant is leased (rented). The lease payments are made a year in advance. This year's payment of $6,000 was made on March 1, 19x6. and covers the period from March 1 to the following February 28.
9) Amortization is calculated using the straight-line method, assuming an average life of 10 years and a residual value of $10,000. This year's amortization expense amounted to $8,000 on the factory equipment and $2,000 on the office equipment that is used primarily in the administrative offices.

10) The note receivable is a note from a customer, and the face amount is due on January 1, 19X7. The note requires semiannual interest payments on July 1, 19X6 and January 1, 19X7. The interest rate stated on the note is 11%.

11) Four quarterly dividends of $7,000 each were declared during 19X6. All but the last quarter's dividend have been paid by December 31, 19X6.

12) Marketable securities costing $5,000 were sold for $5,500.

13) A count of the physical inventory at the end of the year revealed the following balances:

Raw materials	$3,000
Work-in-process	5,500
Finished goods	4,500

14) Property, plant, and equipment with a net book value of $2,000 was sold at a loss of $1,000. The original cost of the equipment was $15,000.

5. Use the information in the balance sheet, income statement, statement of changes in financial position, and note 4 of Telepanel Systems Inc. shown in Exhibit 3-14 to reconstruct the aggregate entries that were made to the fixed assets (furniture and equipment) account and its associated accumulated depreciation during the fiscal year 1995.

CHAPTER

4

Revenue Recognition

PERFORMANCE MEASUREMENT

CASH-TO-CASH CYCLE

REVENUE RECOGNITION

In Chapters 1 through 3, the basic financial statements of a corporation were discussed. Two of those statements, the income statement and the statement of changes in financial position, measure the performance of the corporation across some time horizon. In this chapter, some of the problems inherent in the measurement of performance are considered, and the accounting concepts and guidelines for the recognition of income are discussed. Chapter 5 discusses the statement of changes in financial position and the measurement of performance using cash flows in more detail.

PERFORMANCE MEASUREMENT

After making an investment, investors generally want to know how well their investment is performing. To put this in a simple context, suppose an investment is made in a savings account at a local bank branch. Periodically, statements are received from the bank that detail any new deposits or withdrawals and any interest earned by the savings. The interest earned can then be compared with the balance on the account to give an indication of the performance of the investment. Ratios can help us assess this performance.

The Return on Investment (ROI) Ratio as a Measure of Performance

A common measure of performance used in business is a ratio called the **return on investment** or (**ROI**), which is generally computed as follows (in Chapter 12 we will discuss several other ratios that also calculate returns):

$$ROI = \frac{Return}{Average\ Investment}$$

In the case of the bank account, the numerator is the interest earned during the period, and the denominator is the average amount invested over the time period. By averaging the denominator, additional deposits or withdrawals made during the period are taken into account. A simple average of the beginning balance and the ending balance in the investment is often used; however, more sophisticated averaging methods may be more appropriate.

Suppose the average investment in a bank account was $1,000, and the return was $100. The ROI from the investment would be:

$$ROI = \frac{\$100}{\$1,000} = 10\%$$

Based on this return, two questions might be asked: (1) Is this a good return on investment? and (2) How confident is the investor that this really is the return?

To answer Question (1), the return on this investment should be compared with the returns that could have been earned on other, alternative investments, or with the returns that other, similar investors are earning. If the next best alternative would have returned only 8%, the bank account was a good investment. If, however, other similar investors are earning 12% for investments of similar risk, it would seem that the best investment was not made.

To answer Question (2), the investors must assure themselves that their $1,000 investment plus their $100 return is really worth $1,100 today. Ultimately, the only way to be sure that the investment is worth $1,100 is to sell the investment; that is, to withdraw the $1,100 from the bank. If the investor does not sell the investment, there is still some chance that the bank will not have the money to repay them; the bank might, for example, file for bankruptcy. In the late 1980s and early 1990s, this was not an inconceivable event as several small Canadian banks went out of business. In banks insured by the Canadian Deposit Insurance Corporation (CDIC), small accounts (those up to $60,000) are insured so that, even in the event of a bank collapse, the investor would still be repaid by the CDIC. A bank account of this type is about as safe an investment as can be made. An uninsured account would not give the same comfort level with regard to the failure of the banking institution.

Now suppose that, instead of investing in a savings account, an investment is made in a house. Assume that the house is bought for investment purposes for $200,000. Assume further that there are no further cash outlays or inflows during the year from this investment. To assess the return on the investment, the value of the investment at the end of the period must be determined. This value could be estimated by getting an appraisal of the house by a real estate agent, or by comparing the house with other comparable houses in the area that have recently sold. The selling prices of those houses could serve as a basis for estimating the value of the investment. In either case, the value will be an **estimate**. Confidence in these estimates will surely be lower than the confidence in the estimate of the return earned from the investment in the savings account at the bank. In fact, the only certain way to determine the return on the house would be to sell it; that is, sell the investment. If the investor does not want to sell the investment, however, the only alternative would be to use an estimate of the selling price to measure performance. If the investor estimates the selling price to be $225,000, the ROI will be:

$$ROI = \frac{(\$225,000 - \$200,000)}{\$200,000} = 12.5\%$$

Measuring the performance of a business is much like estimating the return on the investment in a house. The business makes investments in property, plant, equipment, inventory, accounts receivable, and other assets, and periodically measures the performance of these investments. However, It does not want to sell its investment in these assets at the end of every accounting period simply to determine the proper ROI. It must, therefore, estimate any changes in the value of its assets and liabilities that may have occurred during the accounting period, and report these as net income.

Some of the changes in value (returns) are easy to measure, such as the interest earned on a savings account. Other changes, such as the change in the value of property, plant and equipment, are not as easily measured, as the example concerning the investment in a house demonstrates. Because accounting data should be reliable as well as relevant (in Chapter 1 we discussed these terms), accountants have established concepts and guidelines for recognizing the changes in value of assets and liabilities to ensure that the measure of performance most commonly used (net income) provides a reliable measure of the effects of the transactions that took place during the period.

◤◣ Net Income as a Measure of Performance

The income statement measures the return to the shareholders on their investment in the corporation; that is, it measures changes in shareholders' wealth in the corporation. The accounting value of this shareholders' wealth is measured by the value of shareholders' equity accounts. Remember that these accounts include common shares and retained earnings.

Shareholders' equity accounts are typically affected by three general types of transactions: shareholder investment activities, the declaration of dividends, and transactions that result in profits or losses. Shareholders may invest more money in the corporation by buying, for example, new shares when they are issued. This does not directly affect their return on the investment, but does affect the amount of investment they have in the corporation. Second, shareholders may declare themselves a dividend (via a vote of the board of directors), which reduces their wealth in the corporation by reducing the total assets in the corporation. This also does not directly affect the return on investment, but does affect the amount of investment. Finally, those transactions that result in profits or losses will affect shareholders' wealth through their effects on retained earnings. It is this last set of transactions, and their impact on value, that is measured by the income statement.

Because the corporation does not want to sell its investments each period to determine its performance, some concepts and guidelines have been developed to guide how estimates of changes in value can be determined. These guidelines and concepts are sometimes called revenue recognition principles. To understand them, it is useful to understand the correspondence relationship between the **cash-to-cash cycle** of the corporation and the estimation of changes in value.

◖◗ CASH-TO-CASH CYCLE

As we have seen, corporate managers engage in three general types of activities: financing, investing, and operating. Let us focus for a moment on operating activities.

Operating activities include all the normal day-to-day activities of every business, which almost always involve cash. Operating activities involve the normal buying and selling for the purpose of earning profits, for which the business was created. The typical operation of a business involves an outflow of cash that is followed by an inflow of cash, a process commonly called the **cash-to-cash cycle**. In Exhibit 4-1, the cash-to-cash cycle of a typical manufacturing corporation is shown. Each phase in the cash-to-cash cycle is discussed in the following subsections.

EXHIBIT 4-1

Cash-to-Cash Cycle of a Manufacturing Corporation

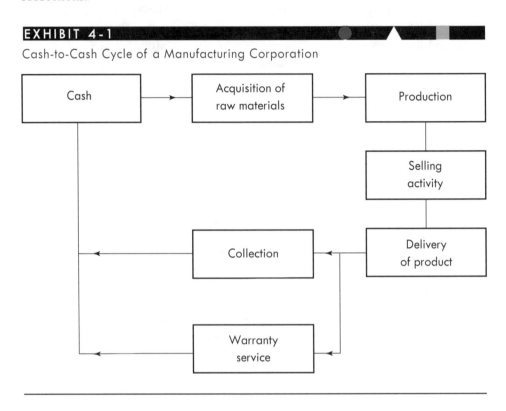

▶◣ Cash

We have already discussed how the initial amount of cash in a corporation comes from the initial investment by shareholders, and from any loans that the corporation may have taken out to provide the initial financing. In Chapter 12, the difference between the return on the investment made by the shareholders and the investment made by the lenders is considered; at this point, however, no distinction will be made between them. To simplify matters, you might think of the corporation as being totally financed by shareholders; that is, there are no loans.

▶◣ Acquisition of Raw Materials

Before the corporation acquires the raw materials needed to make its products or to provide its services, it must first undertake the investing activities of acquiring property, plant and equipment. Next, labour is hired and the basic raw materials to produce the product are purchased (or contracts are signed to acquire them). Note that, in a manufacturing corporation, the costs involved in this initial phase may be more substantial that those of a service-oriented corporation.

Production

In the production phase the property, plant, equipment, labour, and raw materials are converted into a marketable product. Of course the labour and raw materials are used up much more quickly than the property, plant and equipment. The end result of the production process is a stockpile of goods available for sale. These are the finished goods inventories to which we referred in Chapter 3.

Selling Activity

The selling phase includes all those activities designed to promote and sell the product. These may include pricing the products produced, advertising them, hiring and managing a sales force, establishing retail sales outlets, **agency** agreements, signing supply agreements, and attending trade shows, among other activities. The end result of this phase are sales contracts between the buyer and seller. This may be a verbal agreement or a formal written document.

Delivery of Product

Once a sales contract has been achieved, the product must be delivered to the customer. Depending on the type of product, this may be instantaneous (as in a grocery store), or it may take months or years (as with a ship-building corporation producing ships).

Collection

Upon delivery of the product, collection of the sales price in cash may be immediate, such as in a grocery store, or it could take place at some later date, resulting in an amount owing at the time of delivery, which is called an **account receivable**. Payment at a later date is the same as the seller making a loan to the buyer and accepting the risk that the buyer will not pay (this is called credit risk). The loan to the buyer may carry explicit interest charges, but usually no interest is charged if payment is made within a specified period of time. If the buyer does not pay within the specified period of time, the seller may try to obtain the product back (repossession) or may try other methods to collect on the account, such as turning it over to a collection agency.

Other events could also occur that would affect the collection of cash. The goods may be returned for various reasons, resulting in no cash collection. The goods may be damaged in shipment, and the buyer may ask for a price adjustment (generally called a **price allowance**). There may also be an incentive built in to encourage prompt payment of cash, such as a **cash discount**, which means that less than the full amount will be accepted as full payment. For example, a seller may offer a 2% price discount if the account is paid within 10 days. These terms are sometimes stated as "2/10 net 30," which means that a 2% discount is offered if payment is made within 10 days; otherwise, the total amount is due at the end of 30 days.

◤◣ Warranty Service

Some goods carry a written or implied guarantee of quality. Automobiles, for example, are warranted for a certain number of years or for a certain number of kilometers. During this period, the seller is responsible, to some extent, for replacement or repair of the product. This affects the ultimate amount of cash that is available at the end of the cycle.

◤◣ Summary of Cash-to-Cash Cycle

The net amount left in cash after this cycle is completed is then available to produce more goods and services in the next cycle. If the cash inflows are less than the cash outflows, the amount of cash available is reduced, and the corporation may be unable to begin a new cycle. To the extent that cash inflows exceed cash outflows, the corporation can expand its volume of activity, add another type of productive activity, or return some of the extra cash to shareholders in the form of dividends.

Note that the order of the phases in the cash-to-cash cycle may be different from one corporation to the next. For example, a transportation contractor such as Bombardier may do most of its selling activity early in the cycle to obtain contracts to deliver products at a future date, with much of the acquisition of raw materials and production taking place after the contract is signed. Also, in some corporations, the separate phases may take place simultaneously. In a grocery store, for example, the delivery of goods to the customer and the collection of cash take place at the same point in time.

◖◗ REVENUE RECOGNITION

Managers do not want to wait until the end of the cash-to-cash cycle to assess the performance of their corporation because they must make day-to-day decisions that will ultimately affect the final cash outcome. If they wait until the end, they may not be able to make appropriate adjustments. For example, if the first few items sold result in significant uncollected accounts or require significant warranty service, they might want to rethink their policies on granting credit and providing warranties. If the warranty is the problem, they might also want to institute better quality control procedures in the production process. Furthermore, the cash-to-cash cycle is a continual process that is constantly beginning and ending for different transactions.

To measure operating performance as accurately as possible, accountants divide normal operating activities into two groups, called revenues and expenses. **Revenues** are the inflows of cash or other assets from the normal operating activities of the business which mainly involve the sale of goods or provision of services. **Expenses** are the costs incurred to earn revenues. The difference between revenues and expenses, called **net income**, is one of the key measurements of performance.

The need for timely information to make decisions argues for recognizing revenue as early as possible in the cash-to-cash cycle. The earlier in the cycle revenue is recognized, however, the greater the number of estimates needed to measure the net performance. For example, if the corporation chooses to recognize revenue at the time of delivery of the product to customers (a common practice for many businesses), it will have to make estimates regarding the collectibility of the receivables and costs of warranty service. To measure the return (profitability) on the sale of a product accurately, these items should be considered; otherwise, the corporation may be overestimating the return on the sales of its products. To produce the most accurate measurement of net operating performance, all costs incurred to earn revenues are matched to the revenues they helped earn. In accrual accounting, this is called the **matching principle** (refer again to Chapter 1). The matching principle requires that all costs incurred (in the past, present, or to be incurred in the future) to produce the revenue must be recognized at the same time the revenue is recognized.

The earlier in the cash-to-cash cycle the corporation chooses to recognize revenues, the less reliable is the corporation's estimate of the effects of future events. In return, however, the corporation receives more timely information. To reduce the uncertainty inherent in estimating future events, the corporation would need to recognize revenues later in the cash-to-cash cycle when those estimates are more reliable, but the information would be less useful for making management decisions.

There is obviously a conflict between the desire to measure performance on a timely basis (early in the cycle) and the ability to measure performance reliably (late in the cycle). Revenue recognition criteria have been developed within GAAP to resolve this conflict, and to produce a measure of performance that is intended to balance the need for timely information with the need for reliable information. Two of the most fundamental principles are **recognition** and **measurement** criteria.

Revenue Recognition Criteria

By recognition, we mean recognizing an item for inclusion in a financial statement, including both the description and the amount. For revenues, this would mean the inclusion of a line in the income statement for the revenue earned during the period and the amount of the revenue.

Recognition criteria include two aspects. The first criterion requires the item to be **measurable** so that a reasonable estimate can be made of the amount. The second criterion states that any future economic benefit must be *probable* before an item can be listed.

For revenues, these criteria mean that the revenues must be measurable, that they can be reasonably estimated, and that it is probable that the future benefits that will be obtained from earning the revenues will be obtained by the corporation. The future benefits from revenues would normally be the cash that will be received for the account receivable.

◣◣ Revenue Measurement Criteria

Measurement means the process of determining an appropriate amount or value to ascribe to some attribute of the item being measured. For revenues, this means determining the dollar amount that represents the value of the revenue. Several methods can be used to determine the amount at which any item can be measured for inclusion in financial statements, including:

1. **Historical cost** By historical cost, accountants mean the actual cost at the time of acquisition. Cost means the value of whatever is given up to acquire the item.

2. **Replacement cost** By replacement cost, accountants mean the costs that would have to be incurred to replace the item today, with the replacement item having the same productive capacity as the item it replaced.

3. **Net realizable value** By net realizable value, accountants mean the amount of cash that would be received if the item were sold, after considering costs to sell the item. Gold mines commonly record revenues by recording the value of the gold produced at its net realizable value.

4. **Present value of future cash flows** To calculate this value, accountants calculate the amounts of cash that will be received at various times in the future from this item and discount these cash flows back to today. If an item is sold with the cash to be received over an extended period of time, the present value of the future cash flows to be received would be the proper measure of the value of the revenues. For further details of present value, see Appendix 1 (at the end of the text).

Although the methods listed would seem to be more relevant to the valuation of assets, the choice of a particular method has important implications for revenue recognition. For example, if an item of inventory is recorded at historical cost, the only time the corporation records revenue from the inventory is when it is sold to someone outside the corporation. On the other hand, if the item of inventory is recorded at net realizable value, revenue would be recorded as the market value of the item changed, even though it has not yet been sold.

The choice of which method to use for a particular asset or liability is sometimes a difficult and controversial decision. For example, in the late 1970s and early 1980s, there was much concern in Canada that high inflation rates were not being reflected adequately in financial statements based primarily on historical costs. At that time, corporations were encouraged to provide information about the current costs and purchasing power of their assets and liabilities. This recommendation existed for about nine years and was subsequently dropped after much discussion of the pros and cons of producing this type of information. As each specific asset and liability category is discussed in subsequent chapters of this book, the choice of measurement methods will be considered.

Examples of the different revenue recognition methods used by corporations in Canada are given in the next section.

■■ Other Revenue Recognition Criteria

In addition to the general recognition criteria already discussed, two specific factors are generally considered before a revenue can be recognized. The first is whether

AN INTERNATIONAL PERSPECTIVE
REPORTS FROM OTHER COUNTRIES

Income recognition may be based on different attributes in countries other than Canada. For example, in The Netherlands, income is determined on a current-cost basis. The following excerpt from the 1990 annual report of Koninklijke Wessanen NV (Wessanen), a corporation that produces and distributes consumer food products, illustrates the income recognition principles:

General

Income and shareholders' equity are determined on a current cost basis. Current cost is based on the replacement value of assets unless the going-concern value or the net realizable value is lower. Accounting on a current cost basis requires charging to income:

- amortization of property, plant and equipment at their replacement value;
- raw materials and supplies drawn from base inventories, at the purchase price prevailing at the time of sale of the finished product.

Revenues are recognized on delivery of the goods and services. Costs are charged to income in the period in which they are incurred.

the revenue has been **earned**. A revenue is considered to have been **earned** when the corporation has substantially completed what it must do to be entitled to the benefits of the revenues. This is sometimes referred to as "the earnings process being substantially complete." In general, this would mean that there are very few costs yet to be incurred in the cash-to-cash cycle, or that the remaining costs are subject to reasonable estimation or both.

The second factor is whether the revenues have been realized or are realizable. Revenues are **realized** when products, services, or other assets are exchanged for cash or claims to cash. Revenues are **realizable** when the products, services, or other assets are exchanged for assets (not cash or claims to cash) that are readily convertible into cash or claims to cash. Readily convertible assets are assets for which there is an active market in which price quotations are available and in which the asset could easily be traded at the quoted price without affecting the price. For example, if the corporation received shares that are actively traded in exchange for a piece of inventory, the shares would be considered readily convertible into cash.

In conclusion, if revenues have been earned and are realized or realizable, they should be recognized in the financial statements. These conditions are usually met at the time of delivery of the product to the customer, so this is the point at which many corporations recognize their revenues. In the following sections, various methods of revenue recognition are discussed, including the point of sale to the customer as well as at other points on the cash-to-cash cycle.

Revenue Recognition Methods

The revenue recognition criteria can be met at different points on the cash-to-cash cycle. Therefore, the point at which different corporations recognize revenues varies. Several different methods that you will see in practice are discussed in the following subsections.

■ ■ Revenue Recognition at the Time of Sale

The most common point at which revenues are recognized is the time of sale or shipment to the customer, or both. In annual reports, most corporations state their revenue recognition policy as part of the first footnote, which includes a summary of the significant accounting policies of the corporation. For example, Mosaid Technologies Incorporated states its revenue recognition policy in Footnote 1 of the financial statements:

> "Revenue from product sales is generally recognized on shipment. . . . Service revenue is recognized when the service is performed, or, in the case of maintenance contracts, is recognized on a straight-line basis over the term of the contract."

The disclosure by Tyco Toys Inc. states that:

> "Sales are recorded as shipped, F.O.B. point of shipment. The Company provides for returns based upon a percentage of gross sales, based on historical experience."

The term "F.O.B." means "free on board" and is a legal term used to describe the point at which title to the goods passes. In this case, because the goods are shipped F.O.B. shipping point, the title passes after the goods leave the seller' dock. If they were shipped F.O.B. destination, the goods would remain the property of the seller until they reached their destination, the buyer' receiving dock. In this latter case, it would be inappropriate to record goods as having been sold until they reached the buyer.

Another example of this basis for recording revenues occurs in the 1994 financial statements of Haley Industries Limited.

 ALEY INDUSTRIES LIMITED
b) Basis of recording revenue

Revenue from the sale of castings and patterns is recognized at the time title passes to the purchaser, which is usually when the goods are conveyed to a carrier or when the tooling is accepted by the customer.

To illustrate revenue recognition at the time of sale, assume that Hawke Corporation sells 1,000 units of its product during the year 19x1 at $30 per unit. Assume further that the costs of these units totalled $22,000 and that, at the time of sale, Hawke estimated they would cost the corporation an additional $500 in warranty expenses in the future. The income statement for Hawke for 19x1 would appear as in Exhibit 4-2.

EXHIBIT 4-2

Revenue Recognition at Time of Sale

HAWKE CORPORATION
Income Statement
For the period ended December 31, 19x1

Revenues	$30,000
Cost of goods sold	22,000
Gross profit	$ 8,000
Warranty expense	500
Net income	$ 7,500

In some cases, a corporation might receive a deposit on an order for a product to be delivered in the future. Because it is unlikely that the revenue recognition criteria would be met by this transaction (the corporation may still have to manufacture the product), the revenue from this order would not be recorded until the goods are delivered. The deposit is then recorded as revenue received in advance (a liability account as it represents an obligation either to deliver the goods or to return the deposit). For example, if the Hawke Company received a $500 deposit on an order, it would make the following entry:

A – Cash	500	
L – Deposits from Customers		500

When the goods are delivered, the liability to provide the product is satisfied, and the deposit can then be recognized as a revenue with the following entry:

L – Deposits from Customers	500	
SE – Sales Revenue		500

Businesses that require deposits or advance payments on products or services may disclose this in their footnote on revenue recognition. Typical disclosures for this type of situation are shown on page 224 for AIFS Inc. Note that liabilities are created for the obligation to provide the service or product in the future.

▉ ▉ Revenue Recognition at the Time of Contract Signing

Even though the point of sale, or more correctly, the point at which title to the product is transferred to the buyer from the seller, is the most common method used to recognize revenues, several situations exist that require exceptions to this method.

> **A** **IFS INC.**
>
> The Company develops, markets and operates educational and cultural programs worldwide and generally requires deposits and final payments by participants in advance of the time programs take place. Payments received relating to programs of subsequent periods are deferred and reflected in income over the period of each program.
>
> The Company has classified that portion of the deferred revenue representing the estimated costs to earn the revenue as a current liability with the remainder being classified as non-current.

Over the years, certain types of transactions have caused concern among investors and accountants about the revenue recognition practices employed. Two of those were in the areas of franchising and retail land sales.

Both of these industries initially recognized revenues at the date of contract signing. In the case of franchisers, this contract was the initial franchise agreement. In the case of retail land sale corporations, it was the land sale agreement. The problem was that, in both cases, a considerable amount of uncertainty existed with regard to future costs on the seller's part subsequent to contract signing, and to the collectibility of the receivables from buyers.

The uncertainty stemmed from industry practices. Franchisers (such as McDonald's) typically agree to provide a significant amount of service, such as assistance in locating and designing the franchise facility and in training the staff, subsequent to the signing of a franchise agreement and prior to the opening of the business. In addition, the initial franchise fee is typically paid in instalments. Retail land sale corporations often sell land before it is developed and, therefore, have yet to incur the development costs. Sales contracts typically require low down payments and sometimes below-market interest rates to entice buyers to sign contracts. These conditions make it relatively easy for a buyer to back out of the transaction before all the cash is collected, thereby negating the sale.

Given the uncertainties with regard to future costs and the collectibility of the receivables that have resulted from these transactions, revenue for franchisers and retail land sale corporations is now recognized at the time of contract signing only if certain minimum criteria are met. These criteria require, first, that there be only minimal costs yet to be incurred, and, second, that the receivables created in the transaction has a reasonable chance of being collected. These industries have special accounting rules because of the special nature of their revenue recognition practices. The excerpt on page 225 from the financial statements of Comac Food Group Inc. typifies the revenue recognition policies of franchisers.

■ ■ Revenue Recognition at the Time of Production

Revenue recognition at the time of production is common in two different kinds of industries: mining and long-term construction. If the market value and sale of the

C OMAC FOOD GROUP INC.
Income from initial franchise fees and the sale of franchised stores is deferred and is recognized when the franchisee commences store operations.

Franchise royalties are based on the sales of the franchisees and are recorded as earned.

production are both fairly certain at the time of production, as in certain mining operations, then the inventories produced can be valued at their net realizable value and the resulting revenues can be recognized immediately. The reason for this practice is that the critical event in the revenue earning process for a gold mine is not the *sale* of gold, but the *production* of gold. This is because the market for gold is well-established with fairly stable prices, so sale of gold is assured as soon as it is produced. By recording the revenues as soon as possible, these corporations have more timely information for making decisions.

An example of this revenue recognition method is Bema Gold Corporation, which operates gold and silver mines.

B EMA GOLD CORPORATION
Revenue, net of refining and selling costs, is recorded at the estimated net realizable value when the gold and silver is available to be processed by the smelter or refinery. Adjustments to these amounts are made after final prices, weights and assays are established.

The second type of industry that recognizes revenue at the time of production is one where the production period is long, such as in the long-term construction industry. Disclosures below for Western Star Trucks Holdings Ltd. and Mosaid Technologies Incorporated illustrate this type of revenue recognition:

W ESTERN STAR TRUCKS HOLDINGS LTD.
Western Star recognizes income on long-term contracts using the percentage of completion method of accounting.

M OSAID TECHNOLOGIES INCORPORATED
Revenue from design contracts is recognized on a percentage of completion basis.

In the long-term construction industry, two methods of recognizing revenue are generally accepted: the **completed contract method**, and the **percentage of completion method**. The **completed contract method** defers the recognition of revenue until the contract is completed and is generally used for projects that are completed in a reasonably short period of time. Longer-term projects are generally accounted for using the **percentage of completion method**, which recognizes a portion of the revenues and expenses of a project during the construction period based on the percentage of completion. The basis for determining the percent complete is usually the costs incurred relative to the estimated total costs.

As an example, suppose that the XYZ Construction Corporation agrees to construct a building for $200 million that will take three years to build, and the company expects to incur costs of $60 million, $75 million, and $15 million in Years 1, 2 and 3, respectively. The total expected costs are $150 million and, therefore, the profit on the project is expected to be $50 million. If all goes according to plan, XYZ would recognize the revenues and expenses (and related profits) shown in Exhibit 4-3 during the three years with the percentage of completion method.

EXHIBIT 4-3

Revenue Recognition with the Percentage of Completion Method
(Amounts in thousands)

Year	Degree of Completion		Revenue Recognized		Expenses Recognized	Profit
1	$60,000/$150,000 =	40%	40% × 200,000 =	80,000	$ 60,000	$20,000
2	$75,000/$150,000 =	50%	50% × 200,000 =	100,000	$ 75,000	25,000
3	$15,000/$150,000 =	10%	10% × 200,000 =	20,000	$ 15,000	5,000
		100%		200,000	$150,000	$50,000

If XYZ had used the completed contract method, all the revenues and expenses would have been deferred and recognized at the time of completion, that is, the entire $50 million in profit would have been recognized in Year 3.

With either the percentage of completion method or the completed contract method, if an overall loss is projected on the project, Generally Accepted Accounting Principles (GAAP) require that the loss be recognized as soon as it can be estimated. For example, if it turned out that, at the end of Year 2, the total estimated costs to complete the contract of XYZ were $225 million (instead of the original $150 million), an overall loss of $25 million would be indicated for the contract. At the end of Year 2, XYZ would have to recognize a loss of $45 million. This loss would offset the $20 million profit reported in Year 1 and would result in a net loss at this point of $25 million on the contract. If the actual costs equalled the estimated costs in Year 3, no additional profit or loss would be recorded in Year 3, as the overall loss on the contract would already have been recognized.

The recognition of the estimated loss in the preceding example is partially a result of the conservative nature of accounting. Conservatism requires that losses generally be recognized as soon as they can be estimated, but profits are seldom recognized until they are realized.

■ ■ Revenue Recognition at the Time of Collection

It is seldom the case that the revenue recognition criteria will not be met prior to collection. Therefore, for reporting purposes, revenue is almost always recognized prior to the time of collection. There are circumstances, however, that make the collection of the receivable so uncertain that GAAP would require that revenue recognition be postponed until cash is actually collected. In these situations, two methods can be used to recognize revenue at the time of cash collection: the **instalment** method, and the **cost recovery method**. The revenue recognition policies of PGI Inc. and ANDAL Corporation, which follow, refer to the use of these methods in certain circumstances. These methods are used infrequently for reporting purposes. Note that the use of either method postpones the recognition of revenue until cash is collected, which means that the corporation would not record revenues at the normal point of sale.

> ## P GI INC.
> Homesites are generally sold under contracts for deed which provide for a down payment and monthly instalments, including interest, for periods up to ten years. Income from sales of homesites is recorded when minimum down payment (including interest) and other requirements are met. However, because of collectibility problems with certain off-site broker/foreign sales programs, the Company reports homesite instalment sales with down payments of less than 20% under the instalment method.

> ## A NDAL CORPORATION
> Land sales are accounted for by the cost recovery method. Under the cost recovery method, no gain is recognized until cash received exceeds the cost and the estimated future costs related to the land sold.

In an instalment type of sale, the buyer agrees to pay for the goods or service over time, sometimes over many months or years. The seller sets the payments that the buyer makes so that all costs incurred can be recovered, a profit is made on the sale, and suitable interest is charged for the loan the seller is making to the buyer. Therefore, the payments received by the seller can be viewed as covering three things: cost recovery, profits, and interest.

The instalment method and the cost recovery method differ in the order in which cost recovery and profit are recognized. In the instalment method, each payment received is viewed as being part interest, part profit, and part cost recovery. In the cost recovery method, payments are viewed as first recovering costs and then, once all costs have been recovered, applying to profits. The recognition of interest can take place either simultaneously with cost recovery, or after all costs have been recovered. The cost recovery method would be recommended over the instalment method in examples where the recovery of the receivable is in serious doubt.

The instalment method and the cost recovery method can be illustrated with a simple example. Assume that the ABC Land Corporation sells a homesite for

$100,000 that has a cost of $60,000. Further, assume that the buyer has agreed to make three instalment payments over the next three years of $50,000, $40,000, and $40,000, respectively, or a total set of payments of $130,000. The excess of the payments over the selling price, $30,000, represents interest. Assume that ABC decides to recognize interest evenly over the three years, or $10,000 per year. This is not generally done, but it will simplify matters for the purposes of this example. Assume further that interest is recognized in each period with both the cost recovery and instalment methods. Exhibits 4-4 and 4-5 show the amount of income that will be recognized with the two methods.

EXHIBIT 4-4

Revenue Recognition with the Instalment Method

$$\text{Profit \%} = (\$100,000 - 60,000)/\$100,000 = 40\%$$
$$\text{Gross profit} = \text{Payments applied to principal} \times \text{profit \%}$$
$$= (\text{Cash received} - \text{interest}) \times \text{profit \%}$$

Year	Gross Profits	Interest
1	($50,000 − 10,000) × 40% = $16,000	$10,000
2	($40,000 − 10,000) × 40% = $12,000	10,000
3	($40,000 − 10,000) × 40% = $12,000	10,000
Total	= $40,000	$30,000

EXHIBIT 4-5

Revenue Recognition with the Cost Recovery Method

$$\text{Cost recovery} = (\text{Payments} - \text{interest}) \text{ [up to the point at which all costs are recovered]}$$

Year	Cost Recovery	Interest	Profits
1	$50,000 − 10,000 = $40,000	$10,000	$0
2	$40,000 − 10,000 = $20,000°	$10,000	$10,000
3	$0	$10,000	$30,000
Totals	$60,000	$30,000	$40,000

° Note, in year 2, that the remainder of the costs are recovered ($60,000 − 40,000 = $20,000) and that the excess of payments less interest and cost recovery go to profits (40,000 − 10,000 − 20,000 = $10,000).

■ ■ Revenue Recognition with Multiple Lines of Business

In businesses that have multiple lines of business or that sell products in either standard as well as customized models, the revenue recognition criteria may be met at different points for different products. The disclosures for Cara Operations Limited and CHC Helicopter Corporation illustrate this point.

C ARA OPERATIONS LTD.

Generally, revenues from food sales and gift stores and retail sales of office products are recognized upon sale of products. Commercial sales of office products and revenues from wholesale food distribution are recognized at the time of shipment. Income on the sale of franchises is deferred until such time as is considered earned. Revenues from services are recognized as services are rendered.

C HC HELICOPTER CORPORATION

Revenues from helicopter operations are recognized based on the terms of customer contracts which generally provide for revenue on the basis of hours flown at contract rates or fixed monthly charges or a combination of both.

Revenues from engine and component repair and overhaul contracts are recognized on the percentage of completion basis, measured on the basis of the sales value of the actual costs incurred and work performed.

ETHICS IN ACCOUNTING

Pressures to show profit or growth in revenues, or both, can create ethical dilemmas for managers and accountants. Some of these pressures are self-imposed, particularly if the manager's compensation is tied to reported profits or revenues. Other pressures may be externally imposed by someone more senior in the organization. Suppose, for example, that you are the accountant of a division of a corporation and that the manager of the division has asked you to recognize the revenue from a large order just received. Revenue in your corporation is usually recorded when the goods are shipped, not when the order is received. The manager has indicated that this order will bump the division over its sales target for the year and that the bonuses of several managers in the division will be significantly affected. She has also indicated that the company is about to issue more common shares and that her boss would like to show improved results from last year to get the most favourable price for the shares that will be issued. What should you do? Identify the individuals that will be helped and hurt by your decision in order to help you determine what to do.

AN INTERNATIONAL PERSPECTIVE
REPORTS FROM OTHER COUNTRIES

As mentioned earlier in the chapter, revenue recognition principles and attributes may differ among countries. If a country uses a different set of principles, the amounts shown in income could be different. For example, companies in The Netherlands use the current-cost basis to measure income and shareholders' equity. Changes in the carrying values of inventories and property, plant, and equipment will be made in this system to reflect their current costs. The increases in the value of the assets will not yet have been realized but will have to be reflected on the balance sheet. These increases are shown in an account called a "revaluation reserve" account in the shareholders' equity section of the balance sheet. Exhibit 4-6 shows the balance sheet of Royal Ahold, a consumer food products company from The Netherlands. Note the revaluation reserve account in the shareholders' equity section.

EXHIBIT 4-6

ROYAL AHOLD
Consolidated Balance Sheets
(including proposed appropriation of earnings)
(NLG thousands)

	January 1 1995	January 2 1994
ASSETS		
Current assets	535,426	557,329
Cash and cash equivalents	675,329	690,007
RECEIVABLES		
Prepaid expenses	173,212	178,330
Inventories	1,790,991	1,690,777
	3,174,958	3,116,443
Fixed assets		
Tangible fixed assets, net of depreciation		
Land	241,045	233,148
Buildings	1,492,035	1,564,670
Machinery and equipment	865,141	836,653
Other	1,418,895	1,374,024
Under construction	184,113	139,682
	4,201,229	4,148,177
Loans receivable	84,473	27,416
Investment in unconsolidated subsidiaries and affiliates	630,977	625,553
Intangible assets	73,967	66,750
	4,990,646	4,867,896
	8,165,604	7,984,339

EXHIBIT 4-6 (continued)

ROYAL AHOLD
Consolidated Balance Sheets
(including proposed appropriation of earnings)
(NLG thousands)

LIABILITIES AND STOCKHOLDERS' EQUITY

Current Liabilities		
Loans payable	519,700	553,107
Taxes payable	282,896	269,912
Accounts payable	1,594,152	1,548,252
Accrued expenses	503,352	460,219
Other current liabilities	400,384	364,389
	3,300,484	3,195,879
Long-term liabilities		
Subordinated loans	430,000	440,000
Other loans	749,960	842,474
	1,179,960	1,282,474
Capitalized lease commitments	768,798	740,093
Deferred income taxes	99,481	115,594
Other provisions	538,103	464,938
	2,586,702	2,603,099
Minority interests	58,064	47,891
Stockholders' equity		
Cumulative Preferred Shares — NLG 1,000.00 par value;		
authorized — 300,000 shares; issued — none		
Common Shares — NLG 1.25 par value;		
authorized — 240,000,000 shares; issued —		145,600
120,143,985 shares and 116,482,098 shares, respectively	150,180	
Additional paid-in capital	940,252	894,590
Revaluation reserve	132,004	132,827
General reserve	1,033,918	964,450
	2,220,354	2,137,470
	8,165,604	7,984,339

SUMMARY

In this chapter, the concepts underlying the recognition of income were explored to improve your understanding of net income as a measure of performance of the business corporation. While net income is a useful measure of performance, it is not the only measure of performance in which users of financial statements should be interested. In the next chapter, the statement of changes in financial position, which summarizes cash flows, is considered. The construction of the statement itself, as well as the interpretation of the information contained in the statement, is discussed. The implications regarding the health of the corporation above and beyond those shown on the income statement are also discussed.

SUMMARY PROBLEM

Suppose that Saska Construction Corporation is in the construction business and enters into a contract with a customer to produce a building. The contract price is $10 million, and the estimated cost of the building is $6 million. The construction is estimated to take three years to complete. Prepare a schedule of the revenues and expenses that would be recognized in income in each of the three years with each of the following methods:

a. Recognition of income at contract signing

b. Instalment method, assuming the following payment schedule:

Year	Amount
1	$3,000,000
2	5,000,000
3	2,000,000

c. Cost recovery method, assuming the same payment schedule as in part b

d. Percentage of completion method, assuming the following schedule of estimated costs:

Year	Amount
1	$3,000,000
2	1,800,000
3	1,200,000

e. Completed contracts method

SUGGESTED SOLUTION TO SUMMARY PROBLEM

a. Recognizing revenue at the time of contract signing would probably not be allowed under GAAP because of the extended construction period of the contract. If it were allowed, all the profit, $4 million, would be recognized in the first year and none in later years.

b. Instalment method (answers in thousands)

Selling Price	$10,000
Less: Cost	6,000
Profit	$ 4,000

Profit % = $4,000/$10,000 = 40%

Year	Cash Flow (= Revenue)	Profit (Cash Flow × Profit %)	Expenses (Cash Flow − Profit)
1	$ 3,000	$ 3,000 × 40% = $1,200	$ 3,000 − $ 1,200 = $1,800
2	$ 5,000	$ 5,000 × 40% = $2,000	$ 5,000 − $ 2,000 = $3,000
3	$ 2,000	$ 2,000 × 40% = $ 800	$ 2,000 − $ 800 = $1,200
	$10,000	$4,000	$6,000

c. Cost recovery method (answers in thousands)

Year	Cash Flow (= Revenue)	Expense	Profit
1	$ 3,000	$3,000	$ 0
2	5,000	3,000	2,000
3	2,000	0	2,000
	$10,000	$6,000	$4,000

d. Percentage of completion method (answers in thousands)

Year	Degree of Completion	Revenue Recognized	Expenses Recognized	Profit
1	$ 3,000/$6,000 = 50%	50% x 10,000 = $ 5,000	$3,000	$ 2,000
2	$ 1,800/$6,000 = 30%	30% x 10,000 = 3,000	1,800	1,200
3	$ 1,200/$6,000 = 20%	20% x 10,000 = 2,000	1,200	800
	100%	$10,000	$6,000	$4,000

e. Completed contract method (answers in thousands)

Year	Revenue	Expense	Profit
1	0	0	0
2	0	0	0
3	$10,000	$6,000	$4,000
	$10,000	$6,000	$4,000

ABBREVIATIONS USED

GAAP Generally accepted accounting principles

ROI Return on investment

F.O.B. (Shipping point/Destination) Free on board

GLOSSARY

Account receivable An amount owing as a result of the sale of a product or service.

Agency The act of being a legal representative of some other person or corporation. In business terms, agents act as representatives for corporations for many purposes such as sales, repairs, etc.

Cash discount A reduction in the amount that has to be paid on an account payable or account receivable if payment is made within a specified time limit.

Cash-to-cash cycle The operating cycle of the corporation that describes the operating activities of the corporation from the initial outlays of cash to make a product or to provide a service, to the replacement of cash through collections from customers.

Completed contracts method A method of revenue recognition used in the construction industry in which the revenues from a contract are recognized only when the contract is completed.

Cost The value of whatever is given up to acquire an item.

Cost recovery method A method of revenue recognition based on cash collections in which no profits are recognized from a sale until the cash collected equals the costs of the item sold. Cash collected subsequent to the recovery of all costs is considered pure profit.

Earned A term used to indicate that the corporation has completed its earnings process sufficiently to allow the recognition of the revenues from the sale.

Expenses The costs incurred to earn revenues.

Financing activities Those activities that involve acquiring cash from long term loans and investments by owners.

Instalment method A method of revenue recognition based on cash collections in which each payment received is viewed as part profit and part recovery of costs. A fraction of each payment received is recorded as profit.

Investing activities Those activities that involve the buying and selling of long term assets.

Matching principle A concept that requires all expenses related to the production of revenues to be recorded during the same time period as the revenues. The expenses are said to be matched with the revenues.

Measurement The process of determining an appropriate amount or value of some attribute of the item being measured.

Net income The difference between revenues and expenses.

Operating activities Those activities involving the cash effects of the normal operations of a business, such as the buying and selling of goods and services.

Percentage of completion method A method of revenue recognition used in the construction industry in which a percent of the profits that are expected to be realized from a given project is recognized in a given period, based on the percentage of completion of the project. The percent complete is typically measured as the fraction of costs incurred to date relative to the total estimated costs to complete the project.

Price allowance An adjustment made to the selling price of a good or service to satisfy a customer, typically for some defect in the good or service provided.

Realizable Revenues are realizable when the products, services, or other assets are exchanged for assets (not cash or claims to cash) that are readily convertible into cash or claims to cash

Realized A term indicating that a revenue has been received in cash or claims to cash.

Recognition Recognizing an item for inclusion in a financial statement, including both the description and the amount.

Return on investment A measure of performance of an investment, calculated as the ratio of the return from the investment to the average amount invested.

Revenues The inflows of cash or other assets from the normal operating activities of the business which mainly involve the sale of goods or provision of services.

Revenue recognition criteria Criteria developed in GAAP that specify the conditions under which revenue should be recognized.

ASSIGNMENT MATERIAL

Assessing Your Recall

1. Diagram a typical cash-to-cash cycle of a manufacturing corporation, and briefly explain the various components of the cycle.

2. List the two major revenue recognition criteria that exist under GAAP.

3. Describe the concept of a revenue being "earned," and contrast it with the concept of a revenue being "realized."

4. Explain the difference between the percentage-of-completion method and the completed contracts method.

5. Explain the difference between the instalment method and the cost recovery method.

6. Explain what F.O.B. means, and describe why it is important to the concept of revenue recognition.

7. In the recognition of assets and liabilities, four different valuation methods are currently used in practice. List the four methods and, for one of them, discuss the implications of the choice of this method for income recognition.

8. Explain the meaning of the matching principle.

◤◣ Applying Your Knowledge

9. Jones Sales Corporation was incorporated on January 1, 19X6. During 19X6, it bought products costing $126,500 and at midnight on December 31, 19X6 it had $12,200 of the products left in its warehouse. It had recorded sales of $221,000 during 19X6, including a sale of $1,500 sold to Green Corporation with terms F.O.B. destination. These items were still in transit at midnight on December 31, 19X6. Another sale, included in the $221,000, was made on December 31 for $2,300 and was sold to Bill's Corporation with terms F.O.B. shipping point; it was not picked up from the loading dock in the warehouse until January 2, 19X7. The products sold to Green cost Jones $1,100, and those sold to Bill's cost Jones $1,800. The items sold to Bill's were counted in the $12,200 inventory on December 31. The items sold to Green were not included in the December 31 inventory count.

Required:
Prepare as much of the income statement for Jones for 19X6 as you can, showing the proper amount of sales, cost of goods sold, and gross profit. Show all calculations.

10. Brickstone Construction Company signs a contract to construct a building in four years for $40,000,000. The expected costs for each year are:

Year 1:	$ 9,750,000
2:	12,025,000
3:	6,500,000
4:	4,225,000
Total	$32,500,000

The building is completed in Year 4.

Required:
Compute, for each year, the total revenue, expense and profit using each of the following methods:
a. The percentage of completion method
b. The completed contract method

11. Sandra Carlson sold her house costing $210,000 to Bob Fletcher for $300,000. Bob agreed to pay $60,000 per year for a period of five years.

    Required:
    Compute the revenue, expense, and profit for each of the five years (ignoring interest) using each of the following methods:
    a. The instalment method
    b. The cost recovery method

12. Imperial Corporation purchases a factory from Superior Manufacturing Corporation for $1.5 million. The cost of the factory in Superior's records is $975,000. The terms of agreement are that yearly instalment payments of $705,000, $505,000, $455,000, and $255,000 will be made over the next four years. Each of these payments includes an interest payment of $105,000 per year.

    Required:
    Compute the revenue, expense, and profit for each of the four years that Superior Manufacturing Company should report using each of the following methods:
    a. The instalment method
    b. The cost recovery method

13. Cruise Shipping Inc. agreed to rebuild the "Santa Marice," an old cargo ship owned by the Oceanic Shipping Corporation. Both parties signed the contract on November 28, 19x6, for $120 million, which is to be paid as follows:

    $12 million at the signing of the contract
    $24 million on December 30, 19x7
    $36 million on June 1, 19x8
    $48 million at completion, on August 15, 19x9

    The following costs were incurred by Cruise Shipping Inc. (in millions):

19x6:	$19.2
19x7:	38.4
19x8:	24.0
19x9:	14.4
Total	$96.0

    Required:
    a. Compute the revenue, expense, and profit for each of the four years (ignoring interest) that Cruise Shipping Inc. should report using each of the following methods:
       1. Instalment method
       2. Cost recovery method
       3. Percentage of completion method
       4. Completed contract method
    b. Which method do you think should be employed by Cruise Shipping Inc. to show the corporation's performance under the contract? Why?

14. Computronics Corporation received a contract on March 3, 19x7, for setting up a central communication centre for a college. The contract price was $1 million, which is to be paid as follows:

$150,000 at the signing of the contract
$ 60,000 on July 1, 19x7
$ 30,000 on December 31, 19x7
$ 80,000 on March 25, 19x8
$100,000 on August 25, 19x8
$180,000 on December 31, 19x8
$400,000 on June 30, 19x9
The system was completed on June 30, 19x9

Estimated and actual costs were:

$150,000	for the six months ending June 30, 19x7
$225,000	for the six months ending December 31, 19x7
$262,500	for the six months ending June 30, 19x8
$ 75,000	for the six months ending December 31, 19x8
$ 37,500	for the six months ending June 30, 19x9
Total $750,000	

Required:
a. Compute the revenue, expense, and profit that Computronics should report for each of the six months ending June 30 and December 31 using each of the following methods:
   1. Percentage of completion method
   2. Completed contract method
   3. Instalment method
   4. Cost recovery method
b. Which method should be used by Computronics Corporation? Why?

15. Forte Builders Inc., a construction corporation, recognizes revenue from its long-term contracts using the percentage completion method. On March 29, 19x6, the corporation signed a contract to construct a building for $500,000. The corporation estimated that it would take four years to complete the contract and estimated the cost to the corporation at $325,000. The expected costs in each of the four years are as follows:

Year	Cost
19x6	$113,750
19x7	97,500
19x8	81,250
19x9	32,500
Total	$325,000

On December 31, 19x7, the date Forte closes its books, the corporation revised its estimates for the cost in 19x8 and 19x9. It estimated that the contract would cost $200,000 in 19x8 and $100,000 in 19x9 to complete the contract.
Required:
Compute the revenue, expense, and profit/loss for each of the four years.

16. Samson Industries purchased furniture and appliances from the Metal and Wood Corporation for $75,000 under the following payment plan, which called for semi-annual payments over two years:

Payment	Amount
1	$33,600
2	16,800
3	22,400
4	11,200
Total	$84,000

Each payment contains interest (assume that the proportionate share of interest in each payment is the same as the proportion of that payment to the total payments). Assuming that the cost of the furniture and appliances is $60,000, compute the revenue, expense, and profit that Metal and Wood Corporation would report for each of the instalment payments using each of the following methods:
a. The instalment method
b. The cost recovery method

17. On June 21, 19x6, Tristar Electric Corporation signed a contract with Denton Power Incorporated to construct a small hydroelectric generating plant. The contract price was $10 million, and it was estimated that the project would cost Tristar $7,850,000 to complete over a three-year period. On June 21, 19x6, Denton paid Tristar $1 million as a default-deposit. In the event that Denton backed out of the contract, Tristar could keep this deposit. Otherwise, the default-deposit would apply as the final payment on the contract (assume, for accounting purposes, that this is treated as a deposit until completion of the contract). The other contractual payments are as follows:

Date	Amount
October 15, 19x6	$3,150,000
April 15, 19x7	1,350,000
December 15, 19x7	1,800,000
March 15, 19x8	1,755,000
August 10, 19x8	945,000
Total	$9,000,000

Estimated costs of construction were as follows:

Year	Amount
19x6	$3,532,500
19x7	2,747,500
19x8	1,570,000
Total	$7,850,000

The contract was completed on January 10, 19x9. Tristar closes its books on December 31 each year.

Required:

Compute the revenue, expense, and profit to be recognized in each year using each of the following methods:

a. The instalment method
b. The cost recovery method
c. The percentage of completion method
d. The completed contracts method

18. Sonya's Christmas Tree Corporation began operations on April 1, 19X1. She bought a parcel of land on which she intended to grow Christmas trees. The normal growth time for a Christmas tree is six years, so she divided her land into six plots. In 19X1 she planted the first plot with trees and watered, cultivated and fertilized her trees all summer. In 19X2 she planted her second plot with trees and watered, cultivated and fertilized both planted plots. She continued with her plantings and care every year through 19X6, when she planted the last plot. On November 1, 19X6, she harvested the first plot of trees that she had planted in 19X1. In 19X7 she replanted the first plot.

    Required:
    a. Describe Sonya's cash-to-cash cycle.
    b. What revenue recognition options are open to her? Which one would you recommend and why?
    c. Using your recommended revenue recognition policy, how would Sonya account for all of her costs for growing the trees?

19. Terry Park, after graduating with a degree in computer systems and design, set up a business to design and produce computer games for use in arcades. Terry hired two other designers because of the anticipated volume of business. One designer, Kim, is paid an hourly wage. The second, Sandy, is paid 50% of the revenue received by Terry on the games designed or redesigned by Sandy. Terry rents an office where they all work and provides all necessary equipment, supplies, and other items. Terry is not paid a wage but keeps all of the profits earned.

    Terry quickly realized there were two kinds of business: speculative design and custom design. For the speculative designs, Terry or one of the designers would think of a new game, and design, program, and test it. Terry would then try to sell it to a distribution company, for either a fixed price or for a percentage (which ranges from 10% to 25%) of the total revenues earned by the games. To date, Terry has sold three of the four games produced. Terry is currently negotiating the sale of the fourth game.

    For the custom design business, Terry would receive an order from a distribution company for either the design of a new game or the redesign of an existing game (which occurs frequently as games have a useful life of only six months because players quickly get bored with games). Terry negotiates either a fixed fee payable upon completion, or an hourly rate based on the estimated length of time it should take to redesign the game. Terry sets the hourly rate based on the perceived difficulty of the project, but the rate is always at least triple the amount paid to Kim. For the hourly-rate contracts, Terry submits monthly invoices showing the number of hours worked on the project.

Required:
    a. Describe Terry's cash-to-cash cycle.
    b. What revenue recognition options are open to Terry? Which one(s) would you recommend and why?

c. Using your recommended revenue recognition policy, how would you account for all of the costs incurred by Terry?

d. What recommendations would you make to Terry about the running of this business?

▶▲◀ Reading and Interpreting Published Financial Statements

20. Zale Corporation sells fine jewelry and giftware in a chain of stores nationwide. Some of its sales are layaway sales; that is, the customer buys an item but takes delivery and makes payment on that sale at a later date. There may be an initial down payment on the layaway sale. During 1989, Zale changed its method for recognizing the revenues from these sales. The following excerpt is from the first footnote in their annual report for the year ended March 31, 1991:

> "The Company also changed its method of accounting for layaway sales effective April 1, 1989. Prior to that time, sales were not recorded until the final layaway payment is received from the customer. Under the new method, a sale is recorded when the initial layaway payment is received from the customer."

Required:

As the auditor of the financial statements of Zale, how would you respond to this change? Discuss the circumstances under which each method would be appropriate, based on the revenue recognition criteria under GAAP.

21. Eddie Bauer Outdoor Outfitters sells clothing and other items both from retail stores and through catalogue mailings. The cost of catalogue production and mailing is fairly substantial for a corporation such as Eddie Bauer. Discuss how the costs associated with catalogue production and mailing should be treated for accounting purposes. Frame your answer in terms of the revenue recognition criteria and the matching principle discussed in the chapter.

22. The balance sheet, income statement, and Note 2(i) of Imperial Parking Limited at March 31, 1995 are shown in Exhibit 4-7.

Required:

a. Rewrite the balance sheet and income statements for 1994 and 1995 as they would appear if revenues were recognized on a cash basis.

b. Comment on the effects this change in revenue recognition policy would have on these statements.

c. Which set of financial statements better represents Imperial's operations?

23. The revenue recognition policies used by SoftQuad International Inc., a producer of software and system control programs, according to Note 2(e) of its 1994 financial statements, is as follows:

> "(i) Sales of software products are recognized when the product is shipped and accepted by the customer.
> (ii) Revenue from the sale of customized software packages, including implementation and installation services, is recognized on a percentage of completion basis.

(iii) Fees from support agreements for software packages are initially recorded as deferred revenue and recognized as revenue over the terms of the agreements.

(iv) Software license fees are recognized as revenue upon the fulfillment of all significant obligations under the terms of the license agreements."

EXHIBIT 4-7

IMPERIAL PARKING LIMITED
Consolidated Balance Sheets
As at March 31, 1995 and 1994
(stated in thousands of dollars)

	1995	1994
		(note 2(l))
ASSETS		
Current assets:		
Cash and cash equivalents	$ 3,599	$ 11,352
Accounts receivable	4,169	2,182
Inventory	1,944	1,304
Deposits and prepaid expenses	1,395	938
	11,107	15,776
Other assets (note 4)	3,747	2,148
Fixed assets (note 5)	8,224	5,718
Management and lease agreements (note 6)	17,003	3,577
Goodwill (note 7)	11,153	11,491
	$ 51,234	$ 38,710
LIABILITIES AND SHAREHOLDERS' EQUITY		
Current liabilities:		
Bank indebtedness (note 8)	$ 1,700	$ –
Rents payable	6,687	3,496
Trade accounts payable and other accrued liabilities	7,314	4,512
Deferred revenue	1,662	1,045
Current portion of long-term debt	1,095	6,739
	18,458	15,792
Long-term debt (note 9)	4,349	969
	22,807	16,761
Shareholders' equity:		
Share capital (note 10)	31,114	26,163
Deficit	2,687	4,214
	28,427	21,949
Commitments and contingencies (note 12)		
	$ 51,234	$ 38,710

On behalf of the Board:

Director   _Director_

EXHIBIT 4-7 (continued)

IMPERIAL PARKING LIMITED
Consolidated Statements of Income and Deficit
Years ended March 31, 1995 and 1994
(stated in thousands of dollars)

	1995	1994
Revenue:		
Parking revenue	$136,591	$109,691
Parking equipment supplies	2,372	2,190
	138,963	111,881
Direct expenses:		
Direct costs	122,168	98,624
Cost of parking equipment	915	853
	123,083	99,477
Gross margin	15,880	12,404
Other operating expenses:		
General and administrative	10,898	8,566
Depreciation and amortization	2,583	2,149
	13,481	10,715
Income from operations before undernoted	2,399	1,689
Other expenses:		
Interest on long-term debt	639	1,002
Interest on subordinated shareholder loans	–	369
Other interest	233	284
	872	1,655
Net income	1,527	34
Deficit, beginning of year (note 2(l))	4,214	4,248
Deficit, end of year	$ 2,687	$ 4,214

Per share (note 10(h))

IMPERIAL PARKING LIMITED
Excerpted from Notes to the Statements

(i) Revenue recognition:

The Company recognizes the gross revenue collected or due from parking lots which the Company manages. Deferred revenue is derived primarily from revenue received in advance of its due date.

Required:

For each of the four parts of SoftQuad's recognition policy, explain why that policy is suitable for recognizing SoftQuad's revenues and explain why the policy conforms to GAAP.

24. The revenue recognition policy of Queenstake Resources Ltd., a mining company, from Note 1 of its 1995 financial statements is as follows:

"Revenues from the sales of metals are net of royalties and treatment charges, and are recognized when legal title passes to the buyer. Settlement adjustments arising from final determination of metal weights and assays are reflected in sales when received."

Required:

a. Explain why this revenue recognition conforms to GAAP. Include consideration of the treatment of royalties (fees based on actual quantity or value of minerals produced) and settlement adjustments (adjustments caused by selling product based on the actual mineral content when the actual mineral content is not known until a final analysis is undertaken by the purchaser).

b. What alternative revenue recognition policies and recording could Queenstake use that would also conform with GAAP?

EXHIBIT 4-8

REDAURUM LIMITED
Consolidated Balance Sheet
As at December 31, 1994

	1994	1993
Assets		
Current		
Cash and cash equivalents	$ 4,132,014	$ 1,365,425
Other term deposits	758,505	–
Accounts receivable	225,031	26,030
Inventory *(Note 4)*	1,165,537	391,458
	6,281,087	1,782,913
Mining property, plant and equipment *(Note 5)*	4,390,065	2,893,126
Exploration properties *(Note 6)*	2,828,157	1,769,311
Portfolio investments		
(quoted 1994 – $512,500; 1993 – $322,625)	479,885	322,760
Other assets	24,205	–
	$ 14,003,399	$ 6,768,110
Liabilities		
Current		
Bank overdraft	$ 262,715	$ 65,758
Accounts payable and accrued liabilities	1,743,764	1,505,037
Bank loan	526,458	–
Current portion of long-term debt *(Note 7)*	83,679	86,708
	2,616,616	1,959,641
Long-term debt *(Note 7)*	286,235	302,138
	2,902,851	1,959,641
Shareholders' Equity		
Capital stock *(Note 8)*		
Common Shares	10,808,318	4,915,018
Warrants	925,000	–
Deficit	(269,452)	(134,217)
Cumulative translation adjustment	(363,318)	27,668
	11,100,548	4,808,469
	$ 14,003,399	$ 6,768,110

The accompanying notes form an integral part of these consolidated financial statements.

Approved on behalf of the Board:

Director   *Director*

EXHIBIT 4-8 (continued)

REDAURUM LIMITED
Consolidated Statement of Loss
For the year ended December 31, 1994

	1994	1993
Revenue from mining operations	$ 3,280,306	$ 1,079,963
Cost of production	2,075,526	779,000
Gross operating profit	1,204,780	300,963
Administrative expenses, project	1,236,600	468,956
Loss from mining activities	(31,820)	(167,993)
Expenses		
Administration fees	70,898	90,495
Advertising and promotion	52,812	83,081
Consulting fees	136,483	52,839
Directors' fees	56,125	20,412
Legal and audit	76,158	252,088
Listing and filing fees	7,908	40,653
Office and general	75,881	17,130
Rent and secretarial	90,885	18,175
Share transfer expense	13,285	13,444
Shareholders' information	49,640	17,069
Telephone	26,993	22,992
Travel	78,801	120,215
Interest	(201,071)	(15,559)
Foreign exchange	(546,690)	–
Amortization	4,334	–
Financial advisory	20,300	–
	12,742	733,034
Loss for the year before the undernoted	(44,562)	(901,027)
Write-down of portfolio investments	(109,500)	(108,625)
Gain on sale of portfolio investment	18,827	–
	(90,673)	(108,625)
Net loss for the year	$ (135,235)	$ (1,009,652)
Loss per share *(Note 9)*	$ (0.003)	$ (0.045)

Consolidated Statement of Deficit
For the year ended December 31, 1994

	1994	1993
Retained earnings (deficit), beginning of year *(Note 8)*		
As originally reported	$ (134,217)	$ 1,563,482
Adjustment of prior year's income due to change in accounting policy applied retroactively *(Note 3)*	–	(688,047)
As restated	(134,217)	875,435
Net loss for the year	(135,235)	(1,009,652)
Deficit, end of year	$ (269,452)	$ (134,217)

The accompanying notes form an integral part of these consolidated financial statements.

EXHIBIT 4-8 (continued)

REDAURUM LIMITED
Excerpted from Notes to the Statements

Note 1

Revenue recognition
Revenue is recognized in the financial statements when diamonds are sold and delivery takes place.

4. Inventories

	1994	1993
Diamonds held for sale	$　581,998	$　255,565
Ore stockpiles and work in progress	250,071	–
Materials and supplies	333,468	135,893
	$　1,165,537	$　391,458

25. The balance sheet, income statement, and Notes 1 (part) and 4 for Redaurum Limited (a diamond mining company) for 1993 and 1994 are shown in Exhibit 4-8.

Required:

a. Redraft the balance sheet and income statements for 1993 and 1994 to show how they would appear if Redaurum adopted the same revenue recognition policy for diamonds as Bema Gold Corporation uses for gold and silver (discussed previously), which stated "Revenue, net of refining and selling costs, is recorded at the estimated net realizable value when the gold and silver is available to be processed by the smelter or refinery. Adjustments to these amounts are made after final prices, weights and assays are established." Assume that the diamonds held for sale and ore stockpiles earn the same gross operating profits as the average revenues for the year.

b. Why is it not appropriate for Redaurum to use the same revenue recognition policy as Bema Gold?

CASE

QUEBEC SUPERCHEESE CORPORATION (QSC)

Quebec Supercheese Corporation (QSC) produces many varieties of cheese that are sold in every province in Canada, mainly through large grocery stores and specialty cheese shops. The cheese is produced at its factory in Montreal and shipped across Canada using commercial refrigerated trucks that pick up the cheese at the factory loading dock. All cheese is shipped FOB shipping point, meaning the purchasers pay for the trucking and assume responsibility for the cheese as soon as the trucks pick it up at the factory. In accordance with generally accepted accounting principles, QSC recognizes the sale as soon as the trucks load the cheese, as the purchasers have title and responsibility for the cheese at this point.

QSC is not happy with these arrangements because it has received many complaints from purchasers about spoilage. Even though the purchasers and their truckers have full responsibility for this spoilage, many disputes have occurred because the truckers insist the cheese is spoiled when they pick it up. QSC is considering setting up its own fleet of trucks to deliver its cheese across Canada. It estimates the additional freight costs to QSC can be regained through the higher prices it would charge for including shipping in the price (FOB destination).

QSC's president was not happy when she learned that sales would be recognized and recorded only upon delivery to the customer since she knew that an average of five days' sales are in transit at all times because of the distances involved. One day's sales total approximately $100,000 on average. The effect of this change would be an apparent drop in sales of $500,000 and a decrease of $50,000 in net income in the year of the change.

Required:

a. Advise the president about revenue recognition guidelines.

b. Do you see a solution to the problem of changing the shipping method but avoiding the resulting effect on the income statement?

◤◣ Critical Thinking Questions

26. The income statement and Note 1(e) from Big Rock Brewery Ltd. for the year ended March 31, 1995 are shown in Exhibit 4-9.

    Required:
    a. Explain what the "Government Commissions and Taxes" are.
    b. Argue why they should (and should not) be included in the revenues of Big Rock.

27. Alliance Communications Corporation is a fully integrated supplier of entertainment products whose origins are in the television and motion picture production industry. It produces, among other products, series for television that it sells to television networks. Some of these series involve the incurring of costs to develop an idea, and produce a pilot show, followed by attempts to market the show to television stations. If the series is sold, weekly shows are produced for later airing by participating stations.

    Discuss the revenue production process of this kind of television series, emphasizing the critical points in the revenue recognition process and pointing out the similarities and differences between the revenue process for Alliance and for a company manufacturing television sets.

EXHIBIT 4-9

BIG ROCK BREWERY LTD.
Statement of Income and Retained Earnings
Years Ended March 31, 1995 and 1994
(Denominated in Canadian dollars)

	1995	1994
SALES	$ 23,078,655	$ 16,140,745
GOVERNMENT COMMISSIONS AND TAXES	9,388,863	6,572,458
COST OF SALES	6,054,940	4,363,698
GROSS PROFIT	7,634,852	5,204,589
EXPENSES		
Amortization	405,451	414,946
Selling, general and administrative (Schedule)	3,942,690	2,756,846
Interest on long-term debt	43,249	12,891
Total expenses	4,391,390	3,184,683
INCOME BEFORE THE FOLLOWING	3,243,462	2,019,906
GAIN (LOSS) ON DISPOSAL OF CAPITAL ASSETS (Note 7)	(441,130)	79,815
INCOME BEFORE INCOME TAXES	2,802,332	2,099,721
INCOME TAXES (Note 8)	1,060,000	792,000
NET INCOME FOR YEAR	1,742,332	1,307,721
RETAINED EARNINGS BEGINNING OF YEAR	3,053,086	1,745,365
RETAINED EARNINGS END OF YEAR	$ 4,795,418	$ 3,053,086
EARNINGS PER SHARE (Note 9)		
Basic	40¢	30¢
Fully diluted	39¢	29¢

e. **Revenue recognition**

Revenue is recognized at the time of shipment at the gross sales price charged to the purchaser. Invoices for sales to Canadian customers are submitted to the respective provincial Liquor Control Boards who pay the company after deducting Liquor Control Board commissions. Excise taxes are assessed on production. Commissions and taxes are comprised as follows:

	1995	1994
Liquor Control Board commissions	$ 7,023,449	$ 5,135,099
Excise and sales taxes	2,365,414	1,437,359
	$ 9,388,863	$ 6,572,458

Product, which is returned due to expired shelf life and for which the customer is given credit, is netted against gross sales. Product returns totalled $81,226 in 1995 and $185,491 in 1994.

CHAPTER

Management of Cash and

Statement of Changes in Financial Position

In Chapter 4, the basic concepts underlying the recognition of income were discussed from the point of view of the shareholders of the corporation. Although this is an important perspective, there are other measures of performance that affect the overall health of the corporation that are not adequately captured by the income statement. Because the income statement is based on accrual accounting, the flows represented on the income statement do not necessarily correspond to the cash flows of the corporation. Because the corporation cannot operate without cash, it is important to understand its cash-generating performance during the period. This chapter discusses the second major measure of performance, the cash flows that are summarized in the statement called the statement of changes in financial position, or SCFP. The SCFP is quite simple in intent, but a bit more difficult to prepare and understand properly.

WHY ANOTHER FLOW STATEMENT?

The need for another flow statement is probably best conveyed by the use of an example, the Ajax Widget Corporation (a fictitious corporation). The assumptions for the example are listed in the boxes below.

Ajax Widget Corporation

> **PRODUCT LINE**
> The Ajax Widget Corporation makes widgets. A widget is a hypothetical product selected for this example.

> **COSTS/SUPPLIER CREDIT**
> The production process for widgets is such that they cost Ajax Widget $4 each to make. All the costs must be paid in cash at the time of production because Ajax's suppliers do not allow them any credit.

> **SALES/CUSTOMER CREDIT**
> Widgets currently sell for $5 each and Ajax allows its customers up to 30 days to pay for the widgets they buy. For the purpose of this example, it is assumed that all of Ajax's customers pay on the thirtieth day after a sale. Ajax is a relatively new corporation and has been experiencing fairly rapid growth in sales. Exhibit 5-1 shows this growth during the first three months of 19x1. Ajax Widget expects that sales will continue to increase by an additional 600 units per month for at least the next year.

> ## PRODUCTION/INVENTORY POLICY
> Ajax Widget's production process is such that it cannot produce units instantaneously. Therefore, it must maintain a certain level of inventories so that units are available when a customer arrives to buy one. Ajax's policy, at this point, is that it must maintain inventory at the end of the period equal to 50% of the current month's sales. This relationship can be seen in the data in Exhibit 5-1, which lists the sales in each month and the ending inventory.

EXHIBIT 5-1

AJAX WIDGET CORPORATION
Sales/Inventory/Production Data

(Data in units)

	January	February	March
Beginning inventory	250	500	800
Production	1,250	1,900	2,500
Goods available	1,500	2,400	3,300
Sales	1,000	1,600	2,200
Ending inventory	500	800	1,100

Performance Evaluation Using the Income and Cash Flow Statements

As we have discussed earlier in the text, the performance of Ajax can be measured by constructing an income statement. Assuming that the revenues are recognized at the time of sale and that no other expenses are incurred other than production costs, Exhibit 5-2 shows the income statement for each of the first three months of 19X1.

EXHIBIT 5-2

AJAX WIDGET CORPORATION
Income Statement

	January	February	March
Revenues	$ 5,000	$ 8,000	$ 11,000
Cost of goods sold	(4,000)	(6,400)	(8,800)
Net income	$ 1,000	$ 1,600	$ 2,200

As can be seen from Exhibit 5-2, net income is growing at a predictable rate — the shareholders and managers should certainly be happy with this growth. Assuming that sales continue to increase at a rate of 600 units per month, this growth in income should continue. In the long run, the investment in Ajax should be profitable.

Exhibit 5-3 provides some information about the balance sheet of Ajax. The trends in cash, accounts receivable, and inventory shown in Exhibit 5-3 reflect rapid business growth. Accounts receivable reflects an increased level of sales, as does inventory, because ending inventory is a function of sales. The disturbing trend in Exhibit 5-3 is, of course, the decline in the amount of cash on hand for Ajax. To understand the decline in cash, the cash-to-cash cycle of Ajax must be considered. Exhibit 5-4 shows the cycle for Ajax.

EXHIBIT 5-3

AJAX WIDGET CORPORATION
Partial Balance Sheet

	Dec. 31	Jan. 31	Feb. 28	Mar. 31
Cash	$8,000	$5,500	$2,900	$900
Accounts receivable	2,500	5,000	8,000	11,000
Inventory	1,000	2,000	3,200	4,400

EXHIBIT 5-4

AJAX WIDGET CORPORATION
Cash-to-cash Cycle

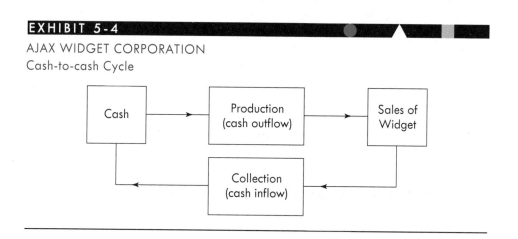

The cash-to-cash cycle illustrates the **lead/lag relationship** between the cash paid out for production costs and the cash coming in from collections of accounts receivable. The lag between production and sale varies depending on which units are involved. Some units are produced and sold in the same month. Other units are produced in one month, remain in ending inventory, and are sold in the following month. This creates a one-month lag between the outflow of production costs and the sale of those widgets that are carried over in ending inventory. Therefore, considering both units produced and units sold in the same period, as well as those that end up in ending inventory, the average lag between production and sale is somewhat less than a month. Once a widget is sold, the lag between sale and collection is one month, because the collection policy is to allow customers 30 days to pay. Consequently, the total lag between cash outflow to cash inflow is somewhere between one and two months.

Because the income statement measures performance at a particular point in the cash-to-cash cycle, it ignores all the timing differences between revenues and expenses recognized and the related cash flows. Therefore, the income statement is not very useful in tracking the cash flows of the corporation. The income statement will continue to be positive as long as sales are increasing for Ajax. The growth in sales, however, forces Ajax to produce more and more units each month. It is possible that the production costs paid in cash in a given month could exceed the cash collections from the previous month's sales. It is evident from the decline in the cash balance in Exhibit 5-4 that this has happened during the first three months of 19x1. Thus, even though net income is increasing each month, the cash position of the corporation is declining. Because Ajax cannot operate without a sufficient amount of cash, it would make sense to prepare a separate statement in addition to the income statement to measure the performance of the corporation on a cash basis. Hence the need for a cash flow statement.

The cash flow statement cannot replace the income statement; they each provide useful information. The income statement summarizes the profitability of the corporation's operations, while the SCFP summarizes the cash flows. To analyze the operations of any corporation properly, you must consider both profits and cash flows. In the long run, the total profits and net cash flows will be very similar, but they may be quite different for any single year or even over a period of several years.

To understand the usefulness of the information provided by the SCFP, think of the management of cash as one of the basic duties of the corporation's management. Management must ensure that sufficient cash is maintained on hand both to generate profits now and to invest in assets that will produce profits in the future. Simply producing profits now is not sufficient to ensure the corporation's long-term survival. Without sufficient cash to make investments in revenue-producing assets, the long-term viability of the corporation may be in doubt.

EXHIBIT 5-5

AJAX WIDGET CORPORATION
Cash Flow Statement

	January	February	March
Receipts (collections)	$ 2,500	$ 5,000	$ 8,000
Disbursements (production costs)	(5,000)	(7,600)	(10,000)
Net cash flow	($2,500)	($2,600)	($2,000)

Exhibit 5-5 shows the cash flow statement for each of the three months in 19x1 for Ajax. As can be seen from Exhibit 5-5, the cash flow of the Ajax Widget Corporation has been negative for the first three months of 19x1. The receipts in the cash flow statement are the collections from the previous month's sales, and the disbursements are the production costs for the month. The production costs can be calculated by taking the units produced in Exhibit 5-1 and multiplying them by the unit cost of $4.

The cash flow statement paints a very different picture of the performance of Ajax during the first quarter of 19X1 compared to the income statement. Cash flow is obviously a problem for Ajax. Because Ajax has only $900 left in its cash account, the question Ajax faces is whether cash will run out in April and, if so, what will it do to continue doing business? In order to decide whether the problem will persist, Ajax should prepare a forecast for the next several months.

Assuming continued growth in sales of 600 units a month and no change in the collection, inventory, and payment policies of the Ajax Widget Corporation, Exhibit 5-6 illustrates the forecast for the next several months.

EXHIBIT 5-6

AJAX WIDGET CORPORATION
Net Income, Cash Flow, and Cash Balance Forecast

	April	May	June
Revenues	$14,000	$17,000	$20,000
Cost of goods sold	(11,200)	(13,600)	(16,000)
Net income	$ 2,800	$ 3,400	$ 4,000
Receipts (collections)	$11,000	$14,000	$17,000
Disbursements (production costs)	(12,400)	(14,800)	(17,200)
Net cash flow	($1,400)	($800)	($200)
End of month cash balance	($500)	($1,300)	($1,500)

As can be seen from Exhibit 5-6, income continues to grow by $600 each month, reflecting the growth in sales of 600 units times the net profit margin of $1 per unit. The cash flow statement indicates that net cash flow will be negative for the next three months, but the trend is that net cash flow is improving and it looks as though it will be positive by July. The ending cash balance is projected to be negative for the next three months and will take longer to return to a positive cash balance. This is a problem because Ajax cannot operate with a negative cash balance. Operating with a negative cash balance if feasible only if the bank permits a corporation to overdraw its bank accounts; that is, if it allows more cash to be withdrawn than was deposited. A negative cash balance is really a loan from the bank.

The problem is perhaps best portrayed by Exhibit 5-7, which graphs the situation with regard to net income, cash flow, and cash balance for the entire year 19X1. Note the cash balance line, which drops below zero in April and returns to a positive balance in September. In reality, the corporation cannot have a negative cash balance without making special arrangements with its bank, and something must be done to prevent the problem from continuing for too long. Nevertheless, the graph clearly shows the magnitude and duration of Ajax's cash flow problem.

Having now forecast that a problem exists, Ajax must find a way to solve it. There are many ways in which Ajax can address this problem. Before you read on, you might want to take a few moments to think about how you would solve Ajax's cash flow problem.

EXHIBIT 5-7

AJAX WIDGET COMPANY

Income, Cash Flow, and Cash Balance Forecast

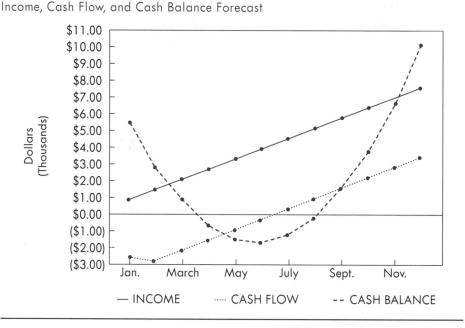

— INCOME   ····· CASH FLOW   -- CASH BALANCE

Solutions to the Cash Flow Problem

The cash flow difficulties that Ajax is experiencing are typical of many new corporations. These problems have three fundamental causes: high growth rates in sales, significant lead/lag relationships in cash inflows and outflows, and under-capitalization. **Capitalization** refers to how much cash the corporation has to start with. Start-up corporations generally experience a rapid rate of growth in sales. This increase in sales requires them to produce more and more units as well as to expand their productive capacity. Increasing production and expanding capacity both require cash.

Compounding the growth problem is the presence of significant lead/lag relationships between the corporation's cash inflows and outflows. If there were no lead/lag relationship, then, as long as the product could be sold for more than it cost to produce, there would be no cash flow problem. Most corporations, however, do have some significant lead/lag relationships in their cash flows, which are magnified in periods of high growth.

Finally, start-up corporations tend to be undercapitalized, that is, they do not have a large pool of cash to start with. When the large cash needs appear, imposed by rapid growth and the lead/lag relationships, the corporation has no cash reserves to get it through prolonged periods of cash outflows. Start-up corporations (as well as other corporations in rapid growth phases) will experience cash flow problems at some point. In Ajax's case, the problems create a crisis during the month of April. Solutions to the three causes of the cash flow problems of Ajax are discussed in the following subsections.

■ ■ Solution 1: Slow The Business Growth

One way to solve Ajax's problem is to slow down the rate of growth of sales. Exhibit 5-8 shows graphically what happens when the rate of growth in sales is 500 units per month rather than 600. All other facts and assumptions are assumed to be unchanged. You can see from the graph that this solves the cash flow problem of Ajax because the cash balance line does not dip below zero in any month. Cash flows are still negative in some early months, but the balance in cash is sufficient to absorb these cash outflows. Limiting growth may not be the proper response in this case because it may be detrimental to the corporation in the long run. Limiting growth is likely to divert customers to competitors, and those customers may develop loyalties to those competitors and reduce the corporation's long-run potential in terms of client base.

EXHIBIT 5-8

AJAX WIDGET CORPORATION
Forecasts: Projections with Growth Set at 500 Units per Month

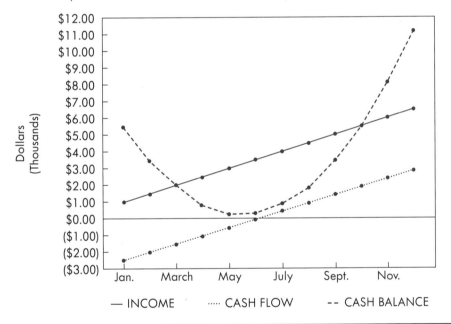

■ ■ Solution 2: Increase Capitalization

A second way to solve the cash problem is to address the undercapitalization problem; that is, to start with a larger amount of cash. This larger amount of cash may be obtained in numerous ways. Two typical ways are either to issue additional shares in the corporation, or to borrow the cash (debt). If Ajax issues new shares, the cash flow projections will have to be adjusted to incorporate the additional cash inflow from the issuance and any subsequent outflows for dividends. If money is borrowed, the cash flow projections will have to be adjusted for the initial inflow from the borrowing as well as for the subsequent payments of principal and interest that will occur in the future. Exhibit 5-9 shows what will happen if an additional $2,000 is obtained at the beginning of January from the issuance of shares. For simplicity, it is assumed that there are no dividends. Note, again, that this solves the cash flow problem.

This solution of increased capitalization is not without its own problems. The first is that Ajax may not be able to convince a lender that it is worthy of a loan. Lenders are typically very skeptical of new ventures. Second, if shares are issued, the current shareholders of Ajax will be giving up control of some portion of their investment in the corporation, and they may not want to do that. It may also be difficult to find additional investors willing to take the risk of buying shares in the corporation.

EXHIBIT 5-9

AJAX WIDGET CORPORATION
Forecasts: Projections with $2,000 More Initial Cash

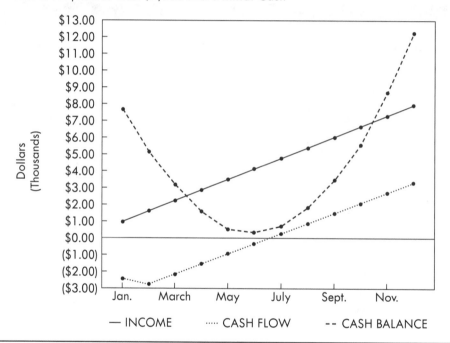

— INCOME   ····· CASH FLOW   -- CASH BALANCE

◼◼ Solution 3: Adjust Lead/Lag Relationships

The third way to solve the cash flow problem of Ajax is to change the lead/lag relationships between the cash inflows and outflows. There are numerous ways to do this. One way to accomplish a change in this relationship is to change the accounts receivable, accounts payable, or inventory policies of Ajax. Collecting on accounts receivable sooner, paying accounts payable later, or reducing the amount of inventory on hand would all have the effect of reducing the difference between the cash outflow and inflow in a given month. Exhibit 5-10, for example, shows what will happen if the accounts receivable policy is changed to require customers to pay within three weeks rather than one month.

EXHIBIT 5-10

AJAX WIDGET CORPORATION
Forecasts: Projections with a Change in Accounts Receivable Policy

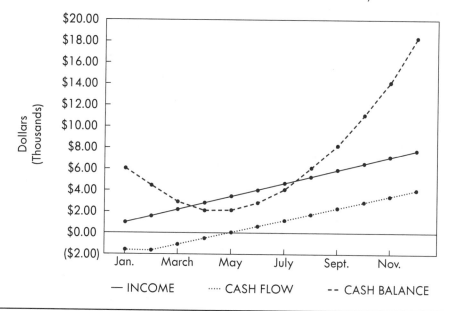

— INCOME   ····· CASH FLOW   −− CASH BALANCE

This change would be sufficient to solve the cash flow problem, assuming everything else remains the same. Of course, everything else may not stay the same. If Ajax institutes this change, it is likely that some customers will no longer do business with Ajax if they can get better payment terms from a competitor. Thus the rate of growth in sales may be affected. Ajax, therefore, may need to make changes in some other assumptions before it can realistically conclude that this will solve its problem. In this case, however, you know from Exhibit 5-8 that slowing the rate of growth will actually help solve the cash flow problem.

Besides changing the receivables, payables, and inventory policies of Ajax, there are other ways to affect the lead/lag relationship. Changing either the price or cost of a widget would affect the amounts in the lead/lag relationship and could therefore solve the problem. Remember, however, that changes in these items may also affect other assumptions, such as sales growth.

To summarize, it is clear that a cash flow statement provides additional information that is not captured by the income statement and balance sheet alone. For a shareholder, manager, or other user of the financial statements, it is important to understand the relationship between the income of the corporation, its cash-to-cash cycle, and its cash flow statement. Also, understanding how receivables, payables, and inventory policies affect the cash flows of the corporation is extremely important in evaluating the performance of the corporation. We discuss how users interpret cash flow information in greater detail later in the chapter.

We now turn to the components of cash flow, then we explain the preparation of a cash flow statement. Finally, we explain how the cash flow statement can be used to assess the financial health of the corporation.

◖◗ DEFINITION OF CASH AND CASH EQUIVALENTS

As we have seen above, proper management of cash is one of the critical tasks that management of all businesses must achieve. Having too little cash on hand results in not being able to pay liabilities and expenses. If this continues, bankruptcy will result. Having too much cash on hand is also a problem in that it is not efficient. Cash held in chequing accounts typically earns little or no interest. It is much better to invest excess cash in some kind of temporary investment that will earn interest. Thus the proper management of cash involves the management of cash, short term borrowings, and temporary investments.

Therefore, in considering cash flows that are to be summarized in the SCFP, rather than restricting our consideration to just cash, we must consider the broader concept of **cash** and **cash equivalents**, sometimes called the **cash position**. We use the term cash equivalents or cash position to include the short-term, highly liquid investments that are readily convertible into known amounts of cash. They also must be close enough to maturity that there is little risk of changes in their value due to changes in interest rates. Items that commonly meet these criteria are Government of Canada Treasury Bills, and demand loans of other corporations. Cash equivalents also include short-term borrowings that corporations use to cover their cash short-ages for short periods of time, such as lines of credit.

◖◗ COMPONENTS OF CASH FLOW

Once again, we refer to the three basic steps the management of any business involves. First, you must find sufficient long-term *financing* from investments by shareholders or long-term borrowings to provide for sufficient capitalization of the business. Next you must *invest* these funds in assets that you will *operate* to produce revenues and profits. Finally, you must operate the business on a profitable basis.

The basic format of the SCFP summarizes all cash flows into these three groups of activities. Exhibit 5-11 shows the SCFP for SoftQuad International Inc. for the years ended December 31, 1994 and 1993. SoftQuad, based in Toronto, Ontario, develops specialized software. Note that the SCFP is divided into these three groups of activi-ties: Operating Activities (which SoftQuad divides into two parts) with a net cash outflow of $1,691,145 for 1994, Investing Activities with a net cash outflow of $5,338,407 for 1994, and Financing Activities with a net cash inflow of $8,572,491 for 1994. The Net Cash Inflow for 1994 is $1,542,939. The final section of the SCFP shows how this net cash inflow, when added to the cash position at the beginning of the year of $130,468, results in a cash position (called Cash and Short-term Deposits by SoftQuad) of $1,673,407 at the end of the year. Thus the SCFP summarizes all the cash flows for 1994 that resulted in the increase in cash position during the year.

▸◣ Financing Activities

Financing activities are described as the activities involved in obtaining resources from shareholders and other investors (generally lenders) and repaying shareholders and investors. Transactions classified as financing typically involve balance sheet

EXHIBIT 5-11

SOFTQUAD INTERNATIONAL INC.
Consolidated Statements of Changes in Financial Position
Years Ended December 31, 1994 and 1993

	1994	1993
NET INFLOW (OUTFLOW) OF CASH RELATED TO THE FOLLOWING ACTIVITIES:		
Operating		
Net loss	$ (3,301,410)	$ (1,823,613)
Items not affecting cash		
Amortization of fixed assets	117,649	72,754
Amortization of deferred development costs	336,875	—
Amortization of goodwill	846,321	647,997
Amortization of acquired software products	1,233,333	—
	(767,232)	(1,102,862)
Changes in non-cash operating working capital items		
Accounts receivable	(892,650)	(216,069)
Investment tax credits receivable	186,705	273,783
Inventory	(46,896)	—
Prepaid expenses	42,278	19,643
Accounts payable and accrued charges	(240,598)	(113,835)
Due to related parties	(64,701)	(16,534)
Deferred revenue	91,949	(17,260)
	(1,691,145)	(1,173,134)
Investing		
Purchase of fixed assets	(326,797)	(134,694)
Acquisition of net assets of subsidiary including bank indebtedness of $86,810 (Note 3)	(3,286,810)	—
Expenditures on development costs	(1,724,800)	—
	(5,338,407)	(134,694)
Financing		
Issuance of common shares (Note 9)	5,871,091	1,172,445
Issuance of common shares on acquisition of subsidiary (Note 9)	3,200,000	—
Repayment of debenture	(525,000)	(75,000)
Proceeds on long-term debt	26,400	—
	8,572,491	1,097,445
Net Cash Inflow (outflow)	1,542,939	(210,383)
Cash and Short-term Deposits, Beginning of Year	130,468	340,851
Cash and Short-term Deposits, End of Year	$ 1,673,407	$ 130,468

accounts classified as long-term liabilities and shareholders' equity. Typical cash inflows would be those from issuing common shares, bonds, mortgages, and other borrowings. Outflows include dividends paid to shareholders, repurchase of shares, and repayment of the principal of any long-term debt obligation.

A special word is needed about interest and dividends. Interest expense and dividends are made to pay lenders and investors for the use of their money by the corporation. Interest expense always appears in the operating section, but dividends usually appear in the financing section (sometimes dividends are shown separately and not as part of the operating, financing, or investing sections). To see the complete picture of all financing activities, you would have to reclassify interest expense and move it from the operating section to the financing section.

In the SCFP of SoftQuad shown in Exhibit 5-11, the items included in the financing activities section are fairly typical:

> Issuance (sale) of common shares: inflows of $5,871,091 and $3,200,000
>
> Repayment of debenture (long-term debt): outflow of $525,000
>
> Proceeds on (issue of) long-term debt: inflow of $26,400.

Not included in the SoftQuad SCFP are dividends paid to shareholders (an outflow of cash). Dividends do not appear in SoftQuad's SCFP simply because they did not pay any in either 1994 or 1993.

Note that SoftQuad has a large net inflow of cash from financing activities. This is typical of a new corporation or a corporation that is growing. A mature corporation will stop growing so rapidly and will begin repaying its long-term liabilities.

Investing Activities

Transactions classified as **investing activities** typically involve balance sheet accounts classified as long-term assets. Typical transactions in this section would be investment in property, plant and equipment and its subsequent sale or disposal, as well as investments in long-term marketable securities. In the SoftQuad SCFP, examples of these types of items are:

> Purchase of fixed assets (property, plant and equipment): outflow of $326,797
>
> Acquisition of net assets of subsidiary (investment in long-term assets): outflow of $3,286,810
>
> Expenditures on development costs (investment in long-term assets): outflows of $1,724,800.

Not included in this SCFP are dispositions (sales) of long-term assets (cash inflows), simply because SoftQuad did not dispose of any long-term assets in 1994 or 1993.

Note that SoftQuad had a large net outflow of cash for investing activities. This is also typical of a new or growing corporation. A mature corporation will invest relatively less in long-term assets.

Operating Activities

Operating activities include all other transactions not covered by financing or investing activities. The operating section typically includes the cash flows that result directly from the sales of goods and services to customers. Transactions classified as operating activities typically involve balance sheet accounts classified as current assets and current liabilities. The major cash inflow is from the collection of revenues from customers. The major cash outflow is the payment to suppliers (for materials, labour, etc.). Interest payments are also included in this section of the cash flow statement.

One other cash flow worth noting in the operating section is related to taxes. Even though taxes are affected by all three types of activities, the net results of the taxes on the corporation are reported in the operating section of the SCFP.

A complete record of the gross amount of cash coming into the corporation from operating activities would show the total amount of cash received from revenues and collections from customers as inflows, and the total amount of cash paid out to suppliers for expenses and accounts payable as outflows. This approach, called the **direct approach**, is theoretically very informative but is rarely used in the SCFP. The method normally used in published SCFPs' is the **indirect approach**. Note that these two approaches differ only in the format and content of the Operating Activities section. The Investing and Financing Activities sections are the same for both approaches.

The indirect approach does not report the full gross cash flows from operating activities; instead, it shows only the net cash flows. Using the indirect approach, the operating section starts with reported net income and then shows adjustments to net income to arrive at the net cash flows from operations.

The adjustments are in two groups. The first group includes items from the income statement that do not involve cash flows. In the SoftQuad SCFP, note that the net loss is adjusted by the items listed under the heading "Items not affecting cash." The main item in this group is amortization. If you think about amortization, it does not involve a cash payment the way other expenses such as wages do. Amortization expense merely involves recognizing the use of a long-term asset. The cash outflow related to that asset occurred when the asset was purchased, which probably happened several years ago and was initially reported in the investing section of the SCFP. Thus the net income figure has been reduced by the amount of the amortization expense that does not represent a current cash outflow. The amortization expenses are thus added back to net income to determine the actual net cash flows from operating activities for the year.

The second group of adjustments are needed because all revenues and expenses do not result in immediate cash flows. If accounts receivable increases, this means that not all of the revenues have been collected in cash; some will be collected later. Thus SoftQuad's SCFP shows an adjustment for Accounts Receivable with a negative $892,650, indicating that this amount of SoftQuad's revenues were not collected this year, but will be in the next fiscal year.

Other adjustments included in this second group follow similar reasoning. If current assets increase, this reflects a decrease in the amount of cash inflow, or a net cash outflow from operating activities. If current liabilities such as accounts payable decrease, this means that cash was used to pay down the liabilities, which is a cash outflow adjustment. If current liabilities increase, this indicates that cash was saved by not paying the liabilities this year. This cash saving is the same as an increase in cash from operations.

◖◗ PREPARATION OF THE CASH FLOW STATEMENT

To illustrate the preparation of a cash flow statement, another example will be used. Exhibit 5-12 shows the balance sheet for Beaver Industries Inc. (a fictitious corporation) for the year ended December 31, 19x1. Exhibit 5-13 shows the income statement for Beaver Industries for the same period.

In addition to the balance sheet and income statement, the following additional information applies to the transactions of Beaver Industries Inc., for 19x1:

1. Beaver Industries is a retailer and, as such, all amounts added to its inventory reflect purchases at wholesale prices. All inventory is purchased on credit from suppliers.

2. Beaver Industries sells its products to customers on credit. There are no cash sales.

3. During the year, Beaver Industries sold (for $500 in cash) property, plant, and equipment that had an original cost of $1,000 and a book value of $200, thus recording a gain on sale of $300.

4. No new long-term debt was issued by Beaver Industries in 19x1.

5. Notes payable were used during 19x1 for short-term financing.

◤◣ T-Account approach

Our objective is to construct a statement of changes in financial position from the information given above, which is typical of most corporations, although simplified for illustrative purposes. We want to determine all of the cash flows that would have occurred to produce the balances shown above. There are several methods that can be used to determine the underlying cash flows, but all of them require, at a minimum, a balance sheet showing balances at the beginning and end of the year, plus an income statement for the current year. In addition, some additional information may be required.

Two of the common methods used to determine the underlying cash flows are by using a set of T-accounts, or using a worksheet. The T-account approach will be used here, but recognize that a worksheet could also be used to accomplish the same task. We will also show the preparation of an SCFP using only the indirect approach, as virtually all published SCFPs use this format. For completeness, we include the T-account preparation of the SCFP using the direct approach in the Appendix to this chapter. (Appendix C)

Exhibit 5-14 shows the set-up of the T-account approach. Note that a large T-account has been included for cash because the objective of this exercise is to reconstruct all the transactions that affected cash in this account. All the accounts from the balance sheet are listed, with their beginning and ending balances included. The objective is to reconstruct the transactions that occurred during 19x1 and to include as much detail as possible regarding the nature of the cash transactions. Within the cash account, the transactions are categorized into the three basic activities discussed above: operating, financing, and investing activities.

EXHIBIT 5-12

BEAVER INDUSTRIES INC.
Balance Sheet

	Dec. 31, 19x0	Dec. 31, 19x1
Cash	$ 20,000	$ 12,500
Accounts receivable	20,000	10,000
Inventory	30,000	40,000
Total current assets	$ 70,000	$ 62,500
Property, plant, and equipment	$100,000	159,000
Accumulated amortization	(50,000)	(69,200)
Net fixed assets	$ 50,000	$ 89,800
Total assets	$120,000	$152,300
Accounts payable	$ 5,000	$ 20,000
Dividends payable	0	1,000
Total current liabilities	$ 5,000	$ 21,000
Notes payable	0	20,000
Bonds payable	$ 50,000	$ 40,000
Common shares	25,000	30,000
Retained earnings	40,000	41,300
Total shareholders' equity	65,000	$ 71,300
Total liabilities and shareholders' equity	$120,000	$152,300

EXHIBIT 5-13

BEAVER INDUSTRIES INC.
Income Statement

For the year ended December 31, 19x1

Sales revenue	$130,000
Cost of goods sold	90,000
Gross profit margin	$ 40,000
Cash operating expenses	15,000
Amortization	20,000
Total expenses	$ 35,000
Income from operations	5,000
Gain on sale of property, plant, and equipment	300
Net income	$ 5,300

With the indirect approach, the operating activities section is constructed by starting with net income and then reconciling it to its net cash flow equivalent. In this approach, net income is initially assumed to increase cash by the amount of the net income (or decrease cash by the amount of a net loss). This is not strictly true because many of the items in income do not represent cash flows. For example, as

EXHIBIT 5-14

BEAVER INDUSTRIES INC.
Cash Flow T-Account Worksheet: Indirect Approach

A – Cash

	✓	20,000			
Operating:				(3)	Inventory increase
Net income	(1)	5,300	10,000	(6)	Gain: Sale of PP&E
A/R decrease	(2)	10,000	300		
A/P increase	(4)	15,000			
Amortization	(5)	20,000			
Investing:				(7)	Purchase of PP&E
Sale of PP&E	(6)	500	60,000		
Financing:				(11)	Bonds payable
Notes payable	(10)	20,000	10,000	(9)	Dividends
Common shares	(12)	5,000	3,000		
	✓	12,500			

A – A/R

✓	20,000		
		10,000	(2)
✓	10,000		

A – Inventory

✓	30,000		
(3)	10,000		
✓	40,000		

A – PP&E

✓	100,000		
(7)	60,000	1,000	(6)
✓	159,000		

XA – Accumulated Amortization

		50,000	✓	
(6)	800	20,000	(5)	
		69,200	✓	

L – A/P

	5,000	✓	
	15,000	(4)	
	20,000	✓	

L – Dividends Payable

		0	✓	
(9)	3,000	4,000	(8)	
		1,000	✓	

L – Notes Payable

		0	✓
0		20,000	(10)
		20,000	✓

SE – Common Shares

		25,000	✓
0		5,000	(12)
		30,000	✓

SE – RE

		40,000	✓	
(8)	4,000	5,300	(1)	
		41,300	✓	

L – Bonds Payable

		50,000	✓
(11)	10,000	0	
		40,000	✓

we discussed on page 263, amortization has no effect on cash. The remaining entries in the operating section are used to adjust all the items that compose the net income to the amount of the cash flows that actually occurred.

In using the T-account method, it is very convenient to reconstruct the summary journal entries that would have been recorded for each of the accounts to determine the resulting net cash flows. These reconstructed journal entries are not essential, but they are a convenient method of determining what happened. For example, the entry to record net income is as follows:

(1)		
A – Cash (Operating)	5,300	
SE – Retained Earnings		5,300

One of the adjustments that must be made when all net income is assumed to increase cash results from the assumption that all the revenues included in net income are collected in cash. The change in the balance of accounts receivable shows the net effect of the difference between the sales revenue recorded during the period, and the cash collected from customers.

In Beaver Industries' case, the accounts receivable balance decreased during the year, which means that more collections (credit entries to the accounts receivable account) were made than sales (debit entries to the accounts receivable account). This means that Beaver collected more cash than its sales figure shows. The adjustment to the cash account, therefore, shows an *increase* in cash over that represented by the revenues included in net income. In effect, this adjustment adds $10,000 to the revenues shown of $130,000 and is included in net income to produce a net of $140,000 in cash received from customers as follows:

Sales revenues	$130,000
Decrease in accounts receivable	$ 10,000
Cash collections from sales	$140,000

The net or summary entry to record this adjustment is as follows:

(2)		
A – Cash (Operating)	10,000	
A – Accounts Receivable		10,000

A second assumption that requires an adjustment is that the cost of goods sold reduced cash during the period by the same amount. There are two reasons why this may be incorrect. The first reason is that the goods sold, represented by the amounts shown in costs of goods sold, may have come from the beginning inventory (i.e., were made last year) and did not require an outflow of cash *this* year (assuming all production costs are paid in cash). The change in the balance of inventory provides information about this potential adjustment.

A second reason would be the assumption that purchases of inventory during the period resulted in accounts payable, assuming all purchases are bought on credit. Therefore, if these accounts were not paid as of year-end, the expenses reported would not yet have resulted in cash outflows. The effects of both these reasons can be corrected by adjusting the net income number by the net change in the inventory balance and the net change in the accounts payable balance. The effect of these two entries is to adjust the cost of goods sold number included in the net income ($90,000) to its cash equivalent of cash paid to suppliers ($85,000) as follows:

Cost of goods sold as reported (assumed cash outflow)	($90,000)
Increase in inventory (requiring extra cash outflow)	(10,000)
Increase in accounts payable (meaning less cash paid out)	15,000
Actual cash paid to suppliers	$(85,000)

The entries to record these adjustments are as follows:

(3) and (4)		
A – Cash (Operating)	15,000	
L – Accounts Payable		15,000
A – Inventory	10,000	
A – Cash (Operating)		10,000

A third type of adjustment results from the assumption that all other expenses represent cash outflows. Amortization expense is not a cash expense. Amortization is merely a recognition that part of the long term assets are used up each year, but no cash flows are associated with amortization expense. The associated cash flow occurred years before when the assets were purchased. Therefore, because amortization expense is included in calculating net income and results in a decrease in net income, its effect must be removed by adding it back to net income to show the net income figure that would have resulted if we had not included amortization expense.

One caveat at this point: because this adjustment is on the debit side of the cash account, it looks as though amortization is a source of cash. This is not true. Cash collections from customers are the source of cash from operations. It is only because the indirect method is attempting to correct the misstatements made by assuming that all net income increases cash that this item appears as if it were a source of cash. Many analysts approximate the cash from operations of a corporation by adding amortization to the net income of the corporation. This is a quick and reasonably close approximation to cash received from operations. However, this method ignores the adjustments due to the other accounts that are shown in Exhibit 5-14.

The entry to adjust for amortization is as follows:

(5)		
A – Cash (Operating)	20, 000	
XA – Accumulated Amortization		20,000

The last adjustment in the operating section adjusts the net income number for the gain from the sale of the property, plant, and equipment. The $300 gain shown in income assumes that $300 was received in cash. However, point #3 from the additional information provided at the outset of the example indicated that $500 cash was received in the disposal of the property, plant, and equipment. Thus the effect on cash is $500, not $300. Therefore, making the assumption that the $300 increase in the net income figure represents the cash inflow is not correct.

The second problem is that, even if this were the right amount, it would be reported in the wrong section of the cash flow statement. Corporations invest in property, plant, and equipment, so cash flows resulting from disposals of property, plant, and equipment are also investing (or, more properly, disinvesting) activities. These are not operating cash flows. The entry to correct for these two misstatements makes two adjustments. It adjusts the amount of cash that actually was received, and it corrects the activity that was affected. The entry is as follows:

(6)		
A – Cash (Investing)	500	
XA – Accumulated Amortization	800	
A – Property, Plant and Equipment		1,000
A – Cash (Operating)		300

The remaining items adjust for the cash flows that resulted from the financing and investing activities. To determine the cash flows for financing and investing activities, look for changes in long-term assets, long-term liabilities, and shareholders' equity accounts.

The amount of the purchases of new property, plant, and equipment can be determined by considering the beginning and ending balances in the property, plant, and equipment summary account and the credit entry made to this account in entry (6). Note that this cash outflow is shown in the investing section. The entry is:

(7)		
A – Property, Plant, and Equipment	60,000	
A – Cash (Investing)		60,000

Because all the income statement transactions have now been explained, attention can be turned to the retained earnings account to determine if the entire change in this account has been explained. The account needs an additional debit of $4,000 to explain the change in the balance. This debit represents the dividends declared during the period. The entry is:

(8)		
SE – Retained Earnings	4,000	
L – Dividends Payable		4,000

When dividends are declared, they become legally payable, but there may be a lag between the time they are declared and the time they are paid. Therefore, the credit side of entry (8) is to a dividend payable account. The cash entry for dividends takes into consideration the change in the balance of the dividends payable account. The balance in the dividends payable account probably reflects the last quarter's dividend, which has yet to be paid. The entry is:

```
(9)
L – Dividends Payable                              3,000
     A – Cash (Financing)                                    3,000
```

The accounts that still have changes that remain to be explained at this point are the notes payable, bonds payable, and common shares accounts. Using the extra information provided, an analysis is now made of each of these accounts.

The entry for notes payable is a net entry. It is net because not enough information is given to determine how many new notes were issued for cash or how many were retired (paid off by paying cash). All that is known is the net change in the notes payable account. The net change indicates that more notes were issued during this period than were retired because the balance in the account increased. This net effect is then shown as increasing the notes payable account. The net cash inflow appears in the financing section. The entry is:

```
(10)
A – Cash (Financing)                              20,000
     L – Notes Payable                                     20,000
```

Entry (11) is similar to that in (10) except that, in this case, the additional information indicated that there were no new long-term borrowings this year. Therefore, there were no new credits to this account. Because the balance in the account decreased, it can be inferred that $10,000 worth of bonds were paid off during the year. The entry is:

```
(11)
L – Bonds Payable                                 10,000
     A – Cash (Financing)                                  10,000
```

In the shares account, credits represent new issuance of shares, and debits represent repurchases of shares. Again, because there is no explicit information that there were new issuances or repurchases, you can only infer the net effect. The net effect is that the account increased, indicating that more shares were issued than were repurchased. The entry is:

(12)		
A – Cash Financing	5,000	
SE – Common Shares		5,000

Entry (12) completes the cash flow analysis. All the net changes in the accounts have been explained. The cash account now contains all the information necessary to produce a cash flow statement. The net cash flows from the three types of activities, as taken from the Cash T-account are as follows:

BEAVER INDUSTRIES INC.
Statement of Changes in Financial Position
For the Year Ended December 31, 19X1

Operating activities	
Net income	$ 5,300
Add back items not representing cash flows:	
Amortization	20,000
Gain on disposal	(300)
Adjustments for working capital items:	
Decrease in Accounts Receivable	10,000
Increase in Accounts Payable	15,000
Increase in Inventory	(10,000)
Cash from operating activities	$ 40,000
Investing activities	
Purchase of Property, Plant, and Equipment	$(60,000)
Sale of Property, Plant, and Equipment	500
Cash used for investing activities	$(59,500)
Financing activities	
Issue of Notes Payable	$ 20,000
Issue of Common Shares	5,000
Payment of Bonds Payable	(10,000)
Payment of Dividends	(3,000)
Cash from financing activities	$ 12,000
Decrease in Cash	$ (7,500)

This information from the Cash T-accounts was used to prepare a proper statement of changes in financial position. The totals of the cash flows from the three types of activities, $7,500 net cash outflow (40,000 − 59,500 + 12,000 = −7,500) must be the same as the net change in cash for the year, a $7,500 reduction (20,000 − 12,500 = −7,500), which it is.

Remember that debits in the cash account represent sources or inflows of cash, and credits represent uses or outflows of cash. The formal cash flow statement shows the operating, investing, and financing activities separately.

AN INTERNATIONAL PERSPECTIVE
REPORTS FROM OTHER COUNTRIES

As mentioned in Chapter 1, the SCFP or cash flow statement is not required in all countries. If a cash flow statement is not produced, the techniques in this chapter can be used to construct one from the balance sheet and income statement as well as other information that is provided in the financial statements. This may require making some assumptions and may result in some inaccuracies, but it will produce a statement that provides a good approximation of the net cash flows of the entity.

Exhibit 5-15 illustrates the conversion from a funds flow statement to a cash flow statement using the data from the Statement of Changes in Financial Position for Royal Packaging Industries Van Leer B. V. and Subsidiaries, a Dutch corporation. Note that even though this statement is called a statement of changes in financial position, it is not a cash flows statement. It is really a statement of changes in working capital items. Note also that the last three columns in the exhibit reclassify the relevant line items into the classifications normally shown in the

EXHIBIT 5-15

ROYAL PACKAGING INDUSTRIES VAN LEER B.V. AND SUSIDIARIES
Statement of Changes in Financial Position
(All amounts in thousands of Dutch Guilders)

	As stated	Reclassified as Operating	Reclassified as Investing	Reclassified as Financing
Source of funds:				
Net Income	73,300	73,300		
Dividend	(28,000)			(28,000)
Depreciation	101,690	101,690		
Movement in Provisions	18,277	18,277		
Funds from other sources				
Capital Contribution from Shareholder	39,000			39,000
Increased bank loans and overdrafts	75,106			75,106
Disposal of intangible assets	14,059		14,059	
New medium and long term loans	9,832			9,832
Movements in minority participations	3,568		3,568	
Redemption of loans granted	3,956		3,956	

⬤ INTERPRETATION OF CASH FLOW INFORMATION

Once the SCFP has been prepared, users will want to interpret what the statement tells them about the corporation. While many users will be interested in what has happened to cash in the current period, they are likely to be more interested in predicting the future cash flows of the corporation. A bank loan officer, for example, wants to be sure that, if money is lent to the corporation, the corporation will be able to pay it back. A stock analyst, on the other hand, will want to know what the

SCFP. Also, note that, after all the items have been reclassified, the total cash flow calculated at the bottom is the same as the net change in cash originally reported by Royal. There are some items that require explanation. "Movements in provisions" refers to adjustments for noncash expenses (similar to amortization). "Movements in minority participation" refers to changes in the investments that Royal has in other companies (those that are not consolidated). In Canada, "participations" would be referred to as investments. The "Exchange rate losses . . ." line item affects all three types of activities used in the SCFP but, without further information, it is impossible to classify this item properly. For simplicity, this amount has been shown in the operating section. "Stocks" refers to inventory, "debtors" refers to accounts receivable, and "creditors" refers to accounts payable in the bottom section of the report.

EXHIBIT 5-15 (continued)

Statement of Changes in Financial Position
(All amounts in thousands of Dutch Guilders)

		Reclassified as		
	As stated	Operating	Investing	Financing
Application of funds				
Investment of tangible assets	(228,233)		(228,233)	
Redemption of medium and long-term loans obtained	(52,565)			(52,565)
Goodwill on acquisition of subsidiaries	(10,523)		(10,523)	
Dividends distributed to outside shareholders	(576)			(576)
Exchange rate losses on shareholders funds, fixed assets and medium and long term loans	(1,547)	(1,547)		
Increase in working capital:				
Increase in stocks	(7,208)	(7,208)		
Increase in debtors	(18,196)	(18,196)		
Decrease in creditors	(10,389)	(10,389)		
Totals		155,927	(217,173)	42,797
Operations		155,927		
Investing		(217,173)		
Financing		42,797		
Net Cash Flow		(18,449)		

cash flows will be over a long period of time to ensure an adequate return on the investment in shares. Users interested in the future of the corporation will try to decide which cash flows will continue in the future and which will not continue.

In addition to deciding which cash flows are likely to continue, users will also want to make sure that cash from continuing operations is sufficient, over the long run, to pay for the continuing investing and financing activities. There is a limit to the cash inflows that can be achieved from investing and financing activities.

Investing inflows are limited by the kinds of returns that can be earned from investments in long-term assets and the level of investment by the corporation. The financing inflows are limited by the willingness of lenders and investors to invest their money in the corporation. At some level of debt, the corporation becomes so risky that no lender will agree to lend more. Because the inflows from investing and financing are limited, the corporation, if it is to remain in business, must generate sufficient cash inflow from operating activities to pay the interest and dividends on the financing activities and to continue investing at appropriate levels in property, plant, and equipment.

Beaver Industries, as an example, generated $40,000 from operations. Assuming that these are continuing operations (as opposed to discontinued operations) and that Beaver is in a fairly stable industry, you would expect this amount of cash flow to continue into the future. One way to evaluate this is to look at the trend in cash flow from operations over the last five years to see how stable this number is. The next question to address is whether this flow is sufficient to cover the continuing cash needs of Beaver.

Looking at the uses of cash in the investing and financing sections, you see that Beaver spent $60,000 to buy new property, plant, and equipment, $3,000 to pay dividends, and $10,000 to pay off debt. It is likely that purchasing new property, plant, and equipment will be a continuing need because buildings and equipment wear out over time. But does the corporation buy $60,000 in property, plant, and equipment every year, or is this year's purchase larger (or smaller) than usual? If Beaver buys $60,000 every year, you could quickly conclude that the cash from operations will not be sufficient in the long run to pay for this one need, not to mention other needs. If, however, Beaver has this large need only once every three years and if, in the other two years, the purchases are, say, $15,000, then the average amount of property, plant, and equipment purchases is $30,000 per year [($60,000 + 15,000 + 15,000)/3 = $30,000]. Cash flow from operations would be sufficient to pay for this need, with $10,000 left over to pay for other needs. Again, this can be learned by looking at the trend in property, plant and equipment spending over the last five years to determine the average spending pattern.

Once started, the payment of dividends is generally a continuing need. Corporations are reluctant to stop or reduce the payment of dividends because such action sends a negative signal to the market about the future profitability of the corporation. The amount of dividends paid, of course, is affected by the number of shares outstanding. If there was an additional issuance of shares in a given year, some growth in the total amount of dividend payments would be expected. Beaver is, in fact, in this position. New shares were issued in 19X1, and this could mean more dividends paid in future years.

The repayment of debt is another generally continuing item, but it is not dependent on cash from operations for repayment. Most corporations maintain a certain amount of debt. The level of debt is sometimes measured by comparing the dollar amount of debt on the balance sheet to the total amount of debt plus shareholders' equity. This measure is called a debt/equity ratio. For Beaver, this ratio, at the end of the year, was $81,000/$152,300 = 53.2%. This measure indicates that 53.2% of Beaver's total financing is in the form of debt. As will be discussed in Chapter 12, there is a theoretical optimal level of debt that will maximize the return to shareholders. Most corporations try to maintain this optimal level of debt. Therefore, if some debt must be paid off in a given year (which would lower the debt/equity ratio), it is generally replaced by a new borrowing (which would bring the debt/equity ratio back to its original value). This process of replacing old debt with new debt is sometimes called the rollover of debt. In the SCFP, this type of transaction would show up as both an inflow of cash and an outflow of cash in the financing activities section.

With regard to debt, Beaver did pay off some long-term debt without rolling it over into additional long-term borrowings. Beaver did, however, take out some additional short-term borrowings to finance the corporation. It is possible that Beaver may be waiting until long-term interest rates are lower to replace this long-term debt and is using short-term debt until it feels the time is right. Recognize that this short-term debt will probably require a cash payoff in a relatively short period of time, whereas the long-term borrowing will require cash payments over a longer period of time. If the corporation has some short-term cash inflow shortages, short-term debt can be a difficult problem. As the reader of the financial statements, you should have some understanding of how soon the debt of a corporation comes due because this will impact its need for cash.

On an overall basis, Beaver required $73,000 in cash to pay for the purchase of property, plant, and equipment, dividends, and the repayment of debt. It generated a total of $65,500 from operations, issuance of notes payable, issuance of common shares, and the sale of property, plant, and equipment. This produced a shortfall of $7,500 for the period, which was covered by the beginning balance of cash. Cash declined during this period from $20,000 to $12,500. If all the items in the cash flow statement were continuing items, Beaver could continue to operate for only another one to two years before it runs out of cash. Nothing definitive can be said about Beaver's cash flow health because not enough historical data are available. You can say that, if all items are continuing, Beaver will be in trouble in a year or two. If, on the other hand, the purchase of property, plant, and equipment does not continue at its present level, then Beaver may be in reasonable shape.

Cash from operations can also be examined further to determine whether there are any problems in the operations of the corporation. This analysis is easily done using the indirect format of the SCFP, where net income is reconciled to cash from operations. For Beaver Industries, the operating section shows that the two reasons for the increase in cash from operations during this period were that accounts receivable decreased and accounts payable increased. This gives some information about the management of the receivables and payables of the corporation, which are critical in determining the lead/lag relationship in the cash-to-cash cycle. In general, these two accounts would be expected to move in unison. When business is growing, the corporation usually generates more receivables and more payables. When business contracts, both these accounts decrease. In the case of Beaver, they are moving in opposite directions with accounts receivable decreasing and accounts payable increasing. This should raise a red flag that should lead the reader of the statement to ask more questions about why these amounts are moving in opposite directions. It could mean that there is a problem in the management of receivables or payables, especially the accounts payable.

Another concern regarding cash from operating activities is that Beaver increased inventories during the period, causing cash from operations to decline. If a business were expanding, you would expect a larger inventory. But increased sales normally means that a larger amount of accounts receivable should also be present, which was not the case. Again, this raises a red flag, which should prompt the user to ask why inventory has increased this much. It is possible that Beaver is stockpiling inventory in anticipation of a strike by employees, or it may be that its product is not selling and it has not adjusted production sufficiently. This situation may lead to obsolete inventory that cannot be sold.

◼◖◗ SUMMARY

In this chapter we outlined the benefits that can be obtained from the cash flows that are summarized in the statement of changes in financial position. Remember that both cash flows and profits must be generated for a business to be successful. In the next chapters, details of the items that appear in the balance sheet are provided so you will have a better understanding of the items that appear in the financial statements.

SUMMARY PROBLEMS

1. The 19x3 balance sheet and income statement of Oxford Industries, Inc. are provided in Exhibit 5-16. Oxford Industries manufactures and distributes a broad range of clothing and related services to retailers. Using these statements, construct the statement of changes in financial position for Oxford for the year ended June 1, 19x3. Use T-accounts and the indirect approach. The following additional information and assumptions are also provided (all numbers in thousands unless otherwise indicated).
   a. The beginning and ending balances in the accumulated amortization account were $65,225 and $69,385, respectively.
   b. Dividends declared in fiscal 19x3 totalled $4,817.
   c. Amortization on tangible assets totalled $6,389 in 19x3. Amortization on intangible assets totalled $171.
   d. Purchases of new property, plant, and equipment totalled $5,849 in 19x3.
   e. Property, plant, and equipment sold in 19x3 produced a gain of $134.
   f. All changes in the shareholders' equity accounts other than earnings and dividends are due to the purchase and retirement of common shares.
   g. No new long-term debt was issued in 19x3.
   h. Changes in the Other Assets account are considered operating items by Oxford.
   i. Changes in the deferred tax account should be made to the operating section.

2. Based on the answer to Question 1 and the previous two years' SCFP for Oxford Industries shown in Exhibit 5-17, answer the following questions:
   a. Discuss the corporation's ability to meet its needs for cash over the last three years. Comment on the continuing nature of the major items that have appeared over the last three years.
   b. Explain why so much cash was generated from operations in 19x2.

EXHIBIT 5-16

OXFORD INDUSTRIES, INC.
Balance Sheet
($ in thousands)

	June 1, 19x3	June 2, 19x2
Assets		
Current Assets:		
Cash and equivalents (Note A)	$ 2,488	$ 10,089
Receivables, less allowances for doubtful accounts of $2,401		
(19x3) and $2,400 (19x2)	74,117	71,991
Inventories (Notes A and B)	90,753	90,332
Prepaid expenses	7,575	5,552
Total Current Assets	174,933	177,964
Property, Plant and Equipment (Notes A, C, and D)	32,824	33,920
Other Assets	672	1,178
Total Assets	$208,429	$213,062
Liabilities and Shareholders' Equity		
Current Liabilities:		
Notes payable (Note D)	$ 10,500	$ —
Trade accounts payable	35,286	40,703
Accrued compensation	9,709	11,610
Other accrued expenses	9,750	9,727
Income taxes	—	1,065
Current maturities of long-term debt	4,726	4,653
Total Current Liabilities	69,971	67,758
Long-Term Debt, less current maturities (Note D)	31,962	36,843
Deferred Income Taxes (Notes A and J)	2,836	885
Commitments (Note E)		
Shareholders' Equity (Notes D and F)		
Common shares	14,313	15,268
Retained earnings	89,347	92,308
Total Shareholders' Equity	103,660	107,576
Total Liabilities and Shareholders' Equity	$208,429	$213,062

EXHIBIT 5-16 (continued)

OXFORD INDUSTRIES, INC.
Income Statement
Consolidated Statements of Earnings
($ in thousands except per share amounts)

	Year Ended		
	June 1, 19x3	June 2, 19x2	June 3, 19x1
Net Sales (Notes A and G)	$550,434	$566,176	$590,603
Costs and Expenses:			
Cost of goods sold	444,105	454,173	495,658
Selling, general and administrative	89,997	91,890	99,813
Restructuring charge (Note H)	—	—	10,000
Interest	3,491	3,981	4,146
	537,593	550,044	609,617
Earnings (Loss) Before Income Taxes	12,841	16,132	(19,014))
Income Taxes (Notes A and J)	4,892	6,257	(9,260)
Net Earnings (Loss)	$ 7,949	$ 9,875	$ (9,754)
Net Earnings (Loss) Per Common Share (Note K)	$ 0.82	$ 0.99	$ (0.93)

EXHIBIT 5-17

OXFORD INDUSTRIES, INC.
Cash Flow Statements
($ in thousands)

	Year Ended	
	June 2, 19x2	June 3, 19x1
Cash Flows From Operating Activities:		
Net earnings (loss)	$ 9,875	$ (9,754)
Adjustments to reconcile net earnings (loss) to net cash provided by operating activities:		
Amortization	7,998	8,731
(Gain) loss on sale of property, plant and equipment	411	(366)
Changes in working capital:		
(Increase) decrease in:		
Receivables, net	3,773	(2,826)
Inventories	9,209	6,367
Prepaid expenses	(975)	502
(Decrease) increase in:		
Trade accounts payable	2,398	5,888
Accrued expenses and other current liabilities	1,477	108
Income taxes payable	1,065	—
(Increase) decrease in prepaid and deferred income taxes	3,646	(4,699)
Decrease in other noncurrent assets	377	1,042
Net cash provided by operations	39,254	4,993

EXHIBIT 5-17 (continued)

OXFORD INDUSTRIES, INC.

Cash Flow Statements

$ in thousands

	Year Ended	
	June 2, 19x2	June 3, 19x1
Cash Flows From Investing Activities:		
Purchase of property, plant and equipment	(5,779)	(7,159)
Proceeds from sale of property, plant and equipment	478	2,158
Net cash used in investing activities	(5,301)	(5,001)
Cash Flows From Financing Activities:		
Increase (decrease) in short-term borrowings	(15,000)	(11,500)
Dividends on common shares	(4,978)	(5,200)
Payments on long-term debt	(4,573)	(2,206)
Addition to long-term debt	—	30,000
Purchase and retirement of common shares	(1,033)	(11,951)
Proceeds from exercise of stock options	—	153
Net cash used in financing activities	(25,584)	(704)
Net Change In Cash	8,369	(712)
Cash At Beginning of Period	1,720	2,432
Cash At End of Period	$10,089	$ 1,720
Supplemental Disclosures of Cash Flow Information		
Cash paid (received) for:		
Interest	$ 3,849	$ 4,794
Income taxes	5,586	782
Income taxes refunded	(5,210)	—

SUGGESTED SOLUTIONS TO SUMMARY PROBLEMS

1. T-Account Worksheet:

A – Cash

✓		10,089			
Operations:					
Net income	(1)	7,949	2,126	(2)	Increase in A/R
Increase in accrued			421	(3)	Increase in inventory
expenses	(7)	23	2,023	(4)	Increase in prepaid expenses
Increase in deferred					
taxes	(17)	1,951	5,417	(5)	Decrease in accounts payable
Amortization	(10)	6,560	1,901	(6)	Decrease in accrued compensation
Decrease in other					
assets	(16)	335	1,065	(8)	Decrease in taxes payable
			134	(12)	Gain on sale of plant, property, and equipment
Investing:					
Proceeds from sale of property, plant, and equipment	(12)	690	5,849	(11)	Acquisition of property, plant, and equipment
Financing:					
Proceeds from issuance of notes payable	(18)	10,500	4,817	(9)	Dividends
			7,048	(13)	Retirement of common shares
			4,808	(15)	Retirement of long-term debt
✓		2,488			

A – Accounts Receivable

✓	71,991	
(2)	2,126	
✓	74,117	

A – Inventories

✓	90,332	
(3)	421	
✓	90,753	

T-Account Worksheet (continued):

A – Prepaid Expenses			
✓	5,552		
(4)	2,023		
✓	7,575		

A – PP&E			
✓	99,145		
(11)	5,849	2,785	(12)
✓	102,209		

A – Other Assets			
✓	1,178		
		171	(10)
		335	(16)
✓	672		

XA – Accumulated Amortization			
		65,225	✓
(12)	2,229	6,389	(10)
		69,385	✓

L – Notes Payable			
		0	✓
		10,500	(18)
		10,500	✓

L – Accounts Payable			
		40,703	✓
(5)	5,417		
		35,286	✓

L – Accrued Compensation			
		11,610	✓
(6)	1,901		
		9,709	✓

L – Other Accured Expenses			
		9,727	✓
		23	(7)
		9,750	✓

L – Taxes Payable			
		1,065	✓
(8)	1,065		
		0	✓

L – Current Portion of Long-term Debt			
		4,653	✓
(15)	4,808	4,881	(14)
		4,726	✓

L – Long-term Debt			
		36,843	✓
(14)	4,881		
		31,962	✓

L-Deferred Taxes			
		885	✓
		1,951	(17)
		2,836	✓

SE – Common Shares			
		15,268	✓
(13)	955		
		14,313	✓

SE – Retained Earnings			
		92,308	✓
(9)	4,817	7,949	(1)
(13)	6,093		
		89,347	✓

Explanations of selected transactions.

Transaction 10. The debit entry to the cash account is a combination of the amortization of property, plant, and equipment and the amortization of the intangible assets. The entry is:

A – Cash (Operating)	6,560	
XA – Accumulated amortization		6,389
A – Other assets		171

Transaction 12. The sale of property, plant, and equipment resulted in a gain of $134. The cost and the accumulated amortization associated with this sale are determined by balancing the accounts in the T-account worksheet. The entry that results is as follows:

A – Cash (Investing)	690	
XA – Accumulated amortization	2,229	
A – Property, plant, and equipment		2,785
A – Cash (Operating)		134

Transaction 13. The purchase and retirement of the common shares would result in the following journal entry:

SE – Common shares	955	
SE – Retained earnings	6,093	
A – Cash (Financing)		7,048

The amounts in this entry are determined by calculating the amounts that will balance the respective accounts in the T-account worksheet.

Transactions 14 and 15. When long-term debt comes within a year of being due, the balance should be transferred to the liability account called "Current portion of long-term debt." Entry (14) accomplishes this. Entry (15) then records the retirement of the debt that came due during the year.

Transaction 17. Adjustments for the changes in deferred taxes are always made to the operating section of the SCFP. (We will discuss deferred taxes in more detail in Chapter 9.)

2. a. Over the last three years, the continuing items appear to be the following (also listed is the average amount per year over the last three years):

Purchase of property, plant, and equipment	6,262
Dividends	4,998
Payments on long-term debt	3,862
Total	15,122

In addition to the preceding three items, which seem to be continuing items, there are also some items that have required fairly significant cash outlays but on a more sporadic basis. These include the short-term borrowings and the purchase and retirement of common shares. It is clear that operations have not been sufficient to meet these needs in any year except 19x2. The shortfalls in 19x1 and 19x3 were covered by additional borrowing, either short-term or long-term as well as from the balance in cash.

b. The large amount of cash generated from operations in 19x2 is due to numerous items that probably cannot be duplicated in another year. Two of the largest items are the decrease in inventories ($9,209) and the decrease in accounts receivable ($3,773). All the changes in the other working capital items, except prepaid expense, caused increases in the cash balance during 19x2. This is a highly unusual event for most corporations. It is clear that it was not duplicated in either of the other two years.

GLOSSARY

Capitalization The amount of resources contributed to the corporation by shareholders and debtholders.

Cash flow The net change in cash that occurs from the beginning of an accounting period to the end of the period.

Direct approach A method of calculating the cash from operations of a corporation in which the direct gross cash receipts and payments are shown.

Financing activities The activities of a corporation that are directed to obtaining resources for the corporation from investors or debtholders. The return of resources to shareholders and debtholders is also considered part of these activities.

Indirect approach A method of calculating the cash from operations of a corporation in which the net income number is adjusted for all noncash revenues or expenses to convert it from an accrual basis to its cash basis equivalent.

Investing activities The activities of a corporation that are directed to investing the resources of the corporation over extended periods of time in long-term assets.

Lead/lag relationship The relationships between the recognition of revenues and expenses for income statement purposes and the recognition of their cash flow effects.

Operating activities The activities of a corporation that are directed to selling goods and services to customers.

ASSIGNMENT MATERIAL

Assessing Your Recall

1. Discuss why it is important for corporations to prepare a statement of changes in financial position in addition to an income statement.

2. Discuss how a corporation's receivables, inventory, and payables policies affect cash flows relative to the income produced in a given period.

3. What is meant by a lead/lag relationship in terms of the SCFP?

4. For a corporation with a cash flow problem, list at least three potential reasons for the problem, and suggest a possible solution for each of these reasons.

5. Describe the three major categories of activities that are shown on the SCFP.

6. Discuss the major difference between the direct approach and the indirect approach for constructing the SCFP.

7. "Amortization is a source of cash." Explain your reasons for agreeing or disagreeing with this statement.

8. In what section of the SCFP (operating, financing, or investing) would each of the following items appear:
   a. Purchase of new property, plant, and equipment
   b. Proceeds from a bank loan
   c. Collections from customers
   d. Dividends to shareholders
   e. Proceeds from the sale of marketable securities
   f. Retirement of debt
   g. Changes in accounts receivable
   h. Net income
   i. Gain or loss on the sale of property, plant, and equipment

▶◤ Applying Your Knowledge

9. For each of the transactions listed in Part b of this question:
   a. Indicate the effect on balance sheet categories by using the following format:

Trans. No.	Cash	Other Current Assets	Noncurrent Assets	Current Liabilities	Noncurrent Liabilities	Shareholders' Equity

   b. For the transactions affecting cash shown below, state whether they relate to an operating, investing, or financing activity.

   Transactions:
   1) Purchases on credit, $10,000
   2) Cash paid to suppliers, $8,000
   3) Sales on credit, $25,000
   4) Cost of goods sold, $15,000
   5) Cash payments received on accounts receivable, $18,000
   6) Salaries accrued, $1,500
   7) Salaries paid (previously accrued), $1,000
   8) Machine purchased for $800 in cash
   9) Amortization expense, $200
   10) Borrowed (long-term) $5,000 to purchase equipment
   11) Interest of $50 accrued and paid on the amount borrowed for the purchase of equipment
   12) Long-term debt worth $1,000 issued
   13) Equipment having a book value of $700 sold for $700 cash
   14) Dividends declared, $350

15) Dividends paid, $200
16) Insurance premium for the next year paid, $175
17) 1,000 shares issued at $1 per share
18) Rent received for building, $250
19) Income taxes accrued and paid, $325

10. For each of the transactions listed in Part b:

a. Indicate the effect on balance sheet categories in the following format:

Trans. No.	Cash	Other Current Assets	Noncurrent Assets	Current Liabilities	Noncurrent Liabilities	Shareholders' Equity

b. For the transactions affecting cash, state whether they relate to an operating, investing, or financing activity.

Transactions:

1) 5,000 common shares are issued at $10 per share.
2) Property, plant, and equipment worth $120,000 are purchased for $50,000 in cash and the balance in common shares.
3) Rent payment of $5,000 is received in advance.
4) Sales contracts for $100,000 are signed, and a $25,000 deposit is received in cash.
5) Merchandise inventory costing $85,000 is purchased on account.
6) Goods costing $15,000 were found defective and returned to suppliers. These goods had been purchased on account.
7) Sales were $175,000, of which $100,000 were on account.
8) Cash is paid to suppliers on account in the amount of $60,000.
9) Equipment recorded at $10,000 was destroyed by fire.
10) The corporation purchased 500 shares of X Corporation at $5 per share for short-term investment purposes.
11) The corporation purchased 2,000 shares of Z Corporation at $8 per share in an effort to buy a controlling interest in the corporation (a supplier).
12) Interest expense for the year amounted to $2,500 and was paid in cash.
13) The sales contract in transaction 4 was cancelled; $10,000 of the deposit was returned and the rest was forfeited.
14) A bank loan for $75,000 was taken out and is due in five years.
15) Equipment with a cost of $50,000 was sold for $60,000. The buyer agreed to pay $60,000 in the future and signed a note receivable.
16) During the year, warranty services costing $3,500 were provided to customers. A provision for warranty services was provided earlier in a separate transaction.
17) Amortization for the year totalled $20,000.
18) Dividends of $10,000 were declared, and $5,000 remained unpaid at year end.
19) Patents on a new manufacturing process were purchased for $5,000.
20) Research and development expenses amounted to $15,000 and were charged to expense as incurred.

11. Compute the cash flow from operations in each of the following cases:

	I	II	III
Sales revenues	$25,000	$35,000	$65,000
Amortization expense	3,000	5,000	20,000
Cost of goods sold	15,000	38,000	41,000
Other expenses	1,500	700	1,200
Dividends paid	3,000	—	1,000
Increase/(Decrease) in:			
Inventories	5,000	(10,000)	15,000
Accounts receivable	3,500	1,000	(2,000)
Prepaid expenses	(500)	(1,000)	1,800
Salaries payable	(10,000)	5,000	(15,000)
Interest payable	(5,000)	(500)	5,000
Other current liabilities	8,000	(10,000)	800

12. Compute the cash flow from operations in each of the following cases:

	I	II	III
Sales revenues	$175,000	$200,000	$225,000
Amortization expense	20,000	15,000	10,000
Cost of goods sold	100,000	185,000	195,000
Interest expense	5,000	25,000	15,000
Dividends paid	8,000	—	5,000
Profit/(loss) on sale of equipment	—	(10,000)	25,000
Increase/(Decrease) in:			
Common shares	10,000	50,000	—
Bonds payable	20,000	(30,000)	(15,000)
Interest payable	(25,000)	(5,000)	10,000
Accounts payable	(25,000)	10,000	15,000
Accounts receivable	50,000	(40,000)	35,000
Inventories	(10,000)	(15,000)	25,000
Property, plant, and equipment	100,000	(50,000)	—

13. Financial statement data for Dennis Corporation for 19x8 are as follows:

DENNIS CORPORATION
Comparative Balance Sheets

	Dec. 31, 19x7	Dec. 31, 19x8
Assets		
Cash	$ 25,500	$ 4,400
Accounts receivable	59,000	35,000
Inventories	30,000	50,000
Total current assets	114,500	89,400
Property, plant, and equipment	165,000	180,000
Accumulated amortization	(61,900)	(80,400)
Total noncurrent assets	103,100	99,600
Total assets	$217,600	$189,000

Liabilities and shareholders' equity

Accounts payable	$ 38,600	$ 28,500
Salaries payable	24,000	12,000
Total current liabilities	62,600	40,500
Bank loan	50,000	40,000
Total liabilities	112,600	80,500
Common shares	100,000	100,000
Retained earnings	5,000	8,500
Total liabilities and shareholders' equity	$217,600	$189,000

Income statement

Sales		$185,500
Expenses		
Cost of goods sold	87,500	
Salaries expense	48,000	
Amortization expense	23,500	
Interest expense	8,000	
Loss on sale of equipment	5,000	
Total expenses		172,000
Net income		13,500

Additional information:

1) Equipment originally costing $35,000 was sold for $25,000.
2) Dividends declared and paid during the year were $10,000.

Required:

Prepare a statement of changes in financial position for Dennis Corporation for the year ended December 31, 19x8, supported by a set of T-accounts.

14. Financial statement data for Matrix Incorporated are as follows:

MATRIX INCORPORATED
Balance sheet

	Dec. 31, 19x3
Assets	
Cash	$ 15,500
Accounts receivable	10,000
Notes receivable	5,000
Inventories	20,500
Total current assets	51,000
Property, plant, and equipment	160,000
Accumulated amortization	(35,500)
Total noncurrent assets	124,500
Total assets	$175,500

Liabilities and shareholders' equity

Accounts payable	$ 5,000
Salaries payable	18,000
Total current liabilities	23,000
Bonds payable	50,000
Total liabilities	73,000
Common shares	100,000
Retained earnings	2,500
Total liabilities and shareholders' equity	$175,500

MATRIX INCORPORATED

Trial Balance for the Year ended December 31, 19x4

	Debits	Credits
Cash	$ 2,900	
Accounts receivable	12,500	
Prepaid rent	6,000	
Inventories	18,900	
Cost of goods sold	275,500	
Amortization expense	10,000	
Rent expense	12,000	
Interest expense	15,000	
Salaries expense	24,000	
Property, plant, and equipment	160,000	
Accumulated amortization		$ 45,500
Accounts payable		13,800
Interest payable		9,000
Salaries payable		6,000
Bonds payable		10,000
Common shares		100,000
Retained earnings		2,500
Sales		350,000
Totals	$536,800	$536,800

Required:

a. Prepare an income statement and a reconciliation of retained earnings for the year ended December 31, 19x4.

b. Prepare a balance sheet as at December 31, 19x4.

c. Prepare a statement of changes in financial position for the year ended December 31, 19x4.

15. The financial statement data for Crescent Manufacturing Corporation are as follows:

CRESCENT MANUFACTURING CORPORATION
Comparative Balance sheets

	Dec. 31, x0	Dec. 31, x1
Assets		
Cash	$ 17,800	$ 12,800
Temporary investments	125,000	25,000
Accounts receivable	38,600	69,600
Prepaid insurance	6,000	
Inventories	43,300	93,300
Total current assets	230,700	200,700
Property, plant, and equipment	225,000	300,000
Accumulated amortization	(36,300)	(86,300)
Total noncurrent assets	188,700	213,700
Total assets	$ 419,400	$ 414,400
Liabilities and shareholders' equity		
Accounts payable	$ 12,600	$ 15,000
Interest payable	8,000	5,600
Dividends payable	20,000	30,000
Total current liabilities	40,600	50,600
Mortgage payable	100,000	75,000
Bonds payable	75,000	75,000
Total long term liabilities	175,000	150,000
Total liabilities	215,600	200,600
Common shares	200,000	190,000
Retained earnings	3,800	23,800
Total shareholders' equity	203,800	213,800
Total liabilities and shareholders' equity	$ 419,400	$ 414,400

Income statement

Sales	$ 508,000	
Interest revenue	12,500	
Gain on sale of temporary investments	25,000	
Total revenues		$ 545,500
Expenses:		
Cost of goods sold	330,000	
Amortization expense	50,000	
Insurance expense	12,000	
Interest expense	43,500	
Salaries expense	60,000	
Total expenses		495,500
Net income		$ 50,000

Additional information:

1) 10,000 shares of Sigma Corporation, which were purchased at a cost of $10 per share, were sold at a price of $12.50 per share.
2) Dividends declared during the year amounted to $30,000 and remained unpaid at year-end.

Required:

Prepare a statement of changes in financial position for Crescent Manufacturing Corporation for the year ended December 31, 19x1. Assume cash position = "cash plus temporary investments."

16. The balance sheets for Simco Corporation as of the beginning and end of 19x1 are shown below:

SIMCO CORPORATION
Balance Sheets

	Dec. 31, x0	Dec. 31, x1
Assets		
Current assets		
Cash	$ 10,000	$ 8,000
Accounts receivable	86,000	100,000
Inventories	102,000	112,000
Total current assets	$ 198,000	$ 220,000
Property, plant, and equipment	485,000	600,000
Accumulated amortization	(125,000)	(150,000)
Total noncurrent assets	$ 360,000	$ 450,000
Total assets	$ 558,000	$ 670,000
Liabilities and shareholders' equity		
Current liabilities		
Accounts payable	$ 78,000	$ 95,000
Wages payable	30,000	40,000
Total current liabilities	$ 108,000	$ 135,000
Bonds payable	100,000	125,000
Total liabilities	$ 208,000	$ 260,000
Shareholders' equity		
Common shares	150,000	175,000
Retained earnings	200,000	235,000
Total shareholders' equity	$ 350,000	$ 410,000
Total liabilities and shareholders' equity	$ 558,000	$ 670,000

Additional Information:

1) No dividends were declared or paid.
2) No property, plant, or equipment was sold.
3) No debt was repaid.
4) Net income was $35,000, including $25,000 of amortization expense.

Required:

Prepare a statement of changes in financial position, for the year ended 19x1.

17. Comparative balance sheets of Marvel Cosmetics Corporation for 19x1 and 19x2 are as follows:

MARVEL COSMETICS CORPORATION
Comparative Balance Sheets

	Dec. 31, x1	Dec. 31, x2
Assets		
Current assets		
Cash	$ 188,000	$ 200,000
Accounts receivable	133,000	120,000
Notes receivable	61,000	70,000
Inventories	326,000	439,000
Total current assets	$ 708,000	$ 829,000
Noncurrent assets		
Land	500,000	525,000
Machinery	238,000	483,000
Accumulated amortization	(97,500)	(143,000)
Total noncurrent assets	$ 640,500	$ 865,000
Total assets	$ 1,348,500	$ 1,694,000
Liabilities and shareholders' equity		
Current liabilities		
Accounts payable	$ 158,000	$ 145,000
Interest payable	10,000	17,500
Total current liabilities	$ 168,000	$ 162,500
Long term debt	200,000	350,000
Total liabilities	$ 368,000	$ 512,500
Shareholders' equity		
Common shares	550,000	650,000
Retained earnings	430,500	531,500
Total shareholders' equity	$ 980,500	$1,181,500
Total liabilities and shareholders' equity	$1,348,500	$1,694,000

Additional information:

1) Net income is $151,000 and includes amortization expenses of $105,500.
2) Dividends declared and paid during the year were $50,000.
3) A machine costing $80,000 was sold at its book value of $20,000.
4) No repayment of long-term debt occurred in 19x2.

Required:

Prepare a statement of changes in financial position, for the year ended 19x2.

18. The financial statement data for Pharmex Pharmaceutical Corporation for 19x5 are as follows:

PHARMEX PHARMACEUTICALS CORPORATION
Comparative Data

	Dec. 31, x4	Dec. 31, x5
Debits		
Cash	$ 80,000	$ 50,000
Accounts receivable	185,000	235,000
Inventories	296,000	325,000
Machinery	545,000	555,000
Totals	$1,106,000	$1,165,000
Credits		
Accumulated amortization	$ 122,500	$ 172,500
Accounts payable	97,500	82,500
Bonds payable	150,000	175,000
Common shares	350,000	400,000
Retained earnings	386,000	335,000
Total credits	$1,106,000	$1,165,000
Income statement data		
Sales		$1,052,000
Gain on sale of machinery		15,000
Cost of goods sold		878,000
Amortization expense		75,000
Interest expense		60,000
Rent expense		85,000

Additional information:

Acquisition cost of new machinery is $135,000. Old machinery having an original cost of $125,000 was sold at a gain of $15,000. Dividends of $20,000 were declared and paid.

Required:

a. Prepare an income statement including a reconciliation of retained earnings for the year ended December 31, 19X5.

b. Prepare a statement of changes in financial position for Pharmex for the year ended December 31, 19X5.

19. The following are the comparative statements of changes in financial position for Sherman Brothers Incorporated:

SHERMAN BROTHERS INCORPORATED
Comparative statements of changes in financial position
($ millions)

	19x3	19x2	19x1
Operating activities			
Net Income	486	415	287
Add back: Amortization	458	327	138
Changes in working capital items:			
Receivables	(150)	(80)	10
Inventories	(5)	(50)	(30)
Prepaid expenses	(5)	(3)	2
Accounts payable	(25)	15	5
Cash from operations	759	624	412
Investing activities			
Acquisition of noncurrent assets	(728)	(464)	(205)
Proceeds from sale of noncurrent assets	37	19	13
Cash used for investing	(691)	(445)	(192)
Financing activities			
Issue in long-term debt	25	450	400
Repayment of long-term debt	(500)	(25)	
Issuance of common shares	1,000		
Repurchase of common shares		(400)	(150)
Dividends paid	(510)	(315)	(200)
Cash flow from financing	15	(290)	50
Net increase (decrease) in cash	83	(111)	270
Cash position at beginning of year	174	285	15
Cash position at end of year	257	174	285

Required:

a. Discuss the corporation's ability to meet its needs for cash over the last three years. Comment on the continuing nature of the major items that have appeared over the last three years.

b. Comment on the accounts receivable, accounts payable, and inventory policies of Sherman Brothers.

c. How did Sherman Brothers finance its repayment of long-term debt and acquisition of noncurrent assets in 19x3?

Reading and Interpreting Published Financial Statements

20. Exhibit 5-18 shows the consolidated balance sheets for Purcell Energy Ltd. at December 31, 1994 and 1993 and the income statements for the same years.

EXHIBIT 5-18

PURCELL ENERGY LTD
Consolidated Balance Sheets
As at December 31

		1994	1993
Assets	**Current**		
	Cash	$ —	$ 140,666
	Accounts receivable	1,084,898	1,206,755
	Prepaid expenses and deposits	14,351	2,000
	Marketable securities, at cost	—	93,875
		1,099,429	1,443,296
	Investments, at cost (Note 2)	66,233	66,273
	Due from Encee Group Ltd. (Note 3)	360,184	—
	Due from affiliated companies (Note 4)	10,944	17,460
	Deferred financing charges, net of accumulated		
	amortization of $8,856	30,997	—
	Capital assets (Note 5)	10,482,981	8,628,246
		$ 12,050,588	$ 10,155,275
Liabilities and Shareholders' Equity	**Current liabilities**		
	Bank indebtedness (Note 6)	$ 130,477	$ —
	Accounts payable and accrued liabilities	1,258,127	915,727
	Accrued interest payable	8,592	1,317
	Promissory note (Note 7)	18,417	36,833
		1,415,613	953,877
	Provision for future site restoration costs	69,372	43,649
	Due to Encee Group Ltd.	—	124,200
	Long term debt (Note 8)	1,020,000	—
		2,504,985	1,121,726
	Shareholders' equity		
	Capital stock (Note 9)		
	Common	11,547,231	11,100,448
	Preferred	128,000	128,000
	Deficit	(2,129,628)	(2,194,899)
		9,545,603	9,033,549
		$ 12,050,588	$ 10,155,275

Director   Director

The accompanying notes are an integral part of these financial statements.

Required:

a. Prepare a statement of changes in financial position for Purcell Energy for the year ended December 31, 1994. State any assumptions you must make to prepare this statement.

b. Comment on the change in cash position and sources and uses of cash during the year, including an explanation of how Purcell financed the large purchase of noncurrent assets during the year.

EXHIBIT 5-18 (continued)

PURCELL ENERGY LTD
Consolidated Statements of Operations and Deficit

	For the Year ended December 31, 1994	For the Nine month period ended December 31, 1993
Revenue		
Oil and gas sales, net of royalties	$ 2,375,603	$ 1,265,050
Other	27,548	8,594
Interest	4,842	459
Consulting and management fees	198,375	—
	2,606,368	1,274,103
Expenses		
Production	672,905	323,806
Depletion, amortization and site restoration	1,299,723	331,517
Amortization of deferred financing charges	8,856	54,841
General and administrative	526,894	338,387
Interest on long term debt	57,710	69,507
	2,566,088	1,118,058
Income from operations	40,280	156,045
Gain on sale of marketable securities	30,040	52,080
Income before income taxes	70,320	208,125
Income taxes (Note 10)		
Current	127,876	136,968
Less utilization of loss carry forwards	(127,876)	(136,968)
	—	—
Net income for the period	70,320	208,125
Deficit, beginning of period	(2,194,899)	(2,403,024)
Dividends on preferred shares	(5,049)	—
Deficit, end of period	$ (2,129,628)	$ (2,194,899)
Earnings per share	$ 0.004	$ 0.016

The accompanying notes are an integral part of these financial statements.

21. Exhibit 5-19 shows the consolidated balance sheets for Telepanel Systems Inc. at January 31, 1995 and 1994 and the income statements for the same years.

EXHIBIT 5-19

TELEPANEL SYSTEMS INC.
Consolidated Balance Sheet
(in Canadian dollars)

	January 31 1995	January 31 1994
Assets		
Current assets		
Cash (Note 2)	$ 3,230,364	$ 3,394,243
Short-term deposits	–	2,000,000
Accounts receivable	592,377	170,418
Inventories (Note 3)	2,228,695	903,565
Prepaid expenses	163,443	37,771
	6,214,879	6,505,997
Fixed assets (Note 4)	568,721	505,743
Deferred expense (Note 5)	243,118	296,105
	$ 7,026,718	$ 7,307,845
Liabilities		
Current liabilities		
Bank and other indebtedness (Note 6)	$ 1,555,524	$ 259,703
Accounts payable and accrued liabilities (Note 7)	868,463	499,424
	2,423,987	759,127
Shareholders' Equity		
Capital stock (Note 8)	23,625,480	22,420,348
Deficit	(19,022,749)	(15,871,630)
	4,602,731	6,548,718
	$ 7,026,718	$ 7,307,845

Approved by the Board

_____   _____
Director   Director

See accompanying notes to financial statements.

Required:

a. Prepare a statement of changes in financial position for Telepanel Systems for the year ended January 31, 1995. State any assumptions you must make to prepare this statement.

EXHIBIT 5-19 (continued)

TELEPANEL SYSTEMS INC.
Consolidated Statement of Operations and Deficit
(in Canadian dollars)

	Year ended January 31		
	1995	**1994**	**1993**
Product sales	$ 3,381,131	$ 433,448	$ 353,578
Expenses			
Manufacturing	4,023,591	814,969	404,896
Selling, general and administration	2,041,725	1,847,006	1,206,915
Research and development	476,041	449,885	287,114
Patent enforcement	–	20,125	138,274
Patent licence fees	–	301,795	122,556
Depreciation	125,663	74,972	30,068
Interest	71,869	12,740	11,074
	6,738,889	3,521,492	2,200,897
Loss from operations before the undernoted item, interest earned and other revenue	(3,357,758)	(3,088,044)	(1,847,319)
Interest earned	206,639	237,805	75,162
Other revenue (Note 9)	–	62,500	889,000
	206,639	300,305	964,162
Loss from operations before the undernoted item	(3,151,119)	(2,787,739)	(883,157)
Unusual items related to issuance of shares (Note 10)	–	–	9,052,137
Loss for the year	(3,151,119)	(2,787,739)	(9,935,294)
Deficit, beginning of year	(15,871,630)	(22,136,028)	(12,200,734)
Reduction of deficit on reduction of capital stock (Note 11)	–	9,052,137	–
Deficit, end of year	$ (19,022,749)	$ (15,871,630)	$ (22,136,028)
Loss per common share	$ (0.22)	$ (0.21)	$(1.09)

See accompanying notes to financial statements.

b. Comment on the change in cash position and sources and uses of cash during the year, including an explanation of how Telepanel was able to finance its net cash outflow from operating activities.

22. The consolidated balance sheets, income statements, and SCFP for Big Rock Brewery Ltd. at March 31, 1995 and 1994 are shown in Appendix A, located at the end of Chapter 1.

Required:

Comment on the change in cash position and sources and uses of cash during the year ended March 31, 1995, including an explanation of how Big Rock is financing its large purchases of capital assets.

23. Exhibit 5-20 shows the consolidated statements of cash flows for Bema Gold Corporation (a mining exploration corporation) at December 31, 1994, 1993, and 1992. The income statement shows no operating revenues for Bema Gold for 1994.

Required:

a. Considering only the information presented in these statements, describe the apparent operations and cash management policies of Bema Gold over these three years.

b. Assume you are considering investing in shares of Bema Gold. What additional information would you require before you could make your decision?

24. Exhibit 5-21 shows the consolidated statements of changes in financial position for Algoma Central Corporation (a shipping and real estate corporation) at December 31, 1994 and 1993.

Required:

Considering only the information presented in these statements, describe the apparent cash management policies of Algoma Central over these two years.

25. Exhibit 5-22 shows the consolidated balance sheets for AT Plastics Inc. at December 31, 1994 and 1993 and the income statements for the same years.

Required:

a. Prepare a statement of changes in financial position for AT Plastics for the year ended December 31, 1994. Assume that the current portion of long-term debt shown at December 31, 1994 was repaid in 1995. State any assumptions you must make to prepare this statement.

b. Comment on the change in cash position and sources and uses of cash during the year, including an explanation of how AT Plastics financed its large repayment of long term debt.

26. The consolidated statements of changes in financial position for Mackenzie Financial Corporation for the years ended March 31, 1995, 1994, and 1993 are presented in Exhibit 5-23. Mackenzie Financial provides investment management and related services to public mutual funds, corporate pension fund clients and other institutional investors.

Required:

Explain why the presentation of this SCFP differs from the presentations discussed in this chapter in the Financing and Investing Activities.

EXHIBIT 5-20

BEMA GOLD CORPORATION
Consolidated Statements of Cash Flows
For the Years Ended December 31
(in thousands of Canadian dollars)

	1994	1993	1992
Operating activities			
Net loss for the year	($ 3,500)	($ 1,103)	($ 8,605)
Non-cash charges (credits)			
Depreciation and depletion	96	121	1,764
Reclamation	189	(1)	341
Equity loss in investees	169	181	272
Amortization of deferred charges	108	351	583
Write-down of mining interest	-	-	243
Interest and other income	-	(713)	-
Other (gains) losses and write-offs	3,038	(950)	3,691
Non-controlling interest	(95)	(313)	-
Change in non-cash working capital			
Accounts and notes receivable	152	(592)	(106)
Inventories	4	440	1,653
Prepaid expenses	15	44	100
Accounts payable	855	(595)	(146)
Cash from (to) operating activities	1,031	(3,130)	(210)
Financing activities			
Common shares issued (Note 12)	21,788	28,451	1,034
Subsidiary's shares issued	8,079	8,347	-
Issue of special warrants	44,336	-	-
Debenture conversions and repayments	(6,419)	(15,636)	(700)
Capital lease repayments	(72)	(1,491)	(424)
Gold loan repayments	-	(611)	(1,164)
Mortgage repayments	(964)	(408)	(128)
Deferred financing costs	(7,345)	(201)	(372)
Restricted cash	(3,139)	-	-
Other	31	(45)	7
Cash from (to) financing activities	56,295	18,406	(1,747)
Investing activities			
Property, plant and equipment, net	(18,120)	(8,046)	(4,018)
Acquisitions	-	(651)	-
Investment purchases	(3,970)	(164)	(1,002)
Note receivable	(322)	(3,311)	-
Proceeds on sale of:			
Subsidiary shares	3,325	1,906	-
Investments	79	1,762	1,909
Equipment	127	1,458	-
Refundable Chilean tax	(711)	(170)	(188)
Other	(540)	(247)	(147)
Cash to investing activities	(20,132)	(7,463)	(3,446)
Increase (decrease) in cash	37,194	7,813	(5,403)
Cash, beginning of year	8,053	240	5,643
Cash, end of year	$ 45,247	$ 8,053	$ 240

See accompanying notes to consolidated financial statements

EXHIBIT 5-21

ALGOMA CENTRAL CORPORATION
Consolidated Statements of Changes in Financial Position
Years Ended December 31

	1994	1993
NET INFLOW (OUTFLOW) OF CASH RELATED TO THE FOLLOWING ACTIVITIES		
OPERATING		
Income from continuing operations	$ 12,233,000	$ 11,342,000
Items not affecting cash		
Depreciation and amortization	17,976,000	15,549,000
Deferred income taxes	6,601,000	(5,130,000)
Gain on sale of fixed assets	(1,312,000)	169,000
Florida real estate project	—	(3,339,000)
Other	(92,000)	693,000
Net change in non-cash operating working capital (Note 8)	(5,114,000)	5,245,000
	30,292,000	24,529,000
INVESTING		
Additions to fixed assets	(22,423,000)	(9,150,000)
Proceeds from sale of Florida real estate	—	4,102,000
Proceeds from sale of fixed assets	1,391,000	13,000
Other	126,000	(282,000)
	(20,906,000)	(5,317,000)
CASH BEFORE FINANCING ACTIVITIES FROM CONTINUING OPERATIONS	9,386,000	19,212,000
FINANCING		
Repayment of long-term debt	(19,865,000)	(13,332,000)
(DECREASE) INCREASE IN CASH FROM CONTINUING OPERATIONS	(10,479,000)	5,880,000
NET CASH FROM DISCONTINUED OPERATIONS	189,000	4,375,000
TOTAL (DECREASE) INCREASE IN CASH FOR YEAR	(10,290,000)	10,255,000
CASH POSITION, BEGINNING OF YEAR	10,205,000	(50,000)
CASH POSITION, END OF YEAR	$ (85,000)	$ 10,205,000

EXHIBIT 5-22

AT PLASTICS INC.
Consolidated Balance Sheets
(as at December 31)

(thousands of dollars)	1994	1993
ASSETS		
CURRENT		
Cash	$ 1,357	$ –
Accounts receivable	25,968	19,756
Inventory (note 2)	26,227	23,987
Prepaids	961	435
Investment tax credits recoverable	577	439
	55,090	44,617
FIXED (note 3)	151,201	152,762
OTHER (note 4)	11,355	9,552
	$217,646	$206,931
LIABILITIES		
CURRENT		
Bank overdraft	$ –	$ 15,355
Accounts payable	24,159	18,619
Current portion of long-term debt (note 5)	5,554	158,107
Obligation under capital leases (note 6)	175	326
	29,888	192,407
LONG-TERM DEBT (note 5)	99,217	17,443
OBLIGATION UNDER CAPITAL LEASES (note 6)	496	87
OTHER LIABILITIES (note 7)	2,414	–
	102,127	17,530
	132,015	209,937
SHAREHOLDERS' EQUITY		
CAPITAL STOCK (note 8)	100,667	25,355
DEFICIT	(15,036)	(28,361)
	85,631	(3,006)
	$217,646	$206,931

See accompanying notes to consolidated financial statements.

Approved by the Board

EGERTON W. KING
Director

JOHN N. ABELL
Director

EXHIBIT 5-22 (continued)

AT PLASTICS INC.
Consolidated Statements of Operations and Deficit
For the years ended December 31

(thousands of dollars, except per share amounts)	1994	1993
SALES	$ 184,558	$ 157,494
COST OF SALES AND OTHER EXPENSES	148,086	126,821
INCOME BEFORE THE UNDERNOTED ITEMS	36,472	30,673
LESS		
Interest on long-term debt	11,617	22,724
Depreciation and amortization	10,433	13,578
Other interest	587	1,079
Other (income) expense (note 10)	(2,345)	509
	20,292	37,890
INCOME (LOSS) BEFORE INCOME TAXES	16,180	(7,217)
INCOME TAXES	1,145	502
NET INCOME (LOSS) FOR THE YEAR	15,035	(7,719)
DEFICIT AT BEGINNING OF YEAR	(28,361)	(20,642)
DIVIDENDS	(1,710)	–
DEFICIT AT END OF YEAR	$ (15,036)	$ (28,361)
NET INCOME (LOSS) PER SHARE (note 12)	$　　1.29	$　　(1.97)

See accompanying notes to consolidated financial statements.

27. The cash flow statements of The Volvo Group, Inc. from its 1994 annual report are provided in Exhibit 5-24. Based on these statements respond to the following questions:
    a. Discuss the company's ability to meet its needs for cash over the last three years. Comment on the continuing nature of the major items that have appeared over the last three years.
    b. Which items would require more investigation or further explanation, or both, to help you understand the company's financial health?
    c. Discuss the ability of Volvo to generate cash from operations over the last three years.

28. The cash flow statements of Bufete Industrial S.A. from its 1994 annual report are provided in Exhibit 5-25. Based on these statements respond to the following questions:
    a. Discuss the company's ability to meet its needs for cash over the last three years. Comment on the continuing nature of the major items that have appeared over the last three years.
    b. Which items would require more investigation or further explanation, or both, to help you understand the company's financial health?
    c. Discuss the ability of Bufete's to generate cash from operations over the last three years.

EXHIBIT 5-23

MACKENZIE FINANCIAL CORPORATION
Consolidated Statements of Changes in Financial Position
For the years ended March 31
(thousands of dollars)

	1995	1994	1993
Operating Activities			
Net earnings for the year	$ 29,450	$ 36,061	$ 17,863
Items not affecting cash –			
Depreciation and amortization	34,241	21,891	15,489
Deferred taxes	25,705	18,215	(1,645)
Equity in earnings of affiliated companies net of dividends			
received of $840 (1994 – $210; 1993 – $Nil)	55	(14,502)	(6,070)
	89,451	61,665	25,637
Net (increase) decrease in non-cash			
balances related to operations (note 12)	11,956	(15,307)	4,268
	101,407	46,358	29,905
Financing Activities			
Proceeds from bank loans	8,245	4,767	–
Proceeds from (repayment of) notes payable	(5,816)	50,000	–
Payment of selling commissions	(32,876)	(97,340)	(7,225)
Increase in customer deposits	34,535	31,684	26,120
Payment of dividends	(7,112)	(6,472)	(5,803)
Issue of common shares	52	5,286	987
	(2,972)	(12,075)	14,079
Investing Activities			
Purchase of capital assets	(15,160)	(12,650)	(7,231)
(Increase) decrease in mortgage loans	(47,905)	7,100	(28,174)
(Increase) in other assets	(2,806)	(1,585)	(3,971)
Purchase of management contracts	–	(1,671)	(7,259)
Purchase price of shares in subsidiary company	(27)	(11,174)	–
Increase in investment in affiliated companies (note 5)	(555)	–	–
	(66,453)	(19,980)	(46,635)
Increase (decrease) in cash and cash equivalents	31,982	14,303	(2,651)
Cash and cash equivalents – beginning of year	112,473	98,170	100,821
Cash and cash equivalents – end of year	$144,455	$ 112,473	$ 98,170
Cash	$ 3,692	$ 4,466	$ 409
Short-term investments	140,763	108,007	97,761
	$144,455	$ 112,473	$ 98,170

(The accompanying notes are an integral part of these consolidated financial statements.)

EXHIBIT 5-24

THE VOLVO GROUP, INC.
Consolidated Statements of Cash Flows
For the Years Ended December 31,
(in millions of SEK)

	1992	1993	1994
Operating activities			
Net income (loss)	(3,320)	(3,466)	(13,230)
Depreciation and amortization	3,119	3,777	5,107
Write-down of shareholdings and fixed assets	315	—	574
Income (loss) from equity method investments after taxes	417	2,815	(1,274)
Dividends received from associated companies	700	717	160
Gain on sale of securities	(131)	(504)	(4,243)
Minority interests after taxes	(1,286)	356	(365)
Decrease (increase) in operating assets:			
Receivables	1,484)	(2,732)	(3,538)
Inventories	2,373	2,209	(2,687)
Increase in current operating liabilities	1,859	6,312	5,915
Increase in accruals for pensions	257	91	17
Decrease in deferred tax liabilities	(2,207)	(989)	(1,343)
Net cash flow provided by operations	3,580	8,586	12,253
Investment activities			
Property, plant and equipment, etc.			
Capital expenditures	(4,267)	(5,143)	(6,769)
Disposals	299	770	1,460
Decrease in investments in bonds	928	—	—
Investments in shares, net	(224)	464	8,182
Long-term receivables and loans	(1,620)	(280)	(1,563)
Acquisitions and sales of companies	323	393	—
Net cash provided by (used in) investment activities	(4,561)	(3,796)	1,310
Financing activities			
Decrease in short-term loans	(298)	(5,104)	(6,233)
Increase (decrease) in long-term loans	3,488	(844)	(2,028)
Withdrawal from restricted deposits in Bank of Sweden	39	2	—
Increase in minority interests	122	15	145
Dividends paid to AB Volvo shareholders	(1,203)	(601)	(601)
Dividends paid to minority shareholders	(81)	0	(132)
Payment of price adjustment to Renault	—	—	(1,422)
Other	78	93	23
Net cash provided by (used in) financing activities	2,145	(6,439)	(10,248)
Translation differences on liquid funds	1,817	1,331	(308)
Increase (decrease) in cash and cash equivalents	2,981	(318)	3,007
Cash and cash equivalents at beginning of year	18,779	21,760	21,442
Cash and cash equivalents at end of year	21,760	21,442	24,449
Cash paid during the year for			
Interest	4,850	4,677	3,165
Income Taxes	525	395	2,388

EXHIBIT 5-25

BUFETE INDUSTRIAL, S.A. AND SUBSIDIARIES
Consolidated Statement of Changes in Financial Position
Years ended December 31
(thousands of new Mexican pesos of December 31, 1994 purchasing power)

	1994[1] (000s US$)	1994	1993	1992
Operations:				
(Loss) income before extraordinary items	(US$1,483)	(NPs7,401)	NPs94,258	NPs29,675
Charges to income not affecting resources:				
Amortization of goodwill	401	2,003	—	—
Amortization off negative goodwill	(2,146)	(10,711)	—	—
Depreciation	5,987	29,873	19,131	20,270
Provision for pension and seniority premiums	675	3,370	5,919	1,050
Net change in:				
Trade receivables	(72,883)	(363,685)	(66,808)	(45,926)
Inventories	2,533	12,642	(36,087)	(198,549)
Other current assets	(8,194)	(40,888)	(58,635)	(11,284)
Accounts payable and accrued expenses	(13,054)	(65,141)	(15,291)	298,208
Advances from customers	(592)	(2,954)	(235,152)	101,961
Other current liabilities	(859)	(4,287)	(11,036)	3,887
Resources (used in) provided by operations before extraordinary item	(89,615)	(447,179)	(303,701)	199,292
Extraordinary items:				
Refund of prior years' asset tax	347	1,736	8,716	—
Realization of prior years' income tax Loss carryforwards	770	3,844	17,944	22,658
Resources (used in) provided by operations	(88,498)	(441,599)	(277,041)	221,950
Financing:				
Capital stock increase	—	—	20,393	—
Premium on issuance of capital stock	(412)	(2,056)	349,833	—
Dividends paid	(1,377)	(6,869)	(5,534)	(5,945)
Bank loans and other financing obtained (repaid) — Net	95,423	476,162	(5,788)	(39,054)
Real estate certificates — Net	177	885	42	(1,509)
Financing (paid) received under capital leases	9,979	49,799	(10,295)	22,326
Minority interest	6,534	32,603	—	—
Resources provided by (used in) financing activities	110,324	550,524	348,651	(24,182)

EXHIBIT 5-25 (continued)

BUFETE INDUSTRIAL, S.A. AND SUBSIDIARIES
Consolidated Statement of Changes in Financial Position
Years ended December 31
(thousands of new Mexican pesos of December 31, 1994 purchasing power)

	1994[1] (000s US$)	1994	1993	1992
Investing:				
Goodwill	(2,007)	(10,016)	—	—
Negative goodwill	4,293	21,422	—	—
Proceeds from sale of assets	254	1,269	885	4,470
Purchase of machinery and equipment	(33,863)	(168,974)	(14,791)	(55,257)
Investment in shares	(345)	(1,724)	(1,015)	(2,981)
Translation adjustment	(745)	(3,717)	—	—
Resources used in investing activities	(32,413)	(161,740)	(14,921)	(53,768)
(Decrease) increase in cash and cash equivalents	(10,587)	(52,815)	56,689	144,000
Cash and cash equivalents at beginning of year	41,197	205,558	148,869	4,869
Cash and cash equivalents at end of year	US$30,610	NPs152,743	NPs205,558	NPs148,869

[1] The U.S. dollar figures at December 31, 1994 have been translated from the new Mexican peso figures at the exchange rate of NPs4.99 per dollar and are not covered by the independent accountants' opinions.

CASE

Atlantic Service Corporation

Atlantic Service Corporation was established five years ago to provide services to the home construction industry. It has been very successful, with assets, sales, and profits increasing each year. However, Atlantic is experiencing serious cash shortages and is in danger of going into bankruptcy because it cannot pay its suppliers and already has a very substantial overdraft at its bank. The president has asked you to analyze the SCFP for the years ended December 31, 19x8 and 19x7, in Exhibit 5-26 to explain what appears to be causing the cash shortage problem, and to recommend a plan to save the corporation from bankruptcy.

◤◣ Critical Thinking Question

As discussed in this chapter, the statement of changes in financial position provides users of financial information with another "flow" measure of a corporation's performance. However, several issues have been raised in both academic and practitioner-oriented research relative to the meaning, usefulness, and calculation of cash flows. For example, Wallace and Collier ("The 'Cash' in Cash Flow Statements: A Multi-Country Comparison," *Accounting Horizons*, December 1991) describe how vari-

EXHIBIT 5-26

ATLANTIC SERVICE CORPORATION
Statement of Changes in Financial Position
Years ended December 31, 19x8 and 19x7

	19x8	19x7
Operating activities		
Net income	$ 150,000	$ 135,000
Add back amortization	25,000	20,000
Plus increase in accounts payable	55,000	45,000
Less increase in accounts receivable	(35,000)	(30,000)
Less increase in inventory	(30,000)	(25,000)
	$ 165,000	$ 145,000
Financing activities		
Increase in one year bank loan	$ 50,000	$ 30,000
Dividends	(15,000)	(10,000)
	$ 35,000	$ 20,000
Investing activities		
Purchase of equipment	$(300,000)	$(250,000)
Net cash used in the year	(100,000)	(85,000)
Cash position, beginning of year	(130,000)	(45,000)
Cash position, end of year	$(230,000)	$(130,000)

ous countries, including Canada, have issued standards regarding the presentation of cash flows but have failed to define the term "cash" either consistently or adequately.

Look up this article in your library, briefly summarize the authors' arguments, and discuss the potential problems associated with the lack of a uniform definition of cash for both companies that have only domestic operations, and for those that have both domestic and foreign operations.

APPENDIX C

SCFP PREPARATION: DIRECT APPROACH

Although the indirect approach for preparing and presenting the statement of changes in financial position is standard practice, a few corporations use the direct approach. The direct approach differs from the indirect approach in its analysis of the operating activities section. While the indirect approach starts with net income and reconciles net income to the net cash flow from operations, the direct approach summarizes all cash inflows and outflows from operations.

In this Appendix, we present the preparation and format of the SCFP using the direct approach. We do this by using the same information for Beaver Industries Inc. we used earlier in the chapter to present the indirect approach.

In Exhibit 5A-26, the completed T-account approach with all the reconstructed transactions for 19x1 for Beaver Industries is shown. The entries in the T-accounts have been given transaction numbers, and each is discussed in this section. The cash flow statement will be constructed using the direct approach for the operating section.

The transactions for 19x1 are reconstructed starting with those that are most easily identifiable because they appear on the income statement. For example, the first transaction that was reconstructed was that for the recognition of sales revenue for the period as follows:

(1)		
A – Accounts Receivable	130,000	
SE – Retained Earnings		130,000

This entry records the sales for the period. The amount is found on the income statement, and an assumption must be made regarding how many of the sales were cash sales and how many were credit sales. A common assumption to make in preparing the cash flow statement is that all sales were on account. The credit entry recognizes that the effect of sales revenue on the balance sheet is to increase retained earnings. Note that there is no need to break out the retained earnings account into temporary accounts because the individual income statement accounts are not important to the calculation of the cash flow statement. The important thing is to make sure that the change in the retained earnings account is fully explained.

The amount of the cash collection is then determined by considering the accounts receivable account. Because the beginning balance was $20,000, the sales (from transaction 1) were $130,000 and the ending balance was $10,000, the collection had to be $140,000 to make the account balance. The cash collections are shown in the operating section as follows:

(2)		
A – Cash (Operating)	140,000	
A – Accounts Receivable		140,000

EXHIBIT 5A-26

BEAVER INDUSTRIES
Cash Flow T-Account Worksheet: Direct Approach

A – Cash

✓	20,000				
Operating:					
Collections	(2)	140,000	85,000	(5)	Payments to suppliers
from customers			15,000	(6)	Other cash expenses
Investing:					
Proceeds from	(8)	500	60,000	(9)	Purchase of PP&E
sale of PP&E					
Financing:					
Issuance of	(12)	20,000	10,000	(13)	Repayment of
notes payable					bonds payable
Issuance of	(14)	5,000	3,000	(11)	Dividends
common shares					
✓	12,500				

A – A/R

✓	20,000		
(1)	130,000	140,000	(2)
✓	10,000		

A – Inventory

✓	30,000		
(4)	100,000	90,000	(3)
✓	40,000		

A – PP&E

✓	100,000		
(9)	60,000	1,000	(8)
✓	159,000		

XA – Accumulated Amortization

		50,000	✓
(8)	800	20,000	(7)
		69,200	✓

L – A/P

		5,000	✓
(5)	85,000	100,000	(4)
		20,000	✓

L – Dividends Payable

		0	✓
(11)	3,000	4,000	(10)
		1,000	✓

L – Notes Payable

		0	✓
	0	20,000	(12)
		20,000	✓

SE – Common Shares

		25,000	✓
	0	5,000	(14)
		30,000	✓

SE – RE

		40,000	✓
(3)	90,000	130,000	(1)
(6)	15,000	300	(8)
(7)	20,000		
(10)	4,000		
		41,300	✓

L – Bonds Payable

		50,000	✓
(13)	10,000	0	
		40,000	✓

To record the cost of goods sold for the period the following entry was made:

```
(3)
SE – Retained Earnings                          90,000
     A – Inventory                                           90,000
```

After making entry (3) and considering the beginning and ending balance in inventory, the purchases for the period can be calculated because, in this corporation, purchases are the only type of item that affects the debit side of the inventory account. All these purchases of inventory are credited to accounts payable because we assumed all purchases were on account. Again, this is a common assumption to make when the percentage of credit purchases is unknown. The entry is:

```
(4)
A – Inventory                                  100,000
     L – Accounts Payable                                  100,000
```

When the credit purchases of $100,00 from entry (4) and the beginning and ending balance in accounts payable ($5,000 and $20,000 respectively) are known, the amount that represents the payments to suppliers on the accounts payable can be calculated ($5,000 + $100,000 − $20,000). Entry (5) then records this amount. The entry is:

```
(5)
L – Accounts Payable                           85,000
     A – Cash (Operations)                                  85,000
```

The amount listed on the income statement as other cash expenses directly reduces cash and retained earnings as follows:

```
(6)
SE – Retained Earnings                          15,000
     A – Cash (Operations)                                  15,000
```

The amount of amortization expense is given on the income statement and it reduces retained earnings as well as increases the accumulated amortization. However, it does not appear on the SCFP using the direct approach. *NOTE CAREFULLY: Amortization does not affect the cash flow of the corporation* because the cash outflow relating to the property, plant, and equipment occurred when the asset was originally purchased (an investing activity). A cash inflow could occur when a piece of property, plant, or equipment is sold, as we will see with entry (6) below. The entry for the amortization is:

(7)		
SE — Retained Earnings	20,000	
XA — Accumulated Amortization		20,000

At this point, all the information on the income statement, with the exception of the gain from the sale of property, plant, and equipment, has been used. Because some information regarding that transaction was given in the statement of the problem, it can now be reconstructed. In the extra information given, the original cost of the equipment is stated as $1,000 (the amount taken out of property, plant, and equipment) and the book value as $200. A book value of $200 means that the balance in the accumulated amortization account must have been $800 because the asset was originally purchased for $1,000. The $800 of accumulated amortization must be removed from the accumulated amortization account. The cash proceeds from this transaction were $500 and, therefore, a gain of $300 must have been reported. The gain appears on the income statement and, as shown earlier, increases retained earnings. Note, in the cash account, that the cash proceeds are shown in the investing section. This is not an operating item. The entry is:

(8)		
A — Cash (Investing)	500	
XA — Accumulated Amortization	800	
A — Property, Plant, and Equipment		1,000
SE — Retained Earnings		300

The final entries, (9) to (14), are identical to those described for the indirect approach, entry numbers (7) to (12).

The cash account now contains all the information necessary to produce an SCFP. The cash from operations can be taken directly from the figures in the cash T-account as follows:

Collections from customers	$ 140,000
Payments to suppliers	(85,000)
Other operating expenses	(15,000)
Net cash from operations	$ 40,000

The net cash from operations of $40,000 is the same amount as was determined under the indirect approach.

The remainder of the SCFP, that is, the financing and investing activities, will be the same as that produced using the indirect approach, as shown previously. The direct and indirect approaches differ only in the format and details of the operating activities section.

CHAPTER

Cash, Temporary Investments,
and Accounts Receivable

Ⅰn this chapter, the accounting methods and principles that apply to cash, accounts receivable, and temporary investments are considered. In each account category, recognition criteria, valuation methods, financial statement analysis considerations, and other issues that are important to understanding the account category are discussed. The complexities of financial statement analysis are discussed in this chapter and each subsequent chapter in a section entitled "Statement Analysis Considerations."

The assets discussed in this chapter have the unique property that they all either are cash or will become cash. In accounting terms, we often call them **monetary assets** because they either are money, or will become money. Obviously they are very important to every business since sufficient cash must be available at all times to pay for purchases and debts as they become due for payment.

◖◗ CASH

In the first chapter of this book, we discussed the criterion that are used to decide if something is an asset for accounting purposes. The simple criteria identified as assets those things: (1) that the corporation owns or has the right to use, and (2) that have probable future value. In this chapter we will use those criteria to decide if and how we will categorize cash as an asset.

Cash certainly meets the ownership/right-to-use criteria. Ownership of currency is generally evidenced by possession; because it is difficult to differentiate except from serial numbers on bills, cash is a very difficult asset to control. All corporations must be very careful how they handle and control their cash and must design appropriate control procedures as part of their internal control systems so that it is not lost or stolen. Auditors design special audit procedures to test whether these controls adequately safeguard the handling and recording of cash.

Cash also meets the probable future value criterion. Cash does not have any intrinsic value other than the value of the paper and the metal from which it is made. It derives its value from its ability to be exchanged for goods and services in the future, which is also called its purchasing power. It serves as the medium of exchange in every economy. The ability of cash to serve as a medium of exchange depends on the faith of the individuals in the economy who use it. If there is a loss of confidence that the medium can be exchanged in the future, the currency loses its value. For example, in Germany after World War I, German currency lost its value as a form of exchange. It did retain some small value, but it lost its ability to serve as a medium of exchange because of high inflation following Germany's loss.

The purchasing power of cash in the future is not the same as its purchasing power today. The future value of cash may be uncertain because it cannot be known for sure whether or not its ability to buy goods and services will be the same as it is today. When an economy goes through a period of inflation or deflation, the value of its currency changes. Under inflation, the same amount of currency will buy fewer goods and services at the end of a period than at its beginning. For example, if $40 is held at the beginning of the period and the price of a barrel of oil is $20, two barrels of oil can be purchased with the cash. If the $40 is still held at the end of the period and prices have doubled (a barrel of oil costs $40), only one barrel of oil can be purchased. The exchangeability of the currency has changed, and a loss in value has occurred relative to oil.

Cash Valuation Methods

Assuming that cash meets the recognition criterion, the next problem is how to record the cash in the accounting system. For this account and for all other accounts discussed in this text, several possible valuation methods will be discussed. Some of these methods are not allowed under Canadian GAAP but are allowed in other countries. The purpose of discussing different methods is to discuss the conceptual framework that underlies current practice. A separate section is devoted to the requirements of Canadian GAAP. In some cases, the methods used under Canadian GAAP are a combination of the various possible valuation methods discussed here.

One possible method of valuing cash is to record it at its face value. This means that as long as cash is held, its value is assumed not to change. Using the example in the previous section of holding $40 in cash, the cash would be valued at $40 at the beginning of the period as well as the end of the period. Note that the valuation principle used also has implications for the income statement during the period. If cash is valued at face value, there will be no gain or loss caused by holding cash during the period because its face value does not change.

As in the example involving the price of oil, even though the face value of the $40 does not change, the ability of cash to be converted into goods and services is affected by the level of inflation or deflation during the period. During periods of inflation, cash is said to have sustained a loss in **purchasing power** because of its relative loss in terms of exchangeability for goods and services. In Chapter 4, several valuation methods that can be used for different attributes of assets were discussed in relation to revenue recognition criteria. In the example we are using here, the attribute of face value does not change, but the attribute of purchasing power does. If the attribute of face value is used to value cash, there will be no income recognition, as stated in the preceding paragraph. If, however, the attribute of purchasing power is used to value cash, then income would have to be recognized for the change in purchasing power during the accounting period (in the oil example, there was a one barrel loss in purchasing power). Consequently, the choice of which attribute of cash to measure is critical in how cash is represented on the balance sheet and how it affects the income statement.

GAAP and Cash

Under GAAP, there is an underlying assumption, called the **unit-of-measure assumption**, which specifies that the results of activities of the corporation should be measured in terms of a **monetary unit** (e.g., the Canadian dollar). This precludes the measurement of activities in terms of purchasing power, and cash is, therefore, measured at its face value rather than by any other method.

While the unit-of-measure assumption requires that Canadian currency be measured at face value, this is not the case for foreign currency. Suppose, for example, that a corporation does business with a German customer and that the agreement with the customer is *denominated* in Deutsche marks (DM). This means that the customer is required to pay in DM rather than Canadian dollars. The corporation will receive DM and will probably hold a certain amount of DM currency at the beginning and the end of the accounting period. Because this asset is measured in a different monetary unit than the rest of the assets of the corporation, a conversion will have to be made from DM into Canadian dollars.

Under GAAP, the conversion of DM into dollars is done using the exchange rate that exists on the date of the balance sheet. For example, suppose the exchange rate is 1.0 DM/$ at the beginning of the year and 1.10 DM/$ at the end of the year. Further, suppose that the corporation holds 1,100 DM at the beginning and the end of the year. Exhibit 6-1 shows how the DM currency would be valued on the balance sheet. You can see that, while there is no gain or loss during the year in terms of DM (the face value does not change), there is a loss in terms of dollars. This loss will appear on the income statement and will be called a *foreign currency transaction loss*.

EXHIBIT 6-1

Foreign Currency Valuation

Date	Amount of Foreign Currency	Exchange Rate	Amount of Cdn. Currency
Jan. 1, 19x1	1,100 DM	1.0 DM/$	$1,100
Dec. 31, 19x1	1,100 DM	1.1 DM/$	$1,000
Loss	0 DM		$100

Reasons for changes in the exchange rates of currencies are difficult to pinpoint precisely but, in theory, one of the major causes is differential inflation rates in the two countries (the economic theory that describes this is called the *purchasing power parity theory*). Individuals who hold currencies in countries with high inflation rates lose more purchasing power than those in countries with low inflation rates. Exchange rates adjust to compensate for these differences in purchasing powers. In effect, GAAP recognizes the changes in purchasing power of foreign currency by allowing the dollar value of the foreign currencies to rise and fall with the exchange rates.

One final note with regard to purchasing power. In the mid-to late 1970s and in the early 1980s, Canada experienced high rates of inflation (by Canadian standards). Accounting regulators became concerned with the problem that income, as measured by GAAP, did not take into consideration the changes in purchasing power of the assets and liabilities of the corporation. In 1982 the CICA adopted guidelines that requested that corporations present supplementary information regarding the effects of changing price levels on the financial results. These requirements were dropped in 1992 when inflation was down to more normal levels. Therefore, in Canada, there is currently no systematic reporting of the effects of inflation or changing prices on the financial results of corporations.

◣◥ Other Issues

There are no major accounting issues related to cash; you simply report how much cash is owned by the corporation. By cash, we mean currency, cheques, money orders, amounts in bank accounts that can be used with very short notice, and deposits ready to be deposited into bank accounts.

The main problems with cash are the control of cash to ensure it is not lost or stolen, and the management of cash balances. Proper control of cash includes very simple policies such as ensuring that all cash is deposited into bank accounts daily or even more frequently, using secure safes and tills to hold cash until it is deposited, writing cheques instead of using cash to pay expenses, and keeping as little cash on hand as possible.

One normal control procedure used by virtually every corporation is the **bank reconciliation**. A bank reconciliation is the procedure used to ensure that the accounting records agree with the bank records. Every bank account has a corresponding general ledger account. Both the corporation's records and bank ledgers reflect the same transactions such as cash deposits and cheques written, except that the bank may record the transactions at a different time. For example, a corporation may write and record a cheque on November 1, mail it to the payee, who receives it on November 7 and deposits the cheque into its bank account on November 8. The payee's bank will forward the cheque to the payer's bank who withdraws the money from the payer's account on November 9. These transactions take a few days to occur, so the cheque will be outstanding from the time the payer records it on November 1 until the bank shows it as a withdrawal from the account on November 9. During the time the cheque is outstanding, the two accounts (general ledger and the bank's records) will be different. The bank reconciliation is the process used to account for all such differences. As an individual, you should be reconciling your personal bank balance every month so that you can manage your cash most effectively.

Bank reconciliations are an important control procedure to ensure that all transactions affecting the bank account have been properly recorded so the corporation knows that no transactions have been missed. They are normally done every month for every bank account as soon as the bank statement is received.

The bank reconciliation procedure consists of reconciling the balance recorded by the corporation to the balance recorded by the bank. The main reconciling items are outstanding cheques, outstanding deposits (deposits recorded by the corporation on one day but not received or recorded by the bank until the next business day), bank service charges that have been deducted from the bank account but not recorded by the corporation, errors in recording items, and any other item that is found.

Another important control point is that the person who reconciles the bank account must not be the person who is in charge of the bank account or the accounting records. This is important so that any error or discrepancy will be found and corrected properly. This also prevents giving an individual the opportunity to take cash and change the books to cover the theft.

Proper cash management includes the maintenance of sufficient cash in readily accessible bank accounts to pay expenses, but also includes not having too much cash either on hand or in bank accounts. Cash is a non-earning asset; that is, it is not earning a return. The corporation will want to keep as much of its cash invested in income-earning assets as possible. Income-earning assets include savings accounts and short-term investments. Cash management policies of corporations are critical to the effective management of their cash position and to the maximization of total earnings. Advanced cash management techniques are not discussed in this book but are very important to the shareholders and management of corporations.

Statement Analysis Considerations

One concern that might be expressed regarding cash is restrictions placed on its use. Sometimes a corporation's cash is restricted with regard to withdrawal from the bank because of a feature known as compensating balances. These are minimum balances that must be maintained in the bank account to avoid significant service charges or, in some cases, to satisfy restrictive loan covenants (which are clauses in loan agreements that are designed to reduce the risk to the lender). A corporation

---

ETHICS IN ACCOUNTING

The handling of cash in any business can be a source of ethical dilemmas for managers and employees. Strict controls must be placed on who within the organization handles cash, and how cash is to be handled. The set of controls put in place by a business to control cash (or any other asset or liability) is sometimes referred to as the internal control system. Internal controls are not based on the assumption that people are basically dishonest. Rather, it is up to management to ensure that employees do not have opportunity to become dishonest.

Suppose, for example, that you own a parking lot and have hired an employee to collect fees from individuals who park in the lot. What controls do you think would be necessary to ensure that all the cash the employee collects is received by you? What characteristics would you look for in the person you hire to do this job?

There are certain basic guidelines on control issues that corporations should consider. By "control," we mean the coordination of activities toward the achievement of corporate objectives, including the identification and mitigation of known risks, the identification and exploitation of opportunities, and the capacity to respond and adapt to the unexpected. Control can provide assurance regarding a broad range of objectives in three general categories: the effectiveness and efficiency of operations, the reliability of financial and management reporting, and compliance with applicable laws and regulations and corporate policies.

The ethical questions arise in thinking of management's attitudes towards their employees. Should they assume all employees are dishonest and will steal if they think they can get away with it? Or should they design controls to ensure employees are not tempted by opportunities?

might also restrict cash to a specific use. In this case, the restricted cash should be segregated from other amounts of cash. Other than these, there are no special considerations with regard to cash for financial statement analysis beyond those that were already discussed in conjunction with the understanding of the statement of changes in financial position (the cash flow statement) in Chapter 5.

◖◗ TEMPORARY INVESTMENTS

As mentioned in the cash section, the management of cash is an important part of managing a corporation. One aspect of the management of cash is the corporation's desire to minimize the corporation's cash balance given that currency or chequing accounts normally earn no returns. One way to convert cash into an earning asset is to invest it in temporary (short-term) investments in marketable securities. **Marketable securities** are **securities** (i.e., assets that are publicly traded) that represent either a debt interest (Treasury Bills, bonds, or Guaranteed Investment Certificates) or an equity interest (shares) in another entity. The more active the trading in the security, the easier it is to convert the security back into cash when the cash is needed for other purposes. The ability to turn an investment back into cash quickly is known as **liquidity** and is an important aspect of managing the corporation's cash position.

Securities that are not marketable would likely not qualify as current assets of the corporation because they might not be easily converted into cash within a year. They would probably be classified as noncurrent investments. The discussion in this section is restricted to marketable securities.

The probable future value associated with marketable securities comes from two sources. One source is the periodic payments that these securities produce while they are being held. If the security is a debt security, these payments represent interest. For convenience, many organizations treat debt securities with short-term maturities, e.g., three months, as equivalent to cash. Payments received from equity securities represent dividends. The second source of value is the value of the securities when sold in the future. If the intention is to hold these securities for the short term (less than one year), then the resale price becomes very important. If the intention is to hold these securities for the long term (more than one year), the resale price is not as important. Securities held for the long term are usually called long-term investments and do not appear under the heading of temporary investments in the balance sheet.

The uncertainty, or risk, associated with the future value from temporary investments relates to both the periodic payments and the ultimate sales value. The issuers of debt, for example, may default on the payments. This not only causes uncertainty with regard to the periodic payments, but also reduces the value of a security in terms of its final price. With regard to equity securities, there is no guarantee that dividends will continue at present levels, nor is there any guarantee of the ultimate sales value. The corporation may fail, making the equity shares worthless.

The uncertainty with regard to the future cash flows of a security is sometimes evidenced by the volatility of the price of the security in the securities markets. If you read the business section of the newspaper, you should be well aware of the volatility of the markets for equity securities (shares). The market prices of shares fluctuate for many reasons. An example of a large fluctuation in share price was Loewen Group Inc. in 1995, when its share price ranged from $54 to $32.75. Loewen is an operator of funeral homes in Canada and the U. S. who was sued in the U. S. for $10,000,000 for breach of contract. The American court found against Loewen and awarded damages against them of $500,000,000 (U. S.). Loewen's share price fell $10 in the first few days after the court decision, an amount roughly equal to the amount of the award if allocated on a per share basis.

A similar volatility has been present in recent years in the markets for debt securities (bond markets). The degree of uncertainty depends on the type of security and on the financial health of the issuing entity. Debt securities, for example, may be viewed as quite safe if they are issued by the government, such as Canadian government bonds. At the other extreme are corporate bonds issued by very highly leveraged corporations (highly leveraged means total liabilities greatly exceed total equities). These bonds are sometimes called *junk bonds*. Junk bonds pay very high interest rates to compensate for the high risk that their principal may not be repaid. Equity securities offer a similar spectrum of risk.

The ownership criterion of these assets is relatively straightforward. For some securities, pieces of paper can be held by the owner that represent ownership (share certificates and bonds). In many cases, however, no certificates are issued and ownership is evidenced by entries in an account maintained by an outside party (such as a broker).

Temporary Investments Valuation Methods

One method that could be used to value temporary investments is to record them at their **historical cost**. With this method, changes in the market value of the investments have no effect on the balance sheet or income statement until the investment is actually sold. Income is recognized at the time the investment is sold and is termed a **realized gain** or **loss**. In addition, income is recognized with this method as periodic payments are received in the form of dividends or interest revenue.

A second method would be to value temporary investments at their market value. In its pure form, this method means that changes in the market value of the investments would cause changes in the carrying value on the balance sheet and corresponding recognition of income on the income statement. The changes in market value are called **unrealized gains** or **losses**. Upon sale of the investments, there will be no further recognition of income because the investment is already valued at its market value at the time of sale. In addition, the periodic receipts of interest and dividends are recognized as income.

A third possible method is to measure the purchasing power of the cash flows received from the investments. Debt securities, for example, represent fixed amounts of cash (interest and principal) that are to be received at specific dates in the future (payment dates). The purchasing power of these future cash flows is subject to the same risk from inflation as cash that is held today. In other words, the cash received a year from now may buy fewer goods than it does today. Assets that represent fixed cash flows in the future (such as the debt security) are called **monetary assets**. This third valuation method measures the changes in purchasing power of the debt security and reports the gain or loss in purchasing power in the income statement.

Nonmonetary assets, such as inventory, do not represent fixed cash flows to be received in the future. The cash to be received from the sale of inventory, for example, could change in response to inflation or the market forces of supply and demand. If the economy has 10% inflation, it may be possible to raise the inventory's selling price by 10% to match the inflation rate. Whether this is possible or not depends on the supply and demand characteristics of the specific type of inventory.

GAAP and Temporary Investments

The accounting for temporary investments is quite simple. Temporary investments are held in place of cash, so the intention is to show them at the amount of cash that is expected to be received from them. However, this intention is modified to show a conservative figure. Therefore, temporary investments are shown at their cost, unless their market value has declined to below cost. If this happens, they are shown at the market value. We call this method the **lower of cost and market** method. This is a hybrid of the two methods discussed earlier, historical cost (i.e., the amount paid for the securities when they were purchased) and market value. The **lower of cost and market** method uses cost, except in situations where the market value of the portfolio is less than the historical cost, and then the market value is used. The gain resulting from a market value higher than cost is not recognized. This one-sided rule with regard to market values was adopted based on the conservative principle in accounting which states, in essence, that losses should be recognized as soon as they can be estimated, but that gains should be deferred until they are realized.

The implementation of this method presents several issues that must be resolved. The first is a classification issue. When a corporation invests in a temporary investment, it must first decide whether to classify the investment as a current or noncurrent asset. The classification is generally based on the intent of management and on the marketability of the asset. If management intends to hold the security for less than one year, and if it is readily marketable, it will be classified as a current asset. Otherwise, it will be classified as noncurrent, in which case the account will be called a long-term investment rather than a temporary or short-term investment.

A second issue that is important in the accounting for investments in marketable equity securities is the amount of control the acquiring corporation will have over the acquired corporation. Most equity securities are shares that carry a vote entitling the owner to vote for the board of directors, which has direct authority over management. For short-term investments, there is usually no intention on the part of the acquiring corporation to exercise control. In fact, the number of shares usually purchased as a short-term investment (a relatively small number) do not allow an acquiring corporation to exercise much control. With long-term investments in shares, there may be some intention to control the corporation. In some cases, for example, the acquiring corporation will buy 100% of the outstanding shares of the corporation. In this case, the acquiring corporation exercises absolute control over the acquired corporation. The accounting for corporations in which a corporation exercises significant control is different from that in which the corporation has little control (i.e., a passive investment). The accounting for investments in which there exists significant control is discussed in Chapter 13. In this chapter, only passive investments in securities are considered.

The data in Exhibit 6-2 for the Clifford Corporation is used to illustrate the application of the lower of cost and market method to short-term investments. You should assume that Clifford's year-end is December 31, and that it prepares income statements on a quarterly basis. You will notice that Clifford buys three securities during the first quarter (the first three months in the year). The exhibit then tracks the performance of the portfolio during the year.

EXHIBIT 6-2

CLIFFORD CORPORATION
Temporary Investments Data

Security	Quarter Acquired	Acquisition Cost	Quarter Sold	Selling Price
A	1	$10,000	3	$14,000
B	1	$20,000	4	$18,000
C	1	$30,000	—	—

Values as of the End of

	Quarter 1		Quarter 2		Quarter 3		Quarter 4	
Security	Cost	Market	Cost	Market	Cost	Market	Cost	Market
A	$10,000	$11,000	$10,000	$13,000	—	—	—	—
B	$20,000	$17,000	$20,000	$21,000	$20,000	$17,000	—	—
C	$30,000	$29,000	$30,000	$28,000	$30,000	$29,000	$30,000	$28,500
Portfolio	$60,000	$57,000	$60,000	$62,000	$50,000	$46,000	$30,000	$28,500

Dividends Received

Quarter	Amount
1	$500
2	$525
3	$420
4	$250

■■ ■ Initial Acquisition

The initial acquisition entry is the same as the entry to acquire any other asset. To illustrate, the following entries would record the acquisition of the temporary investments during the first quarter of the year:

FOR INVESTMENT A:		
A – Temporary Investments	10,000	
A – Cash		10,000
FOR INVESTMENT B:		
A – Temporary Investments	20,000	
A – Cash		20,000
FOR INVESTMENT C:		
A – Temporary Investments	30,000	
A – Cash		30,000

■ ■ Dividend Recognition

Dividend income is recognized each period as dividends are declared. In Exhibit 6-2, the dividends from all three shares have been aggregated into one amount. The entry to record these dividends in Quarter 1 would be as follows:

AT DECLARATION DATE		
A – Dividends Receivable	500	
SE – Dividend Revenue		500
AT PAYMENT DATE:		
A – Cash	500	
A – Dividends Receivable		500

■ ■ Recognition of Unrealized Losses/Recoveries and Realized Gains and Losses

The lower of cost and market rule requires that, at any financial statement date, the corporation compares the aggregate market value of its portfolio to its cost to determine the lower of the two. The corporation is then required to carry its portfolio at this lower value. Note that, for Quarter 1 at March 31 in Exhibit 6-2, the portfolio should be carried at $57,000 because this is the lower of cost and the market value. The write-down from the cost of $60,000 would result in an *unrealized* loss of $3,000, which would appear in the income statement.

The lower of cost and market rule can be applied on one of two bases: either compare the totals for the entire portfolio of investments, or apply the rule to individual securities. For example, if we were to apply the lower of cost and market rule on an individual basis, shares B and C would be written down to their market values, but share A would remain at cost. This would result in an unrealized loss of $4,000, which is larger than the loss that results when the rule is applied on a portfolio basis. This occurs because the portfolio basis allows that unrealized gains on some securities (such as share A) can offset unrealized losses on other securities (shares B and C). Most corporations tend to use the portfolio basis as most corporations manage their temporary investments on a portfolio basis. Therefore, this valuation method better reflects the value of the portfolio to the corporation.

The entry to record the reduction in the carrying value of the temporary investments and the unrealized loss would be:

LOWER OF COST AND MARKET ENTRY AT END OF QUARTER 1 AT MARCH 31:

SE – Unrealized Loss on Valuation of Temporary Investments	3,000	
XA – Valuation Allowance for Temporary Investments		3,000

For the current portfolio, the preceding debit entry affects the income statement; that is, unrealized losses are shown on the income statement. The credit entry is to a contra-asset account (see Appendix B for contra-asset accounts). The account is contra to the temporary investments account and reduces the portfolio of securities to its aggregate market value. **The valuation allowance account** is sometimes called the *allowance for the excess of cost of marketable securities over market value account*. It is similar to an accumulated amortization account in that it preserves the historical-cost amounts in the temporary investments account that are needed for disclosure and tax purposes. The effects on the balance sheet and income statement of the application of the lower of cost and market rule, as well as the other events that affect marketable securities, are summarized in Exhibit 6-3.

EXHIBIT 6-3

CLIFFORD CORPORATION
Financial Statement (Partial)

Income Statement

Quarter	Quarter 1	Quarter 2	Quarter 3	Quarter 4
Unrealized holding loss on valuation of temporary investments	($3,000)	—	($4,000)	—
Recovery of unrealized holding loss on valuation of temporary investments	—	$3,000	—	$2,500
Realized gain (loss) on sale of temporary investments	—	—	$4,000	($2,000)
Dividend revenue	$500	$525	$420	$250
Effect on net income of temporary investments	($2,500)	$3,525	$420	($ 750)

Balance Sheet

Quarter	Quarter 1	Quarter 2	Quarter 3	Quarter4
Temporary Investments (at cost)	$60,000	$60,000	$50,000	$30,000
Less valuation allowance	($3,000)	$0	($4,000)	($1,500)
Temporary Investments (at LCM)	$57,000	$60,000	$46,000	$28,500

In Quarter 2, Clifford again recognizes dividend revenue. At the end of Quarter 2 at June 30, when the corporation applies the lower of cost and market rule again, you should note that the market value of the portfolio has recovered and, in fact, has gone up above the original cost of the securities purchased. GAAP allows that the corporation can recover unrealized losses but can never recognize unrealized gains above the original cost of the securities. This means that Clifford can recover the $3,000 unrealized loss it recorded in the first quarter to bring the portfolio back to its original cost of $60,000 but that it cannot recognize the unrealized gain of $2,000 above the original acquisition cost. The entry to record the recovery would be as follows:

LOWER OF COST AND MARKET ENTRY AT END OF QUARTER 2 AT JUNE 30

XA – Valuation Allowance for Temporary Investments	3,000	
SE – Recovery of Unrealized Loss on Valuation		
of Temporary Investments		3,000

As shown in Exhibit 6-3, the effect of the preceding entries would be to record a recovery (gain) on the income statement in Quarter 2, and the debit entry brings the balance in the valuation allowance account to zero.

In the third quarter, Clifford recognized dividend revenue and sold security A for $14,000. A realized gain is recorded for the sale transaction because security A cost only $10,000 originally. The gain or loss that is recorded equals the difference between the acquisition cost of the investment and its selling price. To record this sale in the third quarter, the following entry would be made:

A – Cash	14,000	
A – Temporary Investments		10,000
SE – Realized Gain on Sale of Temporary Investments		4,000

Realized gains or losses always appear on the income statement as shown in Exhibit 6-3.

At the end of Quarter 3 at September 30, the corporation again applies the lower of cost and market rule. Recognize that the portfolio now has one less security, because security A was sold during the period. The analysis indicated that the portfolio should be carried at market because it is lower than cost. The adjustment to the allowance account is for the full difference between the cost and market because the balance in the valuation allowance account is zero. The entry at the end of Quarter 3 at September 30 is:

LOWER OF COST AND MARKET ENTRY AT END OF QUARTER 3 AT SEPTEMBER 30

SE – Unrealized Loss on Valuation of Temporary Investments	4,000	
XA – Valuation Allowance for Temporary Investments		4,000

In the fourth quarter of the year, Clifford sells security B for $18,000 and continues to hold security C at the end of the quarter, which is also the year-end date of December 31. The sale of security B results in a realized loss of $2,000 because its acquisition cost was $20,000. The amount of unrealized losses is not considered in calculating the realized loss. The following entry is made for the sale of security B:

A – Cash	18,000	
SE – Realized Loss on Sale of Temporary Investment	2,000	
A – Temporary Investments		20,000

The evaluation of the lower of cost and market rule at the end of Quarter 4 indicates that the market value of the portfolio (the portfolio now consists of only one security) is lower than the cost by $1,500. As the balance in the allowance account is $4,000, Clifford will have to recognize a recovery of $2,500 to bring the balance back to $1,500. The following entry will accomplish this:

LOWER OF COST AND MARKET ENTRY AT END OF QUARTER 4 AT DECEMBER 31		
XA – Valuation Allowance for Temporary Investments	2,500	
SE – Recovery of Unrealized Loss on Valuation		
of Temporary Investments		2,500

Again, Exhibit 6-3 summarizes the results of the transactions affecting the marketable securities in Quarter 4.

The disclosure of the effects of transactions involving temporary investments in a typical set of financial statements tends to be somewhat limited because of the insignificant nature of these transactions relative to the other transactions of the corporation. Even though GAAP requires that market value of temporary investments be disclosed, many corporations may simply list a line item for temporary investments on the balance sheet and have a note stating that the securities are carried at cost, which approximates market. No detail may be provided concerning the amount of dividend revenue or the amount of realized and unrealized gains and losses that are recognized. When the amounts are significant, however, a note to the financial statements generally provides the details.

Examples of disclosures of market values of temporary investments are shown in Exhibit 6-4.

■ ■ Long-Term Investments

Accounting rules for noncurrent investments are different from the rules for short-term investments and are discussed in Chapter 13.

EXHIBIT 6-4

EXAMPLES OF DISCLOSURE OF TEMPORARY INVESTMENTS

Imperial Metals Corporation

	December 31 1994	March 31 1994
Marketable securities [Market value $796, 138 (March 31, 1994 – $916, 463)]	508,572	343,968

Bema Gold Corporation

	December 31 1994	December 31 1993
Marketable securities, at cost (Market 1994 – $1,298; 1993 – $926)	1,270	779

AN INTERNATIONAL PERSPECTIVE
REPORTS FROM OTHER COUNTRIES

Most countries use the lower of cost and market rule in the valuation of marketable securities. In some countries, however, the application of the rule varies somewhat. For example, the following disclosure from Note 5 from the 1995 financial statements of Matsushita Electric Co. Ltd. (Japan) illustrates the use of the lower of cost and market for a Japanese Corporation.

Marketable equity securities included in short-term investments and in investments and advances are carried at the lower of cost or market, cost being determined by the average method. Other items included in short-term investments, primarily marketable securities classified as current assets and those included in investments and advances, are carried at cost or less.

In addition to the difference mentioned above, there is conformity in Germany (as there is in several other countries, such as France and Japan) between what is reported to the tax authority and what is reported to shareholders. In the application of the lower of cost and market rule, if the securities are written down in one period, they may be written back up in a subsequent period. However, because of the tax conformity, this would not be in the best interest of the corporation from a tax perspective and, therefore, the write-up may not occur. In the 1990 financial statements of Siemens, an electrical and electronics manufacturer, the following footnote appeared:

(9) Marketable securities and notes

. . . For tax reasons, write-downs of DM24.6 million made in prior years were not reversed in 1989/90, although the market price of such securities increased during the year. This reduced net income by DM 10 million.

◤◣ Statement Analysis Considerations

If marketable securities make up a significant portion of the current assets of the corporation, the potential effects that the unrecognized gains and losses have on the financial health of the corporation being analyzed should be recognized. If the portfolio is being held at the lower of cost and market, you have some idea already of the loss potential of the securities as some portion of it has already been recognized. Remember, though, that, if the lower of cost and market rule is applied on a portfolio basis, gains on some securities can offset losses on others. Also, if the market value of the securities is above the cost, this unrealized gain will not have been recognized. Unrecorded gains or losses could make any ratio using net income misleading. The disclosure requirements for marketable securities are such that you can usually get information about both of these amounts from the notes to the financial statements as Canadian GAAP requires that market values of temporary investments be disclosed.

◖◗ ACCOUNTS RECEIVABLE

Accounts receivable are amounts owed from customers that resulted from the normal business transactions of selling goods and services on credit. The ownership criterion for accounts receivable is evidenced either by a formal contractual agreement or by some other less formal arrangement such as a sales invoice. The probable future value criterion would be met by the fact that a receivable is the right to receive payment at some future date. The cash that is received at that future date can then be exchanged for other goods and services. The value of the cash that is to be received in the future is affected by the same uncertainties that we described in the earlier section on cash. In addition to those uncertainties, there is also the uncertainty that the customer will not pay the cash as agreed. A complete default by the customer would be called a **bad debt**. This makes the valuation of accounts receivables less certain than the valuation of cash.

Other uncertainties with accounts receivable are that the customer might return the goods for credit, the customer may request a price adjustment if the goods are damaged in shipment, or the customer may pay less than what is listed on the bill if allowed a discount for prompt payment. All these factors impact the uncertainty of collecting accounts receivable.

◤◣ Accounts Receivable Valuation Methods

An account receivable is an agreement to pay a certain amount at some point in the future. A simple way to value the receivable is to add up the gross payments called for in the agreement. This *gross payments method* would ignore the effects of bad debts (customers that do not pay), returns, and so forth, as well as the effects of the *time value of money*. The time value of money refers to the concept that a dollar paid tomorrow is worth less than a dollar paid today. The reasoning here is that an investor can invest the dollar received today and have more than a dollar by tomorrow. Therefore, if the corporation has a receivable for $100 to be received a month from now, it is worth less than $100 today.

A second method for valuing an account receivable is to take into consideration the time value of the gross payments to be received. Using the terminology of the time value of money, we would want to compute the *present value* of the future cash flows of the receivable. We would *discount* the future cash flows, using an appropriate interest rate to arrive at this present value. See Appendix 1 at the end of the text, for a full discussion of the computation of present values.

A third method is to take into consideration the possibility that the receivable may not be paid. This could result from a default by the customer, or the return of the goods. Partial payment might also result if the customer pays early, taking advantage of a cash discount, or if the customer demands a price concession. Incorporating these events into the valuation would mean reducing the receivable. This alternative can be used in conjunction with either the first (gross payments) or the second (present value) method of valuing the receivable.

The purchasing power concepts that were discussed in the cash section might be considered as another valuation possibility. An account receivable typically represents the right to receive a fixed amount of cash at a specific point in time; that is, it is a monetary asset (we discussed monetary assets earlier in this chapter). The right to receive a fixed amount of cash is subject to the same kinds of changes in value due to inflation as is cash.

Finally, a valuation method based on the market value of the accounts receivable might also be considered. Accounts receivable can be sold to other parties, who then collect from the customer. The process of selling accounts receivable is referred to as **factoring**. If a ready market is available in which to sell a receivable, a market price can be used as a value for the receivable.

◤◥ GAAP and Accounts Receivable

Most Canadian companies show receivables at the present value of the gross payments less appropriate allowances for bad debts, returns, and so forth. There is, however, a materiality consideration. If there is little difference between the present value and the gross payments, such as occurs with receivables expected to be paid in a relatively short period of time, the gross payments may be used. The use of present value adds some complications to the accounting for receivables and, unless the accounting for present value makes a significant difference, it is probably not worth the effort. For most corporations, the time between sale and collection is relatively short (say, 30 to 60 days). Unless interest rates are extremely high, the difference between the present value and the gross payments for these types of receivables is relatively small. Therefore, most corporations account for their accounts receivable at the gross amount less the allowance for bad debts, returns, and so forth. The adjustment for these allowances are necessary because the corporation does not want to overstate its assets or its income from sales to customers. For example, consider a corporation that sells $10,000 worth of goods during the accounting period, all on account. The entry to record this transaction is:

| A – Accounts Receivable | 10,000 | |
| SE – Sales Revenue | | 10,000 |

If the corporation anticipates that it will collect the entire $10,000, the preceding entry would appropriately state the effects of the transaction on assets and shareholders' wealth. However, if the corporation anticipates that some customers will not pay, this entry overstates the receivables as well as the shareholders' wealth.

The likelihood that a customer will default on payments depends on the customer's credit worthiness. A corporation can improve its chances of receiving payments by performing a credit check on its customers before it grants them credit. The corporation must balance its desire to sell its product to the customer against the likelihood that the customer will pay. Too strict a credit policy means that many customers will be denied credit and will purchase their goods from other suppliers. Too loose a credit policy and the corporation may lose more money from bad debts than it makes from good sales. The corporation should do a cost/benefit analysis to decide what its credit policy should be.

In addition to a policy on bad debts, other policies can affect the amounts collected. One of these is the return policy of the corporation. Can customers return goods, and under what circumstances? Again, the strictness or looseness of the policy will have an effect on whether customers will buy goods from the corporation. A second policy that should be considered is whether the corporation offers a cash discount for early payment. If so, the amount of cash that will be collected from the receivable will depend on how many customers pay early. How many pay early will depend on how attractive the discount is. Both of these policies require some adjustment to the amounts recorded in the receivable as well as in the sales revenue account.

The accounting methods for anticipated bad debts or doubtful (sometimes referred to as "uncollectible") accounts are illustrated in the section that follows. Recognize that similar methods could be used to account for the other adjustments to accounts receivable, such as cash discounts and sales returns. For a more complete description of the accounting for discounts and returns, refer to an intermediate accounting text.

Accounting for doubtful accounts requires adjustments to the accounts receivable account as well as the recognition of the related bad debts expense in the income statement. Some smaller businesses used the direct write-off method, but most corporations use what is called the allowance method to recognize doubtful accounts.

Direct Write-Off Method

The direct write-off method recognizes the loss from the uncollectible account in the period in which the corporation decides the account is, in fact, uncollectible. The decision by the corporation that the account is uncollectible is usually based on a bad debt policy. For example, the policy may state that accounts will be declared uncollectible if they have been outstanding for more than 120 days. This policy is based on the corporation's experience with collecting from its customers and usually means that the probability of collecting the account after 120 days is so small that it is not worth pursuing. The corporation may still try to collect this account, but it will probably turn it over to a collection agency, which will pursue the customer.

Consider the example accompanying the preceding journal entry. Suppose that during the same period in which the $10,000 worth of goods were sold, $300 worth of accounts receivable were identified as being more than 120 days overdue. These accounts should be *written off*. With the direct write-off method, the entry to record this is:

SE – Bad Debt Expense	300	
A – Accounts Receivable		300
(Specific Accounts Receivable would be written off)		

Note that the debit to the bad debt expense account reduces net income in this period. Bad debt expense is somewhat different from other "expenses." It is not accompanied by a related cash outflow. It is more like a reduction in a revenue account in the sense that it represents revenues the corporation will never receive. In recognition of this, a few corporations report this as a direct reduction in the sales revenue amount on the income statement. These corporations report a line item which they call *net sales*, where they mean *net* to mean that the bad debt expense has been netted out against the sales revenue amount. However, almost all corporations show bad debts as an expense grouped with other expenses and not as a reduction of the revenues.

The credit entries to the accounts receivable account are to specific customer accounts; the corporation has identified exactly who it is that has not paid. For example, the $300 might be in two specific accounts, a $180 account from Joe Lee and a $120 account from Mary Smith. The accounts receivable balance is generally supported by what is called a *subsidiary ledger*, in which individual separate receivable accounts are maintained for each customer. This entry would cause reductions in the accounts of both Joe Lee and Mary Smith.

The direct write-off method is a simple way to account for bad debts. The corporation makes every reasonable effort to collect the account, and when it finally decides that an account is uncollectible, it records the preceding entry to remove it from the system. The problem with this method is that it violates the matching concept discussed in Chapter 4. As you will recall, the matching concept states that all expenses related to the production of revenue should be matched with the revenue in the period in which the revenue is recognized. The direct write-off method could result in the revenue being recognized in one accounting period and the associated bad debt expense recorded in the following period. If bad debts are not material, then this mismatching can probably be ignored. If bad debts are significant, however, this mismatching can distort the measurement of performance enough that most accountants would find this method unacceptable. A more appropriate method when bad debts are significant is the allowance method, which is discussed next.

Before we leave the direct write-off method, we should mention that this method is sometimes put into practice because it is very simple to use. For example, when bad debts are a very small amount, the misstatement involved in using the direct write-off method is not large. Small corporations may also use the direct write-off method as it simplifies bookkeeping.

Allowance Methods

Let us sumamrize here two key points. First, the matching concept requires that when a corporation recognizes revenue from a sale, it must also recognize all expenses relating to that sale. Second, bad debts are technically not expenses; they are reductions in revenues. These reductions in revenues should be recognized at the same time as the revenues are recognized. Because, at that point, the corporation does not know which customers will end up as bad debts, it must make some estimates of what dollar amount of sales will ultimately be uncollectible. These estimates are usually based on the corporation's past experience with its customers. New businesses usually have little basis for initial estimates and so must use some other method of making an estimate.

Using the example begun in the section on direct write-offs, assume that the corporation estimates that, of the $10,000 in sales, $325 will ultimately prove uncollectible. One method used to arrive at this estimate is discussed later in the chapter. As the corporation is not able to identify the customers that will not pay, the $325 cannot directly reduce specific accounts receivable. Therefore, the following entry records this amount in an account that is contra to the accounts receivable account. This contra-account, which is usually called the *allowance for doubtful accounts*, reduces that aggregate amount of accounts receivable for the anticipated effects of uncollectible accounts. As in the direct write-off method, the debit is to the bad debt expense account.

The allowance for doubtful accounts normally has a credit balance because its purpose is to show that the full debit balance amount in the accounts receivable will not be collected. In effect it reduces the accounts receivable total to the net amount of cash that the corporation actually expects to receive. Remember that the allowance account is a contra to accounts receivable and is grouped with that current asset.

SE — Bad Debt Expense	325	
XA — Allowance for Doubtful Accounts		325

Note that the effects of this entry are to reduce the net carrying value of the accounts receivable (the accounts receivable balance less the balance in the allowance account) from $10,000 to $9,675 ($10,000 − $325) and to reduce the net income by the same amount. Accounts receivable are now stated at the amount the corporation ultimately expects to collect in cash.

The write-off of accounts receivable, with the allowance method, occurs when the cutoff date specified in the write-off policy is met. Assume that we are using the same policy as with the direct write-off method, that is, that accounts are written off after 120 days. In our example, nonpayments resulted in $300 in write-offs (see the direct write-off method section). With the allowance method, this means that we have now specifically identified customer accounts that are bad, which we were unable to identify at the time we recognized the bad debt expense. No further expense should be recognized. We should simply remove the specific account from the accounts receivable and remove an equivalent amount from the allowance account because some portion of the allowance account is no longer necessary. The entry is:

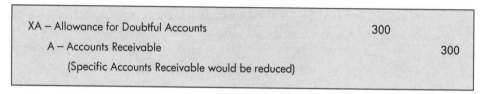

XA – Allowance for Doubtful Accounts	300	
A – Accounts Receivable		300
(Specific Accounts Receivable would be reduced)		

What happens if one of the accounts we have written off is paid? This is called a **recovery**. Recoveries, under the allowance method, are accounted for by reinstating the account receivable. This is accomplished by reversing the write-off entry and then showing the normal cash collection entry. The following two entries would be made if an account worth $50 was recovered after having been written off. Note that, whereas one net entry can be made to accomplish the recording of this transaction, if no entry is made to the accounts receivable account, the customer's account will always be shown in the records as having been a bad debt.

(a) To reverse the write-off entry:		
A – Accounts Receivable	50	
XA – Allowance for Doubtful Accounts		50
(b) To record the cash receipt		
A – Cash	50	
A – Accounts Receivable		50

Assume that this was the first year of this corporation's operations and that the corporation had collected $8,500 from its customers by the end of the year. Exhibit 6-5 illustrates the entries and balances in the accounts receivable and the allowance for doubtful accounts.

The ending balance in the accounts receivable account ($1,200) represents those accounts that have not been collected as of the end of the accounting period. In our example, the maximum amount of time any of these accounts can have been outstanding is 120 days; any account beyond that time is written off. The ending balance in the allowance for doubtful accounts should be the remaining allowance that applies to the ending balance in accounts receivable. In other words, the corporation expects that, of the remaining $1,200 in accounts receivable, $75 will prove to be uncollectible.

EXHIBIT 6-5

Allowance Method for Doubtful Accounts

A – Accounts Receivable

Beginning Balance	0		
Credit sales	10,000	8,500	Cash collections
Recoveries	50	300	Write-offs
		50	Collections from recoveries
Ending balance	1,200		

XA – Allowance for Doubtful Accounts

		0	Beginning balance
Write-offs	300	325	Bad debt expense
		50	Recoveries
		75	Ending balance

In most financial statements, the allowance account is netted against the accounts receivable account to produce a single line item on the balance sheet. Few corporations provide details of the amount of the allowance.

One final point to consider about the accounting for doubtful accounts is the method used to estimate the dollar amounts that are doubtful. A method that is commonly used is called the **percentage of credit sales method.** This method will be described below. Another method that is used is called the **ageing of accounts receivable method.** We will leave the discussion of this method to intermediate accounting texts.

■ ■ Percentage of Credit Sales Method

The **percentage of credit sales method** is based on the assumption that the amount of bad debt expense is a function of the total sales made on credit. It estimates the bad debt *expense* for the period by multiplying the credit sales during the period by an appropriate percentage. The percentage is determined based on the past collection history of the corporation. In the example above, the $325 of bad debt expense that was used could have been the result of using 3.25% of credit sales as an estimate of the bad debts (3.25% of the $10,000 in credit sales would have resulted in the estimate of bad debts expense of $325). In a new corporation, the percentage may be determined initially by considering the bad debt experience of other corporations in the same industry. In an existing corporation, historical data are generally used to estimate this percentage as adjusted for present and anticipated future economic conditions. For example, in a recession, bad debt percentages often rise.

The initial estimate of the percentage must be adjusted from time to time to reflect the recent credit experience of the corporation. If the corporation is experiencing more write-offs than were estimated, the percentage should be increased. Corporations typically do not go back to prior periods to adjust this percentage but adjust it on a prospective basis. Therefore, an overestimate or an underestimate in one period will be adjusted in the following period. The percentage can be affected by the types of customers that the corporations has, a change in credit policy, and general economic conditions, such as recessions and changes in unemployment.

Note that, with the percentage of sales method, the ending balance in the allowance for doubtful accounts results from simply totalling the entries to the account. The percentage relationship between the *ending* balance in the allowance account and the accounts receivable account has nothing to do with the percentage used to estimate bad debt expense. In the example, the ratio of the ending balance in the allowance account to the accounts receivable account is 6.25% ($75/$1,200). This is considerably higher than the 3.25% bad debts the corporation estimated as its percentage of sales. This is not inconsistent, however, as a higher percentage of the accounts receivable that are left at the end of the period may not be paid. For example, many of them may be approaching the 120-day limit, which means that the probability of collecting them is becoming extremely small.

■◑■ NOTES RECEIVABLE

Notes receivable are very similar to accounts receivable in their fundamental characteristics. Therefore, we will not discuss the recognition criteria and valuation methods; they are the same as for accounts receivable. The difference between an account receivable and a note receivable is that the note receivable is evidenced by a more formal agreement referred to as a **promissory note**. A promissory note is a written contract between two parties, the *maker* and the *payee*. The maker promises to pay specific amounts either upon demand by the payee, or at a definite date in the future.

Interest may be shown explicitly as a part of the note, or it may be implicit in the contractual payments. When interest is explicit, it is typically calculated by multiplying the explicit interest rate by the face value of the note times the time factor. The presumption here is that the face value is the amount that has been borrowed via the note. A note in which the interest is implicit specifies the amount to be paid at maturity (the face value), which will be larger than the initial amount borrowed. The interest is the difference between the amount borrowed and the face value. These are sometimes called *discounted notes*.

The maturity of notes is generally longer than accounts receivable, but is usually less than a year; hence, the notes are usually considered current assets. Long-term notes receivable are classified in the noncurrent assets section.

Notes are most commonly arranged with banks or other financial institutions. These financial institutions may require that the maker of the note put up some type of **collateral** for the note. **Collateral** is some asset that the payee has the right to receive if the maker defaults on the note. As an example, think of an individual who purchases a car by using a loan from a bank or finance company. The bank would use the new car as collateral for the loan.

A note secured by collateral is called a **secured** note. The collateral may be some type of real property, such as real estate, or personal property, such as equipment or inventory. Depending on the credit worthiness of the maker, a financial institution may issue an *unsecured* note, which means no collateral is specified.

AN INTERNATIONAL PERSPECTIVE
REPORTS FROM OTHER COUNTRIES

The estimation of uncollectible accounts is accomplished in some countries (e.g., France and Germany) by considering the circumstances of individual accounts rather than by estimating an overall percentage rate such as with the percentage of sales method discussed earlier. Note that this is not the same as the direct write-off method because the estimate of the amount uncollectible from an individual account may precede the actual write-off. This method also seems to be used by some corporations in Japan, as evidenced by the following disclosure in the 1991 financial statement of Mitsubishi Materials Corporation:

MITSUBISHI MATERIALS CORPORATION

Note 11 – Provision for Bad Debts and Write-off of investments—Unconsolidated Subsidiaries

Provisions for bad debts and write-off of investments—unconsolidated subsidiaries for each of the three years ended March 31, 1991 were as follows:

	Millions of yen			Thousands of U.S. dollars (Note 1-a)
	1991	1990	1989	1991
Provision for bad debt allowance:				
Akenobe Mining Co., Ltd.	¥ 116	¥ 233	¥ 350	$ 822
Hosokura Mining and Smelting Co. Ltd.	236	288	198	1,674
Yatani Mining Co., Ltd.	85	266	84	603
Furutobe Mining Co., Ltd.	93	127	58	660
Chitose Mining Co., Ltd.	121	136	123	858
Osarizawa Mining Co., Ltd.	212	114	149	1,504
Katashina Mining Co., Ltd.	(127)	11	14	(901)
Nippon Electronic Materials Corp.	—	—	955	—
Japan High Purity Silica Co., Ltd.	1,140	—	—	8,085
Others	—	21	31	—
Write-off of investments:				
Nippon Electronic Materials Corp.	—	244	—	—
	¥1,876	¥1,440	¥1,962	$13,305

Interest on Notes Receivable

Interest on notes receivable can be either explicit or implied. A note with implied interest might state: "The maker of the note agrees to pay $1,050 at maturity in exchange for $1,000 today." The maker is borrowing $1,000 and, as the maturity payment is $1,050, the difference ($50) is interest. A note with explicit interest might state: "The maker agrees to pay the principal amount of $1,000 at maturity plus interest at a rate of 12% (always stated as an annual rate unless otherwise indicated) in exchange for $1,000 today." The dollar amount of interest in this case depends on how long it is between now and maturity.

Short-term notes receivable generally require that interest payments be calculated using **simple interest** calculations. Long-term notes, on the other hand, generally use **compound interest** calculations. Compound interest calculations are discussed in Appendix 1. Simple interest calculations are demonstrated in the following equation.

Interest charges are calculated based on the amount borrowed, the interest rate, and the amount of time that passes. The formula is:

> Simple Interest Formula: Interest = Principal × Interest Rate × Time

The principal is the amount borrowed, the interest rate is specified in the note and is stated as a yearly amount, and the time is the time that has elapsed, stated as a fraction of a year. The calculation of the time that has elapsed is generally measured in days. While the actual number of days can be used, many lenders simplify the calculation by considering that each month is composed of 30 days and, therefore, 360 days is treated as being equivalent to one year. This convention is used in the calculations that follow.

To illustrate the computation of interest and the accounting for notes, assume the following:

1. On November 30, 19X1, the Staker Corporation agrees to accept a note of $1,000 from the Wilks Corporation to satisfy an outstanding account receivable from Wilks. (This could happen if Wilks is having trouble meeting its payment or temporarily has some more pressing needs for its cash.) The note has a maturity of two months (60 days) and an interest rate of 12%.

2. Staker's fiscal year-end is December 31, and Wilks does not pay the note until maturity.

On acceptance of the note from Wilks, Staker makes the following entry:

A – Notes Receivable	1,000	
A – Accounts Receivable		1,000

Staker's entry reflects receipt of the note from Wilks and the reduction in its accounts receivable.

On December 31, 19X1, one month after receiving the note, Staker must close its books. This means that it must record the accrual of interest on the note from Wilks. The interest through December 31, 19X1 is calculated as follows:

$$
\begin{aligned}
\text{Interest} &= \text{Principal} \times \text{Interest Rate} \times \text{Time} \\
&= \$1,000 \times 12\% \times 30/360 \\
&= \$10
\end{aligned}
$$

The entry to record this amount is:

A – Interest Receivable	10	
SE – Interest Revenue		10

At the end of January, 19x2, Staker will receive payment from Wilks of $1,020. Staker will have to record the accrual of interest for the month of January and the receipt of cash. The calculation of interest is the same as the earlier one because another 30 days has passed. Two entries are shown on January 31, 19x2. The first records the accrual of the interest, and the second records the cash payment. Recognize that one combined entry could have been made. The entries are:

A – Interest Receivable	10	
SE – Interest Revenue		10
A – Cash	1,020	
A – Interest Receivable		20
A – Notes Receivable		1,000

Other entries are possible if the note has been paid off early or if the note is extended for an additional period of time. Another possibility is that the note may be sold to another party. This is the same as factoring accounts receivable. The note may be sold with or without recourse, meaning that if the maker does not pay the note at maturity, the third party that bought the note may or may not have the right to collect the amount owed from the payee.

Relatively few notes receivable appear on balance sheets because they are not common and their amounts are relatively small. Normally notes receivable are grouped with accounts receivable.

◼◐◼ FINANCIAL STATEMENT ANALYSIS CONSIDERATIONS

◼◣◼ Short-Term Liquidity

As discussed in Chapter 1, liquidity refers to the ability of the corporation to convert assets into cash to pay liabilities. An important part of the analysis of short-term liquidity comes from considering the short-term monetary assets on the balance sheet. There are at least two ratios that provide quantitative measures of short-term liquidity: the current ratio, and the quick ratio.

◼◣◼ Current Ratio

The current ratio is measured by comparing the current assets directly with the current liabilities. It is calculated as:

$$\text{Current Ratio} = \frac{\text{Current Assets}}{\text{Current Liabilities}}$$

Remember that current assets are those that are going to be converted into cash in the next year or operating cycle of the corporation, and that current liabilities are going to require the use of cash in the next year or operating cycle. As such, this ratio should normally be greater than 1; otherwise, it is difficult to see how the corporation will remain solvent in the next year. The rule of thumb for this ratio is that, to provide a margin of safety, for most businesses, the ratio should be approximately 2 or greater. However, the size of this ratio depends on the type of business and the type of assets and liabilities that are considered current.

Refer to Exhibit 5-22. The current ratio for AT Plastics in 1994 is:

CURRENT RATIO – AT PLASTICS: 1994

$$\text{Current Ratio} = \frac{\$55,090}{\$29,888} = 1.84$$

One caveat: the current ratio is fairly subject to manipulation by a corporation at the end of the year. This ratio may not, therefore, be a very reliable measure of liquidity. For example, consider a corporation that has $100 in current assets and $50 in current liabilities at the end of a given year. Its current ratio would be 2 ($100/$50). Suppose that $25 of the $100 is in cash and the rest is in inventory. Suppose further that the corporation uses up all its $25 in cash by paying off $25 worth of current liabilities at the end of the year. The current ratio becomes 3 ($75/$25); now the corporation looks more liquid. Notice, however, that the corporation is actually less liquid; in fact it is virtually illiquid, in the short term because it has no cash and must sell its inventory and wait until it collects on those sales before it will have any cash to pay its bills. In this case, the current ratio is deceptive.

Quick Ratio

One of the problems with the current ratio is that some assets in the current section may be much less liquid than others. For example, inventory is less liquid than accounts receivable, which is less liquid than cash. In some industries, inventory is very illiquid because of the long period of time that it may have to be held before sale. Consider, for example, the holding period in the manufacture of 12-year-old scotch whisky. The current ratio in such cases will not adequately measure the short-term liquidity of the corporation. The quick ratio is used in this case to assess the short-term liquidity. It differs from the current ratio only in that inventories are omitted from the numerator. It is calculated as:

$$\text{Quick Ratio} = \frac{\text{Current Assets} - \text{Inventories}}{\text{Current Liabilities}}$$

The rule of thumb for this ratio is that it should be approximately 1 or more. Again, the actual value depends somewhat on the type of industry. For AT Plastics, the calculation results in:

QUICK RATIO – AT PLASTICS: 1994

$$\text{Quick Ratio} = \frac{\$55,090 - 26,227}{\$29,888} = .966$$

Analysis of Accounts Receivable Using the Accounts Receivable Turnover Ratio

A corporation's cash flows are critical to its profitability and even to its survival. Because most corporations receive a significant amount of operating cash from the collection of their accounts receivable, the analysis of a corporation's short-term liquidity should consider its success in collecting its accounts receivable.

One of the common ratios used to assess the management of accounts receivable is the **accounts receivable turnover ratio**. This is calculated by dividing the sales revenue for the period by the average accounts receivable as follows:

$$\text{Accounts receivable turnover ratio} = \frac{\text{Total sales revenue}}{\text{Average accounts receivable}}$$

Calculating this ratio from financial statement data usually requires you to assume that all sales are on account. If the analyst has more detailed information about the composition of sales, then some adjustment can be made in the numerator to include only credit sales. In addition, information in the financial statements may indicate that not all receivables are from customers. Therefore, a more sophisticated calculation might include only customer receivables in the denominator as only these relate to the sales revenue figure in the numerator.

As an example, consider the information provided in Exhibit 6-6 from the 1994 and 1995 financial statements of Big Rock Brewery Ltd.

EXHIBIT 6-6

BIG ROCK BREWERY LTD.
1995 Financial Statements

BALANCE SHEET (Excerpts)

Current assets	1995	1994	1993
Trade accounts receivable	$1,481,068	$1,177,089	$749,834

INCOME STATEMENT (Excerpts)			
Sales	$23,078,655	$16,140,745	$12,730,373

A quick review of this information shows that Big Rock's accounts receivable doubled from $749,834 in 1993 to $1,481,068 in 1995. At first glance, this might appear to indicate that its collection of receivables is much worse in 1995 compared to 1993. But a more detailed analysis shows a very different picture, as indicated in Exhibit 6-7.

EXHIBIT 6-7

BIG ROCK BREWERY LTD.
Accounts Receivable Turnover

$$1995: = \frac{23,078,655}{\frac{(1,481,068 + 1,177,089)}{2}} = \frac{23,078,655}{1,329,078.5} = 17.36$$

$$1994: = \frac{16,140,745}{\frac{(1,177,089 + 749,834)}{2}} = \frac{16,140,745}{963,461.5} = 16.75$$

In this context, "turnover" means how often the accounts receivable are "turned over," meaning how often they are fully paid and replaced by new accounts. Thus the turnover analysis shows that Big Rock's collection record is better in 1995 than in 1994: the turnover increased from 16.75 to 17.36.

Another way to analyze performance of accounts receivable collection is to calculate the **number of days' sales** in the ending balance of the receivables. This analysis assumes that the sales are spread evenly over a 365 day year. Then using this calculation, Big Rock's average daily sales increased from $44,221 ($16,140,745/365) in 1994 to $63,229 ($23,078,655/365) in 1995. Therefore the 1994 accounts receivable balance of $1,177,089 represents 26.6 days' average sales ($1,177,089/$44,221) and the 1995 balance of $1,481,068 represents 23.4 days ($1,481,068/$63,229). Thus Big Rock's 1995 balance of accounts receivable represents 3.2 fewer days' sales than the 1994 balance, indicating it is collecting its receivables relatively faster in 1995. Another comparison that should be made is with the corporation's normal credit terms. If normal credit terms are 30 days, then approximately 30 days' sales would be expected to be uncollected in accounts receivable.

These analyses indicate that Big Rock is collecting cash from its accounts receivables faster in 1995 than in 1994, which is generally a good sign.

In doing these analyses, several complicating factors should be considered. For example, some receivables such as "financing receivables" do not correspond directly to the revenues produced during the period. These financing receivables may reflect loans made by the corporation to its customers. These loans do not immediately generate an equivalent amount of revenue the way sales of goods or services do. Revenue from the financing receivables is earned over time as the loans accrue interest. Therefore, an accounts receivable turnover, based on these receivables, would have little meaning.

Finally, trends over time should be considered. As an example, in the company you are analyzing, you may find that the amounts written off over the last several years have been increasing. Whether this is good or bad depends on how the accounts receivable balance has changed over the same period of time. To address this question, a ratio such as comparing the amounts written off to the balance in the receivables could be calculated. If this ratio is increasing over the last several years, it may represent some relative degradation in the quality of the receivables. If this were to continue, this would not be good news for the corporation.

Another way to address the same issue would be to compare the ratio of the ending balance in the allowance for doubtful accounts to the ending balance in the accounts receivable (before deducting the allowance). An increase in this ratio over time would indicate that a higher percentage of the ending accounts receivable was considered uncollectible. This, too, would be a negative indication.

SUMMARY

In this chapter, we discussed three major types of current assets that are either cash or about to become cash. The next chapter considers the last major component of current assets: inventory. Because of the complexities associated with inventory accounting, an entire chapter is devoted to this discussion. Other current assets that appear on balance sheets from time to time are considered in other chapters in this book. Deferred tax assets, for example, are covered in Chapter 9. For the remaining current assets, reference to the footnotes of the corporation's financial statements or to an intermediate accounting text should help you understand their nature.

SUMMARY PROBLEMS

1. Exhibit 6-8 provides information about the transactions involving short-term investments for the Labbe Corporation. Assuming that Labbe prepares financial statements on a quarterly basis, construct the journal entries that Labbe would make each quarter to record these transactions (do not bother making closing entries for income statement accounts). Assume that all dividends are received in cash during the quarter.

2. The Gujarat Corporation sells goods on credit to its customers. During 19x4, Gujarat sold $150,000 worth of goods on credit and collected $125,000 from its customers. The corporation started the period with a balance of $15,000 in accounts receivable and a balance in the allowance for doubtful accounts of $450. During 19x4, Gujarat wrote off $2,925 of accounts receivable. If Gujarat estimates that $525 of the ending accounts receivable will ultimately be uncollectible, calculate the amount of bad debt expense that should be recorded. Also show all journal entries that would be made during the period that would affect accounts receivable and the related allowance account.

EXHIBIT 6-8

LABBE CORPORATION
Temporary Investments Data

Security	Quarter Acquired	Acquisition Cost	Quarter Sold	Selling Price
Alpha Co.	1	$20,000	—	—
Beta Co.	1	$35,000	4	$29,000
Gamma Co.	1	$15,000	2	$19,000

Values as of the End of

Security	Quarter 1 Cost	Quarter 1 Market	Quarter 2 Cost	Quarter 2 Market	Quarter 3 Cost	Quarter 3 Market	Quarter 4 Cost	Quarter 4 Market
Alpha	$20,000	$21,000	$20,000	$22,000	$20,000	$17,000	$20,000	$15,000
Beta	$35,000	$32,000	$35,000	$36,000	$35,000	$37,000	—	—
Gamma	$15,000	$14,000	—	—	—	—	—	—
Portfolio	$70,000	$67,000	$55,000	$58,000	$55,000	$54,000	$20,000	$15,000

Dividends Received

Quarter	Amount
1	$650
2	$525
3	$550
4	$150

SUGGESTED SOLUTIONS TO SUMMARY PROBLEMS

1. The journal entries that Labbe Corporation would make each quarter are as follows:

QUARTER 1:

Acquisition entry:

A – Temporary Investments	70,000	
A – Cash		70,000

Dividend revenue:

A – Cash	650	
SE – Dividend Revenue		650

Unrealized loss/recovery:

SE – Unrealized Loss on Valuation of Temporary Investments	3,000	
XA – Valuation Allowance for Temporary Investments		3,000

Realized gain/loss on sale:

    No sales this quarter

QUARTER 2:

Acquisition entry:

    No acquisitions this quarter

Dividend revenue:

A – Cash	525	
SE – Dividend Revenue		525

Unrealized loss/recovery:

XA – Valuation Allowance for Temporary Investments	3,000*	
SE – Unrealized Recovery on Valuation of		
Temporary Investments		3,000

Realized gain/loss on sale:

A – Cash	19,000	
A – Temporary Investments		15,000
SE – Realized Gain on Sale of Temporary Investments		4,000

*Because the portfolio has recovered from its loss position in Quarter 1, the portfolio should now be carried at cost, and the balance in the valuation allowance account ($3,000) should be reduced to zero.

QUARTER 3:

Acquisition entry:

    No acquisitions this quarter

Dividend revenue:

A – Cash	550	
SE – Dividend Revenue		550

Unrealized loss/recovery:

SE – Unrealized Loss on Valuation of Temporary Investments	1,000	
XA – Valuation Allowance for Temporary Investments		1,000

Realized gain/loss on sale:

    No sales this quarter

QUARTER 4:

Acquisition entry:

    No acquisitions this quarter

Dividend revenue:

A — Cash	150	
SE — Dividend Revenue		150

Unrealized loss/recovery:

SE — Unrealized Loss on Valuation of Temporary Investments	4,000*	
XA — Valuation Allowance for Temporary Investments		4,000

Realized gain/loss on sale:

A — Cash	29,000	
SE — Realized Loss on Sale of Temporary Investments	6,000	
A — Temporary Investments		35,000

* The market value of the portfolio at the end of quarter 3 was $1,000 below cost. Since the market value is $5,000 below cost at the end of quarter 4, $4,000 must be added to the allowance account to bring it to the total $5,000 difference between cost and market.

2. The following journal entries would be made during the year by Gujarat Corporation:

Credit sales:

A — Accounts Receivable	150,000	
SE — Sales Revenue		150,000

Collections from customers:

A — Cash	125,000	
A — Accounts Receivable		125,000

Write-off bad debts:

XA — Allowance for Doubtful Accounts	2,925	
A — Accounts Receivable		2,925

Bad debt expense:

SE — Bad Debt Expense	3,000	
XA — Allowance for Doubtful Accounts		3,000*

*The bad debt expense figure can be obtained by considering the balances in the allowance account as shown in the following T-account:

XA — Allowance for Doubtful Accounts

		450	Beginning balance
Write-offs	3925	???	Bad debt expense
		525	Ending balance

The credit entry for bad debt expense in the account can be solved for based on the other amounts in the account. A $3,000 credit entry will produce the appropriate ending balance.

GLOSSARY

Accounts receivable Assets of a seller that represent the promise by a buyer to pay the seller at some date in the future.

Allowance method A method used to value accounts receivable by estimating the amount of accounts receivable that will not be collected in the future.

Bank reconciliation The procedure used to reconcile a corporation's record of its bank account balance to the record provided by the bank.

Collateral Something of value that is pledged against a debt. If the borrower defaults on the debt, the lender receives title to the collateral.

Compound interest Interest computed by adding the interest earned in one period to the balance in the account and multiplying the total by the interest rate. The interest earned in one period then earns interest itself in the next period.

Direct write-off method A method of recognizing bad debts. Bad debt expense is recognized under this method at the time the account receivable is written off.

Factor An entity that buys accounts receivable from a corporation.

Factoring The process of selling the accounts receivable of a corporation.

Historical cost A valuation attribute or method that values assets at the price paid to obtain those assets.

Lower of cost and market A valuation method that reports the value of an asset at the lower of its historical cost and its current market value.

Marketable equity securities Investment in shares that actively trade in a market.

Marketable securities Shares or debt securities that actively trade in a market.

Monetary An attribute of an asset or liability that indicates that the asset or liability represents a fixed number of monetary units.

Monetary unit The nominal units used to measure assets and liabilities. The monetary unit used is usually the local currency unit (such as the Canadian dollar).

Non monetary An attribute of an asset or liability that indicates that the asset or liability does not represent a fixed number of monetary units.

Notes receivable An asset that represents the right of the holder of the note to receive a fixed set of cash payments in the future.

Percentage of credit sales method A method of estimating the bad debt expense of a corporation by estimating the expense as a percent of the credit sales for the period.

Promissory note A document in which the issuer of the note agrees to pay fixed amounts to the holder of the note at some point in the future.

Purchasing power An attribute of an asset that measures its ability to be exchanged for goods and services.

Realized gain/loss A gain or loss from the sale of an asset or liability that is the result of a completed transaction (in general, it means that cash or an agreement to pay cash has been exchanged).

Recourse A provision in agreements to sell receivables in which the buyer of the receivables has the right to return the receivable to the seller if the buyer cannot collect the receivable.

Recovery (accounts receivable) The reinstatement and collection of an account receivable that was previously written off.

Recovery (marketable securities) An unrealized gain from revaluing the portfolio of marketable securities according to the lower of cost and market rule.

Security An ownership portion (share) or debt that may be publicly traded.

Simple interest Interest that is calculated by multiplying the interest rate in the agreement by the principal involved. Interest earned in one period does not earn interest in a subsequent period.

Uncollectible accounts Accounts receivable that are deemed to be uncollectible. The point at which they are uncollectible is generally established by the corporation policy.

Unit-of-measure assumption An assumption made under GAAP that all transactions should be measured using a common unit, the Canadian dollar.

Unrealized gain/loss A gain or loss recognized in the financial statements that has not resulted in the receipt of cash or the right to receive cash, but represents a change in value of an asset.

Valuation allowance An account used to hold the adjustments necessary to lower the carrying value of the temporary investments from historical cost to market value when the market value is lower.

Write-off The process by which an account receivable is removed from the books of a corporation when it is deemed uncollectible.

ASSIGNMENT MATERIAL

◤◤ Assessing Your Recall

1. Briefly describe how cash, temporary investments, and accounts receivable meet the criteria of probable future value and ownership to qualify as assets.

2. Explain what the unit of measure assumption means in accounting.

3. Discuss why cash is subject to purchasing power risk and why inventory may or may not be subject to this risk.

4. Discuss the process that accountants use to establish the lower of cost and market value for temporary investments.

5. What are the guidelines accountants use to decide if an investment should be classified as a temporary investment?

6. Describe and compare the direct write-off method and the allowance method for determining bad debt expense. Is either more consistent with GAAP than the other?

7. Describe two ratios that measure current liquidity and compare the information they provide.

8. Describe a ratio that measures the management of accounts receivable and explain what information it provides.

◤◤ Applying Your Knowledge

9. The Ajax Corporation reconciles its bank account every month. At May 31, 19X3, the bank balance according to its general ledger account was $4,643.22 but the bank statement at May 31 showed a balance of $7,582.45. After every item on the bank statement was compared to the detailed transactions recorded in the ledger, the following items were noted. The cheques that were not yet cashed were: cheque number 466 dated May 29 for $1,250.00, cheque number 467 dated May 30 for $520.00, cheque number 468 dated May 31 for $360.50, and cheque number 470 dated May 31 for $2,350.75. The deposit made on May 31 for $1,517.02 was not yet recorded by the bank. The May bank service charges of $25.00 had not been recorded by Ajax.

Required:
a. Prepare a bank reconciliation at May 31.
b. How much cash does Ajax actually have in its account at May 31?
c. Prepare adjusting journal entries to record all necessary adjustments.

10. The following transactions relate to the TinCan Corporation for 19X1 and 19X2. TinCan closes its books on December 31 each year.

Transactions:

March 25, 19X1	TinCan purchased 1,500 shares of Meta-Solid Corp. at $20 per share. It also paid fees to its stockbroker of $0.20 per share.
June 30	The market value of each share of Meta-Solid is $35.
August 15	Meta-Solid declared a dividend of $0.45 per share.
October 25	Dividend cheques received from Meta-Solid Co.
December 31, 19X1	The market value of each share of Meta-Solid is $30.
February 18, 19X2	500 shares of Meta-Solid Corp. are sold at the prevailing market price of $29.50 per share. Brokerage fees are $0.15 per share.

Required:

a. Prepare journal entries for recording all the preceding transactions in the books of TinCan Corporation. Assume the shares purchased are considered to be temporary investments. Note that we have not discussed fees to stockbrokers or brokerage fees. In answering this question, use your knowledge of accounting to determine a logical method of recording them.

b. What amount of temporary investments would appear in TinCan's balance sheets at December 31, 19X1?

11. The Corona Corporation holds a portfolio of temporary investments. The aggregate cost and aggregate market value of the entire portfolio in four years are as follows:

Dates	Aggregate Cost	Aggregate Market Value
Dec. 31, 19x1	$250,000	$210,000
Dec. 31, 19x2	300,000	280,000
Dec. 31, 19x3	320,000	325,000
Dec. 31, 19x4	350,000	345,000

Required:

a. Give the necessary journal entries for each year. The accounting period ends on December 31 each year.

b. What amount of temporary investments would appear in Corona's balance sheets for each of these years?

12. The trial balance of Peters & Scot Inc. shows a $50,000 outstanding balance in the accounts receivable account at the end of its first year of operations, June 30, 19X1. During this fiscal year, 75% of the total credit sales had been collected, and no accounts had been charged off as uncollectible. The corporation estimated that 1.5% of the credit sales would be uncollectible. During the following fiscal year, the account of James Cordon, who owed $500, was judged uncollectible and was written off. At the end of the year, on June 30, 19X2, the amount previously written off was collected in full from Mr. Cordon.

Required:

a. Prepare the necessary journal entries for recording all the preceding transactions in the books of Peters & Scot.

b. Show the accounts receivable section of the balance sheet at June 30, 19X1.

13. The Sabre Razor Corporation's accounts receivables show the following balances at October 31, 19x8, before adjustment: accounts receivable: $1,348,000; allowance for doubtful accounts: $110,000. Total sales for the year then ended were $21,500,000. Sabre has a policy that 1% of its sales on credit would be expected to be uncollectible. Of the total sales, 10% are cash sales and 90% are made on credit.

    Required:
    a. Show the accounts receivables section of Sabre's balance sheet at October 31, 19x8.
    b. What amount of bad debts expense would appear in the income statement for the year ended October 31, 19x8?

14. On March 1, 19x3, the Gamma Corporation receives a note receivable from the Moon Corporation in settlement of its account receivable. The nine-month, 15% note for $10,000 is valued at its face amount. On May 31, 19x3, the Gamma Corporation endorses the note and gives (i.e., sells) it to Varian Corporation to settle an account payable. The note is valued at its face amount, plus accrued interest. On December 7, 19x3, the Varian Corporation notifies the Gamma Corporation that the note was paid by Moon.

    Required (Difficult!):
    Assuming that all three corporations close their books on June 30, what amounts will appear in the balance sheets, income statements, and notes to the financial statements of all three corporations at June 30, 19x3? (This question will require some thought on your part as you must determine how the corporations will show these transactions.)

15. The following information relates to the temporary investments held by Trimex Corp. as current assets.

Security	Acquisition Date	Acquisition Cost	Date Sold	Selling Price	Market Value Dec. 31 19x1	Market Value Dec. 31 19x2	Market Value Dec. 31 19x3
A	Mar. 13/x1	$35,000	Sep. 22/x3	$29,500	$38,000	$30,000	—
B	Jun. 24/x1	65,000	May 27/x2	70,000	60,000	—	—
C	Oct. 8/x2	95,000	—	—	—	100,000	$90,000
D	Aug. 3/x3	100,000	—	—	—	—	102,000

The Trimex Corp. closes its books on December 31 each year.

    Required:
    a. Prepare journal entries relating to these temporary investments for each year.
    b. Show how the marketable securities would be presented on the income statement and balance sheet for each year.

16. The following information relates to Faun & Faun Inc. for the year ended December 31, 19x2.

Balance sheet at December 31, 19x2	
Current assets	
Temporary investments—at cost	$313,000
Less: Valuation allowance for Temporary Investments	13,000
Net balance (lower of cost and market)	$300,000

The income statement includes the following:

	19x1	19x2
Unrealized loss on valuation of Temporary Investments		($3,850)
Recovery of unrealized loss on valuation of		
Temporary Investments	2,000	
Realized gain (loss) on sale of Temporary Investments	(4,950)	(5,650)
Net income	$96,325	$103,825

During 19x2, the corporation sold temporary investments for $50,000 in cash. These investments had a market value of $53,000 on December 31, 19x1. The corporation also purchased new temporary investments at a cost of $85,000.

Required:
a. Compute the cost of the temporary investment sold in 19x2, and create the necessary journal entry to show the sale of the investment.
b. Compute the beginning balance (at cost) of the temporary investment for the year 19x2.
c. Compute the beginning balance in the valuation allowance for temporary investments for the year 19x2.

17. The Ace Corporation's credit sales during the first year of its operations (19x1) were $925,000. On December 31, 19x1, the accounts receivable had a debit balance of $125,000. The management estimated that 2% of all credit sales would probably be uncollectible. The corporation wrote off accounts worth $5,650 at the end of the first year.

On December 31, 19x2, the unadjusted trial balance showed the following:

	Debit	Credit
Accounts receivable	$138,000	
Allowance for doubtful accounts	6,350	
Credit sales		1,250,000
Bad debt expense	—	—

The corporation, because of the debit balance in the allowance account, decided to change its rate of estimating bad debts from 2% of credit sales to 3%.
a. Show the accounts receivable section of the balance sheet at December 31, 19x1 and 19x2.
b. What bad debt expense would appear in the income statements for 19x1 and 19x2?

18. Balance sheets and the income statement of the Dyckman Corporation for the year 19x5 are given here. In addition to these statements, the following information is available:

Transactions:
1. There were no sales of property, plant, and equipment during 19x5.
2. No dividends were declared or paid during 19x5.
3. Temporary Investments costing $75 were sold for $100.

DYCKMAN CORPORATION
Balance Sheet
At December 31,

	19x5	19x4
Assets		
Cash	$540	$500
Accounts receivable	900	850
Allowance for doubtful accounts	(15)	(10)
Temporary investments	600	500
Valuation allowance	(100)	(50)
Inventory	1,800	1,350
Property, plant, and equipment	8,000	5,800
Accumulated amortization	(2,800)	(1,800)
Total assets	$8,925	$7,140
Liabilities and Shareholders' Equity		
Accounts payable	$1,700	$1,550
Common shares	3,000	3,000
Retained earnings	4,225	2,590
Total liabilities and shareholders' equity	$8,925	$7,140

DYCKMAN CORPORATION
Income Statement
For the year ended December 31, 19x5

Revenues	$10,000
Cost of goods sold	6,500
Gross profit	3,500
Expenses:	
Bad debt expense	150
Amortization	1,000
Unrealized loss on valuation of temporary investments	50
Realized gain on sale of temporary investments	(25)
Total expenses	1,175
Income before taxes	$ 2,325
Income taxes	690
Net income	$ 1,635

Required:
Prepare a statement to show why cash increased from $500 to $540.

◤◣ **Reading and Interpreting Published Financial Statements**

19. The balance sheet of Telepanel Systems Inc. at January 31, 1995 shown in Exhibit 3-14 shows a cash balance of $3,230,364. Note 2 to the financial statements states: "Cash includes interest-bearing deposits of $2,936,915 (1994 - $3,195,794) with nonbanking institutions."

Required:

a. Explain why the interest-bearing deposits with nonbanking institutions are included in Cash.

b. Describe what you think the cash management policies of Telepanel are.

20. In the balance sheet of Mosaid Technologies Incorporated, shown in Exhibit 6-9, cash is described as "Cash and short-term marketable securities." Why are cash and short-term marketable securities shown together?

21. Using data for Mosaid Technologies Incorporated (Balance sheet in Exhibit 6-9 and income statement in Exhibit 3-5), calculate the accounts receivable turnover ratios for 1995 and 1994, using balances of accounts receivable at each year end rather than average balances. Comment on the ratios and trend.

22. Comment on the bad debt expense and recovery shown in the Consolidated Statement of Earnings and Retained Earnings for Mosaid Technologies Incorporated for 1994 and 1995 shown in Exhibit 3-5 by explaining what these figures indicate.

23. The following footnote appeared in the 1994 financial statements of BCE Inc.:

7. Accounts Receivable ($ millions) at December 31:

	1994	1993
Trade	$4,885	$4,531
Provision for uncollectibles	(111)	(97)
	$4,774	$4,434
Related parties	58	126
Other	211	676
Total accounts receivable	$5,043	$5,236

Required:

a. What do you think a "trade" receivable is?

b. Why is the trade receivable shown separately from the Related parties and other receivables?

c. Why do you think the "Provision for uncollectibles" is shown immediately below the trade receivables and not below the "other" receivables?

d. Assuming there were no accounts receivable written off in 1994, what amount of bad debt expense would have been recorded in 1994?

e. Knowing that some accounts receivable would have been written off in 1994, how would your answer in (d) have been different if (i) $5 million in accounts were written off, and (ii) $10 million in accounts were written off?

f. Reconstruct the journal entries to record transactions relating to sales and collections of accounts receivable given that the credit sales in 1994 were $21,670 million. Assume accounts receivable written off in 1994 were $10 million.

24. The Consolidated Balance Sheets and Consolidated Statements of Operations and Deficit of Purcell Energy Ltd. at December 31, 1994 are shown in Exhibit 6-10.

Required:

a. Reconstruct the journal entries that would have been made in 1994 relating to marketable securities (i.e. Temporary Investments).

b. Explain why the Gain on sale of marketable securities is shown below the subtotal "Income from operations."

EXHIBIT 6-9

MOSAID TECHNOLOGIES INCORPORATED
(Incorporated under the Ontario Business Corporations Act)
Consolidated Balance Sheets
(in thousands)

	as at April 30	
	1995	1994
Current Assets		
Cash and short-term marketable securities	$ 19,364	$ 18,579
Accounts receivable	7,738	3,550
Revenues recognized in excess of amounts billed	965	628
Income taxes receivable	-	476
Inventories (Note 2)	1,966	889
Prepaid expenses	135	145
	30,168	24,267
Investment Tax Credits (Note 3)	700	285
Capital Assets (Note 4)	2,808	1,043
Other Assets	-	50
	$ 33,676	$ 25,645
Current Liabilities		
Accounts payable and accrued liabilities	$ 3,691	$ 2,121
Income taxes payable	32	-
Deferred income taxes	249	-
Deferred revenue	749	189
Obligations under capital leases – current portion	22	61
	4,743	2,371
Obligations Under Capital Leases	50	9
Deferred Income Taxes	756	-
	$ 5,549	$ 2,380
Shareholders' Equity		
Share capital (Note 7)	19,083	18,705
Retained earnings	9,044	4,560
	28,127	23,265
	$ 33,676	$ 25,645

See accompanying Notes to the Consolidated Financial Statements.

Thomas I. Csathy
Director

Robert F. Harland
Director

EXHIBIT 6-10

PURCELL ENERGY LIMITED
Consolidated Balance Sheets
As at December 31

		1994	1993
Assets	*Current*		
	Cash	$ —	$ 140,666
	Accounts receivable	1,084,898	1,206,755
	Prepaid expenses and deposits	14,351	2,000
	Marketable securities, at cost	—	93,875
		1,099,429	1,443,296
	Investments, at cost (Note 2)	66,233	66,273
	Due from Encee Group Ltd. (Note 3)	360,184	—
	Due from affiliated companies (Note 4)	10,944	17,460
	Deferred financing charges, net of accumulated		
	amortization of $8,856	30,997	—
	Capital assets (Note 5)	10,482,981	8,628,246
		$ 12,050,588	$ 10,155,275
Liabilities and Shareholders' Equity	*Current liabilities*		
	Bank indebtedness (Note 6)	$ 130,477	$ —
	Accounts payable and accrued liabilities	1,258,127	915,727
	Accrued interest payable	8,592	1,317
	Promissory note (Note 7)	18,417	36,833
		1,415,613	953,877
	Provision for future site restoration costs	69,372	43,649
	Due to Encee Group Ltd.	—	124,200
	Long term debt (Note 8)	1,020,000	—
		2,504,985	1,121,726
	Shareholders' equity		
	Capital stock (Note 9)		
	Common	11,547,231	11,100,448
	Preferred	128,000	128,000
	Deficit	(2,129,628)	(2,194,899)
		9,545,603	9,033,549
		$ 12,050,588	$ 10,155,275

Director   Director

The accompanying notes are an integral part of these financial statements.

EXHIBIT 6-10 (continued)

PURCELL ENERGY LIMITED
Consolidated Statements of Operation and Deficit

	For the Year ended December 31, 1994	For the Nine month period ended December 31, 1993
Revenue		
Oil and gas sales, net of royalties	$ 2,375,603	$ 1,265,050
Other	27,548	8,594
Interest	4,842	459
Consulting and management fees	198,375	—
	2,606,368	1,274,103
Expenses		
Production	672,905	323,806
Depletion, amortization and site restoration	1,299,723	331,517
Amortization of deferred financing charges	8,856	54,841
General and administrative	526,894	338,387
Interest on long term debt	57,710	69,507
	2,566,088	1,118,058
Income from operations	40,280	156,045
Gain on sale of marketable securities	30,040	52,080
Income before income taxes	70,320	208,125
Income taxes (Note 10)		
Current	127,876	136,968
Less utilization of loss carry forwards	(127,876)	(136,968)
	—	—
Net income for the period	70,320	208,125
Deficit, beginning of period	(2,194,899)	(2,403,024)
Dividends on preferred shares	(5,049)	—
Deficit, end of period	$ (2,129,628)	$ (2,194,899)
Earnings per share	$ 0.004	$ 0.016

The accompanying notes are an integral part of these financial statements.

25. The balance sheet and income statement for Imperial Metals Corporation (a Canadian mining corporation) from its December 31, 1994 financial statements appear in the Exhibit 6-11. Analyze the temporary investments (Marketable securities in the Current Assets section), noting the Gain on sale of marketable securities in the income statement.

Required:

a. Reconstruct, as much as you can, the summary journal entries that would have been made during the nine months ended December 31, 1994 in the

EXHIBIT 6-11

IMPERIAL METALS CORPORATION
Consolidated Balance Sheets

	December 31, 1994	March 31, 1994
ASSETS		
Current Assets		
Cash and cash equivalents	$17,849,354	$ 17,168,346
Marketable securities [Market value $796,138 (March 31, 1994 - $916,463)]	508,572	343,968
Accounts receivable	896,713	1,394,391
	19,254,639	18,906,705
Investments in and Advances to Affiliates (Note 2)	8,024,418	7,676,726
Oil and Natural Gas Properties (Note 3)	1,290,076	1,339,870
Mineral Properties (Note 4)	9,247,526	9,193,263
Equipment and Leasehold Improvements	166,406	121,738
	$37,983,065	$37,238,302
LIABILITIES		
Current Liabilities		
Accounts payable and accrued charges	$932,419	$ 1,217,448
Future Site Restoration Costs	199,890	206,138
Deferred Income Taxes	2,414,000	2,495,000
	3,546,309	3,918,586
SHAREHOLDERS' EQUITY		
Share Capital (Note 5)	35,549,594	35,377,327
Deficit	(1,112,838)	(1,851,950)
	34,436,756	33,525,377
Common Shares owned by Subsidiary, at Cost	-	(205,661)
	34,436,756	33,319,716
	$37,983,065	$37,238,302

Approved by the Board:

N. Murray Edwards
Director

Pierre B. Lebel
Director

Marketable securities and related accounts. What assumptions must you make to do this?

b. Comment on the success of the operation of the temporary investments portfolio, including its impact on net income.

c. Why do you think Imperial Metals show 1993 figures for nine months only?

EXHIBIT 6-11 (continued)

IMPERIAL METALS CORPORATION
Consolidated Statements of Income and Deficit

	Nine Months Ended December 31, 1994	Year Ended March 31, 1994
REVENUE		
Oil and natural gas, net of royalties	$641,774	$1,037,987
Gold sales, net of royalties	522,810	3,979,925
Uranium sales, net of royalties	-	2,152,563
Management fees	310,877	63,634
Interest	785,134	297,051
	2,260,595	7,531,160
EXPENSES		
Oil and natural gas production	215,088	530,562
Gold production	445,828	2,609,886
Uranium production	-	1,858,502
Depletion, depreciation and amortization	209,218	1,404,118
Administration	1,042,903	2,003,956
Interest	3,714	66,485
	1,916,751	8,473,509
OPERATING INCOME (LOSS)	343,844	(942,349)
Add (Deduct)		
Gain on dilution of interest in subsidiary	-	2,983,548
Gain on sale of uranium subsidiary (Note 1)	-	3,348,040
Writedown of investments and advances	-	(2,346,500)
(Loss) gain on sale and writedown and abandonment of oil and natural gas and mineral properties	(88,125)	31,420
Gain on sale of marketable securities	199,866	699,288
Other	304,948	12,519
	416,689	4,728,315
INCOME BEFORE INCOME TAXES AND MINORITY INTEREST	760,533	3,785,966
(Recovery of) income taxes (Note 6)	(66,507)	2,420,478
Minority interest in income	-	220,849
NET INCOME	827,040	1,144,639
Deficit, Beginning of Period	(1,851,950)	(2,996,589)
Loss on cancellation of common shares on wind-up of subsidiary	(87,928)	-
DEFICIT, END OF PERIOD	$(1,112,838)	$(1,851,950)
Income Per Share (Note 7)	$0.02	$0.02

CASE

SAINTJAY SUPPLIES LIMITED

Saintjay Supplies Limited is concerned about its ability to pay its debts. Analyze the information provided below and explain why Saintjay is experiencing problems with its cash balance. What can Saintjay do to reduce these problems?

Saintjay Supplies Limited
Selected Financial Information (in $1,000)

Years Ended March 31,	19x7	19x8	19x9
Sales on credit	$12,700	$14,100	$17,100
Cash	310	50	10
Temporary Investments	25	—	—
Accounts receivable	1,180	1,510	1,980
Inventories	940	1,250	1,470
Short-term bank loans	—	240	760
Accounts payable	610	390	440
Other short-term liabilities	80	80	80

◤◣ Critical Thinking Questions

26. The balance sheet, statements of income and of changes in financial position, and Note 6 of Petromet Resources Limited at December 31, 1994 are shown in Exhibit 6-12. Analyze the Investments in the Current Assets and related amounts in the other statements and notes.

    Required:
    a. Reconstruct the journal entries that would have been made by Petromet in 1994 relating to these temporary investments.
    b. Explain why the income statement does not show any realized gain on sale of investments, using basic GAAP concepts?

27. The balance sheet and Note 2 of Semi-Tech Corporation at March 31, 1995 are shown in Exhibit 6-13.

    Required:
    a. Describe the policies used by Semi-Tech to record its accounts receivable, paying particular attention to sales that are payable by instalment receivables. Advance reasons why Semi-Tech uses these policies.
    b. What alternative policies could Semi-Tech use to record instalment receivables?

EXHIBIT 6-12

PETROMET RESOURCES LIMITED
Consolidated Balance Sheet

	December 31, 1994	December 31, 1993
ASSETS		
Current		
Cash and term deposits	$ 10,869	$ 8,913,876
Accounts receivable	10,083,645	5,447,698
Investments (market value $3,294,000; 1993–$2,047,000)	2,525,000	125,000
	12,619,514	14,486,574
Property, Plant and Equipment (Note 3)	80,055,512	25,921,770
	$ 92,675,026	$ 40,408,344
LIABILITIES		
Current		
Accounts payable and accrued liabilities	$ 15,230,476	$ 10,003,845
Long Term Bank Debt (Note 4)	16,142,350	–
Convertible Debentures (Note 5)	25,000,000	–
Deferred Gain (Note 6)	2,400,000	–
Future Abandonment and Site Restoration Costs	345,000	182,000
Deferred Income Taxes	222,000	264,000
SHAREHOLDERS' EQUITY		
Share capital (Note 7)	29,602,364	17,169,446
Shares reserved for issuance (Note 7)	–	10,152,705
Retained earnings	3,732,836	2,636,348
	33,335,200	29,958,499
	$ 92,675,026	$ 40,408,344

On Behalf of the Board:

(signature)

(Director)

(signature)

(Director)

EXHIBIT 6-12 (continued)

PETROMET RESOURCES LIMITED
Consolidated Statement of Income

	Year ended December 31, 1994	Year ended December 31, 1993	Eleven months ended December 31, 1992
REVENUE			
Petroleum and natural gas	$ 9,547,723	$ 7,268,209	$ 2,176,598
Royalties, net of Alberta Royalty Tax Credit	(1,473,812)	(1,354,110)	(363,728)
Other income	116,969	149,226	37,493
	8,190,880	6,063,325	1,850,363
EXPENSES			
Operating	1,256,874	795,778	334,649
General and administrative	593,418	404,929	457,709
Depletion and depreciation	3,122,955	2,318,950	518,241
Interest on long term debt	1,315,117	86,489	38,614
Other interest	272,028	–	–
	6,560,392	3,606,146	1,349,213
Income before other items and taxes	1,630,488	2,457,179	501,150
Other items (Note 8)	–	849,169	(1,434,549)
Income (loss) before taxes	1,630,488	3,306,348	(933,399)
Taxes (Note 9)	534,000	670,000	–
NET INCOME (LOSS)	$ 1,096,488	$ 2,636,348	$ (933,399)
Earnings (loss) per share	$ 0.04	$ 0.11	$ (0.07)
Weighted average number of common shares outstanding (Note 1(d))	26,506,240	22,966,413	13,840,173

PETROMET RESOURCES LIMITED
Consolidated Statement of Retained Earnings

	Year ended December 31, 1994	Year ended December 31, 1993	Eleven months ended December 31, 1992
Balance, beginning of period	$ 2,636,348	$ (9,278,154)	$ (8,344,755)
Reduction of deficit against stated share capital (Note 7)	–	9,278,154	–
Net income (loss)	1,096,488	2,636,348	(933,399)
BALANCE, END OF PERIOD	$ 3,732,836	$ 2,636,348	$ (9,278,154)

EXHIBIT 6-12 (continued)

PETROMET RESOURCES LIMITED
Consolidated Statement of Changes in Financial Position

	Year ended December 31, 1994	Year ended December 31, 1993	Eleven months ended December 31, 1992
Cash provided by (used in)			
OPERATING ACTIVITIES			
Net income (loss)	$ 1,096,488	$ 2,636,348	$ (933,399)
Items not affecting cash:			
Depletion and depreciation	3,122,955	2,318,950	518,241
Other items	–	(849,169)	1,434,549
Deferred income tax	401,000	629,000	–
Funds flow from operations	4,620,443	4,735,129	1,019,391
Change in non–cash working capital (Note 10)	590,684	4,324,582	(114,342)
	5,211,127	9,059,711	905,049
INVESTING ACTIVITIES			
Property, plant and equipment, net	(57,093,697)	(22,296,389)	(3,752,679)
Purchase of investments	(2,400,000)	–	–
Sale of investments	2,400,000	1,026,009	1,518,707
	(57,093,697)	(21,270,380)	(2,233,972)
FINANCING ACTIVITIES			
Convertible debentures	25,000,000	–	–
Long term bank debt	16,142,350	–	–
Common shares, net of issuance costs	2,837,250	10,557,493	1,953,971
Convertible debenture issue costs	(1,000,037)	–	–
Shares reserved for issuance	–	9,275,705	600,000
	42,979,563	19,833,198	2,553,971
Increase (decrease) in cash and term deposits	(8,903,007)	7,622,529	1,225,048
Cash and term deposits, beginning of period	8,913,876	1,291,347	66,299
CASH AND TERM DEPOSITS, END OF PERIOD	$ 10,869	$ 8,913,876	$ 1,291,347

PETROMET RESOURCES LIMITED
Excerpted from Notes to the Statement

6. DEFERRED GAIN

During the year the company sold 600,000 common shares of an investment and realized proceeds of $2,400,000. The proceeds were invested in a treasury issue of the same company resulting in a purchase of 600,000 common shares and 300,000 common share purchase warrants. The warrants are exercisable at $5.50 until August, 1996. The gain on the sale has been deferred until the final disposition of the investment.

EXHIBIT 6-13

SEMI-TECH CORPORATION
Consolidated Balance Sheets

(Incorporated under the laws of Ontario)
(In millions of Canadian dollars)

	March 31, 1995	March 31, 1994
Assets		
Current assets:		
Cash and cash equivalents	$ 396.9	$ 356.1
Accounts receivable	588.9	437.4
Inventories	356.0	297.6
Others	10.6	8.6
Total current assets	1,352.4	1,099.7
Investments in equity of Operating Affiliates	485.4	446.3
Property, plant and equipment, net	376.6	300.8
Other assets, including goodwill of $933.4 (1994 – $852.4)	1,015.4	927.5
	$ 3,229.8	$ 2,774.3
Liabilities and Shareholders' Equity		
Current liabilities:		
Bank loans and indebtedness	$ 441.0	$ 300.0
Accounts payable and accrued liabilities	354.0	274.9
Total current liabilities	795.0	574.9
Long-term debt	762.1	661.0
Pension obligations	81.9	73.2
Other non-current liabilities	16.3	8.0
Total liabilities	1,655.3	1,317.1
Minority interests	412.9	332.7
Shareholders' equity:		
Capital stock	925.3	939.6
Contributed surplus	0.5	0.5
Cumulative translation adjustment	85.9	13.8
Retained earnings	149.9	170.6
Total shareholders' equity	1,161.6	1,124.5
	$ 3,229.8	$ 2,774.3

(See accompanying notes to financial statements)

On behalf of the Board:

(signed) Frank E. Holmes
Director

(signed) Douglas A.C. Davis
Director

EXHIBIT 6-13 (continued)

SEMI-TECH CORPORATION
Excerpted from Notes to the Statement
Note 2. — Accounts Receivable

	March 31, 1995	March 31, 1994
Trade:		
Instalment	$ 194.3	$ 122.3
Other	369.7	298.6
Miscellaneous	86.7	51.2
	650.7	472.1
Less:		
Unearned carrying charges	36.4	21.4
Allowances for doubtful accounts	25.4	13.3
	$ 588.9	$ 437.4

CHAPTER

7

Inventory

Inventory is any item purchased by a company for resale to customers, or that is to be used in the manufacture of items to be sold to customers. Inventory is generally the most important asset to a retailer or manufacturer. The success or failure of the corporation is dependent upon buying or making inventory with a unit cost lower than its selling price. It is also dependent upon buying or making the inventory that people want to buy. Management must be very careful to buy or make the right items, at the right price, and in the right quantities so that sufficient profit can be made on their sale to cover all the other necessary business expenditures.

Visualize, for a moment, a music store that sells CDs, tapes, and movies. Imagine the complications that can arise with inventory: the store must select from its supplier the music and movies that people want to buy in quantities that will ensure it does not run out of stock of an item (called a **stockout**) and force buyers to go elsewhere—where they may buy more than just the item that was out of stock at the first store. It must make sure that it does not have too many items in inventory because there are storage and handling costs associated with inventory on hand, as well as the risk of obsolescence, and it must make sure that it sets prices that are competitive but at the same time high enough to provide sufficient profit for the corporation. The store must also provide safeguards so that people cannot steal the inventory. Complicating this activity even further is the variety and volume of items typically sold by any one corporation.

When you think about inventory you probably think about items you have purchased recently in stores. Inventory includes those items, but also much more. To a property developer, inventory is land and buildings; to an oil and gas company, it is oil in the ground; to a recycler, it is old newspapers and aluminum cans. Exhibit 7-1 includes two other examples of inventory.

Investment in inventory can be substantial, so corporations manage inventory levels carefully to maximize their return (profit) and minimize their costs. A variety of accounting methods for estimating the total cost of inventory have been developed and are acceptable under GAAP. This makes the accounting for inventory a fairly complicated process. The basics of inventory accounting are covered in this chapter so that you will have a reasonable understanding of how inventory is measured, recorded and reported. You can then use this information to make informed decisions about corporations.

RECOGNITION CRITERIA

The probable future value associated with inventory is measured by the corporation's ability to sell the inventory in the future, and to use the proceeds to buy other goods and services. Since inventory has not yet been sold, the collection of cash from its sale is even more uncertain than collecting accounts receivable. All the uncertainties associated with the collection of accounts receivable are present with inventory, as well as two others that are unique to inventory: finding buyers, and obsolescence. If a sufficient number of buyers cannot be found at the initial price set for the product or service, the price may have to change in order to attract buyers. A second uncertainty is obsolescence and spoilage. Computer hardware, for instance,

Examples of Inventory

Fletcher Challenge Canada Limited is a forest company headquartered in British Columbia. Exhibit 7-2 shows Note 5 from its 1995 annual report that describes its inventory.

Comac Food Group Inc. owns and holds franchise interests in a chain of retail bakery cafés, retail specialty coffee shops, and restaurants in Canada. Note 3 (Exhibit 7-3) from its 1995 annual report lists its inventory items. Note how the value of franchise stores under construction has greatly increased from the previous year. Comac is obviously expanding!

FLETCHER CHALLENGE CANADA LIMITED
Excerpted from Notes to the Statements

5. Inventories

(in millions of dollars)		1995		1994
Pulp, paper and newsprint	$	73.1	$	114.3
Logs and wood chips		148.0		79.4
Lumber and other wood products		22.7		24.2
Supplies		65.4		64.4
	$	309.2	$	282.3

COMAC FOOD GROUP INC.
Excerpted from Notes to the Financial Statements
March 31, 1995 and 1994

3. Inventories

Inventories are comprised of the following:

	1995 $	1994 $
Franchise stores under construction	296,000	7,000
Stores held for resale	84,000	—
Ingredients, uniforms and selling supplies	54,000	33,000
	434,000	40,000

is at considerable risk of technological obsolescence. Spoilage, on the other hand, is a major factor for food inventories.

Ownership of inventories is evidenced by possession and sometimes by legal title. Usually ownership of low-priced inventories is evidenced by possession because it is impractical to keep track of legal title to such inventories. They are very much like cash in terms of management. Adequate controls must be maintained so that the inventory is not lost or stolen. Ownership of high-priced inventories may also be evidenced by possession, but there are generally legal documents that also prove ownership. The ownership of automobiles, for instance, is evidenced by registration.

Inventory, therefore, meets the recognition criteria for an asset, and should be recorded as such in the corporation's accounts. The amount that is placed in the accounts then depends on the valuation or measurement criteria that are applied.

VALUATION CRITERIA

The valuation method allowed under GAAP is a combination of several valuation approaches. GAAP generally specifies cost, but it recognizes that the cost figure used should not differ materially from recent cost. If it does, the corporation can use one of a number of methods to recognize a decline in inventory value. Before GAAP is discussed in detail, however, we need to examine these different approaches to valuation.

Historical Cost

One possible valuation method is to carry inventory at its historical cost. According to this method, inventory is recorded at its cost on the date it was acquired. In the purest application of this method, no recognition is made of changes in the market value of the inventory while it is held. Income is recognized only when the inventory is sold. At that time, a profit or loss is recorded.

Market Value

A second possible valuation method is to carry inventory at its market value. To apply this method, the term **market** must be more clearly defined. Inventory really has two markets. The first market is the market in which the corporation buys its products. In the case of a retailer, this is called the **wholesale market**. For a manufacturing corporation, there is no one market in which the corporation buys its inventory because numerous costs are incurred instead to construct the product. If the market price can be found in the market where the inventory is bought, the term **replacement cost** is used. Replacement cost refers to what it would cost the corporation to acquire the materials, labour, and overhead to replace the product today. The market in which these inputs are acquired is called the **input market**, or the **entry market** since this is the market in which the products enter the corporation.

Another measure of market value might be obtained from the market in which the corporation sells its products. This is called the **retail market**. The corporation, of course, hopes prices in the retail market are higher than those in the wholesale market so that it can earn a profit. The markets in which corporations sell their products are sometimes referred to as **output markets**, or **exit markets**. In accounting terminology, the exit price is sometimes referred to as the **net realiz-**

able value (NRV), which is defined as the net amount that can be realized from the sale of the product in question. Net realizable value is not the same as the selling price. The *net* part of NRV refers to the corporation's need to net some costs against the selling prices. For example, there are generally some selling costs that must be incurred to sell a product. Net realizable value is then the selling price less the costs necessary to sell the item. In a manufacturing corporation, some inventory is not ready for sale (work in process). Net realizable value, in this case, is the selling price less the costs to sell as well as the costs necessary to complete the item.

One final issue with regard to the definition of market should be noted. The markets referred to in the preceding paragraphs are assumed to be the normal markets in which the corporation does normal business. There also are markets for goods that must be sold quickly (such as in a "fire sale"), or in abnormally large or small quantities. The prices in these markets do not reflect the value of inventory in its normal use and should not be used in valuing inventory of a **going concern** (a corporation that will continue to operate in the foreseeable future). These markets may be important in valuing inventory, however, if the corporation is in bankruptcy or going out of business. Under these distress conditions, normal accounting procedures would not be appropriate because the conditions violate the going-concern assumption that underlies GAAP financial accounting.

■ ■ Replacement Cost

If a corporation uses a pure replacement cost valuation system, inventory is carried at its replacement cost. At acquisition, replacement cost is the same as historical cost. As the corporation holds the inventory, however, unrealized increases and decreases in value are recognized as the replacement cost of the inventory changes. The balance sheet reflects the replacement cost of the inventory at the end of each period, and the income statement shows the unrealized profits and losses. At the time of sale, the only additional profit or loss that is recognized is the difference between the replacement cost at the date of sale and the selling price. This difference is called a **realized profit or loss**.

■ ■ Net Realizable Value

A pure net realizable value system records inventory at its net realizable value. At the date of acquisition, this means that a profit or loss is recorded equal to the difference between the historical cost and the net realizable value. While the inventory is held, this system requires that changes in net realizable value be recognized as unrealized profits or losses. At the time of ultimate sale, no profit is recognized because the item has already been recorded at its net realizable value.

■ ■ Net Present Value

Another possible valuation method values inventory at the net present value of the cash to be received from the ultimate sale of the inventory. This method is somewhat similar to the net realizable value method just discussed in that it uses the ultimate selling prices and all future costs to estimate cash flows to be received in the future. The difference is that it also incorporates the specific timing of the cash flows and then discounts those cash flows, using an appropriate discount rate to produce a net present value. Profits and losses are recognized with this method at the time of inventory acquisition, assuming a difference between the net present value and the acquisition cost. Changes in the amount or timing of the future cash flows or the appropriate discount rate cause the corporation to recognize profits and losses during the holding period. Assuming that the corporation accurately forecasts the ultimate selling price, there is no profit recognition at the time of sale because the inventory is carried at the ultimate selling price at that point.

This method is not used in Canada even for a lower of cost and market decision. The estimates of future cash flows and the discount rate used provide too many subjective variables to users.

■ ■ Purchasing Power

Inventory is not subject to the same risk from inflation as are cash and accounts receivable. Inventory is not fixed in terms of the number of dollars it will produce. It is, therefore, a **nonmonetary asset**. With nonmonetary assets, the price of the inventory item can adjust to changes in the price structure of the economy. For instance, if prices double overnight, then selling prices of the inventory may be doubled to compensate. If inventory prices can be fully adjusted to inflation (or deflation) rates, there is no purchasing power risk. To the extent that inventory prices cannot fully adjust to inflation, inventory suffers some loss of purchasing power.

◢◣ What is GAAP?

GAAP requires the application of cost. When the use of cost results in a figure that is materially different from recent cost figures, companies should apply a lower of cost and market (LCM) rule at the end of the period. Market, as defined here, is most commonly either replacement cost or net realizable value. In Canada, most corporations describe their inventories as being valued at the lower of cost and market. In order to understand the GAAP implications for inventory, we will first discuss what should be included in the cost of inventory, and then consider how to apply the LCM rule.

■ ■ Acquisition Costs

GAAP requires that inventory contain all "**laid-down**" costs. For a retailer, **laid-down** costs include the invoice price as well as any custom, tariff and excise duties, in addition to freight and cartage costs. As a practical matter, it is often difficult to assign the specific dollar amount of freight and cartage to a specific item of inventory. Imagine, for example, that a major grocery store received a new shipment of inventory that contained everything from cereal to heads of lettuce. It would be totally impractical to assign freight costs to a single head of lettuce. Therefore, many corporations do not assign these costs to inventory, but treat them instead as period costs in the period in which they are incurred. The shipping costs, often called

transportation in or **freight in**, may be assigned to inventory, but are more commonly treated as period costs in the cost of goods sold calculation. The calculation becomes:

Beginning inventory
+ Purchases
+ Transportation in
= Goods available for sale
− Ending inventory
= Cost of goods sold

Costs that are to be included in the inventory of manufacturing corporations were discussed in Chapter 3. Manufacturers incur direct material, direct labour, and overhead costs in manufacturing their inventory. All these costs must be included in inventory, as well as the retailer's costs discussed in this section.

■■ ■ Lower of Cost and Market

Because inventory is crucial to the success of corporations in the retail and manufacturing business, users are very interested in its value. When inventory is listed as a current asset on the balance sheet, users assume that it will be sold in the subsequent period for at least its stated value, but more optimistically, at a profit. During an accounting period, economic circumstances may arise that negatively affect the value of the inventory. At the end of every accounting period, most companies compare the cost of the inventory to its market value and apply the lower of cost and market (LCM) rule. The rule is similar to that applied to temporary investments, discussed in Chapter 6. There is, however, one significant difference, which is that any write-down of inventory to a market value that is lower than cost is considered to be

AN INTERNATIONAL PERSPECTIVE
REPORTS FROM OTHER COUNTRIES

Most countries require that overhead costs be included as a part of the carrying value of inventory. Some countries, however, such as India, Chile, and Denmark, require that overhead costs be treated as period expenses. The disclosure from Danisco (an international food industry company in Denmark) illustrates this treatment:

Stock

Raw materials, consumables, and goods for resale are entered at the lower of cost or market price. The value of finished goods and goods in course of production is fixed at the value of the material involved and the direct production costs.

a permanent write-down. No recoveries are made as they were with temporary investments. LCM can be applied to individual items, to pools of similar items or to the inventory as a whole. It is generally impractical to apply it on an individual item basis, so corporations will use either pools of similar items or the total inventory.

The unrealized losses that result from the application of the LCM rule are often hidden in the cost of goods sold expense. Remember that the cost of goods sold calculation is:

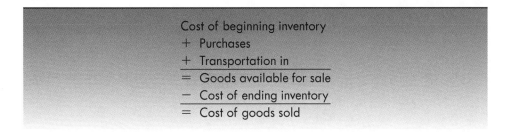

Cost of beginning inventory
+ Purchases
+ Transportation in
= Goods available for sale
− Cost of ending inventory
= Cost of goods sold

If the market value of the inventory is lower than the calculated cost amount, ending inventory is assigned the lower value. If the ending inventory value goes down, the cost of goods sold expense goes up, thereby incorporating the loss. Corporations could disclose the inventory loss in value as a separate item on the income statement if it was a material amount. They could also discuss it in a note to the financial statements.

To determine the appropriate market value to use in applying the LCM rule, we need to go back to the previous discussion about market value. In Canada, corporations usually define market as net realizable value, or net realizable value less a normal profit margin, or replacement cost. The most common is net realizable value. This makes sense because if the selling price has dropped below the cost, the corporation will likely experience a loss next period when the inventory is sold. Because the decline in value occurred in the current period, we reduce the value of the inventory in the current period. Then when it is sold in the next period, it will sell at no profit if the selling price does not change. The option of net realizable value less a normal profit margin reduces the inventory value even more in the current period so that when it is sold in the next period, it will sell at a profit. This option is not used very often, but it is available to corporations under GAAP. When replacement cost is used, it is often with inventory that is used to manufacture items rather than with inventory that is held for resale.

Exhibit 7-4 includes the inventory disclosure for Western Star Trucks Holding Ltd., which designs and assembles highly customized automotive vehicles. Note that it uses net realizable value as well as specific identification and standard and average costs in its inventory disclosure. More will be said about these other costs later in the chapter.

Exhibit 7-5 includes the inventory disclosure for Imperial Parking Limited, which manages parking lots and parkade facilities. Imperial Parking uses replacement cost to determine the market value of its inventory.

In both of these examples, reference is made to a costing method called first-in, first-out. This method will be discussed later in the chapter.

EXHIBIT 7-4

WESTERN STAR TRUCKS HOLDING LTD.
Excerpted From Notes to the Statements

The following is an example of disclosure of the market value equal to net realizable value:

Inventories
Inventories are stated at the lower of cost and net realizable value. Cost is determined for trucks and buses on a specific identification basis and for parts using standard and average costs which approximate costs determined on a first-in first-out basis.

EXHIBIT 7-5

IMPERIAL PARKING LIMITED
Excerpted From Notes to the Statements

The following is an example of the disclosure of market value equal to replacement cost:

Inventory:
The Company's inventory consists of meter parts and supplies and is recorded at the lower of cost determined on a first-in, first-out basis and replacement cost.

INVENTORY SYSTEMS

Now that we have discussed the valuation of inventory in a general way, we need to look at various systems corporations have developed to manage the volume and variety of inventory that they purchase and subsequently sell. Keeping track of inventory units and their associated costs is essential to the profitable management of the corporation. Information concerning the units sold and those in inventory is necessary for intelligent decisions about pricing, production, and reordering. An inventory system is needed to keep track of this information.

AN INTERNATIONAL PERSPECTIVE
REPORTS FROM OTHER COUNTRIES

Most countries require the application of a lower of cost and market rule. The application of this rule, however, can vary across countries. The *market* value used in the rule is interpreted to mean replacement cost in a few countries (Italy and Japan, for example), whereas, in many more countries, it is interpreted as net realizable value (France, Germany and the United Kingdom, for example). Indeed, the **International Accounting Standards Committee (IASC)** defines market value as net realizable value. Very few countries allow the flexibility that is present under Canadian GAAP. Another difference is that Canada and the United States are somewhat alone in viewing the write-down of inventory as permanent. Most other countries either require or permit the recovery of value back to original cost if the market recovers.

At least two types of information about inventory are needed. The first relates to the *number* of units sold during a period, and the *number* that remain. This information is needed to trigger the reordering of inventory or to set the level of production for the current period. It may also be necessary to fill sales orders. The second type of information is data about the *cost* of goods sold during the period, and the *cost* of those that remain. This information is needed to prepare the financial statements, to evaluate performance, and to make pricing decisions.

Some inventory systems keep track of units of inventory but not their cost; others keep track of both units of inventory and cost. Systems that keep track of units but not costs are referred to as **physical inventory systems**. Major grocery chains, for example, have their cash registers connected to computers that record the sale of each item of inventory when the item is scanned for its bar code. The computerized inventory system is programmed to trigger new orders when the number of items remaining drops to a predetermined level. Unless the computer program is very sophisticated, it will not identify the cost of the item sold. Systems that keep track of the number of units and the costs associated with units of inventory are referred to as **cost inventory systems**. A **cost inventory system** can most easily be implemented when the inventory items are uniquely identifiable. For example, a car dealership records the unique characteristics of each vehicle that it buys for resale. When a vehicle is sold, it is relatively easy to record the sale of that specific vehicle, and to record its original cost to the dealer. A grocery store, on the other hand, would not be able to determine the original cost of a can of peas because it would have no way of identifying the case from which the can was sold. The bar code on the can tells the computer simply that it is a can of peas. With the increasing level of computer technology, more businesses will be able to convert to cost inventory systems and to manage their inventories more closely.

In any inventory system it is important to understand how inventory flows through the system. To illustrate these flows, consider the inventory T-account in Exhibit 7-6. The corporation starts the period with a certain amount of beginning inventory which, in a physical inventory system, is the number of units and, in a cost inventory system, is the number of units times the cost of those units. These amounts are known from the end of the last period. The number of units purchased and the cost of those purchases are known from the invoices for the period (in the case of a manufacturer, the debits are for direct materials, labour, and overhead, all of which are known during the period). What is unknown is the cost of goods sold (the number of units sold in a physical system) and the cost (number) of units left in

---

EXHIBIT 7-6

Inventory Information

	A – Inventory		
Beginning balance	KNOWN		
Purchases	KNOWN	?????	Cost of goods sold
Ending balance	?????		

ending inventory. The sum of the cost of the beginning inventory and that of purchases is known as the cost of **goods available for sale**. The problem is deciding how to divide the total cost between the cost of goods sold and those that remain in ending inventory. Whatever inventory system is implemented, it must be able to allocate the goods available for sale between the cost of goods sold and ending inventory.

The type of inventory system used depends on the type and size of inventory involved and the cost of implementing the system. We will discuss two general types of inventory systems: perpetual, and periodic systems.

Perpetual Inventory Systems

Perpetual inventory systems keep track of units or their associated costs, or both, on a continual basis. This means that, as soon as a unit is sold, it (or its cost) is immediately removed from the inventory account. In terms of the T-account in Exhibit 7-6, a credit is made to the account at the time of sale. The ending balance in the account can be computed at any time to provide information about what is left in the account. In this type of system, the ending inventory balance and the cost of goods sold account are always up-to-date in terms of units or costs. Therefore, the information provided by this type of system is the most timely for decision purposes.

Up-to-date information, which is useful in any business, is crucial to some businesses, such as car dealerships. In the car business, the sales personnel must know what stock is still available for sale so that a car is not sold twice. Because selling prices are negotiated and the cost of different cars may vary dramatically, the cost of a specific car must be known at the time of sale so that an appropriate profit margin will be earned on the sale. The dealer's profitability depends on up-to-date information. Luckily, the cost of keeping track of this information on a perpetual basis is not very high because the number of units of inventory is relatively small.

Contrast this with the decisions faced by the owner of a hardware store. Prices are not negotiated at the time of sale, so knowing the cost of each unit on a per-sale basis is not as necessary. The amount of inventory must be known in order to reorder stock, but reordering is probably not done on a daily basis. The cost of keeping track of each inventory item on a perpetual basis would be fairly substantial because the hardware store deals with numerous items in relatively large quantities. Consider, for example, using the perpetual system to keep track of all the types of nuts and bolts the store sells. The cost to implement a perpetual system in this case would probably outweigh the benefits of having up-to-date information. The hardware store would therefore probably develop a periodic inventory system.

Periodic Inventory Systems

In a **periodic inventory system**, there is no entry to record the reduction in inventory at the time of sale. This may be because a perpetual inventory tracking system is too expensive to maintain, or because the cost of the item sold may not be known at the time of sale. In a retail store, for example, clerks know the retail price of an item because it is written on the sales tag, but they probably do not know the cost of the item to the store. To determine the amount sold and the amount left in inventory, the corporation must periodically stop business and physically count the units that are left, then assign costs to them. The cost of goods sold is then determined by subtracting the ending inventory value, established by the count, from the sum of the beginning inventory value and the purchases made during the period. This process assumes that all items included in the cost of goods sold were indeed sold, which may not always be the case. If items were stolen or misplaced they would not be on the shelves or in the warehouse when the inventory was counted, and we would assume they had been sold. With a periodic inventory system, the corporation does not have up-to-date information during the period regarding the level of inventory or the cost of goods sold. It, therefore, needs to develop other methods to determine reorder points.

The counting and costing of ending inventory can be an expensive process, particularly for corporations with large amounts of inventory. The corporation must close during the counting process and thus turn away business. It must also pay individuals to do the counting. Because of the cost, it generally makes sense to count inventory only once a year. For internal control purposes, some corporations count key items of inventory more frequently than once a year and often prepare financial statements more frequently than once a year. Accountants have therefore developed estimation methods that are used to establish inventory values for these interim reports.

A corporation may use a perpetual system to keep track of the physical units (remember the use of bar codes in the grocery store) but, because of the difficulty in determining unit costs, may use a periodic system to assign costs to units. This type of mixed system provides up-to-date information regarding the number of units available to aid in reordering or in production decisions. It does not provide up-to-date cost information. This may be perfectly acceptable to management if up-to-date unit information is more important than cost information.

Costs and Benefits of System Choice

One of the key factors in the choice of inventory systems is the cost of maintaining the system. The perpetual system provides better information than the periodic system but does so at a higher cost. However, as the cost of computer technology continues to decline, the implementation of perpetual systems has become a real possibility for corporations that formerly would not have considered it. For example, the introduction of the bar code scanner in the grocery business has allowed these businesses to keep track of units of inventory on a perpetual basis. Further, with the introduction of **Electronic Data Interchange** (EDI), some retailers use this information for automatic reordering of inventory directly from the wholesaler or manufacturer.

One other advantage of the perpetual basis that we have not discussed is the identification of **inventory shrinkage**. *Shrinkage* is a general term that refers to losses of inventory due to theft, damage, and spoilage. Periodic systems are incapable of identifying shrinkage because shrinkage appears as a part of the cost of goods sold when the ending inventory value is subtracted from the beginning inventory plus purchases. A perpetual system can identify shrinkage because the system tells the corporation what the ending inventory should be. The corporation can then do a count to see what is actually left in its physical inventory. The difference is the shrinkage. Physically counting the inventory is necessary under either system and the fact that shrinkage can be identified under the perpetual system is an added bonus. Corporations with perpetual systems may, however, stagger the counting of inventories so that not all inventories are counted at the same time.

The cost of an inventory system must be balanced against the benefits of the information it provides. The main benefit of the perpetual system is its timely information. When inventory information is needed on a timely basis for pricing, reordering, or other important decisions, the benefits of the perpetual system must be carefully considered even though the system is likely to be more expensive.

COST FLOW ASSUMPTIONS

In order to accurately determine the cost of goods sold and the cost of ending inventory, the cost of specific units must somehow be linked to the actual physical units that either were sold (cost of goods sold) or remain in ending inventory. For some businesses, this is not difficult because the physical units are unique and records are kept that specifically identify the unit and its cost. Under these circumstances, the corporation can match the physical units with their costs using the **specific identification method**. Western Star Trucks (Exhibit 7-4) would be able to identify the cost of each unit in its inventory. Each vehicle would have its own invoice price and registration number and be, therefore, unique.

In some businesses, the ability to specifically identify costs of individual physical units is not feasible. Consider a shoe retailer who buys multiple styles, sizes and colours of shoes in a single order. If the retailer never ordered the same shoe again, it would be possible to determine the cost of a specific pair of shoes. However, once a second order is placed and arrives at the store, it is no longer possible to identify whether a specific pair of shoes came from the first order or from the second unless

ETHICS IN ACCOUNTING

The determination of the ending balance in inventory is crucial not only for determining the balance sheet value for inventory, but also for establishing the cost of goods sold for the income statement. Any overstatement of ending inventory will result in an understatement of cost of goods sold and, therefore, an overstatement in income. There are many situations that put pressure on managers and employees to show higher net income, such as budget targets and bonus plans. There may also be incentives to overstate ending inventory if it is to serve as collateral for loans. Auditors are also interested in establishing ending inventory values and typically are required under audit guidelines to be present at the physical count of ending inventories to make sure they are appropriately determined.

the retailer took the time to mark the second purchase to distinguish it from the first. It is unlikely that retailers would incur the additional cost of specifically identifying each new order. Therefore, in businesses in which specific identification is not feasible, a logical assumption is generally made about how costs flow through the corporation.

Note as we go through the following assumptions that we are discussing *cost* flows, not *physical* flows. We will be suggesting logical assumptions for cost flows that may be entirely opposite to the way inventory physically flows through the corporation. To illustrate these assumptions, we will use the data in Exhibit 7-7 for Ted's Toasters, Inc.

Three cost flow assumptions—first-in, first-out (FIFO), last-in, first-out (LIFO) and weighted average—form three logical ways of assigning costs to units sold or remaining in inventory. FIFO assumes that the first unit purchased is also the first unit sold, hence first-in, first-out. LIFO assumes, however, that the last unit purchased is the first unit sold, hence last-in, first-out. Weighted average assigns an average cost to both cost of goods sold and ending inventory. Let's look at each of these approaches in more detail.

Ted's Toasters starts the period with six toasters in inventory. Note that the beginning inventory cost is $84 or unit cost is $14. Only in the very first period of operations are the beginning values in inventory the same under all three assumptions. Because different cost flow assumptions assign costs to units in different ways, in subsequent periods each assumption will result in different per-unit amounts being assigned to ending inventory, which in turn becomes beginning inventory for the next period. Each of these cost flow assumptions is discussed in the following subsections. Refer to Exhibit 7-7 as each method is discussed.

First-In, First-Out (FIFO)

The **first-in, first-out**, or **FIFO**, method is the method most commonly used in Canada. It assigns the first costs to the first units sold. This means that ending inventory units will be matched to costs for the most *recent* purchases. One way to visualize this

EXHIBIT 7-7

TED'S TOASTERS, INC.
Inventory of toasters

Date		Units	Unit cost	Total
January 1	Beginning inventory	6	$14.00	$ 84.00
January 10	Purchase #1	20	14.25	285.00
January 20	Purchase #2	10	14.50	145.00
Goods available for sale		36		$514.00
Sale record				
		Units	Unit price	Total
January 15	Sale #1	12	$32.00	$384.00
January 25	Sale #2	15	32.50	487.50
		27		$871.50

method is to consider the flow through a pipeline, as shown in Exhibit 7-8. Purchases enter one end of the pipeline. As new purchases are made, they enter the same end of the pipeline, pushing the first purchases further into the pipe. Goods that get sold come out the other end of the pipeline. Therefore, the ones that get sold first are also the ones that entered the pipeline first. The goods still left in the pipeline at the end of the period are the ending inventory. While the acronym FIFO is appropriate for this method, it refers to what happens to the cost of goods sold, not to the ending inventory. A more accurate acronym for ending inventory is LISH, for **last-in, still-here.**

Using Ted's Toasters data (Exhibit 7-7) and the FIFO assumption, we can assign a cost to the cost of goods sold and ending inventory as follows:

Cost of goods sold (27 units)

6 units @ $14.00 (beginning inventory)	$ 84.00
+ 20 units @ $14.25 (first purchase)	285.00
+ 1 unit @ $14.50 (second purchase)	14.50
27 units	$383.50

Ending inventory (9 units)

9 @ $14.50 (second purchase)	$130.50

Note how the sum of units in cost of goods sold and ending inventory (27 + 9) equals the 36 units in goods available for sale. The sum of the dollar amounts ($383.50 + $130.50) equals the dollar amount of the goods available for sale, $514.00. If the dollar amount of ending inventory were to increase, the dollar amount of the cost of goods sold would have to decrease because the sum of the two must add up to the dollar amount of the goods available for sale. Any errors in counting ending inventory or assigning costs will have an immediate impact on the cost of goods sold and, therefore, net income.

FIFO describes fairly accurately the physical flow of goods in most businesses. For example, in grocery stores new items are put behind old items on the shelf so that old items are sold first. If the grocery store did not rotate inventory in this way, some items would sit on the shelf for months, risking spoilage.

Under GAAP, the matching of costs to physical units does not depend on the physical flow of goods. GAAP attempts to provide the best measure of periodic net income, which is not necessarily achieved by choosing a cost flow assumption that matches the physical flow of the goods. Under FIFO, the costs assigned to the cost of goods sold are the costs from beginning inventory and from earlier purchases.

EXHIBIT 7-8

FIFO Visualization

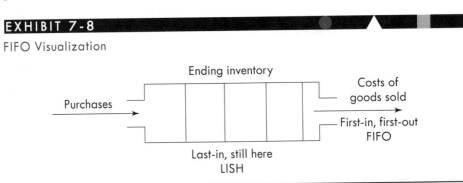

◤◣ Last-In, First-Out (LIFO)

The **last-in, first-out**, or **LIFO,** method is used very infrequently in Canada. It assigns the last costs in (i.e., the costs of the most recent purchases) to the first units sold. That means ending inventory is assigned the costs associated with the first purchases (or beginning inventory). The LIFO method is visualized in Exhibit 7-9. Imagine inventory as something stored in a bin. New purchases are added to the bin from the top, adding new layers of inventory to what is already in the bin (beginning inventory). Goods sold are taken from the top layer of the bin. The costs associated with these units are, therefore, the costs associated with the most recent purchases. Ending inventory, on the other hand, is associated with the cost of the layers at the date each was purchased. The bottom layers could have been purchased in a much earlier period. The acronym used to refer to ending inventory is FISH, for **first-in, still-here**.

Using Ted's Toasters (Exhibit 7-7) and the LIFO assumption, let us now assign a cost to cost of goods sold and ending inventory.

Cost of goods sold (27 units)	
10 units @ $14.50 (second purchase)	$145.00
+ 17 unit @ $14.25 (first purchase)	242.25
27 units	$387.25
Ending inventory (9 units)	
3 units @ $14.25 (first purchase)	$ 42.75
+ 6 unit @ $14.00 (beginning inventory)	84.50
9 units	$126.75

Note again how the sum of the units in cost of goods sold and ending inventory (27 + 9) equals the 36 units in goods available for sale. The sum of the dollar amounts ($387.25 + $126.75) equals the dollar amount of the goods available for sale,

---

EXHIBIT 7-9

LIFO Visualization

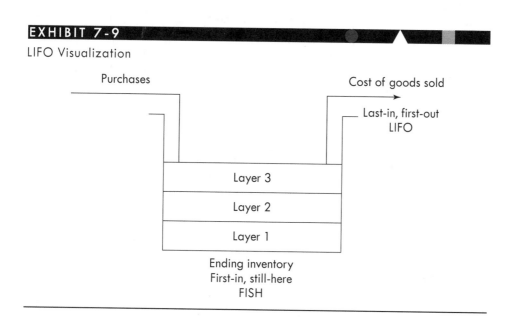

$514.00. Note also that the dollar amount of ending inventory is lower than it is under FIFO and that, therefore, the dollar amount of the cost of goods sold is higher. The unit cost of inventory has been rising through January, and because the cost of goods sold is assigned costs from the most recent purchases, it receives higher unit costs than under FIFO.

The main problem with LIFO is the cost assigned to ending inventory. In Ted's Toasters, the cost was the $14.00 from beginning inventory and the $14.25 from the first purchase. When purchases are made in February, LIFO will assign those new purchase costs to the cost of goods sold, and again assign the $14.00 and $14.25 to ending inventory. Several years from now, the unit cost assigned to ending inventory could still be the $14.00 and the $14.25. These old costs will not show the inventory on the balance sheet at a very realistic value. In fact, if it was left unadjusted the inventory costs could be substantially below market value. Recognizing this problem with LIFO, accountants have developed several techniques to adjust the inventory amount to a more realistic value while still assigning the most recent costs to the cost of goods sold. The discussion of these methods is, however, beyond the scope of an introductory textbook.

Remember that the diagram in Exhibit 7-9 is concerned with the flow of costs, not the physical flow of inventory. Not very many inventories actually follow a LIFO physical flow, although there are a few examples: using steel plates from the top of a pile, or for example, selling nails from a keg of nails. This, however, does not prevent corporations from using the LIFO cost assumption to assign costs. LIFO represents a logical way of assigning costs. In fact, the cost of goods sold on the income statement includes the most recent cost and is, therefore, a good match to the revenue of the period.

LIFO and FIFO represent the two extremes of cost assumptions. LIFO will produce the highest cost of goods sold and, therefore, the lowest net income when unit costs are rising. This might be of interest to a manager who wants to discourage shareholders from requesting cash dividends. FIFO, on the other hand, will produce the lowest cost of goods sold and, therefore, the highest net income under the same condition. This might be of interest to a manager who wants to attract new investors. Because these two assumptions produce dramatically different financial results, it is important for users of financial statements to know which method is being used and to understand the managerial objectives that might underlie the selection of that method.

Of the three methods we have examined thus far (specific identification, FIFO, and LIFO), LIFO is used the least often in Canada for several reasons. First, it produces the lowest net income when costs are rising. Second, the value of inventory on the balance sheet quickly becomes an unrealistic value. Third, Revenue Canada does not accept it as a method for determining inventory costs for tax purposes, probably because it produces the lowest net income and would therefore produce the lowest taxable income. We now turn our attention to the fourth and final potential cost flow assumption: the weighted average method.

Weighted Average

The weighted average method computes an average cost for all the units available for sale in a given period and assigns that average cost to both the units that are sold during the period, and to those that remain in ending inventory. Exhibit 7-10 provides a visualization of this method. Imagine inventory as a liquid stored in a tank, such as gasoline at a filling station. Purchases are dumped into the tank and mixed with beginning inventory and previous purchases. Inventory that is sold is therefore a mixture of beginning inventory and recent purchases. In Ted's Toasters, the average cost is computed by taking the total cost of the goods available for sale ($514.00) and dividing it by the number of toasters available (36) to produce an average cost of $14.278 per unit. This unit cost is then assigned to all the units in ending inventory (9 × $14.278 = $128.50), and to the 27 units sold (27 × $14.278 = $385.51). Note that when the ending inventory of $128.50 is added to the cost of goods sold of $385.51, the total is $514.01—a one-cent difference from the total value of goods available for sale. This error occurred because we had to round the unit cost. When using the weighed average method, use the calculated unit cost to determine either the ending inventory or the cost of goods sold. Determine the other amount by subtracting your calculated amount from the value of goods available for sale.

Note that the weighted average method produces results on the income statement and balance sheet that are somewhere in-between those of LIFO and FIFO. Because it produces a lower net income than FIFO, many corporations in Canada choose it for tax purposes. They like the higher net income produced by FIFO for reporting purposes and so will maintain two sets of inventory records. This is acceptable practice.

Cost Flow Assumption Choice

All three of the cost flow assumptions we have discussed are in accordance with GAAP. Given free choice, which method should Ted's Toasters use to represent the operating results for the period? This depends on the fundamental objectives of

EXHIBIT 7-10

Weighted Average Visualization

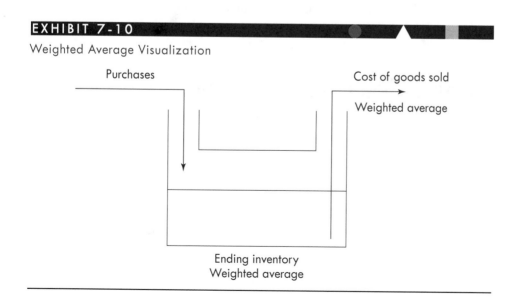

management. Examine Exhibit 7-11 to see the different financial statement effects of each of the three assumptions.

Ted's Toasters would probably like to use LIFO because it produces the smallest amount of profit and would therefore result in the smallest amount of tax liability. However, because Revenue Canada will not allow it, Ted's tax adviser would instead recommend weighted average.

Management in Ted's Toasters, however, may be more interested in getting a bonus to increase their own compensation. If Ted's calculates their bonuses based on reported net income, they would be more likely to choose FIFO, which produces the highest amount of net income. Management may also be tempted to use FIFO if the company has a loan agreement with a lender that requires the company to maintain a specified current ratio (current assets / current liabilities) and the corporation is in danger of not meeting the required ratio test. First-in, first-out produces the highest value of inventory that goes into the numerator of the current ratio.

Political sensitivity may also influence the cost flow decision. Suppose the corporation is in the oil and gas industry, and that recent disturbances in world oil markets have caused the price of oil to rise significantly. Consumer advocates have been criticizing the oil and gas industry for profiting from this situation by raising prices beyond what is required by the change in world prices. They advocate an excess profits tax on the industry. In this situation, the corporation may want to avoid reporting income at any higher level than is necessary. Last-in, first-out may be the best choice to minimize the income effects of these changing prices.

Constraints on Selection

The choice of inventory methods is not entirely without constraints. First of all, GAAP requires the corporation to select the method that is the fairest matching of costs with revenues regardless of the actual physical flow of inventory. To understand what is meant by fair matching, consider the situation at Ted's. Ted's has been experiencing a rise in its costs; that is, a period of inflation. Presumably, it has been able to adjust the prices it charges to customers to reflect this rise in costs.

EXHIBIT 7-11

TED'S TOASTERS, INC.
Financial statement effects

| | Cost flow assumption | | |
	FIFO	Weighted Average	LIFO
Sales revenue	$871.50	$871.50	$871.50
Cost of goods sold	383.50	385.50	387.25
Gross profit	$488.00	$486.00	$484.25
Balance sheet			
Inventory	$130.50	$128.50	$126.75

Consider the income reported using the LIFO method. The $484.25 in the gross margin is a result of matching the cost of $387.25 (the most recent purchases) with the current revenue of $871.50. If prices were to stabilize at this point, Ted's could continue to produce a steady profit margin on future sales because it can continue to buy goods at $14.50. On the other hand, the gross margin of $488.00 produced by using FIFO matches a cost of $383.50 (old costs) against the current revenue. Considering that the current replacement cost of that unit is $14.50, the income produced under FIFO can be split up into a **current gross margin** and a **realized holding gain** as shown in Exhibit 7-12. The sum of the current gross margin and the realized holding gain is the amount of profit reported in Exhibit 7-11 under GAAP. The presentation in Exhibit 7-12 is shown for illustration purposes and is not used under GAAP. It does illustrate that income produced using FIFO is a combination of a gross margin that can be expected to continue into the future, and a realized holding gain that cannot be duplicated in the future. The holding gain is often referred to as a paper profit. Users should be aware that because lower older costs form part of the cost of goods sold, some of the resulting gross margin is not a true profit because some of the profit must be used to replace the sold inventory with more expensive units.

As indicated in Exhibit 7-12, holding gains on inventory are, in fact, recognized at the time the item is sold. Holding gains on items in ending inventory are not recognized under GAAP. Holding losses on items in ending inventory are recognized to the extent that write-downs occur in the application of the lower of cost and market rule. Therefore, under GAAP, the only changes in the value of inventory that are not recognized are the unrealized holding gains on ending inventory. These holding gains are probably small for corporations using FIFO because ending inventory is stated at the most recent prices. With LIFO, however, these unrealized holding gains can be large.

Given Ted's circumstances, it could be argued that LIFO produces a better measure of periodic net income because the realized holding gains that are contained in net income using FIFO will not persist into the future. It is generally true that, during periods of inflation, LIFO produces a better measure of net income. Note, however, that LIFO may also produce the least accurate measure of the value of ending inventory under such circumstances because the prices in inventory may be very old and very low compared to current prices.

EXHIBIT 7-12

FIFO Income and Holding Gains

Sales revenue	$871.50	
Replacement cost of goods sold	391.50 (27 @ $14.50)	
Current gross margin		$480.00
Replacement cost of goods sold	$391.50	
Historical cost of goods sold	383.50	
Realized holding gain		8.00
Reported net income		$488.00

Under another set of circumstances, LIFO might not be the best choice. For example, if prices had been stable throughout the period (say, all units had a cost of $14), then all the cost flow assumptions would produce the same income. The least expensive inventory method should be applied under these circumstances.

COST FLOW ASSUMPTIONS AND CHANGING PRICES

As the Ted's Toasters example illustrates, the use of LIFO during periods of rising prices generally produces the lowest net income, whereas the use of FIFO produces the highest net income. The reverse would be true during periods of deflation. In Canada, there have been virtually no sustained periods of deflation in recent memory. However, that is not to say that some corporations have not faced periods of decreasing unit prices in the goods they use or produce. Take, for example, the microchip industry, which has seen significant drops in the cost per unit of its product. For these types of businesses, FIFO would make sense for tax purposes: in cases of declining costs, FIFO would produce the highest cost of goods sold and the lowest net income.

In periods of stable prices, all three cost flow assumptions produce the same values for cost of goods sold and ending inventory. The differences among the assumptions are driven by changes in prices across time. The magnitude of the effect depends on the size of the change in prices and on the size and turnover characteristics of the inventory. Users of financial statements, therefore, need to know more than just the inventory method that is being used. They must also know the type of inventory being sold, and how the economy may be affecting the cost of that inventory.

Consider the use of FIFO and the effects of changing prices. The balance sheet reflects the most recent prices. The cost of goods sold reflects older prices. How old

AN INTERNATIONAL PERSPECTIVE
REPORTS FROM OTHER COUNTRIES

The predominant practice with regard to cost flow assumptions around the world is to assume either FIFO or weighted average. LIFO either is not permitted (France and the United Kingdom), or is used only in limited situations in most countries other than the United States. The significant use of LIFO in the United States is partially driven by the LIFO conformity rule and its acceptability for tax purposes. The LIFO conformity rule states that if LIFO is used for tax purposes, it must also be used for financial statement reporting. In Germany, the reporting books are essentially the same as the tax books, and until recently LIFO was not permitted under the tax code. German law has recently changed, however, to allow LIFO. The following disclosure from BASF (a German chemical company) illustrates this change:

. . . the valuation of raw materials, work in process and finished products and merchandise was generally changed from the average cost method to the LIFO method, which is now permissible for German tax purposes. This change resulted in a decrease of net income by DM 52.3 million . . .

can these prices be? The oldest costs in the cost of goods sold figure are those that existed in beginning inventory. Those costs may have been incurred in the last month of the last year or even earlier, depending how often the company turns over its inventory. **Inventory turnover** measures the number of times the total inventory is sold during the period. (see chapter 3).

If the inventory turnover ratio is 12, the inventory turns over once a month, and the ending inventory costs come from the purchases made in the last month of the year. If inventory turnover is four, the company turns over its inventory once a quarter, and the oldest costs in ending inventory could come from the beginning of the last quarter of the year. Therefore, while these costs are viewed as "old," in reality they are not very old. When prices are not rising very rapidly, the differences between current year prices and those from the end of the last year will be relatively small.

Now, consider LIFO. Cost of goods sold reflects the most recent prices. Inventory, on the other hand, reflects old prices. How old can these old prices be? The oldest prices in ending inventory are associated with the oldest layer of inventory, which could have been acquired in the first year the company was in business. For a 100-year-old company, these unit prices could be from 100 years ago. Even with small levels of annual inflation, the cumulative difference in prices for these layers and current prices can be very substantial. The effects of inflation can cause the LIFO inventory value of a corporation to be very different from the current replacement cost of the inventory. For this reason, LIFO corporations often provide information in the footnotes to their annual reports to inform the reader of the current cost of their inventories.

The choice of cost flow assumption depends on the nature of the inventory, but the same assumption does not have to apply to all inventories held by the corporation. For corporations that have international operations, for example, LIFO may be used for the international operations while FIFO is used in Canada. The inventory footnote for Cominco Ltd. in Exhibit 7-13 makes reference to foreign inventories.

INVENTORY ESTIMATION

There are several circumstances in which a corporation needs the cost of goods sold or inventory value, but either chooses not to count inventory or simply cannot

EXHIBIT 7-13

COMINCO LTD., 1994
Excerpted from Notes to the Statements

Finished goods, raw materials and partially processed materials are valued generally at the lower of cost (determined on the monthly average amount) and net realizable value with certain exceptions. Inventories of the Highland Valley Copper partnership, consisting principally of copper concentrates and related by-products, are determined on the last-in, first-out method and valued at estimated net realizable value at time of accumulation, and inventories of precious metals are stated at market value less a provision for estimated refining and delivery charges. Stores and operating supplies are valued at average cost less appropriate allowances for obsolescence.

count it. In these cases, the corporation may attempt to estimate the cost of goods sold figure if it wants to prepare monthly income statements. It may need to estimate the amount and value of inventory for insurance purposes if the inventory is destroyed or stolen. As mentioned earlier, it is difficult to determine inventory shrinkage when using the periodic system. Corporations will often estimate the inventory before they start the annual physical inventory count so that they can determine if shrinkage has occurred.

Using the Cost-To-Sales Ratio

One way to estimate the cost of goods sold is to multiply the sales revenue for the period (a figure that is readily determinable) by the normal cost-to-sales ratio. The normal cost-to-sales ratio reflects the normal markup that the corporation applies to its products. For example, a corporation that normally marks up its products by 50% prices an item that costs $60 at $90. The cost-to-sales ratio then is 67% ($60/$90). If the sales for a given month are $12,000, the estimated cost of goods sold is $8,000 (67% × $12,000).

This cost-to-sales ratio can be used to estimate ending inventory as well. The corporation would be able to determine the cost of the goods available for sale by referring to the accounting records and finding the beginning inventory and the purchases for the period. For example, if the beginning inventory is $2,000 and the purchases for the period were $9,000, the goods available for sale would be $11,000. If we use the cost-to-sales ratio and the sales amount from the previous paragraph, we can determine that the cost of goods sold is $8,000 for the period. Because we know that goods available for sale must equal cost of goods sold plus ending inventory, all we need to do is subtract the calculated cost of goods sold ($8,000) from the goods available for sale ($11,000) to find the cost of ending inventory ($3,000). This method is often referred to as the **gross margin estimation method**.

STATEMENT ANALYSIS CONSIDERATIONS

Because of the diversity of cost flow assumptions that can be made by corporations and the significant differences that these assumptions can cause in the financial statements of the corporations, adjustments must be made when inventory ratios are compared across corporations. Cross-industry analyses are most affected by cost flow assumptions. Analyses of the same corporation over time are not affected as much, as long as the inventory method has been consistently applied (the corporation used FIFO or weighted average all the time). Changes in the cost flow assumption across time make time series analyses difficult. When using the inventory or cost of goods sold amounts in ratio analysis keep these points in mind as you evaluate your results.

The one ratio that looks exclusively at inventory is the inventory turnover ratio. This ratio tells the user how fast inventory is sold or how long it is held before it is sold. It is calculated as:

$$\text{Inventory turnover} = \frac{\text{Cost of goods sold}}{\text{Average inventory}}$$

The numerator contains the cost of goods sold which measures the costs assigned to all the items of inventory that were sold. Inventory turnover for AT Plastics Inc. for 1994 was

$$\frac{\$148,086}{\dfrac{(\$26,227 + \$23,987}{2}} = 5.9$$

If the turnover is 5.9, it takes AT Plastics approximately 2 months to sell a batch of inventory the size of the average inventory. In order to determine if a turnover of 5.9 is reasonable for AT Plastics, you would need to calculate the ratio for previous years so that you could see if it was changing. You should also compare AT's ratio with other corporations in the same industry to see how it compares with its competitors.

Another way of evaluating this ratio is to calculate the number of days that inventory is held. If you divide the number of days in a year (365) by the inventory turnover, you will know approximately how many days inventory is held before it is sold. For AT Plastics the number of days inventory was held in 1994 was

$$\frac{365}{5.9} = 62 \text{ days}$$

We had already estimated that inventory turned over every two months. This calculation makes the estimate more exact at 62 days.

One concern about this ratio exists when LIFO is used. The ratio attempts to provide information about how fast the physical inventory turns over. Ideally, the ratio would put the number of units sold in the numerator and the number of units in ending inventory in the denominator. Because information about the number of units sold or in ending inventory is not provided in the financial statements, we use the cost figures provided in the statements and divide cost of goods sold by the average cost of inventory. Because LIFO assigns the most recent costs to the cost of goods sold, the units in the numerator are stated at current prices. The units in the denominator, however, may be stated at very old unit prices because of the layers that exist with LIFO. Because of this, during periods of rising prices, the ratio is likely to overstate the turnover since higher-priced units are in the numerator and lower-price units are in the denominator. Because very few corporations in Canada use LIFO, this will not pose a problem for most of the analyses that you do.

◤◥ Other Ratios

Other ratios are affected by the use of LIFO versus FIFO if they contain inventory figures or the cost of goods sold. The most dramatic effects are in those ratios that use balance sheet information. The ratio that is probably most affected is the current ratio, which compares current assets to current liabilities (current assets / current liabilities). If costs are rising, the choice of LIFO can cause this ratio to be significantly lower than it would be with FIFO. Also, remember that the current ratio is used in many debt agreements. If a corporation using LIFO is in danger of violating the requirement for this ratio, a switch to FIFO might solve the problem.

On the income statement, the gross profit percentage (gross profit / sales) is also affected by the choice of FIFO versus LIFO. In Exhibit 7-11, the gross profit for Ted's Toasters varied from $488.00 under FIFO to $484.25 under LIFO. The difference is less than $4.00 but remember that we are dealing with the sale of only 27 units of a single type of inventory. The gross margin percentage is 56% under FIFO and 55% under LIFO. With a greater fluctuation in unit costs and more years of application of the individual methods, the difference between the two would be more dramatic.

◖◗ SUMMARY

This chapter discussed inventory, the current asset that is vital to the health of a corporation. Because of the many kinds of inventory, managing all aspects of inventory is a very complex task. Managers need to order the right kind and amount of inventory, price it competitively (but high enough to ensure that the corporation makes a profit), and safeguard it so that it cannot be stolen. Over time, accountants have developed two major systems for accounting for inventory: the perpetual system that keeps a continuous record of the inventory on hand, and the periodic system that records the purchase of inventory but does not cost the amount that has been sold until the end of an accounting period. Within these two systems, four methods have developed for assigning costs to inventory: specific identification, FIFO, LIFO and weighted average. Each of these methods results in a different cost for ending inventory and cost of goods sold. Users need to be aware of how these methods are used so that they can factor their effect into any ratio analysis that they perform. Because counting inventory to determine the amount on hand is a costly endeavour, accountants have developed methods for estimating inventory. Estimates are used for interim reports and for establishing a pre-count value against which management is able to compare the actual physical count of inventory.

At this point, all the major current asset accounts have been covered, and attention turns next to the noncurrent assets, which have longer lives than current assets. The benefits of these assets are received over much longer periods of time than the current assets. The next chapter considers all noncurrent asset accounts, with the major emphasis on the property, plant and equipment accounts.

SUMMARY PROBLEM

The income statement, balance sheet and Note 2 from the 1995 annual report of Meridian Technologies Inc. are shown in Exhibit 7-14. Meridian is a Canadian

EXHIBIT 7-14

MERIDIAN TECHNOLOGIES INC.
Consolidated Balance Sheets
As at March 31

	1995	1994
	($000)	($000)
Assets		
Cash	3,979	4,591
Accounts receivable	44,555	27,181
Inventory (note 2)	25,896	16,799
Prepaid expenses	8,804	8,158
Total current assets	83,234	56,729
Investments and loans (note 3)	220	1,322
Land, buildings and equipment (note 4)	143,708	92,956
Goodwill	3,022	3,302
	230,184	154,309
Liabilities and Shareholders' Equity		
Accounts payable and accrued liabilities	45,319	25,505
Current portion of long-term debt (note 5)	3,914	2,006
Total current liabilities	49,233	27,511
Long-term debt (note 5)	44,163	18,394
	93,396	45,905
Deferred income taxes		1,630
Common shares (note 6)	133,079	95,489
Retained earnings	2,544	10,287
Cumulative translation adjustment	1,165	998
Total shareholders' equity	136,788	106,774
	230,184	154,309

See accompanying notes

On behalf of the Board:

[signature]

Director

[signature]

Director

EXHIBIT 7-14 (continued)

MERIDIAN TECHNOLOGIES INC.
Consolidated Statements of Operations
Years ended March 31

	1995	1994
	($000)	($000)
Revenues	**199,372**	147,539
Expenses:		
Cost of sales	**185,756**	126,810
Selling and general	**12,739**	9,002
Depreciation and amortization	**8,319**	5,027
	206,814	140,839
Operating (loss) earnings before interest and taxes	**(7,442)**	6,700
Interest expense (note 5)	**(2,620)**	(1,199)
(Loss) earnings before income taxes	**(10,062)**	5,501
Income tax recovery (expense) (note 7)	**2,319**	(2,195)
Net (loss) earnings	**(7,743)**	3,306
(Loss) earnings per share	**$ (0.33)**	$ 0.19
Weighted average number of shares	**23,190,634**	17,579,387

Consolidated Statements of Retained Earnings
Years ended March 31

	1995	1994
	($000)	($000)
Retained earnings, beginning of year	**10,287**	6,981
Net (loss) earnings	**(7,743)**	3,306
Retained earnings, end of year	**2,544**	10,287

Excerpted from Notes to the Statements
March 31, 1995 and 1994

2. Inventory

	1995	1994
	($000)	($000)
Raw materials and supplies	**7,004**	4,602
Work in process	**2,677**	2,922
Finished goods	**4,615**	3,932
Tooling	**11,600**	5,343
	25,896	16,799

company that supplies manufactured parts and components to the automotive and service industries. Note 1 of the report states that "inventory is valued at the lower of cost and net realizable value. Cost is determined substantially on a first-in, first-out basis."

1. What are the implications of the word "substantially" in Note 1?

2. In Note 2, you will see that Tooling makes up nearly half the total inventory amount. What kind of inventory is Tooling?

3. In 1995, Meridian had a loss of $7.7 million. Based solely on the sale of inventory, can you suggest reasons why it may have experienced a loss?

4. Calculate the inventory turnover for Meridian for 1995. Provide a brief discussion about what this ratio means.

5. Calculate the current ratio for Meridian for 1994 and 1995. How important is the inventory value in this ratio?

SUGGESTED SOLUTION TO SUMMARY PROBLEM

All figures in the solution are in thousands.

1. The word "substantially" implies that most of the inventory is assigned a cost under the first-in, first-out assumption, but that some of the inventory is likely assigned a cost using some other assumption. The note does not state the nature of that other assumption.

2. Meridian manufactures automotive parts, so tooling probably refers to tool and die masters. These items are used to cut precision shapes.

3. In 1994, the gross margin on $147,539 of revenues was $20,729 or 14%. In 1995, the revenues increased to $199,372, an increase of $51,833 or 35%. The gross margin on the 1995 revenue was $13,616 or 7%. In other words, although revenues increased, the cost of sales increased more than proportionately to the revenue. The drop in the margin from 14% to 7% makes it more difficult for Meridian to cover all of its other costs.

4.
$$\frac{\$185,756}{\frac{(\$25,896 + \$16,799)}{2}} = 8.7$$

$$\frac{365}{8.7} = 42 \text{ days}$$

Meridian's inventory turnover is 8.7. It takes about 42 days for it to sell its inventory. Without additional information about Meridian's activities in previous years or about its competitors, it is not possible to comment further on this ratio.

5.
$$\text{Current ratio (1994)} = \frac{56,729}{27,511} = 2.06$$

$$\text{Current ratio (1995)} = \frac{82,234}{49,233} = 1.67$$

Inventory represents approximately 30% of the current assets in both 1994 and 1995. This means that it is has a significant impact on this ratio. Without the inventory, the ratio in both years would be close to one. The corporation could meet its current liabilities without selling inventory, but it could not do it as easily as it can with the sale of inventory.

ABBREVIATIONS USED

EDI	Electronic data interchange
FIFO	First-in, first-out
FISH	First-in, still-here
IASC	International Accounting Standards Committee
LCM	Lower of cost and market
LIFO	Last-in, first-out
LISH	Last-in, still-here
NRV	Net realizable value

SYNONYMS

Entry market/Input market/Wholesale market
Exit Market/Output market/Retail market
Entry price/Input price/Replacement cost
Exit price/Output price/Net realizable value
Freight in/Transporation in

GLOSSARY

Cost flow assumption An assumption made as to how the costs of inventory should be assigned to individual units when it is impossible or impractical to assign costs specifically to units.

Current gross margin The difference between the current selling price of a unit of inventory and its current replacement cost.

Electronic data interchange The linkage of two corporations with computers such that inventory is ordered directly over the computer connection.

Entry market The market from which goods or materials enter the corporation; sometimes also referred to as the wholesale market.

Exit market The market in which goods exit the corporation; sometimes also referred to as the retail market.

FIFO An acronym (first-in, first-out) for cost flow assumption that assigns the cost of the first unit into the corporation to the first unit sold.

FISH An acronym (first-in, still-here) that describes the ending inventory units with the LIFO cost flow assumption.

Freight in The transportation cost paid when inventory is acquired.

Going-concern assumption An assumption made in GAAP that the corporation for which the financial statements are being prepared will continue to exist into the foreseeable future.

Goods available for sale The units of inventory available to be sold during the period. These units include those available from the beginning inventory plus those produced during the current period.

Input market Another name for the entry market, the market from which goods or materials enter the corporation.

Inventory shrinkage The losses of inventory due to spoilage, damage, thefts, etc.

Laid-down cost The costs including invoice cost, plus customs, tariff and excise duties and transportation. In a manufacturing corporation, the laid-down cost is direct material, direct labour and overhead.

LIFO An acronym (last-in, first-out) for cost flow assumption that assigns the cost of the last unit purchased by the corporation to the first unit sold.

LISH An acronym (last-in, still-here) that describes the ending inventory units using the FIFO cost flow assumption.

Market Net realizable value or replacement cost.

Net realizable value A selling price of a unit of inventory less any costs necessary to complete and sell the unit.

Nonmonetary asset An asset that is not fixed in terms of the number of monetary units it represents. Examples include inventory or property, plant, and equipment.

Output market Another name for the exit market, the market in which inventory exits the corporation.

Periodic inventory system An inventory system in which cost of goods sold is determined by counting ending inventory, assigning costs to these units and then subtracting the ending inventory value from the sum of the beginning inventory plus purchases for the period.

Perpetual inventory system An inventory system in which the cost of goods sold is determined at the time of sale of the unit.

Realized holding gain A gain that results from the sale of a unit of inventory that had been held during a period of time during which prices increased. The profits that result from the change in price are the portion referred to as a holding gain.

Replacement cost The current price at which a unit of inventory can be replaced by the corporation.

Retail market Another term for exit market. See exit market.

Specific identification A method of assigning costs to units of inventory in which the cost of a unit can be specifically identified from the records of the corporation.

Stockout A situation that arises when a corporation sells all of a specific item of inventory and has no more in stock.

Transportation in A synonym for freight in.

Weighted average costing A method of assigning costs to units of inventory in which each unit is assigned the average cost of the units available for sale during the period.

Wholesale market Another name for the entry market. See entry market.

ASSIGNMENT MATERIAL

Assessing Your Recall

1. Describe the valuation methods for inventory allowed under GAAP.

2. Describe how the lower of cost and market rule is applied to inventory under GAAP and how this application differs from that used for temporary investments.

3. Define and explain the difference between "replacement cost" and "net realizable value."

4. Describe the basic differences between periodic and perpetual inventory systems.

5. Discuss the advantages and disadvantages of the periodic inventory system versus the perpetual inventory system.

6. Describe the three major cost flow assumptions for inventory that are most commonly used in Canada.

7. Discuss the incentives a corporation may have for choosing one cost flow assumption over another. Be sure to include a discussion of the choice from both a reporting and a tax perspective.

8. Explain the term "holding gain," and discuss how it might arise with various cost flow assumptions.

9. Under what circumstances would a corporation want or need to estimate cost of goods sold or inventory?

10. Describe the effects the choice of LIFO or FIFO may have on the ratios related to inventory. Discuss specifically the inventory turnover ratio and the current ratio.

◼️▲ Applying Your Knowledge

11. The Halo Company, a manufacturer of soaps and cosmetics, had raw material inventory worth $30,000 at a unit cost of $15 on March 31. The purchases made during the month of April are as follows:

Date	Units Purchased	Total Cost
April 3	3,000	$45,000
April 10	1,000	18,000
April 14	4,000	80,000
April 23	2,500	55,000
April 29	1,000	30,000

A physical count of inventory showed that 2,500 units were still left on April 30. Compute the cost of ending inventory on April 30 using each of the following cost flow assumptions:
a. FIFO
b. LIFO
c. Weighted average

12. The Brendt Company's information about merchandise inventories is as follows:

			Ending Inventory	
Year	Purchases	Sales	Cost	Market Value
1	$175,000	$145,000	$75,000	$70,000
2	85,000	175,000	40,000	25,000
3	155,000	193,000	62,000	75,000
4	104,000	225,000	19,750	19,750

There was no beginning balance in inventories prior to Year 1.
a. Compute the gross margin for each year using the acquisition cost basis for valuing inventory.
b. Compute the same gross margin using the lower of cost and market basis for valuing inventory.
c. Compare the gross margin for each year using the two methods, and explain the reason(s) for any differences you observe.

13. The following information relates to the merchandise inventory of Apen Corporation for the month of May:

May 1	Beginning inventory	6,000 units	$60,000
May 3	Purchased	3,000 units	$36,000
May 7	Sold	4,000 units	
May 15	Sold	2,000 units	
May 23	Purchased	1,000 units	$18,000
May 29	Sold	3,500 units	

Compute the cost of goods sold and ending inventory as of May 31 using the following inventory systems and cost flows assumptions:

a. Periodic FIFO

b. Periodic LIFO

c. Periodic weighted average

14. Although the use of LIFO and FIFO under the perpetual system was not illustrated in this chapter, use the information for the Apen Corporation provided in Problem 13 and your own understanding of the perpetual system (that is, when inventory is purchased it increases the inventory, and when it is sold its cost is removed from inventory) to calculate the cost of goods sold under the FIFO and LIFO cost flow assumptions.

15. In mid-September, Trojan Incorporated needed to decide how many units should be produced for the balance of the accounting year, which ends on December 31. The company began its operations in the current year with an inventory of 35,000 units, at a cost of $15 per unit. During the year, it produced 65,000 units at a unit cost of $18. The annual capacity of the plant is 200,000 units. It is estimated that the unit cost of producing additional units (for the remaining part of the year) will be $25. The company, after doing time-series and cross-industry analyses, expects the annual sales to be 125,000 units at a selling price of $28 per unit. The company uses a periodic LIFO inventory system.

a. Assume the company produces just enough units to cover the 125,000 units it sells. Determine the cost of goods sold and the gross profit at this level of production.

b. Assume the company produces the maximum that the plant can produce, but still sells only 125,000 units. Determine the cost of goods sold and the gross profit at this level of production.

c. If the company sold the same number of units under assumptions (a) and (b), why is there a difference in the value of cost of goods sold and gross profit?

16. Demolkin Records Ltd. has an inventory count every December 31. It closes its store on that day and hires several university students to help with the counting. Although it has installed an electronic detection device in the doorway of the store to stop people from taking CDs and tapes for which they have not paid, the corporation is still concerned that it is losing some inventory to theft. Demolkin uses the periodic inventory system. While the inventory is being counted, the accountant decides to estimate the amount of inventory that should be on hand. In the accounting records she finds the following information:

Sales for the year	$390,000
Beginning inventory	20,000
Transportation in	800
Purchases	160,000

From previous years, she determines that the normal cost-to-sales ratio is 40%.

a. Complete the calculation for the accountant and determine how much inventory should be on hand.

b. Assume that when the count is complete, the accountant determines that there is $23,500 in ending inventory. Is there a problem of missing inventory? What criteria would you use to determine if this is a serious problem or not? Outline what options may be open to Demolkin if it wishes to do something about the problem.

17. On May 31, Year 7, Cedar Grove Ltd. had a major fire in its main lumber yard. All the inventory was destroyed. In order to complete the insurance claim, the accountant needed an estimate of the inventory that had been in the lumber yard at the time of the fire. A search through the accounting records (which, luckily had been kept in another building that was not destroyed by the fire) produced the following information:

A cost-to-sales ratio of 64%

Purchases for the year up to May 31	$ 74,000
Sales for the year up to May 31	110,000
Inventory on hand on January 1, Year 7	28,000

a. Calculate how much inventory should be on hand.

b. Cedar Grove had two other small lumber yards. On June 1, it counted the inventory in the other yards and determined that there was $9,500 in inventory in the other yards. How much should the company claim from the insurance company?

c. What factors could make the estimate of ending inventory inaccurate?

18. The Sintex Company had merchandise inventory consisting of 3,500 units at a cost of $250 per unit at the beginning of the year. During the year, the company produced 5,000 units at an average cost of $400 per unit. The company sold 4,000 units for $600 each. The replacement cost of units on December 31 was $500 per unit.

a. Compute the cost of goods sold and gross margin using both FIFO and LIFO cost flow assumptions.

b. Separate the gross margin on sales into operating gross margin and realized holding gains using both FIFO and LIFO.

c. Compute the unrealized holding gains and the total gains (operating margin + realized gain + unrealized gain) using both FIFO and LIFO.

d. Compare the total gains and explain any variance using both cost flow assumptions.

19. The following presentation relates to the inventory valuations of Aurora Inc. using different inventory methods (the company started operations in 19x1):

Period	LIFO	FIFO	Lower of FIFO Cost and Market
December 31, 19x1	$ 65,000	$ 60,000	$ 55,000
December 31, 19x2	135,000	125,000	120,000
December 31, 19x3	150,000	143,000	130,000
December 31, 19x4	100,000	125,000	125,000

There was no beginning balance of inventory in 19x1.

a. For 19X1, state whether the prices went up or down.
b. For 19X4, state whether the prices went up or down.
c. State which method would show the highest income in each year.
d. Which method would show the lowest income for the four years combined?

Reading and Interpreting Published Financial Statements

20. Big Rock Brewery Ltd.'s balance sheet, income statement and notes on inventory are in Exhibit 7-15. Using the information in these exhibits, answer the following questions:

a. Calculate the inventory turnover for 1994 and 1995. Instead of using average inventory in the ratio, use the inventory value for the year end. Convert the inventory turnover into days. Knowing that Big Rock is a brewery company, how would you interpret the ratios that you calculated?

EXHIBIT 7-15

BIG ROCK BREWERY LTD.
Balance Sheet
March 31, 1995 and 1994
(Denominated in Canadian Dollars)

STATEMENT 1

	1995	1994
ASSETS		
CURRENT ASSETS		
Cash	$ 42,317	$ 311,960
Accounts receivable	1,481,068	1,177,089
Inventories (Note 2)	1,653,042	943,033
Prepaid expenses and other	85,865	67,138
Total current assets	3,262,292	2,499,220
CAPITAL ASSETS (Note 3)	10,596,468	7,959,570
OTHER	29,535	10,000
	$ 13,888,295	$ 10,468,790
LIABILITIES		
CURRENT LIABILITIES		
Bank indebtedness (Note 4)	$ 408,071	$
Accounts payable	462,739	609,357
Income taxes payable	238,809	392,663
Current portion of long-term debt (Note 5)	220,476	80,400
Total current liabilities	1,330,095	1,082,420
LONG-TERM DEBT (Note 5)	956,498	89,000
DEFERRED INCOME TAXES	1,403,500	881,500
COMMITMENTS (Note 11)		
Total liabilities	3,690,093	2,052,920
SHAREHOLDERS' EQUITY		
SHARE CAPITAL (Note 6)	5,402,784	5,362,784
RETAINED EARNINGS (Statement 2)	4,795,418	3,053,086
Total shareholders' equity	10,198,202	8,415,870
	$ 13,888,295	$ 10,468,790

Approved by the Board:

E.E. McNally, Director

J.A. McKee, Director

EXHIBIT 7-15 (continued)

BIG ROCK BREWERY LTD.
Statement of Income and Retained Earnings
Years ended March 31, 1995 and 1994
(Denominated in Canadian Dollars)

STATEMENT 2

	1995	1994
SALES	$ 23,078,655	$ 16,140,745
GOVERNMENT COMMISSIONS AND TAXES	9,388,863	6,572,458
COST OF SALES	6,054,940	4,363,698
GROSS PROFIT	7,634,852	5,204,589
EXPENSES		
Amortization	405,451	414,946
Selling, general and administrative (Schedule)	3,942,690	2,756,846
Interest on long-term debt	43,249	12,891
Total expenses	4,391,390	3,184,683
INCOME BEFORE THE FOLLOWING	3,243,462	2,019,906
GAIN (LOSS) ON DISPOSAL OF CAPITAL ASSETS (Note 7)	(441,130)	79,815
INCOME BEFORE INCOME TAXES	2,802,332	2,099,721
INCOME TAXES (Note 8)	1,060,000	792,000
NET INCOME FOR YEAR	1,742,332	1,307,721
RETAINED EARNINGS BEGINNING OF YEAR	3,053,086	1,745,365
RETAINED EARNINGS END OF YEAR	$ 4,795,418	$ 3,053,086
EARNINGS PER SHARE (Note 9)		
Basic	40¢	30¢
Fully diluted	39¢	29¢

Excerpted From Notes to the Statements
March 31, 1995 and 1994

b. Inventories

Inventories of raw materials and supplies are valued at the lower of cost (first-in, first-out method) and replacement cost. Inventories of brews in process and finished product are valued at the lower of cost (including direct materials, labour and overhead costs) and net realizable value.

Returnable glass containers are initially recorded at cost. In order to charge operations for wear and disappearance the cost of bottles are charged to operations over their estimated useful life.

---

b. The Note on inventory in Chapter 1 Appendix shows the components of the inventory amount. Three of those items are part of the manufacturing process, the other two are not. What impact do these other two items have on your calculations and interpretations in part (a)?

c. One of the items listed as a component of the inventory is returnable bottles. Some of these bottles will be returned and reused. Suggest some alternative ways that Big Rock could account for these bottles.

d. Big Rock values its raw materials and supplies at the lower of cost (FIFO) and replacement cost. Assume that for 1995, the replacement cost for the raw materials was $925,435. Recalculate the inventory turnover for 1995 using this new information. What impact does this have on the turnover ratio?

21. Imperial Metals Corporation is a mining company that sells base metals, oil and gas and precious metals. Exhibit 7-16 shows Note 4 from its 1994 set of financial statements. Note that it lists costs associated with gold, supplies and other, and uranium concentrates as the components of its inventory. Exhibit 7-16 also shows Imperial's balance sheet and income statement for the same year. Using these pieces of information answer the following questions:

a. In 1993, Imperial listed uranium concentrates as one of the components of its inventory. In 1994, however, the company no longer carried uranium. On the income statement in Exhibit 7-16, uranium sales are listed for year ended March 31, 1994, as are uranium production expenses. If you compare the uranium production expense to March 1994 with the cost of uranium inventory listed in Note 4 at the end of 1993, you will see that the two amounts do not agree. If Imperial does not have any more uranium inventory and it was not recorded as sold in 1994, what happened to it?

b. Using the information from the income statement, determine the gross profit for the sale of each type of inventory (oil and gas, gold and uranium) for March 31, 1994 and December 31, 1994. Has there been any change in any of these over the two year period?

c. Treating the three types of inventory together for cost of goods sold, calculate the inventory turnover for March 31, 1994 and December 31, 1994. Instead of using average inventory, use the inventory value for the year end. Should the fact that inventory is composed of three very distinct and different types of inventory be taken into consideration when you evaluate the inventory turnover ratio? Explain.

22. Mosaid Technologies Incorporated is a high technology company that designs advanced memory chips and designs, manufactures and distributes engineering test systems for memory chips. Note 2 in its 1995 financial statements reads as follows:

2. Inventories (in thousands of dollars)
Inventories comprise the following:

	1995	1994
Repair inventory	$ 132	$ 60
Raw materials	1,103	602
Work in process	731	227
	$1,966	$889

The list of these components tells you that this is a manufacturing company. Mosaid's balance sheet and income statement for 1994 are given in Exhibit 7-17. Using information from these three sources, answer the follow questions:

EXHIBIT 7-16

IMPERIAL METALS CORPORATION
Consolidated Balance Sheets

	December 31, 1994	March 31, 1994
ASSETS		
Current Assets		
Cash and cash equivalents	$17,849,354	$ 17,168,346
Marketable securities [Market value $796,138 (March 31, 1994 - $916,463)]	508,572	343,968
Accounts receivable	896,713	1,394,391
	19,254,639	18,906,705
Investments in and Advances to Affiliates (Note 2)	8,024,418	7,676,726
Oil and Natural Gas Properties (Note 3)	1,290,076	1,339,870
Mineral Properties (Note 4)	9,247,526	9,193,263
Equipment and Leasehold Improvements	166,406	121,738
	$37,983,065	$37,238,302
LIABILITIES		
Current Liabilities		
Accounts payable and accrued charges	$932,419	$ 1,217,448
Future Site Restoration Costs	199,890	206,138
Deferred Income Taxes	2,414,000	2,495,000
	3,546,309	3,918,586
SHAREHOLDERS' EQUITY		
Share Capital (Note 5)	35,549,594	35,377,327
Deficit	(1,112,838)	(1,851,950)
	34,436,756	33,525,377
Common Shares owned by Subsidiary, at Cost	-	(205,661)
	34,436,756	33,319,716
	$37,983,065	$37,238,302

Approved by the Board:

N. Murray Edwards
Director

Pierre B. Lebel
Director

EXHIBIT 7-16 (continued)

IMPERIAL METALS CORPORATION
Consolidated Statements of Income and Deficit

	Nine Months Ended December 31, 1994	Year Ended March 31, 1994
REVENUE		
Oil and natural gas, net of royalties	$641,774	$1,037,987
Gold sales, net of royalties	522,810	3,979,925
Uranium sales, net of royalties	-	2,152,563
Management fees	310,877	63,634
Interest	785,134	297,051
	2,260,595	7,531,160
EXPENSES		
Oil and natural gas production	215,088	530,562
Gold production	445,828	2,609,886
Uranium production	-	1,858,502
Depletion, depreciation and amortization	209,218	1,404,118
Administration	1,042,903	2,003,956
Interest	3,714	66,485
	1,916,751	8,473,509
OPERATING INCOME (LOSS)	343,844	(942,349)
Add (Deduct)		
Gain on dilution of interest in subsidiary	-	2,983,548
Gain on sale of uranium subsidiary (Note 1)	-	3,348,040
Writedown of investments and advances	-	(2,346,500)
(Loss) gain on sale and writedown and abandonment of oil and natural gas and mineral properties	(88,125)	31,420
Gain on sale of marketable securities	199,866	699,288
Other	304,948	12,519
	416,689	4,728,315
INCOME BEFORE INCOME TAXES AND MINORITY INTEREST	760,533	3,785,966
(Recovery of) income taxes (Note 6)	(66,507)	2,420,478
Minority interest in income	-	220,849
NET INCOME	827,040	1,144,639
Deficit, Beginning of Period	(1,851,950)	(2,996,589)
Loss on cancellation of common shares on wind-up of subsidiary	(87,928)	-
DEFICIT, END OF PERIOD	$(1,112,838)	$(1,851,950)
Income Per Share (Note 7)	$0.02	$0.02

EXHIBIT 7-16 (continued)

IMPERIAL METALS CORPORATION
Excerpted from Notes to the Statements
March 31, 1994 and 1993

4. Inventory

	1994	1993
Costs associated with gold ore under leach	$176,166	$ 518,361
Supplies and other	11,469	72,761
Uranium concentrates	–	2,273,005
	$187,635	$2,864,127

EXHIBIT 7-17

MOSAID TECHNOLOGIES INCORPORATED
Consolidated Statement of Earnings and Retained Earnings
Years ended April 30, 1995 and 1994
(in thousands, except per share amount)

	1995	1994
Revenues		
Operations	$ 23,202	$ 14,348
Interest	1,084	369
	$ 24,286	$ 14,717
Expenses		
Labour and materials	5,275	3,979
Research and development (Note 8)	4,741	3,228
Selling and marketing	4,576	2,573
General and administration (Note 8)	2,578	1,618
Foreign exchange loss (gain)	147	(222)
Bad debt (recovery) expense	(19)	74
	17,298	11,250
Earnings before income taxes	6,988	3,467
Income tax expense (Note 3)	2,504	542
Net earnings	4,484	2,925
Retained earnings, beginning of year	4,560	1,635
Retained earnings, end of year	$ 9,044	$ 4,560
Earnings per share (Note 11)		
Basic	$ .66	$ .59
Fully diluted	$ .60	$ .51

See accompanying Notes to the Consolidated Financial Statements.

EXHIBIT 7-17 (continued)

MOSAID TECHNOLOGIES INCORPORATED
(incorporated under the Ontario Business Corporations Act)
Consolidated Balance Sheets
(in thousands)

| | as at April 30 | |
	1995	1994
Current Assets		
Cash and short-term marketable securities	$ 19,364	$ 18,579
Accounts receivable	7,738	3,550
Revenues recognized in excess of amounts billed	965	628
Income taxes receivable	-	476
Inventories (Note 2)	1,966	889
Prepaid expenses	135	145
	30,168	24,267
Investment Tax Credits (Note 3)	700	285
Capital Assets (Note 4)	2,808	1,043
Other Assets	-	50
	$ 33,676	$ 25,645
Current Liabilities		
Accounts payable and accrued liabilities	$ 3,691	$ 2,121
Income taxes payable	32	-
Deferred income taxes	249	-
Deferred revenue	749	189
Obligations under capital leases – current portion	22	61
	4,743	2,371
Obligations Under Capital Leases	50	9
Deferred Income Taxes	756	-
	$ 5,549	$ 2,380
Shareholders' Equity		
Share capital (Note 7)	19,083	18,705
Retained earnings	9,044	4,560
	28,127	23,265
	$ 33,676	$ 25,645

See accompanying Notes to the Consolidated Financial Statements.

Thomas I. Csathy
Director

Robert F. Harland
Director

a. Calculate the current ratio (CA/CL) for both 1994 and 1995. Comment on the impact that inventory has on this ratio in each year.

b. Calculate the inventory turnover for 1994 and 1995. Instead of average inventory, use the inventory value for the year end. As the repair inventory is not part of normal manufacturing, calculate the turnover with only the raw materials and work-in-process inventories. Use the "labour and materials" from the income statement in place of "cost of goods sold." Make whatever comments you can about the results that you get. Remember to consider what you know about the kind of inventory Mosaid sells.

c. Calculate the gross profit percentage on the income statement using "Revenues: operations" for the Sales amount, and "Labour and materials" for the Cost of Goods Sold amount. Calculate it for both 1994 and 1995. It is obvious from the income statement that sales have increased since 1994. What effect has this had on the gross profit? What conclusions can you draw from the results that you found?

CASE

BEMA GOLD CORPORATION

Bema Gold Corporation is a Canadian company headquartered in Vancouver, British Columbia. It explores and develops gold properties in South America. Raj, a Business Administration student, has recently inherited some money from a grandparent. She intends to create a diversified portfolio of share investments. On the riskier side, she has heard that investing in gold properties can be quite profitable. She is contemplating investing in Bema Gold Corporation. She has the annual report which includes the financial statements (see Exhibit 7-18). She is confused because she cannot see any gold inventory on the balance sheet. She is also concerned because the corporation has not shown a profit for the last three years, yet issued 5,000,000 new shares in 1994 and 7,968,539 in 1993. If other investors are willing to buy almost 13,000,000 new shares over the last two years, they obviously have confidence in this company.

a. Knowing that Bema explores and develops gold properties, explain why it does not have any gold inventory on its balance sheet. There can be several reasons for this, so try to find more than one.

b. Review the three financial statements and draw up a list of questions you would like to ask an investment advisor about this corporation.

◤◥ Critical Thinking Question

You and two of your friends have decided to apply some of the knowledge that you are learning in your business classes. You plan to start a wholesale business, buying goods in the Czech Republic and selling them to small specialty stores in the city. One of your friends has an aunt in the Czech Republic who has some contacts that will enable you to buy the merchandise you want. Another friend has an uncle who

EXHIBIT 7-18

BEMA GOLD CORP.
Consolidated Balance Sheets
As at December 31
(in thousands of Canadian dollars)

Assets

	1994	1993
Current		
Cash (Notes 2 & 7)	$ 45,247	$ 8,053
Marketable securities, at cost (Note 3)		
(Market 1994 - $1,298; 1993 - $926)	1,270	779
Accounts and notes receivable	1,062	1,232
Refundable Chilean tax	2,370	1,547
Prepaid expenses	49	64
	49,998	11,675
Restricted cash (Note 2)	3,139	-
Investments (Note 3)	3,594	1,028
Note receivable (Note 4)	3,953	3,415
Property, plant and equipment (Notes 5 & 9)	65,654	47,645
Other assets (Note 6)	14,076	2,638
	$ 140,414	$ 66,401

Liabilities

	1994	1993
Current		
Accounts payable	$ 7,326	$ 1,353
Provision for reclamation costs	890	545
Current portion of long-term debt (Note 7)	1,086	4,913
	9,302	6,811
Provision for reclamation costs	-	156
Long-term debt (Note 7)	-	3,767
Other liabilities (Note 6.i)	2,491	26
Non-controlling interest	14,306	5,874
	26,099	16,634

Special Warrants & Shareholders' Equity

	1994	1993
Special warrants (Note 11)	46,260	-
Shareholders' equity		
Capital stock (Notes 7, 12 & 20)		
Authorized: 300,000,000 common shares with no par value		
Issued: 62,083,485 common shares (1993 - 51,434,093)	92,667	70,879
Deficit	(24,612)	(21,112)
	68,055	49,767
	114,315	49,767
	$ 140,414	$ 66,401

Approved by the Directors

Director   Director

See accompanying notes to consolidated financial statements

EXHIBIT 7-18 (continued)

BEMA GOLD CORP.
Consolidated Statements of Loss and Deficit
For the Years Ended December 31
(in thousands of Canadian dollars, except shares and per share amounts)

	1994	1993	1992
Gold and silver revenue	$ -	$ 683	$ 4,627
Operating costs	-	557	3,088
Gross profit from mine operations	-	126	1,539
Expenses			
Depreciation and depletion	96	121	1,967
Mining taxes and royalty	-	(6)	477
Reclamation	515	179	376
General and administrative	2,231	1,773	1,967
General exploration	561	243	128
Interest on long-term debt	594	673	1,017
Amortization of deferred financing costs	76	255	333
Write-down of mining interest	-	-	243
	4,073	3,238	6,508
Loss before the following	(4,073)	(3,112)	(4,969)
Interest and other income	1,803	1,049	280
Other gains (losses) and (write-offs) (Note 8)	(984)	918	(3,611)
Non-controlling interest	95	313	-
Equity loss in investees	(169)	(181)	(272)
Loss before taxes	(3,328)	(1,013)	(8,572)
Capital taxes	(172)	(90)	(33)
Net loss	(3,500)	(1,103)	(8,605)
Deficit, beginning of year	(21,112)	(20,009)	(11,404)
Deficit, end of year	($ 24,612)	($ 21,112)	($ 20,009)
Net loss per common share	($0.06)	($0.03)	($0.28)
Weighted average common shares outstanding (in thousands)	55,634	35,887	31,185

See accompanying notes to consolidated financial statements

owns a trucking company that transports merchandise all over Europe. You hope to use the trucking company to transport your merchandise from the Czech Republic to Amsterdam for shipment to Canada.

You are going to have a meeting to discuss the necessary details surrounding the buying and selling of the inventory. In preparation for the meeting, write a short report outlining the items that you think should be discussed. To make this more realistic and your task easier, decide on what types of inventory you are going to buy. The type of inventory you import will affect some of the decisions you make.

EXHIBIT 7-18 (continued)

BEMA GOLD CORP.
Consolidated Statements of Cash Flows
For the Years Ended December 31
(in thousands of Canadian dollars)

Operating activities	1994	1993	1992
Net loss for the year	($ 3,500)	($ 1,103)	($ 8,605)
Non-cash charges (credits)			
Depreciation and depletion	96	121	1,764
Reclamation	189	(1)	341
Equity loss in investees	169	181	272
Amortization of deferred charges	108	351	583
Write-down of mining interest	-	-	243
Interest and other income	-	(713)	-
Other (gains) losses and write-offs	3,038	(950)	3,691
Non-controlling interest	(95)	(313)	-
Change in non-cash working capital			
Accounts and notes receivable	152	(592)	(106)
Inventories	4	440	1,653
Prepaid expenses	15	44	100
Accounts payable	855	(595)	(146)
Cash from (to) operating activities	1,031	(3,130)	(210)

Financing activities			
Common shares issued (Note 12)	21,788	28,451	1,034
Subsidiary's shares issued	8,079	8,347	-
Issue of special warrants	44,336	-	-
Debenture conversions and repayments	(6,419)	(15,636)	(700)
Capital lease repayments	(72)	(1,491)	(424)
Gold loan repayments	-	(611)	(1,164)
Mortgage repayments	(964)	(408)	(128)
Deferred financing costs	(7,345)	(201)	(372)
Restricted cash	(3,139)	-	-
Other	31	(45)	7
Cash from (to) financing activities	56,295	18,406	(1,747)

Investing activities			
Property, plant and equipment, net	(18,120)	(8,046)	(4,018)
Acquisitions	-	(651)	-
Investment purchases	(3,970)	(164)	(1,002)
Note receivable	(322)	(3,311)	-
Proceeds on sale of:			
Subsidiary shares	3,325	1,906	-
Investments	79	1,762	1,909
Equipment	127	1,458	-
Refundable Chilean tax	(711)	(170)	(188)
Other	(540)	(247)	(147)
Cash to investing activities	(20,132)	(7,463)	(3,446)

	1994	1993	1992
Increase (decrease) in cash	37,194	7,813	(5,403)
Cash, beginning of year	8,053	240	5,643
Cash, end of year	$ 45,247	$ 8,053	$ 240

See accompanying notes to consolidated financial statements

CHAPTER

8

Capital Assets

In the previous two chapters, assets whose value would be realized within one year (or operating cycle) of the corporation were considered. In this chapter, all assets whose value will be realized over a period of time longer than a year (or operating cycle) are discussed. Property, plant, and equipment are the most recognizable of these **capital assets**. These are a type of noncurrent asset called **tangible assets**, which are usually defined as those assets with some physical form ("tangible" comes from the Latin word meaning "to touch"). **Intangible assets** are noncurrent capital assets that are associated with certain rights or privileges of the corporation, such as patents, trademarks, leases, and goodwill.

In the sections that follow, the recognition and valuation issues for capital assets are discussed, much as they were for current assets. Because of the long-term nature of these assets, the issue of how to show the income statement effects (expensing of the cost) of the purchase of these assets over time must be addressed. The expense that is recorded is referred to as **amortization**.

◖◗ RECOGNITION CRITERIA

The probable future value of noncurrent assets takes at least two forms. Capital assets are used, first and foremost, to produce products or to provide services. Therefore, the future value is represented by the cash that will be received from sales of those products and services in the future. Because of the long-term nature of capital assets, these cash flows will be received over several future periods. This type of value is sometimes referred to as **value in use.**

The second source of value for capital assets is their ultimate sales value. Many capital assets are used until the corporation decides to replace them with a new asset. For example, a business may use a truck for three or four years and then trade it in on a new one. This type of value is called **residual value** and can be very important, depending on the type of asset.

Value in use is normally the most appropriate concept for capital assets because corporations usually invest in them to use them, not to sell them. Residual value cannot be totally ignored because it affects the value of the asset at the end of the period for which the corporation uses the asset. You saw in Chapter 2 how we use residual value to determine amortization.

The uncertainty of the value in use for capital assets is the inherent uncertainty with regard to future sales of the product or service produced. The corporation does not know with certainty whether the demand for its products or services will continue into the future. It also does not know what prices the corporation will be able to command for its products or services. Other uncertainties relate to the production technology. Equipment can become obsolete as a result of technological change. New technology can give competitors a significant advantage in producing and pricing the product. Technological change can also eliminate the need for the corporation's product. Consider the disadvantages of a typewriter manufacturer with the advent of the personal computer.

The uncertainty of the ultimate residual value is similar to that of the value in use because the ultimate residual value depends on whether the asset has any value in use to the ultimate buyer. It also is uncertain whether a buyer can even be found.

Equipment that is made to the original buyer's specifications may not have much of a residual market because it may not meet the needs of other potential users.

VALUATION CRITERIA

In the sections that follow, the discussion is limited to valuation issues regarding property, plant, and equipment, which are similar to those relating to other noncurrent capital assets. At the end of the chapter, specific concerns and issues with regard to intangible assets are discussed.

Canadian GAAP requires that property, plant, and equipment be valued at their historical cost with no recognition of market value unless there is a permanent decline in the value of the asset. Some countries do allow for the recognition of changes in market values of property, plant, and equipment and there have been historical instances of corporations disclosing information about the market values of their property, plant, and equipment. Before GAAP is discussed in detail, several possible valuation methods are considered.

Historical Cost

In an historical-cost value system, the original cost of the asset is recorded at the time of acquisition. Changes in the market value of the asset are ignored in this system. During the period in which the asset is used, its cost is expensed (amortized) using an appropriate amortization method (these methods are discussed later). Market values are recognized only when the asset is sold. The corporation then recognizes a gain or loss on the sale, where the gain or loss is determined by the difference between the proceeds from the sale and the net book value of the asset at the time of sale. The net book value is the original cost less any amortization that had been taken to the point of sale. This net book value is sometimes called the **amortized cost** of the asset.

Market Value

Another possible valuation method records noncurrent assets at their market value. There are at least two types of market values: **replacement cost** and **net realizable value.**

Replacement Cost

In a **replacement cost** valuation system, the asset is carried at its replacement cost. By replacement cost, accountants mean the amount that would be needed to acquire an equivalent asset. At acquisition, the historical cost is recorded because this is the replacement cost at the time of purchase. As the asset is used, the carrying value of the asset is adjusted upward or downward to reflect changes in the replacement cost. Unrealized gains and losses are recognized for these changes. The periodic expensing of the asset, in the form of amortization, has to be adjusted to reflect the changes in the replacement cost. For example, if the replacement cost of the asset goes up, the amortization expense will also have to go up to reflect the higher replacement cost. A gain or loss is also recognized upon disposal of this asset. The amount of the gain or loss is determined by the difference between the proceeds from the sale, and the amortized replacement cost at the time of sale. The CICA at one time recommended that corporations report supplementary information on the replacement cost of its property, plant, and equipment. In countries experiencing extreme rates of inflation, capital assets may be recorded at replacement value to provide a better measure of the results for the period. For example, in Mexico, replacement cost of property, plant, and equipment is required for corporations whose shares trade on stock exchanges.

Net Realizable Value

With a net realizable value system, assets are recorded at the amount that could be received by converting the asset to cash in the normal course of business. During the periods in which assets are being used, gains and losses are recognized as the net realizable values change over time. Amortization in this type of system is based on the net realizable value and is adjusted every year for the change in this value. At the time of sale, there is no further recognition of gain or loss as the asset should be carried at net realizable value at the date of sale. This system is not consistent with the notion of value in use of the asset, which assumes the corporation has no intention of selling the asset. Therefore, this method is generally not used in Canada.

The word *market* must be used with some care. The preceding discussions assume that both the replacement market and the selling market are the markets in which the corporation normally trades. There are, however, special markets for assets if the corporation must liquidate its assets quickly. The values in these markets can be significantly different from those in the normal market. As long as the corporation is a going concern, these specialty markets are not appropriate markets to establish values for the corporation's assets. On the other hand, if the corporation is bankrupt or going out of business, these specialty markets may be the most appropriate places to obtain estimates of the market values of the corporation's assets.

Net Present Value

Another possible valuation system is to record assets at their net present value. By present value, accountants mean the discounted amount of future cash flows expected to be received from the asset. This valuation system is, in fact, used by many businesses to make the initial decision about whether to buy an asset. Estimates are made of the cash in flows that will be received and cash out flows that will be incurred from the use of the asset. These estimated cash flows are then "present-valued" (see the Appendix to the text for a full discussion of present value) and compared to the cost. If the present value is more than the cost, the asset is worth more to the corporation than its cost. If the present value is less than the cost, the asset will not be worth the cost.

When a present value system is used for accounting purposes, the present value at the date of acquisition is recorded. If this amount differs from the cost at the date of acquisition, a gain or loss is reported for the difference. Gains and losses may also be recognized as the assumptions underlying the present-value calculation change. These assumptions include the amounts and timing of the cash flows as well as the interest rate used to discount the cash flows. Amortization under a present-value system can be viewed as the net change in the present value of the asset from the beginning of the period to the end of the period. At the time of disposal of an asset, a gain or loss is recognized based on the difference between the proceeds and the net present value at the time of disposal.

The present value method has significant appeal when the initial decision to buy the asset is made on the basis of its net present value. In fact, this method provides the most consistent way to measure the performance of the investment in the asset after its purchase. However, the net-present-value method requires numerous estimates and accountants generally feel that the resulting values are too unreliable to be used for reporting purposes.

▶️🔺 What is GAAP?

Capital assets are normally valued at their historical cost (their original acquisition cost). During the period of use, the cost of the asset is expensed using an amortization method that is rational, systematic, and appropriate to the asset. The estimated period of use is generally assumed to have a maximum period of 40 years because estimates longer than 40 years tend to be very uncertain. Changes in market values of the assets are generally not recognized. If it is ever anticipated that the net recoverable amount is less than the net carrying value, the difference is recognized as an expense and the carrying value of the asset must be written down. The net recoverable amount is the total of all future cash flows without discounting them to present values.

■ ■ Capitalizable Costs

At the date of acquisition, the corporation must decide which costs associated with the purchase of the asset should be included or capitalized as a part of the asset's cost. The general guideline under GAAP is that any cost that is necessary to acquire and get the asset ready for use is a **capitalizable cost**. The following is a partial list of costs that would be considered capitalizable costs:

CAPITALIZABLE COSTS UNDER GAAP:

Purchase price (less any discounts)

Installation costs

Transportation costs

Legal costs

Direct taxes

Interest cost (self-constructed assets)

The determination of which costs appropriately belong in an asset account is not always an easy one. For example, the cost associated with the salaries of the employees who manage the acquisition of the asset are normally not included in the acquisition cost itself. This is true even though the time spent by the employees is necessary to acquire the asset.

Deciding which costs to capitalize is also influenced by the rules used for tax purposes. For tax purposes, the corporation would like to expense as many costs as possible to reduce taxable income and save on taxes. Capitalizing a cost means that the corporation will have to wait until the asset is amortized before the cost can be deducted for tax purposes. There is, therefore, an incentive to expense rather than to capitalize costs that are only indirectly related to the acquisition of the asset. A corporation may decide to expense the cost for reporting purposes to bolster their argument that the cost is an expense for tax purposes. The materiality criterion also plays a part in which costs are capitalized. Small expenditures related to the purchase of the asset may be expensed rather than capitalized because it is easier to expense them.

■■ Basket Purchases

Sometimes a corporation acquires several assets in one transaction. For example, when a forest products corporation acquires timberland, it is buying both land and timber. The price paid for the timberland must then be divided between the land and the timber. Under GAAP, the price paid for these two assets must be divided between them on the basis of their relative fair values at the time of acquisition for two reasons. First, full disclosure requires that each important type of asset should be shown separately. Second, each type of asset that has a different rate of amortization should be separated in the accounts.

Suppose that the purchase price of the timberland was $1 million and the relative fair values of the land and timber were assessed at $300,000 and $900,000 respectively. In this case, 25% [$300,000/($300,000 + $900,000)] of the cost, or $250,000, should be assigned to the land and the remaining 75%, or $750,000, should be assigned to the timber. In the case of timberland, splitting the cost has significant implications for the corporation because the cost of land is not amortized and the cost of timber can be expensed as the timber is harvested.

■■ Interest Capitalization

Interest capitalization deserves special consideration. Interest is capitalized when accountants include the interest paid on money borrowed to finance a capital asset in the cost of the asset, rather than expensing it. This is an issue for corporations that construct some of their own capital assets. For example, some utility corporations construct their own buildings. In addition to the costs incurred in the actual construction of the asset, such as raw materials, labour, and overhead, the corporation may also incur interest costs if it has to borrow money to pay for the materials, labour, and overhead. Canadian GAAP permits corporations to capitalize interest costs for capital assets that are constructed or acquired over time if the costs are directly attributable to the acquisition, although no detailed guidelines are set. For assets that are purchased rather than constructed, interest costs are not capitalized.

AN INTERNATIONAL PERSPECTIVE
REPORTS FROM OTHER COUNTRIES

While most countries value property, plant, and equipment at historical cost, a few (the United Kingdom, France, and Switzerland) allow for revaluation of these assets based on current replacement costs. In France, these revaluations are seldom done because there is a conformity between the reporting and tax books that would make these revaluations taxable. In the United Kingdom, such revaluations are quite common. The footnote disclosure from the 1994 financial statement of Guinness PLC (a distiller and brewer), as shown in Exhibit 8-1, illustrates this point. The increase in the valuation of assets that occurs under replacement cost valuation does not typically pass through income but is instead recorded directly in the shareholders' equity section in an account called a revaluation reserve. More will be said about these reserves in Chapter 11.

EXHIBIT 8-1

GUINNESS PLC
Excerpted from Notes to the Statements

14. Tangible Fixed Assets

	Land and buildings (Note (A)) £m	Plant and machinery £m	Casks, containers and road vehicles £m	Total £m
Cost or valuation				
At 1 January 1994	845	1,142	246	2,233
Additions	44	125	52	221
Subsidiaries acquired	4	3	—	7
Disposals	(1)	(35)	(26)	(62)
Exchange adjustments	(1)	(17)	(3)	(21)
At 31 December 1994	891	1,218	269	2,378
Depreciation				
At 1 January 1994	28	409	71	508
Charge for the year	18	90	33	141
Disposals	—	(22)	(24)	(46)
Exchange adjustments	—	(7)	(2)	(9)
At 31 December 1994	46	470	78	594
Net book amount				
At 31 December 1994	845	748	191	1,784
At 31 December 1993	817	733	175	1,725

EXHIBIT 8-1 (continued)

GUINNESS PLC
Excerpted from Notes to the Statements

(A) Land and Buildings
(I) The amount shown at cost or valuation includes the following:

	1994	1993
	£m	£m
At cost	348	301
At valuation in 1992	543	544
	891	845

AMORTIZATION CONCEPTS

Amortization is a systematic and rational method of allocating the cost of capital assets to the periods in which the benefits from the assets are received. This matches, in some systematic way, the expense of the asset to the revenues earned from its use. The allocation of any cost across multiple periods will always be somewhat arbitrary. GAAP requires only that the amortization method used be a rational and systematic method appropriate to the nature of the capital asset with a limited life and to its use by the enterprise. In addition, the method of amortization and estimates of the useful life should be reviewed on a regular basis.

Amortization as used in accounting does not refer to valuation. While it is true that the capital assets of a corporation generally decrease in value over time, amortization does not attempt to measure this change in value.

Matching some portion of a capital asset's cost to the revenues of the corporation, along with the other expenses of the corporation, results in a net profit or loss during the period. The corporation does not show the entire cost of the capital asset as an expense in the period of acquisition because the asset is expected to produce revenues over multiple future periods. If these revenues do not materialize, the corporation will have overstated its profitability in earlier periods and will have to write off the remaining cost of the asset.

To allocate the expense systematically to the proper number of periods, the corporation must estimate the **useful life** of the asset, that is, the periods over which the corporation intends to use the asset to produce revenues. The corporation must also estimate the ultimate residual sales value of the asset at the end of its useful life.

Once the useful life and residual value of the asset have been estimated, the **amortizable cost** (cost minus the residual value) must then be allocated in a systematic and rational way to the years of useful life. Even though Canadian GAAP does not specify which amortization methods may be used, most Canadian corporations use one of three methods. These methods are discussed in the next section.

◖◗ AMORTIZATION METHODS

As GAAP developed in the twentieth century, "rational and systematic" methods of amortizing capital assets were developed. The simplest, and most commonly used method (used by about 50% of Canadian companies) is the **straight-line** method (illustrated in Chapter 2), which allocates the amortizable cost of the asset evenly over the useful life of the asset. Many accountants have argued in favour of this method for two reasons. First, it is a very simple method to apply. Second, they argue that it properly matches expenses to revenues for costs associated with assets that generate revenues evenly throughout their lives. It might also be argued that, if an asset physically deteriorates evenly throughout its life, then straight-line amortization would capture this physical decline.

For certain assets, decline in revenue-generating capabilities (and physical deterioration) do not occur evenly over time. In fact, many assets are of most benefit to the corporation during the early years of their useful lives. In later years, when an asset is wearing out and requires more maintenance and perhaps produces inferior products, the value to the corporation declines significantly. This scenario argues for a more rapid amortization in the early years of the asset's life when a larger amortization expense is matched to the larger revenues produced. Methods that match this pattern are known as **accelerated** or **diminishing balance amortization** methods.

A third type of amortization recognizes that the usefulness or benefits derived from some capital assets can be measured fairly specifically. These methods are called **production** or **unit of production methods**. Their use requires that the output or usefulness that will be derived from the asset be measurable as a specific quantity. For example, a new truck might be expected to be used for a specific number of kilometres, such as 500,000. Then the amortization cost per kilometre can be calculated and used to determine amortization expense based on the number of kilometres driven in the accounting period.

A fourth but rarely used amortization method argues that, for some assets, the greatest change in usefulness and/or physical deterioration takes place in the last years of the asset's life rather than in the first few years. A method that captures this pattern is called **decelerated amortization**. Although this type of amortization method is not used much in practice, it is conceptually consistent with a present-value method of valuation of the asset. **Present-value amortization methods**, also sometimes called **compound interest methods**, are of this type.

Exhibit 8-2 illustrates the pattern of decline in the carrying value of an asset under the three basic types of methods: **straight-line**, **accelerated**, and **decelerated**. Exhibit 8-3 illustrates the pattern of amortization expense recognition with the same methods. The graphs are based on a 40-year useful life, a zero residual value, and a $10,000 original cost. The methods used are the **straight-line**, **accelerated**, and **decelerated** methods. These methods are discussed in detail later. Note that Exhibits 8-2 and 8-3 do not show production methods because there is no consistent pattern with production methods. The amount of amortization expense depends on the actual usage each year.

EXHIBIT 8-2

Amortization Methods

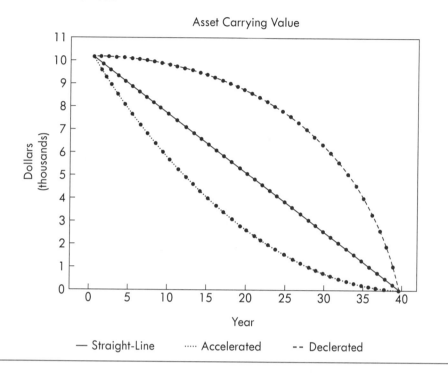

Asset Carrying Value

— Straight-Line   ····· Accelerated   -- Declerated

In Exhibit 8-2, note that using the straight-line method produces an even (or straight-line) decline in the carrying value of the asset. The accelerated method produces a more rapid decline in the carrying value, and the decelerated method (present value) shows a less rapid decline. Note that all methods start and end at the same value.

In Exhibit 8-3, you can see that the expense for each period is the same with the straight-line method. Using an accelerated method, the amortization expenses are higher in the earlier years of the asset's life, corresponding to the more rapid decline in carrying value as seen in Exhibit 8-2. A decelerated method, on the other hand, shows a slower decline in the carrying value of the asset and hence small amounts of amortization expense in the earlier years compared to the later years. Although the pattern of recognition is different, the total amount of the expense taken over the life of the asset is the same for all methods.

Straight-Line Method

The most common method used for financial reporting is the **straight-line method**. It assumes that the cost of the asset should be allocated evenly over the life of the asset. Estimates must be made of the useful life and residual value. To illustrate the straight-line calculation and the calculation of amortization using other methods, a simple example is used. Assume that the corporation buys an asset for $10,000, with an estimated useful life of five years and an estimated residual value of $1,000. Straight-line amortization would be computed as shown in Exhibit 8-4.

EXHIBIT 8-3

Amortization Methods

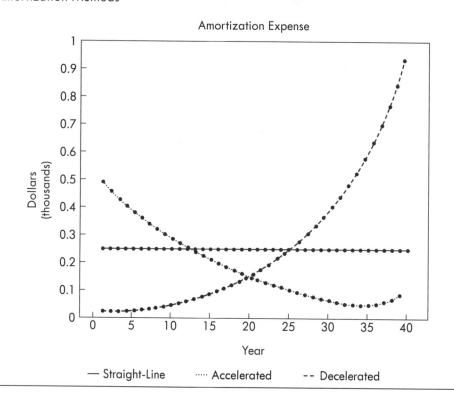

Amortization Expense

Straight-Line ·····*Accelerated* -- *Decelerated*

The $1,800 of amortization expense is recorded each year for five years so that, by the end of the useful life of the asset, the entire amortizable cost ($9,000 = $10,000 − 1,000) will have been expensed and the residual value of $1,000 will remain on the books of the corporation.

Whereas the straight-line method can be described by the estimated useful life and estimated value, it is sometimes characterized by a rate of amortization. The rate of amortization with the straight-line method is determined by taking the inverse of the number of years, 1/N, where N is the number of years of estimated useful life. In the case of the asset in the example, amortizing it over five years means a rate of 0.2 (1/5) or 20% per year. This will be referred to as the **straight-line rate.**

Accelerated Methods

Most accelerated methods are computed by multiplying the carrying value of the asset by a fixed percentage. Because the carrying value (cost less accumulated amortization) decreases each year (because the accumulated amortization increases each year by the amount of the amortization recorded), the computed amount of amortization to be recognized as an expense decreases each year.

The percentage used in these computations is selected by management based on their judgement of the rapidity of the decline in usefulness of the asset. The faster

EXHIBIT 8-4

Straight-Line Method

Assumptions:

Original Cost	$10,000
Estimated Residual Value	$ 1,000
Estimated Useful Life	5 years

Calculation:

Straight-line Amortization

$$\text{Amortization Expense} = \frac{\text{Original Cost} - \text{Estimated Residual Value}}{\text{Estimated Useful Life}}$$

$$= \frac{\$10,000 - \$1,000}{5 \text{ years}}$$

$$= \$1,800 \text{ per year}$$

Amortization schedule:

Year	Book Value Beginning	Amortization Expense
1	$10,000	$1,800
2	8,200	1,800
3	6,400	1,800
4	4,600	1,800
5	2,800	1,800
		$9,000

the decline, the higher the percentage selected. Different types of capital assets have different percentages. A capital asset with a relatively long expected useful life (such as a building) would have a fairly small percentage (such as 5% or 10%). A capital asset with a relatively short expected useful life (such as equipment) would have a larger percentage (such as 20% or 30%).

One method of establishing the percentage rates to be used is called the **double declining balance method**. With this method, the percentage selected is double the straight-line rate. Thus, using the example shown above in Exhibit 8-4, the 5-year expected useful life of an asset would be amortized over 5 years on a straight-line basis (that is, 1/5 per year, or 20%), but would be amortized at 40% using a double declining balance method (2 × 20%). However, even though this method appears to be based on fairly concrete numbers, it must be remembered that the 40% rate is still only an estimate.

Double declining balance amortization is calculated for our example asset in Exhibit 8-5. Note that the residual value of the asset does not enter into the computation of the amortization expense. In accelerated methods, the estimated residual value serves as a constraint. In the example in Exhibit 8-5, this means that in Year 5 the corporation would not take the full amortization expense determined by the calculation because this would reduce the carrying value of the asset below the estimated residual value. In other cases, the residual value may not be reached prior to

EXHIBIT 8-5

Double Declining Balance Method

Assumptions:

Original Cost	$10,000
Estimated Residual Value	1,000
Estimated Useful Life	5 years
200% Declining Balance Method	

Calculation:

$$\text{DB rate} = \text{DB\%} \times \text{SL rate}$$
$$= 200\% \times 1/n$$
$$= 200\% \times 1/5 = 40\%$$

Amortization schedule:

At the beginning of the year

Year	Balance in PP&E	Accumulated Amortization	Net Book Value	Calculation of Expense		Amortization Expense
1	$10,000	$0	$10,000	40% × 10,000	=	$4,000
2	10,000	4,000	6,000	40% × 6,000	=	2,400
3	10,000	6,400	3,600	40% × 3,600	=	1,440
4	10,000	7,840	2,160	40% × 2,160	=	864
5	10,000	8,704	1,296	40% × 1,296	=	296
a						
						$9,000

a The calculation of amortization expense in Year 5 results in a calculated amortization expense of $518, which would reduce the balance below the residual value. Therefore, only the amount of expense necessary to bring the balance to the residual value ($1,000) is allowed.

the end of the useful life so that additional amortization must be taken in the year of disposal of the asset. Alternatively, a loss on disposal could be recognized. In the example in Exhibit 8-5, suppose that the residual value was $500. The amortization schedule would be the same as in Exhibit 8-5 except that in Year 5 the corporation would have to recognize $796 in amortization expense so the carrying value of the asset would be $500, which is the amount of the residual value.

Production Methods

Another method used to calculate amortization is based on the assumption that benefits derived from a capital asset are related to the output or use of that asset. Note that the straight-line and accelerated methods of amortization assume that benefits derived from capital assets are related to time, disregarding how much the assets are actually used during the time period. **Production methods** relate benefits to actual usage.

Use of **production methods** requires that the useful life of the assets must be known or can be estimated and expressed as units of output. For example, trucks can be amortized using a production method if their expected useful life can be expressed in kilometres driven or hours used. Machinery used in producing products may have an expected useful life based on the total number of units of output. Amortization expense is determined by calculating the amortization cost per unit, then multiplying this cost per unit by the actual number of units produced for the time period. The formula for calculating amortization expense per unit for production methods is as follows:

$$\text{amortization expense per unit} = \frac{(\text{cost} - \text{residual value})}{\text{estimated total units of output}}$$

To calculate total amortization expense, simply multiply this per-unit cost by the total number of units produced.

■ ■ Recording amortization expense

For any amortization method, the recording of the expense is similar. Amortization expense is debited and accumulated amortization is credited. The credit side of the entry is made to an accumulated amortization account and not to the asset account. The accumulated amortization account is a contra-asset account that is used to accumulate the total amount of amortization expense that has been recorded for the capital asset. It might help you to think of the asset account being used to show the original historical cost of the asset, and the accumulated amortization account being used to show how much of the asset has already been used.

In financial statements, corporations normally show the total original costs of all tangible capital assets separately by category, (such as land, buildings, and equipment) with accumulated amortization for each category. Some corporations show only one total for accumulated amortization for all the various categories of assets. Some corporations show capital assets grouped not by category but by operating division. Many corporations show only the total net book value (cost less accumulated amortization) in the balance sheet, with the details provided in a note to the financial statements.

Examples of disclosure of capital assets (sometimes called fixed assets) and related accumulated amortization (sometimes called depreciation) are shown in Exhibits 8-6 and 8-7.

◖◗ DEFERRED TAXES

The issue of deferred taxes, which is discussed in greater depth in Chapter 9, arises quite naturally at this point and is therefore introduced here. Deferred taxes arise because Revenue Canada does not allow corporations to deduct amortization expense when calculating taxable income. However, they do allow a similar type of deduction, called **capital cost allowance**. Capital cost allowance (CCA) is calculated in a manner similar to accelerated amortization, with several exceptions.

EXHIBIT 8-6

CARA OPERATIONS
Excerpted from Notes to the Statements

Disclosure of Capital Assets by Category
3. Capital Assets

(In thousands of dollars)	Cost	Accumulated Amortization	1995 Net	Cost	Accumulated Amortization	1994 Net
Land	$ 39,864	$ —	$ 39,864	$ 40,362	$ —	$ 40,362
Buildings	95,032	31,228	63,804	93,734	29,146	64,588
Equipment	138,160	59,491	78,669	132,374	56,385	75,989
Leasehold improvements	43,937	20,464	23,473	43,678	18,376	25,302
Equipment under capital leases	22,115	3,169	18,946	13,430	1,587	11,843
	$ 339,108	$ 114,352	$ 224,756	$ 323,578	$ 105,494	$ 218,084

EXHIBIT 8-7

ALGOMA CENTRAL CORPORATION
Excerpted from Notes to the Statements

Disclosure of Capital Assets by Operating Division
4. Fixed assets

		1994		
	Land	Depreciable Assets	Accumulated Depreciation	Net
Marine Group	$ 171,000	$ 352,364,000	$ 224,634,000	$ 127,901,000
Real Estate Group	936,000	46,809,000	12,996,000	34,749,000
Corporate	—	519,000	358,000	161,000
	$ 1,107,000	$ 399,692,000	$ 237,988,000	$ 162,811,000
		1993		
	Land	Depreciable Assets	Accumulated Depreciation	Net
Marine Group	$ 69,000	$ 330,690,000	$ 208,639,000	$ 122,120,000
Real Estate Group	1,294,000	46,728,000	11,610,000	36,412,000
Corporate	—	515,000	263,000	252,000
	$ 1,363,000	$ 377,933,000	$ 220,512,000	$ 158,784,000

Deferred taxes result mainly from differences in the timing of the recording of the amortization expense and the deduction of the related capital cost allowance.

While it is not the purpose of this text to teach you about income taxes, which are subject to very complex rules, you should understand the basic rules of how capital cost allowance works. For tax purposes, capital assets are grouped into classes as defined by Revenue Canada. For example, most vehicles are grouped into Class 10 and most equipment into Class 8. Each class has a prescribed rate used to calculate the maximum amount that may be deducted. For example, Class 10 has a maximum rate of 30% and Class 8 has a 20% rate. Corporations may deduct any amount of the **undepreciated capital cost** (UCC) in the class up to the stated maximum in a year, except for assets acquired in the current year. The maximum CCA that may be deducted for new assets is restricted to 50% of the normal amount.

As an example, assume that Central Corp. purchases new equipment (Class 8) in Year 1 with a total cost of $20,000. For tax purposes, they may deduct a maximum of $2,000 (50% × $20,000 × 20%) CCA in Year 1. In Year 2, they may deduct a maximum of $3,600 (20% × ($20,000 − $2,000)). In Year 3, the maximum would be $2,880 (20% × ($20,000 − $2,000 − $3,600)). Note that the UCC declines each year by the amount of CCA claimed.

The cost of new capital assets is added to the class to increase the UCC. When capital assets are sold, the lesser of the cost or the proceeds is deducted from the UCC.

These differences between tax and financial statement amounts can produce significant differences between the income measured in accordance with GAAP and the taxable income reported to Revenue Canada. For example, assume that a corporation has only one asset. Assume further that there are no other differences in the revenues and expenses for accounting and tax purposes. For tax purposes, assume the maximum capital cost allowance rate is 30%. For financial statement purposes, assume the use of straight-line, and use the deductions shown in Exhibit 8-4. Exhibit 8-8 presents some additional data for this hypothetical corporation and the computation of income before taxes for the first year of the asset's life.

EXHIBIT 8-8

Deferred Tax Computation

Income Statement

	Accounting	Tax
Revenues	$9,000	$9,000
Expenses (except amortization)	5,000	5,000
Income before amortization & taxes	$4,000	$4,000
Amortization/CCA	$1,800	1,500
Income before taxes	$2,200	$2,500
Tax expense (30%)	$660	
Taxes payable (30%)		$750

If the tax rate is 30%, the corporation will owe Revenue Canada $750 ($2,500 × 30%) in taxes based on the income reported to Revenue Canada. What should the corporation report as tax expense to the shareholders? Some accountants would argue that the tax expense should be calculated based on the accounting income times the tax rate. In this case, the tax expense would be $660 ($2,200 × 30%). Others would argue that the corporation should report the actual taxes payable to Revenue Canada, $750, as the expense. In the second case, the tax expense for accounting purposes would not bear any relationship to the income before taxes; that is, $750/$2,200 = 34% would not reflect the actual tax rate of 30%.

Canadian GAAP requires that the tax expense reported in the income statement be based on the accounting income before taxes multiplied by the tax rate, that is, the $660 just discussed. The entry that would be recorded for our example corporation would therefore be:

SE – Tax Expense	660	
L – Deferred Tax	90	
L – Income Taxes Payable		750

As you can see in the preceding entry, the debit to tax expense would then be less than the credit to the taxes payable account, because the latter is based on what is actually owed to Revenue Canada. The difference between these two entries is called the deferred tax. If the deferred tax has a debit balance, it represents tax that is paid to Revenue Canada before it appears in the income statement as an expense. If deferred tax has a credit balance, it represents taxes that will eventually have to be paid by the corporation later in the asset's life, when the amortization for tax purposes is significantly less than the deduction for reporting purposes.

Deferred tax, therefore, arises from differences in the methods used to compute either revenues or expenses for tax purposes compared to financial statement purposes. The discussion of income taxes is continued in more detail in Chapter 9.

CHOICE OF AMORTIZATION METHOD

Corporations are free to choose from the amortization methods that have been discussed. The majority of corporations use the straight-line method, probably because of its simplicity and possibly because it produces the highest net income in the early years of an asset's life. Some small corporations choose to calculate amortization expense in the same amount as CCA to simplify bookkeeping.

CHANGES IN AMORTIZATION ESTIMATES AND METHODS

Because the amounts used for useful life and residual values are estimates, the assumptions used in their estimation may change over time. For example, after an asset has been in service for several years, the corporation may change its estimate about the remaining useful life of the asset. The asset may last longer or deteriorate faster than originally anticipated. Changes in the estimates used to calculate amortization expense are *accounting estimate changes*. As discussed in Chapter 3, accounting estimate changes are handled prospectively.

To illustrate a prospective change in amortization assumptions, the amortization example in Exhibit 8-4 will be used. Assume that, at the end of Year 3, the corporation decides that the asset has three more years of useful life left (i.e., it should have had an original life of six rather than five years), and that the residual value at the end of the sixth year will be $400. The corporation recalculates the amortization for Years 4, 5, and 6 based on these new assumptions. The new calculation is based on the remaining book value at the end of Year 3 of $4,600 [$10,000 − (3 × $1,800)]. The entire schedule of amortization, then, is as shown in Exhibit 8-9. Note that there is no restatement of prior periods with a change of estimate.

The disclosure of changes in estimates in financial statements usually describes the nature of the change and the effects on the current year. An example of a change in accounting estimate for Bally Manufacturing Corporation is shown on the following page.

EXHIBIT 8-9

Straight-Line Method
Change in Estimate of Useful Life and Residual Value

Assumptions:

Original Cost	$10,000
Estimated Residual Value	$ 1,000
Estimated Useful Life	5 years

At end of year 3:

Remaining Estimated Useful Life	3 years
Estimated Residual Value	$400

Calculation of Remaining Amortization (years 4–6):

Straight-Line Amortization

$$\text{Amortization Expense} = \frac{\text{Remaining Book Value} - \text{Estimated Residual Value}}{\text{Estimated Useful Life}}$$

$$= \frac{\$4,600 - 400}{3 \text{ years}}$$

$$= \$1,400 \text{ per year}$$

Amortization Schedule:

Year	Book Value Beginning	Amortization Expense
1	$10,000	$1,800
2	8,200	1,800
3	6,400	1,800
4	4,600	1,400[a]
5	3,200	1,400
6	1,800	1,400
		$9,600

[a] Year of change in accounting estimates.

BALLY MANUFACTURING CORPORATION

Depreciation of property, plant, and equipment is provided principally on the straight-line method. Depreciation expense was $130,943,000, $127,766,000, and $117,770,000 for 1990, 1989, and 1988. Effective January 1, 1989, the company extended, by one to two years, the estimated useful lives of furniture, fixtures and equipment in the three casino properties it acquired in 1986 and 1987. The change was made to more accurately reflect the service period of these assets. The change had the effect of increasing income before extraordinary item and net income by $4,504,000 or $.17 per share in 1989.

Amortization amounts can also change as new costs are added to the asset account for major repairs and improvements. These generally will require new estimates of useful life and residual value. These are handled as changes in accounting estimates.

Changes in amortization *methods* are handled in a similar fashion to any other change in accounting methods. As discussed in Chapter 3, such changes require the corporation to make the changes retroactively and to restate the financial statements to make them appear as they would have appeared had the new method always been used. This topic is discussed in more detail in more advanced accounting courses.

⬤ DISPOSAL OF PROPERTY, PLANT, AND EQUIPMENT

At the end of an asset's useful life, the corporation usually sells the asset for another asset of similar productive capacity, especially if the line of business is growing and prospering. In lines of business that are on a decline or discontinued, old assets are not replaced and assets may be sold or written off before they reach the end of their useful lives.

Normally, at the end of an asset's life, the asset is sold. If the corporation has accurately projected the residual value, there is no gain or loss on the transaction. If the residual value was not estimated accurately, either a gain or a loss results from this transaction. For example, suppose that the asset in Exhibit 8-4 is sold at the end of its useful life for $1,200. Recall that its original cost was $10,000 and that its residual value was $1,000. The following entry would be made to record the transaction.

A – Cash	1,200	
XA – Accumulated Amortization	9,000	
A – Property, Plant, and Equipment		10,000
SE – Gain on Sale of Property, Plant, and Equipment		200

In this entry, the accumulated amortization is removed from the account as well as the original cost. Note that the net of these two amounts is the carrying value of the asset at the point of sale, $1,000 ($10,000 − 9,000). This amount is also known as the **book value** or the **net book value** at the time of sale. Note also that you cannot credit the property, plant, and equipment account for the amount of the book value of $1,000 as that would leave $9,000 in the asset account and $9,000 in the accumulated amortization, even though the asset is no longer owned by the corporation.

If the asset had been worthless at the end of its useful life, the disposal of the asset would be recorded as above, except that no cash is received. If we assume that no cash is received, then the *write-off* of the asset in our example results in the following entry: Note that the remaining book value of $1,000 is recorded as a loss on disposal and not as an adjustment to the amortization that has been recorded.

SE – Loss on disposal of Property, Plant, and Equipment	1,000	
XA – Accumulated Amortization	9,000	
A – Property, Plant, and Equipment		10,000

NATURAL RESOURCES

Corporations that deal with natural resources face some unique problems not associated with investments in property, plant, and equipment. For example, consider the situation of an oil exploration corporation. The corporation incurs large costs to find oil. Some explorations are successful in finding oil and others are not. Should the costs of unsuccessful exploration be capitalized on the balance sheet as assets, or should they be written off? If these costs are capitalized as assets, that implies they have future value. But do they? On successful explorations, if the costs are capitalized, how should they be expensed? That is, what is the useful life of the asset created, and what is a reasonable pattern of expense allocation across the useful life? The amortization of natural resources is sometimes referred to as depletion.

Under GAAP, oil exploration companies have a choice of two methods to account for exploration costs: the **full costing method,** and the **successful efforts method**. The full costing method capitalizes the costs of all explorations, both successful and unsuccessful, as long as the expected revenues from all explorations are estimated to exceed the total costs. The successful efforts method, on the other hand, capitalizes only the cost of successful explorations, and expenses unsuccessful exploration costs. Sufficient time is allowed to determine whether an effort is or is not successful. Generally, smaller oil corporations use the full costing method as use of the successful efforts method would make their income appear to be very uneven from year to year, depending on the results of the wells they drilled in the year. Larger oil corporations drill more wells every year, so they tend to use the successful efforts method as it is simpler to apply.

With either method, the capitalized costs are then expensed over the life of the exploration site. The amortization method most commonly used is the **units-of-production method**. With this method, the total number of barrels of oil (in the case of an oil field) that exists in the field is estimated. The amortization expense is then calculated by dividing the number of barrels extracted during the period by the estimated total and multiplying this ratio by the capitalized costs. If, for example, the corporation estimates a field to have 2,000,000 barrels of oil, that 500,000 barrels are extracted in a given period, and that the capitalized costs are $6 million, then the amortization expense during the period would be $1.5 million ($6,000,000/ $2,000,000 × 500,000).

INTANGIBLE ASSETS

As discussed earlier in the chapter, some assets can have probable future value to the corporation but may not have any physical form. The knowledge gained from research and development, or the customer loyalty and awareness spawned by a well-run advertising campaign, are examples of intangible assets. The corporation certainly hopes that it benefits from having spent money on these things. The difficulty in trying to quantify the benefits and to assess the costs of producing intangible assets, such as research and development or advertising, is what makes intangible assets a troublesome area for accountants. Although accountants would generally agree that these might constitute assets, the inability to provide reliable data concerning their costs and future value prevents them from recording these items objectively on the books of the corporation.

The capitalization guideline for intangible assets is that if an intangible asset is developed internally by the corporation, the costs associated with its production are generally expensed as incurred. If the intangible asset is purchased from an independent third party, however, the intangible asset can be capitalized at its acquisition cost.

An exception to this general guideline occurs with the development costs for a product or process. If certain guidelines are met, these development costs may be capitalized and amortized over the useful life of the product. However, the basic research costs that might have led to the product are still expensed. The guidelines are intended to ensure that costs will be capitalized only if the product or process is actually marketable. The guidelines stipulate that the product or process be clearly definable, that technical feasibility be established, that management intend to market the product in a defined market, and that the corporation have the resources needed to complete the project.

The **amortization** of the cost of an intangible asset is similar to the amortization of other capital assets. The corporation must estimate the useful life and residual value (if any) of the asset. Because of the estimation problems associated with intangible assets, this is sometimes very difficult to do. Typically, the method used to amortize intangibles is the straight-line method, with an estimated residual value of zero. The useful life depends on the type of intangible.

One point is worth noting. When estimating the useful life of an intangible asset, both economic life and legal life should be considered. Many intangible assets, such as patents, copyrights, and trademarks, have very well-defined legal lives, but may have less well-defined and much shorter economic lives. For intangible assets that have indeterminate lives, GAAP requires that a maximum of 40 years be used for amortization purposes.

Several types of intangible assets involve special problems. They are discussed in the following section.

Advertising

Corporations spend enormous amounts of money advertising their products to increase current and future sales. Does the incurrence of advertising costs create an asset for the corporation? If the advertising is successful, then the answer is likely to be yes. But how will the corporation know if the advertising is successful, and what time periods will receive the benefits from advertisements that were purchased during the current period? The answers to these questions are very difficult to address. The intent of advertising is clearly to create an asset, but measuring its value can be extremely difficult. These measurement uncertainties are so severe that accountants generally expense all advertising costs. If a corporation does capitalize this cost, it has to provide very strong evidence to support the creation of an asset.

▶◣ Patents, Trademarks, and Copyrights

Patents, trademarks, and copyrights are legal agreements that give the owner rights to use protected information. If the protected information is valuable, then the agreements are considered assets. Of course, determining whether they have value or not is a difficult task, as is estimating the period over which the agreements will continue to have value. Each agreement has a legal life associated with it. For example, a patent has a legal life of 20 years, but this does not mean that it will have an economic life of 20 years. The patent on a computer chip, for example, may have a useful economic life of only a year or two as a result of technological innovation.

A corporation records these types of intangible assets only when it buys them from a third party. Development costs of most internally developed patents, trademarks, and copyrights are expensed. Some minor costs, such as registration and the legal costs of filing a patent, trademark, or copyright can be capitalized. The costs are then usually amortized on a straight-line basis over the estimated useful life of the asset. Legal life serves as a maximum in the determination of the asset's useful economic life.

▶◣ Goodwill

Conceptually, **goodwill** can result from a number of factors. Above-average management expertise, for example, could give a corporation an advantage over another corporation in the same industry. An excellent location could provide a comparative advantage in another situation. Excellent employee or customer relations can also create an advantage in the marketplace.

Corporations incur costs to create these types of goodwill. Advertising campaigns, public service programs, charitable gifts, and employee training programs all require outlays that to some extent develop goodwill. This type of goodwill is sometimes referred to as internally developed goodwill.

As with other intangible assets, the costs of developing internally developed goodwill are expensed as they are incurred. Under GAAP, goodwill is recorded as an asset only when it is part of the purchase price paid to acquire another corporation. Goodwill is not an easily identifiable asset, but is represented by the dollar figure paid by the acquiring company for various valuable — but intangible — characteristics of the acquired corporation (such as good location, good management, etc.). These characteristics, in effect, give the acquired company more value than its identifiable assets. Recorded goodwill arises only in situations in which one corporation buys ownership rights in another corporation. When the cost of the ownership right exceeds the fair value of the identifiable net assets acquired, then the corporation has purchased goodwill.

The recording of goodwill and its computation will be discussed in more detail in Chapter 13. Once recorded, it is amortized over a maximum of 40 years, because of the indeterminate nature of its useful life. Note that, if goodwill can be traced to a specific cause and its useful life is known to be shorter than 40 years, then it should be amortized over its useful life rather than over 40 years.

EXHIBIT 8-10

COMAC FOOD GROUP INC.
Balance Sheets
As at March 31

	1995 $	1994 $
ASSETS		
Current		
Cash and short term deposits *[note 16]*	197,000	51,000
Accounts receivable *[notes 8 and 9]*	309,000	211,000
Inventories *[note 3]*	434,000	40,000
Prepaid expenses and deposits	69,000	25,000
Current portion of notes receivable *[notes 4, 8 and 9]*	23,000	35,000
	1,032,000	362,000
Notes receivable *[notes 4, 8 and 9]*	29,000	130,000
Capital assets *[note 5]*	65,000	68,000
Goodwill and deferred charges *[note 6]*	833,000	804,000
	1,959,000	1,364,000
LIABILITIES AND SHAREHOLDERS' EQUITY		
Current		
Bank indebtedness *[note 8]*	—	45,000
Accounts payable and accrued liabilities *[note 10]*	560,000	372,000
Current portion of capital lease obligations *[note 7]*	9,000	7,000
Current portion of long term debt *[note 9]*	36,000	42,000
Deferred revenue	208,000	93,000
	813,000	559,000
Capital lease obligations *[note 7]*	11,000	10,000
Accrued dividends *[note 11]*	247,000	179,000
Long term debt *[note 9]*	454,000	455,000
Shareholders' equity		
Share capital *[note 11]*	3,318,000	3,187,000
Deficit	(2,884,000)	(3,026,000)
	434,000	161,000
Commitments and contingency *[note 13]*		
	1,959,000	1,364,000

See accompanying notes

On behalf of the Board:

Director   Director

EXHIBIT 8-10 (continued)

COMAC FOOD GROUP INC.
Excerpted from Notes to the Statements
March 31, 1995 and 1994

6. Goodwill and Deferred Charges

| | 1995 | | | 1994 | | |
	Cost $	Accumulated Amortization $	Net $	Cost $	Accumulated Amortization $	Net $
Goodwill	1,012,000	184,000	828,000	937,000	136,000	801,000
Other deferred charges	61,000	56,000	5,000	56,000	53,000	3,000
	1,073,000	240,000	833,000	993,000	189,000	804,000

During the year, amortization of $51,000 (1994 – $53,000) related to goodwill and deferred charges.

ACQUISITION OF PASTEL MINORITY INTEREST:
On March 31, 1995, the Company acquired an additional 6.5% of the outstanding common shares of International Pastel Food Corporation (Pastel) to hold 100% of the Pastel common shares for consideration of 179,109 Class B common shares of Comac, valued at $52,000. Costs incurred to complete the transaction totalled $23,000. Total purchase costs of $75,000 have been allocated to goodwill.

Effective March 31, 1995, Pastel was wound-up into the Company.

Examples of the disclosure of goodwill and other intangible assets are shown in Exhibit 8-10 for Comac Food Group Inc., and in Exhibit 8-11 for AT Plastics Inc.

STATEMENT ANALYSIS CONSIDERATIONS

The use of different amortization methods for capital assets can produce significantly different results in the financial statements of two otherwise similar corporations. A corporation using the straight-line method will show higher carrying values for its capital assets than a similar corporation using the double declining balance method for the first few years. This affects the balance sheet value as well as the amortization expense that is reported in the income statement. Unfortunately, there is no easy way for the user to convert from one method to another to make the statements more comparable.

Probably the biggest concern in the analysis of capital assets is understanding which assets have been left out, and what market values can be assigned to the assets listed. The historical cost figures for property, plant, and equipment can be very old. Even though the corporation is not holding these assets for resale, it will have to

EXHIBIT 8-11

AT PLASTICS INC.
Consolidated Balance Sheets
As at December 31

(thousands of dollars)	1994	1993
ASSETS		
CURRENT		
Cash	$ 1,357	$ –
Accounts receivable	25,968	19,756
Inventory (note 2)	26,227	23,987
Prepaids	961	435
Investment tax credits recoverable	577	439
	55,090	44,617
FIXED (note 3)	151,201	152,762
OTHER (note 4)	11,355	9,552
	$217,646	$206,931
LIABILITIES		
CURRENT		
Bank overdraft	$ –	$ 15,355
Accounts payable	24,159	18,619
Current portion of long-term debt (note 5)	5,554	158,107
Obligation under capital leases (note 6)	175	326
	29,888	192,407
LONG-TERM DEBT (note 5)	99,217	17,443
OBLIGATION UNDER CAPITAL LEASES (note 6)	496	87
OTHER LIABILITIES (note 7)	2,414	–
	102,127	17,530
	132,015	209,937
SHAREHOLDERS' EQUITY		
CAPITAL STOCK (note 8)	100,667	25,355
DEFICIT	(15,036)	(28,361)
	85,631	(3,006)
	$217,646	$206,931

See accompanying notes to consolidated financial statements.

Approved by the Board

EGERTON W. KING
Director

JOHN N. ABELL
Director

EXHIBIT 8-11 (continued)

AT PLASTICS INC.
Excerpted from Notes to the Statements

4. Other Assets

(thousands of dollars)	COST	ACCUMULATED AMORTIZATION	1994 NET BOOK VALUE
Deferred exchange	$ 5,060	$ 352	$ 4,708
Deferred pension costs	3,148	–	3,148
Development costs	2,748	358	2,390
Goodwill	1,109	–	1,109
	$ 12,065	$ 710	$ 11,355

(thousands of dollars)	COST	ACCUMULATED AMORTIZATION	1993 NET BOOK VALUE
Deferred exchange	$ 3,118	$ 1,748	$ 1,370
Deferred pension costs	3,138	–	3,138
Development costs	1,827	133	1,694
Organization costs	9,638	8,469	1,169
Deferred charges - ethylene contract	1,007	124	883
Trademarks, patents and licences	2,404	1,771	633
Investment in associated company	665	–	665
	$ 21,797	$ 12,245	$ 9,552

replace them at some point in time and, therefore, the replacement cost may be relevant. Under current GAAP, corporations are not required to disclose replacement cost information.

Another problem is that many intangible assets that have been developed internally do not appear on the books of the corporation because their costs have been expensed under GAAP. The large dollar amounts that corporations are willing to pay for goodwill when taking control of other corporations testifies to the substantial value of these unrecorded assets. A failure to consider these assets can lead two different analysts to significantly different conclusions about the value of a corporation.

One final general concern with regard to statement analysis is whether the capital assets listed on the corporation's balance sheet are really worth the amounts recorded. For example, the conditions that gave rise to goodwill at the date of acquisition may have changed since acquisition. Suppose the goodwill was due to the technical expertise of a key employee of the business that was acquired. If the employee dies or otherwise leaves the corporation after acquisition, then the goodwill could be worthless. For this reason, analysts generally have a healthy skepticism about the value of goodwill and other intangibles.

AN INTERNATIONAL PERSPECTIVE
REPORTS FROM OTHER COUNTRIES

In some countries, goodwill is not allowed as an asset. It is written off at the date of acquisition, yet does not typically appear on the income statement. The write-off is made to a separate account in the shareholders' equity section. This type of accounting is used in France, the United Kingdom, and Switzerland. In the U.K., corporations prepare a statement outlining the movements in shareholders' equity combined with a statement of recognized gains and losses. In effect, this is a statement of comprehensive income. To illustrate this type of statement, consider the disclosure by Cadbury Schweppes PLC in Exhibit 8-12. Note the line item for goodwill written off. This is the deduction from shareholders' equity of the amount of goodwill acquired during the year. The following disclosure in the footnotes of Cadbury's financial statements reflects the goodwill policy:

EXHIBIT 8-12

CADBURY SCHWEPPES PLC AND SUBSIDIARIES
Recognised Gains and Losses
Movements in Shareholders' Equity
For the 53 weeks ended January 2, 1993 and the 52 weeks ended January 1, 1994 and December 31, 1994
(In millions)

	1992	1993	1994
Statement of Total Recognised Gains and Losses			
Cadbury Schweppes plc	(£)24.5	(£)140.1	(£)135.3
Subsidiary companies	168.7	92.8	122.8
Associated companies	2.4	3.9	3.8
Net income for Ordinary Shareholders	195.6	23.8	261.9
Currency translation differences	72.6	(43.2)	(48.4)
Total recognised gains and losses for the year	(£)268.2	(£)193.6	(£)213.5
Reconciliation of Movements in Shareholders' Equity			
Total recognised gains and losses for the year	(£)268.2	(£)193.6	(£)213.5
Dividends to Ordinary Shareholders	(98.0)	(116.4)	(130.5)
New share capital subscribed	159.1	341.4	14.1
Adjustment for UESDA (see Note 17)	-	-	80.9
Goodwill written off	(119.7)	(138.3)	(42.6)
Adjustments to minority interests	(0.3)	-	(0.8)
Other	(0.1)	0.1	(0.1)
Net increase in Shareholders' Equity	209.2	280.4	134.5
Shareholders' Equity at beginning of year	874.9	1,084.1	1,364.5
Shareholders' Equity at end of year	(£)1,084.1	(£)1,364.5	(£)1,499.0

The historical cost net income for the financial year was (£)263.5m (1993: (£)238.6m, 1992: (£)196.3m) and the historical cost retained profit (including the impact of the UESDA) was (£)213.9m (1993: (£)122.2m, 1992: (£)98.3m).

(continued)

Results of subsidiary companies acquired during the financial year are included in the consolidated statements of income from the effective date of control and those of companies disposed of up to the effective date of disposal. For this purpose the separable net assets, both tangible and intangible other than goodwill, of newly acquired subsidiaries are incorporated into the financial statements on the basis of the fair value to the company as at the effective date of control. Any excess of the consideration over that fair value is written off against reserves on consolidation.

Using the Return on Assets (ROA) Ratio

An important ratio that is used to calculate how well management managed the assets used in the corporation is the return on assets ratio, or ROA. This ratio simply expresses the total return earned as a percentage of total assets. The return on the investment in assets should be computed prior to any payments or returns to the debtholders or shareholders. Net income has interest expense already deducted, but not dividends. Therefore, the net income, if it is to be used as a measure of return on assets, must be adjusted for the effects of interest expense so it is treated on a basis that is similar to the treatment of dividends.

A complicating factor exists because interest is a deductible expense in the computation of income tax expense. Therefore, if interest expense is to be removed from the net income figure, we must also adjust the amount of income tax expense that would result. In other words, the tax savings (i.e., the reduction in income tax expense) associated with this interest deduction must also be removed. The ROA ratio is then calculated as the ratio of the return (income before interest) divided by the investment in total assets as follows:

$$ROA = \frac{\text{Income Before Interest}}{\text{Average Total Assets}}$$

$$= \frac{\text{Net Income} + \text{Interest Expense} - \text{Tax Savings of Interest Expense}}{\text{Average Total Assets}}$$

$$= \frac{\text{Net Income} + \text{Interest Expense} - (\text{Tax Rate} \times \text{Interest Expense})}{\text{Average Total Assets}}$$

$$ROA = \frac{\text{Net Income} + [\text{Interest Expense} \times (1 - \text{Tax Rate})]}{\text{Average Total Assets}}$$

As with many ratios, the ROA by itself is not as meaningful as a comparison over time or among corporations. However, before using ROA to compare different corporations, you should be sure their amortization policies are comparable, as different amortization policies will affect the total assets figure.

AN INTERNATIONAL PERSPECTIVE
REPORTS FROM OTHER COUNTRIES

Before the twentieth century, the regular deduction of an expense for amortization for either reporting or tax purposes was usually not done. Corporations deducted amortization in years when sufficient income was generated to cover the expense. In years when income was insufficient, little or no deduction was taken. Under current GAAP, such an arrangement is not appropriate. In certain foreign tax jurisdictions, however, this sporadic deduction of amortization is still allowed for tax purposes, as illustrated by the the following quotation from the 1989 financial statements of the Puerto Rican Cement Co. Inc. Note that allowing corporations to make this kind of deduction will permit them to minimize their income taxes payable as long as they keep buying capital assets.

PUERTO RICAN CEMENT CO. INC., 1991

The Puerto Rico Income Tax Law provides for a flexible depreciation system whereby a taxpayer may claim, for tax return purposes only, depreciation at any rate without reference to useful lives. Such depreciation, however, is limited to an amount not greater than income before taxes (determined without taking into consideration the depreciation deduction).

ETHICS IN ACCOUNTING

The valuation, amortization, and disclosure of capital assets in financial statements is one area susceptible to the manipulation of earnings by management. The idea of "earnings management" is very controversial, since the reliability of information produced by accounting systems is one of the most important qualitative characteristics underlying GAAP. The possibility that management may be able to manage earnings has been studied by many researchers who have attempted to determine if it occurs and, if it does, to estimate its effects. In a research study along these lines, Bruns and Merchant ("The Dangerous Morality of Managing Earnings," *Management Accounting*, August 1990, pp. 22-25) surveyed 649 managers using a questionnaire that described 13 earnings-management situations and asked respondents to judge the situations as ethical, questionable, or unethical. To quote the authors directly on their results:

"We found striking disagreement among managers in all groups. Furthermore, the liberal definitions revealed in many responses of what is moral or ethical should raise profound questions about the quality of financial information that is used for decision-making purposes by parties both inside and outside a company. It seems many managers are convinced that if a practice is not explicitly prohibited or is only a slight deviation from rules, it is an ethical practice regardless of who might be affected either by the practice or the information that flows from it. This means that anyone who uses information on short-term earnings is vulnerable to misinterpretation, manipulation, or deliberate deception."

The write-off of property, plant, and equipment is but one way that management can manipulate earnings. The reader of financial statements must be aware of the possibility of management manipulation as they read and analyze the statements. The preparers of accounting reports may also find themselves in ethical dilemmas when they are told by management to "manage" earnings by selecting different accounting techniques or changing estimates strictly for the purpose of producing desired numbers.

SUMMARY

In this chapter, we described the recording of capital assets and the related amortization expense. Capital assets include land, buildings, vehicles, equipment, and any other assets that have a useful life of more than one year. Capital assets are normally recorded at historical costs. Amortization of capital assets is an estimate of the expense that relates to the use of the assets each year. As an estimate, it is up to management to determine appropriate amortization rates.

SUMMARY PROBLEM

XYZ Trucking Corporation has a fleet of 10 large trucks that cost a total of $1,410,000. The trucks have an estimated useful life of 10 years and have an estimated residual value of 10%. For tax purposes, their Capital Cost Allowance (CCA) rate is 30%. The trucks are expected to be driven 1,000,000 kilometres each. At the end of the tenth year the trucks were sold for $5,500 each.

Required:

1. Prepare a schedule showing the straight-line amortization that would be recorded over the life of these trucks.

2. Prepare a schedule showing the amortization that would result if XYZ had used the double declining balance method.

3. Prepare a schedule showing amortization on a production basis if the following usage was recorded:

Year 1:	125,000 km
Year 2:	120,000 km
Year 3:	115,000 km
Year 4:	110,000 km
Year 5:	105,000 km
Year 6:	100,000 km
Year 7:	90,000 km
Year 8:	80,000 km
Year 9:	70,000 km
Year 10:	60,000 km

4. Prepare journal entries to record the disposal of the trucks, assuming:
   a. XYZ used straight-line amortization

b. XYZ used double declining balance amortization
c. XYZ used production method of amortization

5. Compare the difference in tax saving in the first two years if Revenue Canada accepted straight-line amortization rather than CCA. Assume a 34% tax rate.

SUGGESTED SOLUTION TO SUMMARY PROBLEM

1. The residual value of the equipment would be $141 thousand (10% of $1,410 thousand rounded to the nearest thousand). The straight-line amortization would be:

$$\text{Amortization Expense} = \frac{\text{Original Cost} - \text{Estimated Residual Value}}{\text{Estimated Useful Life}}$$
$$= (\$1,410 - 410 \text{ thousand})/10 \text{ years}$$
$$= \$126.9 \text{ thousand/year}$$

2. Double declining balance method:

$$\text{Declining balance rate} = 200\% \times \text{straight-line rate}$$
$$= 200\% \times 1/10 = 20\%$$

The amortization schedule for double declining balance is (in thousands):

Year	Asset Balance			Calculation	Amortization Expense
1			1,410.0	20% × 1,410.0	$282.0
2	(1,410.0 − 282.0)	=	1,128.0	20% × 1,128.0	225.6
3	(1,128.0 − 225.6)	=	902.4	20% × 902.4	180.5
4	(902.4 − 180.5)	=	721.9	20% × 721.9	144.4
5	(721.9 − 144.4)	=	577.5	20% × 577.5	115.5
6	(577.5 − 115.5)	=	462.0	20% × 462.0	92.4
7	(462.0 − 92.4)	=	369.6	20% × 369.6	73.9
8	(369.6 − 73.9)	=	295.7	20% × 295.7	59.1
9	(295.7 − 59.1)	=	236.6	20% × 236.6	47.3
10	(236.6 − 47.3)	=	189.3	See note	48.3

Note: The calculation in Year 10 would result in amortization of $37.8 thousand, which would be insufficient to reduce the carrying value of the asset to its residual ($141 thousand). Therefore, additional amortization would be taken in Year 10 to bring the asset to its residual value of $141 thousand at the end of Year 10.

3. Cost per km: $(1,410,000 - 141,000)/1,000,000 = \$1.269$

Amortization in Year 1: $1.269 × 125,000 =	$	158,625
Amortization in Year 2: $1.269 × 120,000 =	$	152,280
Amortization in Year 3: $1.269 × 115,000 =	$	145,935
Amortization in Year 4: $1.269 × 110,000 =	$	139,590
Amortization in Year 5: $1.269 × 105,000 =	$	133,245
Amortization in Year 6: $1.269 × 100,000 =	$	126,900
Amortization in Year 7: $1.269 × 90,000 =	$	114,210
Amortization in Year 8: $1.269 × 80,000 =	$	101,520
Amortization in Year 9: $1.269 × 70,000 =	$	88,830
Amortization in Year 10: $1.269 × 60,000 =	$	76,140
		$1,237,275

4. a. Straight-line method:

Cash	55,000	
Accumulated amortization	1,269,000	
Loss on disposal	86,000	
Trucks		1,410,000

b. Double declining balance method:

Cash	55,000	
Accumulated amortization	1,269,000	
Loss on disposal	86,000	
Trucks		1,410,000

c. Production method:

Cash	55,000	
Accumulated amortization	1,237,275	
Loss on disposal	117,725	
Trucks		1,410,000

5. Year 1: Straight-line Amortization: 126,900
    CCA: $50\% \times 30\% \times 1,410,000$ $\underline{211,500}$
    $\underline{\underline{\$\ 84,600}}$

Difference in tax: $34\% \times 84,600 = \$28,764$ less tax paid.
Year 2: Straight-line Amortization: 126,900
CCA: $30\% \times (1,410,000 - 211,500) =$ $\underline{359,550}$
    $\underline{\underline{\$232,650}}$

Difference in tax: $34\% \times 232,650 = \$79,101$ less tax paid.

ABBREVIATIONS USED

CCA	Capital cost allowance
UCC	Undepreciated capital cost

SYNONYMS

Amortization/depreciation
Amortized cost/net book value/carrying value

GLOSSARY

Accelerated amortization A method of amortization that allocates higher expenses to the earlier years of an asset's life than does the straight-line method.

Amortizable cost The amount of an asset that can be amortized over its useful life. It is calculated as the original cost less residual value.

Amortized cost The amount of an asset's cost that remains after it has been amortized. It is another term for net book value or carrying value.

Amortization The allocation of the cost of capital assets to expense over their useful lives.

Basket purchase A purchase of assets in which more than one asset is acquired for a single purchase price.

Book value The value of an asset or liability carried on the books of a corporation. For capital assets, this value is the original cost of the asset less the accumulated amortization of the asset.

Capital assets Assets that have expected useful lives of more than one year (or normal operating cycle, if longer) that are used in the business and are not intended for resale.

Capital cost allowance The deduction permitted by Revenue Canada for tax purposes in place of amortization.

Capitalizable cost A cost that can be recorded as an asset on the financial statements rather than being expensed immediately.

Compound interest amortization An amortization method that calculates the amortization expense for a period by the change in the present value of the asset.

Decelerated amortization A method of amortization that allocates lower expenses to the earlier years of an asset's life than to the later years.

Declining balance amortization Amortization methods that calculate the amortization each period by multiplying rate of amortization by carrying value of the asset.

Deferred tax An asset or liability account that arises under GAAP when there is a difference between the revenues or expenses used for tax purposes and book purposes.

Depletion A term sometimes used to describe amortization of the cost of natural resources to expense over the useful life of the resource.

Depreciation A term sometimes used for amortization, especially for tangible assets that are not natural resources.

Double declining balance amortization A particular type of declining balance amortization method that is calculated by using a percentage rate that is double the rate that would be used for straight line amortization.

Full costing method A method of accounting for the drilling and exploration costs of an oil exploration corporation in which all costs of exploration are capitalized and amortized without regard to the success or failure of individual wells. Common in smaller oil and gas companies.

Goodwill An intangible asset that arises when a corporation acquires another corporation and pays more for the corporation than the fair market value of its identifiable net assets.

Intangible asset A nonphysical capital asset that usually involves a legal right.

Interest capitalization The recording of interest as a part of the construction cost of an asset.

Net book value The carrying value of an asset on the books of a corporation.

Net realizable value The selling price of an asset less any costs to complete and sell the asset.

Net recoverable amount The estimated future net cash flow from use of a capital asset together with its residual value.

Present value amortization An amortization method that calculates the amortization expense for a period by the change in the present value of the asset.

Production method A method of amortization that allocates the amortizable cost of the asset to the years of its useful life as a function of the volume of production or usage for the period.

Rate of amortization A ratio or percent that describes the amount of amortization that may be taken during a given period. For straight-line amortization, the rate is the reciprocal of the number of years of useful life ($1/N$).

Replacement cost A market value of an asset determined from the market in which the asset can be purchased by the corporation. In a manufacturing corporation, replacement cost is the cost to reproduce the asset based on current prices of the inputs.

Resale value The market value of an asset in the market in which it can be sold.

Residual value The estimated net realizable value of a capital asset at the end of its useful life to the corporation.

Straight-line amortization A method of amortization that allocates the amortizable cost of the asset evenly over its useful life.

Straight-line rate The rate of amortization for the straight-line method; calculated as the reciprocal of the number of years of useful life (1/N).

Successful efforts method A method of accounting for the drilling and exploration costs of an oil exploration corporation in which the costs of exploration are capitalized and amortized only for successful wells.

Tangible asset An asset that has a physical substance.

Undepreciated capital cost The amount in a class

that has not yet been deducted as capital cost allowance for tax purposes.

Useful life An estimate of the period of time over which an asset will have economic value to the corporation.

Value in sale The value of an asset if the intent is to sell the asset.

Value in use The value of an asset if the intent is to use the asset rather than sell it.

ASSIGNMENT MATERIAL

Assessing your Recall

1. Describe what is meant by "value in use" versus "value in sale" as applied to capital assets.

2. Discuss the types of costs that should be capitalized for a piece of equipment.

3. Describe the procedure used under GAAP to allocate the cost of a basket purchase of assets to the individual assets.

4. Describe why interest can be capitalized as a part of the construction costs of an asset.

5. Discuss the purpose of amortization expense and the various patterns of amortization that might be taken by a corporation.

6. Discuss the motivations that a corporation might have for choosing one amortization method over another.

7. Describe how residual value and useful life are used in the calculation of amortization under the following methods: straight-line, production method, and declining balance.

8. Describe the differences between Capital Cost Allowance compared to accelerated amortization.

9. Discuss the nature of deferred taxes in the context of differences between amortization and CCA.

10. Under GAAP, describe the conditions under which intangible assets can be recorded on the books of a corporation, and the guidelines under which that value can then be expensed over the life of the asset. Specifically, discuss goodwill, research and development, and patents.

Applying your Knowledge

11. On June 30, 19x5, Sherman Bros. Corp. purchased a new machine for $20,000. A useful life of 10 years and a residual value of $500 were estimated. On September 30,

19x6, another machine was acquired for $50,000. Its useful life was estimated to be 15 years and its residual value $2,000. On April 30, 19x7, the first machine was sold for $17,000. Sherman Bros. closes its books on December 31 each year and uses the straight-line method of amortization.

Required:
Give the necessary journal entries for the years 19x5 through 19x7 for both machines.

12. On March 31, 19x4, Hammer & Holding Inc. purchased new machinery. The corporation acquired the new machinery by trading in its old machine, paying $22,975 in cash, and issuing a 12% note payable for $5,000. The old machinery was acquired on June 30, 19x1, for $30,000. At that time, its estimated useful life was 10 years, with a $1,000 residual value. The asset's market value was approximately the same as its book value at the date of trade-in. The new machinery's estimated life is five years, with a residual value of $2,500. The corporation uses a straight-line method of amortization and closes its books on December 31.

Required:
a. Give the necessary journal entries for 19x4.
b. On March 31, 19x9, the machinery acquired in 19x4 could not be sold, and the corporation decided to write it off. Give the necessary journal entries for 19x9.

13. On October 31, 19x3, the Steelman Cupboard Corporation acquired a new machine for $85,000. The corporation estimated the useful life to be 10 years and expected a residual value of $1,000. During 19x6, the corporation decided that the machine was to be used for another 10 years including all of 19x6 and that the residual value would be $800. On June 30, 19x8, the machine was sold for $45,000. The corporation uses the straight-line method of amortization and closes its books on December 31.

Required:
Give the necessary journal entries for 19x3, 19x6, and 19x8.

14. The Vector Corporation builds its own machinery, which it later uses for the production of its products. On January 1, 19x4, the corporation borrowed $5 million at an annual interest rate of 9% for a period of six years. Interest is paid on January 1 for the interest incurred in the previous year. The corporation borrowed the money specifically to finance the construction of this machinery. On July 1, 19x4, the corporation began construction of this machine. An average amount of $3.5 million was invested in making the machine in 19x4. On January 1, 19x5, the corporation borrowed another $5 million for general purposes, not strictly related to construction of the equipment, at an interest rate of 10% for a period of five years. On average, an additional amount of $2 million was invested in the manufacture of the equipment in 19x5. The construction process was completed on March 31, 19x6. The additional average amount of construction costs incurred in 19x6 was $75,000. The Vector Corporation makes all its interest payments on time and closes its books on December 31. This corporation traditionally capitalizes interest cost.

Required (a difficult problem!):
Give the necessary journal entries for 19x4, 19x5, and 19x6 for all these transactions.

15. A machine is purchased on January 1, 19X3, for $50,000. It is expected to have a useful life of five years and a residual value of $2,000. The corporation closes its books on December 31.

    Required:
    Compute the amount of amortization to be charged each year using each of the following methods:
    a. Straight-line method
    b. Double declining balance method

16. The Pure Oil Corporation estimated that the new oil field that it acquired has five million barrels of oil. The corporation extracted 500,000 barrels in the first year, 600,000 barrels in Year 2, and 1 million barrels in Year 3. The costs capitalized for the oil field total $25 million. The corporation amortizes oil field capital costs using the production method.

    Required:
    Compute the amortization expense for each year.

Reading and Interpreting Published Financial Statements

17. Exhibit 8-6 provided a summary of the capital assets of Cara Operations Limited at April 2, 1995 and April 3, 1994. The 1995 Consolidated Statements of Cash Flow is shown in Exhibit 8-13.

    Required:
    Using the information provided in Exhibits 8-6 and 8-13, prepare summary journal entries to reconstruct the changes that occurred in the capital asset accounts and related accumulated amortization accounts for the 1995 fiscal year.

18. Mosaid Technologies Incorporated incurs substantial costs in researching and developing computer software. Mosaid's income statements for 1995 and 1994 are shown in Exhibit 3-5.

    Required:
    a. Rewrite this income statement to show the results if Mosaid were to capitalize these costs. Assume Mosaid amortizes intangible capital assets at 20% straight line.
    b. Explain why Mosaid is not allowed to capitalize these costs.

19. The income statement from the 1990 financial statements of Union Camp Corporation is shown in the Exhibit 8-14. Union Camp's primary business is paper, paperboard, and packaging. Included in the 1990 financial statements was the following footnote:

    Capitalized Interest
    Interest is capitalized on major capital expenditures during the period of construction. Total interest costs incurred and amounts capitalized were (in thousands):

	1990	1989	1988
Total Interest	$ 99,742	$ 69,767	$ 63,975
Interest Capitalized	(68,514)	(21,967)	(13,268)
Net Interest Expense	$ 31,228	$ 47,800	$ 50,707

EXHIBIT 8-13

CARA OPERATIONS LIMITED
Consolidated Statements of Cash Flow
For the years ended April 2, 1995 and April 3, 1994

	52 weeks	53 weeks
(In thousands of dollars)	1995	1994
CASH PROVIDED BY (USED IN)		
Operations		
Net earnings for the year	$ 26,844	$ 30,754
Amortization of capital assets	19,478	17,139
Loss (Gain) on disposal of capital assets	4,443	(142)
Amortization of goodwill	3,598	3,406
Deferred income taxes	(2,978)	26
Amortization of contracts and trademarks	609	401
	$ 51,994	$ 51,584
Change in operating working capital	(2,425)	(4,618)
	$ 49,569	$ 46,966
Investing		
Purchase of capital assets	$ (30,733)	$ (31,002)
Purchase of contracts and trademarks	(3,755)	(323)
Goodwill arising on earn-out (note 8 (c))	(1,917)	(1,414)
Change in mortgages and notes	(889)	(1,291)
Change in investments	(243)	18
Repayment of employee stock plan loan	242	271
Proceeds on disposal of capital assets	140	998
Acquisitions (note 9)	–	(17,294)
	$ (37,155)	$ (50,037)
Financing		
Change in long-term debt	$ (19,429)	$ 2,308
Dividends	(9,395)	(9,395)
Increase in obligations under capital leases	7,102	7,090
	$ (21,722)	$ 3
Change in Net Cash	(9,308)	(3,068)
Net Cash – Beginning of Year	7,287	10,355
Net Cash – End of Year	$ (2,021)	$ 7,287
Net Cash defined as:		
Cash and Cash Equivalents	$ 1,079	$ 7,287
Bank Indebtedness	(3,100)	–
	$ (2,021)	$ 7,287

EXHIBIT 8-14

UNION CAMP CORPORATION
Income Statement
Consolidated Income

	($ in thousands, except per share)		
For The Years Ended December 31,	1990	1989	1988
Net sales	$2,839,704	$2,761,337	$2,660,918
Cost and other charges:			
Cost of products sold	1,983,338	1,813,209	1,733,462
Selling and administrative expenses	268,263	248,780	243,191
Depreciation and cost of company			
timber harvested	217,416	204,572	190,611
Income from Operations	370,687	494,776	493,654
Interest expense	31,228	47,800	50,527
Other (income) — net	(26,559)	(22,302)	(24,882)
Income before Income Taxes	366,018	469,278	468,009
Income taxes	136,427	169,878	172,863
Net Income	$ 229,591	$ 299,400	$ 295,146
Net Income Per Share	$3.35	$4.35	$4.25

Required:

a. Calculate the times interest earned ratio (a measure of the "cushion" of earnings available to pay interest, calculated as Income before Interest and Taxes/Interest Expense) for each of the three years based on the interest expense reported in the income statement.

b. Recalculate the times interest earned ratio for each of the three years based on the total interest expense information given in the footnote.

c. Discuss which of the ratios calculated in parts (a) and (b) would be a better predictor of Union Camp's ability to make interest payments in the future.

20. The 1994 balance sheet and income statement of Purcell Energy Ltd. was shown in Exhibit 5-18. Note 1 relating to their accounting policies for capital assets is shown in Exhibit 8-15.

Required:

a. Explain in your own words how Purcell records and amortizes capital assets relating to oil and gas properties.

b. Explain how Purcell's policies would be different if it used successful efforts policies.

21. The 1995 annual report, including the complete financial statements for Big Rock Brewery Ltd. at March 31, 1995, are shown in the Appendix to Chapter 1.

Required:

What changes would result in the balance sheet and income statement if Big Rock did not capitalize interest? (Hint: Consider Note 3.)

EXHIBIT 8-15

PURCELL ENERGY LIMITED
Excerpted from Notes to the Statements

Capital Assets The Company follows the full cost method of accounting for oil and gas operations whereby all costs of exploring for and developing oil and gas reserves are initially capitalized. Such costs include land acquisition costs, geological and geophysical expenses, carrying charges on non-producing properties, costs of drilling and overhead charges directly related to acquisition and exploration activities.

Costs capitalized, together with the costs of production equipment, are depleted on the unit-of-production method based on the estimated gross proved reserves. Petroleum products and reserves are converted to equivalent units of natural gas using their relative energy content.

Costs of acquiring and evaluating unproved properties are initially excluded from depletion calculations. These unevaluated properties are assessed periodically to ascertain whether impairment has occurred. When proved reserves are assigned or the property is considered to be impaired, the cost of the property or the amount of the impairment is added to costs subject to depletion calculations.

Proceeds from a sale of petroleum and natural gas properties are applied against capitalized costs, with no gain or loss recognized, unless such a sale would significantly alter the rate of depletion. Alberta Royalty Tax Credits are included in oil and gas sales.

In applying the full cost method, the Company performs a ceiling test which restricts the capitalized costs less accumulated depletion and amortization from exceeding an amount equal to the estimated undiscounted value of future net revenues from proven oil and gas reserves, as determined by independent engineers, based on sales prices achievable under existing contracts and posted average reference prices in effect at the end of the year and current costs, and after deducting estimated future general and administrative expenses, production related expenses, financing costs, future site restorations costs and income taxes.

Joint Venture Operations All of the Company's petroleum and natural gas exploration activities are conducted jointly with others. These financial statements reflect only the Company's proportionate interest in such activities.

Site Restoration Costs The Company accrues for site restoration costs on the basis of actual production. The accrual is based on Management's best estimate of these future costs allocated on the ratio of actual production to proved producing reserves. The current period accrual for these costs is $25,723 (1993 - $12,517).

CASE

ONTA AND KEWBEE SALES CORPORATIONS

Summary balance sheet and income statement information for Onta Sales Corporation and KewBee Sales Corporation for the year ended December 31, 19x9 (the first year of operations for both corporations) are shown below. Both corporations have similar businesses. Upon investigation, you find that Onta is financed mainly by shareholders' equity while KewBee is financed mainly by long-term debt. Onta amortizes all equipment at 10% straight-line and buildings at 5% straight-line while KewBee amortizes equipment at 20% declining balance and buildings at 10% declining balance. Both have effective corporate income tax rates of 25%.

Required:

a. Which corporation has the higher return on assets without adjusting for differences in amortization policy?

b. Which corporation has the higher return on assets after adjusting for differences in amortization policy? (Do this using two different calculations.)

c. Explain why, using numbers from this example, the ROA adjusts for interest after taxes in the numerator.

d. Explain why, using numbers from this example, you should adjust for differences in amortization policy when comparing different corporations.

	Onta	KewBee
Balance Sheet Information		
Total current assets	$ 75,000	$ 80,000
Capital assets		
Land	150,000	125,000
Equipment	200,000	200,000
Accumulated amortization	(20,000)	(40,000)
Buildings	500,000	500,000
Accumulated amortization	(25,000)	(50,000)
Total assets	$ 880,000	$ 815,000
Total liabilities	300,000	700,000
Total shareholders' equity	580,000	115,000
Total liabilities and equity	$ 880,000	$ 815,000
Income Statement Information		
Revenues	$1,000,000	$1,000,000
Expenses:		
Amortization	45,000	90,000
Interest	30,000	70,000
Other	770,000	770,000
Income taxes	38,750	17,500
Net income	$ 116,250	$ 52,500

◢◣ Critical Thinking Question

22. The balance sheet, income statement, and Notes of H. Jager Developments Inc. at December 30, 1995 and 1994 are shown in Exhibit 8-16. Jager develops and sells real estate.

    Required:

    a. Explain why Jager does not classify land, housing, and other properties as capital assets.

    b. Explain why Jager does not split its assets or liabilities into current and non-current sections.

EXHIBIT 8-16

H. JAGER DEVELOPMENTS INC.
Consolidated Balance Sheet
February 28

	1995	1994
ASSETS		
Accounts receivable	$ 242,818	$ 575,314
Prepaid expense and deposits	75,324	44,508
Land and housing under development	8,925,941	2,997,798
Due from related party (Note 3)	365,664	—
Other (Note 4)	248,394	216,518
Investment in H. J. Forest Products Inc. (Note 5)	4,578,405	4,600,000
	$ 14,436,546	$ 8,434,138
LIABILITIES		
Bank indebtedness	$ 52,564	$ 113,218
Accounts payable and accrued liabilities	1,312,209	1,144,742
Customer and mortgage advances	632,810	1,073,955
Due to related parties (Note 6)	246,183	281,054
Mortgages and loans (Note 7)	5,582,523	154,955
	7,826,289	2,767,924
SHAREHOLDERS' EQUITY		
Capital stock (Note 8)	7,641,385	6,876,385
Deficit	(1,031,128)	(1,210,171)
	6,610,257	5,666,214
	$ 14,436,546	$ 8,434,138

On behalf of the Board

_____Harvey Jager_____   _____
Director   Director

See accompanying notes to the financial statements.

EXHIBIT 8-16 (continued)

H. JAGER DEVELOPMENTS INC.
Consolidated Statement of Operations
Year Ended February 28

	1995	1994
SALES	$ 6,526,506	$ 4,383,373
DIRECT COSTS	5,701,235	4,313,040
	825,271	70,333
EXPENSES		
General and administrative	532,531	845,255
Depreciation and amortization	35,151	41,343
Interest	6,087	28,769
	573,769	915,367
EARNINGS (LOSS) BEFORE UNDERNOTED	251,502	(845,034)
Loss on sale of securities	(904)	—
Gain on sale of fixed and other assets	27,540	—
Write-down of land and housing under development	(99,095)	(260,000)
EARNINGS (LOSS) BEFORE INCOME TAXES	179,043	(1,105,034)
INCOME TAXES (Note 10)	—	—
NET EARNINGS (LOSS)	179,043	(1,105,034)
DEFICIT, beginning of year	(1,210,171)	(105,137)
DEFICIT, end of year	$ (1,031,128)	$ (1,210,171)
EARNINGS (LOSS) PER SHARE	$ 0.01	$ (0.11)

See accompanying notes to the financial statements.

EXHIBIT 8-16 (continued)

H. JAGER DEVELOPMENTS INC.
Notes to the Consolidated Financial Statements
February 28, 1995

1. OPERATIONS

H. Jager Developments Inc. is a real estate developer concentrating primarily in the development and construction of villa housing, residential and resort development.

2. SUMMARY OF SIGNIFICANT ACCOUNTING POLICIES

PRINCIPLES OF CONSOLIDATION

These financial statements include the accounts of the Company and its wholly-owned subsidiaries, Country Rose Restaurant Inc. and Lake Newell Utility Corporation Limited.

LAND AND HOUSING UNDER DEVELOPMENT

Land development costs and housing under construction are carried at the lower of cost and estimated net realizable value. Cost includes the cost of land, construction costs, carrying costs and other direct costs associated with development. Carrying costs include interest on borrowings directly related to land development and construction in progress as well as property taxes and the applicable portion of general and administrative overheads. During the year, overhead costs and interest of $354,000 and $218,157 respectively were capitalized.

The cost of land is pro-rated to each phase of a project on an acreage basis up to and including the time that a plan of subdivision is established. Cost of land sold, including development and capitalized costs, are allocated, generally within each subdivision to saleable lots or acreage in proportion to anticipated revenues. Housing units sold are costed on an individual basis whereby specific and identifiable costs are applied to each unit.

REVENUE RECOGNITION

Revenues and earnings on housing unit sales are recognized when the purchaser becomes entitled to occupancy. Revenues and earnings from the sale of land and other properties is recorded when the collection of the sale proceeds is reasonably assured and all other significant conditions of sale are met.

EQUIPMENT AND INTANGIBLES

Equipment and intangibles, which are included in other assets, are recorded at cost and are depreciated and amortized respectively as follows:

Equipment	-	declining balance at rates from 20% to 30% per annum
Licensing rights	-	straight-line over 10 years
Goodwill	-	straight-line over 10 years

CHAPTER

Liabilities

Chapters 6 and 7 discussed current assets; in this and the next two chapters, our attention turns to the credit side of the balance sheet and the accounting for liabilities and shareholders' equity. Both liabilities and shareholders' equity can be viewed as sources of assets. Shareholders contribute assets to the corporation in return for an ownership interest and the right to share in the future profits of the corporation. Liability holders contribute assets in return for a promise of repayment at some future date, usually with interest.

The general nature of liabilities is discussed first, followed by a discussion of current liabilities, contingent liabilities, and deferred taxes. Chapter 10 covers major noncurrent liabilities, such as bonds, leases, and pensions. In Chapter 11, shareholders' equity transactions are discussed.

RECOGNITION CRITERIA FOR LIABILITIES

As there are recognition criteria for assets, so too there are general recognition criteria for liabilities. In Section 1000.33 of the *CICA Handbook*, the essential characteristics of liabilities are discussed:

1. A liability embodies a duty or responsibility to transfer assets or services at a determinable future date, on the occurrence of a specified event or on demand.

2. The duty or responsibility must obligate the entity, leaving it little or no discretion to avoid the obligation.

3. The transaction giving rise to the obligation must have already occurred.[1]

[1] CICA Handbook, Section 1000.33.

The transfer of assets or services criterion is similar to the probable future value criterion for assets. The uncertainty associated with liabilities concerns the dollar value of assets to be sacrificed, and when that sacrifice will be made. The use of the terms "assets" and "services" indicates that the obligation is not always settled in cash. Some obligations will require settlement in goods or services.

To avoid uncertainty about the amount and timing of the settlement, some liabilities have fixed payments and fixed due dates. Most loans and accounts payable are of this type. The interest and principal payments are specified in the loan agreement, as are the dates on which those payments will be made. Other liabilities, such as warranty liabilities, may have neither fixed payments nor fixed dates. The incidence of warranty expenses will depend on when the customer detects a warranty problem, and the extent of that problem. Liabilities, therefore, differ in the amount of uncertainty with which they are associated.

If the uncertainty associated with either the amount or the timing of the future transfer is sufficiently high, the liability will probably not be recognized in the financial statements. Suppose, for example, that the corporation is under investigation by the government for an alleged chemical spill into the river. Does the corporation have an obligation to transfer assets in the future? If the corporation is found negligent, there could be a significant liability if a fine is imposed or if the corporation cleans up the spill, or both. The corporation may have a difficult time, however, predicting whether it will be found negligent and, if found negligent, how much it will cost to satisfy the obligation. In this case, it is likely that no liability will be recorded.

The ownership criterion that is used for assets does not strictly apply to liabilities, but a similar notion is present. Corporations should record only those obligations that they will be required to satisfy. For example, if a customer falls on the corporation's sidewalk, sues the corporation for medical costs, and wins, the corporation may not be obligated to make the payment. If the corporation is insured against such claims, the insurance company will pay the claim. The corporation, therefore, does not record the obligation to pay this liability on its books because it is the insurance company's obligation. If insurance does not cover all the obligation, the corporation needs to record any excess obligation.

The third characteristic of a liability, that is, proving that the transaction that gave rise to the obligation has already occurred, is sometimes difficult to evaluate. For example, in the case of the lawsuit mentioned in the preceding paragraph, what is the event that gave rise to the obligation? Is it the customer falling on the sidewalk, the filing of a lawsuit, or the decision of the court? In this case, the certainty of the obligation increases as each subsequent event occurs. However, the event that gives rise to the ultimate obligation depends on the sequence of events.

Another difficulty that can make evaluation difficult arises when the corporation signs a binding contract. Suppose, for example, that the corporation signs a contract to purchase 1,000 units of inventory at $30 per unit, to be delivered 30 days from now. Is the signing of the contract the event that gives rise to the obligation to pay for the inventory, or is it the delivery of the inventory? The obligation of the corporation is contingent upon the seller performing its part of the contract by delivering the goods on time. If the goods are not delivered, then the corporation is not obligated to pay. The signing of the contract creates what is known as a **mutually unexecuted contract** because, at the time of signing, neither the buyer nor the seller has performed its part of the contract. The seller has not delivered any inventory, and the buyer has not paid any cash. Under GAAP, such contracts are normally not recorded in the books.

A **partially executed contract** is one in which one party has performed all or part of its obligation. In the example just given, the contract would be viewed as partially executed if the buyer had made a deposit of $3,000. Under GAAP, a partial transaction would then be recorded. In this case, the seller would show an inflow of cash of $3,000, and create a liability account to represent its obligation to deliver inventory valued at $3,000. The liability account would be called *unearned revenue*. Once inventory valued at $3,000 was delivered to the customer, the obligation would be satisfied and the revenue would be earned. Note that only the amount of the deposit is recorded at this time, not the full amount of the contract ($30,000 = 1,000 units × $30 per unit). The buyer would show an outflow of cash of $3,000, and create an asset account for the right to receive the inventory valued at $3,000. The account would be called *deposits on purchase commitments*.

VALUATION CRITERIA

Just as there are different possible methods for valuing assets, there are several possible methods for valuing liabilities. Theoretically, liabilities are valued at their net present value as at the date they are incurred. There are, however, several possible valuation methods to be considered before GAAP is discussed in depth.

Valuation Methods

One way to value a liability is to record it at the *gross amount* of the obligation, that is, the total of the payments to be made. For example, if an obligation requires the corporation to pay $1,000 each month for the next three years, the gross obligation would be $36,000. While this amount accurately measures the total payments to be made, it may not accurately measure the obligation of the corporation as at the date it is recorded on the balance sheet. For example, suppose that the obligation is a rental agreement for a piece of machinery. If the corporation can cancel the rental agreement at any time, it is obligated to pay only $1,000 each month. The remaining payments are an obligation only if it decides to keep using the asset. If the contract was noncancellable, the full $36,000 would make more sense.

Another reason why the gross obligation may not adequately measure the value of the liability is that it ignores the time value of money. Suppose that, in the example, the $1,000 a month is to repay a loan. The total payments of $36,000 include both the repayment of principal and the payment of interest. Interest is an obligation only as the corporation uses the money over time. If the corporation has the option to pay off the loan early, it merely has to pay off the principal balance and any accumulated interest. It does not have to pay the full amount of the payments. Suppose, for example, that the principal of the loan is $31,000. The difference ($5,000) between this amount and the gross amount is the interest that accrues over time. The corporation could settle the obligation today with a payment of $31,000. Therefore, recording the liability at $36,000 would overstate the obligation of the corporation at the present time.

To recognize the time value of money, a corporation may record its obligations at their **net present value**. Under this valuation system, the corporation records interest expense to recognize the interest that accrues with the passage of time. In the full implementation of a present-value system, gains and losses on the liabilities of the corporation are also recognized as the assumptions underlying the present-value calculation change. These assumptions include the amount and timing of the future cash flows, and the interest rate used to discount the cash flows.

Just as there is concern about the purchasing power of monetary assets, there is concern about liabilities because most are also **monetary items** (i.e., they are fixed in terms of the cash flows that are required to settle them). They are, therefore, subject to changes in purchasing power. As the purchasing power of the dollar changes, the "cost" (in terms of purchasing power) to the corporation of repaying the obligation changes. For example, suppose the corporation takes out a fixed payment loan to buy a piece of equipment. If inflation takes place during the period of time that the corporation is paying off the loan, the purchasing power of the dollar decreases, and the corporation pays off the obligation with "cheaper" dollars. It experiences a *purchasing power* gain during this period. Recording liabilities using some measure of purchasing power is another valuation possibility.

What is GAAP?

Under GAAP, liabilities should be recorded at the present value of the future payments. The interest rate used depends on the type of liability, and the corporation's creditworthiness. It should be the appropriate interest rate for an arms-length transaction of the type that gives rise to the obligation. However, accountants do not use present-value calculations for short-term liabilities such as accounts payable because the time to maturity is so short. Instead, current liabilities such as accounts payable and wages payable are recorded at the gross amount that is owed. Short-term notes payable that have an interest component are recorded at the total principal amount. The interest is recorded as it accrues.

Once a liability is recorded, the carrying value is not usually adjusted except when the liability is paid. One exception occurs when a corporation is in financial trouble and restructures its debt in negotiations with its creditors. Based on the concessions that the corporation may obtain from the lender, it may be able to reduce the amount owed on the obligation, or to reduce the interest rate used to calculate interest expense on the existing balance, or to extend the period over which the debt is to be paid. This is called **troubled debt restructuring**.

CURRENT LIABILITIES

Current liabilities are those obligations that require the transfer of assets or services within one year, or one operating cycle, of the corporation. As just discussed, most of them are carried on the books at the gross amount. In order for a corporation to stay solvent (able to pay its debts as they fall due), the corporation must have sufficient current assets and operations to pay the current liabilities. Creditors, like bankers, will often use total current liabilities to assess the corporation's ability to remain viable. The most frequently encountered current liabilities are discussed in the following subsections.

Working Capital Loans and Lines of Credit

As mentioned in the preceding paragraph, corporations need to have sufficient current assets or inflows of cash from operations to pay debts as they fall due. However, some of those current assets may not be converted into cash fast enough to meet current debt obligation deadlines. To manage this shortfall, corporations have a few options. For example, they can arrange a **working capital loan** with a bank. This short-term loan is often secured by customer balances in accounts receivable, or by inventory. As money is received from accounts receivable, or as the inventory is sold, the amounts received are used to pay off the loan.

Another way that corporations can deal with cash shortages is to arrange a **line of credit** with a bank. In this scenario, the bank assesses the corporation's ability to repay short-term debts and establishes a short-term debt balance that it feels is reasonable for the corporation. This provides the corporation with more freedom to take advantage of opportunities and/or to settle debts. If cheques written by the corporation exceed the current cash balance in the bank, the bank covers the excess by immediately activating the line of credit and establishing a short-term loan. Subsequent cash deposits by the corporation are used by the bank to draw down the loan. A corporation that is using a working capital loan or has activated a line of credit might have a negative cash balance, which must be shown with the current liabilities. This negative cash balance would be obvious to users on the statement of changes in financial position because the end cash balance would also be negative. For example, Big Rock Brewery Ltd. has a "revolving line of credit to a maximum limit of $750,000 and which bears interest at Royal Bank prime plus 1/8% per annum" (Big Rock's Annual Report, p. 13, included as the Appendix to Chapter 1). On March 31, 1995, its short-term loan balance was $408,071, whereas its cash balance was $42,317. This resulted in the cash deficiency of $365,754 that was reported on the Statement of Changes in Financial Position. The line of credit limit of $750,000 shows that the Royal Bank is fairly confident about the financial health of Big Rock.

Accounts Payable

Accounts payable occur when a corporation buys goods or services on credit. These are sometimes referred to as **trade accounts payable.** (For an example, see the excerpt from the liability section of Imperial Parking Ltd., Exhibit 9-1). Payment is generally deferred for a relatively short period of time, such as 30 to 60 days. These accounts generally do not carry explicit interest charges and are sometimes thought of as "free" debt. Under some agreements, there can be either a penalty for late payment, or a discount provision for early payment. The penalty and the difference between the discounted payment and the full payment can both be viewed as interest charges for delayed payments on these liabilities.

Wages and Other Payroll Payables

Wages owed to employees can be another significant current liability. The magnitude of the liability depends somewhat on how often the corporation pays its employees because the balance in the account reflects the accrual of wages as of the last pay period. In addition to the wages themselves, the corporation may also provide fringe benefits for employees that must also be quantified. These accruals for health care, pensions, vacation pay, and other benefits also need to be recognized in the periods in which they occur. Because these may be paid in periods other than those in which they are earned, liabilities have to be recorded.

Additionally, the corporation acts as a government agent (federal and provincial) in the collection of certain taxes. For example, income taxes must be withheld from employees' wages and remitted to the government. While this is not an expense to

EXHIBIT 9-1

IMPERIAL PARKING LTD.
Excerpted from the Consolidated Balance Sheets
As at March, 31, 1995 and 1994
(in thousands of dollars)

Liabilities and Shareholders' Equity

	1995	1994
Current liabilities:		
Bank indebtedness (note 8)	$ 1,700	$ —
Rents payable	6,687	3,496
Trade accounts payable and other accrued liabilities	7,314	4,512
Deferred revenue	1,662	1,045
Current portion of long-term debt	1,095	6,739
	18,458	15,792
Long-term debt (note 9)	4,349	969
	22,807	16,761

the corporation, the corporation must nevertheless keep track of the amounts deducted from employees' earnings and show the liability to pay these amounts to the government. The liability to pay the employee is reduced by the amount withheld. Other deductions, such as Canada Pension Plan (CPP) or Quebec Pension Plan (QPP) amounts and Employment Insurance (EI), are also deducted from employees' total wages and remitted to the government. This further reduces the amount paid to employees. Corporations must also make additional payments to the government for CPP or QPP, EI and Workers' Compensation. These amounts are shown as an expense to the employer and are recorded as liabilities until they are remitted to the government.

As an example, assume that Angelique's Autobody Shop has a two-week payroll of $7,500 for its seven employees. Income tax of $990 is deducted from the employees' cheques, as well as 2.7% for CPP and 3% for EI. The employer has to submit an additional 2.7% for CPP and 4.2% for EI on behalf of its employees. The journal entries to record the payroll would be:

DEDUCTIONS FROM EMPLOYEES' EARNED INCOME:

SE – Wages expense	7,500.00	
L – Employee income tax payable		990.00
L – CPP contribution payable		202.50
L – EI taxes payable		225.00
A – Cash		6,082.50

ADDITIONAL DEDUCTIONS PAID BY EMPLOYER:

SE-Wages expense	517.50	
L – CPP contribution payable		202.50
L – EI taxes payable		315.00

The amounts in the three liability accounts are remitted periodically to the government according to its regulations. Note that the total amount recorded by the employers as an expense ($8,017.50) exceeds the amount they have agreed to pay the employees ($7,500.00). Because of these extra amounts the government requires corporations to remit, businesses complain each time the government makes changes to the Canada Pension Plan or Employment Insurance. The additional amounts must always be considered by an employer whether it is considering hiring new employees, or maintaining its current number.

Short-Term Notes and Interest Payable

Short-term notes payable represent borrowings of the corporation that require repayment in the next year or operating cycle. They either carry explicit interest rates, or are structured such that the difference between the original amount borrowed and the amount repaid represents implicit interest. Interest expense and interest payable should be recognized over the life of these loan agreements.

Assume that the Checkerboard Taxi Corporation borrowed $10,000 at 9% from the local bank. The loan was to be repaid by monthly instalments of $1,710.70 over six months. The monthly instalments included reductions of the principal ($10,000) as well as interest at 9% per annum. The following amortization table illustrates the interest component and the reductions of the principal.

Month	Payment	Interest	Principal reduction	Principal balance
				$10,000.00
1	$1,710.70	$75.00[a]	$1,635.70	$ 8,364.30
2	$1,710.70	$62.73	$1,647.97	$ 6,716.33
3	$1,710.70	$50.37	$1,660.33	$ 5,056.00
4	$1,710.70	$37.92	$1,672.78	$ 3,383.22
5	$1,710.70	$25.37	$1,685.33	$ 1,697.89
6	$1,710.70	$12.81[b]	$1,697.89	–0–

[a] $10,000 × .09 / 12 = $75.00
[b] rounding error of $.08

The journal entry at the end of the first month to record the first payment would be:

SE – Interest expense	75.00	
L – Short-term note payable	1,635.70	
A – Cash		1,710.70

Try to reconstruct the journal entries for the remaining months. The short-term note payable would initially have been recorded at the principal amount of $10,000, then gradually reduced as monthly payments were made.

Income Taxes Payable

Corporations are subject to both federal corporate income taxes, and provincial corporate taxes. As mentioned earlier in the book, the rules governing the calculation of income for tax purposes may differ from the rules under GAAP. The discussion in Chapter 8 concerning deferred taxes highlighted this difference (deferred taxes are discussed in great detail later in this chapter). The taxes that become payable under the rules of Revenue Canada must be recorded as a liability of the corporation. Multinational corporations may also be subject to taxation in the countries in which they operate.

The payment of taxes does not always coincide with the incurrence of the tax. In Canada, corporations are required to make monthly tax payments, usually based on taxes paid the previous year, so that the government has a steady flow of cash during the year on which to operate. The deadline for filing the yearly tax return is six months after the corporate year-end, but the balance of taxes owed for a year must be paid within two months of the year-end. Penalties are imposed if the corporation significantly underestimates the amount of tax payable.

Warranty Payable

When a corporation sells a good or service, there are either explicit or implicit guarantees to the buyer. If the product or service fails to satisfy the customer, the seller may have to provide **warranty service**. Because the amount of warranty service is unknown at the time of sale, the corporation should estimate an amount in order to match the expense of the warranty to the revenue from the sale. If the corporation has been in business for a reasonable length of time, this can be accomplished fairly easily, based on the past history of defects in the product. For new products and new corporations, this may be much more difficult.

As warranty service is provided (paid for by cash or other resources), the estimated liability amount is reduced. For tax purposes, corporations claim a deduction when warranty service is actually provided. This creates a difference between the recognition of warranty expense for book and tax purposes. The difference between estimated warranty expense and the actual amounts spent on warranty work gives rise to deferred taxes in much the same manner as does accounting amortization and CCA.

As an example of a warranty situation, let us consider Hubble Appliance Company Ltd. It sells large appliances such as stoves and refrigerators. During the month of January, 19x6, it sold eight refrigerators, each of which carried a three-year warranty against mechanical defects. If the refrigerators sold for an average price of $950, Hubble would record revenues of $7,600 ($950 × 8). Although Hubble buys quality merchandise from its supplier, it is possible that within three years of sale, one or more of these refrigerators may break down. In reviewing its past record of mechanical breakdowns, Hubble estimates that, over the long term, it costs approximately 5% of every sticker price to fix all units that ultimately require repair work. Over the next three years, Hubble therefore expects to spend about $380 ($7,600 × .05) to fix one of more of the eight refrigerators just sold. Depending on the quality of the eight refrigerators, it may spend more than $380, or less than $380. Experience and knowledge of the merchandise make it possible for corporations to make reasonably accurate estimates. To record the estimated warranty obligation, Hubble makes the following journal entry:

| SE – Warranty expense | 380 | |
| L – Estimated warranty obligation | | 380 |

If Hubble needed to spend $126 in 19X7 to replace a leaking seal on one of the refrigerators, it would record the repair work by reducing the liability account.

| L – Estimated warranty obligation | 126 | |
| A – Cash | | 126 |

As you can see, an expense is not recorded when actual repair costs are incurred. By estimating its potential future obligation at the same time that it records revenue from the sale, Hubble is able to record the warranty expense in the same period that it records the revenue. This way, users get a clearer picture of the actual amount of revenue earned on the sale. If Hubble had delayed recognizing an expense until it actually incurred some warranty costs, that expense could easily appear in a period other than the one in which the revenue was recognized. The profit reported for the sale would then have been overstated. For this reason, corporations are asked to estimate the potential future warranty obligation and to record it at the time of sale, if the amount of warranty costs are material.

Unearned Revenues

In many businesses, customers are required to make down payments prior to the receipt of goods or services. This creates partially executed contracts between buyers and sellers. Because the sellers have not performed on their part of the contract, it would be inappropriate for them to recognize revenue from the sale. Therefore, sellers must defer the recognition of revenue from down payments. These deferrals create liabilities that are known as unearned revenues, or deferred revenues.

Businesses that require prepayments generally show unearned revenues as a part of the liability section. Magazine and newspaper publishers are among these types of businesses. The current liability section of Imperial Parking Limited in Exhibit 9-1 (earlier in this chapter) illustrates this and several other types of current liabilities. Remember that Imperial Parking Limited manages parking lots and parkades. According to Note 1 (i.), the Deferred Revenue shown among the liabilities arises from parking lot fees collected in advance of their due date. Note as well, that Imperial Parking Limited has the "Trade accounts payable and other accrued liabilities" to which we referred earlier.

Current Portion of Long-Term Debt

When long-term debt (discussed in Chapter 10) comes within a year of being due, it must be reclassified as a current liability. This reclassification enables users to better estimate the outflow of cash expected during the following year. Therefore, this account category, known as **current portion of long-term debt**, is used for all the debt that was originally long-term, but that is now within one year, or one operating cycle, of being paid off or retired. This account is also referred to as the *current maturity* of long-term debt. In the case of long-term mortgages or other debt obligations requiring monthly or annual payments, the current maturity part that is shown with the current liabilities represents the amount of principal that will be paid off in the next year. Remember that the interest paid on this debt is only recorded as it accrues or is paid. Note in Exhibit 9-1 that in 1995, about 20% of Imperial Parking's long-term debt is due to be paid within the next year.

◖◗ COMMITMENTS

In the course of business, many corporations sign agreements committing them to certain transactions. A common type of commitment transaction is a **purchase commitment**, which is an agreement to purchase items in the future for a negotiated price. As discussed earlier, this is an example of a mutually unexecuted contract and, under GAAP, is therefore not recorded on the books of the corporation. The corporation would, however, discuss it in a note to the financial statements if it felt that the commitment would have a material effect on future operations. An example of this type of disclosure can be seen in Exhibit 9-2, which is the inventory footnote for AT Plastics Inc.

AT Plastics likely disclosed this information because of the type of contract involved, and because it is committed for the next four years. A **take or pay contract** means that the corporation must pay for the 70,290 tonnes of ethylene whether it actually takes that much from the supplier or not. No monetary amounts are discussed because the contract price varies according to the cost of the service provided.

When the financial statements of a corporation are analyzed, undisclosed purchase commitments are a significant risk to be considered. The problem this can pose for the reader of financial statements is illustrated by an international example from Westinghouse Corporation in the United States in the mid-1970s. Westinghouse was in the business of building nuclear power plants for utility companies. To secure the construction business, utility companies were offered fixed-price contracts by Westinghouse to supply them with uranium after the plants were completed and running. The average prices stated in these contracts were approximately $8 − $10 U.S. per pound of uranium. By the mid-1970s, Westinghouse was committed to providing a total of approximately 70 million pounds over a 20-year

EXHIBIT 9-2

AT PLASTICS INC., 1994
Excerpted from Notes to the Statements

Note 13. Commitments

Purchases:
The Company has agreed to purchase 70,290 tonnes of ethylene per year until the end of 1998, under a cost of service, take or pay contract.

period. Since these were mutually unexecuted contracts, they were not recorded or disclosed in the financial statements.

When the market price of uranium was close to the fixed price in the contracts, these mutually unexecuted contracts were a break-even proposition for Westinghouse (i.e., no gain or loss would occur when the contracts were satisfied), and no disclosure was required. The problem began when a cartel formed in the uranium supply market and drove up the price of uranium. When the price reached $26 U.S. per pound in September 1975, Westinghouse informed the utility companies that it was to be excused from performing on its contracts because of a legal doctrine called "commercial impracticability." The utility companies then brought lawsuits against Westinghouse, alleging breach of contract. By 1978, the price of uranium had risen to $45 U.S. per pound.

Because the price escalated so significantly above the contract price of $8–$10 U.S. per pound, Westinghouse had to disclose the loss on these commitment contracts. In 1975, the estimated cost to Westinghouse of settling the contracts approached $2 billion, which was about 75% of its total equity at the time. Over the next 15 years, Westinghouse settled most of the suits, the first of which was settled in 1977 for $20.5 million. The audit opinion of Westinghouse was qualified by the auditors for several years until 1979, when Westinghouse accrued a loss of $405 million (net of taxes) to cover the estimated costs of settling the remaining suits. Remember that auditors qualify their opinion about a corporation's financial statements if the corporation does not follow GAAP. Failing to accrue the potential liability for the lawsuits would have led to such a qualification. The effects of these suits lingered for 15 years as indicated by the note in Exhibit 9-3, excerpted from the Westinghouse 1990 annual report.

CONTINGENCIES

Contingent liabilities (also referred to as **contingent losses**) arise when the incurrence of the liability is contingent upon some future event. The settlement of a lawsuit, for example, is a situation in which the corporation may or may not incur a

---

EXHIBIT 9-3

WESTINGHOUSE, 1990
Excerpted from Notes to the Statements

Note 20: Contingent Liabilities and Commitments

The Corporation had previously provided for all estimated future costs associated with the resolution of all uranium supply contract suits and related litigation. The remaining balance at December 31, 1990 is deemed adequate considering all facts and circumstances known to management. The future obligations require providing specific quantities of uranium and products and services over a period extending beyond the year 2010. The net cost of meeting these obligations and other related settlement transactions are applied to the balance of the liability and are not reflected in results of operations. Variances from estimates which may occur will be considered in determining if an adjustment of the liability is necessary.

liability, depending upon the judgment in the case. The note in Exhibit 9-4, from the 1994 annual report of Queenstake Resources Ltd., outlines one such contingency.

EXHIBIT 9-4

QUEENSTAKE RESOURCES LTD.
Excerpted from Notes to the Statements

Note 11. Contingency

Queenstake Resources U.S.A., Inc. ("QTI"), a dormant subsidiary of the Company, has responded to a request from the United States Forest Service (the "Forest Service") for information to enable a determination of whether QTI is a Potentially Responsible Party ("PRP") with respect to the costs of remediation of operations in the 1940s at the Buckskin, Nevada property conducted by others. QTI optioned the Buckskin property in 1986, conducted an exploratory drilling program and subsequently reclaimed the surface disturbed areas to the satisfaction of the Forest Service. QTI returned the property to its owners in 1992. The Forest Service has had an Engineering Evaluation/Cost Analysis of a non-time critical removal action for the Buckskin property prepared by EnviroSearch International in which they recommend a total clean-up program of the 1940s tailings and waste rock to cost approximately U.S. $325,000. QTI believes that it is not one of the PRPs on the Buckskin property and that any claim against it is without merit. However, there is no assurance that QTI will not be held liable for some portion of the total cost in the future.

Another example of a contingency is the guarantee of one corporation's loan by another corporation. This happens many times when a subsidiary corporation takes out a loan and the parent corporation (the corporation that owns most of the shares of the subsidiary) guarantees repayment of the loan. The liability to repay the loan is a contingent liability to the parent corporation because it is contingent upon the default of the subsidiary. Such a contingency is illustrated in the 1994 annual report for Cominco Ltd., shown in Exhibit 9-5.

EXHIBIT 9-5

COMINCO LTD.
Excerpted from Notes to the Statements

Note 15. Commitments and contingencies

(b) Red Dog Mine
Under the terms of an agreement between the Alaska Industrial Development and Export Authority (AIDEA) and Cominco Alaska Incorporated (CAK), a subsidiary company, CAK provided a letter of credit for U.S. $120,000,000 as collateral security to permit AIDEA to finance the road and port facilities to service the Red Dog mine in north-western Alaska. The remaining term of the letter of credit, which the Corporation has guaranteed, is six years and U.S. $72,000,000 is currently outstanding. The agreement gives CAK certain non-exclusive priority rights for the transportation of concentrates for a minimum term of 50 years with a renewal provision of five additional 10-year terms. Once commercial production commenced, CAK was required to pay a minimum annual user fee based on AIDEA's cost to construct the system plus an investment return. After the earlier of 35 years or repayment of AIDEA's investment base plus interest, the toll fee will be recalculated as defined in the agreement. The estimated minimum annual toll fee will approximate U.S. $12,000,000.

As a third and final example, the selling of accounts receivable with recourse creates a contingent liability for the selling corporation because it may be required to buy back the receivable under the recourse provision if the customer defaults on the payments. A further discussion of the sale of receivables is located in Chapter 6.

Under GAAP, a contingent loss should be recognized as a loss on the income statement and a liability on the balance sheet if it meets the following criteria:

1. It is likely that some future event will result in the corporation incurring an obligation which will require the use of assets or the performance of a service.

2. The amount of the loss can be reasonably estimated.

If either of these criteria are not met, but the potential for loss is significant, the corporation should provide users with information about the potential loss in a note disclosure similar to the two examples already quoted.

DEFERRED TAXES

Deferred taxes arise because, although the corporation uses accounting revenues and expenses to determine income tax expense on the income statement, it also uses Revenue Canada's calculations of revenues and expenses to determine the income tax payable (that is, the amount that must actually be paid to the government). In Chapter 8, deferred taxes were mentioned because corporations must use capital cost allowance (CCA) for tax purposes. They can, however, use one of several amortization methods to prepare financial statements.

Other areas that create differences between what is taxed and what is reported include the warranty costs we mentioned earlier in this chapter. The warranty expense on the income statement is based on an estimate of future warranty costs based on revenue that was recognized in the current period. For a deduction for tax purposes, the actual amount that the corporation paid in the current period to repair items under warranty is used. Amortization and warranties are examples of how the tax expense reported on the income statement—as calculated based on the accounting revenues and expenses reported on the statement—will be different from the actual taxes payable to the government.

Two methods are currently used to calculate deferred taxes: the **deferral method**, and the **liability method**. The deferral method is used in Canada, but the Accounting Standards Board is considering a switch to the liability method. The liability method is used in the United States, and is also under consideration by the International Accounting Standards Committee. Because Canada still uses the deferral method, this section will concentrate on that method. Following this discussion, the liability method will be briefly described.

AN INTERNATIONAL PERSPECTIVE
REPORTS FROM OTHER COUNTRIES

In Italy, commitments and contingencies are explicitly shown in a formal statement in the annual report. The following statement from the 1990 annual report of Dalmine SPA (an Italian iron tubing company) illustrates this statement.

Memorandum Accounts, Commitments and Contingencies
As of 31st December 1990 and 1989

Debit Balances

	31.12.90	31.12.89
Third parties for assets held		
Third parties for goods in deposit	10,429,742,694	38,185,640,672
Third party notes as guarantee	—	546,613,617
Leased assets	812,136,419	1,010,380,979
	11,241,879,113	39,742,635,268
Company assets held by third parties:		
Third parties for goods or assets	3,812,139,541	3,316,204,802
Third parties for goods and work in process	13,810,027,848	978,522,397
Third parties for fixed assets in bailment	150,256,800	166,952,000
	17,772,424,189	4,461,679,199
Commitments		
Third party shares for collection	445,400	445,400
Guarantees given by the Company on behalf of third parties	148,076,396,127	103,517,909,544
Guarantees	23,286,057,496	42,413,385,812
Third parties for gurantees given on behalf of the Company	20,685,493,402	43,828,239,515
Subsidiaries and associated companies for guarantees	9,970,937,911	6,444,003,937
Third parties for liens and mortgages	221,925,458,000	221,925,458,000
Liens and mortgages from associated companies	13,200,000,000	13,200,000,000
	437,144,788,336	431,329,442,208
Risks:		
Risks on notes credited with recourse	184,159,327	93,784,276
Risks on ntoes financed	—	277,873,191
	184,159,327	371,657,467
Total	466,343,250,965	475,905,414,142

◤◣ Deferral Method

The **deferral method** calculates the amount of tax expense to be reported to shareholders by using the income reported to shareholders and the tax rates in effect at the time of the calculation. Because the income reported to shareholders may differ from that reported to Revenue Canada, the amount of tax expense reported can differ from the amount payable to Revenue Canada. The difference between the expense and the amount payable becomes the amount of deferred tax. It is merely a "plug" to reconcile the expense reported to shareholders, and the liability owed to the taxing authority.

Some users misunderstand deferred taxes on the balance sheet. They incorrectly assume that deferred taxes represent an amount owed by the corporation to Revenue Canada. It does not. The amount owed is shown as *taxes payable*. Deferred taxes on the balance sheet represent an amount that will *likely* become payable in the future, if conditions continue unchanged into the future. In the early period of a capital asset's life, CCA could be larger than accounting amortization, which means that the corporation will pay less tax today than is measured for tax expense on the income statement. However, in the latter part of the asset's life, CCA will be less than the accounting amortization, which means that the corporation will pay more in tax than is measured for tax expense on the income statement. Over the life of any asset, the total tax expense will be the same as total taxes payable.

To understand the deferral method, consider the data and calculations in Exhibit 9-6. Assume that amortization is the only difference between the book and tax accounting methods of the corporation.

You can see in the tax calculation for Year 1 in Exhibit 9-6 that the tax expense reported for book purposes ($1,840) is the income before taxes multiplied by the tax rate ($4,000 × 46%). The taxes for tax purposes ($1,610) then represents the amount payable to Revenue Canada ($3,500 × 46%). The entry to record these amounts in the books is:

SE – Tax expense	1,840	
L – Tax payable		1,610
L – Deferred tax		230

EXHIBIT 9-6

Deferral Method Computations

Assumptions (in thousands):

Income before tax and amortization	$5,000
Capital asset purchased in Year 1:	
Original cost	$10,000
Estimated useful life	10 years
Estimated residual value	$0
Straight-line method used for book purposes	
Class 10 asset at 30% for tax purposes	
Tax rate	46%

Income Statement (Year 1):

	Book	Tax
Income before amortization and taxes	$5,000	$5,000
Amortization*	1,000	1,500
Income before taxes	$4,000	$3,500
Taxes	1,840	1,610
Net income	$2,160	$1,890

*CCA = 10,000 × .30 × .5 = 1,500

The question that should be raised at this point is: Why is the credit of $230 for deferred tax considered a liability? To answer this, consider the criteria for a liability: (1) there is a responsibility to transfer assets or services in the future; (2) the obligation cannot be avoided; and (3) the event giving rise to the obligation has already occurred. Is there a responsibility to transfer assets in the future? Some would argue that there is. For example, consider what will happen through the rest of the life of the asset. Exhibit 9-7 shows the computation of the deferred taxes over the 10-year life of the asset, assuming that the same income before taxes and amortization occurs in each year and that the tax rate remains fixed at 46%.

From the data in Exhibit 9-7, you can see how the difference between the amortization and CCA causes the deferred tax account to rise to a balance of $1,419, and then to decline all the way down until it takes on a debit balance in Year 10. Because the CCA is always calculated as 30% of the reduced balance, the deferred tax account

EXHIBIT 9-7

Deferred Taxes
Income Statement (book purposes):

	Year 1	Year 2	Year 3	Year 4	Year 5	Year 6	Year 7	Year 8	Year 9	Year 10
Income before amortization and taxes	$5,000	$5,000	$5,000	$5,000	$5,000	$5,000	$5,000	$5,000	$5,000	$5,000
Amortization	$1,000	$1,000	$1,000	$1,000	$1,000	$1,000	$1,000	$1,000	$1,000	$1,000
Income before taxes	$4,000	$4,000	$4,000	$4,000	$4,000	$4,000	$4,000	$4,000	$4,000	$4,000
Tax expense	$1,840	$1,840	$1,840	$1,840	$1,840	$1,840	$1,840	$1,840	$1,840	$1,840
Net income	$2,160	$2,160	$2,160	$2,160	$2,160	$2,160	$2,160	$2,160	$2,160	$2,160

Income Statement (tax purposes):

	Year 1	Year 2	Year 3	Year 4	Year 5	Year 6	Year 7	Year 8	Year 9	Year 10
Income before CCA and taxes	$5,000	$5,000	$5,000	$5,000	$5,000	$5,000	$5,000	$5,000	$5,000	$5,000
CCA	$1,500	$2,550	$1,785	$1,249	$875	$612	$429	$300	$210	$147
Income before taxes	$3,500	$2,450	$3,215	$3,751	$4,125	$4,388	$4,571	$4,700	$4,790	$4,853
Tax expense	$1,610	$1,127	$1,479	$1,725	$1,898	$2,018	$2,103	$2,162	$2,203	$2,232
Net income	$1,890	$1,323	$1,736	$2,026	$2,227	$2,370	$2,468	$2,538	$2,587	$2,621

Balance sheet:

	Year 1	Year 2	Year 3	Year 4	Year 5	Year 6	Year 7	Year 8	Year 9	Year 10
Change in deferred tax (difference between taxes for book and tax purposes)	$230	$713	$361	$115	($58)	($178)	($263)	($322)	($363)	($392)
Balance in deferred taxes (beginning of year)	$0	$230	$943	$1,304	$1,419	$1,361	$1,183	$920	$598	$235
Balance in deferred taxes (end of year)	$230	$943	$1,304	$1,419	$1,361	$1,183	$920	$598	$235	($157)

does not decline to exactly zero. In the years beyond Year 10, there will be no further amortization on the income statement, but the corporation can continue to claim a deduction for 30% of the remaining balance for tax purposes as long as the corporation still has the asset. The total income that would be reported for accounting purposes over the 10 years would be $21,600, whereas the total disposable income remaining after taxes are paid would be $21,786. The difference represents the remaining amount of CCA ($343) that can still be claimed for tax purposes times 54% (1 − .46). The total impact on income is the same, but the timing of the tax expense and the taxes payable are different over the life of the asset.

The difference between the tax expense reported to shareholders and the taxes payable to Revenue Canada is a result of the timing difference between when the amortization expense is reported for tax purposes, and when it is reported for book purposes. According to the deferral method, the differences are referred to as **timing differences**. Differences in the first half of the life of the asset (referred to as **originating differences**) increase the balance in deferred taxes. These differences are reversed in the last half of the life of the asset (referred to as **reversing differences**), causing the balance in deferred taxes to decline. The taxes that are "deferred" in the first half of the life of the asset are paid in the last half of the life of the asset. Because of this, some would argue that the credit entry to deferred taxes in the entry shown earlier is a liability.

Others argue that it is not a liability because the obligation to transfer assets in the future may not occur. For example, Revenue Canada might change its tax rules and/or its rates, which would change the amount of tax the corporation would have to pay or, the corporation could continue to purchase capital assets, which could result in the potential deferral being delayed for many years if not indefinitely. This aspect of deferred taxes is explained in more detail later in this section.

The change in the deferred tax balance can also be shown graphically, as in Exhibit 9-8. Note that the graph represents a single asset and illustrates how the balance in deferred taxes starts at zero and returns past zero at the end of the 10 years.

If the corporation had only one asset at a time, the originating balance and reversing of that balance would occur as shown in the example. However, corporations often have several assets that have varying estimated lives and residual values. Because most growing corporations are continually replacing old assets with new assets (usually costing more), the reversing activities of one asset are often offset by the larger originating differences. Instead of a declining credit balance in the deferred tax account, therefore, it is often an increasing balance. For example, look at the liability section of Big Rock Brewery Limited in Exhibit 9-9.

Big Rock has a substantial investment in capital assets. In 1995, it increased its investment in capital assets by almost $3 million. Big Rock uses straight-line amortization for reporting purposes, but like every other corporation in Canada, must use CCA for tax. You can see that the deferred tax balance rose by $500,000. A note disclosure tells us that "The company follows the tax allocation method of accounting for the tax effect of the timing differences between taxable income and accounting income. Timing differences result principally from claiming capital cost allowance for income tax purposes in excess of amortization on capital assets."

Although the difference between amortization and CCA is not the only timing difference that causes deferred taxes, it usually has the most impact. The warranty expense mentioned earlier also creates deferred taxes. However, the originating dif-

EXHIBIT 9-8

Deferred Tax Balance, Single Asset

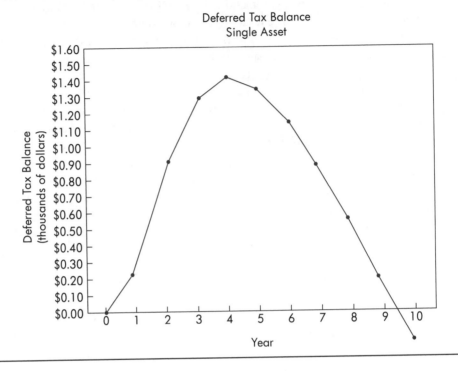

ferences for warranties create debits to deferred taxes, and the reversing entries are credits—the opposite of amortization/CCA.

Deferred taxes can represent a significant amount on the balance sheet. It is therefore important that you understand what they are, and what they are not. They are the difference between the tax expense as calculated on accounting income, and the tax payable as calculated on taxable income. They are not the amount owed to the government for the current period. In fact, whether or not the corporation ever pays the amount to the government depends on the future activities of the business, and on whether or not the government keeps the same tax rules.

Deferred taxes can appear in various parts of the balance sheet as current assets or liabilities, or as long-term assets or liabilities. Where they appear is a function of the differences that caused them, and whether they have a debit or credit balance. Deferred taxes that arise from warranty costs are often classified as current because the actual costs for warranties (those that are tax deductible for tax purposes) are usually incurred during the same year as the expense, or in the following year. This is true if the warranty is a one-year warranty. For three-year warranties, the deferred taxes would take longer to reverse, and are therefore classified as noncurrent. Deferred taxes that result from the CCA/amortization situation are classified as noncurrent because it takes several years for the deferred taxes to reverse. Because of the difficulty in determining whether or not deferred taxes are actually a liability, you will often see them classified on their own at the end of the noncurrent liabilities section.

EXHIBIT 9-9

BIG ROCK BREWERY LTD.
Excerpted From the Balance Sheet
March 31, 1995 and 1994
(Denominated in Canadian Dollars)

Liabilities

	1995	1994
CURRENT LIABILITIES		
Bank indebtedness (Note 4)	$ 408,071	$
Accounts payable	462,739	609,357
Income taxes payable	238,809	392,663
Current portion of long-term debt (Note 5)	220,476	80,400
Total current liabilities	1,330,095	1,082,420
LONG-TERM DEBT (Note 5)	956,498	89,000
DEFERRED INCOME TAXES	1,403,500	881,500
COMMITMENTS (Note 11)		
Total liabilities	3,690,093	2,052,920

Before the liability method is discussed, one more issue regarding the deferral method should be considered because it also applies to the liability method. Some differences between the methods used for book and tax purposes are considered **permanent differences**. One example is the recognition of dividend revenue received from an investment in another Canadian corporation. This is a legitimate revenue for book purposes. For tax purposes, however, it is not taxable income because the corporation that paid the dividends already paid taxes on it. To tax the recipient of the dividend would, in effect, tax the same income twice. If deferred tax were to be computed on this permanent difference, it would never reverse, and the balance in the deferred tax account would never disappear. For this reason, GAAP requires that permanent differences be ignored for the computation of deferred taxes. This applies to both the deferral method and the liability method.

Liability Method

Although the deferral method is GAAP today in Canada, the Accounting Standards Board of the CICA is considering a change from the deferral method to the liability method. The liability method focuses on the balance sheet, not on the income statement. It attempts to measure the liability to pay taxes in the future based on a set of assumptions about future revenues and expenses. It measures the future tax liability based on future tax rates, rather than on the current rates used by the deferral method. The liability method is used in the United States and is being proposed by the International Accounting Standards Committee. If Canada adopts this method, it will bring our GAAP more in line with both of these groups. Because the actual details of the liability method are a topic for an intermediate course, we will not go into any more detail here.

◖◗ OTHER TAX DISCLOSURES

Included in the usual tax disclosure of a corporation are three basic types of disclosures. The first is a breakdown of the tax expense (sometimes referred to as the tax provision) into the amounts currently payable, and the amounts deferred. If the corporation has significant foreign operations, foreign taxes are sometimes broken out in this disclosure. In Western Star Trucks Holdings' financial statements, this is disclosed in Note 13, where the breakdown of the tax expense occurs in the first table and the foreign tax effects occurs in the second table under "Foreign tax rate differentials" in Exhibit 9-10.

The second tax disclosure is a discussion of the items that cause the deferred tax amounts. In Exhibit 9-10, Western Star Trucks Holdings has not provided this breakdown. Instead, it has moved directly into the third type of disclosure.

The third major disclosure in the footnotes is a reconciliation of the difference between the tax expense reported, and the amount that would have been reported based on statutory rates. This disclosure takes into consideration the tax credits and other items that cause the average (effective) rate to be different from the statutory Revenue Canada rate. The second table in Exhibit 9-10 shows that the differences are substantial, and are due mainly to a manufacturing deduction which is an example of a permanent deduction, and unrecorded tax loss benefits and foreign tax rate differentials which affect the deferred taxes.

EXHIBIT 9-10

WESTERN STAR TRUCKS HOLDINGS LTD.
Excerpted from Notes to the Statements

13. Income Taxes

Income tax expense is comprised as follows:

	1995	1994
[in thousands of dollars]		
Current	15,616	9,988
Deferred	3,919	738
Benefit of loss carryforward	[6,204]	[6,140]
	13,331	4,586

The following table reconciles the reported income tax expense to the income tax provision which would have been obtained by applying the combined basic Canadian federal and provincial income tax rate of 45% [1994 – 45%] to accounting income.

	1995	1994
[in thousands of dollars]		
Provision for income taxes based on combined basic Canadian federal and provincial income tax rate	24,651	11,570
Increase [decrease] in taxes resulting from		
Manufacturing and processing profits deduction	[1,865]	[869]
Foreign exchange on translation of subsidiaries	299	420
Minority interest	–	710
Benefit of loss carryforward realized in the year	[6,204]	[6,140]
Benefit of loss carryforward applied to reduce deferred income tax credits	[1,706]	–
Foreign tax rate differentials	[2,561]	[1,103]
Other	717	[2]
	13,331	4,586

AN INTERNATIONAL PERSPECTIVE
REPORTS FROM OTHER COUNTRIES

In some countries, such as Italy, Norway and Chile, accounting practices follow the tax requirements of the country. Therefore, no deferred tax account is necessary since there are no differences between book and tax calculations. In most other countries, such as Denmark, France, and Japan, the provision for income taxes is based on taxable income and not on the book income reported to shareholders. Therefore, these countries also do not show deferred taxes. A relatively small number of countries including South Africa and the United States compute deferred taxes on all timing differences (excluding permanent differences). The United Kingdom follows the Canadian practice, except that differences that will not reverse in the foreseeable future are not recorded as deferred taxes. Instead, they are treated like permanent differences.:

SUMMARY

This chapter opened with a description of commonly reported current liabilities. It also described some of the anomalies that can affect the decisions made by users, but that may or may not be actually reflected on the balance sheet or income statement. These items are commitments (often described in notes to the financial statements) and loss contingencies (reported on the financial statements if likely to occur and measurable, but in the notes to the financial statements only if likely but not measurable). The chapter concluded with a discussion about deferred income taxes, an item that can be confusing to users because it can be either current or noncurrent, depending on its source. Unlike previous chapters, this one did not include a discussion of financial statement analysis concerns regarding liabilities. This topic is deferred until the discussion of the remaining liabilities in Chapter 10 is complete. In Chapter 10, attention turns to the noncurrent liabilities, of which the primary accounts are bonds payable, pension liabilities, and lease liabilities.

SUMMARY PROBLEM

The Lundkvist Corporation purchased a piece of equipment on January 1, 19x8 for $21,000. The corporation will amortize the asset straight-line for book purposes over its useful life, which is estimated to be seven years. The residual value is estimated to be $0. The asset qualifies as a class 10 asset for tax purposes, with a 30% CCA rate. During 19x8, Lundkvist generated $4,500 in income before amortization and taxes. The tax rate in 19x8 is 25%. The amortization of the asset purchased in 19x8 is the only difference between the book methods and the tax methods used by Lundkvist.

Required:

1. Construct the entry for taxes that Lundkvist will make in 19x8 using the deferral method of calculating deferred taxes.

2. Prepare a footnote to accompany the 19x8 financial statements.

SUGGESTED SOLUTION TO SUMMARY PROBLEM

1. The tax expense and taxes payable for 19x8 are calculated as shown in Exhibit 9-11 under the deferral method.

    The entry to record taxes in 19x8 is, therefore:

SE – Tax Expense	375	
L – Tax Payable		338
L – Deferred Tax (plug)		37

2. The following footnote could be included with Lundkvist Corporation's financial statements:

    Income Taxes

    Income taxes for 19x8 consist of:

Current	$338
Deferred	37
	$375

    Deferred income taxes arise as a result of timing differences from claiming capital cost allowance for income tax purposes in excess of amortization on capital assets.

Statutory rate	25.0%
Effect on taxes of capital cost allowance	(2.5)
Effective tax rate	22.5%

EXHIBIT 9-11

Deferral Method Computations

Assumptions:

Income before tax and amortization	$4,500

Capital asset purchased in Year 19x8:

Original cost	$21,000
Estimated useful life	7 years
Estimated residual value	$0

Straight-line method used for book purposes

Class 10 asset with a CCA rate of 30%

Tax rate (19x8)	25%

Income Statement (19x8):

	Book	Tax
Income before amortization and taxes	$4,500	$4,500
Amortization[a]	3,000	3,150
Income before taxes	$1,500	$1,350
Taxes	375	338
Net income	$1,125	$1,012

[a] Refer to Chapter 8 for the calculation of straight-line amortization and CCA.

ABBREVIATIONS USED

CCA	Capital Cost Allowance
CPP	Canada Pension Plan
EI	Employment Insurance
QPP	Quebec Pension Plan

SYNONYMS

Contingent liability/Contingent loss
Current maturities of long-term debt/Current portion of long-term debt

GLOSSARY

Commitments Obligations to which a company has agreed, but that do not yet meet the recognition criteria for liabilities under GAAP.

Contingencies Events or transactions whose effects on the financial statements depend on the outcome of some future event.

Contingent liability A liability of a corporation that is contingent on some future event, such as the resolution of a lawsuit.

Contingent losses A loss to the corporation that is contingent upon some future event.

Current portion of long-term debt That portion of long-term debt that is within one year of being due.

Deferral method A method of computing deferred taxes in which the tax expense to shareholders is calculated by multiplying the current tax rate by the income before taxes reported to shareholders. The entry to the deferred tax account is then the difference between this expense and the taxes owed to the taxing authority on the corporation's tax return.

Deferred taxes Accounts used to reconcile the differences between the taxes reported to Revenue Canada (taxes payable) and those reported to shareholders (tax expense).

Liability An obligation that will require a probable future sacrifice of resources of the corporation.

Liability method A method of computing deferred taxes in which the balance in the deferred tax account is calculated based on the tax calculation of future years at future tax rates. The tax expense reported to shareholders is then determined based on the calculated deferred tax amount and the taxes owed to the taxing authority.

Line of credit A credit limit established by a bank that allows the corporation to write cheques for amounts greater than the amount of cash in a bank account.

Monetary liability A liability that is fixed in terms of the number of currency units it represents.

Mutually unexecuted contract A contract between two entities in which neither entity has performed its part of the agreement.

Net present value The value today of an amount or series of amounts to be received or paid in the future.

Originating differences The initial differences between book and tax reporting that arise in the accounting for the transactions of the corporation. When these differences reverse themselves, the reversals are referred to as reversing differences.

Partially executed contract A contract between two entities in which one or both of the parties has performed a portion of its part of the agreement.

Permanent differences Differences between book and tax reporting that never reverse themselves; that is, they are "permanent." For example, a manufacturing deduction that reduces taxable income but is not an accounting expense.

Purchase commitment A contract between two entities in which one entity agrees to buy goods or services from another entity, but neither party has executed the contract.

Reversing differences Timing or temporary differences that are reversals of previously recognized originating differences.

Take or pay contract A contract in which the buyer must pay for a minimum level of merchandise whether delivery of those goods is taken or not.

Timing differences Differences that arise in the accounting for the transactions of a corporation between the tax rules and the GAAP guidelines. The differences are restricted to those that involve only timing issues, that is, the period in which the items are reported. The term is used in the deferral method of computing deferred taxes.

Troubled debt restructuring The renegotiation of the terms of a debt agreement when the debtor is financially distressed.

Unearned revenues Cash receipts from customers that have not yet met the criteria for revenue recognition.

Working capital loan A short-term loan, often a demand loan, that is arranged with a bank to cover short-term cash shortages experienced by a corporation.

ASSIGNMENT MATERIAL

◤◥ Assessing your Recall

1. List the three essential characteristics of a liability.

2. Explain the meaning of a mutually unexecuted contract, and how it is accounted for under GAAP.

3. Describe the appropriate valuation method for liabilities under GAAP. Include a discussion of both current and noncurrent liabilities in your answer.

4. Describe the nature of an account called unearned revenues, and provide an example.

5. Explain the circumstances under which a commitment would be recognized in the financial statements under GAAP.

6. Explain the circumstances under which a loss contingency would be recognized in the financial statements under GAAP.

7. Describe how deferred taxes are calculated in the deferral method.

8. Describe or discuss the meaning of the following terms: timing differences, permanent differences, originating differences, and reversing differences.

◤◥ Applying Your Knowledge

9. Some accountants do not believe that deferred taxes meet the criteria for recognition as a liability. Discuss deferred taxes in terms of the three criteria for a liability, and provide your own arguments in support of whether or not they meet the criteria.

10. Sam's Cycle Shop had the following transactions involving current liabilities:

   1) It ordered bicycle repair parts from a supplier for $206,445. The parts were ordered on credit. During the year $189,500 was paid to suppliers.

2) Sam offered his customers a one-year warranty on bicycles. He estimated that warranty costs would total 2% of sales. Sales for the year were $2,488,200. During the year, he actually spent $31,040 for parts and labour to repair bicycles under warranty.

3) Sam has four employees involved in sales, and two involved in assembly and repairs. During the year, they earned gross wages of $132,000. From this amount, Sam deducted 25% for income tax, 2.7% for Canada Pension deductions, and 3% for Employment Insurance Contributions before giving the cheques to his staff. As an employer, he was also required to make an additional contribution of 2.7% for Canada Pension, and 4.2% for Employment Insurance on behalf of his employees.

Required:

a. Journalize the above transactions.

b. Prepare the current liability section of the balance sheet as it would appear at the end of the year after these transactions.

11. The University Survival Magazine was a small operation run by two enterprising university students. They published a magazine once a month from September through April. The magazine reported on various university activities, providing tidbits of knowledge on how to get the best tickets, where the best beer was sold for the best price, where the good study spots were located, and how to get library personnel to help with research. They sold their magazine by single copy in the bookstore for $3.00 an issue, or by subscription for $20.00 per year for eight issues. In August, they canvassed various local businesses and managed to raise $15,000 in advertising for the magazine. The advertisements were to be included in all eight issues of the magazine. In early September of 19x7, they sold 4,000 subscriptions. Up to the end of December, they sold 6,000 single copies in each of the four months. The cost of printing the first four issues of the magazine was $76,000.

Required:

a. Journalize all of the transactions for August through to the end of December. Where there are alternative ways of recording a transaction, explain why you chose to record it the way you did.

b. Prepare any necessary adjusting entries on December 31.

c. Prepare an income statement for the students for the period up to the end of December.

d. Write a brief memo to the students explaining why the net income amount on the balance sheet will not equal the cash balance in the bank account.

12. On April 10, 19x7, while looking for new furniture for his home, Dr. Cutter, a surgeon, cut his right index finger because some of the nails on the table he was looking at were not hammered in properly. On June 10, 19x7, Dr. Cutter sued the furniture store for $5 million. The case came to trial on September 13, 19x7, and the jury reached a decision on December 13, 19x7, finding the store liable and awarding Dr. Cutter a sum of $3.5 million. On February 3, 19x8, the furniture store, dissatisfied by the judgment, appealed to a higher court. The higher court reheard the case beginning on July 18, 19x8. On November 25, 19x8, a jury again found the store liable and awarded $5 million to Dr. Cutter. On January 15, 19x9, the furniture store paid $5 million to Dr. Cutter.

Required:

Using the stated events in the case, identify the various times at which a loss could be recognized. Using the criteria for a contingent liability, recommend and justify which of those times would be the most appropriate for reporting a note to the financial statements and for making an actual journal entry on the books. Assume the corporation's year-end is December 31.

13. The Air Cool Air Conditioning Company services air conditioners on a quarterly basis. It offers its customers a service plan that costs $500 per year and includes four service visits during the year. The company collects the entire $500 when the contract is signed, and recognizes the revenue on a quarterly basis when each of the four service visits is completed. On January 1,800 contracts were outstanding. Of these, 300 expired at the end of the first quarter, 200 at the end of the second quarter, 150 at the end of the third quarter, and 150 at the end of the fourth quarter. Sales of new contracts and expenses during the year are as follows:

Quarter	Contracts Sold	Expenses
1	300	$80,000
2	250	66,000
3	350	98,000
4	400	115,000

Assume that the sale of new contracts takes place at the beginning of each quarter.

Required:
a. Give the necessary journal entries for each of the four quarters.
b. How many contracts were still outstanding at the end of the fourth quarter, and what is the value of these contracts?
c. Determine the amounts that would appear on the balance sheet and income statement on December 31 with respect to the above activities. Prepare a partial balance sheet and income statement to show how these amounts would be reported.

14. On January 1, 19x7, the Fitwell Nuts & Bolts Company purchased a new machine costing $8,000. The company uses straight-line amortization for book purposes and CCA for tax purposes. The machine has an estimated useful life of four years and zero residual value. For tax purposes, the machine is in the 20% asset class, and the company is in the 25% marginal tax bracket and closes its books on December 31.

Required:
a. Calculate the amount of deferred tax each year from 19x7 to 2000, and give the necessary journal entries for recording the tax expense for each year. Assume that income before amortization and taxes is constant at $20,000 each year. Also, prepare a deferred tax T-account for each of the years, using the deferral method.
b. What amount would appear on the balance sheet for deferred taxes for 19x7 to 2000? Where on the balance sheet would these amounts be reported?

c. If you were a banker reviewing this corporation's financial statements in anticipation of granting it a loan, what importance would you place on the deferred tax balance? Explain.

15. On January 1, 19x6, the Canadian Works Company purchased a new capital asset costing $15,000. The company estimated the useful life of the asset to be five years with a $3,000 residual value. The company uses straight-line amortization for book purposes and the asset qualifies for a 30% CCA rate for tax purposes. The company closes its books on December 31. The income before amortization and taxes in 19x6 is $50,000.

Required:
a. Calculate the deferred tax amount, income tax expense, and taxes payable for 19x6 using the deferral method. Assume a tax rate for 19x6 of 40%. Give the necessary journal entry.
b. Calculate the deferred tax amount to the end of years 19x7 and 19x8.
c. Explain why the deferred tax account has changed over the three years.

16. On July 1, 19x7, the Hudson Manufacturing Corporation signed a contract with Forte Turbine Corporation to purchase 10 machines costing $20,000 each. The machines will be purchased one every year for 10 years. Hudson estimates the useful life of the machines to be eight years, with zero salvage value. The corporation uses the straight-line method for book purposes, and CCA for tax purposes. The machines are in the 30% asset class for tax purposes. The corporation closes its books on June 30.

Required:
a. Calculate the amount of deferred tax under the deferral method for the first seven years, assuming that the tax rate is 40% and that it remains constant throughout the 10-year period.
b. Calculate the balance in deferred tax at the end of the seventh year.
c. Repeat parts (a) and (b) for Year 8, and compare the balance in deferred tax at the end of Year 8 with that of Year 7. Explain what is happening in the eighth year.

◤◣ Reading and Interpreting Published Financial Statements

17. Imperial Metals Corporation is a Canadian mining company with operations in Canada and the United States. In the notes to the financial statements of its 1994 annual report, Imperial Metals states:

Future Site Restoration Costs
The estimated costs for restoration of producing resource properties are accrued and charged to operations over commercial production based upon total estimated site restoration costs and recoverable reserves. The estimated costs for restoration of non-producing resource properties are accrued as liabilities when the costs of site clean-up and restoration are likely to be incurred and can be reasonably estimated. Actual site restoration costs will be deducted from the accrual.

Required:

a. Explain how and why Imperial Metals treats future restoration costs for producing properties different from non-producing properties.
b. Using accounting concepts, explain why it is not appropriate for Imperial Metals to wait until it actually incurs restoration costs before it recognizes an expense on its income statement for restoration.

18. Note 4 of Enerflex System Ltd.'s 1994 financial statements (Exhibit 9-12) describes in more detail its debt situation.

Required:

Using the information included in Exhibit 9-12, answer the following questions:
a. Enerflex has a $40,000,000 line of credit. What is a line of credit?
b. The line of credit carries interest at the bank prime rate. What is a prime rate? What does the prime rate tell you about the bank's estimate of this line of credit?
c. The lines of credit are "secured by general assignments of accounts receivable and inventory." What do you think that this means?

19. Mackenzie Financial Corporation's balance sheets for March 31, 1995 and 1994 are included in Exhibit 9-13. Mackenzie provides investment management and related services to public mutual funds, corporate pension fund clients and other institutional investors.

EXHIBIT 9-12

ENERFLEX SYSTEMS LTD.
Excerpted from Notes to the Statements

4. Debt

	1994	1993
Current:		
Bank loans (a)	$ 12,002	$ 7,837
Long-term:		
Mortgage (b)	$ 4,792	$ 4,862
Less current portion	76	70
	$ 4,716	$ 4,792

(a)   Operating bank lines of credit totalling $40,000,000 with interest at bank prime secured by general assignments of accounts receivable and inventory.

(b)   Interest at 8.21%, amortization 25 years, maturing in 1997, secured by land and buildings.

The Company entered into an interest rate swap amounting to $1,000,000 with an effective interest rate of 11.1% which matured on January 4, 1995.

Long-term debt is due in the following years: $76,000 in 1995, $82,000 in 1996 and the remaining $4,634,000 in 1997.

Interest on long-term debt was $396,500 for 1994 ($402,000 for 1993).

EXHIBIT 9-13

MACKENZIE FINANCIAL CORP.
Consolidated Balance Sheets
As at March 31
(thousands of dollars)

	1995	1994
Assets		
Cash and short-term investments	$ 144,455	$ 112,473
Accounts and other receivables	52,187	46,599
Income taxes receivable	–	10,854
Mortgage loans	189,932	142,027
Deferred selling commissions and investment		
in related partnerships *(note 3)*	112,757	100,526
Investment in affiliated companies	56,039	55,539
Management contracts	17,534	20,708
Capital assets *(note 4)*	22,705	16,760
Goodwill *(note 5)*	8,293	9,463
Other assets *(note 6)*	14,661	11,865
	$ 618,563	$ 526,814
Liabilities		
Bank loans *(note 7)*	$ 13,012	$ 4,767
Accounts payable and accrued liabilities	34,592	38,159
Income taxes payable	10,257	–
Customer deposits *(note 8)*	213,880	179,345
Notes payable *(notes 3 and 9)*	44,184	50,000
Deferred taxes	48,423	22,718
	$ 364,348	$ 294,989
Commitments and Contingencies *(notes 7 and 13)*		
Shareholders' Equity		
Capital Stock *(note 10)*		
Authorized – Unlimited number of common shares		
Issued and outstanding		
– 59,264,115 (1994 – 59,254,115) common shares	$ 38,813	$ 38,761
Retained earnings	215,402	193,064
	$ 254,215	$ 231,825
	$ 618,563	$ 526,814

(The accompanying notes are an integral part of these consolidated financial statements.)

Signed on behalf of the Board

Alexander Christ
Director

F. Warren Hurst
Director

Required:

a. Mackenzie has a liability called "customer deposits" among its liabilities. What does this liability represent? It does not distinguish between current and noncurrent liabilities. Which do you think it is, and why?

b. Mackenzie has an asset called "mortgage loans". Usually accounts called mortgage loans are liabilities. What is this item and why is it listed with the assets?

20. The 1994 financial statements of Purcell Energy Ltd. include the current liability "Bank indebtedness" in the amount of $130,477. This liability is further described in the following note:

6. Bank Indebtedness

The bank loan bears interest at prime plus 1 3/4% and is supported by a fixed charge on the oil and gas properties. This loan is part of a $500,000 credit policy.

Required:

a. If the interest is prime plus 1 3/4%, how much is it? Does the bank consider this corporation to be a good credit risk?

b. Is a credit policy the same as a line of credit?

c. What does it mean if the loan is "supported by a fixed charge on the oil and gas properties"?

21. In Exhibit 9-14, Note 12 of Doman Industries Limited's 1994 financial statements describes how the income tax on the income statement is determined.

Required:

a. Doman Industries' tax at statutory rates of 44.5% in 1994 is adjusted by various items to arrive at an actual income and capital taxes expense of $44,176.

EXHIBIT 9-14

DOMAN INDUSTRIES LIMITED

Excerpted from Notes to the Statements

12. Income and Capital Taxes

	1994	1993
	($000's)	
Income and capital taxes expense on pre-tax earnings based on the combined basic Federal and Provincial income rates of 44.5% in 1994 and 44% in 1993	$44,487	$32,512
Differences resulting from:		
Large Corporations and other capital taxes	4,900	5,521
Manufacturing and processing profits deduction	(7,388)	(3,673)
Federal surtax	947	614
Non-taxable incomes, including equity in operating earnings of associated companies	(71)	(1,769)
Other, primarily non-deductible items	1,301	488
Income and capital taxes expense	$44,176	$33,693
Comprised of:		
Current income and capital taxes	$ 6,865	$ 7,963
Deferred income taxes	37,311	25,730
	$44,176	$33,693

Deferred income taxes arise principally from timing differences between the amortization of property, plant and equipment and deferred charges against earnings and the related amounts claimed for income tax purposes.

Determine the actual tax rate. Review the adjustments that caused the change and determine which of the items represent permanent differences, and which represent timing differences. To answer this question you will need to refer to the table in Exhibit 9-14 and to the statement at the very bottom of the exhibit.

b. In 1994, how much did Doman Industries actually pay to Revenue Canada for income taxes? Explain how you calculated the amount.

22. During December of 1990, Harley-Davidson Inc. in the United States was found liable for damages in a lawsuit brought by a former supplier of aftermarket motorcycle parts. The jury awarded the supplier compensatory and punitive damages of $7.2 million. The company, in its 1990 annual report, indicated that it had appealed the verdict and planned to aggressively seek its reversal. Also in the 1990 annual report of Harley-Davidson, the following footnote appeared:

> At December 31, 1990, the Motorcycles and Related Products segment (the Motorcycle segment) and the Transportation Vehicles segment (the Transportation segment) estimate that they were contingently liable under repurchase agreements for an approximate maximum of $53.0 million and $27.4 million, respectively, to lending institutions that provide wholesale floor plan financing to the dealers. These agreements are customary in both the motorcycle and recreational vehicle industry. The Company's loss exposure on repurchase is limited to the difference between the resale value of the vehicle and the amount required to be paid the lending institution at the time of repurchase.

Required:

a. Should Harley-Davidson record the $7.2 million loss from this lawsuit and a related liability in 1990? In your answer, identify the criteria that you would evaluate to arrive at your conclusion.

b. How should Harley-Davidson report on its contingent liability with regard to the wholesale floor plan financing agreements?

23. In the 1995 annual report of Imperial Parking Limited, the following note was included under Commitments and Contingencies:

> Revenue Canada has completed a series of goods and services tax audits primarily with regard to the taxability of violation notice receipts. Management has calculated that the maximum potential exposure to the Company from the series of audits, excluding any penalties or interest that may be claimed by Revenue Canada, will not exceed $900,000. While the Company intends to appeal all assessments received, it has provided in the accounts the expected costs of resolution.
>
> As part of its regular operations, the Company periodically becomes involved with legal claims or potential claims related to damage to vehicles or personal injuries for which the Company carries insurance, or disagreements with individual employees or on the interpretation of management or lease agreements.

Required:

a. What criteria should be evaluated in determining how Imperial Parking should handle the liability associated with the potential Revenue Canada assessment?

b. Imperial Parking's net incomes in 1995 and 1994 were $1,527,000 and $34,000 respectively. Does the reassessment have the potential to be materially significant for Imperial Parking? Explain your reasoning.

c. How should Imperial Parking handle the various legal claims described in the second paragraph?

CASE

THE BIGGER MOTOR CORPORATION

The Bigger Motor Corporation manufactures and sells outboard motors for pleasure boats. Sales are relatively constant from February through November. December and January are very slow months and the corporation usually has its employees take holidays in these months. The corporation has recently signed a contract with Henley Leisure Products Ltd., in North Battleford, a large dealership that sells everything from campers to boats and motors to life jackets. Bigger was given the contract because it was willing to offer extended credit terms to Henley. Because the credit terms were longer than normal, Bigger needs about $60,000 in additional working capital. The senior manager has identified three possible ways of acquiring these funds.

1. *Line of credit.* The bank would agree to extend a line of credit to Bigger for $75,000. The cost of the line of credit would be 9% per annum, with equal repayments expected in each of the four months after an amount was drawn on the line of credit.

2. *Accounts payable.* The corporation purchased about $50,000 per month on credit with terms of 2/30, net 90. Up to this point, the corporation had always taken advantage of the cash discount of 2% and paid all accounts within 30 days. The corporation could forfeit the discount and take 90 days to pay.

3. *Short-term bank loan.* The bank would agree to loan the corporation $75,000 at 7% interest. Payments could be made over 10 months. As security for the loan, the bank would require that the corporation maintain a cash balance equal to 15% of the loan amount.

Required:

a. Evaluate each of the three alternatives.

b. Recommend one of the alternatives and write a memo to the president of the corporation explaining why your recommendation would be the best one for the corporation.

◤◣ Critical Thinking Question

An issue discussed in Chapter 9 is financial statement recognition and disclosure of contingent liabilities, such as the potential claims associated with litigation. Loss and liability recognition is a function of whether it is likely that an asset has been impaired—or that a liability has been incurred—and the degree to which a loss can reasonably be estimated. Evaluating whether these conditions exist is often a matter of judgement by management and auditors, more so than perhaps in any other issue of recognition or disclosure. Research has shown that reliance on judgement leads to differences among companies in whether and how contingencies associated with lawsuits are disclosed.

1. In today's environmentally conscious world, regulatory bodies are making more demands on resource companies to be environmentally responsible. For example, companies involved in mineral exploration are often required to plan for the cleanup and restoration of resource sites. A review of several resource companies' annual reports reveals that some companies create liabilities each year in anticipation of this future event, some companies mention a contingent liability in the notes to the financial statements, and some companies say nothing about it. In a brief essay, discuss the criteria that a company should use when deciding on the kind of disclosure necessary to account for future cleanup and restoration costs.

2. As discussed in this chapter, some long-term liabilities are measured using present values. Discuss the appropriateness of using present values for long-term liabilities, and examine whether liabilities that are recorded for lawsuits are, or should be, subject to present value measurement.

CHAPTER

10

Long-Term Liabilities

In the previous chapter, liabilities that were due within a year or within an operating cycle were discussed. In this chapter, liabilities that must be satisfied over a longer period of time are considered. The three major obligations discussed are bonds payable, lease liabilities, and pension and other employment benefit liabilities. The general nature of liabilities was discussed in Chapter 9, along with the recognition and valuation criteria for liabilities. You might want to refresh your memory before moving on.

BONDS

When a public corporation wants to raise long-term funds to support its operations, it has two basic alternatives: the equity (stock) market, or the debt market. Issuing shares in the equity market is discussed in Chapter 11. Issuing debt in the debt market is the subject of this section. Within the debt market, there are various sources of funds. The corporation may borrow money from a commercial bank, much as individuals borrow money from the bank to buy a new home or car. These are often listed on a corporation's financial statements as notes payable. The term of the note can be short-term or long-term, and carry a fixed or floating interest rate. Another source of funds is what is known as the **commercial paper** market. Commercial paper is an unsecured promissory note that is generally sold to other businesses by a corporation that has a fairly high credit rating. In effect, one corporation borrows from another.

Another market in which the corporation may borrow money is the **bond market**. Generally, bonds are sold initially to institutional and individual investors through an investment banker (who gets a commission for handling the transaction). The **investment banker**, or a group of investment bankers (sometimes known as a **syndicate**), works with the corporation to decide which bond terms will be most attractive to investors. Once all the bonds have been sold by the investment bankers, they can be freely traded between investors in a bond market much the same as shares are traded on the stock market. Some bonds are sold to investors through what is referred to as **private placement**. These types of bonds do not trade in public markets. Private placements are usually made to institutional investors such as trustees in charge of pension funds.

A full understanding of how the various debt markets differ is beyond the scope of this book. Various markets are mentioned so that you can gain some appreciation of the disclosures you will typically find as you read annual reports. Publicly traded bonds in Canada are used to illustrate the accounting issues surrounding long-term debt. There are some complex issues related to **foreign-denominated debt** that we will mention briefly, but in-depth coverage falls outside the parameters of this book.

Basic Bond Characteristics

A bond is a formal agreement between a borrower (the corportion) and a lender (the investor) that specifies how the borrower is to pay back the lender and any conditions that the borrower must meet during the period of the loan. The conditions of the loan are stated in a document called the **indenture agreement**. The indenture agreement may specify certain restrictions on the corporation that are known as **bond covenants**. These covenants may limit the corporation's ability to borrow additional amounts, to sell or acquire assets, or to pay dividends. The restrictions placed in the bond convenants are intended to provide protection to the investor against default on the loan by the corporation.

Bonds that are traded in public markets are fairly standardized. The indenture agreement will state a **face value** for the bonds which, in almost all cases, is $1,000 per bond. Unless stated otherwise, you should assume that the face value of a bond is $1,000. The face value specifies the cash payment the borrower will make to the lender at the **maturity date** of the bond (which is also specified in the indenture agreement). In addition to the cash payment at maturity, most bonds make semi-annual interest payments to the lender. The amount of these payments is determined by multiplying the bond interest rate times the face value and dividing by two (because they are semi-annual payments). The bond interest rate is stated as an annual percentage and is *not* an effective or true interest rate, but simply a rate that determines the periodic amount of the interest payments.

One other important item described in the indenture agreement is the collateral the corporation pledges to the lenders. Some bonds specify particular assets as collateral. A bond known as a **mortgage bond** has some type of real property as collateral. A **collateral trust bond** provides shares and bonds of other corporations as collateral. A bond that carries no specific collateral but is backed by the general creditworthiness of the corporation is known as a **debenture bond**. General debenture bonds can be either **senior debenture bonds** or **subordinated debenture bonds**. The distinction between *senior* and *subordinated* is the order in which creditors are paid in the event of bankruptcy: Senior creditors are paid first.

Some indenture agreements specify special provisions of the bond that are designed to make the bonds more attractive to investors. **Convertible bonds**, for example, are convertible to a specified number of common shares in the corporation issuing the bond. In the 1970s and 1980s, investors became concerned about the effects of inflation on the fixed payments, particularly the large final payment, that characterize bond agreements. Remember from earlier chapters that, in a period of inflation, fixed payments decline in terms of their purchasing power. Therefore, the payment the investor receives at the maturity date may be worth considerably less (in terms of purchasing power) than the dollars lent to the corporation initially. To protect investors from the effects of inflation, some corporations have issued bonds that index the final payment to a commodity. Sunshine Mining Corporation issued one of the first of these bonds in 1980. It indexed the maturity payment to be the larger of $1,000 (the normal maturity payment of a bond) or the market value of 50 ounces of silver. If inflation was significant, the market value of silver would rise, and the investor would get the market value at maturity. Since that time, other bonds have indexed maturity values to oil and other commodities.

Public Bond Issues

When a corporation decides to issue bonds in the public bond market, it contacts an **investment banker**, who will assist the corporation in issuing the securities. The investment banker will consult the corporation about its objectives, and will help design an issue that will both meet the corporation's objectives, and attract investors. All the basic features of the bond that have been discussed will be considered when structuring the offering.

The investment bankers will not only help design the bond issue, but will also be responsible for the initial sale of the issue to their investor clients. Because most issues involve larger amounts than one investment banker can easily sell, the investment banker usually forms a syndicate with other investment bankers, who will be jointly responsible for selling the issue. The members of the syndicate are sometimes known as the **underwriters** of the issue.

The syndicate will agree on a price for the bond issue and will attempt to sell all the bonds to their clients. The price of the bond is fixed at this point and will not change until the syndicate has sold all its bonds. If events occur that make the price unattractive to the clients of the investment bankers, then it is likely that the syndicate will not sell the entire issue. In some cases, the syndicate agrees to sell the issue on what is known as a **best efforts basis**. If the syndicate cannot sell all the securities, it simply returns the securities to the corporation, which means that the corporation will not be able to raise the amount of money it had hoped for. For financially strong corporations, however, the syndicate guarantees to sell the entire issue, thereby accepting the risk that it will not be able to sell all the issue to its clients.

Once all the bonds have been sold to the clients of the syndicate, the bonds are "thrown on the open market." This means that holders of the bonds are free to trade them with any other investors. Prices of the bonds can then fluctuate with changes in economic conditions.

▶◣ Bond Markets

All financial newspapers and several local newspapers provide information about bond prices to interested investors. Bond prices are quoted in *The Financial Post* in a section entitled "Bonds." An excerpt from this section is shown in Exhibit 10-1. You will notice that it lists Canada, Provincial, Corporate and International bonds. Look for a moment at the Corporate section. The first column of the listing shows who is issuing each bond. An abbreviation of the corporate name is given, followed by a set of numbers and a date in the next two columns. These columns identify the bond interest rate of the issue, the maturity year, then in the final two columns, the current selling price and the expected rate of return at that selling price. For instance, locate the line "Northern Tel 7.45 Mar 10/98 102.11 6.05." This is a bond from Northern Telecom that bears a 7.45% interest rate and that matures on March 10, 1998. Prices in the market are quoted as a percent of the face value. The bond is currently selling at 102.11, which means that investors are paying $1,021.10 for a $1,000 bond. As you will see in the next section of this chapter, this means that the bond is selling at a premium. When investors buy this bond at a premium they will earn a return of 6.05 %. The return is less than the actual interest on the bond because the bond sold for more than the face or principal value.

Another disclosure you will see in business publications is what is known as a **tombstone ad**. A tombstone ad is an announcement by the underwriters that a bond issue has been arranged by them and is being sold through them. Exhibit 10-2 shows

EXHIBIT 10-1

CANADIAN BOND MARKET QUOTES
(Source: *The Financial Post,* July 31, 1996, p. 41)

Bonds

Supplied by Securities Valuation Co. from RBC Dominion Securities Inc./International from Reuters

Benchmark issues, as designated by the Bank of Canada, are listed in boldface. (N)–new benchmark, (O)–old benchmark

Canada

	Coupon	Mat. Date	Bid $	Yld%
CMHC	6.00	Dec 1/98	99.56	6.20
CMHC	8.25	Aug 3/99	104.61	6.53
CMHC	8.50	Dec 1/99	105.41	6.66
CMHC	8.80	Mar 1/00	106.42	6.75
CMHC	8.20	Jun 30/00	104.67	6.82
CMHC	7.75	Dec 1/00	102.95	6.95
Canada	7.50	Jul 1/97	102.00	5.23
Canada (N)	**7.00**	**Sep 15/97**	**101.70**	**5.41**
Canada (O)	**6.25**	**Feb 1/98**	**100.71**	**5.75**
Canada (N)	**10.75**	**Mar 15/98**	**107.51**	**5.82**
Canada	6.50	Sep 1/98	100.74	6.11
Canada (N)	**8.00**	**Nov 1/98**	**103.70**	**6.21**
Canada	5.75	Mar 1/99	98.60	6.34
Canada	7.75	Sep 1/99	103.33	6.54
Canada	9.25	Dec 1/99	107.74	6.62
Canada	8.50	Mar 1/00	105.58	6.72
Canada (O)	**7.50**	**Sep 1/00**	**102.27**	**6.85**
Canada (N)	**7.50**	**Mar 1/01**	**102.08**	**6.96**
Canada	9.75	Jun 1/01	111.02	7.02
Canada	9.50	Oct 1/01	110.30	7.08
Canada	9.75	Dec 1/01	111.65	7.08
Canada	8.50	Apr 1/02	106.18	7.15
Canada	7.25	Jun 1/03	99.38	7.36
Canada	7.50	Dec 1/03	100.35	7.43
Canada (O)	**10.25**	**Feb 1/04**	**115.87**	**7.45**
Canada	6.50	Jun 1/04	94.03	7.52
Canada	9.00	Dec 1/04	108.85	7.55
Canada (O)	**8.75**	**Dec 1/05**	**107.50**	**7.61**
Canada (N)	**7.00**	**Dec 1/06**	**95.01**	**7.71**
Canada	9.50	Jun 1/10	113.13	7.92
Canada	9.00	Mar 1/11	108.93	7.95
Canada	10.25	Mar 15/14	120.86	8.02
Canada	9.75	Jun 1/21	117.61	8.09
Canada (O)	**8.00**	**Jun 1/23**	**98.95**	**8.09**
Canada (N)	**9.00**	**Jun 1/25**	**109.77**	**8.12**

Provincial

	Coupon	Mat. Date	Bid $	Yld%
Alberta	5.75	Sep 3/96	100.07	4.82
Alberta	6.00	Mar 1/99	99.19	6.34
Alberta	8.50	Sep 1/99	105.36	6.55
Br Columbia	7.00	Mar 2/98	101.73	5.84
Br Columbia	7.00	Jun 9/99	101.57	6.38
Br Columbia	10.15	Aug 29/01	112.75	7.11
Br Columbia	9.00	Jan 9/02	107.95	7.21
Br Columbia	7.75	Jun 16/03	101.47	7.47
Br Columbia	9.00	Jun 21/04	108.02	7.63
Br Columbia	9.50	Jan 9/12	111.75	8.15
Br Columbia	8.50	Aug 23/13	102.79	8.19
Br Columbia	9.00	Aug 23/24	107.79	8.28
New Brunswick	9.12	Apr 1/02	108.49	7.27
Newfoundland	10.00	Jul 25/01	110.85	7.36
Newfoundland	11.00	Feb 15/12	120.85	8.55
Nova Scotia	9.87	Mar 1/98	105.88	5.92
Nova Scotia	8.25	Dec 1/05	102.56	7.85
Nova Scotia	9.60	Jan 30/22	112.07	8.44
Ont Hyd	7.25	Mar 31/98	102.14	5.87
Ont Hyd	9.62	Aug 3/99	108.19	6.58
Ont Hyd	9.00	Apr 16/02	107.97	7.27
Ont Hyd	9.00	Jun 24/02	108.09	7.29
Ont Hyd	10.12	Oct 15/21	118.52	8.35
Ont Hyd	8.90	Aug 18/22	105.57	8.37
Ontario	8.75	Apr 16/97	102.45	5.15
Ontario	8.00	Mar 11/03	102.77	7.46
Ontario	8.75	Apr 22/03	106.65	7.47
Ontario	7.75	Dec 8/03	101.13	7.54
Ontario	9.00	Sep 15/04	107.81	7.69
Ontario	8.10	Sep 8/23	97.21	8.36
Ontario	7.50	Feb 7/24	90.79	8.36
PEI	9.75	Apr 30/02	110.84	7.40
PEI	9.25	Mar 18/13	107.99	8.35
Quebec	8.50	Apr 1/97	102.15	5.15
Quebec	8.00	Mar 30/98	103.23	5.92
Quebec	10.25	Apr 7/98	106.80	5.93
Quebec	6.00	Apr 1/99	98.84	6.48
Quebec c97	10.25	May 4/01	111.55	7.33
Quebec	10.25	Oct 15/01	112.55	7.30
Quebec	9.25	Apr 1/02	108.20	7.45
Quebec	7.50	Dec 1/03	98.54	7.76
Quebec	9.37	Jan 16/23	107.75	8.63
Quebec	9.50	Mar 30/23	109.05	8.63
Quebec Hydro	10.87	Jul 25/01	114.88	0.00
Saskatchewan	8.12	Feb 4/97	101.46	5.15

Corporate

	Coupon	Mat. Date	Bid $	Yld%
AGT	9.50	Aug 24/04	110.02	7.80
Alta Nat Gas	8.40	Jul 15/03	103.36	7.76
Avco Fin	8.75	Mar 15/00	105.23	7.08
B C Gas	8.50	Aug 26/02	104.25	7.61
B C Gas	8.15	Jul 28/03	101.73	7.82
B C Tel	7.25	Jul 15/98	101.78	6.26
B C Tel	9.65	Apr 8/22	111.86	8.50
BCE	9.00	Aug 28/97	103.49	5.59
BCE	7.12	May 1/98	101.71	6.07
BCE	8.95	Apr 1/02	106.62	7.49
Bell	9.50	Jun 15/02	109.64	7.44
Bell c04	9.45	Mar 1/11	106.50	8.37
Bell	9.70	Dec 15/32	112.73	8.55
Bk of Montreal	8.85	Jun 1/03	106.14	7.67
Bk of Montreal	10.85	Dec 20/08	119.78	8.26
Bk of N S	8.10	Mar 24/03	102.48	7.61
Bk of N S	8.90	Jun 20/25	103.99	8.52
Bombardier	8.30	Jul 28/03	103.23	7.69
CIBC	7.10	Mar 10/04	96.58	7.70
CIBC	9.65	Oct 31/14	110.99	8.45
Cdn Utilities	8.43	Jun 1/05	103.90	7.81
Cdn Utilities	9.40	May 1/23	110.39	8.41
Cons. Gas	7.55	Dec 15/97	102.45	5.66
Imasco Ltd	8.37	Jun 23/03	103.20	7.76
Interprov Pipe	8.20	Feb 15/24	96.98	8.48
Molson Brew	8.20	Mar 11/03	102.36	7.73
Northern Tel	7.45	Mar 10/98	102.11	6.05
Nova	8.30	Jul 15/03	102.83	7.76
Nova Scotia Pw	7.70	Oct 15/03	99.15	7.85
Oshawa Group	8.25	Jun 30/03	102.55	7.76
Pancan Pet	8.75	Nov 9/05	105.56	7.89
Royal Bank	10.50	Mar 1/02	114.05	7.38
Seagram Ltd	9.00	Dec 15/98	105.54	6.44
T-D Bank c97	9.10	May 15/02	102.89	5.28
Talisman Energ	9.45	Dec 22/99	107.78	6.83
Talisman Energ	9.80	Dec 22/04	111.04	7.97
Teleglobe	8.35	Jun 20/03	102.96	7.78
Thomson	7.90	Sep 17/02	101.73	7.54
Thomson	9.15	Jul 6/04	107.01	7.94
Tr Cda Pipe	9.45	Mar 20/18	108.11	8.61
Transalta Util	8.35	Dec 15/03	103.85	7.65
Union Gas	9.70	Nov 6/17	110.68	8.59
Union Gas	8.75	Aug 3/18	101.42	8.60
Westcoast Ener	9.90	Jan 10/20	112.40	8.65

International

	Coupon	Mat. Date	Bid $	Yld%
Australia	12.50	15 JAN 1998	106.69	7.55
Australia	8.75	15 JAN 2001	102.53	8.06
Australia	6.75	15 NOV 2006	88.20	8.49
Britain	7.00	30 MAR 1998	101.56	6.24
Britain	7.00	06 NOV 2001	98.46	7.34
Britain	7.50	07 DEC 2006	97.22	7.89
France	4.50	12 OCT 1998	99.75	4.62
France	5.50	12 OCT 2001	99.36	5.64
France	6.50	25 OCT 2006	100.44	6.44
Germany	5.75	20 AUG 1998	103.16	4.11
Germany	5.25	21 FEB 2001	99.66	5.32
Germany	6.25	26 APR 2006	98.85	6.40
Italy	9.50	01 FEB 1999	102.20	8.66
Italy	9.50	01 FEB 2001	102.41	9.01
Italy	9.50	01 FEB 2006	100.58	9.61
Japan	4.60	22 JUN 1998	106.09	1.27
Japan	6.60	20 JUN 2001	118.71	2.32
Japan	3.00	20 SEP 2005	97.90	3.30
U.S.	6.25	31 JUL 1998	99.91	6.30
U.S.	6.38	15 MAY 1999	99.81	6.45
U.S.	6.63	31 JUL 2001	99.88	6.66
U.S.	6.88	15 MAY 2006	100.00	6.87
U.S.	7.00	15 JUL 2006	100.88	6.88
U.S.	6.88	15 AUG 2025	97.50	7.08
U.S.	6.00	15 FEB 2026	87.19	7.04

a replica[1] of an advertisement for two issues of IBM bonds in 1979. Although this ad appeared almost 20 years ago, it is a "classic." The ad states the face amount of the issues, which is two $500 million issues totaling $1 billion. The ad stipulates the bond interest rates of 9 1/2% and 9 3/8%, and the maturity years of 1986 and 2004. At the bottom of the ad is a listing of the underwriters (investment bankers) that offered this security for sale.

EXHIBIT 10-2

IBM CORPORATION, 1979
Tombstone Ad

This announcement is neither an offer to sell nor a solicitation of an offer to buy these securities
The offer is made only by the Prospectus
New Issues/October 9, 1979
$1,000,000,000
International Business Machine Corporation
$500,000,000
9 1/2% Notes Due 1986
Price 99.40% and accrued interest, if any, from October 16, 1979
$500,000,000
9 3/8% Notes Due 2004
Price 99.625% and accrued interest, if any, from October 16, 1979
Copies of the Prospectus may be obtained in any State in which this announcement is circulated only from such of the undersigned as may legally offer these securities in such State.

Salomon Brothers   Merrill Lynch White Weld Capital Markets Group
Merrill Lynch, Pierce, Fenner & Smith Incorporated

Morgan Stanley & Co. Incorporated	The First Boston Corporation	Goldman, Sachs & Co.
Bache Halsey Stuart Shields Incorporated	Bear, Stearns & Co.	Blyth Eastman Dillon & Co. Incorporated
Dillon, Reed & Co. Inc.	Donaldson, Lufkin & Jenrette Securities Corporation	Drexel Burnham Lambert Incorporated
E. F. Hutton & Corporation Inc.	Kidder, Peabody & Co. Incorporated	Lazard Freres & Co.
Lehman Brothers Kuhn Loeb Incorporated	Paine, Webber, Jackson & Curtis Incorporated	
L. F. Rothschild, Unterberg, Towbin	Shearson Hayden Slone Inc.	
Smith, Barney, Harris Upham & Co. Incorporated	Warburg Paribas Becker	A. G. Becker
Wortheim & Co. Inc.	Dean Witter Reynolds Inc.	

[1] The data were taken from an advertisement that appeared in the November 5, 1979, issue of *Fortune*; similar ads appeared in *The Wall Street Journal*, *The New York Times*, and *Barrons* during October, 1979. The list of underwriters was more extensive in the ads in these other publications.

The IBM ad is of historic interest because it marked the first time IBM had gone to the public debt market to raise money. It is also of interest because the issuance of these bonds caused major losses to the underwriters. The underwriters initially tried to sell the bonds to their customers at the prices quoted in the ad (99.4% and 99.625%). After about 60% of the bonds had been sold, the Federal Reserve Board made a surprise announcement that imposed tough new credit restrictions. These restrictions drove market interest rates up significantly. As you can understand from the earlier discussion of interest rates and prices, the fixed prices stated in the ad quickly became unattractive to investors. The underwriters were unable to sell the rest of the issue at the prices quoted. Since this was not a "best efforts" issue, the underwriters were left holding the remainder of the issue. The underwriters were then forced to throw the issue on the open market, at which point the market price of the bonds fell approximately 5 points, from around 99 to 94. This meant that each bond suffered a $50 loss. The number of bonds remaining in the hands of the underwriters totalled approximately 400,000, which translates to a loss of $20 million.

Bond Pricing

The prices of bonds are established in the marketplace by negotiations between buyers and sellers. At the initial issuance of the bonds, the buyers are institutional and individual investors, and the seller is the corporation issuing the bonds. The buyers calculate the present value of the cash flows they will receive from the bond, then decide the amount they are willing to pay for the bond. The seller does a similar calculation to decide what it is willing to accept for the bond. The buyer weighs the discount rate against the rate that could be earned from the next best alternative investment, and also against the risk involved with the particular bond issue. The higher the risk, the higher the discount rate should be. In other words, if buyers are going to accept a higher risk of default, they want to be compensated for that risk with a higher return. In addition to the calculation of the present value, the buyer also has to factor in any special features of the bond such as convertibility into shares or any indexing of the maturity value to a commodity. In the rest of this section, these special features are ignored as we discuss bond pricing.

The starting point in determining the value of a bond is to calculate the cash flows that will be received by the buyer (and paid by the seller). To illustrate the calculation of interest payments, assume a corporation issues bonds on January 1, 19X1 with a total face value of $100,000 and a bond interest rate of 10%. The corporation issues 100 bonds, each has a face value of $1,000, and each is due on December 31, 19X7. The corporation must make a $100,000 payment to the lenders on December 31, 19X7 and must make interest payments every six months of $5,000 each. The $5,000 amount is calculated as follows:

$$\text{Interest Payment} = \text{Face Value} \times \text{Bond Interest Rate} \times 1/2$$
$$= \$100,000 \times 10\% \times 1/2 = \$5,000$$

There will be a total of 14 interest payments because there are seven years to maturity and two interest payments per year. The interest payments of a bond are typically structured to come at the end of each six-month period. This means that the stream of interest payments is an **annuity in arrears**, meaning the payments are made at the end of the period.

To illustrate the pricing of a bond, we will use a very simple example. Suppose the Baum Corporation wishes to issue a $1,000 bond (a single bond will be used to make it simple) with two years to maturity. The bond is to have a bond interest rate of 10% and pay interest semi-annually. Suppose that Baum expects the investor to demand a return of 8% compounded semi-annually from an investment in its bonds. What price can Baum expect to get from this offering? The cash flows that Baum will pay must be discounted using the desired rate of return of 8%. Exhibit 10-3 shows the time line and the cash flows that would result from this bond.

EXHIBIT 10-3

BAUM CORPORATION
Bond Cash Flows

Assumptions:

Face value $1,000

Bond interest rate 10%

Time to maturity   2 years

Discount rate 8%

Calculation:

Number of periods

$$= \text{Time to maturity} \times 2$$
$$= 2 \text{ years} \times 2 = 4 \text{ periods}$$

Discount rate per period $= $ Discount rate $/ 2$
$$= 8\% / 2 = 4\%$$

Interest payments $= $ Face amount $\times$ bond interest rate $\times 1/2$
$$= \$1,000 \times 10\% \times 1/2 = \$50$$

				$1,000
Cash flows	$50	$50	$50	$50
End of period	1	2	3	4
(Semi-annual periods)				

Note that the interest payments (the four payments of $50 each) are an annuity in arrears and that the maturity payment ($1,000) is a lump sum cash flow at the end of the fourth period. There are four periods because interest payments are made at the end of each six-month period. The total net present value of the bond, based on an 4% discount rate, is calculated on the following page. To calculate the net present value, we will use the Time Value of Money tables found in Appendix 1 to the text.

The result of this calculation means that Baum should expect buyers to pay up to $1,036.30 for this bond. If buyers pay exactly this amount, they will earn an 8% return (compounded semi-annually). If they pay more for this bond, they will earn less than 8% and, if they pay less than this amount, they will earn more than 8%. Note that, because the payments to be paid by Baum are fixed by the terms of the bonds, the only way buyers of the bonds can change the return is by changing the amount they invest initially (i.e., the price they pay). If Baum thinks that 8% is too high an interest rate to pay, it should not offer these bonds at the price calculated here. It should offer them at a higher price (which will lower the interest rate).

We need to calculate the present value of each of the future cash flows.

				$1,000
	$50	$50	$50	$50
1	4%			
2		4%		
3			4%	
4				4%

For illustrative purposes we will use Table 2, Present Value of $1, found in Appendix 1.

($50 × 0.96154) + ($50 × 0.92456) + ($50 × .88900) + ($50 × 85480) + ($1,000 × 0.85480)

48.08   +   46.23   +   44.45   +   42.74   +   854.80

= $1,036.30

Recognize, however, that buyers may not be willing to buy the bonds at that higher price.

An easier way to arrive at the above amount of $1,036.30 is to treat the interest payments of $50 as an annuity (calculate the present value by using Table 3 from Appendix 1, Present Value of an Annuity in Arrears) and add to this calculation the present value of the payment at maturity ($1,000). The calculation would be as follows:

$50 × 3.62990 (Present value for 4 periods at 4%) + ($1,000 × 0.85480)
181.50 + 854.80 = $1,036.30

This is the method we will use for subsequent calculations of the present value of a bond issue. These calculations can also be made using a financial calculator which has present value and future value functions.

How does a different discount rate affect the value of the bond? Suppose that, instead of 8%, buyers demand a 12% return from this type of investment. The only thing that would change in the calculation would be the factors that enter the present-value calculation. The computation would then be:

Present value of the Baum Corporation bond at 12%:
PV of bond = PV of interest payments + PV of maturity payment
           = PV of the annuity of $50 for 4 periods at 6% + PV of the $1,000 for 4 periods at 6%
           = ($50 × 3.46511) + ($1,000 × 0.79209)
           = $965.35

Consistent with the preceding explanation, if buyers pay less for the bond (in this case, $965.35), they earn a higher return (12%). Baum Corporation, in this case, receives a lower amount from this borrowing and pays a higher interest rate (12%).

According to the terminology used to describe bond pricing, when the bond is issued (or sells) at a price higher than its face value (i.e., greater than $1,000), it is issued (sells) at a **premium**. When the bond is issued for less than its face value, it is issued at a **discount**. If it is issued for exactly its face value, it is said to be issued at **par**. You should avoid placing any connotations on the words *premium* and *discount.* They do not mean either that buyers paid too much or that they got a good deal. The price they pay, whether it is par, premium, or discount, is the appropriate value for the bond, given the discount rate used.

A question that might be asked is: What rate would have to be used to discount the cash flows in the example for the bonds to be issued at par? The answer is 10%. Whenever the discount rate of a bond is exactly equal to the bond interest rate, the bond will sell at par. Consequently, if the discount rate is higher than the bond interest rate, the bond sells at a discount and, when the discount rate is lower than the bond interest rate, it sells at a premium. This relationship is represented in the table in Exhibit 10-4, which shows the price of the bond in the example for various combinations of bond interest rates and discount rates.

Note that, in Exhibit 10-4, all the prices on the diagonal, which represent situations in which the bond interest rate equals the discount rate, are at par. Prices below the diagonal represent premium price situations, where the discount rate is below the bond interest rate, and the area above the diagonal represents discount prices.

Bond Accounting

The accounting for bonds will be illustrated using the simple examples just developed earlier for a bond issued at par, at a discount, and at a premium. For each of the bonds, the entries made at issuance to recognize the interest accrual and payments, and to record the final payment of the face amount at maturity, will be illustrated.

Bonds Issued at Par

Consider the issuance of the Baum Corporation bond (see data in Exhibit 10-3) when bond interest rates were 10%. To record the bond issued at par, the cash proceeds must be recorded in the cash account and the present value of the bond in the liability account. Because the cash proceeds equal the present value at issuance, the

EXHIBIT 10-4

Relationship of Bond Price to Bond Interest and Discount Rates

		Discount Rates			
		6%	8%	10%	12%
Bond	6%	$1,000.00	$963.70	$929.08	$896.05
Interest	8%	$1,037.17	$1,000.00	$964.54	$930.70
Rates	10%	$1,074.34	$1,036.30	$1,000.00	$965.35
	12%	$1,111.51	$1,072.60	$1,035.46	$1,000.00

following entry is made (any commissions that are paid to the underwriters are ignored to keep the entries simple):

BAUM CORPORATION BOND ISSUED AT PAR — ISSUANCE ENTRY

(at issuance date)

A – Cash	1,000	
L – Bond Payable		1,000

No interest is recognized on the date of issuance because interest accrues as time passes. The recognition of interest requires two entries. The first is to accrue the interest expense for the period and the amount payable to the bondholders. The second is to record the cash payment made. The recognition of expense should be based on a time value of money computation using the discount rate (10% for the Baum Corporation bond sold at par) and the carrying value of the loan ($1,000 when sold at par). The amount payable to the bondholders is dictated by the bond interest rate. The following calculations and entries would be made at the end of the first interest payment period (six months):

BAUM CORPORATION BOND ISSUED AT PAR — INTEREST ENTRIES

(at end of first interest period)

SE – Interest Expense[a]	50	
L – Interest Payable[b]		50
L – Interest Payable	50	
A – Cash		50

[a]Interest expense = Carrying Value × Discount Rate × Time
= $1,000 × 10% × 6/12 = $50
[b]Interest payable = Face Amount × Bond Interest Rate × Time
= $1,000 × 10% × 6/12 = $50

The calculation of the interest expense (the interest incurred during the coupon period) and interest payable (the cash amount owed based on the bond contract) results in the same number for a bond sold at par. This is not the case for bonds issued at a premium or a discount.

The calculation of the interest payable amount will be the same in all four interest periods over the life of the bond. The calculation of interest expense in each period will depend on the carrying value of the bond at the beginning of each period. The carrying value will equal the face value of the bond less the discount or the face value of the bond plus the premium. The carrying value (book value) at the end of each period can be calculated using the following formula:

Carrying value (ending) = Carrying value (beginning) + Interest Expense − Payments

In the first period:

$$\text{Carrying value (ending)} = \$1,000 + 50 - 50 = \$1,000$$

Because the expense and the cash payment are the same in every period, a bond sold at par will have a carrying value of $1,000 at the end of every period. The entries for interest recognition, therefore, would be exactly the same at the end of each of the four interest periods.

At the end of the fourth period, the corporation will make the final payment of the face value. The entry will be:

BAUM CORPORATION BOND ISSUED AT PAR — MATURITY PAYMENT ENTRY

(at maturity date)

L – Bond Payable	1,000	
A – Cash		1,000

The accrual of interest and the related payments can be shown graphically as in Exhibit 10-5. Note that the balance in the liability account increases each period as the interest accrues. The balance then drops abruptly at the end of the period when a cash payment is made. Note that the balance in the liability account at the end of

EXHIBIT 10-5

Carrying Value of a Bond Issued at Par

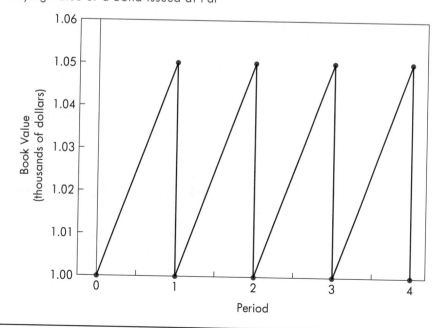

the four interest periods is $1,000. This is the balance prior to the maturity payment and, therefore, should be exactly $1,000.

Sometimes, the change in the value of a bond over its life is also summarized in what is known as an amortization table. Exhibit 10-6 shows a typical amortization table for the bond issued at par.

■ ■ Bonds Issued at a Discount

In this section, assume that investors demanded a 12% return for the bonds issued by Baum. As calculated earlier in the chapter, the bonds would be issued at a price of $965.35 under these conditions. The following entry would then be made by Baum Corporation at issuance:

BAUM CORPORATION BOND SOLD AT A DISCOUNT — ISSUANCE ENTRY		
(at date of issuance)		
A – Cash	965.35	
XL – Discount on Bond Payable	34.65	
L – Bond Payable		1,000

In this case, the present value of the liability is $965.35, and this is the amount that should be recorded on the books of Baum. This amount could be credited directly to the bond payable account. However, generally accepted procedures are to credit the bond payable account with the face value of the bond and then to reduce the amount by creating a contra-liability account called *discount on bond payable*. The contra-account (note that the XL notation in the journal entry represents a contra-liability account) is most commonly reported directly with the bond payable account. The net of these two amounts is the present value, that is, $1,000 − $34.65 = $965.35. Note that this presentation allows for both the disclosure of the face amount of the bonds and the net present value at the date of issuance.

The interest entries for the bond issued at a discount are shown in the following box. Notice that the interest expense is now different from the amount payable. The reason for this is that the discount rate and the carrying value are now different from the bond interest rate and the face amount. The difference between the expense and the interest payable is credited to the discount account, which decreases the balance in the account. This is known as the **amortization of the discount**.

EXHIBIT 10-6

Amortization Table — Bond Issued at Par

Period	Beginning Carrying Value	Interest	Payment	Ending Carrying Value
1	$1,000.00	$50.00	$50.00	$1,000.00
2	$1,000.00	$50.00	$50.00	$1,000.00
3	$1,000.00	$50.00	$50.00	$1,000.00
4	$1,000.00	$50.00	$1,050.00	$0.00

**BAUM CORPORATION BOND ISSUED AT A DISCOUNT —
INTEREST ENTRIES**

(at end of the first interest period):

SE — Interest Expense[a]	57.92	
XL — Discount on Bonds Payable		7.92
L — Interest Payable[b]		50.00
L — Interest Payable	50.00	
A — Cash		50.00

[a]Interest expense = Carrying Value × Discount Rate × Time
             = $965.35 × 12% × 6/12 = $57.92
[b]Interest payable = Face Amount × Bond Interest Rate × Time
             = $1,000 × 10% × 6/12 = $50.00

Because the discount is being amortized each period, the net carrying value changes from period to period. The amortization of the discount can be done in a straight-line fashion, that is, the same amount each period, as long as the effect on the financial statements is not materially different from applying the effective interest method, which is illustrated in this section. The carrying value at the end of the period would be calculated as before:

$$\text{Carrying Value (ending)} = \text{Carrying Value (beginning)} + \text{Interest Expense} - \text{Payments}$$

In the first period:

$$\text{Carrying Value (ending)} = \$965.35 + 57.92 - 50.00 = \$973.27$$

Notice that the carrying value increases a little by the end of the first period. This new carrying value balance is used to calculate the interest expense in the second period. Therefore, the interest expense will increase slightly each period to reflect the increase in the carrying value. The ending carrying value could also be calculated by subtracting the balance in the discount account from the face amount in the bond payable account. The discount account will have a balance of $26.73 ($34.65 − 7.92) at the end of the first period. The face amount minus this discount will give the carrying value of $973.27, the same amount as calculated in the preceding equation.

Exhibit 10-7 shows graphically how the value of the liability changes over time. Notice that because this bond is issued at a discount, the beginning value is below $1,000. As time passes, the discount is amortized (decreases) and the carrying value increases, eventually reaching $1,000 by the maturity date, when the final payment of $1,000 is made.

At the maturity date, the final maturity payment is made with the same entry as that made in the par case because the final carrying value is the same ($1,000). Recognize that what is happening is that the payments made at the interest dates are

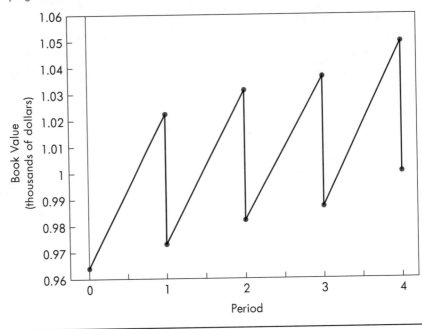

EXHIBIT 10-7

Carrying Value of a Bond Issued at a Discount

not sufficient to pay for the interest that has accrued during the period. The excess of the interest expense over the payment then adds to the principal, creating the rising balance in the principal shown in the graph. Exhibit 10-8 shows the amortization table for the bond issued at a discount.

■■ ■Bond Issued at a Premium

If the interest rate demanded by investors is 8%, then the Baum Corporation bonds would be issued at a premium. The issue price in this scenario was calculated earlier in the chapter as $1,036.30. The following entry would be made at issuance by Baum Corporation:

BAUM CORPORATION BOND ISSUED AT A PREMIUM— ISSUANCE ENTRY		
(at date of issuance)		
A – Cash	1,036.30	
L – Premium on Bonds Payable		36.30
L – Bond Payable		1,000.00

As in the case of the bond issued at a discount, the $1,000 face value is credited to the bond payable account. The excess of the proceeds over the face amount is credited to an account called *premium on bond payable*. This account is a liability

EXHIBIT 10-8

Amortization Table — Bond Issued at a Discount

Period	Beginning Carrying Value	Interest	Payment	Ending Carrying Value	Beginning Discount
1	$965.35	$57.92	$50.00	$973.27	($34.65)
2	$973.27	$58.40	$50.00	$981.67	($26.73)
3	$981.67	$58.90	$50.00	$990.57	($18.33)
4	$990.57	$59.43	$1,050.00	$0.00	($9.43)

account, but is also known as an **adjunct account**. The balance in this account is reported directly with the bond liability account; that is, the accounts are linked together. Adjunct accounts are used when they contain balances that add to a related account in the same way that contra-accounts subtract from related accounts. The sum of the two accounts creates a liability that is measured at its net present value.

The interest entries for the bond issued at a premium would be:

BAUM CORPORATION BOND ISSUED AT A PREMIUM — INTEREST ENTRIES

(at end of the first bond interest period):

SE — Interest Expense[a]	41.45	
L — Premium on Bond Payable	8.55	
L — Interest Payable[b]		50.00
L — Interest Payable	50.00	
A — Cash		50.00

[a]Interest expense = Carrying Value × Discount Rate × Time
= $1,036.30 × 8% × 6/12 = $41.45
[b]Interest payable = Face Amount × Bond Interest Rate × Time
= $1,000 × 10% × 6/12 = $50.00

The premium on the bond payable is amortized in much the same way as is the discount. As the premium is amortized, the premium account is reduced and, conse-

AN INTERNATIONAL PERSPECTIVE
REPORTS FROM OTHER COUNTRIES

The amortization of the discount on a bond in Canada and the United States is calculated using present-value methods as described earlier. In some countries (Australia and Denmark, for example), the discount is typically amortized in a straight-line fashion, in much the same way as straight-line amortization. Straight-line amortization of the discount (and premium) is acceptable in Canada and the United States as long as the results of doing so are not materially different from the use of the present-value methods.

Also, in some countries, the amount of discount is written off in the year of issuance rather than being amortized to income over the life of the bond.

quently, the carrying value of the bond is reduced from period to period. This should make sense because the cash payments made each period are more than enough to pay for the interest expense. The excess of the payments over the expense (i.e., the **amortization of the premium**) reduces the carrying value of the debt. The carrying value at the end of the period would be calculated as before:

$$\text{Carrying Value (ending)} = \text{Carrying Value (beginning)} + \text{Interest Expense} - \text{Payments}$$

In the first period:

$$\text{Carrying Value (ending)} = \$1{,}036.30 + 41.45 - 50.00 = \$1{,}027.75$$

Exhibit 10-9 shows how the carrying value of the liability changes over time. Notice that, because this bond is issued at a premium, the beginning carrying value is above \$1,000. As time passes, the premium is amortized (decreases), and the carrying value decreases, eventually reaching \$1,000 by the maturity date. At the maturity date, the final maturity payment is made with the same entry as that made in the par case in that the final carrying value is the same (\$1,000). Exhibit 10-10 shows the amortization table for the bond issued at a premium.

EXHIBIT 10-9

Carrying Value of a Bond Issued at a Premium

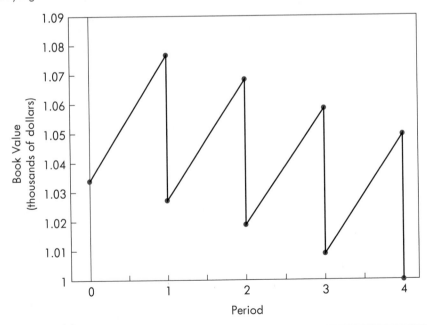

EXHIBIT 10-10

Amortization Table — Bond Issued at a Premium

Period	Beginning Carrying Value	Interest	Payment	Ending Carrying Value	Beginning Premium
1	$1,036.30	$41.45	$50.00	$1,027.75	($36.30)
2	$1,027.75	$41.11	$50.00	$1,018.86	($27.75)
3	$1,018.86	$40.75	$50.00	$1,009.62	($18.86)
4	$1,009.62	$40.38	$1,050.00	$0.00	($9.62)

■ ■ Early Retirement of Debt

Although a corporation does not have to pay off its debts until maturity, there are times when it makes sense for it to pay the debt earlier than the maturity date. This transaction is known as **early retirement**, or **early extinguishment**, of debt. Retiring bonds can be accomplished by buying the bonds in the bond market or by calling the bonds. The bonds may have a call feature that allows the corporation to buy them back from the investors at a predetermined price. If the intention is to buy them in the bond market, it is likely that interest rates in the economy have changed between the issuance date and the date at which the corporation wants to buy back the debt. Because the interest rate used to account for the bond is fixed at the issuance date, it is likely that the carrying value of the bond will be different from the market value. A gain or loss will, consequently, result from this transaction. The gains and losses from the early retirement of debt are shown on the income statement.

To demonstrate the accounting for an early retirement, suppose the Baum Corporation bond we discussed in the last section was issued when interest rates were 8%. Further, suppose that, after one year, Baum wishes to retire the bond. Interest rates in the economy have increased to 12% by this time. The carrying value at the end of Year 1 would be $1,018.86, as shown in Exhibit 10-10. The market value of the bond based on the 12% interest would be determined by discounting the remaining two coupon payments and the maturity value at 12%. This value would be the same as the value from the amortization table shown in Exhibit 10-8 for the bond as if it were originally issued at 12%. Therefore, the market value would be $981.67. If Baum buys back the bond at this price, it will be satisfying an obligation on its books at $1,018.86 with a cash payment of $981.67. A gain will, therefore, result from this transaction. The entry to record this transaction would be:

EARLY RETIREMENT ENTRY		
L – Bond Payable	1,000.00	
L – Premium on Bond Payable	18.86	
A – Cash		981.67
SE – Gain on Early Retirement of Bond		37.19

■ ■ Debt for Equity Swaps

Some debt issues have provisions written into the indenture agreement that makes them convertible into common shares under certain conditions. When the conversion takes place, the carrying value of the bonds is removed from the bond accounts and transferred to the common shares accounts. If the Baum Corporation bond retired in our last entry was, instead, converted into common shares, the following entry would be made:

CONVERSION OF BONDS TO SHARES		
L – Bond Payable	1,000.00	
L – Premium on Bonds Payable	18.86	
SE – Common Shares		1,018.86

Note that no gain or loss is recognized on this transaction. There is some controversy about whether the shares should be recorded at fair market value at the date of conversion and a gain or loss recognized on the transaction. Under GAAP at the time of writing of this book, no such gain or loss is recognized. The AcSB of the CICA is considering changing the initial recording of a convertible bond. The new guidelines would divide the initial issue price of the bond between its debt component and its equity component. When the bonds are converted, the journal entry would remove the debt accounts and transfer them and the equity accounts to common shares, making the journal entry slightly more complicated. In the next chapter, the credit entry to record the issuance of shares is discussed in more detail.

◖◗ LEASING

When a corporation needs to use an asset, such as a piece of machinery, it can obtain the use of the asset in two ways. One is to purchase the asset outright. A second is to enter into a **lease agreement** in which another corporation (the **lessor**) buys the asset and the corporation (the **lessee**) makes periodic payments to the lessor in exchange for the use of the asset over the length of the lease agreement (**lease term**).

There are benefits and costs to both alternatives. One benefit of ownership of the asset is that the corporation can amortize the asset for tax purposes and, in some cases, obtain an investment tax credit for the purchase. Investment tax credits are incentives provided by Revenue Canada to encourage investment in certain types of assets. These credits usually take the form of a direct reduction in the corporation's tax bill based on a fixed percentage of the asset's acquisition cost.

Profit from appreciation in the value of the asset is another benefit of ownership. Loss from the amortization of the asset, which could be dramatic if the asset becomes technologically obsolete, is the downside. If the corporation has to borrow to buy the asset, the corporation's debt/equity and interest coverage ratios will change, which could affect its future borrowing capabilities (these ratios are discussed later in this chapter as well as in Chapter 12). This also ties up capital that might be used for other projects.

To the lessee, the benefits of leasing are several. The lessee does not have to put up its own capital to buy the asset. It also does not have to borrow to buy the asset, which means that its debt/equity and interest coverage ratios will not be affected. If the corporation is in a tax situation in which little taxable income is generated, the tax advantages of amortizing the asset or claiming an investment tax credit would be of limited value to the lessee. If the lessor can take advantage of the capital cost allowance deduction, then the lease payments that the lessee makes will be reduced as a result of the decrease in the lessor's costs. Because the lessee does not own the asset, the risk of loss from obsolescence falls on the lessor. Another advantage, along these same lines, is that the lessee may not want to use the asset for its full useful life. If the corporation wants to use the asset for only a short time, there is significant risk associated with the resale value if the corporation decides to buy the asset rather than to lease it.

Lessee Accounting

The accounting issues for a lessee can be illustrated using two extreme examples. At one extreme, suppose that the lease contract is signed for a relatively short period of time, say, two years, whereas the useful life of the asset leased is eight years. In this case, it is clear that the lessee is not buying the asset, but is instead renting it for only a short period of time. The lease contract may be viewed as a mutually unexecuted contract, and the cash payments required by the lease are recorded by the lessee as rent expense and an outflow of cash. This type of lease is known as an **operating lease**.

Suppose, at the other extreme, that the lease contract was signed for the entire useful life of the asset and that the title to the asset passes to the lessee at the end of the lease term (not an uncommon event). In this case, the substance of the transaction is that the lessee has bought an asset and has agreed to pay for it in instalments. There is essentially no difference between this arrangement and one in which the lessee borrows the money and buys the asset for cash. The lender, in this case, is the lessor. It seems appropriate for the lessee to account for this as a borrowing and as a purchase of an asset. The asset is therefore recorded at its cost (in this case, the present value of the lease payments), and is amortized over time. The obligation to the lessor is recorded as a liability, and interest expense is recognized over time. This type of lease is known as a **capital lease**.

Although the appropriate accounting procedures for these extreme situations seem fairly clear, the question arises: What does the corporation do when the lease is somewhere in between these extremes? Suppose, for example, that the lease term is for 70% of the useful life of the asset and the corporation has an option to buy the asset at the end of the lease term. Should this qualify as a capital lease? In terms of the financial statement effects, a corporation would generally prefer to treat the lease as an operating lease. This would keep the lease obligation off the books, and there would be no effect on the debt/equity and interest coverage ratios. To address this issue, criteria have been developed within GAAP to distinguish capital leases from operating leases. From the lessee's point of view, the lease qualifies as a capital lease if one of the following criteria is met:

> ## CAPITAL LEASE CRITERIA
> 1. The title to the asset passes to the lessee by the end of the lease term.
> 2. The lease term is equal to or greater than 75% of the useful life of the asset.
> 3. The present value of the minimum lease payments is greater than 90% of the fair value of the leased asset.

If the transaction does not meet any of the three criteria, the lease is an operating lease.

Criterion 1 indicates that the corporation will own the asset by the end of the lease term and, hence, is buying an asset. Many leases provide an option for the lessee to buy the asset at the end of the lease term. If the price to buy the asset is considered a bargain (i.e., it is likely that the corporation will exercise its option and buy the asset), then Criterion 1 would be met. Criterion 2 means that the corporation will have use of the asset during most of its useful life, even though it may not retain title to it at the end of the lease term. The third criterion means that if the price the lessee pays to lease the asset is close to the price it would pay to buy the asset, it should account for the transaction as a purchase.

To illustrate the differences in accounting under a capital lease and an operating lease, let's consider the following simple situation. Suppose that an asset is leased for five years and requires quarterly lease payments of $2,000 each, payable in advance. The title does not pass at the end of the lease term, and there is no purchase option. The interest rate that is appropriate for this lease is 12%.

If the lease qualifies as an operating lease, the only entry to be made would be to record the payments as rent expense each quarter. The following entry would be made each quarter:

> ### OPERATING LEASE ENTRY
> | | | |
> |---|---|---|
> | SE – Rent Expense (lease expense) | 2,000 | |
> | A – Cash | | 2,000 |

If the lease qualifies as a capital lease, the transaction must be recorded as the purchase of an asset, and a related obligation. Both the asset and the obligation would be recorded at the present value of the lease payments. This transaction is structured as an annuity in advance (the first payment is made immediately and then there are 19 more payments). Because there are quarterly payments and the lease term is five years, there would be a total of 20 payments. The interest rate per period for use in discounting would be 3% (the quarterly rate based on the 12% annual rate). Using Table 3 from Appendix 1 for the present value of an annuity, the following would be the computation of the present value:

$$\text{PV of lease payments} = \text{First payment} + \text{PV of 19 payments at 3\%}$$
$$= \$2,000 + (\$2,000 \times 14.32380)$$
$$= \$2,000 + \$28,647.60$$
$$= \$30,647.60$$

The entry to record the purchase of the asset and the related obligation at the time of contract signing would be:

CAPITAL LEASE ENTRY
(at date of signing)

A – Asset under Lease	30,647.60	
L – Lease Obligation		30,647.60

Subsequent to acquisition, the asset would be amortized over its useful life (in this case, the lease term, since the title does not pass at the end of the lease term). Assuming the corporation uses straight-line amortization, the amortization for the first quarter would be $1,532.38 ($30,647.60/20 quarters). Note that the residual value is zero in this calculation because the lessee does not retain title to the asset at the end of the lease term. The entry to record amortization would be:

CAPITAL LEASE EXPENSE ENTRY
(last day of quarter)

SE – Amortization Expense	1,532.38	
XA – Accumulated Amortization		1,532.38
(on leased assets)		

In addition, the lease obligation would result in the recognition of interest expense similar to that generated by a bond. In the first quarter, two things happen. The first is that a payment is made at the beginning of the quarter (the first payment). This entire payment reduces the principal of the obligation because no time has passed and no interest has accrued. The principal at the beginning of the quarter is, therefore, $28,647.60 ($30,647.60 − 2,000). Interest is then calculated on this principal in the amount of $859.43 ($28,647.60 × 12% × 3/12). The entries to record these transactions in the first quarter are:

CAPITAL LEASE PAYMENT ENTRY
(on first day of the quarter)

L – Lease Obligation	2,000	
A – Cash		2,000

CAPITAL LEASE EXPENSE ENTRY
(on last day of the quarter)

SE – Interest Expense	859.43	
L – Lease Obligation		859.43

An amortization table of the lease obligation could be prepared that is similar to those constructed earlier for bonds. By the end of the lease term, the lease obligation would be zero. Note that, in the case of a lease, the interest is added directly to the lease obligation account, and the cash payments directly reduce the balance.

This transaction has certain effects on the financial statements. If the asset qualifies as a capital lease, the assets and liabilities of the corporation would be higher by $30,647.60 than under an operating lease. On the income statement, the corporation would report both amortization expense and interest expense with the capital lease, whereas, with the operating lease, the corporation would report only rent expense. In the first quarter, the amortization plus interest would be $2,391.81 ($1,532.38 + 859.43). The expense under the operating lease would be $2,000. Therefore, in the first quarter, the capital lease reports higher expenses (they would be even higher if the corporation used an accelerated method of amortization). The total expenses reported over the life of the lease would be the same, however, regardless of which method is used to record the transaction. With the operating lease, the total expenses would be $40,000: ($2,000 × 20 payments). The total capital lease expenses would also be $40,000: $30,647.60 in amortization and $9,352.40 in interest (total payments minus principal = $40,000 − 30,647.60). The difference, then, is in the pattern of expense recognition over the life of the lease, with operating leases showing a level amount of expense but with capital leases showing larger expenses in the early years (when amortization and interest are high), and smaller expenses in later years. Exhibit 10-11 graphs the pattern of expense recognition over the life of the lease, treating the lease as an operating lease versus a capital lease.

Because no asset or liability is recorded under operating leases, GAAP requires corporations that have significant operating leases to disclose their commitments to pay for these leases. Corporations are required to disclose the future lease payments to be made in total and for each of the next five years. Capitalized leases also require

EXHIBIT 10-11

Patterns of Expense Recognition for Leases

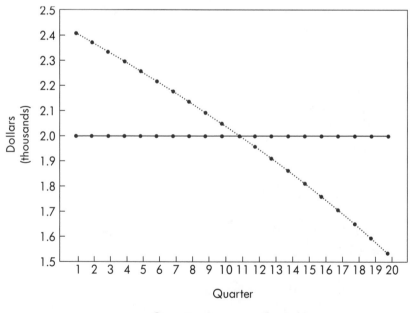

Quarter

— Operating Lease ····· Capital Lease

similar disclosure. The obligations associated with leases would typically be shown in a footnote that relates either to long-term debt, or to commitments or contingencies. In the financial statements for BCE Inc., these disclosures can be found in Note 17 (Exhibit 10-12). Assets under capital leases are sometimes also segregated in the plant, property, and equipment section of the balance sheet.

Lessor Accounting

Lessor accounting is designed to be a mirror image of the accounting by the lessee. If the lessee qualifies for capital lease treatment, then the lessor should be viewed as having provided an asset to the lessee (the lessor will replace the capital asset with a receivable asset). If the lessee must treat the lease as an operating lease, then the lessor should retain the asset on its books as the owner and record lease revenue from the lease payments. In either of these situations, the lessor does not have a long-term liability (the subject of this chapter) on its books. Your intermediate financial accounting courses will discuss lease accounting in more detail.

EXHIBIT 10-12

BCE INC.

Excerpted from Notes to the Statements

17. Commitments and contingent liabilities

a) Lease commitments

At December 31, 1994, the future minimum lease payments under capital leases and operating leases with initial non-cancellable lease terms in excess of one year were:

	Capital leases	Operating leases
		($ millions)
1995	14	299
1996	12	229
1997	7	165
1998	6	129
1999	6	75
Thereafter	26	377
Total future minimum lease payments	71	1,274
Less: estimated executory costs	2	
Net minimum lease payments	69	
Less: imputed interest	24	
Total capital leases as at December 31, 1994	45	

Rental expense applicable to operating leases for the year 1994 was $423 million, $417 million in 1993 and $405 million in 1992.

AN INTERNATIONAL PERSPECTIVE
REPORTS FROM OTHER COUNTRIES

A significant number of countries (such as France, Italy, and Japan) do not require the capitalization of leased assets. In other countries, the capitalization of leases is required or is the predominant practice (United States, United Kingdom, and Canada).

PENSIONS

Pensions are agreements between employers and employees that provide employees with specified benefits (income) upon retirement. To the extent that the corporation is obligated to make payments under these agreements, some recognition should be given of the cost of these benefits in the years when the corporation receives the benefits from the work of its employees. Because the payments to retired employees occur many years in the future, pensions represent an estimated future obligation. Two kinds of pension plans are commonly used by employers: **defined contribution plans**, and **defined benefit plans**.

Defined Contribution Plans

In a **defined contribution plan**, the employer agrees to make a set (defined) contribution to a retirement fund for the employee. The amount is usually set as a percentage of the employee's salary. Employees sometimes make their own contributions to the same fund to add to the amounts invested. The benefits to the employee at retirement depend on how well the investments in the retirement fund perform. The employer satisfies its obligation to the employee upon payment into the fund. The fund is usually managed by a trustee, and the assets are legally separated from the assets of the corporation, which means they are not reported with the other assets on the balance sheet of the corporation.

The accounting for defined contribution funds is relatively straightforward. The corporation accrues the amount of its obligation to the pension fund, and then records a payment. Because the liability is settled, no other recognition is necessary in the financial statements. The entry to recognize pension expense and the related payment is:

SE — Pension Expense	XXX	
L — Pension Obligation		XXX
L — Pension Obligation	XXX	
A — Cash		XXX

Corporations generally make cash payments that coincide with the accruals because they cannot deduct the cost for tax purposes if no cash payment is made. Therefore, no net obligation usually remains with a defined contribution plan.

Defined Benefit Plans

A **defined benefit plan** guarantees to pay an employee a certain amount of money during each year of retirement. The formula used to calculate how much is paid usually takes into consideration the amount of time an employee has worked for the corporation as well as the highest salary (or an average of the highest salaries) that the employee earned while working for the corporation. For example, a plan might guarantee that the employee will receive 2% of the average of the highest three years of salaries for each year that the employee works for the corporation. If the employee worked for the corporation for 30 years and had an average salary of $40,000 for the highest three years, the pension benefit would be $24,000 per year [($40,000 × 2%) × 30 years].

Each year, as employees provide service to the corporation, they earn pension benefits which obligate the corporation to cash payments at some point in the future. To estimate the present value of the liability, factors to be considered include projections of how long the employee will work for the corporation, at what age the employee will retire, what the employee's average salary will be at retirement, how long the employee will live after retiring, and whether the employee will work for the corporation until retirement. All these factors will affect the amount and timing of the cash flows. In addition, the corporation must choose an appropriate rate of interest at which to calculate the net present value.

A given employee may leave the corporation at some point prior to retirement. If the pension benefits belong to employees only as long as they remain in the employment of the corporation, then there may be no obligation on the part of the corporation to pay out pension benefits. In most plans, however, there is a provision for **vesting** the benefits. Benefits that are vested belong to employees, regardless of whether they leave the corporation. In addition, while one employee may leave, many others will stay. Thus, even without vesting, it is likely that some fraction of the employees will continue to work for the corporation until retirement. The total obligation of the pension plan may, therefore, have to be estimated based on the characteristics of the average employee rather than on particular employees.

Calculating the present value of the future pension obligation generally requires the services of an **actuary**. The actuary is trained in the use of statistical procedures to make the types of estimates required for the pension calculation.

The accounting entries for defined benefit pension plans are essentially the same as the preceding entry for defined contribution plans. The corporation must make an accrual of the expense and the related obligation to provide pension benefits. The amounts are much more difficult to estimate in the case of defined benefit plans, but the concept is the same as for defined contribution plans. The entry made to recognize the pension expense is called the **accrual entry**. Setting aside cash to pay for these future benefits is done by making a cash entry. This is sometimes called the **funding entry**. Many employee pension plan agreements have clauses that require the corporation to fund the pension obligation. Because of the uncertainties associated with the amounts of the liabilities, some corporations have been somewhat reluctant to fully fund their pension obligations. There is no requirement that the amount expensed be the same as the amount funded. Therefore, a net pension obligation may result if more is expensed than funded, or a net pension asset may exist if funding is larger than the amount expensed. The actual calculation of the pension expense incorporates many factors and is beyond the scope of this book. To keep the problem simple, we will provide you with information about the pension expense.

Pension funds are described as **overfunded** if the assets in the fund exceed the present value of future pension obligations. In **underfunded** pension plans, the present value of future obligations exceeds fund assets. Funds in which the assets actually equal the present value of the future obligations are called **fully funded** plans.

The pension fund itself is usually handled by a trustee, and contributions to the fund cannot be returned to the employer except under extraordinary circumstances. To provide sufficient funds to pay benefits, the trustee invests the assets contributed to the fund. Benefits are then paid out of these fund assets.

■ ■ Annual Statement Disclosures

In Canada, for a defined contribution plan, GAAP requires the disclosure of contribution amounts for the period. For a defined benefit plan, the required disclosure is the present value of the future obligations of the corporation plus the value of the pension fund assets. In light of the fact that the dollar values of future obligations and fund assets are usually substantial, this appears to be barely adequate. Some corporations comply strictly to this required disclosure, but others offer more information about their plans. BCE Inc., for example, provides extensive disclosure about its plan (a defined benefit plan) and the components of its pension expense (see Exhibit 10-13).

◖◗ OTHER EMPLOYMENT BENEFITS

Employers sometimes offer other types of benefits in addition to pensions. Health-care benefits and life insurance are two of the most commonly offered benefits. The obligation to provide these benefits has, for the most part, been ignored in the financial statements of corporations in Canada. The benefits have been recorded on a pay-as-you-go basis; that is, the costs have been expensed as the cash is paid out to insurance companies who cover the costs of the benefits. To date, corporate exposure in Canada has been limited because of publicly funded health care. This may not be true in the future.

Employers also sometimes offer extended health-care benefits to retired employees. Most employers also record these on a pay-as-you-go basis. In the United States, they have recently required corporations to accrue the obligation for future benefits from these post-retirement benefits in much the same way as regular future pension benefits are accrued. As a result, several corporations reported losses in the first year the accrual was made. In Canada, we do not yet have such a requirement.

For the many corporations that have made no liability provision for these benefits, any new standard could have significant effects on their financial statements. The standard would likely cause liabilities to increase and shareholders' equity to decrease. Some of the effects would be deferred and amortized to income and the balance sheet over future periods in a manner similar to the amortization provisions of other components of the pension expense.

◖◗ STATEMENT ANALYSIS CONSIDERATIONS

Two ratios that are commonly used to evaluate a corporation's ability to repay its obligations are the debt/equity ratio and the times interest earned ratio. Using the

EXHIBIT 10-13

BCE INC.
Excerpted from Notes to the Statements

19. Pensions

The following table sets forth the financial position of the pension plans and BCE's net pension asset:

		($ millions)
At December 31	**1994**	**1993**
Net assets available for plan benefits **– at market-related value**	12,076	11,478
Actuarial present value of plan benefits		
Accumulated plan benefits		
Vested	8,374	7,362
Non-vested	857	912
	9,231	8,274
Effect of salary projections	1,970	2,066
Projected plan benefits	11,201	10,340
Excess of plan assets at market-related value **over projected plan benefits**	875	1,138
Unrecognized net experience gains	(962)	(1,153)
Unrecognized net assets existing at January 1, 1987	(97)	(98)
Other unrecognized plan amendments	337	334
Net pension asset reflected on the consolidated **balance sheets**	153	221
Deferred pension asset (included in deferred charges)	436	497
Deferred pension obligation (included in other long-term liabilities)	(283)	(276)
Net pension asset	153	221

Experience gains and losses, the unrecognized net plan assets existing at January 1, 1987 and plan amendments are amortized over the employees' average remaining working lives (14 years at December 31, 1994).

The components of BCE's pension expense follow:

			($ millions)
	1994	**1993**	**1992**
Service cost – benefits earned	298	298	273
Interest cost on projected plan benefits	879	831	798
Expected return on plan assets	(956)	(954)	(913)
Net amortization	8	(2)	(21)
Pension expense	229	173	137

Pension expense was calculated using a value of assets adjusted to market over periods ranging from 3 to 5 years. The weighted average discount rate used in determining the accumulated and accrued plan benefits, and the weighted average assumed long-term rate of return on plan assets, was 8.4% in 1994, 8.5% in 1993 and 8.7% in 1992.

In addition to pension benefits, the Corporation and most of its subsidiary companies provide certain health care and life insurance benefits for retired employees. The costs of such benefits amounted to $35 million in 1994, $34 million in 1993 and $29 million in 1992.

AN INTERNATIONAL PERSPECTIVE
REPORTS FROM OTHER COUNTRIES

While a significant number of countries require accrual of pension cost, many other countries require only that the costs of pension plans be recognized as benefits are paid, the pay-as-you-go method. Countries with this type of accounting include Belgium, India, Norway, and Spain.

EXHIBIT 10-14

ENERFLEX SYSTEMS LTD.
Consolidated Statements of Financial Position

(Thousands)

	December 31 1994	1993
Assets		
Current Assets		
Accounts receivable	$ 50,171	$ 26,106
Inventory (note 1)	18,925	16,780
Total current assets	69,096	42,886
Rental Equipment (note 2)	18,078	9,515
Property, Plant and Equipment (note 3)	13,770	8,012
Goodwill, net of accumulated amortization	1,561	1,607
	$ 102,505	$ 62,020
Liabilities and Shareholders' Equity		
Current Liabilities		
Bank loans (note 4)	$ 12,002	$ 7,837
Accounts payable and accrued liabilities	37,935	18,850
Income taxes payable	6,094	3,614
Deferred income taxes - current	(1,067)	(664)
Current portion of long-term debt (note 4)	76	70
Total current liabilities	55,040	29,707
Long-term Debt (note 4)	4,716	4,792
Deferred Income Taxes	1,156	1,063
	60,912	35,562
Shareholders' Equity		
Share capital (note 5)	34,158	34,158
Retained earnings (deficit)	7,435	(7,700)
	41,593	26,458
	$ 102,505	$ 62,020

Commitments and Contingencies (note 6)

On behalf of the Board:

Director   Director

balance sheet and income statement (Exhibit 10-14) of Enerflex Systems Ltd., a Calgary based corporation that manufactures, services and leases compressor packages for the production and processing of natural gas, we will demonstrate how these two ratios can provide insights into the riskiness of a corporation.

The formula for the debt/equity ratio is:

EXHIBIT 10-14 (continued)

ENERFLEX SYSTEMS LTD.
Consolidated Statements of Income

(Thousands, except per share amounts)

	Year Ended December 31	
	1994	1993
Sales (note 7)	**$ 217,342**	$ 119,983
Cost of Goods Sold	**166,055**	92,149
Gross Margin	**51,287**	27,834
Expenses (Income)		
Selling, general and administrative (note 8)	**20,646**	13,570
Interest (note 4)	**1,345**	1,114
Gain on sale of rental equipment	**(872)**	(438)
	21,119	14,246
Income before Income Taxes	**30,168**	13,588
Income Taxes (note 9)	**12,389**	5,893
Net Income	**$ 17,779**	$ 7,695
Net Income per Common Share (note 10)	**$ 2.35**	$ 1.02*
*Pro forma		

$$\frac{\text{Total Liabilities}}{\text{Total Liabilities} + \text{Shareholders' Equity}}$$

The 1993 and 1994 debt/equity ratios of Enerflex Systems Ltd. are:

$$\frac{\$35,562}{\$35,562 + \$26,458} = 57.3\% \qquad \frac{\$60,912}{\$60,912 + \$41,593} = 59.4\%$$

These calculations demonstrate that in 1993 just over half of Enerflex Systems' assets were financed through debt. The ratio climbed a little higher in 1994. From the balance sheet we can see that Enerflex Systems increased its short-term liabilities by approximately $25 million and its shareholders' equity by approximately $14 million, all of which was from having sufficient income to reverse a previous year's deficit. The increase in the short-term liabilities in 1994 puts increased demands on the corporation's cash flows. It would be important to follow this ratio for more than two years before too many conclusions can be drawn about any major shifts in financing strategy by the corporation.

The times interest earned ratio provides a measure of the corporation's ability to make interest payments out of earnings. It is calculated by the following formula:

$$\frac{\text{Income before interest and taxes}}{\text{Interest}} = \frac{\text{Net income} + \text{Taxes} + \text{Interest}}{\text{Interest}}$$

The calculation of the times interest earned ratio for Enerflex Systems Ltd. for 1993 and 1994 would be:

$$1993: \quad \frac{\$13,588 + 1,114}{\$1,114} = 13.2$$

and

$$1994: \quad \frac{\$30,168 + \$1,345}{\$1,345} = 23.4$$

In 1993, Enerflex Systems Ltd. could pay its interest obligation 13 times out of earnings. This is a very comfortable position. The risk of nonpayment of interest is very low. By the end of 1994, earnings had improved such that Enerflex could now pay its interest obligations 23 times out of earnings. Any creditor would likely be very confident about lending funds to Enerflex Systems. The increase in the times interest earned ratio, coupled with the small increase in the debt/equity ratio, demonstrates to creditors that the risk of nonpayment of interest or principal of the debt has declined in the two years.

The biggest concern for analysts regarding liabilities is the possibility of unrecorded liabilities. As seen in the last chapter, commitments and contingent liabilities can have significant effects on the health of a corporation. In this chapter, obligations of the corporation for operating leases and other postretirement health-care benefits are examples of liabilities that are not reported on the financial statements. Unrecorded liabilities will cause the debt/equity ratio to be understated and the times interest earned ratio to be overstated. Certain disclosures give the analyst some help in understanding the effects of these unrecorded liabilities. For example, the disclosure of the next five years of lease payments for operating leases allows an analyst to approximate the present value of these lease payments for inclusion in ratio analysis. The effects of commitments and other off-balance-sheet liabilities such as health care are difficult to estimate, but the analyst should have a good understanding of the corporation and the type of contracts it enters into with suppliers, customers and employees so that these liabilities do not come as surprises.

Another concern is whether the book values of liabilities reflect their current market values. Because GAAP requires that liabilities be recorded at the interest rates that were in effect when the debt was issued, changes in market rates can cause changes in the value of these liabilities that are not reflected on the corporation's books. This is particularly important when one corporation is trying to buy another. Book value can be adjusted either by looking at the market value of the debt (for publicly traded debt) or by recalculating the present value of the debt based on current market interest rates. This, of course, requires some detailed information about the terms of the outstanding debt.

Another risk that the analyst should consider is that posed by debt that is denominated in a foreign currency. As you can imagine, if the corporation is required to repay a debt in a foreign currency, fluctuations in the exchange rate for that currency can cause increases or decreases in the liability as expressed in dollars. Another risk is that the corporation may enter into debt agreements in which the interest rate is not fixed but floats with interest rates in the economy (sometimes called variable-rate debt). If interest rates go up, the corporation can find itself paying significantly higher interest payments. Both these risks can be managed through the use of sophisticated hedging techniques involving financial instruments such as interest rate and foreign currency options and swaps. To help readers of financial statements understand these complex transactions and the risks posed to the corporation, the Accounting Standards Board has recently issued a new guideline, 3860, which requires corporations to disclose these types of transactions and to provide some details concerning the risks the corporation faces because of them. Many of these risks are associated with amounts that are off-balance-sheet. As an example, consider the disclosure made by Meridian Technologies Inc., in its 1995 annual report (Exhibit 10-15):

EXHIBIT 10-15

MERIDIAN TECHNOLOGIES INC. 1995
Excerpted from Notes to the Statements

Note 5
Long-term debt

The Company utilizes interest rate and cross-currency swap agreements to hedge its interest rate and foreign currency exposure on its existing and future bank term loans and U.S. investments. At March 31, 1995, the Company had entered into an interest rate swap converting a notional U.S. $20,000,000 of floating rate debt to 8.45% fixed rate debt, maturing in 1997. At March 31 1995, the Company had also entered into cross-currency swaps converting a notional Canadian $42,000,000 of floating rate debt to a notional U.S. $30,205,000 fixed rate debt at an average rate of 8.55%, maturing as to one-third in each of 1998, 1999 and 2000. Interest differential amounts arising from the swaps are charged or credited to interest expense. Translation gains or losses arising from the cross-currency swaps are included in the cumulative translation adjustment.

SUMMARY

This chapter completes the discussion of liabilities. The risks associated with long-term liabilities are more extensive than those associated with the short-term liabilities discussed in the previous chapter because of the longer time frame and the uncertainty of the future. Bonds, leases and pensions have major impacts on the financial health of corporations. Understanding what these items are and how they are recorded and reported on the financial statements is essential to any evaluation of the future profitability of an organization.

The discussion of balance sheet accounts concludes in the next chapter with a discussion of shareholders' equity. Following that chapter, we provide a complete review of the ratio analysis used in this book. In the final chapter, we discuss complex organizations and include some additional comments about the presentation of debt and equity that affect the analysis of these organizations.

SUMMARY PROBLEMS

1. The Higgins Corporation issued $100,000 face value bonds with a bond interest rate of 8% on January 1, 19x1. The bonds mature on December 31, 19x10 (i.e., there are 10 years to maturity) and pay interest semi-annually on June 30 and December 31. The price set for these bonds reflected an assumption that investors would need a 10% return in order to be convinced to buy the bonds.

   a. What price was set for these bonds under the assumptions set forth above? (Ignore commissions to the underwriters in your answer.)

   b. If the bonds were issued at the price calculated in part (a), what entries would the Higgins Corporation make during 19x1 to account for these bonds?

   c. If, prior to the issuance of the bonds, interest rates increase in the economy such that investors demand a 12% return from investments such as Higgins' bonds, what price would they be willing to pay on January 1, 19x1 for these bonds?

2. The Acme Rental Corporation enters into a lease for the use of a computer system. The lessor paid $35,000 for the computer system and will lease the computer system to Acme for five years. At the end of the lease term, the computer will be returned to the lessor, who estimates that the computer will have a zero residual value. The lease contract will call for monthly payments to be made at the end of each month.

   a. What equal monthly payments will the lessor require from Acme if it is to produce a return of 12% to the lessor?

   b. Based on the facts, how should Acme account for this lease?

   c. Construct the entries that Acme should make during the first two months of the lease, assuming that the lease is signed on January 1, 19x1 and that payments are made on the last day of each month.

3. Exhibit 10-16 shows the pension footnote for Cominco Ltd. (an integrated natural resource corporation involved in mineral exploration, mining, smelting and refining).

   a. What kind of pension plan does Cominco Ltd. have?

   b. What is the estimated future obligation of the pension plan and the value of the pension assets at the end of 1994? Is the plan over or under funded?

   c. Why did Cominco Ltd.'s pension expense decrease in 1994?

SUGGESTED SOLUTIONS TO SUMMARY PROBLEMS

1. a. Present Value of the Higgins Corporation Bond at 10%:

> PV of Bond = PV of Interest Payments + PV of Maturity Payment
> = ($4,000 × 12.46221 (Table 3)) + ($100,000 × 0.37689(Table 2))
> = $87,537.84

EXHIBIT 10-16

COMINCO LTD.
Excerpted from the Notes to the Statements

14. Pensions

Cominco maintains both defined benefit and defined contribution pension plans.

Benefits from the defined benefit plans are based on either years of service and highest average remuneration in a specified period or a stated amount for each year of service. The pension costs are determined annually by independent actuaries and include current service costs and a provision for the amortization of prior service costs. Pension costs for current services are charged to earnings in the year incurred. The liability for past service is charged to earnings over the remaining service lives of the employees.

Benefits from the defined contribution plan are based on the accumulated plan value, interest rates and type of life annuity chosen at date of annuity purchase. Pension costs for current services are funded by Cominco and charged to earnings in the year incurred.

Total pension expense including past service cost was $19,900,000 for 1994 and $23,100,000 for 1993. In 1993, the pension expense was higher as a result of the introduction of the defined contribution pension plan and settlement of union agreements at Trail Operations.

The date of the most recent actuarial valuation for most defined benefit pension plans is December 31, 1992. At December 31, 1994, actuarial estimates of the present value of accumulated pension benefits amounted to $464,500,000 and the actuarial value of assets calculated on adjusted market values was $413,100,000.

b.

HIGGINS CORPORATION BOND — ISSUANCE ENTRY
(at date of issuance)

A – Cash	87,537.84	
XL – Discount on Bond Payable	12,462.16	
L – Bond Payable		100,000.00

HIGGINS CORPORATION BOND — INTEREST ENTRIES

(at the end of the first interest period)

SE – Interest Expense[a]	4,376.89	
XL – Discount on Bond Payable		376.89
L – Interest Payable[b]		4,000.00
L – Interest Payable	4,000.00	
A – Cash		4,000.00

[a] Interest Expense = Carrying Value × Discount Rate × Time
$$= \$87,537.84 \times 10\% \times 6/12 = \$4,376.89$$
[b] Interest Payable = Face Amount × Bond Interest Rate × Time
$$= \$100,000 \times 8\% \times 6/12 = \$4,000.00$$

HIGGINS CORPORATION BOND — INTEREST ENTRIES

(at the end of the second interest period)

SE – Interest Expense[a]	4,395.74	
XL – Discount on Bond Payable		395.74
L – Interest Payable[b]		4,000.00
L – Interest Payable	4,000.00	
A – Cash		4,000.00

[a] Interest Expense = Carrying Value × Discount Rate × Time
$$= \$87,914.73 \times 10\% \times 6/12 = \$4,395.74$$
Ending Carrying Value = Beginning Carrying Value + Interest − Payment
$$= \$87,537.84 + 4,376.89 - 4,000.00 = \$87,914.73$$
[b] Interest Payable = Face Amount × Bond Interest Rate × Time
$$= \$100,000 \times 8\% \times 6/12 = \$4,000.00$$

c. Present Value of the Higgins Corporation Bond at 12%:

PV of Bond = PV of Interest Payments + PV of Maturity Payment
$$= (\$4,000 \times 11.46992 \text{ (Table 3)}) + (\$100,000 \times 0.31180 \text{(Table 2)})$$
$$= \$77,059.68$$

2. a. The lease represents an annuity in arrears type of problem. The investment in the asset is the present value, and the payments can be determined using the formula for the present value of an annuity in arrears as shown below. Because there are 60 monthly payments in the lease period, N = 60 and r = 1%.

PV = Payment × PV of an annuity in Arrears for 60 periods at 1%
$$\$35,000 = PMT \times 44.95504$$
$$PMT = \frac{\$35,000}{\$44.95504}$$
$$PMT = \$778.56/\text{month}$$

b. Because the lease covers more than 75% of the useful life of the asset, Acme should account for it as a capital lease.

c. The following entries should be made in the first two months:

CAPITAL LEASE ENTRY
(at January 1, 19x1)
A — Asset under Lease   35,000
   L — Lease Obligation   35,000

Assuming that the corporation amortizes its leased assets straight-line over the lease term, the following entry would be made at the end of the first month:

CAPITAL LEASE EXPENSE ENTRY
(on January 31, 19x1)
SE — Amortization Expense   583.33[a]
   XA — Accumulated Amortization   583.33
   (on leased assets)

[a] Straight-line Amortization = $35,000/60 months = $583.33/month

---

The amortization of the obligation must also be recorded in the first month. Because this is an annuity in arrears, the first payment reduces the principal of the obligation at the end of the month. The following entries would be made:

CAPITAL LEASE EXPENSE ENTRY
(on January 31, 19x1)
L — Lease Obligation   778.56
   A — Cash   778.56
SE — Interest Expense   350.00[a]
   L — Lease Obligation   350.00

[a] Interest Expense = Carrying Value × Interest Rate × 1/12
                 = $35,000 × 12% × 1/12
                 = $350.00

In the second month, similar entries would be made as follows:

CAPITAL LEASE EXPENSE ENTRY
(on February 28, 19x1)
SE — Amortization Expense   583.33[a]
   XA — Accumulated Amortization   583.33
   (on leased assets)

[a] Straight-line Amortization = $35,000/60 months = $583.33/month

---

CAPITAL LEASE EXPENSE ENTRY
(on February 28, 19x1)

L – Lease Obligation	778.56	
A – Cash		778.56
SE – Interest Expense	345.71ᵃ	
L – Lease Obligation		345.71

ᵃ Interest Expense = Carrying Value × Interest Rate × 1/12
$$= (\$35{,}000 - \$778.56 + \$350.00) \times 12\% \times 1/12$$
$$= \$34{,}571.44 \times 12\% \times 1/12$$
$$= \$345.71$$

3. a. Cominco Ltd. has both defined benefit and defined contribution pension plans.

b. The estimated future obligation of the pension plan is $464,500,000. The value of the pension assets is $413,100,000. The plan is underfunded by $51,400,000.

c. Cominco Ltd.'s pension expense decreased in 1994 because in 1993 the corporation introduced the defined contribution plan and settled union agreements at Trail Operations which caused increased expenses in 1993.

SYNONYMS

Bond interest rate/coupon rate/stated rate
Early retirement of debt/Early extinguishment of debt
Market rate of interest/yield rate/effective rate/discount rate

GLOSSARY

Accrual entry In the context of pension accounting, this is the entry to accrue pension cost and create the pension obligation.

Actuary A professional trained in statistical methods who can make reasonable estimates of pension costs.

Adjunct account An account that adds to a related account; that is, it has the same type of balance as the related account. In this chapter, an example of this type of account is the premium on bond payable account.

Amortization of discount The systematic reduction of the discount account balance over the life of a bond. The reduction of the discount account each period adds to the interest expense recorded during the period.

Amortization of premium The systematic reduction of the premium account balance over the life of a bond. The reduction of the premium account each period reduces the interest expense recorded during the period.

Best efforts basis The basis on which underwriters sometimes sell bonds for corporations. The underwriter makes its "best effort" to sell the bonds but, if they cannot be sold, the bonds are returned to the corporation.

Bond A long-term borrowing of a corporation that is evidenced by a bond certificate. The borrowing is characterized by a face value, interest rate, and maturity date.

Bond covenants Restrictions placed on a corporation that issues bonds. The restrictions usually apply to the ability of the corporation to pay dividends or require that the corporation maintain certain minimum ratios.

Bond interest rate An interest rate specified in a bond used to determine the interest payments that are made by the bond.

Bond market A market in which bonds of corporations are actively traded.

Capital lease A lease that the lessee must record as an asset and a related borrowing as if the transaction represented the purchase of the asset.

Collateral trust bond A bond that provides marketable securities as collateral in the event of default by the corporation.

Commercial paper A short-term borrowing in which the lender is another corporation.

Convertible bond A bond that is convertible under certain conditions into common shares.

Debenture A bond that is issued with no specific collateral.

Defined benefit plan A pension plan that specifies the benefits that retirees will receive upon retirement. The benefits are usually determined based on the number of years of service and the highest salary earned by the employee.

Defined contribution plan A pension plan that specifies how much the corporation will contribute to the pension fund of its employees. No guarantee is made of the amount that will be available upon retirement.

Discount A term used to indicate that a bond is sold or issued at a value below its face value.

Early extinguishment of debt The retirement of debt prior to its scheduled maturity date.

Early retirement of debt The retirement of debt prior to its scheduled maturity date.

Face value A value specified in a bond that determines the cash payment that will be made on the maturity date of the bond. The face value is also used to determine the periodic interest payments made by the bond.

Foreign-denominated debt Borrowing of a corporation that must be repaid in a foreign currency.

Fully funded Refers to a pension plan in which the pension plan assets equal the projected benefit obligation.

Funding entry In the context of pensions, this is the entry made to show the cash payment made to the pension plan to fund the obligation.

Indenture agreement An agreement that accompanies the issuance of a bond specifying all the terms and restrictions of the borrowing.

Interest payment The periodic interest payments made by a bond. The payments are typically made semi-annually. The amount is calculated by multiplying the face value of the bond by the bond interest rate.

Investment banker The intermediary who arranges the issuance of a bond in the public debt market on behalf of a corporation. The investment banker sells the bonds to its clients before the bond is traded in the open market.

Lease agreement An agreement between a lessee and a lessor for the rental or purchase of an asset, or both.

Lease term The period or term over which a lessee makes payments to a lessor in a lease.

Lessee The party or entity that is renting or purchasing the asset in a lease.

Lessor The party or entity that is selling or lending the asset in a lease.

Maturity date A date specified in a bond that determines the final payment date of the bond.

Mortgage bond A bond that provides some type of real asset as collateral in the event of default by the corporation.

Note A long-term borrowing.

Operating lease A lease in which the lessee does not record an asset and related obligation but treats the lease as a mutually unexecuted contract. Lease expense is then recognized as payments are made per the lease contract.

Other post-employment benefits Benefits provided to retirees other than pensions. These benefits are typically health-care or life insurance benefits.

Overfunded Refers to a pension plan in which the plan assets exceed the projected benefit obligation.

Par A term used to indicate that a bond is sold or issued at its face value.

Pension A plan that provides benefits to employees upon retirement.

Premium A term used to indicate that a bond is sold or issued at a value above its face value.

Private placement A borrowing arranged privately between two corporations or entities.

Projected benefit obligation The present value of the pension obligations under a defined benefit plan. The calculation includes all necessary actuarial assumptions and an assumption with regard to the escalation of salaries.

Public bond market A market in which bonds are publicly traded.

Senior debenture A general borrowing of the corporation that has priority over other types of long-term borrowings in the event of bankruptcy.

Subordinated debenture A general borrowing of the corporation that has a lower priority than senior debentures in the event of bankruptcy.

Syndicate A group of underwriters that collectively helps a corporation sell its bonds.

Tombstone ad An advertisement that indicates the essential terms of an initial bond issuance.

Underfunded A pension plan in which the plan assets are less than the projected benefit obligation.

Underwriter An investment bank that arranges and agrees to sell the initial issuance of a corporation's bonds.

Unguaranteed residual value The value of an asset at the end of the lease term of the asset when the asset reverts back to the lessor.

Vesting An event by which employees are granted pension benefits even if they leave the employ of the corporation.

ASSIGNMENT MATERIAL

Assessing Your Recall

1. Describe the following terms that relate to a bond: indenture agreement, bond covenants, face value, maturity date, bond interest rate, interest payments, and collateral.

2. Discuss the role of the investment banker in the issuance of bonds by a corporation.

3. Describe what the term "best efforts basis" means in the issuance of bonds and why it is important to a corporation.

4. Discuss how bonds are priced and how the price is affected by changes in market interest rates.

5. Describe the following terms as they relate to the issuance and sale of bonds: par, premium and discount.

6. Discuss the meaning of the term bond discount and what is meant by the amortization of a bond discount.

7. Explain the procedure for the retirement of debt before maturity. Why would a corporation retire debt early?

8. Discuss the benefits of leasing from both the lessee and the lessor's point of view.

9. List and discuss the criteria used to distinguish capital leases from operating leases for lessees.

10. Differentiate defined contribution pension plans from defined benefit plans.

11. Define the following terms: overfunded, underfunded, and fully funded.

12. Explain what the following ratios tell you about a corporation's financial health: debt/equity ratio, and times interest earned.

▶️◣ Applying Your Knowledge

13. The Standard Mills Corporation issues 100 bonds each with a face value of $1,000 that mature in 30 years. The bonds carry a 10% interest rate and are sold to yield 12%. They pay interest semi-annually.

    Required:
    a. Compute the issuing price of the bonds, and show the journal entry to record the issuance of the bonds.
    b. Compute interest expense for the first year, and show the journal entries to record this expense and the corresponding interest payments.

14. Emkay Inc. issues 100, $1,000, 12% bonds maturing in 10 years. The bonds pay interest semi-annually and are issued to yield 10%.

    Required:
    a. Compute the issue price of the bonds, and give the journal entry to record the issuance.
    b. Compute the book value of the bonds five years after issuance, that is, at the beginning of the sixth year.
    c. Compute the market value of the bonds five years after issuance if the market yield has increased to 14%.
    d. Compare the book value (calculated in part (b)) and the market value (calculated in part (c)) at the end of five years, and explain why a difference exists.

15. The Spartan Tech Corporation issued 8% bonds with a face value of $100,000, maturing in three years. The bonds pay interest twice a year. Prepare an amortization table for the three years under each of the following conditions:

    Required:
    a. Market yield at issuance is 8%.
    b. Market yield at issuance is 10%.
    c. Market yield at issuance is 6%.

16. On July 1, 19x7, the Turlotec Manufacturing Corporation leased one of its machines costing $500,000 to Start Mechanical Corporation. The 10-year lease was classified as a capital lease for accounting purposes. The lease agreement required equal semi-annual payments of $50,926 payable on December 31 and June 30 each year, and an interest rate of 16%. Both corporations close their books annually on December 31.

    Required:
    Show the necessary journal entries relating to the lease in the books of Start Mechanical Corporation during 19x7. Assume the machine has a useful life of 10 years and zero residual value. Further assume that both companies use straight-line amortization.

17. Bagel Boys, Ltd. has decided to lease a truck to deliver its bagels. The corporation signs an agreement on January 1, 19x8 to lease a truck for $350 per month for the next three years. The title to the truck reverts to the lessor at the end of the lease term. The lease calls for payments on the first of the month starting on February 1, 19x8. Bagel Boys, Ltd. closes its books monthly and believes that 9% is an appropriate discount rate for the lease.

Required:

a. Assuming that the market value of the truck is $20,000 and that the lessor believes its useful life is five years, how should Bagel Boys account for this lease?

b. Show the appropriate accounting entries for the first two months of 19x8 for the lease under both the operating lease method and the capital lease method. Assume that Bagel Boys amortizes its assets using the straight-line method.

◤◣ Reading and Interpreting Published Financial Statements

18. Refer to Exhibit 10-2 to answer the following questions concerning the bonds issued by IBM Corporation in 1979.

Required:

a. Show the issuance entry and the first two interest payment (and interest recognition) entries that IBM would have made for the 9 1/2% notes issued. Assume the original issuance price stated in the ad. The price in the ad implies a yield of 9.62%.

b. Suppose that the appropriate yield at issuance was 10% instead of 9.62%. What would have been the issuance price of the bonds?

c. Given your answer in part (b) and the original issuance price, what would you estimate the yield of the bonds was when the market value of the bonds fell by $50 apiece after the Federal Reserve Board issued their tough credit restrictions (see the discussion at the end of the subsection entitled "Bond Markets" for more details)?

19. In August of 1997, Niagara Corporation issued $920 million of zero coupon bonds that were due in 2012. Zero coupon bonds pay no interest payments and make a maturity payment of only the face value. Interest is still compounded semi-annually as with an ordinary bond. Answer the following questions with regard to this offering:

Required:

a. If bond buyers demand a return of 8% from the investment in these bonds, what would be the issue price of the bonds? The following present-value factors may be useful:

> Present value of $1:
> 15 periods @ 8% = 0.31524
> 30 periods @ 4% = 0.30831
>
> Present value of an annuity in arrears:
> 15 periods @ 8% = 8.55948
> 30 periods @ 4% = 17.29199

b. The bonds were actually issued at a price of 31.393, which implies a yield of 7.875%. Assuming the bonds were issued on August 1, 1997, construct the entries that would be made during 1997 to account for these bonds. Indicate the net book value of the bonds at the end of 1997. Niagara closes its books on December 31.

20. Note 7 to the 1995 financial statements of CHC Helicopter Corp. (Exhibit 10-17) describes its senior subordinated notes which were issued during 1994.

Required:

a. What are senior subordinated notes?

b. Were the notes issued at par, below par or above par? (Hint: these notes were issued in U.S. dollars but the financial statements are in Canadian dollars.)

c. The notes pay interest each January 15 and July 15. CHC Helicopter Corp.'s year end is April 30. Assume interest was paid on January 15, 1994 as required. Prepare the journal entry to accrue the interest to April 30, 1994 and then prepare the journal entry on July 15, 1994 to pay the second instalment of interest.

d. During 1995, some of the notes were repurchased by the corporation. Calculate how much was paid to buy them on the market.

21. On March 31, 1995, Comac Food Group Inc. had two long-term bank loans and two long-term notes payable outstanding (see Exhibit 10-18). The notes consist of two notes, one for $7,000 and one for $25,000.

Required:

a. The monthly instalments of principal and interest on the $25,000 note are $700. Prepare the journal entries for the April and May payments assuming that they are made on April 30 and May 31. (Hint: part of the $700 goes to interest and the remainder against the principal.)

EXHIBIT 10-17

CHC Helicopter Corp.

Excerpted from Notes to the Financial Statements

(Tabular amounts in thousands of Canadian dollars, except per share amounts)

7. Senior subordinated notes

During 1994, the Company completed a note issue of U.S. $85,000,000 through the issuance of 85,000 units with each unit consisting of U.S. $1,000 principal amount of senior subordinated notes and eight warrants for the purchase of Class A subordinate voting shares. The notes bear interest from December 9, 1993, at a fixed rate of 11½% per annum, payable semi-annually on each January 15 and July 15, commencing July 15, 1994. The notes are unsecured and will mature on July 15, 2002.

During 1995 the Company repurchased U.S.$4,000,000 of these notes at an average of 88.625% of face value, and wrote-off a proportionate amount of the related deferred costs. No significant net gain was realized on the repurchase.

The outstanding balance at April 30 is as follows:

	1995	1994
Principal amount	$ 115,600	$ 117,300
Repurchased and held by the company	5,440	–
Net amount outstanding		
(1995 - U.S.$81,000,000; 1994 - U.S.$85,000,000)	$ 110,160	$ 117,300

EXHIBIT 10-18

COMAC FOOD GROUP INC.
Excerpted from the Notes to the Financial Statements
March 31, 1995 and 1994

9. Long Term Debt
Long term (debt) is comprised of the following

	1995 $	1994 $
Bank loan	401,000	361,000
Bank loan	57,000	80,000
Bank loan	—	18,000
Notes payable	32,000	38,000
	490,000	497,000
Less current portion	36,000	42,000
	454,000	455,000

The first loan is collateralized by assets pledged by Company's Coming Publishing Limited (Publishing), a significant shareholder, and bears interest at the bank's prime rate. At March 31, 1995 the loan facility limit was $600,000. The facility was reduced to $400,000 effective April 26, 1995 and will be further reduced by $100,000 each year to April 30, 1999. There are no principal repayment terms and the Company must pay monthly interest payments. The bank has indicated that they would not demand payment of the loan principal below $400,000 prior to March 31, 1996 as long as the collateral remains in place. As Publishing has indicated that it does not intend to remove or reduce the collateral below $400,000 prior to March 31, 1996, the loan is classified as long term.

The second loan has a general assignment of book debts pledged as collateral, bears interest at the bank's prime rate plus 2% and the bank has indicated it will accept principal repayments of $2,000 per month over the period to September 1997.

At March 31, 1995 the Company has notes payable of $7,000 and $25,000. The first note, payable to Publishing, bears interest at 7% and is repayable in equal monthly instalments of principal and interest of $1,700. The second note bears interest at 11% and is repayable in equal monthly instalments of principal and interest of $700.

b. For both of the bank loans, the note describes items used as collateral. What is collateral? What impact would the type of collateral have on a corporation's ability to borrow money?

c. The first bank loan has interest at "prime". The second bank loan has interest at "prime plus 2%". What factors could you suggest for why the corporation must pay more interest for the second loan?

EXHIBIT 10-19

AT PLASTICS INC.
Consolidated Balance Sheets
As at December 31

(thousands of dollars)	1994	1993
ASSETS		
CURRENT		
Cash	$ 1,357	$ –
Accounts receivable	25,968	19,756
Inventory (note 2)	26,227	23,987
Prepaids	961	435
Investment tax credits recoverable	577	439
	55,090	44,617
FIXED (note 3)	151,201	152,762
OTHER (note 4)	11,355	9,552
	$217,646	$206,931
LIABILITIES		
CURRENT		
Bank overdraft	$ –	$ 15,355
Accounts payable	24,159	18,619
Current portion of long-term debt (note 5)	5,554	158,107
Obligation under capital leases (note 6)	175	326
	29,888	192,407
LONG-TERM DEBT (note 5)	99,217	17,443
OBLIGATION UNDER CAPITAL LEASES (note 6)	496	87
OTHER LIABILITIES (note 7)	2,414	–
	102,127	17,530
	132,015	209,937
SHAREHOLDERS' EQUITY		
CAPITAL STOCK (note 8)	100,667	25,355
DEFICIT	(15,036)	(28,361)
	85,631	(3,006)
	$217,646	$206,931

See accompanying notes to consolidated financial statements.

Approved by the Board

EGERTON W. KING
Director

JOHN N. ABELL
Director

EXHIBIT 10-19 (continued)

AT PLASTICS INC.
Excerpted from Notes to Consolidated Financial Statements

6. Obligation under Capital Leases

Included in fixed assets is computer equipment with a cost of $2,216,900 and accumulated depreciation of $1,319,171 under capital leases which expire by December 1998. Interest is imputed at 8%. The Company is committed to the following payments under the leases:

(thousands of dollars)		
1995	$	221
1996		218
1997		170
1998		165
Total lease payments		774
Less amount representing imputed interest		(103)
Balance of obligation		671
Less current portion		175
Long-term obligation under capital leases	$	496

22. The balance sheet and obligation under capital leases footnote from the 1994 annual report of AT Plastics Inc. are included in Exhibit 10-19 for this problem.

    Required:
    a. Reconstruct the entries made by the AT Plastics during fiscal 1994 to account for the liability portion of its capital lease. Assume that no new leases were signed in 1994 and state any other assumptions used to reconstruct these entries.
    b. AT Plastics develops and manufactures specialty plastics, raw materials and fabricated products. It amortizes its computer equipment over three to five years. Knowing these two facts, suggest reasons why AT Plastics leases its computer equipment instead of buying it directly.
    c. Calculate the debt/equity ratios for AT Plastics for 1993 and 1994. Write a short report evaluating your findings. Include comments on the changes in the components of the debt and the impact of the deficit on the ratios.

EXHIBIT 10-20

FLETCHER CHALLENGE CANADA INC.
Excerpted from Notes to the Statements

17. Employee Retirement Plans

The Company and its Canadian subsidiaries maintain pension plans open to all salaried employees and hourly employees not covered by union pension plans. To December 31, 1993, these pension plans were defined benefit plans which provided pensions based on years of service and earnings.

Effective January 1, 1994, the Canadian defined benefit plan was reorganized to provide a defined contribution segment as well as a defined benefit segment. Employees were offered the option of converting to the defined contribution segment. Those employees who did not opt to convert to the defined contribution segment remain in the defined benefit segment. Employees hired subsequent to January 1, 1994 enrol in the defined contribution segment. The defined contribution segment does not provide a minimum pension based on years of service and earnings; instead, contributions are based on a percentage of an

employee's earnings with the employee's pension benefits based on these contributions along with earnings from these contributions. For the defined contribution segment, the Company's obligations are satisfied upon crediting contributions to the employees' accounts.

The Company's U.S. subsidiaries maintain various defined benefit pension plans which cover substantially all of their employees. Benefits are based on years of service and earnings for salaried employees and a specified dollar amount per year of service for hourly employees.

Based on the most recent actuarial valuations of these plans as of December 31, 1994 and April 1, 1995, respectively, there was no unfunded liability for past services.

Utilizing management estimates, which include the effect of plan amendments made to June 30, 1995, the status of the defined benefit pension plans is as follows as at June 30:

(in millions of dollars)	1995	1994
Present value of accrued pension benefits	$ 338.5	$ 337.2
Pension fund assets	$ 374.0	$ 404.5

---

23. The note on employee retirement plans from the 1995 financial statements of Fletcher Challenge Canada is included in Exhibit 10-20.

    Required:

    a. Describe the pension plan structure of Fletcher Challenge Canada.

    b. Suggest reasons why Fletcher Challenge made the change it did in 1994.

    c. Is the pension plan overfunded or underfunded? To which plan are these amounts attributed? Why are you not given any amounts for the other plan?

24. The balance sheet and income statement from the 1995 annual report of Western Star Trucks Holdings Ltd. are included in Exhibit 10-21.

    Required:

    a. Calculate the debt/equity ratios and the times interest earned ratios for 1994 and 1995. Ignore the "Minority Interest" amount included with the 1995 liabilities.

    b. Write a short report evaluating the ratios that you calculated in part (a).

EXHIBIT 10-21

WESTERN STAR TRUCK HOLDINGS LTD.
Consolidated Balance Sheets

As at June 30 [in thousands of dollars]	1995	1994
ASSETS		
Current		
Cash and short-term investments	58,834	20,863
Cash collateral deposits – LSVW Contract [notes 8 and 9]	2,480	8,488
Accounts receivable	47,320	41,945
Prepaid expenses and deposits	4,944	589
Inventories [note 5]	66,519	52,902
Deferred LSVW account [note 4]	7,314	10,076
Total current assets	187,411	134,863
Capital assets [note 6]	37,893	10,967
Deferred costs [note 7]	21,978	14,056
	247,282	159,886
LIABILITIES, MINORITY INTEREST AND SHAREHOLDERS' EQUITY		
Current		
Accounts payable	64,148	80,167
Accrued liabilities	31,966	11,538
Income taxes payable	5,845	4,485
Customer deposits	16,491	–
Loans and advances and capital lease obligations [note 8]	10,893	5,683
Total current liabilities	129,343	101,873
Deferred income tax	1,794	–
Customer deposits – non-current	3,438	–
Loans and advances and capital lease obligations – non-current [note 8]	14,316	13,318
Total liabilities	148,891	115,191
Commitments and contingencies [note 9]		
Minority interest [note 10]	15,000	–
Shareholders' equity		
Share capital [note 12]	32,166	31,633
Retained earnings	51,225	13,062
Total shareholders' equity	83,391	44,695
	247,282	159,886

See accompanying notes

On behalf of the Board:

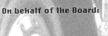

Director   Director

EXHIBIT 10-21 (continued)

WESTERN STAR TRUCK HOLDINGS LTD.

Consolidated Statements of Operations and Retained Earnings

Years ended June 30	1995	1994
[in thousands of dollars except per share amounts]		
Revenue	726,022	426,974
Expenses		
Cost of sales	645,301	384,769
Selling and administrative	25,912	14,462
Interest [income] expense – net	[81]	457
	671,132	399,688
Net income before minority interest and taxes	54,890	27,286
Minority interest [note 10]	–	[1,578]
Net income before taxes	54,890	25,708
Income tax expense [note 13]	13,331	4,586
Net income	41,559	21,122
Retained earnings [deficit], opening balance	13,062	[5,317]
Share issue costs	271	[2,743]
Dividends paid	[3,667]	–
Retained earnings, closing balance	51,225	13,062
Net income per share [note 16]	3.73	2.61
Fully diluted net income per share	3.58	2.61

c. Western Star Trucks' amount of debt and shareholders' equity increased between 1994 and 1995. Analyze the components that caused this increase and comment on how these items might affect your evaluation of the health of this corporation.

25. The balance sheet and income statement from the 1994 annual report of Petromet Resources Limited are included in Exhibit 10-22.

Required:

a. Petromet has made many changes to its debt structure between 1993 and 1994. Calculate the debt/equity ratios and the times interest earned ratios for 1993 and 1994.

b. Write a short report evaluating the ratios you calculated in part (a).

c. One of the material components of the change is a "deferred gain" of $2,400,000. What is a deferred gain? Comment on how this component might affect how you evaluated the ratios in part (a).

EXHIBIT 10-22

PETROMET RESOURCES LIMITED
Consolidated Balance Sheet

	December 31, 1994	December 31, 1993
ASSETS		
Current		
Cash and term deposits	$ 10,869	$ 8,913,876
Accounts receivable	10,083,645	5,447,698
Investments (market value $3,294,000; 1993—$2,047,000)	2,525,000	125,000
	12,619,514	14,486,574
Property, Plant and Equipment (Note 3)	80,055,512	25,921,770
	$ 92,675,026	$ 40,408,344
LIABILITIES		
Current		
Accounts payable and accrued liabilities	$ 15,230,476	$ 10,003,845
Long Term Bank Debt (Note 4)	16,142,350	—
Convertible Debentures (Note 5)	25,000,000	—
Deferred Gain (Note 6)	2,400,000	—
Future Abandonment and Site Restoration Costs	345,000	182,000
Deferred Income Taxes	222,000	264,000
SHAREHOLDERS' EQUITY		
Share capital (Note 7)	29,602,364	17,169,446
Shares reserved for issuance (Note 7)	—	10,152,705
Retained earnings	3,732,836	2,636,348
	33,335,200	29,958,499
	$ 92,675,026	$ 40,408,344

On Behalf of the Board:

(signature)

(Director)

EXHIBIT 10-22 (continued)

PETROMET RESOURCES LIMITED
Consolidated Statement of Income

	Year ended December 31, 1994	Year ended December 31, 1993	Eleven months ended December 31, 1992
REVENUE			
Petroleum and natural gas	$ 9,547,723	$ 7,268,209	$ 2,176,598
Royalties, net of Alberta Royalty Tax Credit	(1,473,812)	(1,354,110)	(363,728)
Other income	116,969	149,226	37,493
	8,190,880	6,063,325	1,850,363
EXPENSES			
Operating	1,256,874	795,778	334,649
General and administrative	593,418	404,929	457,709
Depletion and depreciation	3,122,955	2,318,950	518,241
Interest on long term debt	1,315,117	86,489	38,614
Other interest	272,028	–	–
	6,560,392	3,606,146	1,349,213
Income before other items and taxes	1,630,488	2,457,179	501,150
Other items (Note 8)	–	849,169	(1,434,549)
Income (loss) before taxes	1,630,488	3,306,348	(933,399)
Taxes (Note 9)	534,000	670,000	–
NET INCOME (LOSS)	$ 1,096,488	$ 2,636,348	$ (933,399)
Earnings (loss) per share	$ 0.04	$ 0.11	$ (0.07)
Weighted average number of common shares outstanding (Note 1(d))	26,506,240	22,966,413	13,840,173

Consolidated Statement of Retained Earnings

	Year ended December 31, 1994	Year ended December 31, 1993	Eleven months ended December 31, 1992
Balance, beginning of period	$ 2,636,348	$ (9,278,154)	$ (8,344,755)
Reduction of deficit against stated share capital (Note 7)	–	9,278,154	–
Net income (loss)	1,096,488	2,636,348	(933,399)
BALANCE, END OF PERIOD	$ 3,732,836	$ 2,636,348	$ (9,278,154)

CASE

WASSELEC'S MOVING AND STORAGE CORPORATION

Wasselec's Moving and Storage Corporation is a small company based in the Halifax area. It operates in both the residential and business markets. To service its various clients, Wasselec's Moving and Storage owns two large moving trucks (tractor and trailer units), six medium-sized cartage trucks, two large vans and two cars. Because its business relies on its vehicles, it has always been the policy of the corporation to purchase new vehicles on a regular rotation basis. Its accountant and vehicle service manager have established guidelines that trigger when a new vehicle should be purchased. For example, the large vans are replaced every 100,000 kilometres, the tractors every nine years, and the trailers every fifteen years. The President of the corporation recently read an article about the increasing trend toward leasing. She wonders if Wasselec should start leasing its vehicles instead of buying them, and has asked the accountant for some guidance in this matter. The accountant has asked you, a recent addition to the accounting department, for a summary of the advantages and disadvantages of ownership versus leasing.

Required:

Draft a memo to the accountant summarizing the advantages and disadvantages of ownership versus leasing. Be sure to draft your memo specifically about the assets currently owned by Wasselec. Remember as well that the accountant is very busy and, therefore, your memo should be concise.

◤◣ Critical Thinking Question

A formula has been created for defined benefit pension plans to calculate the pension expense for each accounting period. When the calculated pension expense is compared to the amount of cash transferred to a trustee to invest to handle the future obligations of the pension plan, there could be a difference between the two amounts. If the amount of cash transferred is less that the pension expense, a liability for the difference is created. If the amount of cash transferred is greater, an asset is created. The difference between the two amounts is a partial reflection of whether the pension plan is overfunded or underfunded. These amounts are insignificant compared to the total liability of the corporation with respect to the pension plan. Describe the current GAAP disclosure requirements for pensions. Should corporations be required to include a liability on the balance sheet which reflects the future obligation of the corporation with respect to its pension plan? What impact would such a requirement have on the debt/equity ratio? Are users being given enough information about pension plans to make informed decisions?

C H A P T E R

11

Shareholders' Equity

In this chapter, our exploration of balance sheet line items concludes with a discussion of the accounts that constitute the shareholders' equity section. Alternative forms of organizations and the differences that can be expected in shareholders' equity are considered first. This is followed by a detailed discussion of the transactions that affect shareholders' equity in corporations.

FORMS OF ORGANIZATIONS

Sole proprietorship

As discussed briefly in Chapter 1, the simplest form of business is the **sole proprietorship**. The sole proprietorship is a single-owner business. All profits and losses belong to the owner, and all decisions are made by the owner. Because the sole proprietor does not have to report to shareholders, there is less concern in a sole proprietorship about preparing reports according to GAAP. The sole proprietor might want to follow GAAP if the business is trying to obtain a loan from a bank, since bankers would probably insist on financial statements prepared according to GAAP. GAAP statements might also be required if the sole proprietorship is regulated. The owner prepares information that is useful in making the decisions that need to be made to run the business.

Revenue Canada also wants information about the financial results of a sole proprietorship. Sole proprietors are required to combine the results of their businesses with their personal income for tax purposes. There is no separate taxation for sole proprietorships as there is for corporations. The rules for reporting income to Revenue Canada are, therefore, likely to be the single most important motivator for producing financial statements. The accounting methods used by the sole proprietor are more likely to follow those used for tax purposes than those set forth under GAAP.

With regard to owners' equity accounts, there is little reason for the owner to distinguish the initial investment from the income retained in the business. For this reason, the owners' equity section of the sole proprietorship typically has only one account, which is sometimes called owner's capital. Cash withdrawn from the business for personal use is usually referred to as a withdrawal by the owner. These withdrawals are the equivalent of dividends in a corporation. Because the owner is taxed on the combined basis of personal income and business income, these withdrawals are not taxed in the same manner as corporate dividends.

Partnership

A second form of business that is very similar to a sole proprietorship is a **partnership**. In a partnership, two or more individuals agree to conduct business under one name. The involvement of the partners in the partnership can vary greatly. The rights and responsibilities of the partners are generally specified in a document called a **partnership agreement**. This document is very important because it specifies how the partners will share in the profits and losses of the partnership, as well as how the assets of the partnership will be distributed if the partnership dissolves. In the absence of a partnership agreement, the distribution of assets and profits is assumed to be equal for all partners. If the partners intend to share profits in some other proportion, this must be stated in a partnership agreement. For tax purposes, partnerships are not taxable entities; the income earned by the partners is passed through to them and must be reported on their personal tax returns, similar to the treatment of sole proprietorship income.

One of the major accounting problems in a partnership is distinguishing the roles that partners play as owners, creditors, and employees. For example, should the compensation paid to a partner who works as an employee of the partnership be treated as an expense of the partnership, that is, all partners share in this expense, or should it be treated as a part of the partner's share of the profits from the business? As another example, suppose a partner lends money to the partnership. Should this be viewed as a liability of the partnership, or as part of the equity contributed by this partner? If the partnership liquidates, should this partner get paid back first as a creditor and then share in whatever is left, or should the loan be considered a part of the partner's equity? There is no one right answer to these questions. These issues should all be addressed in the partnership agreement.

The accounting for the owners' equity section of a partnership requires that the partnership keep a separate account for each partner, usually called the partner's **capital account**. Each period, the profits or losses of the partnership must be distributed among the partners' capital accounts. This is usually a relatively complex process that takes into consideration the issues discussed in the preceding paragraph. Sometimes there is also an account for each partner called a **drawing account**. This is an account that keeps track of the amounts withdrawn by the partner during the period. It is similar to a dividends declared account in a corporation. It is a reduction in the capital account of the specific partner. As with sole proprietorships, such withdrawals are not taxable.

Detailed accounting rules for partnerships are generally covered in advanced accounting texts and will not be discussed here. The accounting for the transactions of a partnership other than owners' equity is essentially the same as that discussed in this book for corporations.

◤◣ Corporations

The third major form of business organization is the **corporation**, which has been the focus of most of this book. It differs from sole proprietorships and partnerships in at least two significant ways. The first is that the corporation is legally separate from the shareholders. While the owners of sole proprietorships and partnerships can be held liable for the debts of their businesses, corporate shareholders have limited liability for the debts of the corporations they own. Corporate shareholders cannot be made to pay for the debts of the corporation out of their personal assets. Sole proprietors and partners do not enjoy this limited liability.

The second significant way in which corporations differ from proprietorships is the manner in which they are taxed. Because the corporation is viewed as a separate legal entity, Revenue Canada and provincial governments impose a corporate tax on the income earned by the corporation. This corporate tax is in addition to the personal income tax that shareholders pay on their personal income when they receive dividends or when they sell their shares and experience a gain or loss.

The basics of accounting for shareholders' equity in a corporation have been covered in earlier chapters of the book. Later in this chapter, more details are provided concerning more complex transactions that involve shareholders' equity in a corporation.

Advantages and Disadvantages of the Different Forms of Organization

While there are many differences among sole proprietorships, partnerships, and corporations, the two primary differences just mentioned, legal liability and taxes, are sufficiently important to warrant detailed discussion here. With regard to legal liability, the owners of a sole proprietorship or partnership are fully liable for the debts of the business. If the business does not have sufficient assets to pay its debts, creditors have the right to try to collect from the personal assets of the owners. This feature is sometimes referred to as **unlimited liability**. The shareholders of corporations, on the other hand, enjoy **limited liability**. The most a shareholder can lose is the amount of the investment in the shares. Creditors cannot seek satisfaction of their claims from the personal assets of corporate shareholders.

Limited liability is obviously an advantage of the corporate form of organization. There are some forms of partnerships, called **limited partnerships**, that also share some of this advantage. In limited partnerships, there are **general partners** and **limited partners**. General partners have unlimited liability, whereas limited partners have limited liability. The downside for the limited partners is that they also have limited say in making decisions within the partnership.

Where taxes are concerned, income of partnerships and sole proprietorships is not taxed at the business level because the income flows through to the individuals. Personal tax is then assessed according to the tax bracket of the individual owner. Corporations, on the other hand, are subject to corporate taxation. Income to the individual shareholders, in the form of dividends or capital gains (if they sell their shares), is then taxed at the individual level. Corporate income is, therefore, subject to double taxation, although the income tax rules include methods intended to reduce the impact of this double taxation. This is obviously a disadvantage of the corporate form.

There are other advantages and disadvantages to each form of business. For example, incorporation requires a significant amount of paperwork and regulation, which makes a sole proprietorship or partnership easier to form. Although partnerships can be formed without any written agreement, a written partnership agreement prepared with legal assistance is advisable in order to avoid the possibility of disagreements among the partners. Corporations, on the other hand, can raise additional capital much more easily than partnerships; they simply issue more shares or bonds. Partnerships and sole proprietorships are limited by the assets contributed by the owners, or earned and not withdrawn.

In Canada, corporations own the vast majority of business assets and almost all large businesses are organized as corporations. That is why we focus on accounting for corporations in this text.

CORPORATIONS

Shareholders of corporations require certain types of legal protection, especially because the owners of most corporations are absentee shareholders; that is, they are not intimately involved in the day-to-day business of the corporation. This protection is provided by the laws of the jurisdiction under which the corporation is incorporated. In Canada, corporations may be incorporated under the federal **Canada Business Corporations Act**, or under similar provincial acts that have been established in all 10 provinces. When investors decide to establish a business in the form of a corporation, they first must decide under which act they want to be incorporated. Normally, most corporations in Canada are incorporated under the provincial laws in which the business, or at least the head office of the corporation, is to be located. After this has been decided, the founding investors prepare a document called the **articles of incorporation**. The articles of incorporation include information about what type of business the corporation will conduct, how the Board of Directors will be organized, who the management will be, details of the shares that will be issued, and other information. The exact content of the articles will depend on the decisions of the incorporating shareholders. Once the corporation has been incorporated, the articles of incorporation can generally be amended only by a vote of the shareholders.

SHARES

For accounting purposes, the most important section of the articles of incorporation is the description of the shares that will be issued. The maximum number of shares that the corporation can issue is specified in the articles. These are referred to as the **authorized shares**. In the past, the articles could also specify a dollar amount that was attached to each share, which was known as the **par value**. Under most jurisdictions in Canada, par value shares are no longer permitted.

The original purpose of par value was to protect the corporation's creditors by setting a limit on the dividends the corporation could pay. In most jurisdictions, a corporation was able to declare dividends up to only the value of the retained earnings. It could not pay dividends out of par value (i.e., the balance in the common shares account). If a corporation were allowed to declare a dividend equal to the total of retained earnings and the balance in the equity accounts, the shareholders might then pay themselves a dividend of this amount (sometimes called a **liquidating dividend** because it liquidated the shareholders' investment). This might have left creditors with insufficient assets to satisfy their claims. Corporations were able to avoid this constraint by setting very low par values and selling the shares at prices above the par value. Only the total of the par values was credited to the shares account; the excess was credited to an account called paid-in capital or premium on shares. Dividends paid out of this account were in fact liquidating dividends since they reduced the paid-in equity of the corporation.

While this is still theoretically true about par values today, the practical value of a par value is almost nonexistent. The par value of most shares was so small compared to the level of other shareholders' equity accounts and the level of liabilities that it provided very little protection to creditors. For this reason, par value shares can no longer be issued in most jurisdictions in Canada, and most new shares have no par value. Today the total amount received for shares is put into one account. This total amount is referred to as the legal capital and must be kept intact and cannot be paid out as dividends. This provides more protection for creditors.

The articles of incorporation also specify the *classes* or *types* of shares that can be issued by the corporation if more than one class of shares is to be issued. In many corporations, more than one class is authorized so that the corporation has more flexibility in attracting different kinds of investors. For example, some investors want the assurance of regular dividends to provide a steady income; others prefer no regular dividends but hope for increasing share values so that they can earn capital gains when they eventually sell the shares.

The different classes of shares differ in the rights that accrue to their holders. Two major classes of shares, **common shares** and **preferred shares**, are discussed in the following subsections. Different classes of shares can be authorized within each of these two major types. For example, some corporations have multiple classes of common shares and multiple classes (sometimes these are called issues) of preferred shares. BCE Inc., for example, has one class of common shares and four series of preferred shares (Series a, b, c, and d), as shown in Exhibit 11-1. Note that BCE's Board of Directors has the power to set specific terms and conditions for each series. This allows for a great deal of flexibility in attracting investment in BCE.

Common Shares

If a corporation issues just one class of shares, they are called **common shares**. Corporations generally issue common shares through a firm of investment bankers, known as underwriters, in much the same way that bonds are issued (see Chapter 10 for a discussion of this process). When common or preferred shares are issued, the details and features of the shares being issued are discussed in a legal document called a **prospectus**, which is issued to potential investors when shares (or a bond) are initially issued (sold).

Common shares carry a basic set of rights, that allow the owner to share proportionately (based on the number of shares held) in:

1. Profits and losses
2. The selection of management of the corporation
3. Assets upon liquidation
4. Subsequent issues of shares (although not all jurisdictions in Canada provide for this basic right)

Rather than establishing complex income-sharing rules the way a partnership does, a corporation retains all of its profits. However, it is sometimes useful to think of a corporation's profits or losses as being allocated to its shares, even if

EXHIBIT 11-1

BCE INC.
Consolidated Balance Sheets

At December 31	Notes	1994	($ millions) 1993
Assets			
Current assets			
Cash and short-term investments		1,367	121
Accounts receivable	(7)	5,043	5,236
Inventories	(8)	1,624	1,610
Prepaid expenses		312	286
Deferred income taxes		451	427
		8,797	7,680
Investments in associated and other companies	(9)	3,889	2,745
Property, plant and equipment, net	(10)	22,157	22,308
Long-term notes and other receivables		738	1,239
Deferred charges		1,657	1,002
Goodwill		854	1,734
Total assets		38,092	36,708
Liabilities			
Current liabilities			
Accounts payable and accrued liabilities		6,087	6,277
Income and other taxes payable		199	104
Debt due within one year	(11)	2,019	2,591
		8,305	8,972
Long-term debt	(12)	11,434	10,449
Deferred income taxes		2,025	2,000
Other long-term liabilities		999	859
Total liabilities		22,763	22,280
Non-controlling interest		3,977	3,505
Preferred shares	(13)	1,229	1,229
Common shareholders' equity			
Common shares	(14)	5,813	5,728
Common share purchase warrants	(15)	38	39
Contributed surplus	(14)	1,003	1,007
Retained earnings		3,136	2,908
Foreign currency translation adjustment	(16)	133	12
		10,123	9,694
Commitments and contingent liabilities	(17)		
Total liabilities and shareholders' equity		38,092	36,708

On behalf of the Board of Directors:

Warren Chippindale   E. Neil McKelvey   David A. Lazzarato
Director   Director   Vice-President and Comptroller

Excerpted from Notes to the Statements

13. Preferred Shares

Authorized
The articles of incorporation of the Corporation provide for an unlimited number of First Preferred Shares and Second Preferred Shares. The articles authorize the Directors to issue such shares in one or more series and to fix the number of shares of each series, and the conditions attaching thereto, prior to their issue.

At December 31	1994		1993	
Outstanding	Number of shares	Stated capital ($ millions)	Number of shares	Stated capital ($ millions)
First Preferred Shares				
Series J shares (a)	600	300	600	300
$1.95 shares, Series M (b)	8,000,000	200	8,000,000	200
Series N shares (c)	700	350	700	350
Series O shares (d)	10,000,000	379	10,000,000	379
Total outstanding (e)		1,229		1,229

EXHIBIT 11-1 (continued)

BCE Inc.

Excerpted from Notes to the Statements

13. Preferred Shares (continued)

(a) Series J shares

The Cumulative Redeemable First Preferred Shares, Series J were issued in March 1989, by way of private placement at $500,000 per share to yield 7.64%. The Series J preferred shareholders were entitled to cumulative annual dividends of $38,200 per share, payable quarterly, to September 29, 1994. After that date, the dividend rate is determined by one of: direct negotiation between BCE Inc. and holders of the shares; bids solicited from investment dealers; or an auction procedure. The dividend rate is currently determined pursuant to the auction procedure under which it may not exceed 0.40% plus the Bankers' Acceptance Rate as such term is defined in the Articles of Amendment creating the Series J shares. These shares, which are non-voting except in certain circumstances where Series J preferred shareholders are entitled to 5,000 votes per share, were not redeemable prior to September 30, 1994. From that date, they are redeemable, at the Corporation's option, at a price of $500,000 per share.

(b) $1.95 shares

The $1.95 Cumulative Redeemable Retractable First Preferred Shares, Series M were issued in April 1989, at $25 per share to yield 7.80%. The $1.95 preferred shareholders are entitled to cumulative annual dividends of $1.95 per share, payable quarterly. These shares, which are non-voting except in certain circumstances where $1.95 preferred shareholders are entitled to one vote per share, are redeemable at the holder's option on April 30, in each of the years 1995 and 1996, at $25 per share, and on or after April 30, 1995, at the Corporation's option, at $25 per share. BCE Inc. may elect, on or before March 16, 1995, to create a further series of preferred shares into which the $1.95 shares will be convertible on a share for share basis, at the option of the holder, on April 30, 1995.

(c) Series N shares

The Cumulative Redeemable First Preferred Shares, Series N were issued in October 1989, by way of private placement at $500,000 per share to yield 7.55%. The Series N preferred shareholders were entitled to cumulative annual dividends of $37,750 per share, payable quarterly, to November 29, 1994. After that date, the dividend rate is determined by one of: direct negotiation between BCE Inc. and holders of the shares; bids solicited from investment dealers; or an auction procedure. The dividend rate is currently determined pursuant to the auction procedure under which it may not exceed 0.40% plus the Bankers' Acceptance Rate as such term is defined in the Articles of Amendment creating the Series N shares. These shares, which are non-voting except in certain circumstances where Series N preferred shareholders are entitled to 5,000 votes per share, were not redeemable prior to November 30, 1994. From that date, they are redeemable, at the Corporation's option, at a price of $500,000 per share.

(d) Series O shares

On April 26, 1990, BCE Inc. issued 10,000,000 Variable Rate Cumulative Redeemable Retractable and Convertible First Preferred Shares, Series O. The Series O preferred shareholders are entitled to receive quarterly cumulative dividends in an amount equal to the greater of the quarterly dividend declared on common shares of BCE Inc. and $0.65 per share. The Series O preferred shares, which are non-voting except in certain circumstances where the Series O preferred shareholders are entitled to one vote per share, are retractable at the option of the holders on April 27, 1995, at a price of $41.75 per share. After April 28, 1995, Series O preferred shares will be redeemable, at the Corporation's option, at $41.75 per share. On April 28, 1995, holders of Series O preferred shares may acquire, for each Series O preferred share held, one common share of BCE Inc. by the combined effect of the tendering for conversion of one Series O preferred share and the exercise of one warrant together with a cash payment of $4.00 per warrant (see note 15 for a description of the warrants).

(e) As set forth in (b) and (d) above, the $1.95 and the Series O preferred shares which totalled $579 million are redeemable at the option of their holders on April 30, 1995 and 1996 and on April 27, 1995, respectively.

these earnings or losses are not actually paid out. The resulting per-share figure is useful in determining if the corporation's profits are increasing or decreasing on an individual share basis. This **earnings per share** figure that corporations calculate provides a measure of performance that all shareholders can use. Recall from Chapter 3 that this is a calculation that consists of dividing the net income of the corporation by the average number of common shares outstanding during the year. A weighted-average is used if the number of common shares outstanding changed during the year. Different classes of shares are entitled to different portions of the earnings. Normally, preferred shares are restricted to the amounts of their dividends, and no more. Common shares normally have no restrictions on their rights to share in earnings once the claims of the creditors and the preferred shares have been satisfied.

If a corporation opts to pay dividends (they are not obligated to do so), shareholders share proportionately in the distribution of earnings in the form of dividends. Corporations, in addition to reporting earnings per share, often report dividends per share. As will be seen shortly, this right may be amended for different classes of shares, especially, for preferred shares.

Common shareholders also have the right to vote in the selection of management for the corporation. The standard rule for voting is one share, one vote. The more shares an individual owns, the greater the influence of the individual in the corporation. One of the shareholders' most important votes is to elect members of the Board of Directors. The Board of Directors then represents the shareholders, and most decisions are made by a vote of the Board of Directors rather than by a vote of all shareholders. The Board of Directors hires (and fires) top-level management of the corporation. The Board also declares the dividends that are paid to shareholders.

The third right of common shareholders is to share in assets upon liquidation. If a corporation goes bankrupt or otherwise liquidates, there is an established order in which creditors and shareholders are paid. Common shareholders come last on that list; whatever is left after creditors are paid is then split proportionately among them based on their relative number of shares. This means that common shareholders bear the highest risk, since there may be nothing left over for them.

The fourth right of common shares is to share proportionately in any new issuance of shares. This is sometimes called the **preemptive right**. Preemptive rights are not automatic. They must be explicitly stated in the articles of incorporation. This right allows current holders of shares to retain their proportionate interest in the corporation when new shares are issued. For example, if a shareholder owns 20% of a corporation's shares, then that shareholder has the preemptive right to purchase 20% of any new shares of that class that may be issued. Without this right, an investor that had a **controlling interest** in a corporation (i.e., more than 50% of the outstanding shares) could lose that controlling interest if the new shares were issued to another investor. Of course this scenario is unlikely as controlling interest includes the right to vote for the directors of the corporation, so directors who support the majority owner can be elected. The greatest protection is for shareholders who own a minority interest in a corporation. Preemptive rights prevent their ownership interest from being diluted.

When more than one class of common shares is issued, each class of common shares is distinguished by some amendment to the fundamental rights just described. For example, a second class of nonvoting common shares might be issued that may be entitled to conversion to voting common shares under certain conditions. This obviously affects the control that holders of the voting common shares have over the operations of the corporation. There might also be differences in the rights to share in the liquidation values of the assets. Comac Food Group Inc. provides an example of a corporation with two classes of common shares, Class A performance shares and Class B common shares, as shown in Exhibit 11-2.

Dividends paid to different classes of common shares may also be paid on a different basis, although each outstanding share of any class of shares will be paid the same amount.

EXHIBIT 11-2

COMAC FOOD GROUP INC.
Excerpted from Notes to the Statements
March 31, 1995 and 1994

11. Share Capital

AUTHORIZED

Class A performance shares

1,500,000 authorized Class A non-voting performance shares are convertible on a one to one basis in increments of 150,000 shares to Class B common shares upon the Company reaching certain performance levels measured by cash flow from operations. Each performance level increases in increments of $100,000 with the first performance level starting at $300,000 per annum.

Common shares – Class B

An unlimited number of Class B voting common shares are authorized, without nominal or par value.

Preferred shares – Class A

200,000 authorized Class A non-voting preferred shares are without nominal or par value and are convertible on a one to one basis to Class B common shares. The shares are retractable by the holder and redeemable by the Company for $1 each plus unpaid accrued dividends. Cumulative dividends of 7% of the redemption amount are compounded and payable annually.

Preferred shares – Class B

An unlimited number of Class B non-voting preferred shares are authorized, without nominal or par value.

The first series of 131,434 Class B preferred shares bear cumulative 7% dividends and retractable by the Company at any time, for $1 each plus unpaid accrued dividends.

The second series of 400,000 Class B preferred shares are convertible on a 1 to 3.21 basis to Class B common shares, at any time. The shares are retractable by the holder, at $1.124 plus unpaid accrued dividends and redeemable by the Company, for $1.124 plus unpaid, accrued dividends. Cumulative dividends compounded and payable on a monthly basis which fluctuated from 6.43% to 9.34% for 1995 [1994 – 5.81% to 6.43%], based on the prime interest rate and adjusted annually for changes in Federal and Provincial dividend tax rates.

Preferred Shares

Preferred shares are shares that have preference over common shares with regard to dividends. This does not mean that preferred shareholders are *guaranteed* a dividend. However, if dividends are declared, they will receive dividends before common shareholders. Many times, in addition to the preference for dividends, there is also some preference with regard to assets in the event of liquidation.

The amount of the preferred dividend is usually stated as a dollar amount per share, such as a $2 preferred shares issue. Such an issue would pay a dividend of $2 per share per year. You can see examples of this type in the balance sheet of BCE Inc. in Exhibit 11-1, where the corporation lists a $1.95 Series M and a $0.65 Series O preferred shares, among others.

EXHIBIT 11-2 (continued)

COMAC FOOD GROUP INC.
Excerpted from Notes to the Statements

Issued and Outstanding

	1995		1994	
	Number	Amount $	Number	Amount $
Performance shares				
Issued and outstanding throughout the year	1,500,000	2,000	1,500,000	2,000
Class B common shares				
Issued beginning of year	11,262,217	2,405,000	11,237,217	2,402,000
Issued to acquire Pastel [note 6]	179,109	52,000	—	—
Issued under options	945,375	78,000	25,000	2,000
Outstanding at end of year	12,386,701	2,535,000	11,262,217	2,404,000
Preferred shares				
Class A	200,000	200,000	200,000	200,000
Class B – series one	131,434	131,000	131,434	131,000
– series two	400,000	450,000	400,000	450,000
Issued and outstanding throughout the year	731,434	781,000	731,434	781,000
Total consideration		3,318,000		3,187,000

At March 31, 1995, dividends on the Class A and Class B preferred shares were in arrears in the amount of $247,000 [1994 – $179,000].

The Company's cash flow for the year ended March 31, 1995 has reached the first performance level required to convert Class A performance shares to Class B common shares. Conversion of these shares has no effect on either basic or fully diluted earnings per share, for the year ended March 31, 1995.

Besides the difference in priority for dividends, another difference between common and preferred shares is that preferred shares are usually nonvoting. One of the troubling issues in accounting is how to deal with securities, such as preferred shares, that have characteristics that make them look more like debt than common shares. Nonvoting preferred shares with a fixed dividend amount are not much different from debt (which is also nonvoting) that has a fixed interest payment. The only real difference is that the corporation is not obligated to pay the preferred dividend, whereas the interest on the debt is a true obligation and a legal liability.

There are other features of preferred shares with which you should be familiar. Preferred dividends may be **cumulative**. Cumulative means that if a dividend is not declared on the preferred shares in one year, the dividends carry over into the next year. In the second year, both the prior year's preferred dividend and the current year's preferred dividend must be declared before any common dividends can be declared. Dividends from prior years that have not been declared for these types of preferred issues are called **dividends in arrears**. Note that for BCE, all four Series of preferred shares have cumulative dividends. In fact, most preferred shares are cumulative.

Another feature is participation. **Participating preferred shares** are preferred shares that not only have a preference with regard to dividends but, if dividends are declared to common shareholders beyond the level declared to the preferred shareholders, the preferred shareholders share in the excess dividends. For example, the BCE Series O preferred shares mentioned in Exhibit 11-1 are entitled to receive a quarterly preferred dividend of $0.65 per share. If the common shares receive a larger dividend, however, then the Series O preferred shares are entitled to receive the same larger amount. Thus, if the common shares receive a quarterly dividend of $0.75 per share, the Series O preferred shares will receive an extra $0.10 dividend per share ($0.75 − $0.65). Most preferred shares are nonparticipating.

Convertible preferred shares are convertible at the option of the shareholder into common shares based on a ratio stated in the articles of incorporation. Note that for BCE, the Series O preferred shares are convertible into common shares with certain conditions attached. Most preferred shares are not convertible. **Redeemable preferred shares** can be sold back to the corporation (retired) at a price and at times specified in the articles at the option of the shareholder. **Retractable preferred shares** can be bought back by the corporation (retired) at a price at and times specified in the articles at the option of the issuing corporation.

While the features of various classes of shares differ, the accounting issues relating to them are primarily the same. Therefore, in the sections that follow, we limit the discussion to common shares.

Issuance of Common Shares

When common shares are issued for cash, the corporation accounts for the proceeds from the issuance by debiting the cash account. The credit entry is then to a common shares account. This common shares account is sometimes referred to as **paid-in capital** or **legal capital**. Remember that to provide protection for creditors the amount credited to the common shares account cannot be paid out as dividends.

To illustrate the issuance entry, suppose that Rosman Corporation issues 1,000 common shares for $20 a share. The following entry would be made:

SHARES ISSUANCE ENTRY:		
A − Cash	20,000	
SE − Common shares		20,000

Historically, corporations were permitted to issue shares that had a stated or par value. The terms stated or par value were originally intended to indicate the underlying value of the shares. With stated or par value shares, only the total of the stated or par value was credited to the common shares account, and any remaining amount was credited to another equity account. The use of stated and par values is generally no longer permitted in most jurisdictions in Canada, although you may find that some corporations may be incorporated in jurisdictions that permit them and some corporations from other jurisdictions still have some par value shares that were issued in the past and not converted to no-par shares.

To illustrate the issuance entry for par value shares, suppose that Green Corporation issued 1,000 common shares for $15 a share that had a par value of $10 per share. The following entry would have been made:

SHARES ISSUANCE ENTRY:

A – Cash	15,000	
SE – Common shares		10,000
SE – Contributed capital		5,000

◤◣ Treasury Shares

Subsequent to issuance, the corporation may decide to buy back some of its own shares. It might do this because it wants to reduce the number of shares outstanding, or because it wants to use the shares to satisfy its stock option plans rather than issue new shares. Shares that have been repurchased by the issuing corporation are called **treasury shares**. In most jurisdictions in Canada, treasury shares are cancelled immediately upon purchase. In some jurisdictions, they are not cancelled immediately and are considered to be issued but not outstanding.

Three terms are used to refer to the number of shares of corporations: **authorized shares**, **issued shares**, and **outstanding shares**. The maximum number of shares that can be issued by the corporation according to the articles of incorporation are the **authorized** shares. Many corporations avoid the possible limitations that might result from an authorized limit by stating that they have the right to issue an unlimited number of shares. Those that have been sold by the corporation are considered **issued** shares, and the issued shares less those held as treasury shares that have not yet been cancelled are the **outstanding** shares. Examples of the use of these terms can be found in Note 11 of the financial statements of Comac Food Group Inc. shown in Exhibit 11-2. For Class A Performance Common Shares, there are 1,500,000 shares authorized and outstanding. For Class B Common Shares, there are an unlimited number of shares authorized and 12,386,701 shares issued at March 31, 1995.

When a corporation repurchases its own shares, a credit is made to cash for the cost of the shares. The debit entry then has to reduce shareholders' equity since the shares are no longer outstanding. A problem arises if the cost of the shares repurchased is different from the amount received when the shares were originally issued. Shares issued at different times will likely have been issued for different amounts. If this is the case, then the average issue price must be determined by dividing the total amount in the shares account by the total number of shares outstanding before the repurchase.

As an example, suppose that Lee Industries Ltd. had 150,000 common shares outstanding and a balance of $1,500,000 in its Common Shares account. The average issue price is $10 ($1,500,000/150,000). If Lee repurchases 1,000 shares for $9 each, then it is paying $1 less than the average issue price. This $1 per share is not considered to be a profit or gain, and therefore does not appear in the income statement. The reason for this is that the $1 does not result from an activity that is part of the normal operations of the corporation. The corporation was not incorporated to earn money by trading in its own shares. As a general rule, corporations never earn revenues or incur losses from transactions involving their own equities. Rather, the $1 is still part of shareholders' equity and is credited to a separate account called "Contributed Surplus." The entry to record this repurchase would be as follows:

SE – Common Shares	10,000	
A – Cash		9,000
SE– Contributed surplus		1,000

If Lee had paid $12 per share, it would have paid $2 more than the average issue price per share of $10. In this case, the $2 extra per share would reduce shareholders' equity. Normally the $2 is debited to Retained Earnings as follows:

SE – Common Shares	10,000	
SE – Retained Earnings	2,000	
A – Cash		12,000

Further details on the accounting for treasury share transactions can be found in more advanced accounting texts.

DIVIDENDS, STOCK SPLITS, AND OPTIONS

Dividends

Dividends are payments to shareholders from the total net incomes retained in a corporation in the Retained Earnings account. Dividends are a payment in return for the use of the shareholders' money by the corporation. Dividends are paid to shareholders only if the Board of Directors has voted to declare a dividend. The declaration of a cash dividend by the Board of Directors makes the dividend a legal liability of the corporation. Dividends are not paid on treasury shares because these are held internally by the corporation, and corporations cannot pay dividends to themselves.

Three dates are important in the dividend declaration process. The first is the **date of declaration**. This is the date on which the Board votes to declare a dividend. On the date of declaration, the corporation records its obligation to pay the dividend and reduces retained earnings. Suppose the Rosman Corporation had declared a cash dividend of $1.50 per share when there were 1,000 shares outstanding. The entry to record the declaration would be:

DIVIDEND DECLARATION ENTRY:		
SE – Dividends Declared (Retained Earnings)	1,500	
L – Dividends Payable		1,500

The debit is usually to a Dividends Declared account, which is a temporary account that is closed to Retained Earnings at the end of the accounting period.

Dividends Declared does not appear on the income statement. It is *not* an expense of doing business; it is a return to shareholders of part of their investment. Corporations typically declare dividends quarterly. Therefore, the Dividends Declared account accumulates all four quarterly dividends by the end of the fiscal year. Not all corporations use a Dividends Declared account, but instead debit dividends directly to Retained Earnings.

In the declaration of the dividend, the Board of Directors specifies that the dividend is payable to shareholders of record on the **date of record**. This second important date is the date on which a shareholder must own the shares in order to receive the dividend. The date of record is typically two weeks after the declaration date. This delay is needed because most public corporations' shares are traded every day, so a corporation has no up-to-date record of the owners of its shares. The delay also allows new owners time to inform the corporation that they are new owners of the shares. If the shareholder sells shares before the date of record, the new owner of the shares will then be entitled to receive the dividend.

In the shares market, traders talk about the **ex-dividend day**. The **ex-dividend day** is the day on which shares are sold without the right to receive the dividend. Purchasing the shares on the ex-dividend day means that the buyer will not receive the dividend; it belongs to the seller. As you might expect, the price of the shares decreases on the ex-dividend day to reflect the loss of this dividend. A couple of weeks after the date of record, the corporation pays the dividend. This third important date is called the **date of payment**. Again, a delay is needed so the corporation can update its list of shareholders and calculate the total amount of dividends owed to each shareholder. This total amount is calculated as dividends per share times the number of shares owned.

At the date of record, no entry is made. The corporation is simply trying to find out who owns the shares on this date to determine who is entitled to receive a dividend cheque. On the payment date, the corporation writes a cheque and must make an entry to record the reduction in cash and the payment of the liability. Rosman would make the following entry for the payment of the dividend declared:

DIVIDEND PAYMENT ENTRY:		
L – Dividend Payable	1,500	
A – Cash		1,500

◤◣ Property Dividends

It is also possible for a corporation to declare a dividend that will be settled with some resource other than cash. Dividends of this type are called **property dividends** or **dividends in kind**. These dividends are rare because the assets other than cash that can be paid out are necessarily limited to assets that can be divided into small, equal parts. A story is told of a liquor company that was short on cash but long on excess inventory who declared a dividend of one bottle per share. Whether this actually happened or not is not as important as the concept it illustrates.

The major accounting question for property dividends is how to value the dividend. Should the property be valued at its fair market value, or at its cost? GAAP requires that the property be valued at its fair market value because this represents the value the corporation is giving up to pay the dividend. This means that if the property is currently being carried at cost, a gain or loss must be recognized to bring the property to its fair market value. Suppose that Rosman declares a property dividend that it will make by transferring inventory with a fair market value of $1,200 to its shareholders. The inventory is carried on Rosman's books at $900. The following entries would be made:

PROPERTY DIVIDEND ENTRIES:

Declaration of Dividend (at fair market value)

SE — Property Dividend Declared	1,200	
L — Dividend Payable		1,200

Recognition of Fair Market Value on Declaration Date and Payment of Dividend on Payment Date:

L — Dividend Payable	1,200	
A — Inventory		900
SE — Gain on Inventory		300

Stock Dividends

Stock dividends are dividends that are satisfied by issuing to shareholders additional shares of the corporation instead of cash or property. Stock dividends thus can be used to issue dividends even when the corporation does not want to, or is not in a position to use any of its assets for dividends. Shareholders who receive stock dividends have the option of keeping the new shares received, or of selling them for cash. As with property dividends, the question is: What value should be attached to the shares that are issued? Should the fair market value of the shares be used, or should some other value be selected?

To answer this question, consider the following extreme situations. When a stock dividend is declared, it is stated as a percent of the outstanding shares. Suppose a corporation declares a 100% stock dividend. This means that each shareholder will receive an additional share for each one that is currently held. No cash changes hands in this transaction. What would you expect to happen to the market value of the shares? It is likely that the value of a share would be cut in half. There is no change in the value of the assets or liabilities of the corporation, only a doubling of the number of shares that represent ownership. If there is no change in the value of the corporation, then the price per share should adjust for the number of new shares that have been issued. This suggests that the value of the new shares issued is zero.

At the other extreme, suppose the corporation issues one additional share as a stock dividend. The recipient of the share can probably sell the share for the fair market value of the existing shares on that date. It is unlikely, assuming that there are large numbers of shares already on the market, that the price per share would adjust for the issuance of this one additional share. In this case, then, the fair market value of the share issued would seem to measure adequately the value of the dividend. In theory, the market price should adjust for the issuance of new shares in a stock dividend, regardless of the number of shares issued. As a practical matter, however, it is unlikely that the market will fully adjust for very small stock dividends, which makes the fair market value of the shares a reasonable measure of the value given up by the corporation.

How, then, does the corporation value the shares that are issued in a stock dividend? Since most stock dividends are for relatively small percentages of the shares issued (similar to the second extreme example), most corporations account for them by using the fair market value of the shares as at the date of declaration.

The market price that is used to record the issuance of a **small stock dividend** should be the market price on the date the dividend is declared. The Board of Directors has the power to revoke the stock dividend at any time prior to its actual issuance. This means that the dividend does not represent a legal liability to the corporation on the date of declaration, unlike a cash dividend. For this reason, some corporations do not record an entry on the date of declaration. If an entry is recorded, the credit part of the entry is made to a shareholders' equity account called Stock Dividends Issuable and not to a Dividends Payable account. Upon issuance, the credit is made to the shares account and the Stock Dividends Issuable account is removed.

To illustrate, let's suppose that the Rosman Corporation decides to issue a 15% stock dividend when 1,000 shares are outstanding and the market price of a share is $30 per share. The following entries would be made for the declaration and issuance:

SMALL STOCK DIVIDEND ENTRIES:

Declaration

SE – Dividends Declared	4,500[a]	
SE – Stock dividend Issuable		4,500

Issuance

SE – Stock dividend Issuable	4,500	
SE – Common Shares		4,500

[a](1,000 shares × 15% × $30 per share) = $4,500

Stock Splits

Another transaction that is very similar to a stock dividend is a **stock split**. A stock split is usually stated as a ratio. A two-for-one stock split is one in which each share currently held by shareholders is exchanged for two new shares. When this is done, the numbers of shares authorized and outstanding are adjusted to compensate for the increase in the number of shares. In a two-for-one split, the number of shares outstanding is doubled. Splits typically involve large numbers of shares, and the arguments discussed earlier with regard to large stock dividends apply here as well. The additional shares mean no increase in value to the corporation, so the shares' market price simply adjusts to compensate for the split.

In accounting for a stock split, there is no change in the dollar amounts of any of the shareholders' equity accounts. The only change is that the number of shares issued and outstanding changes. This can be done only with an informal or **memorandum entry** to the accounting system.

A corporation sometimes reasons that a stock split improves the marketability of a corporation's shares. As a corporation grows, the market value of its shares generally rises. The price per share of the shares can get quite high. At a certain level, some investors (particularly individuals) may not have enough funds to invest to be able to buy these high-priced shares. To appeal to these investors, the corporation may split its shares, which will cut the market price per share of the shares. IBM, for example, split its shares numerous times since its incorporation as its price per share escalated.

Stock Options

An **option** on common shares is an agreement between two parties to either buy or sell a share at a fixed price at some future date. There are two types of options related to common shares of which you should be aware. One type of option is granted by a corporation to an employee, which allows the employee to purchase the corporation's shares at fixed prices. This type of option is generally used as a form of compensation and as an incentive to employees. For example, it was reported in many newspapers in 1996 that an executive with the Potash Corporation of Saskatchewan earned almost $3,000,000 by cashing in stock options, buying 12,900 shares at $17.50 and selling them the same day at $102.50 and buying 22,500 shares at $25.50 and selling them at $104.125.

A second type of option is a contract between two investors that grants one investor the option to buy (referred to as a **call option**) or to sell (referred to as a **put option**) a corporation's shares at a fixed price. The shares are bought from, or sold to, the other investors. These options have no effect on the corporation. They are simply a way for investors to speculate on the share price of a given corporation. This type of option is traded in open markets, and price quotations for these options appear in newspapers and other financial publications. Because puts and calls have no effect on the corporation's accounting records, the discussion in this section is restricted to the first type of option, employee stock options.

Employee stock options are generally granted to employees as part of their incentive compensation plan. The idea is to grant employees options to buy the corporation's shares at a price (called the **exercise price**, **strike price**, or sometimes simply **option price**) that is above the current market price. The incentive is for the employees to work hard to improve the performance of the corporation so that the market price of the shares exceeds the exercise price. When the time comes for employees to exercise their options, they pay the exercise price, obtain the shares, and can either sell them for the current market price and realize a profit, or continue to hold the shares in hopes that the price will go up even further. Obviously, if the share price never exceeds the exercise price, the employees will not exercise their options.

One of the major questions for accounting purposes is whether to record compensation expense for this type of incentive-based plan. When options are granted, most of them are not immediately worth anything since the exercise price is above the current share price. This situation is sometimes referred to as the option being **"out of the money."** In addition, some options allow employees to exercise them only after a certain period of time, and only if they are still employed by the corporation. So, even if the option is **"in the money,"** an employee may not be able to benefit immediately from the granting of the option.

If an option is out of the money, does that mean it is worthless? The answer is a qualified no. Employees may not be able to, nor do they have to, exercise the options immediately. There is generally an extended period of time over which the employees can exercise the option. There may, however, be an **expiration date** specified, after which the option can no longer be exercised. The option will be of some value (in present-value terms) if there is some probability that the share price will exceed the exercise price before the expiration date. The more likely this is, the higher the value of the option. In finance, researchers have developed option pricing models, the most famous of which is the **Black–Scholes model**. Option pricing models establish theoretical values for options based on the time to expiration, the exercise price, the volatility of the shares' price, and other parameters. Research has shown that these models provide a reasonable prediction of the prices of options that are traded in option markets.

However, employee stock options generally cannot be traded because they are restricted to the employees to whom they are issued. Therefore, the value of employee stock options is difficult to establish. Because they do not trade, the value of employee stock options can only be estimated. Under current GAAP, employee stock options are viewed as having no accounting value at the time of granting them (when they are out of the money), and no entry is made to record these options. Options that are in the money — that is, when the share price is greater than the exercise price as at the date of granting — may be recognized as compensation expense on the date of granting. The expense is measured by the difference between the shares' price as at the date of grant, and the exercise price.

On the date of exercise, the corporation normally recognizes the receipt of the proceeds from the employee and the issuance of common shares. This entry is no different from any other issuance entry, and the shares are valued at the amount received by the corporation. No recognition is made of the fair value of the shares as at the date of exercise.

Corporations normally disclose details regarding their stock option plans. For example, the disclosure made by Big Rock Brewery Ltd. on March 31, 1995 in Note 6 to the financial statements is shown in Exhibit 11-3.

EXHIBIT 11-3

BIG ROCK BREWERY LIMITED, 1995
Excerpted from Notes to the Statements

6. Share Capital

Authorized
Twenty million (20,000,000) common shares.
One million (1,000,000) preferred shares which may be issued in one or more series with rights, privileges, restrictions and conditions as fixed by the directors prior to the issue of each series.

Common Shares Outstanding

	1995		1994	
	Shares	Amount	Shares	Amount
Beginning of year	4,406,200	$ 5,362,784	4,406,200	$ 5,362,784
Stock options exercised in the year	10,000	40,000		
End of year	4,416,200	$ 5,402,784	4,406,200	$ 5,362,784

As of March 31, 1995, 310,000 (1994 - 120,000) common shares were reserved for the exercising of stock options by staff, two of the directors and a consultant to the company. These options are exercisable as follows:

Expiry Date	# of Shares	Exercise Value
October 31, 1997	110,000	$ 4.00
December 15, 1999	200,000	$14.65

Big Rock provides an interesting example. Note that the options that expire in 1997 will have no value unless Big Rock's share prices go above $4.00 per share. For the options that expire in 1999, the share price must exceed $14.65 before the options have any value. This increase of $10.65 ($14.65 − 4.00) will encourage employees to work hard to increase the value of Big Rock's shares.

STATEMENT OF RETAINED EARNINGS

In the preceding discussions of shares and dividends, we made several references to the use of the retained earnings account. Many corporations summarize the changes to their retained earnings in a separate statement, the Statement of Retained Earnings. The format of this is very simple. It starts with the opening balance of the retained earnings at the beginning of the year. Then it shows the net income or loss for the year, which comes directly from the income statement. This is followed by the dividends declared in the year. Next appear any other items that affect retained earnings. Finally, the balance of the retained earnings at the end of the year appears. The end balance is the one that appears on the current balance sheet.

An example is shown in Exhibit 11-4 for BCE Inc. Note that the balance of the retained earnings at the beginning of the 1994 fiscal year was $2,908,000,000, net income for the year was $1,178,000,000, and dividends of $922,000,000 were declared. Cancellation of common shares (Treasury Shares) resulted in a charge of $28,000,000 to retained earnings, which left the balance at the end of the year of $3,136,000,000.

EXHIBIT 11-4

BCE INC.

Consolidated Statements of Retained Earnings

	Notes	1994	1993	($ millions) 1992
For the years ended December 31				
Balance at beginning of year		2,908	4,475	4,165
Net earnings (loss)		1,178	(656)	1,390
		4,086	3,819	5,555
Deduct:				
Dividends				
Preferred shares		92	94	95
Common shares		830	814	801
		922	908	896
BCE Inc. common shares purchased for cancellation	(14)	28	–	183
Costs related to issuance and redemption of share capital of BCE Inc. and of subsidiaries		–	3	1
		950	911	1,080
Balance at end of year		3,136	2,908	4,475

FINANCIAL STATEMENT ANALYSIS

The Price/Earnings Ratio

A key ratio that involves shareholders' equity is **earnings per share**. We introduced this ratio in Chapter 3, and discussed it in this chapter as well. Earnings per share provides a measure of the earnings relative to the number of common shares outstanding. It is useful for tracking the return earned by the corporation per share over time. It can also be related to the current market price per share by calculating the multiple or **price/earnings ratio**. This is calculated as market price per share/earnings per share and is a convenient way of relating the accounting earnings to the stock market price.

The Return on Shareholders' Equity Ratio

Another useful indicator of return is **return on shareholders' equity**. This is a more general measure than earnings per share because it relates the net income available to common shares to the total of the common shareholders' equity. It is calculated as follows:

$$ROE = \frac{Net\ Income - Preferred\ Dividends}{Average\ Common\ Shareholder'\ Equity}$$

More detailed discussion of other analyses that involve shareholders' equity are found in Chapter 12.

SUMMARY

This chapter discussed the most common forms of business organization, emphasizing corporations. Particular attention was paid to shares and dividends of corporations. This concludes the discussion of the primary accounts on the balance sheet. In the final chapters of the book, financial statement analysis is summarized and complex corporations are discussed. Discussion of complex organizations has been left to the end as they involve more complex issues that require an understanding of the more basic issues that we have already discussed.

AN INTERNATIONAL PERSPECTIVE
REPORTS FROM OTHER COUNTRIES

The accounting for issuance and retirement of common shares is fairly standard across various countries. The biggest difference between Canada and some other countries is in the establishment of reserves. Reserves in other countries are used either to set aside otherwise unappropriated retained earnings so that they are not available to pay dividends, or to record changes in the value of assets or liabilities that do not pass through the income statement. In Canada, these reserves do not affect earnings for the period. In the United Kingdom property, plant, and equipment can be revalued based on current market values. The increases (or decreases) in value do not pass through the income statement, but are instead recorded in a separate account in shareholders' equity. This is similar to the separate accounts in shareholders' equity for translation adjustments under Canadian GAAP.

In Japan, several types of reserves are permitted in the shareholders' equity section. A portion of the balance sheet and several related footnotes of Nippon Steel Corporation are shown in Exhibit 11-5. These disclosures illustrate the use of shareholders' equity reserves. Note also that the word "reserve" is used in the Nippon report for various liabilities. Some of these are also discussed in the footnotes of Nippon. In Canada, use of the word "reserve" is generally discouraged because readers of financial statements may believe it refers to cash that has been set aside, which is erroneous. In Canada, its use is limited to references to appropriations of retained earnings.

EXHIBIT 11-5

NIPPON STEEL COMPANY

	Millions of yen		Thousands of dollars (Note 3)
	1990	1989	*1990*
LIABILITIES			
Current liabilities:			
Short-term loans and long-term loans due within one year (Note 6)	¥ 458,871	¥ 527,910	$ 2,904,249
Bonds and notes due within one year (Note 6)	4,800	54,285	30,379
Payables:			
Notes payable	52,661	49,126	333,299
Accounts payable — trade	260,174	225,908	1,646,673
Accounts payable	72,687	42,497	460,048
	385,523	317,532	2,440,021
Accrued expenses	260,049	226,593	1,645,883
Advances received	117,510	165,505	743,735
Accrued income taxes and enterprise taxes (Note 14)	779	43,315	4,931
Reserve for estimated loss on rationalization of steel production facilities (Note 9)	—	11,080	—
Other	6,607	5,387	41,817
Total current liabilities	1,234,140	1,351,609	7,811,018
Fixed liabilities:			
Bonds and notes (Note 6)	338,883	317,845	2,144,831
Convertible bonds (Note 6)	298,479	—	1,889,107
Long-term loans (Note 6)	253,024	364,775	1,601,423
Deferred translation gains (Note 10)	27,760	38,288	175,697
Reserve for retirement allowances	217,778	220,926	1,378,347
Reserve for special repair (Note 7)	77,074	76,489	487,814
Reserve for estimated loss on planned disposal of tangible fixed assets (Note 8)	11,274	16,867	71,354
Reserve for accrued income taxes on translation gains (Note 10)	6,000	—	37,974
Other	2,632	6,070	16,662
Total fixed liabilities	1,232,907	1,041,262	7,803,213
Total liabilities	2,467,048	2,392,872	15,614,231
SHAREHOLDERS' EQUITY			
Common stock:			
Authorized — 10,000,000,000 shares			
Issued and outstanding, par value ¥50 per share:			
6,888,397,193 and 6,636,705,453 shares at March 31, 1990 and 1989, respectively	418,846	331,835	2,650,929
Legal reserve:			
Additional paid-in capital	122,343	35,583	774,323
Revenue reserve (Note 11)	72,770	69,451	460,575
	195,113	105,035	1,234,898
Special tax-purpose reserve (Note 13)	42,031	40,847	266,022
Voluntary reserves	100,000	80,000	632,911
Retained earnings (Notes 12 and 17)	108,064	68,877	683,951
Total shareholders' equity	864,056	626,594	5,468,713
Total liabilities and shareholders' equity	¥3,331,105	¥3,019,467	$21,082,944

EXHIBIT 11-5 (continued)

NIPPON STEEL COMPANY

7. Reserve for Special Repair

The Company's blast furnaces and hot blast stoves including related machines periodically require substantial component replacements and repairs. Such replacements and repairs will be made generally every seven to ten years in the case of blast furnaces, and every 14 to 20 years in the case of hot blast stoves. The estimated future costs of such work are provided for and charged to income on a straight-line basis over the periods to the dates of the anticipated replacements and repairs. The difference between such estimated costs and actual costs is charged or credited to income at the time the work is carried out.

8. Reserve for Estimated Loss on Planned Disposal of Tangible Fixed Assets

Under the "Comprehensive Medium-Term Plan for Steel Production" for the restructuring of the Company's steel production operations, several of the Company's blast furnaces and the related steel production facilities are scheduled to be shut down. In connection therewith, the Company estimated the loss on disposal of the designated steel production facilities (estimated book value less salvage value at the time of the plant shut-down) and provided for the estimated loss.

9. Reserve for Estimated Loss on Rationalization of Steel Production Facilities

In connection with the "Comprehensive Medium-Term Plan for Steel Production", the Company recognized estimated loss on rationalization programs for its steel production facilities in the year ended March 31, 1989. During the year ended March 31, 1990, the reserve was entirely reversed and credited against actual expenses incurred for the rationalization programs.

10. Deferred Translation Gains and Reserve for Accrued Income Taxes on Translation Gains

The company has entered into a long-term forward foreign exchange contract with banks covering the 3.25% U.S. Dollar Bonds with warrants due July 1992 and the 4.125% U.S. Dollar Bonds with warrants due February 1993. Consequently, the bonds were translated at the contracted exchange rates. The resulting translation gains are deferred and being amortized ratably over a period up to maturity.

The deferred translation gains arising from the U.S. Dollar Bonds were amortized to income in an amount of ¥10,686 million during the year ended March 31, 1990, and are included in "Miscellaneous" in Non-operating loss of the accompanying Non-Consolidated Statements of Income. The unamortized balance is shown as "Deferred translation gains" of the Non-Consolidated Balance Sheets.

Under the current Japanese Income Tax Law, such translation gains are not taxable until such time as the forward exchange contract is eventually executed at the contracted date. The Company has provided for the income taxes and enterprise taxes attributable to earned translation gains to be paid in future years.

As a result, income taxes and enterprise taxes in respect of the translation gains which were recognized as earned during the year ended March 31, 1990 are shown in the accompanying Non-Consolidated Balance Sheets as "Reserve for accrued income taxes on translation gains", and the corresponding provisions for accrued enterprise taxes and accrued income taxes are included in "Selling, general and administrative expenses" and "Accrued on translation gains", respectively, in the accompanying Non-Consolidated Statements of Income.

11. Legal Reserve — Revenue Reserve

Under the Japanese Commercial Code, the Company is required to appropriate a portion of earned surplus as a revenue reserve in amounts equal to at least 10 per cent of cash dividends and exactly 10 per cent of interim cash dividends until such reserve equals 25 per cent of the amount of capital stock account. This reserve is not available for dividends but may be used to reduce a deficit by resolution of the shareholders' meeting or may be capitalized by resolution of the Board of Directors.

12. Appropriation of Retained Earnings

Under the Japanese Commercial Code and the Articles of Incorporation of the Company, the plan for appropriation of retained earnings (including cash dividend payments) proposed by the Board of Directors must be approved by the shareholders' meeting which must be held within three months after the end of each financial year. The appropriation of retained earnings reflected in the accompanying Non-Consolidated Financial Statements represents the results of such appropriations applicable to the immediately preceding financial year which were approved by the shareholders' meeting and carried out, during that year. Dividends are paid to shareholders on the shareholders' register at the end of each financial year. Interim cash dividends are also distributed to shareholders of record at September 30 of each year pursuant to a resolution of the Board of Directors. As is the customary practice in Japan, the payment of bonuses to directors and statutory auditors is made out of retained earnings instead of being charged to income of the year and constitutes a part of the appropriations described above.

13. Special Tax-Purpose Reserve

Special tax-purpose reserve, which is allowed as a deduction for one year and is reversed into taxable income in subsequent years, is provided for by the Company through appropriation of retained earnings pursuant to the provisions of the Special Taxation Measures Law of Japan. Essentially, the reserve results in the deferral of income tax payments.

SUMMARY PROBLEM

The Balukas Corporation had the following shareholders' equity section balances at December 31, 19x7:

Common shares	$4,700,000
(500,000 shares authorized, 240,00 shares issued)	
Retained earnings	4,000,000
Total shareholders' equity	$8,700,000

During 19x8, the following transactions occurred:

a. On January 2, 19x8 Balukas purchased 5,000 treasury shares at $35 per share and immediately cancelled them.

b. On March 15, 19x8, Balukas issued 10,000 new shares and received proceeds of $40 per share.

c. On June 29, 19x8, Balukas declared and paid a 10% stock dividend. The market price of Balukas' shares on June 29, 19x8 was $45 per share.

d. On June 30, 19x8, Balukas declared a cash dividend of $3.00 per share to shareholders of record on July 15, 19x8, payable on July 31, 19x8.

e. On September 1, 19x8, Balukas issued 100,000 new shares at a price of $50 per share.

f. On December 31, 19x8, Balukas declared a four-for-one stock split. On the same date, the authorized number of shares was increased to 2 million shares.

Required:

1. Construct journal entries for each of the transactions as they occurred during 19x8.

2. Construct the journal entry for transaction (f) if, instead of declaring a stock split, this transaction had been a 300% stock dividend.

SUGGESTED SOLUTION TO SUMMARY PROBLEM

1. a. Treasury Shares Purchase and Cancellation Entry:

SE – Common Shares	97,917[a]	
SE – Retained earnings	77,083	
A – Cash		175,000

[a]($4,700,000/240,000 × 5,000) = $97,917

b. Common Shares Issuance Entry:

A – Cash	400,000	
SE – Common Shares		400,000

    c. Small Stock Dividend Entries:

Declaration

SE – Dividends Declared	1,102,500[b]	
SE –Stock dividend Issuable		1,102,500

Issuance

SE – Stock dividend Issuable	1,102,500	
SE – Common Shares		1,102,500

[b]Number of shares = 240,000 − 5,000 + 10,000 = 245,000 shares
245,000 shares × 10% × $45 per share = $1,102,500

    d. On June 30, 19x2

SE – Dividends Declared	808,500[c]	
L – Dividends Payable		808,500

On July 31, 19x2

L – Dividends Payable	808,500	
A – Cash		808,500

[c](245,000 shares × 110%) = 269, 500 shares
269,500 shares × $3.00 per share = $808,500

    e. Issue of new shares

A – Cash	5,000,000	
SE – Common Shares		5,000,000

    f. No entry is needed. However, a memorandum entry could be made to indicate that the number of shares outstanding has changed from 369,500 to 1,478,000.

2. If transaction (f) had been a 300% stock dividend, no entries would be made, since the transaction would be treated as a stock split rather than a stock dividend.

ABBREVIATIONS USED

GAAP   Generally Accepted Accounting Principles

SYNONYMS

Exercise price/Strike price/Option price

GLOSSARY

Articles of incorporation A document filed with federal or provincial regulatory authorities when a business incorporates under that jurisdiction. The articles include, among other items, the authorized number of shares and dividend preferences for each class of shares that is to be issued.

Authorized shares The maximum number of shares that a corporation is authorized to issue under its articles of incorporation.

Black–Scholes model A theoretical model used to price options.

Call option An option that gives the holder the right to buy shares at a fixed price stated in the contract.

Capital account An account used in a partnership or proprietorship to record the investment and accumulated earnings of each owner.

Common shares Certificates that represent portions of ownership in a corporation.

Convertible preferred shares Preferred shares that are exchangeable or convertible into a specified number of common shares.

Corporation A form of business in which the shareholders have limited liability and the business entity is taxed directly. Shareholders receive distributions from the entity in the form of dividends.

Cumulative preferred shares Preferred shares that accumulate dividends that are not declared from one period to the next. These accumulated dividends, called dividends in arrears, must be paid before a dividend can be declared for common shareholders.

Date of declaration The date the Board of Directors votes to declare a dividend. On this date, the dividend becomes legally payable to shareholders.

Date of record The date on which a shareholder must own the shares in order to receive the dividend from a share.

Dividend declaration An action by the Board of Directors of a corporation that makes payment of a dividend a legal obligation of the corporation.

Dividends in arrears Dividends on cumulative preferred shares that have not yet been declared from a prior year.

Drawing account An account used in a partnership or proprietorship to record the cash withdrawals by owners.

Employee stock option An option granted to an employee to buy shares at a fixed price, usually as part of an incentive compensation plan.

Ex-dividend day A date specified in the shares market on which the shares are sold without the most recently declared dividend.

Exercise price The price per share that is required to be paid by the holder of a stock option upon exercise.

Expiration date In the context of stock options, the date on which the option holder must either exercise the option or lose it.

General partners The partners that have unlimited liability in a limited partnership.

In-the-money option An option that would be worth something if exercised immediately.

Issued shares The shares of a corporation that have been issued.

Limited liability A feature of share ownership that restricts the liability of shareholders to the amount they have invested in the corporation.

Limited partners The partners in a limited partnership that have limited liability.

Limited partnership A partnership that allows some partners to have limited liability (limited partners) and others to have unlimited liability (general partners).

Memorandum entry An entry made to record a stock split. No amounts are affected; only the record of the number of shares issued is affected.

No-par shares Shares that have no par value associated with them.

Option A contract that grants the holder an option to engage in certain types of transactions. In the case of stock options, the contract usually grants the holder the right to buy (call option) or sell (put option) shares at a fixed price (strikeprice).

Out-of-the money option An option that would be worthless if exercised immediately because the market value is less than the exercise price.

Outstanding shares The number of shares of a corporation that are held by individuals or entities outside the corporation (i.e., does not include treasury shares).

Par value A value per share of common shares set in the articles of incorporation.

Participating preferred shares Preferred shares that can also participate in dividends declared beyond the level specified by the preferred shares, that is, beyond the fixed dividend payout specified in the preferred shares contract.

Partnership A form of business in which the owners have unlimited legal liability and the business entity is not taxed directly, but the income from the entity passes through to the partners' individual tax returns.

Partnership agreement An agreement between the partners in a partnership that specifies how the individual partners will share in the risks and rewards of ownership of the partnership entity.

Payment date The date on which dividend payment is actually made.

Preemptive right The right of shareholders to share proportionately in new issuances of shares.

Preferred shares An ownership right in which the shareholder has some preference as to dividends; that is, if dividends are declared, the preferred shareholder receives them first. Other rights that normally are held by common shareholders may also be changed in preferred shares; for example, many issues of preferred shares are nonvoting.

Property dividend A dividend that is satisfied with the transfer of some type of property other than cash.

Prospectus A document filed with a securities commission by a corporation when it wants to issue public debt or shares.

Put option An option that provides the holder with the option to sell something at a fixed price (strike price).

Redeemable preferred shares Preferred shares that can be bought back (redeemed) by the corporation under certain conditions and at a price stated in the articles of incorporation.

Sole proprietorship A form of business in which there is a single owner (sole proprietor). This form is characterized by unlimited liability to the owner and its exemption from corporate taxation.

Stated value A value per share of common shares set in the articles of incorporation.

Stock dividend A distribution of additional common shares to shareholders. Existing shareholders receive shares in proportion to the number of shares they already own.

Stock split A distribution of new shares to shareholders. The new shares take the place of existing shares, and existing shareholders receive new shares in proportion to the number of old shares they already own.

Treasury shares Shares that are repurchased by a corporation and held internally. Treasury shares are normally cancelled immediately upon purchase.

Unlimited liability A characteristic of sole proprietorships and partnerships that means the owners are personally responsible for the liabilities incurred by the business entity.

ASSIGNMENT MATERIAL

Assessing Your Recall

1. Characterize the following forms of business in terms of the legal liability of the owners and their tax status: corporations, sole proprietorships, partnerships, and limited partnerships.

2. Discuss the purpose of a partnership agreement.

3. Describe what is contained in the articles of incorporation and what significance they have for the accounting system.

4. List and briefly describe the four rights that common shareholders typically have in a corporation.

5. Discuss how preferred shares differ from common shares.

6. Briefly describe what each of the following features means in a preferred shares issue:
   a. Participating
   b. Cumulative
   c. Convertible
   d. Redeemable

7. Briefly describe each of the following terms: authorized shares, issued shares, and outstanding shares.

8. Describe the process of declaring and paying a cash dividend, including information about the declaration date, date of record, and payment date.

9. Discuss the nature of a stock dividend and why a distinction is made between small and large stock dividends.

10. Compare and contrast a 100% stock dividend with a two-for-one stock split.

11. Discuss why companies issue employee stock options and what immediate and potential effects these options have on the financial results of the corporation.

12. Explain why corporations might declare a stock dividend rather than a cash dividend.

Applying Your Knowledge

13. Give journal entries for the following transactions:
    a. 10,000 common shares are issued at $25 per share.
    b. 10,000 preferred shares are issued at $35 per share.
    c. A dividend of $2 per share is declared for the preferred shareholders. The corporation is authorized to issue 25,000 preferred shares, and has issued a total of 10,000 shares.
    d. The dividend declared in part (c) is paid.
    e. The corporation described in parts (a) to (d) purchased 500 of its own common shares at a market price of $50 per share and immediately cancelled them.
    f. The corporation purchased 100 of its own common shares at a market price of $20 per share and immediately cancelled them.

14. Give journal entries for the following transactions:
    a. A two-for-one stock split has been declared by a corporation that has 80,000 common shares authorized and 40,000 shares outstanding. The shares were originally issued for $5 each and have a market value of $50 each.
    b. A 10% stock dividend is declared when 40,000 shares are outstanding and the market value of each share is $30.
    c. Stock dividends declared in part (b) are satisfied with the issuance of shares.
    d. The corporation purchases 20,000 of its own shares at a market price of $100 per share and cancels them. (HINT: Calculate the average carrying value per share.)

15. The Timmerman Corporation has 45,000 common shares outstanding. The corporation has decided to issue stock dividends to its shareholders. The market price of each of the Timmerman Corporation's shares is $50. Give the journal entries for recording the issuance of the stock dividend if:
    a. The corporation decides to issue an 18% stock dividend.
    b. The corporation decides to issue a 30% stock dividend.

16. The following information relates to the shareholders' equity section of the Rodgers Corporation (in thousands):

	December 31, 19x7	December 31, 19x8
Preferred shares (10,000 shares outstanding)	$1,000	$1,000
Common shares (375,000 shares outstanding)	7,500	?
Retained earnings	3,750	4,400
Total shareholders' equity	$12,250	?

During 19x8, 10,000 common shares were issued at a price of $30 per share. Cash dividends of $750,000 and $100,000 were paid to common shareholders and preferred shareholders, respectively. The corporation acquired 15,000 treasury shares during the year at $25 per share and held them. The corporation issued 5,000 common shares under employee stock option plans at $22 per share.

Required:
a. Calculate the ending balance in common shares at the end of 19x8.
b. Calculate the amount of net income reported in 19x8.

17. Give the journal entries for the following shareholders' equity transactions of the Globe Apparel Corporation:
    a. On January 10, 19x7, the articles of incorporation are filed with the provincial secretary. The corporation is authorized to issue 100,000 common shares and 50,000 cumulative preferred shares at $10.00 per share.
    b. On January 12, 19x7, the corporation issues 50,000 common shares at $50 each.
    c. On January 15, 19x7, the assets of the Tritex Knits Corporation are acquired in exchange for 10,000 common shares and 10,000 preferred shares. The market value of the common shares was $50 and the preferred shares was $100 on this date. The assets acquired and their relative fair market values are: land, $500,000; equipment, $250,000; inventory, $200,000; building, $500,000; and accounts receivable, $50,000.
    d. On January 20, 19x7, 25,000 of the $10 cumulative preferred shares are issued at $100 per share.
    e. No dividends are declared in 19x7.
    f. On December 2, 19x8, stock dividends are declared for the preferred shares, payable as new common shares to the preferred shareholders on December 31, 19x8 to make the preferred shares current with regard to dividends in arrears. On December 2, 19x8, the common shares are trading at $70 per share.
    g. On December 2, 19x8, a 10% stock dividend is declared for the common shares. The shares are issued on December 15, 19x8, when the market price per share is $75.

18. The Mattle Corporation was formed on January 1, 19x7, and the shareholders' equity section of the balance sheet on December 31, 19x7 appeared as follows:

Shareholders' Equity as of December 31, 19x7:	
Common Shares	$380,000
$4 Preferred Shares	250,000
Retained Earnings	130,000
Total Shareholders' Equity	$760,000

During 19x7, the following transactions took place:
1) Common shares were issued at a price of $40 a share.
2) Preferred shares were issued at $50 per share.
3) 1,000 treasury shares were acquired at $50 per share and immediately cancelled.
4) A preferred dividend was declared and paid for the year.
5) A cash dividend of $5 per share was declared and paid to common shareholders at year-end.

The transactions just listed were the only capital shares transactions that occurred during the entire year. Given this information, answer the following questions:

a. How many common shares were issued?

b. How many preferred shares were issued?

c. How much net income was reported during the year?

◤◣ Reading and Interpreting Published Financial Statements

19. The balance sheets of Alliance Communication Corporation and Note 7 at March 31, 1995 and 1994 are shown in Exhibit 11-6.

    Required:

    a. Reconstruct all journal entries that affected shares for the year ended March 31, 1995.

    b. Reconstruct all journal entries that affected shares for the year ended March 31, 1994.

    c. Calculate the balance in the common shares account as at March 31, 1993.

    d. Reconcile the number of shares outstanding from March 31, 1994 to March 31, 1995.

    e. Calculate how many common shares were outstanding on March 31, 1993.

    f. Calculate the return on shareholders' equity for the year ended March 31, 1995. Net income for the year ended March 31, 1995 was $12,975,000.

20. The balance sheets, income statements (called Statement of Operations), and Note 8 of H. Jager Developments Inc. as at February 28, 1995 and 1994 are shown in Exhibit 11-7.

    Required:

    a. Note that Jager had a number of stock options and share purchase warrants outstanding at February 28, 1995. Explain what stock options and warrants are.

    b. Who holds the options and warrants?

    c. Why would Jager have issued these options and warrants?

    d. Assume that all of the options and warrants were exercised on March 1, 1994 for the prices specified (for the purposes of this question ignore when the options and warrants were actually issued). How much additional cash would Jager have had to invest during the 1995 fiscal year?

    e. Assume that Jager could earn 10% after taxes on additional investments. Calculate the net income Jager would have earned for 1995 in this case.

    f. Calculate the revised basic earnings per share that Jager would have reported for 1995 in this case. (HINT: Remember that both net income and the number of shares outstanding change.)

    g. Calculate the return on shareholders' equity for the year ended February 28, 1995.

21. The 1995 and 1994 balance sheets for Mackenzie Financial Corporation and Note 10 as at March 31, 1995 are shown in Exhibit 11-8.

    Required:

    a. Reconstruct all journal entries that affected common shares for the year ended March 31, 1995. At what price were the 10,000 shares issued?

EXHIBIT 11-6

ALLIANCE COMMUNICATION CORPORATION
Consolidated Balance Sheets
As at March 31

	1995	1994
ASSETS		
Cash and short-term investments	$ 18,860	$ 31,936
Accounts receivable	47,140	46,956
Distribution contracts receivable	42,672	22,093
Investment in film and television programs (note 2)	60,652	51,376
Film and television programs in progress	31,358	24,586
Program exhibition rights	9,625	–
Development costs and investment in scripts	4,336	3,400
Capital assets (note 3)	9,162	2,930
Other assets (note 4)	4,365	744
Goodwill	1,188	1,492
	229,358	185,513
LIABILITIES		
Accounts payable and accrued liabilities	$ 49,391	$ 41,849
Distribution revenues payable	32,770	19,547
Loans payable (note 5)	1,371	285
Deferred income taxes	9,314	5,777
Deferred revenue	34,741	47,811
Minority interest	1,419	–
	129,006	115,269
CONVERTIBLE DEBENTURE (note 6)	16,500	–
SHAREHOLDERS' EQUITY		
Capital stock (note 7)	$ 50,892	$ 29,074
Warrants	–	20,984
Retained earnings	32,340	19,365
Cumulative translation adjustments	620	821
	83,852	70,244
	$ 229,358	$ 185,513

ON BEHALF OF THE BOARD

ELLIS JACOB   HAROLD P. GORDON

Director   Director

b. Assuming that all holders of stock options exercise all warrants outstanding on March 31, 1995, what is the minimum amount of cash that Mackenzie will receive? What is the maximum amount of cash that Mackenzie could receive?

c. Assume that all of the warrants outstanding as at March 31, 1995 were actually exercised on March 31, 1995 for the minimum exercise prices. Redraft the March 31, 1995 balance sheet to include this transaction (this is called a

EXHIBIT 11-6 (continued)

ALLIANCE COMMUNICATION CORPROATION
Excerpted from Notes to the Statements

7. Capital Stock

a) The authorized capital stock of the Company consists of an unlimited number of common shares.

b) During fiscal 1995, the following transactions occurred:

In May, 1994, 1,530,000 shares were issued pursuant to the exercise of 1,530,000 warrants to acquire common shares and the receipt of proceeds of $20,984,000 released from escrow net of issue expenses and income tax benefits;

In October, 1994, 13,900 shares were issued in connection with the purchase of 75% interest in Partisan Music Productions Inc. at $16.33 per share for aggregate proceeds of $227,000;

During the year, 51,936 employee stock options were exercised pursuant to the Company stock option plan for proceeds of $607,651.

c) During fiscal 1994, the following transactions occurred:

In June, 1993, the common shares were split on an 8 for 1 basis;

In July, 1993, 228,320 common shares were issued for $400,000 cash, pursuant to a stock option;

In August, 1993, 1,888,400 common shares were issued pursuant to an initial public offering, at a price of $13 per share for cash proceeds of $23,259,000, net of expenses and income tax benefits;

In September, 1993, 227,300 common shares were issued pursuant to an over-allotment option at $13 per share for cash proceeds of $3,415,000, net of expenses and income tax benefits;

In November, 1993, 78,431 shares were issued in connection with the buyout of the non-control interest in a subsidiary company at $12.75 per share for aggregate proceeds of $1,000,000.

d) As a result, the issued capital stock is as follows:

(IN THOUSANDS OF DOLLARS)	1995	1994
9,776,287 common shares (1994 – 8,180,451)	$ 50,892	$ 29,074

e) The Company has an employee stock option plan which allows for an exercise price based on market price. As of March 31, 1995, options for 1,192,036 shares had been granted to employees and directors of the Company.

"pro forma" balance sheet). Comment on the changes in the pro forma balance sheet compared to the actual March 31, 1995 balance sheet.

d. Calculate the return on shareholders' equity for the year ended March 31, 1995. Net income for the year was $29,450,000.

22. The balance sheets for 1994 and 1993 for Petromet Resources Limited and Notes 5 and 7 as at December 31, 1994 are shown in Exhibit 11-9.

Required:

a. Reconstruct all journal entries that affected common shares for the year ended December 31, 1994.

b. What is the maximum number of common shares that could be outstanding on December 31, 1994 if all possible conversions and options were exercised on December 31, 1994? (Ignore the actual dates these conversions and options are actually exercisable.)

c. If all possible conversions and options were exercised on December 31, 1994 as assumed in part (b), what assets, liabilities, equities, revenues, and expenses would be affected?

d. Calculate the return on shareholders' equity for the year ended December 31, 1994. Net income for the year was $1,096,488.

EXHIBIT 11-7

H. JAGER DEVELOPMENTS INC.
Consolidated Balance Sheet
February 28, 1995

	1995	1994
ASSETS		
Accounts receivable	$ 242,818	$ 575,314
Prepaid expense and deposits	75,324	44,508
Land and housing under development	8,925,941	2,997,798
Due from related party (Note 3)	365,664	—
Other (Note 4)	248,394	216,518
Investment in H. J. Forest Products Inc. (Note 5)	4,578,405	4,600,000
	$ 14,436,546	$ 8,434,138
LIABILITIES		
Bank indebtedness	$ 52,564	$ 113,218
Accounts payable and accrued liabilities	1,312,209	1,144,742
Customer and mortgage advances	632,810	1,073,955
Due to related parties (Note 6)	246,183	281,054
Mortgages and loans (Note 7)	5,582,523	154,955
	7,826,289	2,767,924
SHAREHOLDERS' EQUITY		
Capital stock (Note 8)	7,641,385	6,876,385
Deficit	(1,031,128)	(1,210,171)
	6,610,257	5,666,214
	$ 14,436,546	$ 8,434,138

On behalf of the Board

Harvey Jager

Director

[signature]

Director

EXHIBIT 11-7 (continued)

H. JAGER DEVELOPMENTS INC.
Consolidated Statement of Operations
February 28, 1995

	1995	1994
SALES	$ 6,526,506	$ 4,383,373
DIRECT COSTS	5,701,235	4,313,040
	825,271	70,333
EXPENSES		
General and administrative	532,531	845,255
Depreciation and amortization	35,151	41,343
Interest	6,087	28,769
	573,769	915,367
EARNINGS (LOSS) BEFORE UNDERNOTED	251,502	(845,034)
Loss on sale of securities	(904)	—
Gain on sale of fixed and other assets	27,540	—
Write-down of land and housing under development	(99,095)	(260,000)
EARNINGS (LOSS) BEFORE INCOME TAXES	179,043	(1,105,034)
INCOME TAXES (Note 10)	—	—
NET EARNINGS (LOSS)	179,043	(1,105,034)
DEFICIT, beginning of year	(1,210,171)	(105,137)
DEFICIT, end of year	$ (1,031,128)	$ (1,210,171)
EARNINGS (LOSS) PER SHARE	$ 0.01	$ (0.11)

EXHIBIT 11-7 (continued)

H. JAGER DEVELOPMENTS INC.
Excerpted from the Notes to the Statements
February 28, 1995

8. CAPITAL STOCK

(a) Authorized:

Unlimited common voting shares

Unlimited preferred shares

(b) Common shares issued:

	1995		1994	
	Number	Amount	Number	Amount
Balance, beginning of year	12,624,733	$ 6,876,385	10,149,360	$ 1,357,240
Shares issued:				
On exercise of options	300,000	290,000	220,000	244,400
Pursuant to private placement	626,582	475,000	-	-
For services	—	—	60,973	138,425
On acquisition of shares of				
H. J. Forest Products Inc. (Note 5)	—	—	2,000,000	4,600,000
On settlement of debt owing				
to H. J. Forest Products Inc.	—	—	194,400	536,320
	13,551,315	$ 7,641,385	12,624,733	$ 6,876,385

(c) Stock options:

As at February 28, 1995 the following options, granted to directors and employees, to acquire common shares of the Company, are outstanding:

1995			1994		
Number of Shares	Exercise Price Per Share	Expiry Date	Number of Share	Exercise Price Per Share	Expiry Date
100,000	$ 1.00	April 12, 1995	362,500	$ 1.48	April 12, 1995
262,500	$ 1.00	Nov. 4, 1996	300,000	$ 2.55	Nov. 4, 1996
50,000	$ 1.00	Feb. 15, 1997	50,000	$ 1.64	Feb. 15, 1997
185,000	$ 1.00	Sept. 30, 1997	712,500		
697,500					

EXHIBIT 11-7 (continued)

H. JAGER DEVELOPMENTS INC.
Excerpted from Notes to the Statements
February 28, 1995

8. CAPITAL STOCK (Continued)

d) Share purchase warrants:

During the year the Company issued an aggregate of 896,333 share purchase warrants, of which 803,833 remain outstanding at February 28, 1995, including 482,500 warrants issued to the president and a corporation owned by the president of the Company. The warrants entitle the holder to subscribe for common shares of the Company as outlined below.

Number of Warrants	Exercise Price Per Share	Expiry Date
63,000	$ 1.40	Aug. 31, 1995
249,167	$ 1.40	April 30, 1996
333,333	$ 0.75	April 30, 1996
133,333	$ 1.00	June 30, 1996
25,000	$ 1.00	Nov. 15, 1996

23. The balance sheets for 1994 and 1993 for Queenstake Resources Ltd., and Note 4 as at December 31, 1994 are shown in Exhibit 11-10.

    Required:

    a. Reconstruct all journal entries that affected common shares and warrants for the year ended December 31, 1994.

    b. Reconstruct all journal entries that affected common shares and warrants for the year ended December 31, 1993.

    c. Calculate the average issue price per share for each type of common share issuance during 1993 and 1994. Comment on the average prices received for each type of placement.

    d. Comment on the trends in share prices found in part (c). Which type of average issue price best reflects Queenstake's operating success and prospects? Justify your answer.

EXHIBIT 11-8

MACKENZIE FINANCIAL CORPORATION
Consolidated Balance Sheet
As at March 31
(thousands of dollars)

	1995	1994
Assets		
Cash and short-term investments	$ 144,455	$ 112,473
Accounts and other receivables	52,187	46,599
Income taxes receivable	–	10,854
Mortgage loans	189,932	142,027
Deferred selling commissions and investment in related partnerships *(note 3)*	112,757	100,526
Investment in affiliated companies	56,039	55,539
Management contracts	17,534	20,708
Capital assets *(note 4)*	22,705	16,760
Goodwill *(note 5)*	8,293	9,463
Other assets *(note 6)*	14,661	11,865
	$ 618,563	$ 526,814
Liabilities		
Bank loans *(note 7)*	$ 13,012	$ 4,767
Accounts payable and accrued liabilities	34,592	38,159
Income taxes payable	10,257	–
Customer deposits *(note 8)*	213,880	179,345
Notes payable *(notes 3 and 9)*	44,184	50,000
Deferred taxes	48,423	22,718
	$ 364,348	$ 294,989
Commitments and Contingencies *(notes 7 and 13)*		
Shareholders' Equity		
Capital Stock *(note 10)*		
Authorized – Unlimited number of common shares		
Issued and outstanding		
– 59,264,115 (1994 – 59,254,115) common shares	$ 38,813	$ 38,761
Retained earnings	215,402	193,064
	$ 254,215	$ 231,825
	$ 618,563	$ 526,814

(The accompanying notes are an integral part of these consolidated financial statements.)

Signed on behalf of the Board

Alexander Christ
Director

F. Warren Hurst
Director

EXHIBIT 11-8 (continued)

MACKENZIE FINANCIAL CORPORATION
Excerpted from Notes to the Statements

10. Capital Stock

(a) Stock Options
The Corporation has granted options to purchase common shares to employees and others, at a minimum of the market price on the date the options were granted.

A maximum number of 2,344,011 common shares has been reserved for future options under the share option plans. The maximum number of shares to be allocated to each employee is 5% of the issued and outstanding common shares of the Corporation.

Year Granted	Expiry Date	Exercise Price $	Outstanding March 31, 1994	Issued During Year	Exercised During Year	Cancelled During Year	Outstanding March 31, 1995
1992	1997	4.95 – 5.50	1,007,000		10,000		997,000
1993	1998	7.625 – 12.00	1,885,000			27,500	1,857,500
1994	1999	7.50 – 9.50		625,500		1,000	624,500
			2,892,000	625,500	10,000	28,500	3,479,000

EXHIBIT 11-9

PETROMET RESOURCES LIMITED
Consolidated Balance Sheet

	December 31, 1994	December 31, 1993
ASSETS		
Current		
Cash and term deposits	$ 10,869	$ 8,913,876
Accounts receivable	10,083,645	5,447,698
Investments (market value $3,294,000; 1993–$2,047,000)	2,525,000	125,000
	12,619,514	14,486,574
Property, Plant and Equipment (Note 3)	80,055,512	25,921,770
	$ 92,675,026	$ 40,408,344
LIABILITIES		
Current		
Accounts payable and accrued liabilities	$ 15,230,476	$ 10,003,845
Long Term Bank Debt (Note 4)	16,142,350	–
Convertible Debentures (Note 5)	25,000,000	–
Deferred Gain (Note 6)	2,400,000	–
Future Abandonment and Site Restoration Costs	345,000	182,000
Deferred Income Taxes	222,000	264,000
SHAREHOLDERS' EQUITY		
Share capital (Note 7)	29,602,364	17,169,446
Shares reserved for issuance (Note 7)	–	10,152,705
Retained earnings	3,732,836	2,636,348
	33,335,200	29,958,499
	$ 92,675,026	$ 40,408,344

On Behalf of the Board:

(signature)

(Director)

(signature)

(Director)

Excerpted from Notes to the Statements

5. Convertible Debentures

The 6.5% convertible subordinate debentures are due March 31, 2004. The debentures are convertible into common shares at $9.50 per share and are non redeemable until March 31, 1999, unless the closing price of the common shares for 30 consecutive trading days is $15.25 per share or more. After March 31, 1999, the debentures are redeemable in the event that the weighted average price at which the common shares are traded during a 30 consecutive trading day period is not less than 130% of the conversion price.

EXHIBIT 11-9 (continued)

PETROMET RESOURCES LIMITED
Excerpted from Notes to the Statements

7. Share Capital

(a) Authorized

The authorized share capital consists of an unlimited number of common shares.

(b) Issued

	Shares	Amount
Balance, January 31, 1992	12,238,066	$13,348,136
Issued for cash:		
·Pursuant to flow–through share agreements	428,550	150,000
Pursuant to a private placement	3,636,363	2,000,000
Issued upon debenture conversion	1,428,572	500,000
Less: issue costs	–	(196,029)
Balance, December 31, 1992	17,731,551	$15,802,107
Issued for cash:		
Pursuant to flow–through share agreements	1,300,000	1,275,000
Upon stock option exercise	1,685,000	731,250
Pursuant to a private placement	1,000,000	2,250,000
Upon exercise of warrants	500,000	1,250,000
Acquisitions of subsidiaries (Note 2)	1,570,588	5,250,000
Less: issue costs, net of tax benefits	–	(110,757)
Reduction of deficit (Note 7(c))	–	(9,278,154)
Balance, December 31, 1993	23,787,139	$17,169,446
Issued on warrant conversion	2,000,000	10,500,000
Issued for cash:		
Upon stock option exercise	1,145,000	2,837,250
Less: share and convertible debenture issue costs, net of tax benefits	–	(904,332)
Balance, December 31, 1994	**26,932,139**	**$29,602,364**

(c) At the annual and special meeting of the shareholders held June 14, 1993 a special resolution was passed to eliminate the December 31, 1992 deficit of $9,278,154 against the stated capital account attributable to the common shares.

(d) Stock option plan

The company's stock option plan reserves up to 10% of the outstanding common shares of the company for issuance to eligible participants. At December 31, 1994, options to purchase 2,495,000 common shares were outstanding. These options are exercisable at a price ranging from $0.31 to $8.875 and expire on various dates between 1997 and 1999.

(e) Shares reserved for issuance

At December 31, 1993 shares reserved for issuance were pursuant to 2,000,000 outstanding special warrants. The special warrants were converted into common shares in May, 1994 upon the qualification of such shares for distribution pursuant to a prospectus.

EXHIBIT 11-10

QUEENSTAKE RESOURCES LTD.
Consolidated Balance Sheet
(in Canadian Dollars)

	December 31 1994	December 31 1993
ASSETS		
Current assets		
Cash	$ 6,336,971	$ 3,504,302
Accounts receivable	138,671	78,745
	6,475,642	3,583,047
Investments (Note 2)	256,319	34,609
Mineral properties and equipment (Note 3)	6,842,281	3,976,265
	$ 13,574,242	$ 7,593,921
LIABILITIES		
Current liabilities		
Accounts payable and accrued liabilities	$ 146,781	$ 121,216
Minority interest	-	45,286
	146,781	166,502
SHAREHOLDERS' EQUITY		
Share capital (Note 4)		
Authorized: 50,000,000 common shares without par value		
Issued: 19,751,532 shares	19,168,687	11,328,666
(1993 - 17,032,531 shares)		
Share purchase warrants (Note 4)	189,600	211,000
Deficit	(5,930,826)	(4,112,247
	13,427,461	7,427,419
	$ 13,574,242	$ 7,593,921

Commitments (Notes 3 and 8)
Contingency (Note 11)

Approved by the Board of Directors

Director

Director

EXHIBIT 11-10 (continued)

QUEENSTAKE RESOURCES LTD.
Excerpted from Notes to the Statements

4. Share Capital

(a) During the years ended December 31, 1994, 1993, and 1992, changes in share capital were as follows:

	1994		1993		1992	
	Shares	Amount	Shares	Amount	Shares	Amount
Balance beginning of year	17,032,531	$11,328,666	11,810,867	$3,832,033	11,064,200	$3,569,937
Issued during the year (net of issue costs)						
For cash:						
Private placements	2,250,000	6,665,828	3,375,000	5,340,262	500,000	223,579
Exercise of options	105,001	22,150	481,664	456,709	246,667	38,517
Exercise of warrants	214,000	663,400	1,015,000	853,910	-	-
For mineral properties	150,000	488,643	200,000	575,000	-	-
For debt settlement	-	-	150,000	270,752	-	-
Balance end of year	19,751,532	$19,168,687	17,032,531	$11,328,666	11,810,867	$3,832,033

(b) Under the Company's incentive stock option plan, options were granted to employees and directors at market value at the date of grant. These options, which expire in 2001 to 2004, may be exercised by employees as to 33 1/3% per year, on a cumulative basis, and by directors at any time. The incentive plan includes share appreciation rights, whereby an optionee may, if permitted by the Board of Directors, have the right, when entitled to exercise an option, to terminate such option in whole or in part by notice in writing to the Company, and in lieu of receiving that number of shares permitted to be exercised under the option, to instead receive shares equal in value to the "profit" portion of the option only (the difference between the exercise price and the market price of the option shares). Options outstanding under this plan are as follows:

December 31, 1994			
Number of Shares	Exercise Price	Year Exercisable	
		1995	1996
448,334	$0.15	448,334	-
5,000	$0.22	5,000	-
163,334	$1.30	163,334	-
20,000	$2.80	20,000	-
272,000	$0.70	188,000	84,000
155,000	$3.50	103,333	51,667
1,063,668		928,001	135,667

EXHIBIT 11-10 (continued)

QUEENSTAKE RESOURCES LTD.
Excerpted from Notes to the Statements

4. Share Capital continued

Year ended December 31	1994	1993	1992
Balance beginning of year	821,669	863,333	745,000
Granted	407,000	440,000	485,000
Exercised	(105,001)	(481,664)	(246,667)
Cancelled	(60,000)	-	(120,000)
Balance end of year	1,063,668	821,669	863,333

(c) The Company has outstanding 1,896,000 warrants, each exercisable at $3.00 until they expire on April 2, 1996 and 1,125,000 warrants, each exercisable at $3.70 until they expire on March 18, 1997, with an aggregate assigned value of $189,600 (1993 - $211,000), each of which entitles the holder to purchase one common share.

Warrant activity for the three preceding years is as follows:

Year ended December 31	1994	1993	1992
Balance beginning of year	2,860,000	500,000	-
Issued	1,125,000	3,375,000	500,000
Exercised	(214,000)	(1,015,000)	-
Expired	(750,000)	-	-
Balance end of year	3,021,000	2,860,000	500,000

(d) The total number of common shares that would have been outstanding if all share commitments were met, and all warrants and options were exercised, would have been 23,986,200 as at December 31, 1994.

CASE

Manonta Sales Corporation

Manonta Sales Corporation's summary balance sheet and income statement as at December 31, 19x8 are shown below.

Balance Sheet (in thousands)

Current assets	$178,000
Investments	1,000
Net property, plant and equipment	56,000
Total assets	$235,000
Current liabilities	115,000
Long-term debt	93,000
Shareholders' equity	27,000
Total liabilities and shareholders' equity	$235,000

Income Statement (in thousands)

Sales	$550,000
Cost of goods sold, operating, and other expenses	525,000
Earnings before income taxes	$25,000
Income taxes	10,000
Net income	$15,000
Earnings per share	$1.00

The long-term debt has an interest rate of 10% and is convertible into 9,300,000 common shares. You own 100 common shares of Manonta and are trying to decide if you should keep or sell them. After carefully analyzing all available information about Manonta, you decide the following events are likely to happen. First, you believe Manonta will increase its earnings before income taxes by 10% next year because of increased sales. Second, you believe the effective tax rate will stay the same. Third, the holders of long-term debt will convert it into shares on January 1, 19x9. Fourth, you believe the current multiple of earnings per share to market price of 20 will increase to 22 if the debt is converted because of the reduced risk.

You decide you will sell the shares if you think their market price will not increase by 10% next year. Should you keep the shares or sell them? Support your answer with a detailed analysis.

◤◣ Critical Thinking Question

Corporate executives are normally compensated by a package that consists of a combination of one or more of the following:

a. Salary

b. "Perks" ("perks" is a shortened term commonly used for "perquisites") such as cars, paid vacations, nice offices, and club memberships

c. Bonuses based on reported net income

d. Bonuses based on gross sales

e. Stock option plans

Argue the impact of each of the above items on the actions of executives. What would each item encourage the executive to achieve? Which of these actions might be beneficial to the corporation? Which might be harmful? If you were designing a compensation package for executives running a corporation you owned, what would you include?

CHAPTER

12

Financial

Statement Analysis

In the first 11 chapters of this book, we described the basic components of the financial reporting system and how accounting numbers are accumulated and recorded. In most of these chapters we identified ratios that use the material that was being discussed. In this chapter, we pull all those ratios together and summarize how financial information can be analyzed. Here you will see how the various components of the reporting system work together.

To analyze financial information effectively, you need more than a basic understanding of what each individual statement means. You need to understand the relationships among the three major financial statements, and the methods that produce the numbers. You also need to compare and contrast these relationships over time, and among different corporations. We left this discussion until near the end of the book as proper analysis requires a good understanding of all components of all the financial statements.

This chapter provides an overview of financial statement analysis, and a discussion of the basic ratios used. However, because financial statement analysis is very complex, it can serve only as an introduction. Remember two basic facts as you work through this chapter. First, there is no definitive set of rules or procedures that dictate how to analyze financial statements. Second, every analysis should be tailored to suit the underlying reason for making the analysis. These two features make comprehensive analysis quite complex. A more detailed discussion of financial statement analysis is left to more advanced texts.

OVERVIEW OF FINANCIAL STATEMENT ANALYSIS

Financial statements are typically analyzed for a specific purpose. An investment analyst or a stock broker, for example, may undertake an analysis in order to recommend that a client buy or sell a stock. A bank lending officer may perform an analysis of a client's financial statements to decide whether the client will be capable of paying back a loan if the bank decides to lend the money. A student looking for a job may perform an analysis of a corporation to decide whether it is a suitable corporation for which to work.

Depending on the type of decision to be made, the analyst will tailor the analysis to the demands of the decision. For example, a banker trying to decide whether to make a short-term loan may restrict the analysis to the short-term cash-producing capabilities of the corporation. The investment analyst, on the other hand, may focus on the long-term financial health of the corporation.

In this chapter, we take a very general approach to financial statement analysis. No particular decision is considered as the various ratios are discussed. However, we do attempt to discuss decision contexts in which a particular ratio may be more helpful than others in assessing the health of the corporation. Whatever the decision, one of the first things you have to do is come to some understanding of the business.

Understanding the Business

Understanding the business means more than understanding a corporation's financial statements. It means that you must have a grasp of the underlying economics of the business, the risks involved, and the economic factors that are crucial to the long- and short-run health of the corporation. It means that you must understand the various types of businesses in which the corporation is engaged. For example, a large corporation such as BCE Inc. (Bell Canada) is involved in more than just telephones. It has businesses in many communications areas such as production (Northern Telecom), research (Bell-Northern Research), satellite mobile communications (TMI Communications), satellite television signals (Expressvu Inc.), cable television (Jones Intercable), and many other areas. An analyst who thinks that BCE is only in the telephone business has a very inaccurate view of the risks involved in lending BCE money, or in buying its shares.

A basic understanding of the range of businesses in which a corporation is engaged can be obtained by reading the first section of the annual report. In most annual reports, the first sections are devoted to describing the various businesses in which the corporation is involved, with their associated achievements and expectations. Usually the financial statements are found in the second half of most annual reports. Although this descriptive section of most annual reports does not explain everything you need to know about the corporation, it does provide some insight into what the corporation does and the types of risks it faces.

Once you have an overall view of the kinds of businesses operated by the corporation, you should next read the financial statements, including the auditor's report and the notes to the financial statements.

Reading the Financial Statements

The first thing that should be read in the financial statements is the auditor's report attached to them. The auditor's report confirms that appropriate accounting policies were followed and that the statements "present fairly" the financial condition of the corporation. This report is important because the auditor is an independent third party who is stating a professional opinion on the fairness of the numbers and disclosures reported in the financial statements. Remember that the auditor's report is not a guarantee of the accuracy of the information contained in the financial statements. Financial statements are prepared by management, and management has primary responsibility for them. Auditors express their opinion on whether the financial statements present the information fairly according to generally accepted accounting principles. The auditor's report does not indicate if the information contained in the financial statements is good or bad. It is the reader's responsibility to interpret the information provided.

An example of a typical unqualified auditor's opinion provided by Coopers & Lybrand, Chartered Accountants for the 1995 financial statements of Cara Operations Limited, is shown in Exhibit 12-1.

The second step is to read each of the major financial statements to make sure that the results make sense for the types of activities in which the corporation is engaged. Use your knowledge from this course to look for unusual account titles and unusually large dollar items. If there is a large loss item on the income statement, for example, the nature of the loss is important. Is it an item that should be expected to continue into the future, or is it a noncontinuing item? Unusual account titles may indicate that the corporation is involved in a line of business that is new, which could have serious implications for future operations. For example, if a manufacturer suddenly shows

EXHIBIT 12-1

CARA OPERATIONS LIMITED
Excerpted from the 1995 Annual Report

Auditors' Report

To the Shareholders of Cara Operations Limited

We have audited the consolidated balance sheets of Cara Operations Limited as at April 2, 1995 and April 3, 1994 and the consolidated statements of earnings, retained earnings and cash flow for the years then ended. These financial statements are the responsibility of the corporation's management. Our responsibility is to express our opinion on these financial statements based on our audit.

We conducted our audits in accordance with generally accepted auditing standards. Those standards require that we plan and perform an audit to obtain reasonable assurance whether the financial statements are free of material misstatement.

An audit includes examining, on a test basis, evidence supporting the amounts and disclosures in the financial statements. An audit also includes assessing the accounting principles used and significant estimates made by management, as well as evaluating the overall financial statement presentation.

In our opinion, these consolidated financial statements present fairly, in all material respects, the financial position of the corporation as at April 2, 1995 and April 3, 1994 and the results of its operations and the changes in its financial position for the years then ended in accordance with generally accepted accounting principles.

Coopers & Lybrand
Chartered Accountants
Toronto, Canada
May 9, 1995

Coopers & Lybrand

---

lease receivables on its balance sheet, this probably indicates that it has started to lease assets as well as sell them. The leasing business is very different from the manufacturing business and exposes the corporation to different types of risks. You must take this new information into consideration in an evaluation of the corporation.

A reading of the financial statements is not complete unless the notes to the financial statements are read carefully. Because the major financial statements provide summary information only, there is not much room in the statements to provide all the details necessary for a full understanding of the corporation's transactions. Therefore, the notes provide a place for more details and discussion about many items on the financial statements. Also pay attention in the notes to the summary of the significant accounting policies used by the corporation. Remember that GAAP allows quite a large amount of flexibility in choosing accounting principles, so you should be aware of the choices that were made by management. These will generally be listed in the first note to the financial statements.

Once you have an overall understanding of the business and the financial statements, you can begin a detailed analysis of the financial results.

Retrospective Versus Prospective Analysis

As discussed earlier, most analysis is done with a particular objective in mind. Most objectives involve making decisions that have future consequences. Therefore, almost every analysis of a set of financial statements is, in one way or another, concerned with the future. Because of this, you should make a **prospective** (forward-looking) analysis of the corporation to try to determine what the future will bring. For example, bank lending officers try to forecast future cash flows of corporations to ensure that loans will be repaid.

The problem with prospective analysis is that the world is an uncertain place; no one can predict the future with complete accuracy. Analysts, however, are expected to make recommendations based on their predictions of what the future outcomes will be for specified corporations. In trying to predict the future, one of the most reliable sources of data you have is the results of past operations of a corporation as summarized in the financial statements. To the extent that the future follows the trends of the past, you can use these **retrospective** data to assist in predicting the future. You must also understand the economics of a corporation well enough to know when something fundamental has changed in the economic environment to make it unlikely that the past results of the corporation will predict the future. In such a situation, you cannot rely on the retrospective data.

If you believe that retrospective data may be useful in predicting the future, a complete analysis of that retrospective data is in order. Two major types of analysis of retrospective data are times-series and cross-sectional analyses.

Time-Series Versus Cross-Sectional Analysis

In a **time-series analysis**, the analyst examines information from different time periods for the same corporation to look for any pattern in the data over time. For example, you may look at the sales data over a five-year period to determine if sales are increasing, decreasing, or remaining stable. This would have important implications for future sales of the corporation. The assumption underlying a time-series analysis is that there is some predictability in the time series; that is, past data can be used to predict the future. Without this assumption, there is no reason to do a time-series analysis.

Many corporations provide five- or ten-year summaries to assist in making this analysis. An example is shown in Exhibit 12-2, from Alliance Communications Corporation's 1995 annual report.

A **cross-sectional analysis** compares the data from one corporation with the data from another corporation for the same time period. Usually, the comparison is with another corporation in the same industry (a competitor perhaps), or with an average of the other corporations in the industry. For example, you might look at the growth in sales for General Motors Canada compared to the growth in sales for Ford Canada or Chrysler Canada. Other cross-sectional analyses might compare corporations across different industries (General Motors Canada compared to BCE), countries (General Motors Canada compared to Nissan), and so forth. However, any such cross-sectional comparisons must consider that different industries may have slightly different accounting principles (for example, accounting principles for banks and insurance companies are slightly different from most other industries). Comparing across countries is much more difficult because of different accounting methods and sets of standards used in different countries. However, investment analysts want to recommend the best investment

EXHIBIT 12-2

ALLIANCE COMMUNICATIONS CORPORATION
Excerpted from the 1995 Annual Report

FIVE YEAR COMPARATIVE EARNINGS STATEMENTS

(IN THOUSANDS OF DOLLARS – EXCEPT FOR PER SHARE INFORMATION)	YEAR ENDED MARCH 31 1995	YEAR ENDED MARCH 31 1994	YEAR ENDED MARCH 31 1993	9 MONTHS ENDED MARCH 31 1992	YEAR ENDED JUNE 30 1991
REVENUES	$233,811	$108,985	$132,161	$83,874	$113,301
EXPENSES					
Operating	212,328	97,394	123,481	78,735	108,538
Amortization	5,164	1,494	1,126	417	577
Interest	282	369	809	853	508
	217,774	99,257	125,416	80,005	109,623
EBITDA	$ 21,483	$ 11,591	$ 8,680	$ 5,139	$ 4,763
NET EARNINGS	$ 12,975	$ 7,345	$ 5,065	$ 3,509	$ 2,349
BASIC EARNINGS PER SHARE	$ 1.36	$ 1.01	$ 0.96	$ 0.69	$ 0.46

strategy to their clients out of as wide a range of investments as possible. To make the best recommendation, they must consider the return versus risk trade-off across many corporations. They must, therefore, directly compare corporations in different industries and different countries.

The choice of which type of analysis to conduct is driven, in part, by the type of decision that motivated the analysis. In a lending situation, for example, the lending officer is not so concerned about other companies, but is concerned about the time-series of the data for the particular corporation under consideration. Actually, the lending officer has uses for both types of analysis. The lender must be aware of industry trends in the analysis of a particular corporation to get an overall assessment of how well this corporation performs relative to its competitors to ensure its future viability. The investment analyst must also couple the cross-corporation comparison with a time-series analysis of the financial health of the corporation selected for investment.

Data to be Used

The type of data used in a time-series or cross-sectional analysis will vary depending on the purpose of the analysis. Three general types of data that are frequently used are raw financial data, common size data, and ratio data.

Raw Financial Data

Raw financial data are the data that appear directly in the financial statements. An example of a time-series analysis of this type of data might be the time-series of data from income statements, as shown for Alliance Communications Corporation in Exhibit 12-2, or the time-series of total assets for the past five years. Cross-sectional analysis can also be used with this type of data. For example, you might compare total revenues across corporations in the same industry for the past five years.

Time-series data is almost always available directly from financial statements, since they usually show data for a two-year period. In addition to the main financial statements, some annual reports contain additional time-series data in the form of a five- or ten-year summary such as that shown in Exhibit 12-2. Note that this summary does not include all items that appear on the income statement. Annual reports may also contain data other than strictly financial data, such as numbers of employees or sales volumes expressed in physical units rather than dollars.

In the remainder of the chapter, data from a set of financial statements will be used to illustrate various types of analyses. For purposes of illustration, the financial statement data of Fletcher Challenge Canada Limited for the year ended June 30, 1995 will be used. Fletcher Challenge, with headquarters in Vancouver, British Columbia, is a large producer of pulp and paper. The raw financial statement data for Fletcher Challenge appear in Exhibit 12-3, which includes the balance sheet, income statement, and statement of changes in financial position (SCFP).

■ ■ Common Size Data

Although the raw data of a corporation can reveal much about its performance, some relationships are more easily understood when some elements of the raw data are compared with other elements. For example, in the income statement for Fletcher Challenge in Exhibit 12-3, you can see that the sales revenue for Fletcher Challenge increased from $1,675.4 million in 1994 to $2,153.9 million in 1995. Cost of goods sold has also increased over this same period from $1,397.6 million to $1,649.0 million. The question is, what happened to profit margins on a relative basis? This is a question of the relationship of the costs to the revenues. One way to address this question is to compare the cost of goods sold expressed as a proportion of the sales revenue. Often, this is done by preparing a set of financial statements called **common size statements**.

In a common size income statement, all line items are expressed as percentages of net revenues. In the case of Fletcher Challenge, a common size income statement is shown in Exhibit 12-4 with every item calculated as a percentage of net sales.

This common size income statement makes several significant changes very obvious. It is obvious that the cost of goods sold decreased from 83.4% of net sales in 1994 to 76.6% in 1995. This decrease, combined with a decrease in amortization expenses from 9.2% to 6.8% of net sales, results in an increase in Operating earnings by a full 10 percentage points, from 2.6% to 12.6% of net sales. The increase in income taxes from 0.1% to 5.4% results from an increase in net earnings from 1.6% to 5.6% of net sales. Thus we can determine that the increase in net earnings results mainly from a smaller cost of goods sold as expressed as a percentage of net sales.

Common size statements could also be prepared for the balance sheet and the SCFP. The common size data can then be used in a time-series analysis, as they were earlier, or they could be used in a cross-sectional analysis of different companies. In fact, in cross-sectional analysis, common size statements allow for a comparison of corporations of different sizes.

EXHIBIT 12-3

FLETCHER CHALLENGE CANADA LIMITED
Consolidated Balance Sheets

As at June 30 (in millions of dollars)		1995		1994
Assets				
Current assets				
Cash and short term investments	$	5.6	$	35.7
Accounts receivable (note 4)		282.2		158.2
Inventories (note 5)		309.2		282.3
Prepaid expenses		17.3		9.0
		614.3		485.2
Fixed assets (note 6)				
Property, plant and equipment		1,927.8		1,981.9
Timberlands and logging roads		272.5		266.8
		2,200.3		2,248.7
Other assets (note 7)		116.6		84.8
	$	2,931.2	$	2,818.7
Liabilities and shareholders' equity				
Current liabilities				
Accounts payable and accrued liabilities	$	345.4	$	295.7
Income taxes payable		5.0		3.3
Current portion of long term debt (note 8)		66.2		52.6
		416.6		351.6
Silviculture liability (note 9)		18.8		12.4
Long term debt (note 8)		227.6		391.5
Deferred income taxes		190.0		113.2
Preferred shares issued by subsidiaries (note 10)		34.3		39.8
Non-controlling interest		174.5		143.4
		1,061.8		1,051.9
Shareholders' equity				
Share capital (note 11)		1,262.6		1,262.6
Retained earnings		564.1		456.4
Foreign currency adjustment		42.7		47.8
		1,869.4		1,766.8
	$	2,931.2	$	2,818.7

Commitments (note 16)

Approved by the directors:

John A. Hood, Director

Douglas W. G. Whitehead, Director

EXHIBIT 12-3 (continued)

FLETCHER CHALLENGE CANADA LIMITED
Consolidated Statements of Earnings

For the years ended June 30 *(in millions of dollars, except per share amounts)*	1995	1994
Net sales	$ 2,153.9	$ 1,675.4
Operating costs and expenses		
Cost of products sold	1,649.0	1,397.6
Depreciation, depletion and amortization	146.9	154.4
Selling and administrative	87.0	79.1
	1,882.9	1,631.1
Operating earnings	271.0	44.3
Other income (expense)		
Interest expense (note 12)	(40.5)	(47.1)
Gain on sale of interest in subsidiary (note 2)	–	60.1
Countervailing duty recovery (note 3)	19.5	–
Investment and other income (expense)	19.6	(12.3)
Earnings before income taxes and non-controlling interest	269.6	45.0
Income taxes (note 13)	115.4	2.3
Net earnings before non-controlling interest	154.2	42.7
Non-controlling interest	34.1	16.3
Net earnings	$ 120.1	$ 26.4
Net earnings per weighted average common share	$ 0.97	$ 0.21
Weighted average common shares outstanding (000)	124,189	124,189

Consolidated Statements of Retained Earnings

for the years ended June 30 (in millions of dollars)	1995	1994
Balance at beginning of year	$ 456.4	$ 464.2
Net earnings	120.1	26.4
Dividends declared	(12.4)	(34.2)
Balance at end of year	$ 564.1	$ 456.4

EXHIBIT 12-3 (continued)

FLETCHER CHALLENGE CANADA LIMITED
Consolidated Statements of Changes in Financial Position

For the years ended June 30 *(in millions of dollars, except per share amounts)*	1995	1994
Cash provided by (used for)		
Operations		
Net earnings	$ 120.1	$ 26.4
Items not requiring (providing) cash		
Depreciation, depletion and amortization	146.9	154.4
Income taxes	99.5	(2.3)
Non-controlling interest	34.1	16.3
Gain on sale of interest in subsidiary		
and fixed assets (note 2)	(1.0)	(62.2)
Other	20.4	11.6
	420.0	144.2
Increase in operating working capital	(107.8)	(20.7)
	312.2	123.5
Per weighted average common share	$ 2.51	$ 0.99
Financing		
Increase (decrease) in long term debt	(146.7)	3.4
Net redemption of preferred shares issued		
by subsidiaries	(5.0)	(237.2)
Repurchase of common shares		
by a subsidiary (note 14)	(3.3)	–
Issue of common shares by a subsidiary	–	185.4
Dividends paid	(12.4)	–
	(167.4)	(48.4)
Investment		
Additions to fixed assets	(113.9)	(81.6)
Proceeds from sale of fixed assets	7.6	8.3
Increase in other assets	(68.6)	(40.5)
	(174.9)	(113.8)
Decrease in cash	(30.1)	(38.7)
Cash at beginning of year	35.7	74.4
Cash at end of year	$ 5.6	$ 35.7

(Cash includes cash and short term investments)

EXHIBIT 12-4

FLETCHER CHALLENGE CANADA LIMITED
Common Size Income Statement

	1995	1994
Net sales	100%	100%
Operating costs and expenses		
Cost of goods sold	76.6%	83.4%
Depreciation, depletion and amortization	6.8%	9.2%
Selling and administrative	4.0%	4.7%
	87.4%	97.4%
Operating earnings	12.6%	2.6%
Other income (expense)		
Interest expense	(1.9%)	(2.8%)
Gain on sale of interest in subsidiary	—	3.6%
Countervailing duty recovery	0.9%	—
Investment and other income (expense)	0.9%	(0.7%)
Earnings before income taxes and non-controlling interest	12.5%	2.7%
Income taxes	5.4%	0.1%
Net earnings before non-controlling interest	7.2%	2.6%
Non-controlling interest	1.6%	1.0%
Net earnings	5.6%	1.6%

■ ■ Ratio Data

Common size data are useful for making comparisons of data items within a given financial statement. They are not useful for making comparisons across the various financial statements. Ratios compare one data element from one statement with an element in another statement, or with an element within the same statement. These ratios can then be used in a time-series or cross-sectional analysis. Ratio data are potentially the most useful data because they reveal information about relationships between the financial statements. Therefore, the remainder of the chapter is devoted to discussing various ratios, their computation, and interpretation. Most of these have already been introduced throughout the book in previous chapters.

◖◗ RATIOS

Ratios explain relationships among data in the financial statements. The relationships differ across corporations, if for no other reason than that the underlying transactions may be different across corporations. For example, a manufacturing corporation is very concerned about the management of inventory, and focuses on various ratios related to inventory. A bank, on the other hand, has no inventory and would not be able to compute a ratio involving inventory. It might, however, be very concerned about the loans that it makes, whereas the manufacturer would not have any items comparable to loans.

Because of the differences across corporations, it is impossible for us to address all the ratio issues related to all types of industries. The main focus of our discussion will, therefore, be restricted to Fletcher Challenge. Most of our discussions are also applicable to other corporations in other industries, such as retailing. At the end of the chapter, we include a brief discussion of ratio analysis of non-manufacturing corporations in areas where there may be differences in interpretation.

The ratios that will be discussed are divided into three general categories, but you will see that they are all related. The categories are performance, short-term liquidity, and long-term liquidity. Most of these ratios apply to any corporation regardless of the nature of its business, but some (such as inventory ratios) apply only to certain types of businesses.

Before the calculations of the various ratios are presented, one general caveat should be made about the calculation of ratios. There often are several ways that can be used to compute a given ratio. Therefore, it makes sense to understand the basis of a calculation before you attempt to interpret it. The use of ratios in this book will be consistent with the definitions given. However, if you use similar ratios from other sources, you should check the definition used in that source to make sure that it is consistent with your understanding of the ratio.

Performance Ratios

Net income and cash flow as measures of performance have already been discussed in Chapters 4 and 5. Although much can be learned from studying the income statement and statement of changes in financial position, both in their raw data and common size forms, the ratios discussed in this section complement that understanding and also draw out some of the relationships between these statements and the balance sheet.

For example, in Chapter 4, a performance ratio called the return on investment (ROI) was briefly discussed. In that chapter, ROI was discussed in generic terms as a measure of performance of an investment. The generic form of the ROI calculation can be used to formulate several different ratios depending on the perspective taken in measuring performance. For example, one perspective is that of the shareholders, who make an investment in the corporation and want to measure the performance of their investment. A form of the ROI measure that captures the return to shareholders is referred to as the **return on equity (ROE)**.

A second perspective is that of the debtholders, who make an investment in the corporation by lending money to it. The return they receive is the interest paid by the corporation. The interest rate paid to them is a measure of their ROI. This type of ROI calculation is not explicitly discussed in this chapter.

The third perspective is that of management. Management obtains resources from both shareholders and debtholders. Those resources are then invested in assets. The return generated by the investment in assets is then used to repay the debtholders and the shareholders. The performance of the investment in assets is, therefore, very important. This type of ROI is captured in a ratio referred to as the **return on assets (ROA)**.

In this chapter, both ROE and ROA are considered. In addition to these two overall measures of performance, three additional ratios, referred to as **turnover ratios**, are discussed. These turnover ratios provide additional insights into three major policy decisions management of corporations makes regarding accounts receivable, inventory, and accounts payable policies.

■ ■ Return on Assets (ROA)

Management of a corporation must make two fundamental decisions regarding the corporation. The first is the type of assets in which the corporation should invest (sometimes referred to as the *investment decision*), and the second is whether to seek more financing to increase the amount the corporation can invest in assets (referred to as the *financing decision*). The ROA ratio, in this book, separates the investment decision from the financing decision. Regardless of the mix of debt and shareholder financing, this ratio asks: What type of return is earned on the investment in assets? From this perspective, the return on the investment in assets should be computed prior to any payments or returns to the debtholders or shareholders. Net income is a measure of return on assets that is computed prior to any returns to shareholders, but after the deduction of interest to the debtholders. Therefore, the net income, if it is to be used as a measure of return on assets, must be adjusted for the effects of interest expense so it is treated on a basis that is similar to the treatment of dividends.

A complicating factor exists because interest is a deductible expense in the computation of income tax expense. Therefore, if interest expense is to be removed from the net income figure, we must also adjust the amount of income tax expense that would result. In other words, the tax savings (i.e., the reduction in income tax expense) associated with this interest deduction must also be removed. The ROA ratio is then calculated as the ratio of the return (income before interest) divided by the investment in total assets as follows:

$$\text{ROA} = \frac{\text{Income Before Interest}}{\text{Average Total Assets}}$$

$$= \frac{\text{Net Income} + \text{Interest Expense} - \text{Tax Savings of Interest Expense}}{\text{Average Total Assets}}$$

$$= \frac{\text{Net Income} + \text{Interest Expense} - (\text{Tax Rate} \times \text{Interest Expense})}{\text{Average Total Assets}}$$

$$\text{ROA} = \frac{\text{Net Income} + [\text{Interest Expense} \times (1 - \text{Tax Rate})]}{\text{Average Total Assets}}$$

Based on the data for Fletcher Challenge in 1995, the computation of the ROA results in the following computations. The income tax rate of 42.8% is found in a note to the financial statements.

ROA — FLETCHER CHALLENGE, 1995

$$\text{ROA} = \frac{\text{Net Income} + [\text{Interest} \times (1 - \text{Tax rate})]}{\text{Average Total Assets}}$$

$$= \frac{\$120.1 + [\$40.5 \times (1 - 42.8\%)]}{\dfrac{\$2,931.2 + 2,818.7}{2}}$$

$$= 5.0\%$$

This 5% ROA indicates that Fletcher Challenge earned 5% on the average total assets before making any payments to the suppliers of capital. This 5% should be compared to the ROA earned by other similar corporations and to Fletcher Challenge's ROA in the previous years to determine the trend.

The computation of the appropriate tax rate to use in the ROA formula is somewhat problematic. The rate that should be used is the marginal tax rate of the corporation. The marginal rate is the rate of tax the corporation would pay on an additional dollar of income before taxes. This marginal rate would be a combination of the federal and provincial corporate income tax rates. Many analysts use the average tax rate, which is computed by dividing the tax expense by the income before taxes. Many corporations, including Fletcher Challenge, show the average tax rates in a note to the financial statements.

The ROA is useful as an overall measure of the performance of the investment in the assets of the corporation. However, cross-sectional comparisons of ROAs across industries must be made with care. The level of ROA reflects, to some extent, the risk inherent in the type of assets in which the corporation invests. Investors trade off the risk of an investment for the return on the investment. The more risk the investor takes, the higher the return demanded by the investor. If the corporation invested its assets in a bank account (a very low-risk investment), it would expect a lower return than if it invested in oil exploration equipment (a high-risk business). Although this factor cannot explain all the variations in ROA between corporations, it must be kept in mind. It may be more appropriate either to do a time-series analysis of this ratio, or to compare it cross-sectionally with a direct competitor in the same business. Data obtained from a source of industry ratios such as Dun and Bradstreet can provide you with median measures of ROA that can be used for comparison purposes to determine if the calculated ROA is good or bad.

In addition, there is another useful breakdown of the ROA ratio that can provide insight into the cause of a change in this ratio. The most common breakdown of this ratio is as follows:

$$\text{ROA} = \frac{\text{Net Income} + [\text{Interest Expense} \times (1 - \text{Tax Rate})]}{\text{Average Total Assets}}$$

$$= \frac{\text{Net Income} + [\text{Interest Expense} \times (1 - \text{Tax Rate})]}{\text{Sales Revenue}}$$

$$\times \frac{\text{Sales Revenue}}{\text{Average Total Assets}}$$

$$= \text{Profit Margin Ratio} \times \text{Total Asset Turnover}$$

This breakdown of the ratio into a **profit margin ratio** and a **total asset turnover** allows the analyst to assess some of the reasons why the ROA of a corporation has gone up or down. The profit margin ratio is, of course, affected by the level of the corporation's costs relative to its revenues. Changes in this ratio would indicate a change in the profitability of the product and may indicate changes in the cost structure or pricing policy. The total asset turnover ratio is the ratio of sales to total assets, or the dollars of sales generated per dollar of investment in assets. Changes in this ratio could reflect an increase or decrease in sales volume, or major changes in the level of investment in assets of the corporation.

The breakdown for Fletcher Challenge in 1995 would be as follows:

ROA (BREAKDOWN) — FLETCHER CHALLENGE, 1995

$$ROA = \frac{Net\ Income + [Interest\ Expense \times (1 - Tax\ Rate)]}{Sales\ Revenue}$$

$$\times \frac{Sales\ Revenue}{Average\ Total\ Assets}$$

$$ROA = \frac{\$120.1 + [\$40.5 \times (1 - 42.8\%)]}{2,153.9}$$

$$\times \frac{2,153.9}{\dfrac{\$2,931.2 + 2,818.7}{2}}$$

$$= 6.65\% \times 0.749 = 5.0\%$$

These calculations indicate that Fletcher Challenge earned the 5% ROA by achieving a profit margin ratio of 6.65% and a total asset turnover of 0.749. Note that the 5% could be increased by increasing either the profit margin ratio or the total asset turnover, or both.

Note that the same ROA could be achieved by corporations in the same industry with different strategies. For example, a discount retailer operates on smaller profit margins and hopes to make that up by a larger volume in sales relative to investment in assets. Discounters generally have less invested in their retail stores. Other full-price retailers have a much larger investment in assets relative to their sales volume and, therefore, must charge higher prices to achieve a comparable ROA. Both businesses face the same general sets of risks and should earn comparable ROAs.

■ ■ Return on Equity (ROE)

Return on equity (ROE), discussed earlier in this section, is the return the shareholders are earning on their investment in the corporation. There is one additional quirk that must be understood in computing this ratio. If there is more than one class of shares (generally the second class of shares would be preferred shares), the ROE calculation should be done from the point of view of the common shareholders. This means that any payments to the other class of shares (preferred dividends, for example) should be deducted from net income in the numerator of this ratio because these amounts are not available to common shareholders. The denominator in such cases should include only the shareholders' equity accounts that belong to common shareholders. This usually means that the preferred shares equity account is subtracted from the total shareholders' equity to arrive at the common shareholders' equity.

The computation of the ROE for a corporation is as follows:

$$ROE = \frac{Net\ Income - Preferred\ Dividends}{Average\ Common\ Shareholders'\ Equity}$$

For Fletcher Challenge, which has no preferred shares outstanding, the calculation is the following:

ROE (BREAKDOWN) — FLETCHER CHALLENGE, 1995

$$ROE = \frac{Net\ Income - Preferred\ Dividends}{Average\ Common\ Shareholders'\ Equity}$$

$$= \frac{120.1 - 0}{\dfrac{1869.4 + 1,766.8}{2}}$$

$$= \frac{120.1}{1818.1} = 6.6\%$$

This calculation shows that Fletcher Challenge earned 6.6% ROE, indicating that it earned an average of 6.6% on the average common shareholders' equity balances. Again, this 6.6% could be compared with other similar corporations, or with the results of Fletcher itself over time.

Cross-sectional comparisons (between different corporations) are also difficult with regard to ROE for the same reason that ROA is difficult. Differences in the risks involved should result in differences in returns. Differences in the risks cannot, however, always explain large differences in return as there are many factors that affect ROE.

◼◼ Leverage

Comparing the ROE computed for Fletcher Challenge with the associated ROA shows that the corporation, while earning only a 5.0% return on assets, showed a return of 6.6% on the common shareholders' equity. This increase in return to equity results from the corporation successfully applying *financial leverage*. Financial leverage simply means that some of the funds obtained to invest in assets came from debtholders rather than from shareholders. A corporation that has a larger proportion of debt to shareholders' equity is said to be highly leveraged.

In the case of a totally shareholder-financed corporation, that is, a corporation with no debt, the ROE (assuming only one class of shares) would equal the ROA. There would be no interest expense and, therefore, the numerators of both ratios would be the same. The denominators would be the same because of the accounting equation (Assets = Liabilities + Shareholders' Equity) as adjusted given the assumed absence of any liabilities (Assets = Shareholders' Equity).

To understand the effects of leverage, consider first the data in Exhibit 12-5 for a 100% equity-financed corporation, the Baker Corporation (a fictitious corporation). To keep the illustration simple, all liabilities are considered to be interest-bearing for Baker Corporation. Note that, in this example, Baker generates a 16.67% return on its assets before taxes (income before interest and taxes/assets = $166.67/$1,000). After

EXHIBIT 12-5

BAKER CORPORATION (100% Owner-Financed)

Baker Corporation (100% Owner-Financed)
Balance Sheet

Assets	Liabilities
$1,000	$ 0
	Shareholders' equity
	$1,000

Income Statement

Income before interest and taxes	$166.67
Interest	0.00
Income before taxes	166.67
Taxes (40%)	66.67
Net income	$100.00

ROA = $100/$1,000 = 10%
ROE = $100/$1,000 = 10%

the 40% corporate income taxes, this translates into a 10% after-tax return (ROA). Note also that the ROE is the same as the ROA because there is no debt.

Now consider the data in Exhibit 12-6 for Baker Corporation, which now assume that the corporation is only 90% shareholder-financed.

In Exhibit 12-6, note several things. The first is that the ROA is the same as in Exhibit 12-5, because the mix of assets has not changed; only the amount of debt in

EXHIBIT 12-6

BAKER CORPORATION (90% Owner-Financed) — Interest Rate = 16.667%

Baker Corporation (90% Owner-Financed)
Balance Sheet

Assets	Liabilities
$1,000	$100
	Shareholders' equity
	$900

Income Statement (assuming an interest rate of 16.667%)

Income before interest and taxes	$166.67
Interest	16.67
Income before taxes	150.00
Taxes (40%)	60.00
Net income	$ 90.00

ROA = [$90 + 16.67 × (1 − .4)]/$1,000 = $100/$1,000 = 10%
ROE = $90/$900 = 10%

the balance sheet has changed. The assets should be earning exactly what they would have earned in a 100% shareholder-financed corporation. Second, note that the ROE is the same as the ROA. This will be the case only if the after-tax borrowing rate is the same as the after-tax ROA. Note that the before-tax borrowing rate is 16.67%. To adjust the rate to an after-tax rate, multiply it by 1 minus the tax rate, or 16.67% $\times$ (1 − 40%) = 10%. This means that the corporation borrowed $100 at a net cost of 10% (the after-tax borrowing rate) and invested the $100 in assets that return 10% after taxes (ROA). Therefore, the corporation breaks even on the money it borrowed. The shareholders' return of 10% is the income after taxes ($90) divided by their investment ($900).

Next, consider Exhibit 12-7, in which a lower interest rate is assumed (12%). In Exhibit 12-7, note that the ROE is greater than the ROA. This occurs because the corporation was able to borrow at a rate that was less than the rate it could earn by investing in assets. The after-tax cost of borrowing is 7.2% [12% $\times$ (1 − 40%)], whereas the after-tax return on the assets is 10% (ROA). Therefore, when the corporation borrowed $100, it cost the corporation $7.20 in interest, but it was able to generate $10 in income. The difference is $2.80, which goes to the shareholders as an incremental return. Therefore, the shareholders earn a 10% (or $90) return on their investment of $900, plus they get the excess return of $2.80 that is earned on the money that was borrowed, for a total ROE of 10.3%. This improves their percentage return (ROE) over what they could have earned as a 100% shareholder-financed corporation without any further investment on their part.

This, then, is the advantage of leverage. The shareholders can improve their return (ROE) if the corporation can borrow funds at an after-tax borrowing rate that is less than the after-tax ROA. This is a big "if." The corporation that leverages itself is committed to making fixed interest payments to debtholders prior to earning a return on its assets. It is betting that the return on assets will be higher than the

---

EXHIBIT 12-7

BAKER CORPORATION (90% Owner-Financed) — Interest Rate = 12%

Baker Corporation (90% Owner-Financed)
Balance Sheet

Assets	Liabilities
$1,000	$100
	Shareholders' equity
	$900

Income Statement (assuming an interest rate of 12%)

Income before interest and taxes	$166.67
Interest	12.00
Income before taxes	154.67
Taxes (40%)	61.87
Net income	$ 92.80

ROA = [$92.80 + 12 $\times$ (1 − .4)]/$1,000 = $100/$1,000 = 10%
ROE = $92.80/$900 = 10.3%

after-tax cost of its borrowing. If it is wrong, the return to the shareholders (ROE) could fall below what they could have earned with no debt at all. Consider, for example, the results of Baker Corporation in Exhibit 12-8, where the corporation commits to paying lenders 20% (before taxes). Return on equity in this case falls below the ROA to 9.8%. This is the risk of leveraging a corporation.

If leveraging the corporation a little is potentially a good thing, as Exhibit 12-7 llustrated, why not leverage it a lot? In other words, why not borrow funds to buy most of the corporation's assets? In Exhibit 12-7, why not have 90% debt and 10% equity in the corporation? Exhibit 12-9 illustrates the kind of return the corporation could expect given 90% debt and the same interest rate as in Exhibit 12-7. A return of 35.2% is certainly a very attractive return compared to the ROA of 10% that could be achieved with a 100% shareholder-financed corporation. The problem with this financing strategy is that lenders will find the riskiness of their investment much higher in Exhibit 12-9 than they would in Exhibit 12-6. As the corporation adds more and more debt to its capital structure, it is committing itself to higher and higher fixed interest payments. Therefore, lenders will start demanding higher and higher returns from their investments as the risk increases. The interest rates will rise, and Baker Corporation will no longer be able to borrow at the 12% that was assumed in Exhibit 12-7. When its average borrowing costs start to equal or exceed the ROA of the corporation, it will become unattractive to borrow any further funds.

In theory, the increase in the borrowing rate would be an increasing function of the amount of leverage employed by the corporation. Return on equity would improve over that of a 100% shareholder-financed corporation, up to some point. Exhibit 12-10 graphs the change (at least in theory) in ROE for various levels of leverage. Based on this graph, you can see that there is a point (at the top of the curve) at which ROE would be maximized. The amount of leverage that corresponds to this point has sometimes been called the **optimal capital structure** of the corporation.

EXHIBIT 12-8

BAKER CORPORATION (90% Owner-Financed) — Interest Rate = 20%

Baker Corporation (90% Owner-Financed)
Balance Sheet

Assets	Liabilities
$1,000	$100
	Shareholders' equity
	$900

Income Statement (assuming an interest rate of 20%)

Income before interest and taxes	$166.67
Interest	20.00
Income before taxes	146.67
Taxes (40%)	58.67
Net income	$ 88.00

ROA = [$88.00 + 20 × (1 − .4)]/$1,000 = $100/$1,000 = 10%
ROE = $88/$900 = 9.8%

EXHIBIT 12-9

BAKER CORPORATION (10% Owner-Financed) — Interest Rate = 12%

Baker Corporation (10% Owner-Financed)
Balance Sheet

Assets	Liabilities
$1,000	$900
	Shareholders' equity
	$100

Income Statement (assuming an interest rate of 12%)

Income before interest and taxes	$166.67
Interest	108.00
Income before taxes	58.67
Taxes (40%)	23.47
Net income	35.20

ROA = [$35.20 + 108 × (1 − .4)]/$1,000 = $100/$1,000 = 10%
ROE = $35.20/$100 = 35.20%

For the hypothetical corporation illustrated in the graph, the optimal capital structure would be to have approximately 40% debt and the rest equity. This point exists in theory, but is more difficult to determine in the real world. It is true, however, that as you look across industries, different industries have different average levels of leverage. This would indicate that, based on the risk characteristics of those indus-

EXHIBIT 12-10

Leverage and Optimal Capital Structure

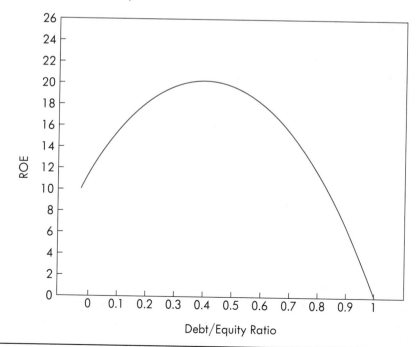

tries, the corporations in those industries borrow to the point they think is profitable, and no further.

The use of leverage by a corporation can be judged, to some extent, by the difference in the ROE of the corporation versus the ROA, as illustrated by the graph. In addition, several other ratios are used to measure the amount of leverage the corporation employs, as well as how well it uses that leverage. These ratios include the debt/equity ratio and times interest earned ratios, which are discussed in a later section on liquidity.

■ ■ Turnover Ratios

In addition to the overall measures of performance, ROA and ROE, there are other measures that are helpful in understanding more specific items that make up the overall performance of the corporation. Three turnover measures are discussed in this book. They relate to the three policy decisions that were discussed in Chapter 5 with regard to the cash flow performance of the corporation. They are **accounts receivable**, **inventory**, and **accounts payable turnovers**. These ratios provide some quantitative measures of the lead/lag relationships that exist between the revenue and expense recognition and the cash flows related to these three items.

ACCOUNTS RECEIVABLE TURNOVER

The accounts receivable turnover ratio attempts to provide information about the accounts receivable policy of the corporation. This ratio measures how many times during a year the accounts receivable balance "turns over," that is, how many times old receivables are collected and replaced by new receivables. It is calculated as follows:

$$\text{Accounts Receivable Turnover} = \frac{\text{Sales on Account}}{\text{Average Accounts Receivable}}$$

When data from financial statements are used, the assumption is usually made that all sales were on account because there is usually no information in the financial statements about the percentage of sales on account versus cash sales. If the turnover ratio was being prepared for internal use by management, this type of information would be available and would be used in the computation of this ratio.

When the data from Fletcher Challenge are used, the ratio for 1995 is:

ACCOUNTS RECEIVABLE TURNOVER — FLETCHER CHALLENGE, 1995

$$\text{Accounts Receivable Turnover} = \frac{\$2,153.9}{\frac{\$282.2 + \$158.2}{2}}$$

$$= 9.8 \text{ times}$$

The level of turnover of accounts receivable depends on several factors, especially the normal credit terms granted by the corporation. If the corporation normally gives 30 days to the customers to pay, and if customers pay in 30 days, the resulting accounts receivable turnover would be 12 because there would be 30 days' of sales always outstanding in accounts receivable. If the normal credit term is 60 days, the resulting accounts receivable turnover would be 6. With an accounts receivable turnover of 9.8, it appears that much of Fletcher Challenge's receivables have 30-day credit terms.

The turnover number can also be converted into a measure of the days necessary to collect the average receivable by dividing the numbers of days in one year by the turnover ratio. To simplify calculations, the number of days in a year is often assumed to be 360 rather than 365. The average days to collect for Fletcher Challenge are:

DAYS TO COLLECT ACCOUNTS RECEIVABLE — FLETCHER CHALLENGE, 1995

$$\text{Days to collect} = \frac{365}{\text{Accounts Receivable Turnover}}$$

$$= \frac{365}{9.8}$$

$$= 37 \text{ days}$$

You cannot simply look at the 37 days and decide if it is bad or good. You need to know what the normal credit terms are, if the average monthly sales are fairly equal (large sales in the last month of the fiscal year would result in an apparently lower turnover and higher number of days' sales in the year-end balance), and what proportion of total sales are made on credit. To analyze this 37 days, we should also consider a time-series analysis (the trend compared to previous years) and a cross-sectional analysis (a comparison with Fletcher competitors).

INVENTORY TURNOVER

The inventory turnover ratio gives the analyst some idea of how fast inventory is sold or, alternatively, how long inventory is held prior to sale. The calculation of the turnover is similar to that of accounts receivable turnover, with a measure of the flow of inventory in the numerator (top number) and a measure of the balance in inventory in the denominator (bottom number). It is calculated as follows:

$$\text{Inventory Turnover} = \frac{\text{Cost of Goods Sold}}{\text{Average Inventory}}$$

Note that the numerator contains the cost of goods sold, not the sales value of the goods sold (revenues). Total sales revenue, while it does measure the flow of goods sold to customers, would be inappropriate in the numerator because it is based on the selling price of the inventory while the denominator is measured at cost. Cost of goods sold measures at cost and so is more appropriate.

The number of days for which inventory is held can be calculated from the turnover ratio in the same way as was the accounts receivable turnover ratio.

INVENTORY TURNOVER — FLETCHER CHALLENGE, 1995

$$\text{Inventory Turnover} = \frac{\$1{,}649.0}{\dfrac{\$309.2 + \$282.3}{2}}$$

$$= 5.6 \text{ times}$$

$$\text{Days inventory held} = \frac{365}{\text{Inventory Turnover}}$$

$$= \frac{365}{5.6}$$

$$= 65 \text{ days}$$

The average number of days that inventory is held depends on the type of inventory produced and how long the production process takes. In the ratio just calculated, the total inventories of Fletcher Challenge were used. This includes raw materials, work-in-process, and finished goods. The 65 days, therefore, refers to the average length of time that costs remain in inventory from original purchase or incurrence to ultimate sale. The ratio could also be calculated using only finished goods in the denominator of the turnover ratio to assess how long it takes from completion of production to sale. Fletcher Challenge produces wood pulp, boards, and paper. From a note to its financial statements, the value of its inventory of pulp, paper and newsprint at June 30, 1995 and 1994 was $73.1 and $114.3 million respectively. Assuming this item represents Fletcher's finished goods ready for sale, we can calculate its finished goods inventory turnover as follows:

FINISHED GOODS INVENTORY TURNOVER — FLETCHER CHALLENGE, 1995

$$\text{Inventory Turnover} = \frac{\$1{,}649.0}{\dfrac{\$73.1 + \$114.3}{2}}$$

$$= 17.6 \text{ times}$$

$$\text{Days inventory held} = \frac{365}{\text{Inventory Turnover}}$$

$$= \frac{365}{17.6}$$

$$= 21 \text{ days}$$

Based on these numbers, it seems obvious that the total production process takes approximately 65 days, but the finished goods are not held for very long before they are sold (21 days). As with the accounts receivable turnover figures, deciding whether this is good or bad would require either a time-series or a cross-sectional analysis, as well as some detailed knowledge of the industry.

ACCOUNTS PAYABLE TURNOVER

The accounts payable turnover ratio is similar to the accounts receivable ratio, but provides information about the payables policy of the corporation. In its ideal form, it would be calculated as follows:

$$\text{Accounts Payable Turnover} = \frac{\text{Credit Purchases}}{\text{Average Accounts Payable}}$$

The problem with the preceding formulation is that the credit purchases of a corporation do not appear directly in the financial statements. It may be possible to approximate the credit purchases by finding the cash payments made to suppliers in the cash flow statement, assuming that the balance in accounts payable did not change drastically during the period. However, this requires that the corporation prepare its SCFP using the direct approach. As mentioned in Chapter 5, almost all corporations use the indirect approach to the SCFP, and cash payments to suppliers do not appear directly in that statement.

Another alternative is to use the cost of goods sold figure in place of purchases on credit because cost of goods sold appears in the income statement. To the extent that the purchase of goods is the main item that affects cost of goods sold, this would be appropriate. In a retailing corporation, this would probably be a good approximation, again assuming that the level of inventories did not change dramatically during the period. For a manufacturing corporation, however, many items other than credit purchases affect the cost of goods sold. As discussed in Chapter 3, amortization on manufacturing equipment, for example, is considered an overhead cost and is included in the cost of goods sold. Therefore, for a manufacturer, this ratio probably has less meaning. When this ratio is calculated, most analysts would use the cost of goods sold in the numerator. It would therefore be calculated as:

$$\text{Accounts Payable Turnover} = \frac{\text{Cost of Goods Sold}}{\text{Average Accounts Payable}}$$

For Fletcher Challenge in 1995, this ratio is:

ACCOUNTS PAYABLE TURNOVER — FLETCHER CHALLENGE, 1995

$$\text{Accounts Payable Turnover} = \frac{\$1,649.0}{\dfrac{\$345.4 + \$295.7}{2}}$$

$$= 5.1 \text{ times}$$

$$\text{Days to pay} = \frac{365}{\text{Accounts Payable Turnover}}$$

$$= \frac{365}{5.1}$$

$$= 72 \text{ days}$$

For Fletcher Challenge, the calculation of this ratio and the average days to pay appears to be high if the normal credit terms received by Fletcher Challenge are 30 days. In this case, it may not be appropriate to use the cost of goods sold as an approximation of purchases on credit if the cost of goods sold includes significant amounts that are not purchased on credit from suppliers. However, we cannot really understand these numbers without knowing more details of the operations and the amounts that are included in the cost of goods sold. Again, cross-sectional and time-series analyses should be undertaken.

◢◣ Short-Term Liquidity Ratios

As discussed in Chapter 1, liquidity refers to the ability of the corporation to convert assets into cash to pay liabilities. A basic understanding of the short-term liquidity position of the corporation should result from a consideration of the financial statements, particularly the statement of changes in financial position, as well as the turnover ratios discussed in the performance section. Understanding the liquidity position requires a knowledge of the leads and lags in the corporation's cash-to-cash cycle. Additionally, there are at least two ratios that provide quantitative measures of short-term liquidity: the current and the quick ratios.

■ ■ Current Ratio

The **current ratio** is calculated by comparing the total current assets to the total current liabilities. It is calculated as follows:

$$\text{Current Ratio} = \frac{\text{Current Assets}}{\text{Current Liabilities}}$$

Remember that current assets are those that are going to be converted into cash in the next year (or operating cycle of the corporation if it is longer than one year), and that current liabilities are going to require the use of cash in the next year. As such, this ratio should be greater than 1; otherwise, it is difficult to see how the corporation will remain solvent in the next year. The rule of thumb for this ratio for most industries is that it should be 1 or more, but, to be conservative, this ratio should be approximately 2 or more. However, the size of this ratio depends on the type of business and the type of assets and liabilities that are considered current.

One caveat: The current ratio is subject to manipulation by a corporation at the end of the year. This ratio may not, therefore, be a very reliable measure of liquidity. For example, consider a corporation that has $100 in current assets and $50 in current liabilities at the end of a given year. Its current ratio would be 2 ($100/$50). Suppose that $25 of the $100 is in cash and the rest is in inventory. Suppose further that the corporation uses up all of its $25 in cash to pay $25 of current liabilities at the end of the year. The current ratio becomes 3 ($75/$25); now the corporation looks more liquid. Notice, however, that the corporation is actually less liquid; in fact, it is virtually illiquid in the short term because it has no cash and must sell its inventory and wait until it collects on the sale of that inventory before it will have any cash to pay its bills. In this case, the current ratio is deceptive.

The current ratio for Fletcher Challenge in 1995 is:

CURRENT RATIO — FLETCHER CHALLENGE, 1995

$$\text{Current Ratio} = \frac{\$614.3}{\$416.6} = 1.5$$

This current ratio of 1.5 is below the 2 that is often desired as a conservative number, but it may be quite acceptable in this industry.

■ ■ Quick Ratio

One of the problems with the current ratio is that some assets in the current section are less liquid than others. For example, inventory is less liquid than accounts receivable, which is less liquid than cash. In some industries, inventory is very illiquid because of the long period of time that it may have to be held before sale. Consider, for example, the holding period in the manufacture of 12-year-old scotch whisky. The current ratio in such cases will not adequately measure the short-term liquidity of the corporation because the inventory will not be converted into cash for a long period of time. In this case, the **quick ratio** is a better measure to assess short-term liquidity. It differs from the current ratio only in that inventories (and sometimes prepaid expenses) are omitted from the numerator. It is calculated as:

$$\text{Quick Ratio} = \frac{\text{Current Assets} - \text{Inventories}}{\text{Current Liabilities}}$$

The rule of thumb for this ratio is that it should be approximately 1 or more. A quick ratio of 1 means that the very short-term current assets are equal to the total of the current liabilities. Again, the actual value depends on the type of industry. For Fletcher Challenge, the calculation results in:

QUICK RATIO — FLETCHER CHALLENGE, 1995

$$\text{Quick Ratio} = \frac{\$614.3 - \$309.2}{\$416.6} = .73$$

This calculated quick ratio of 0.73 is less than the rule of thumb that it should be 1 or more. This low number is consistent with the fairly high accounts payable turnover number of 72 days and the slightly low current ratio of 1.5. Taken together, these numbers may indicate that Fletcher Challenge may be experiencing a cash flow problem at June 30, 1995. However, we cannot really understand these numbers without knowing more details of its operations. Again, cross-sectional and time-series analyses should be undertaken.

◣◤ Long-Term Liquidity Ratios

Long-term liquidity refers to the ability of the corporation to pay its obligations in the long term (meaning more than one year in the future). This means its ability to pay its long-term debt. A time-series analysis of the SCFP and the patterns of cash flow over time should provide a lot of the insight one needs to assess a corporation's abilities in this regard. There are at least two ratios that are generally used in the assessment of long-term liquidity: the debt/equity ratio, and the times interest earned ratio.

■ ■ Debt/Equity Ratio

The debt-to-equity ratio is really a set of ratios that are used to assess the extent to which the corporation is leveraged. From our earlier discussion about leverage, you know that the more leverage a corporation has, the riskier its situation and the more fixed are its commitments to pay interest. Comparing the amount of debt to the amount of equity in a corporation is important in assessing its ability to pay off these debts in the long term.

Of the many different definitions of the debt-to-equity ratios that could be used here, we shall use three. They will be referred to as D/E(I), D/E(II), and D/E(III). D/E(I) expresses the total debt of the corporation as a percent of total liabilities plus shareholders' equity (the same as total assets). The total liabilities are assumed to include all liabilities of the corporation, and the shareholders' equity to include all shareholders' equity accounts. This ratio is calculated as:

$$\text{D/E(I)} = \frac{\text{Total Liabilities}}{\text{Total Liabilities} + \text{Shareholders' Equity}}$$

$$\text{or } \frac{\text{Total Liabilities}}{\text{Total Assets}}$$

For Fletcher Challenge in 1995, this ratio is:

D/E(I) — FLETCHER CHALLENGE, 1995

$$\text{D/E(I)} = \frac{\$1,061.8}{\$2,931.2}$$

$$= .36$$

The second debt-to-equity ratio provides the same information, but in a slightly different form. It is calculated as the ratio of the total liabilities to the total shareholders' equity, as follows:

$$\text{D/E(II)} = \frac{\text{Total Liabilities}}{\text{Total Shareholders' Equity}}$$

For Fletcher Challenge in 1995, this ratio is:

D/E(II) — FLETCHER CHALLENGE, 1995

$$D/E(II) = \frac{\$1,061.8}{\$1,869.4}$$

$$= .57$$

The third debt-to-equity ratio focuses on the long-term debt of the corporation relative to its equity. It is calculated as the ratio of the total long-term liabilities to the sum of the total long-term liabilities plus the shareholders' equity of the corporation, as follows:

$$D/E(III) = \frac{\text{Total Long-Term Liabilities}}{\text{Total Long-Term Liabilities} + \text{Shareholders' Equity}}$$

For Fletcher Challenge in 1995, this ratio is:

D/E(III) — FLETCHER CHALLENGE, 1995

$$D/E(III) = \frac{\$1,061.8 - 416.6}{\$1,061.8 - 416.6 + 1,869.4}$$

$$= .26$$

Is the level of debt represented in these ratios appropriate for Fletcher Challenge? Again, a cross-sectional analysis of these ratios could reveal whether or not Fletcher Challenge has excessive debt compared to other corporations. A time-series analysis could reveal the trend over time. As a general guide, however, the average of corporate debt on the books of nonfinancial corporations is somewhere between 45% and 50%. Fletcher Challenge, with a ratio of 36%, appears to have slightly less debt than average. An inspection of the long-term debt of Fletcher Challenge shows that 18% of the total liabilities ($190.0/$1,061.8) is deferred income taxes which, if you recall, are not contractual obligations with a fixed payment date. Therefore, the long-term liquidity position of Fletcher Challenge appears to be quite good, in contrast with its short-term liquidity position.

■ ■ Times Interest Earned

The final ratio in the long-term liquidity section is the **times interest earned (TIE) ratio**. It compares the amount of earnings available to pay interest to the level of interest expense. Because interest is tax-deductible, the earnings available to pay interest would be the earnings prior to the payment of interest or taxes. One complication in the computation of this ratio is that some corporations capitalize interest when they construct long-term assets. This means that, instead of expensing interest, a corporation can record the interest in an asset account. This generally happens only when a corporation is constructing an asset and incurs interest on money borrowed to finance the construction. The adjustment to the ratio is that the amount of interest capitalized should be added to the denominator. The numerator does not require adjustment if the amount of interest expensed is added back to net income. The ratio is therefore calculated as:

$$\text{Times Interest Earned} = \frac{\text{Income Before Interest \& Taxes}}{\text{Interest}}$$

$$= \frac{\text{Net Income} + \text{Taxes} + \text{Interest}}{\text{Interest}}$$

Fletcher Challenge indicates in a note to the financial statements that its policy is to capitalize interest on "the equivalent amount of borrowed funds during the period of construction." However, the financial statements do not indicate how much, if any, interest was capitalized in 1995. Thus to calculate this ratio for 1995, we must assume that no interest was capitalized in 1995.

TIMES INTEREST EARNED — FLETCHER CHALLENGE, 1995

$$\text{TIE} = \frac{\text{Net Income} + \text{Taxes} + \text{Interest}}{\text{Interest}}$$

$$= \frac{\$120.1 + \$115.4 + \$40.5}{\$40.5}$$

$$= 6.8$$

This figure indicates that Fletcher Challenge earned 6.8 times the amount it needed to pay its interest expense in 1995. Income would have to drop to one-sixth before Fletcher Challenge have trouble paying its interest. To the extent that interest may have been capitalized in 1995, these figures are overstated. When any corporation shows a times interest earned figure of close to 1, this indicates that the payment of its interest may be at risk.

◤◣ Earnings Per Share Ratios

The **earnings per share ratio** is one that is quoted quite often in the financial press and one in which shareholders are very interested. In its simplest form, it is the earnings of the corporation divided by the weighted-average number of common shares outstanding. Although this ratio may be of some help in analyzing a corporation's results, its usefulness is limited. The major problem with using it as a measure of performance is that it ignores the level of investment. Corporations with the same earnings per share might have very different profitabilities, depending on their investment in net assets. The other limitation is that the shares of different corporations are not equivalent, and corporations with the same overall profitability may have different earnings per share figures because they have a different number of shares outstanding that represent ownership. The best use of the earnings per share figure is in a time-series analysis rather than in a cross-sectional analysis.

The earnings per share calculation represents the earnings per *common share*. Therefore, if the corporation also issues preferred shares, the effects of the preferred shares must be removed in calculating the ratio. With preferred shares outstanding, this means that any dividends that are paid to preferred shareholders should be deducted from net income because that amount of income is not available to common shareholders. The number of preferred shares outstanding should also be left out of the denominator. The calculation of **basic earnings per share** then becomes:

$$\text{Basic Earnings per share} = \frac{\text{Net Income} - \text{Preferred Dividends}}{\text{Weighted-Average Number of Common Shares Outstanding}}$$

The preferred dividends that should be deducted are the cumulative preferred dividends, whether they are declared in the year or not, and any non-cumulative preferred dividends that have been declared in the year. Recall from Chapter 11 that cumulative means that if a dividend is not declared on the preferred shares in one year, the dividends then carry over into the next year. In the second year, both the prior year's preferred dividend and the current year's preferred dividends must be declared before any common dividends can be declared.

In addition to preferred shares, another complicating factor in the calculation of earnings per share arises when the corporation issues any securities that are convertible into common shares. Examples of these types of securities are convertible debt, convertible preferred shares, and share option plans. The key feature of these securities is that they are all convertible into common shares under certain conditions. If additional common shares are issued upon their conversion, the earnings per share number could decrease because of the larger number of shares that would be outstanding. This is called the potential dilution of earnings per share.

At the end of a given accounting period, the presence of convertible securities creates some uncertainty about how to report the earnings per share number. Should the corporation report earnings per share without considering the potentially dilutive effects of the convertible securities, or should it disclose some information that would allow readers of the financial statements to understand these effects? The best information that can be provided to users of financial statements is that information should be disclosed that provides some information about the dilutive effects of convertible securities. Thus financial statements may include several earnings per share figures, the main ones being the **basic earnings per share** and **fully diluted earnings per share.**

■ ■ Basic Earnings Per Share

Basic earnings per share is a very simple number that considers only the net income, preferred dividends, and the weighted average number of common shares outstanding. Every published financial statement shows this figure. Note in Exhibit

12-3 (the income statement for Fletcher Challenge) that there were 124,189,000 weighted-average number of common shares outstanding, and net earnings of $120,100,000. There were no preferred shares outstanding. This results in a basic earnings per share of $0.97.

■ ■ Fully Diluted Earnings per Share

Fully diluted earnings per share is calculated under the worst-case scenario set of assumptions. It assumes that all convertible securities are converted (assuming that they are dilutive) and produces the lowest earnings per share number that could result given full conversion of all convertible securities.

Fletcher Challenge has no convertible securities, so there is no fully diluted earnings per share figure.

■ ■ Price/Earnings Ratio

The **price/earnings ratio,** or **multiple**, is a comparison of the price per share on the stock market with the earnings per share of the corporation. Many analysts think of this ratio as the price investors are willing to pay for a dollar's worth of earnings. The interpretation of this ratio is somewhat difficult because stock market price levels are not well understood. It might help to think of the multiple in terms of its inverse. If a corporation is earning $1.00 per common share and the shares are selling for $20 on the stock market, this indicates that the current multiple is 20. The inverse of this multiple is 1/20, or 5%. This indicates that the shares are returning 5% in the form of earnings per share compared to the market price.

Many factors affect the level of stock market prices, including the interest rates prevailing in the economy and the future prospects of the corporation. It is sometimes useful to think that the market price reflects the present value of all future expected earnings of the corporation. The earnings per share figure serves as an important link between the accounting numbers produced in the financial statements and the stock market price of the corporation's shares.

◖◗ NON-MANUFACTURING CORPORATION ANALYSIS

Although the above discussion is applicable to most corporations in most industries, some differences for non-manufacturing corporations should be noted. As an example of a non-manufacturing corporation, consider the analysis of a financial services corporation such as a bank, an insurance corporation, or a finance company. These types of corporations invest in very different kinds of assets than manufacturers, and they obtain their financing from different sources.

The assets of financial services corporations consist of almost no inventories and relatively little property, plant, and equipment. The majority of their assets consists of loans that they made to their customers or other investments. The assets of most nonfinancial corporations consist mainly of property, plant, and equipment, inventories, and receivables.

The liability sections of financial services corporations are also very different from those of manufacturers. The first major difference is the debt-to-equity ratio. Financial services corporations tend to have considerably higher debt-to-equity ratios than manufacturers because of the large amounts of cash received from depositors. In the insurance industry, the high ratio results from amounts owed to policyholders. Second, liabilities of financial services corporations such as banks tend to be predominantly short-term in nature because of the deposits received from customers, which are normally payable upon demand.

The higher leverage employed by financial services corporations reflects, in part, the lower risk of the types of assets in which these corporations invest. Manufacturers, in addition to employing financial leverage, also employ something called **operating leverage**. Operating leverage involves investing in large amounts of property, plant, and equipment (capital assets with fixed amortization costs). The property, plant, and equipment allows manufacturers to make their own inventory rather than buying it from an outside supplier (variable costs). The risk is that the manufacturers must operate at a sufficient volume to allow their profit from the sale of goods to cover their fixed costs. At large volumes, this makes manufacturing corporations very profitable but, at low volumes, the corporations generate large losses because the fixed costs must be paid from the lower sales volumes. Partially because of the amount of operating leverage, lenders generally do not lend to manufacturers as much as they lend to financial services corporations.

The complete analysis of financial services corporations is beyond the scope of this book. It is hoped that this brief discussion of some of the differences between financial services corporation and manufacturers will provide some insights into how an analysis of the two types of companies may differ.

SUMMARY

At this point in the book, we have discussed all the major financial statements and specific accounting methods and principles that apply to each category within the asset, liability, and shareholders' equity sections of the balance sheet. We restricted the discussions to fairly simple corporations to make it easier for you to learn the basics. The final chapter of the book considers more complex organizations. These are corporations (usually called parent corporations) that buy an interest in other corporations (called subsidiaries) to obtain control of the resources of the subsidiary. Complex issues then face the accountant, such as how to represent the resources controlled by the shareholders of the parent corporation. These issues are discussed in Chapter 13.

Ratio Summary

Exhibit 12-11 summarizes the ratios that were developed in the chapter.

EXHIBIT 12-11

Ratio Summary

$$\text{ROA} = \text{Profit Margin Ratio} \times \text{Total Asset Turnover}$$

$$= \frac{\text{Net Income} + [\text{Interest Expense} \times (1 - \text{Tax Rate})]}{\text{Sales Revenue}} \times \frac{\text{Sales Revenue}}{\text{Average Total Assets}}$$

$$\text{ROE} = \frac{\text{Net Income} - \text{Preferred Dividends}}{\text{Average Shareholders' Equity}}$$

$$\text{Inventory Turnover} = \frac{\text{Cost of Goods Sold}}{\text{Average Inventory}}$$

$$\text{Accounts Receivable Turnover} = \frac{\text{Credit Sales}}{\text{Average Accounts Receivable}}$$

$$\text{Accounts Payable Turnover} = \frac{\text{Cost of Goods Sold}}{\text{Average Accounts Payable}}$$

$$\text{Current Ratio} = \frac{\text{Current Assets}}{\text{Current Liabilities}}$$

$$\text{Quick Ratio} = \frac{\text{Current Assets} - \text{Inventory}}{\text{Current Liabilities}}$$

$$\text{D/E(I)} = \frac{\text{Total Liabilities}}{\text{Total Liabilities} + \text{Shareholders' Equity}}$$

$$\text{D/E(II)} = \frac{\text{Total Liabilities}}{\text{Shareholders' Equity}}$$

$$\text{D/E(III)} = \frac{\text{Total Long-Term Liabilities}}{\text{Total Long-Term Liabilities} + \text{Shareholders' Equity}}$$

$$\text{Times Interest Earned (TIE)} = \frac{\text{Net Income} + \text{Taxes} + \text{Interest}}{\text{Interest}}$$

$$\text{Price/Earnings Ratio} = \frac{\text{Stock Market Price}}{\text{Earnings Per Share}}$$

SUMMARY PROBLEM

The income statement, balance sheet, and statement of changes in financial position of AB Breweries Corporation for 19x9, 19x8, and 19x7 are shown in Exhibit 12-12. Calculate the following ratios for 19x9 based on the data in the financial statements. Comment on what the ratios tell us about the financial position of AB Breweries Corporation and what further analyses you should undertake.

Performance Ratios:
  1. ROA (Break down into profit margin ratio and total asset turnover.)
  2. ROE
  3. Accounts receivable turnover
  4. Inventory turnover (both total inventory and finished goods)
  5. Accounts payable turnover

Short-Term Liquidity Ratios:
  6. Current ratio
  7. Quick ratio

Long-Term Liquidity Ratios:
  8. Debt/equity ratios
  9. Times interest earned

EXHIBIT 12-12

AB BREWERIES CORPORATION
Consolidated Statement of Inome
(in millions, except per share data)

Year Ended December 31,	19X9	19X8	19X7
Sales	$12,634.2	$11,611.7	$10,283.6
Less federal excise taxes	1,637.9	868.1	802.3
Net sales	10,996.3	10,743.6	9,481.3
Cost of products and services	7,148.7	7,093.5	6,275.8
Gross profit	3,847.6	3,650.1	3,205.5
Marketing, distribution and administrative expenses	2,126.1	2,051.1	1,876.8
Operating income	1,721.5	1,599.0	1,328.7
Other income and expenses:			
Interest expense	(238.5)	(283.0)	(177.9)
Interest capitalized	46.5	54.6	51.5
Interest income	9.2	7.0	12.6
Other income/(expenses), net	(18.1)	(25.5)	11.8
Income before income taxes	1,520.6	1,352.1	1,226.7
Provisions for income taxes:			
Current	479.1	429.9	357.0
Deferred	101.7	79.8	102.5
	580.8	509.7	459.5
Net Income	$ 939.8	$ 842.4	$ 767.2
Earnings Per Share			
Basic	$ 3.26	$ 2.96	$ 2.68
Fully diluted	$ 3.25	$ 2.95	$ 2.68

EXHIBIT 12-12 (continued)

AB BREWERIES CORPORATION
Consolidated Balance Sheet
Assets (in millions)

December 31,	19X9	19X8
Current Assets:		
Cash and marketable securities	$ 97.3	$ 95.3
Accounts and notes receivable, less allowance for		
doubtful accounts of $5.5 in 19X9 and $6.2 in 19X8	654.8	562.6
Inventories		
Raw materials and supplies	397.2	344.7
Work-in-process	92.5	104.7
Finished goods	145.9	117.8
Total inventories	635.6	576.2
Other current assets	240.0	201.2
Total current assets	1,627.7	1,426.3
Investments and Other Assets:		
Investments in and advances to affiliated		
companies	116.9	100.8
Investment properties	159.9	151.4
Deferred charges and other non-current assets	365.9	358.4
Excess of cost over net assets of acquired		
businesses, net	519.9	533.6
	1,162.3	1,144.2
Plant and Equipment:		
Land	308.9	307.7
Buildings	3,027.8	2,825.2
Machinery and equipment	6,583.9	6,080.3
Construction in progress	669.0	803.5
	10,589.6	10,016.7
Accumulated amortization	(3,393.1)	(2,952.9)
	7,196.5	7,063.8
	$ 9,986.5	$ 9,634.3

EXHIBIT 12-12 (continued)

AB BREWERIES CORPORATION
Consolidated Balance Sheet
Liabilities and Shareholders' Equity (in millions)

December 31,	19X9	19X8
Current Liabilities:		
Accounts payable	$ 709.8	$ 711.2
Accrued salaries, wages and benefits	223.3	247.3
Accrued interest payable	58.5	72.3
Due to customer for returnable containers	44.5	44.6
Accrued taxes, other than income taxes	110.9	71.5
Estimated income taxes	45.2	79.2
Other current liabilities	210.6	185.8
Total current liabilities	1,402.8	1,411.9
Long-Term Debt	2,644.9	3,147.1
Deferred Income Taxes	1,500.7	1,396.2
Common Shares and Other Shareholders' Equity:		
Common Shares, authorized 400,000,000 shares	993.0	894.6
Retained earnings	5,209.8	4,563.3
Foreign currency translation adjustment	20.7	29.3
	6,223.5	5,487.2
Treasury stock, at cost	(1,324.2)	(1,323.1)
ESOP debt guarantee offset	(461.2)	(485.0)
	4,438.1	3,679.1
Commitments and Contingencies	—	—
	$9,986.5	$9,634.3

EXHIBIT 12-2 (continued)

AB BREWERIES CORPORATION
Consolidated Statement of Changes in Financial Position
(in millions)

Year Ended December 31,	19X9	19X8	19X7
Cash Flow From Operating Activities:			
Net income	$ 939.8	$ 842.4	$ 767.2
Adjustments to reconcile net income to net cash provided by operating activities:			
Amortization expense	534.1	495.7	410.3
Increase in deferred income taxes	104.5	80.3	103.4
Decrease/(increase) in non-cash working capital	(208.5)	122.8	(90.6)
Other, net	24.8	(24.3)	(50.2)
Cash provided by operating activities	1,394.7	1,516.9	1,140.1
Cash Flow From Investing Activities:			
Capital expenditures	(702.5)	(898.9)	(1,076.7)
Business acquisitions	(15.7)	(12.1)	(1,117.9)
Cash used for investing activities	(718.2)	(911.0)	(2,194.6)
Cash Flow from Financing Activities:			
Increase in long-term debt	.6	178.6	1,328.3
Decrease in long-term debt	(479.1)	(427.8)	(32.3)
Dividends paid to shareholders	(301.1)	(265.0)	(226.2)
Acquisition of treasury shares	(1.1)	(86.3)	(624.4)
Shares issued to ESOP	—	—	500.0
Shares issued under stock plans and conversion of Convertible Debentures	106.2	53.5	81.6
Cash provided by/(used for) financing activities	(674.5)	(547.0)	1,027.0
Net increase/(decrease) in cash and marketable securities during the year	2.0	58.9	(27.5)
Cash and marketable securities at beginning of year	95.3	36.4	63.9
Cash and marketable securities at end of year	$ 97.3	$ 95.3	$ 36.4

SUGGESTED SOLUTION TO SUMMARY PROBLEM

ROA:

ROA (BREAKDOWN) — AB BREWERIES CORPORATION, 19X9

$$ROA = \frac{\text{Net Income} + [\text{Interest Expense} \times (1 - \text{Tax Rate})]}{\text{Sales Revenue}}$$

$$\times \frac{\text{Sales Revenue}}{\text{Average Total Assets}}$$

$$ROA = \frac{\$939.8 + [\$192^* \times (1 - 580.8/1,520.6)]}{\$12,634.2}$$

$$\times \frac{\$12,634.2}{\dfrac{\$9,634.3 + \$9,986.5}{2}}$$

$$= 8.38\% \times 1.29 = 10.8\%$$

---

* The interest expense was calculated by netting the interest expense with the interest capitalized.

ROE:

ROE — AB BREWERIES CORPORATION, 19X9

$$ROE = \frac{\text{Net Income} - \text{Preferred Dividends}}{\text{Average Shareholders' Equity}}$$

$$ROE = \frac{\$939.8 - 0}{\dfrac{\$3,679.1 + \$4,438.1}{2}}$$

$$ROE = 23.2\%$$

ACCOUNTS RECEIVABLE TURNOVER:

A/R TURNOVER — AB BREWERIES CORPORATION, 19X9

$$\text{Accounts Receivable Turnover} = \frac{\$12,634.2}{\dfrac{\$562.6 + \$654.8}{2}}$$

$$= 20.8 \text{ times}$$

$$\text{Days to Collect} = \frac{365 \text{ days}}{\text{Receivable Turnover}}$$

$$= \frac{365 \text{ days}}{20.8}$$

$$= 18 \text{ days}$$

INVENTORY TURNOVER — TOTAL INVENTORY:

INVENTORY TURNOVER — AB BREWERIES CORPORATION, 19X9

$$\text{Inventory Turnover} = \frac{\$7,148.7}{\dfrac{\$567.2 + \$635.6}{2}}$$

$$= 11.9 \text{ times}$$

$$\text{Days Inventory Held} = \frac{365 \text{ days}}{\text{Inventory Turnover}}$$

$$= \frac{365 \text{ days}}{11.9}$$

$$= 31 \text{ days}$$

INVENTORY TURNOVER — FINISHED GOODS INVENTORY:

INVENTORY TURNOVER — AB BREWERIES CORPORATION, 19X9

$$\text{Inventory Turnover} = \frac{\$7,148.7}{\dfrac{\$117.8 + \$145.9}{2}}$$

$$= 54.2 \text{ times}$$

$$\text{Days Inventory Held} = \frac{365 \text{ days}}{\text{Inventory Turnover}}$$

$$= \frac{365 \text{ days}}{54.2}$$

$$= 7 \text{ days}$$

ACCOUNTS PAYABLE TURNOVER:

A/P TURNOVER — AB BREWERIES CORPORATION, 19X9

$$\text{Accounts Payable Turnover} = \frac{\$7,148.7}{\dfrac{\$711.2 + \$709.8}{2}}$$

$$= 10.1$$

$$\text{Days to Pay} = \frac{365 \text{ days}}{10.1} = 36 \text{ days}$$

CURRENT RATIO:

CURRENT RATIO — AB BREWERIES CORPORATION, 19X9

$$\text{Current Ratio} = \frac{\$1,627.7}{\$1,402.8} = 1.16$$

QUICK RATIO:

QUICK RATIO — AB BREWERIES CORPORATION, 19X9

$$\text{Quick Ratio} = \frac{\$1,627.7 - 635.6}{\$1,402.8} = 0.71$$

D/E(I):

D/E(I) — AB BREWERIES CORPORATION, 19X9

$$\text{D/E(I)} = \frac{\$5,548.4^*}{\$9,986.5} = 55.6\%$$

---
* Calculated as total liabilities and shareholders' equity minus total shareholders' equity ($9,986.5 − $4,438.1).

D/E(II):

D/E(II) — AB BREWERIES CORPORATION, 19X9

$$\text{D/E(II)} = \frac{\$5,548.4}{\$4,438.1} = 1.25$$

D/E(III):

D/E(III) — AB BREWERIES CORPORATION, 19X9

$$\text{D/E(III)} = \frac{\$2,644.9 + \$1,500.7}{\$2,644.9 + \$1,500.7 + \$4,438.1} = 0.48$$

TIMES INTEREST EARNED:

TIE — AB BREWERIES CORPORATION, 19X9

$$\text{TIE} = \frac{\text{Net Income} + \text{Taxes} + \text{Interest}}{\text{Interest}}$$

$$= \frac{\$939.8 + 580.8 + 192.0}{238.5^*} = 7.2$$

---
* The interest in the denominator is the total interest expense, and the addback in the numerator is the net interest expense with the amount of interest capitalized netted out.

◖◗ PERFORMANCE RATIOS

In analyzing the performance of any corporation, first consider the net income and its trend. For AB, the net income is positive and increasing. This is a good sign, which is confirmed by the increasing earnings per share. Next, consider the ROA and ROE ratios. ROA is 10.8% and the ROE is 23.2%. The ROA of 10.8% indicates AB is earning a reasonable return on assets, at least somewhat larger than could be earned if the assets were invested in other securities or bank deposits. From the breakdown in the ROA calculation, the reasonable performance by AB can be seen to be in its profit margin (8.38%) and not the total asset turnover ratio (1.29). The ROE of 23.2% is quite good and indicates good use of leverage.

The turnover figures are also good. The accounts receivable turnover of 20.8 times indicates only 18 days' sales in accounts receivable. This compares very favourably to the normal credit terms of 30 days, and implies there should be no significant collection problems. The inventory turnover of 11.9 times indicates there are 31 days' sales of inventory on hand. This seems to indicate there are no potential problems with obsolete inventory. The finished goods inventory turnover of 54.2 times indicates finished goods are on hand only for seven days. This is a very good figure and indicates that AB is selling its product just one week after it is ready for sale. This is important for a brewery because of the relatively short shelf-life of its products. The accounts payable turnover of 10.1 times indicates it pays its suppliers an average of 36 days after incurring the obligation. This compares to the normal credit terms of 30 days. We might want to try to obtain further information on why AB is slightly above the 30 days figure.

Further analyses would include common size financial statements to determine the trends in the cost of goods sold and other expenses (shown in Exhibit 12-13), and trend analyses of the ROA and ROE.

These common size statements show that net income remained basically unchanged in the three years. The most striking item is the increase in the excise taxes in 19x9, which, of course, goes to government. The apparent drop in cost of goods sold is mainly a reflection of the increased sales figure because of the increase in excise taxes.

◣◤ Short-Term Liquidity

The short-term liquidity ratios are both reasonable, although just slightly on the low side. It would be better if the current ratio of 1.16 were closer to 2 and the quick ratio of 0.71 were closer to 1, but the good finished inventory and accounts receivable turnovers produce a reasonable cash flow. The cash flow from operations is positive and not decreasing when 19x9 is compared to 19x7.

◣◤ Long-Term Liquidity

The fairly high debt-to-equity ratios result in the favourable leverage and increase in the ROE above the ROA. High debt-to-equities requires a stable market for the prod-

EXHIBIT 12-13

AB BREWERIES CORPORATION
Common Size Income Statement

	19X9	19X8	19X7
Sales	100.0%	100.0%	100.0%
Less — federal beer excise taxes	13.0%	7.5%	7.8%
	87.0%	92.5%	92.2%
Cost and Expenses:			
Cost of goods sold	56.6%	61.1%	61.0%
Marketing, distribution and administrative	16.8%	17.7%	18.3%
	73.4%	78.8%	79.3%
Operating Income	13.6%	13.7%	12.9%
Other (income) expense:			
Interest income	−0.1%	−0.1%	−0.1%
Interest expense (net of capitalized)	1.5%	2.0%	1.2%
Miscellaneous	0.1%	0.2%	−0.1%
	1.5%	2.1%	1.0%
Income before income taxes	12.1%	11.6%	11.9%
Income taxes	4.6%	4.4%	4.5%
Net income	7.5%	7.2%	7.4%

ucts sold, and the three years of results appear to indicate that AB's market is reasonably stable. AB earns 7.2 times the interest costs, so there appears to be no real problem in paying interest.

An interesting trend can be seen in the SCFP. Cash inflow from operating activities is positive, as it should be. Cash is being used for investing activities to invest in new long-term assets, which is also a good sign. The interesting aspect is the financing activities section, which shows a net cash outflow. AB is paying down the long-term debt, using cash provided by operations to do so. Reducing long-term debt decreases the likelihood that long-term liquidity will be a problem, but it will also decrease the leverage effect on ROE. Reductions in long-term liabilities also normally indicate a mature corporation, meaning one that is not growing very quickly.

ABBREVIATIONS USED

P/E Ratio	Price/earnings ratio
ROA	Return on assets
ROE	Return on equity
TIE	Times interest earned

GLOSSARY

Accounts payable turnover The number of times that accounts payable are replaced during the accounting period. It is usually calculated as the cost of goods sold divided by the average accounts payable.

Accounts receivable turnover The number of times that accounts receivable are replaced during the accounting period. It is calculated as the sales divided by the average accounts receivable.

Common size data Data that are prepared from the financial statements (usually the income statement and balance sheet) in which each element of the financial statement is expressed as a percentage of some denominator value. On the income statement, the denominator value is usually the net sales revenues for the period and, on the balance sheet, the denominator is the total assets for the period.

Cross-sectional analysis A type of financial statement analysis in which one corporation is compared with other corporations, either within the same industry or across industries, for the same time period.

Current ratio A measure of the short-term liquidity of the corporation. It is measured as the ratio of the current assets of the corporation divided by the current liabilities.

Debt/equity ratios Measures of the leverage of the corporation. There are numerous definitions of these ratios, but all of them attempt to provide a comparison of the amount of debt in the corporation compared to the amount of equity.

Earnings per share A measure of the performance of the corporation, calculated by dividing the earnings for the period available to common shares by the weighted-average number of common shares that were outstanding during the period.

Fully diluted earnings per share A type of earnings per share calculation that provides the lowest possible earnings per share figure under the assumption that all convertible securities and options of the corporation are converted into common shares. It measures the maximum potential dilution in earnings per share that would occur under these assumed conversions.

Inventory turnover The number of times that inventory is replaced during the accounting period. It is cal-culated as the cost of goods sold divided by the average inventory.

Leverage The use of debt in a corporation to improve the return to the shareholders.

Multiple See Price/earnings ratio.

Operating leverage The replacement of variable costs with fixed costs in the operation of the corporation. If a sufficient volume of sales is achieved, the investment in fixed costs can be very profitable.

Optimal capital structure A theoretical point at which the leverage of the corporation maximizes the return to the shareholders (ROE).

Price/earnings ratio A performance ratio that compares the market price per share with the earnings per share.

Profit margin ratio A performance measure that compares the after-tax but before-interest income of a corporation with the revenues of the corporation.

Prospective analysis A financial statement analysis of a corporation that attempts to look forward in time to predict future results.

Quick ratio A measure of the short-term liquidity of a corporation calculated by dividing the current assets less inventories (and, in some cases, prepaid items) by the current liabilities.

Retrospective analysis A financial statement analysis of a corporation that looks only at historical data.

Return on assets A measure of performance that measures the return on the investment in assets of the corporation. It is calculated by dividing the income after tax but before interest by the average total assets of the corporation during the accounting period. The ratio can be split into the profit margin ratio and the total asset turnover ratio.

Return on equity A measure of performance that measures the return on the investment made by common shareholders. It is calculated by dividing the net income less dividends for preferred shares by the average common shareholders' equity during the accounting period.

Time-series analysis A financial statement analysis in which data are analyzed over time.

Times interest earned ratio A measure of long-term liquidity of a corporation. It measures the ability of the corporation to make its interest payments. It is calculated by dividing the income before interest and taxes by the interest expense.

Total asset turnover A measure of performance of a corporation that shows the number of dollars of sales that is generated per dollar of investment in total assets. It is calculated by dividing the sales revenue by the average total assets for the accounting period.

ASSIGNMENT MATERIAL

Assessing Your Recall

1. Explain the difference between a retrospective analysis and a prospective analysis of a corporation.

2. Compare and contrast time-series analysis with cross-sectional analysis.

3. Describe the three major types of data that could be used in a time-series or a cross-sectional analysis.

4. For each of the following ratios, reproduce the formula for their calculation:
   a. ROA (Break down into profit margin ratio and total asset turnover ratio.)
   b. ROE
   c. Accounts receivable turnover
   d. Inventory turnover
   e. Accounts payable turnover
   f. Current ratio
   g. Quick ratio
   h. D/E(I)
   i. D/E(II)
   j. D/E(III)
   k. Times interest earned

5. Explain how the turnover ratios relate to the cash produced from operations of a corporation.

6. Describe leverage, and explain how it is evidenced in the ROA and ROE ratios.

7. Explain, using the profit margin and total asset turnover ratios, how two corporations in the same business (use retail clothing stores as an example) can earn the same ROA, yet may have very different operating strategies.

8. What is the advantage of preparing common size statements in financial statement analysis?

9. Explain why the current ratio is subject to manipulation as a measure of liquidity.

10. Discuss the problems associated with calculating an accounts payable turnover ratio that make it difficult to interpret.

11. Describe how earnings per share are calculated, and discuss the purpose of producing basic and fully diluted earnings per share for a corporation.

▶◀ Applying Your Knowledge

12. The financial data for Nova Electronics Corporation and Pulsar Electrical Ltd. for the current year are as follows:

	Annual sales	Accounts receivable, Jan. 1	Accounts receivable, Dec. 31
Nova Electronics	$3,893,567	$1,103,879	$1,140,251
Pulsar Electrical	1,382,683	357,934	243,212

a. Compute the accounts receivable turnover for each corporation.
b. Compute the average number of days required by each corporation to collect the receivables.
c. Which corporation is more efficient in terms of handling its accounts receivable policy?

13. Information regarding the activities of Polymer Plastics Corporation is as follows:

	Year 1	Year 2	Year 3	Year 4	Year 5
Cost of goods sold	$363,827	$411,125	$493,350	$579,686	$608,670
Average inventory	60,537	76,560	107,338	156,672	202,895

a. Do a time-series analysis for the inventory turnover for each year, and also compute the average number of days that inventories are held for the respective years.
b. Is Polymer Plastics Corporation managing its inventories efficiently?

14. The following financial information relates to Delocro Mechanical Inc. (amounts in thousands):

	Year 1	Year 2	Year 3	Year 4
Sales	$2,000	2,200	2,420	2,662
Average total assets	1,111	1,222	1,344	1,479
Average shareholders' equity	620	682	750	825
Net income	200	230	264	304
Interest expense	50	55	61	67
Tax rate	40%	40%	40%	30%

For each year, calculate:
a. Return on shareholders' equity (ROE)
b. ROA
   1) Profit margin ratio
   2) Total asset turnover
c. Comment on the profitability of Delocro Mechanical Inc.

15. Empire Corporation's summarized balance sheet is as follows:

Total assets	$500,000	Liabilities	$100,000
		Shareholders' equity	$400,000
	$500,000		$500,000

The interest rate on the liabilities is 10% and the income tax rate is 30%.

a. If the ROE is equal to the ROA, compute the net income.

b. Compute the ROE, using the net income determined in part (a).

c. Compute the income before interest and taxes for the net income derived in part (a).

d. Assume that total assets remain the same (i.e., at $500,000) and that loans increase to $300,000 while shareholders' equity decreases to $200,000. Assume that the interest rate is now 8%, and the income tax rate remains at 30%. What is the ROE if the ROA is the same as calculated in part (b), i.e., when ROA = ROE?

e. Compare the ROE in both situations, and comment on your findings.

16. Spectrum Associates financial data are as follows (amounts in thousands):

	Year 1	Year 2	Year 3	Year 4
Current assets				
Accounts receivable	$ 700	$ 800	$ 600	$ 650
Cash	200	100	200	150
Other current assets	100	100	250	100
Inventories	500	1,000	1,450	2,100
	$1,500	$2,000	$2,500	$3,000
Current liabilities				
Accounts payable	$ 600	$ 700	$ 825	$ 800
Accrued salaries	300	400	495	400
Other current liabilities	100	150	165	300
	$1,000	$1,250	$1,485	$1,500

a. Compute the current and quick ratios for Years 1 through 4.

b. Comment on the short-term liquidity position of Spectrum Associates.

17. Artscan Enterprises' financial data are as follows:

	Year 1	Year 2	Year 3
Income before interest and taxes	$ 400	$ 600	$ 800
Interest	70	100	135
Current liabilities	375	475	750
Noncurrent liabilities	625	1,125	1,600
Shareholders' equity	1,000	1,500	2,000

a. Compute the debt/equity ratios (I, II, and III) and times interest earned ratio.

b. Comment on the long-term liquidity position of Artscan Enterprises.

18. State the immediate effect (increase, decrease, no effect) of the following transactions on:

a. Current ratio

b. Quick ratio

c. Working capital

d. ROE

e. Debt/equity ratio (D/E(I))

Transactions:

1. Inventory costing $25,000 is purchased on credit.

2. Inventory costing $125,000 is sold on account for $158,000.

3. Payments of $65,000 are made to suppliers.

4. A machine costing $120,000 is purchased; $30,000 is paid in cash, and the balance will be paid in equal instalments for the next three years.

5. Common shares worth $100,000 are issued.

6. Equipment costing $80,000 with accumulated amortization of $50,000 is sold for $40,000 in cash.

7. Goods that cost $35,000 were destroyed by fire. The residual value of some of the partly burned goods was $3,000, which is received in cash. The goods were not insured.

▶◣ Reading and Interpreting Published Financial Statements

19. The 1995 financial statements of CHC Helicopter Corporation (headquartered in St. John's, Newfoundland) are shown in Exhibit 12-14. Based on these financial statements, answer each of the following questions:
    a. Compute the following ratios for 1995:
       1) ROA (split into profit margin ratio and total asset turnover). Assume that the corporate income tax rate is 43%. (The additional taxes included in the "Income taxes" figure include large corporations tax and foreign taxes.)
       2) ROE (there are no preferred shares outstanding).
       3) Inventory turnover (assume that 50% of Operating Expenses relate to inventory).
       4) Accounts Receivable Turnover.
    b. Compute the following ratios for both 1995 and 1994
       1) Current ratio
       2) Quick ratio
       3) D/E(I)
       4) Times interest earned.
    c. Comment on the use of leverage by CHC.
    d. Assume you are considering investing in CHC. Comment on the pros and cons of doing so. Use not only the ratios, but also the information from the three financial statements in your analysis.
    e. A significant proportion of CHC Helicopter's operations is conducted in other countries. The Canadian dollar has decreased in value relative to the currencies used in most of the countries in which CHC operates. Assume that the Canadian dollar will continue to decrease in value, and that CHC has the ability to choose the currency in which it can receive revenues, pay expenses, and borrow money. How should CHC use this ability to maximize its profits?

EXHIBIT 12-14

CHC HELICOPTER CORPORATION
Consolidated Balance Sheet
April 30, 1995 (in thousands of Canadian dollars)

	1995	1994
Assets		
Current		
Receivables	$ 75,595	$ 71,950
Inventory	73,083	61,742
Prepaid expenses	5,011	5,966
	153,689	139,658
Property and equipment, at cost (Note 3)	336,223	324,507
Less: Accumulated depreciation	81,239	75,381
	254,984	249,126
Other assets (Note 4)	30,386	38,068
	$ 439,059	$ 426,852
Liabilities		
Current		
Bank indebtedness (Note 5)	$ 15,562	$ 11,571
Payables and accruals	57,894	51,836
Current portion of long term debt	12,174	9,992
	85,630	73,399
Long term debt (Note 6)	106,371	100,496
Senior subordinated notes (Note 7)	110,160	117,300
Convertible subordinated debentures (Note 8)	15,000	15,000
Deferred credits (Note 9)	44,829	41,157
Shareholders' Equity	77,069	79,500
	$ 439,059	$ 426,852

Commitments (Note 18)
Contingent liabilities (Notes 2(b) and 19)

On Behalf of the Board

_____ Director _____ Director

See accompanying notes to the financial statements.

EXHIBIT 12-14 (continued)

CHC HELICOPTER CORPORATION
Consolidated Statement of Earnings
Year Ended April 30, 1995
(in thousands of Canadian dollars, except per share amounts)

	1995	1994
Revenue	**$ 366,920**	$ 230,999
Operating expenses	327,694	200,177
Earnings before undernoted items	**39,226**	30,822
Depreciation and amortization	**(17,255)**	(10,879)
Gain on disposal of assets	**5,846**	427
Earnings from operations	**27,817**	20,370
Interest (Note 12)	**26,976**	15,052
Earnings before the following	**841**	5,318
Equity in earnings of associated company (Note 2(a))	**–**	2,363
Debt restructuring (Note 13)	**–**	(10,827)
Earnings (loss) before income taxes	**841**	(3,146)
Income taxes (Note 14)	**1,936**	801
Net loss	**$ (1,095)**	$ (3,947)
Net loss per share (Note 15)	**$ (0.09)**	$ (0.41)

See accompanying notes to the financial statements.

20. The 1995 financial statements of Western Star Trucks Holdings Ltd. (based in Kelowna, British Columbia) are shown in Exhibit 12-15. Based on these financial statements, answer each of the following questions:
    a. Compute the following ratios for 1995:
        1) ROA (split into profit margin ratio and total asset turnover). What assumption should you make about interest expense in 1995?
        2) ROE (there are no preferred shares outstanding).
        3) Inventory turnover.
        4) Accounts receivable turnover.
    b. Compute the following ratios for both 1995 and 1994:
        1) Current ratio
        2) Quick ratio
        3) D/E(I)
        4) Times interest earned

EXHIBIT 12-14 (continued)

CHC HELICOPTER CORPORATION
Consolidated Statement of Cash Flows
Year Ended April 30, 1995
(in thousands of Canadian dollars, except per share amounts)

	1995	1994
Operating activities		
Earnings from operations	$ 27,817	$ 20,370
Items not involving cash		
Depreciation and amortization	17,255	10,879
Gain on disposal of assets	(5,846)	(427)
Other	(166)	–
Cash flow from operations before interest and taxes	39,060	30,822
Interest	(26,976)	(15,052)
Current taxes (Note 14)	(1,069)	(1,637)
Cash flow from operations	11,015	14,133
Change in non-cash working capital (Note 16)	(7,973)	(19,866)
	3,042	(5,733)
Financing activities		
Long term debt - increase	16,883	112,201
- reduction	(10,483)	(135,066)
Senior subordinated notes (Note 7)	(5,440)	117,300
Government grant	555	21
Capital stock	(14)	19,124
Dividends	(1,161)	(952)
	340	112,628
Cash available for investing activities	3,382	106,895
Investing activities		
Business acquisition (Note 2(a))	–	(42,437)
Property and equipment - additions	(40,189)	(48,163)
- proceeds from sale	32,750	5,980
Foreign exchange adjustment (Note 11)	(164)	1,624
Deferred charges	230	(21,656)
	(7,373)	(104,652)
Change in cash during the year	(3,991)	2,243
Short term bank indebtedness, beginning of year	(11,571)	(13,814)
Short term bank indebtedness, end of year	$ (15,562)	$ (11,571)
Cash flow from operations per share (Note 15)	$ 0.95	$ 1.46

See accompanying notes to the financial statements.

EXHIBIT 12-15

WESTERN STAR TRUCK HOLDINGS LTD.
Consolidated Balance Sheet

As at June 30	1995	1994
[in thousands of dollars]		
ASSETS		
Current		
Cash and short-term investments	58,834	20,863
Cash collateral deposits – LSVW Contract [notes 8 and 9]	2,480	8,488
Accounts receivable	47,320	41,945
Prepaid expenses and deposits	4,944	589
Inventories [note 5]	66,519	52,902
Deferred LSVW account [note 4]	7,314	10,076
Total current assets	187,411	134,863
Capital assets [note 6]	37,893	10,967
Deferred costs [note 7]	21,978	14,056
	247,282	159,886
LIABILITIES, MINORITY INTEREST		
AND SHAREHOLDERS' EQUITY		
Current		
Accounts payable	64,148	80,167
Accrued liabilities	31,966	11,538
Income taxes payable	5,845	4,485
Customer deposits	16,491	–
Loans and advances and capital lease obligations [note 8]	10,893	5,683
Total current liabilities	129,343	101,873
Deferred income tax	1,794	–
Customer deposits – non-current	3,438	–
Loans and advances and capital lease obligations – non-current [note 8]	14,316	13,318
Total liabilities	148,891	115,191
Commitments and contingencies [note 9]		
Minority interest [note 10]	15,000	–
Shareholders' equity		
Share capital [note 12]	32,166	31,633
Retained earnings	51,225	13,062
Total shareholders' equity	83,391	44,695
	247,282	159,886

See accompanying notes

On behalf of the Board:

Director   Director

c. Assume you are thinking of investing in Western Star. Comment on the financial health of Western Star, and highlight any areas that might be of concern. Use not only the ratios, but also the information from all the three financial statements in your analysis.

d. Comment on the use of leverage by Western Star.

e. Western Star builds its heavy-duty highway transport trucks in Canada and exports many of them to the U.S. and other countries. It buys parts in both Canada and other countries. Assume first that the Canadian dollar strengthens

EXHIBIT 12-15 (continued)

WESTERN STAR TRUCK HOLDINGS LTD.

Consolidated Statements of Operations and Retained Earnings

Years ended June 30 [in thousands of dollars except per share amounts]	1995	1994
Revenue	726,022	426,974
Expenses		
Cost of sales	645,301	384,769
Selling and administrative	25,912	14,462
Interest [income] expense – net	[81]	457
	671,132	399,688
Net income before minority interest and taxes	54,890	27,286
Minority interest [note 10]	–	[1,578]
Net income before taxes	54,890	25,708
Income tax expense [note 13]	13,331	4,586
Net income	41,559	21,122
Retained earnings [deficit], opening balance	13,062	[5,317]
Share issue costs	271	[2,743]
Dividends paid	[3,667]	–
Retained earnings, closing balance	51,225	13,062
Net income per share [note 16]	3.73	2.61
Fully diluted net income per share	3.58	2.61

See accompanying notes

Consolidated Statements of Cash Flows

Years ended June 30 [in thousands of dollars except per share amounts]	1995	1994
OPERATING ACTIVITIES		
Net income	41,559	21,122
Adjustment for items not involving cash		
Depreciation and amortization	2,183	1,895
Minority interest	–	1,258
Deferred income tax	1,794	–
Cash flow from operations	45,536	24,275
Changes in non-cash working capital balances relating to operations	[3,942]	[16,089]
Cash provided by operating activities	41,594	8,186
FINANCING ACTIVITIES		
Dividends paid	[3,667]	–
Decrease in cash collateral deposits	6,008	1,442
Loans and advances and capital lease obligations	240	563
Issuance of common shares	533	31,533
Share issue costs	271	[2,743]
Increase [decrease] in minority interest	15,000	[10,208]
Increase in customer deposits	9,104	–
Cash provided by financing activities	27,489	20,587
INVESTING ACTIVITIES		
Capital asset additions	[18,363]	[3,513]
Increase in deferred costs	[8,405]	[5,377]
Acquisition of Orion Assets [note 2]	[25,344]	–
Share purchase incentive [note 2]	21,000	–
Cash used in investing activities	[31,112]	[8,890]
Increase in cash and short-term investments	37,971	19,883
Cash and short-term investments, beginning of year	20,863	980
Cash and short-term investments, end of year	58,834	20,863
Cash flow from operations per share [note 16]	4.09	2.99
Fully diluted, cash flow from operations per share	3.90	2.99

See accompanying notes

against the U.S. dollar, and second that it weakens. Comment on the effect these changes would have on Western Star's revenues and expenses.

21. The 1994 financial statements of Tritech Precision Inc. (with headquarters in Toronto, Ontario) are shown in Exhibit 12-16. Based on these financial statements, answer each of the following questions:

    a. Compute the following ratios for 1994:
       1) ROA (split into profit margin ratio and total asset turnover). What assumption should you make about interest expense in 1994?
       2) ROE (There are no preferred shares outstanding).
       3) Inventory turnover.
       4) Accounts receivable turnover.

    b. Compute the following ratios for both 1994 and 1993 pro forma:
       1) Current ratio
       2) Quick ratio
       3) D/E(I)
       4) Times interest earned

    c. Assume you are thinking of investing in Tritech. Comment on the financial health of Tritech, and highlight any areas that might be of concern. Use not only the ratios, but also the information from all the three financial statements in your analysis.

    d. Comment on the use of leverage by Tritech. Include comments on the average interest rates paid by Tritech on both long-term and short-term debt (assume the "Other Interest" relates to the "Current Bank Indebtedness" and be sure to include the "Current Portion of Long-Term Debt" in your calculations). What changes to your leverage calculations would have resulted if Tritech had no "Current Bank Indebtedness," but had obtained the same amount of financing from "Long-Term Debt" at the same long-term interest rates?

    e. Tritech produces specialized parts for several industries, including the automotive and defense industries. Approximately 75% of sales are made in the U.S. Most of the costs and liabilities are in Canadian dollars. Calculate the effects on "Income Before Minority Interest and Income Taxes" under the following assumptions: (i) the Canadian dollar strengthens against the U.S. dollar by 5%; and (ii) the Canadian dollar decreases in value by 5% against the U.S. dollar. Comment on the effect of these changes.

22. The 1994 financial statements of Enerflex Systems Ltd. (with headquarters in Calgary, Alberta), who produces compressor equipment used in the natural gas industry, are shown in Exhibit 12-17. Based on these financial statements, answer each of the following questions:

    a. Compute the following ratios for 1994:
       1) ROA (split into profit margin ratio and total asset turnover).
       2) ROE (there are no preferred shares outstanding).
       3) Inventory turnover.
       4) Accounts receivable turnover.

    b. Compute the following ratios for both 1994 and 1993:
       1) Current ratio
       2) Quick ratio
       3) D/E(I)
       4) Times interest earned

EXHIBIT 12-16

TRITECH PRECISION INC.
Consolidated Balance Sheet

As at December 31 (in thousands of dollars)	1994	Proforma 1993 (note 1)	1993
ASSETS			
Current			
Cash and short-term deposits	$ 1,444	$ –	$ –
Accounts receivable	20,913	12,175	3,585
Inventory *(note 3)*	11,864	11,132	5,483
Prepaids and other assets	964	817	614
Total current assets	35,185	24,124	9,682
Long-term investment *(note 4)*	8,791	9,267	9,267
Fixed assets *(note 5)*	27,189	19,994	5,995
Goodwill	4,731	4,863	4,863
	$ 75,896	$ 58,248	$ 29,807
LIABILITIES AND			
SHAREHOLDERS' EQUITY			
Current			
Bank indebtedness *(note 6)*	7,194	7,579	440
Accounts payable and accrued liabilities	20,654	13,744	4,342
Income taxes payable	102	105	105
Current portion of long-term debt *(note 7)*	1,673	3,887	–
Total current liabilities	29,603	25,315	4,887
Long-term debt *(note 7)*	5,337	4,675	–
Deferred income taxes	851	98	98
Minority interest	1,730	1,514	191
Shareholders' equity *(note 1)*			
Share capital *(note 9)*	32,187	26,193	–
Divisional equity	–	–	24,631
Appraisal increase	431	453	–
Retained earnings	5,757	–	–
Total shareholders' equity	38,375	26,646	24,631
	$ 75,896	$ 58,248	$ 29,807

See accompanying notes

On behalf of the Board:

[signature]

Director

[signature]

Director

EXHIBIT 12-16 (continued)

TRITECH PRECISION INC.
Consolidated Statements of Income

Years ended December 31 (in thousands of dollars)	1994	Proforma 1993	1993
		(note 1)	
Sales	$ 99,566	$ 71,289	$ 32,293
Cost of goods sold	79,736	58,714	25,092
Gross profit	19,830	12,575	7,201
Expense			
Selling and administration	7,984	6,193	4,137
Depreciation and amortization	3,499	2,289	754
	11,483	8,482	4,891
Income from operations	$ 8,347	$ 4,093	$ 2,310
Equity in loss of Haley Industries Limited	476	923	923
Interest on long-term debt	485	591	35
Other interest	605	443	–
Write-down of investment in Haley Industries Limited	–	1,117	1,117
	1,566	3,074	2,075
Income before minority interest and income taxes	6,781	1,019	235
Income taxes (note 8)			
Current	84	125	125
Deferred	753	765	65
	837	890	190
Minority interest	209	43	27
Income before extraordinary item	5,735	86	18
Extraordinary item (note 12)	–	1,040	–
Net income for the year	$ 5,735	$ 1,126	$ 18
Earnings per share			
Basic	1.04	0.18	–
Fully diluted	1.03	0.18	–

See accompanying notes

EXHIBIT 12-16 (continued)

TRITECH PRECISION INC.

Consolidated Statements of Changes in Financial Position

Years ended December 31 (in thousands of dollars)	1994	1993
OPERATING ACTIVITIES		
Net income for the year	$ 5,735	$ 18
Add items not involving a current outflow of cash		
Depreciation and amortization	5,499	754
Deferred income taxes	753	65
Equity in loss of affiliate	476	923
Minority interest	209	27
Write-down of investment in Haley Industries Limited	–	1,117
	10,672	2,904
Net change in non-cash equivalent working capital related to continuing operations	(1,760)	381
Cash provided by operating activities	8,912	3,285
INVESTING ACTIVITIES		
Net purchase of fixed assets	(10,585)	(1,259)
Purchase of subsidiaries *(note 1)*	(7,160)	(1,479)
Cash used in investing activities	(17,745)	(2,738)
FINANCING ACTIVITIES		
Repayment of long-term debt	(2,151)	–
Issuance of shares	13,260	–
Funds transferred from division	–	(905)
Cash provided by (used in) financing activities	11,109	(905)
Increase (decrease) in cash and cash equivalents for the year	2,276	(358)
Bank indebtedness assumed during the year *(note 1)*	(7,586)	–
Net bank indebtedness, beginning of year	(440)	(82)
Net bank indebtedness, end of year	(5,750)	(440)
REPRESENTED BY		
Cash and short-term deposits	1,444	–
Bank indebtedness	(7,194)	(440)
	(5,750)	(440)

See accompanying notes

EXHIBIT 12-17

ENERFLEX SYSTEMS LTD.
Consolidated Statements of Financial Position
Year Ended December 31 (thousands)

	1994	1993
Assets		
Current Assets		
Accounts receivable	$ 50,171	$ 26,106
Inventory (note 1)	18,925	16,780
Total current assets	69,096	42,886
Rental Equipment (note 2)	18,078	9,515
Property, Plant and Equipment (note 3)	13,770	8,012
Goodwill, net of accumulated amortization	1,561	1,607
	$ 102,505	$ 62,020
Liabilities and Shareholders' Equity		
Current Liabilities		
Bank loans (note 4)	$ 12,002	$ 7,837
Accounts payable and accrued liabilities	37,935	18,850
Income taxes payable	6,094	3,614
Deferred income taxes - current	(1,067)	(664)
Current portion of long-term debt (note 4)	76	70
Total current liabilities	55,040	29,707
Long-term Debt (note 4)	4,716	4,792
Deferred Income Taxes	1,156	1,063
	60,912	35,562
Shareholders' Equity		
Share capital (note 5)	34,158	34,158
Retained earnings (deficit)	7,435	(7,700)
	41,593	26,458
	$ 102,505	$ 62,020

Commitments and Contingencies (note 6)

On behalf of the Board:

Director

Director

EXHIBIT 12-17 (continued)

ENERFLEX SYSTEMS LTD.
Consolidated Statement of Shareholders' Equity
(thousands)

	Preferred Shares	Common Shares	Retained Earnings (Deficit)	Total Shareholders' Equity
Balance at January 1, 1993	$ 2,800	$ 6,249	$ 14,357	$23,406
Net income			7,695	7,695
Redemption of preferred shares, January 1993	(2,800)			(2,800)
Cash dividends, January 1993				
Preferred shares			(24)	(24)
Common shares			(2,600)	(2,600)
Gross proceeds from the public issue of common shares on September 22, 1993		36,000		36,000
Expenses of issue ($3,094) less income taxes ($1,252)		(1,842)		(1,842)
Distribution to shareholders (note 5)		(6,249)	(27,128)	(33,377)
Balance at December 31, 1993	–	34,158	(7,700)	26,458
Net income			17,779	17,779
Cash dividends			(2,644)	(2,644)
Balance at December 31, 1994	$ –	$ 34,158	$ 7,435	$41,593

Consolidated Statements of Income
Year Ended December 31 (thousands, except per share amounts)

	1994	1993
Sales (note 7)	$ 217,342	$ 119,983
Cost of Goods Sold	166,055	92,149
Gross Margin	51,287	27,834
Expenses (Income)		
Selling, general and administrative (note 8)	20,646	13,570
Interest (note 4)	1,345	1,114
Gain on sale of rental equipment	(872)	(438)
	21,119	14,246
Income before Income Taxes	30,168	13,588
Income Taxes (note 9)	12,389	5,893
Net Income	$ 17,779	$ 7,695
Net Income per Common Share (note 10)	$ 2.35	$ 1.02*

*Pro forma

EXHIBIT 12-17 (continued)

ENERFLEX SYSTEMS LTD.
Consolidated Statements of Changes in Financial Position
Year Ended December 31 (thousands)

	1994	1993
Operating Activities		
Net income	$ 17,779	$ 7,695
Depreciation and amortization	2,326	2,313
Deferred income taxes	(310)	(706)
Gain on sale of rental equipment	(872)	(438)
Funds from operations	18,923	8,864
Changes in non-cash working capital	(4,645)	(7,016)
	14,278	1,848
Investment Activities		
Acquisition of property, plant and equipment	(7,161)	(1,561)
Acquisition of rental equipment	(8,568)	(2,677)
	(15,729)	(4,238)
Financing Activities		
Net proceeds from public issue of common shares	–	34,158
Redemption of preferred shares	–	(2,800)
Distribution to shareholders of record prior to public issue	–	(33,377)
Dividends paid	(2,644)	(2,624)
Mortgage repayments	(70)	(64)
	(2,714)	(4,707)
Bank Loans		
Increase in bank loans during year	4,165	7,097
Beginning of year	7,837	740
End of year	$ 12,002	$ 7,837

c. Assume you are thinking of investing in Enerflex. Comment on the financial health of Enerflex, and highlight any areas that might be of concern. Use not only the ratios, but also the information from all three financial statements in your analysis.

EXHIBIT 12-18

MOSAID TECHNOLOGIES INCORPORATED
(Incorporated under the Ontario Business Corporations Act)
Consolidated Balance Sheets
As at April 30 (in thousands)

	1995	1994
Current Assets		
Cash and short-term marketable securities	$ 19,364	$ 18,579
Accounts receivable	7,738	3,550
Revenues recognized in excess of amounts billed	965	628
Income taxes receivable	-	476
Inventories (Note 2)	1,966	889
Prepaid expenses	135	145
	30,168	24,267
Investment Tax Credits (Note 3)	700	285
Capital Assets (Note 4)	2,808	1,043
Other Assets	-	50
	$ 33,676	$ 25,645
Current Liabilities		
Accounts payable and accrued liabilities	$ 3,691	$ 2,121
Income taxes payable	32	-
Deferred income taxes	249	-
Deferred revenue	749	189
Obligations under capital leases – current portion	22	61
	4,743	2,371
Obligations Under Capital Leases	50	9
Deferred Income Taxes	756	-
	$ 5,549	$ 2,380
Shareholders' Equity		
Share capital (Note 7)	19,083	18,705
Retained earnings	9,044	4,560
	28,127	23,265
	$ 33,676	$ 25,645

See accompanying Notes to the Consolidated Financial Statements.

Thomas I. Csathy
Director

Robert F. Harland
Director

EXHIBIT 12-18 (continued)

MOSAID TECHNOLOGIES INCORPORATED
Consolidated Statement of Earnings and Retained Earnings
Years Ended April 30, 1995 and 1994
(in thousands, except per share amounts)

	1995	1994
Revenues		
Operations	**$ 23,202**	$ 14,348
Interest	**1,084**	369
	$ 24,286	$ 14,717
Expenses		
Labour and materials	**5,275**	3,979
Research and development (Note 8)	**4,741**	3,228
Selling and marketing	**4,576**	2,573
General and administration (Note 8)	**2,578**	1,618
Foreign exchange loss (gain)	**147**	(222)
Bad debt (recovery) expense	**(19)**	74
	17,298	11,250
Earnings before income taxes	**6,988**	3,467
Income tax expense (Note 3)	**2,504**	542
Net earnings	**4,484**	2,925
Retained earnings, beginning of year	**4,560**	1,635
Retained earnings, end of year	**$ 9,044**	$ 4,560
Earnings per share (Note 11)		
Basic	**$ .66**	$ .59
Fully diluted	**$ .60**	$ .51

See accompanying Notes to the Consolidated Financial Statements.

d. Comment on the use of leverage by Enerflex. Include comments on the average interest rates paid by Enerflex on both long-term and short-term debt (interest on long-term debt in 1994 totalled $397,000; assume the remaining interest relates to the Current Bank Loan and be sure to include the "Current portion of long-term debt" in your calculations). What changes to your leverage calculations would have resulted if Enerflex had no long-term debt but had issued sufficient common shares to provide the same amount of financing?

e. Calculate the net income and earnings per share figures in 1994 assuming that Enerflex had issued common shares as assumed in part (d) and had issued them at the same average price per common share as for the existing common shares. Enerflex had 7,557,000 common shares outstanding at December 31, 1994. Assuming a multiple (price/earnings ratio) of 20, what difference in share price would this change cause? Comment on the use of long-term debt by Enerflex.

EXHIBIT 12-18 (continued)

MOSAID TECHNOLOGIES INCORPORATED
Consolidated Statement of Changes in Financial Position
Year Ended April 30 (in thousands)

	1995	1994
Operating		
Net earnings	$ 4,484	$ 2,925
Items not affecting cash		
Amortization	912	485
Loss (gain) on disposal of capital assets	7	(24)
Investment tax credits	(415)	-
Deferred income taxes	1,005	-
	5,993	3,386
Change in non-cash working capital items	(2,954)	(461)
	3,039	2,925
Investing		
Acquisition of capital assets – net	(2,618)	(789)
Proceeds from disposal of capital assets	2	42
Acquisition of capital assets under capital leases	(68)	-
Other assets	50	(50)
	(2,634)	(797)
Financing		
Increase in obligations under capital leases	68	-
Repayment of obligations under capital leases	(66)	(73)
Issue of common shares (net of costs of $29; 1994 – $1,345)	378	16,438
	380	16,365
Net cash inflow	785	18,493
Cash position, beginning of year	18,579	86
Cash position, end of year	$ 19,364	$ 18,579
Cash comprises the following:		
Cash	$ 3,879	$ 735
Marketable securities	15,485	17,844
	$ 19,364	$ 18,579

See accompanying Notes to the Consolidated Financial Statements.

23. The 1995 financial statements of Mosaid Technologies Incorporated (with head-quarters in Kanata, Ontario) are shown in Exhibit 12-18. Based on these financial statements, answer each of the following questions:
    a. Compute the following ratios for 1995:
       1. ROA (split into profit margin ratio and total asset turnover). What assumption should you make about interest expense in 1995?
       2. ROE (there are no preferred shares outstanding).
       3. Accounts receivable turnover

b. Mosaid is involved in custom computer memory chip design and chip testing. The 1995 inventory of $1,966,000 consists of Repair Inventory of $132,000; Raw Materials of $1,103,000; and Work in Process of $731,000. Explain why there is no Finished Goods Inventory, and why inventory turnover would not be meaningful.

c. Compute the following ratios for both 1995 and 1994:
   1) Current ratio
   2) Quick ratio
   3) D/E(I)

d. Comment on the use of leverage by Mosaid. Compare the ratios calculated for Mosaid with the ratios calculated in Problem 22 for Enerflex Systems Ltd. Compare the use of leverage by the two corporations.

e. Assume it is May 1, 1995 and Mosaid is considering a major expansion that would cost $30,000,000 and wants to raise $10,000,000 of this from outside sources, either by issuing more shares or by long-term debt. Assume Mosaid would maintain its current ROA and income tax rates.
   (i) If it borrowed this $10,000,000 as long-term debt, what is the maximum interest rate it should pay?
   (ii) Assume it could sell additional common shares at the current market price (assume its multiple is 20 and there would be no issuing costs). How many new shares would Mosaid have to issue?
   (iii) Assume Mosaid could borrow the $10,000,000 at 10% before taxes. Should Mosaid use debt or shares to finance this expansion?

24. The 1994 financial statements of Fundy Cable Ltd. (with headquarters in Saint John, New Brunswick) are shown in Exhibit 12-19. Based on these financial statements, answer each of the following questions:
   a. Compute the following ratios for 1994:
      1) ROA (split into profit margin ratio and total asset turnover).
      2) Accounts receivable turnover.
   b. Fundy Cable's business is primarily in cable television distribution. Explain why inventory turnover would not be meaningful.
   c. Compute the following ratios for both 1994 and 1993:
      1) Current ratio
      2) Quick ratio
      3) D/E(I)

EXHIBIT 12-19

FUNDY CABLE LTD./LTÉE
Consolidated Balance Sheets
As at August 31, 1994 and 1993

(in thousands of dollars)	1994	1993
Assets (Note 6)		
Current Assets		
Accounts receivable	$2,891	$2,464
Due from affiliated companies	66	188
Inventory	415	487
Prepaid expenses	390	263
	3,762	3,402
Investment in an Affiliated Company (Note 3)	10,167	9,513
Fixed Assets (Note 4)	31,392	23,197
Other Assets (Note 5)	55,599	17,573
	$100,920	$53,685
Liabilities and Shareholders' Equity		
Current Liabilities		
Bank advances (Note 6)	$5,090	$1,353
Accounts payable and accrued liabilities	6,419	4,433
Income taxes payable	358	55
Prepaid subscriber balances	1,579	764
Current portion of long-term debt	1,170	3,069
	14,616	9,674
Long-Term Debt (Note 6)	70,069	49,613
Deferred Income Taxes	517	1,129
	85,202	60,416
Shareholders' Equity		
Capital Stock (Notes 6 and 7)	23,906	970
Deficit	(8,188)	(7,701)
	15,718	(6,731)
	$100,920	$53,685

See accompanying Notes to Consolidated Financial Statements

On Behalf of the Board

Director   Director

EXHIBIT 12-19 (continued)

FUNDY CABLE LTD./LTÉE

Consolidated Statements of Income

For the Years Ended August 31, 1994 and 1993

(in thousands of dollars, except per share amounts)	1994	1993
Revenue	$43,221	$34,680
Expenses		
Operating	16,723	13,043
Administrative and selling	11,069	10,194
Programming	1,104	830
	28,896	24,067
Operating Income Before the Following	14,325	10,613
Interest on long-term debt	6,202	4,838
Other interest	122	96
Amortization of bond discount	(1,071)	(775)
Depreciation	4,360	3,597
Amortization	1,788	1,192
Gain on disposal of fixed assets	(88)	-
	11,313	8,948
Income Before Income Taxes and Share of Losses of an Affiliated Company	3,012	1,665
Provision for (Recovery of) Income Taxes (Note 8)	789	(82)
	2,223	1,747
Share of Losses of an Affiliated Company	(2,446)	(2,286)
Loss for the Year	($223)	($539)
Loss applicable to Multiple Voting Shares and Subordinate Voting Shares	($523)	($882)
Basic Earnings (Loss) per Share (Note 9)	($0.13)	($0.30)
Weighted Average Number of Outstanding Shares	3,926,000	2,929,000

See accompanying Notes to Consolidated Financial Statements

Consolidated Statements of Deficit

For the Years Ended August 31, 1994 and 1993

(in thousands of dollars)	1994	1993
Balance - Beginning of Year	($7,701)	($6,819)
Adjustments on amalgamation - February 1, 1994	36	-
Loss for the year	(223)	(539)
Dividends - Preferred	(300)	(343)
	(487)	(882)
Balance - End of Year	($8,188)	($7,701)

See accompanying Notes to Consolidated Financial Statements

EXHIBIT 12-19 (continued)

FUNDY CABLE LTD./LTÉE

Consolidated Statements of Changes in Financial Position

For the Years Ended August 31, 1994 and 1993

(in thousands of dollars, except per share amounts)	1994	1993
Operating Activities		
Net income before share of losses of an affiliated company	$2,223	$1,747
Items not affecting cash -		
Depreciation	4,360	3,597
Amortization	1,788	1,192
Amortization of bond discount	(1,071)	(775)
(Gain) loss on disposal of fixed assets	(88)	72
Deferred income taxes	377	(175)
Cash flow from operations before the following	7,589	5,658
Change in non-cash working capital balances	2,643	595
	10,232	6,253
Investing Activities		
Net fixed asset additions	(8,407)	(4,337)
Fixed assets acquired on purchase of CSL	(4,060)	-
Net increase in other assets	(38,814)	(83)
Deposit on aquisitions	(1,000)	(2,000)
Increase in deferred tax liability	210	-
Increase in investment in an affiliated company	(2,029)	(1,108)
	(54,100)	(7,528)
Financing Activities		
Increase in long-term debt - net	18,557	856
Issue of capital stock - net	21,874	-
Redemption of shares	-	(358)
Dividends - Preferred	(300)	(343)
	40,131	155
Increase in Bank Advances	(3,737)	(1,120)
Bank Advances - Beginning of Year	(1,353)	(233)
Bank Advances - End of Year	($5,090)	($1,353)
Cash Flow from Operations, net of Dividends on Preferred Shares	$7,289	$5,315
Cash Flow per Share (Note 9)	$1.86	$1.81

See accompanying Notes to Consolidated Financial Statements

Critical Thinking Question

One of the qualitative characteristics underlying financial accounting is comparability. As you will recall, comparability refers to similarities of financial information between different corporations, and consistency of the financial information produced by a corporation over time. Two of the many ways of achieving comparability is by limiting the number of different ways transactions may be recorded, or by specifying how assets, liabilities, equities, revenues, and expenses will be disclosed in the financial statements.

One of the arguments against comparability is that it limits the ability of corporations to choose among accounting methods, which may result in disclosures that may not be preferred by management.

Discuss the pros and cons of comparability, with reference to the analysis of financial statements.

CHAPTER

13

Complex Organizations

Throughout this text we have shown you excerpts from financial statements from various Canadian and international corporations. Without exception, all of those financial statements were *consolidated* financial statements. Consolidated financial statements become necessary when one corporation buys a controlling ownership interest in another corporation, thus creating a complex organization. Before we end this text, we want to provide you with a broad understanding of how financial statements become consolidated, and the implications of using consolidated statements for decision-making. Because an investment in the common shares in a corporation carries with it a right to vote, one corporation can influence and, under the right circumstances, control the activities of another corporation. In this chapter, we also consider accounting issues related to organizations that are considered complex due to intercorporate investments. We start with a brief discussion of the purpose of such intercorporate investments, and then turn to their accounting and analysis aspects.

PURPOSE OF INTERCORPORATE INVESTMENTS

A corporation may have many reasons for acquiring an ownership interest in another corporation. Investment in the shares of the corporation may be viewed as a good short-term or long-term investment. The equity securities that a corporation carries in its current asset account, called temporary investments, are an example of this type of investment. If the shares are bought for this reason, the number of shares purchased is usually small compared to the number of outstanding shares. Consequently, the acquiring corporation has little influence or control over the affairs of the acquired corporation. Such investments are sometimes called **passive investments** or **portfolio investments** because the acquiring corporation cannot exercise any control over the decisions of the acquired corporation. Some passive investments can also be long-term if the intention of management is to hold the security for long-term returns.

A second major reason for obtaining ownership of the shares of another corporation is to influence or control the decisions made by that other corporation. Common targets for this kind of purchase are competitors, suppliers, and customers. Acquiring a block of shares in a supplier or customer allows the acquiring corporation to exercise some influence over the production, buying, and selling decisions of the acquired corporation, which may benefit the acquiring corporation. If the block of shares purchased is large enough, the acquiring corporation could have a controlling interest in a competitor, which would allow it to increase its market share by increasing its productive capacity or its geographic market, or both. Combining with a competitor is sometimes referred to as **horizontal integration**. Horizontal integration may also offer other benefits that come from economies of scale. The corporation may be able to reduce its work force or use the same distribution system to avoid duplication of effort. Buying a controlling interest in a supplier or customer allows the corporation to ensure a market in which to buy its raw materials (in the case of a supplier), or to sell and distribute its product (in the case of a customer). Buying a supplier or customer is sometimes referred to as **vertical**

integration. Fletcher Challenge Canada Limited is an example of a company that is vertically integrated. It, together with the various corporations that it controls, is involved in lumber, pulp and paper and sales, and handles all aspects of the forest industry from the initial cutting of trees, through the making of lumber and paper products, to the sale of these items to customers.

Another reason for buying and controlling another corporation is **diversification**. If a corporation is in a cyclical business, it can protect itself from cyclical declines in one business by investing in another business that is counter-cyclical. **Cyclical businesses** are those that have significant peaks and valleys of activity. A greeting card corporation is an example of a cyclical business. Some of the cards, like birthday cards, are purchased relatively evenly throughout the year. Other cards, like Christmas cards and Valentine cards, cause peaks in the revenue generation. Such a corporation may wish to diversify by buying into an automobile dealership business. The peak times for the dealership are likely to be the late summer when the new cars are introduced and early spring when people are anticipating travelling over the summer. The greeting card business and the automobile dealership would be having peak activities at different times which would help to even out the revenue flows for the whole business.

Algoma Central Corporation is an example of a diversified Canadian business. Its main focus of operation is marine transportation. It operates several ships, and organizes the transportation of goods, provides for the repair and maintenance of ships, and provides marine-engineering services. This business is dependent not only upon the type of goods shipped, but also upon the economic environment of the countries from which goods are transported and to which the goods are shipped. Algoma has countered some of the cyclical nature of the shipping business by investing in the commercial real estate business. It owns and manages various shopping centres, office buildings and apartment buildings in Ontario. This business is also subject to the economic environment, but is much more localized and would be unlikely to experience the same peaks and valleys as marine transportation.

◖▮ METHODS OF OBTAINING INFLUENCE AND CONTROL

Perhaps the simplest way to obtain control of the assets of another corporation is to purchase the assets directly from that corporation. This is called an **asset purchase.** The accounting for asset purchases is discussed in Chapter 8. If several assets are acquired at one time, such as in the acquisition of an entire division or plant, a single price may be negotiated. As discussed in Chapter 8, this type of purchase is called a basket purchase. The total cost of the assets purchased must be allocated to the individual assets acquired on the basis of their relative fair market values. If one corporation buys all of the assets of another corporation, it is not able either to influence or control the second corporation. Because it has purchased the assets, it controls only the assets it has purchased. The corporation from which it has purchased the assets can continue to operate, but now it has different assets that it must use to generate revenue. An asset purchase does not require consolidated financial statements. Once the new assets are recorded, there are no further accounting complications.

The only way to obtain influence or control over another corporation is to buy common shares in a **share acquisition**. For the sake of this discussion, we will refer to the acquiring corporation as the **investor,** and to the corporation whose shares are acquired as the **investee.**

One way the shares can be obtained is through payment of cash from the investor to the shareholders of the investee (i.e., the shares are bought in the stock market). Another way is an exchange of the investor's shares for shares of the investee. This form of investment is called a **stock swap.** A variation of this is an exchange of the investor's debt (bonds) for shares of the investee in a transaction that may be called a **debt for equity swap.** In fact, some investments involve the exchange of all three (cash, shares, and debt) for the shares of the investee.

In a share acquisition, the investor can obtain a large degree of influence or control over the investee by buying (or swapping) more shares. That influence or control is obtained by exercising the voting rights that the investor obtains when buying the shares. Ultimate control over the assets and liabilities of the investee will occur when the percentage ownership of the voting rights is greater than 50%. This is called a **controlling interest**. An investor can sometimes effectively control an investee even though it owns less than 50% of the shares. This can occur in situations in which the remainder of the shares are owned by a large number of investors, none of whom have a very large percentage ownership in the investee (the shares are said to be **widely held** in such situations). Therefore, if an investor owns 30% to 50% of an investee and the rest of the shares are widely held, the investor may be able to effectively control the assets and liabilities of the investee. Because it is possible to control with less than 50%, GAAP defines control as occurring without the cooperation of others. If a corporation owns 40% of the shares of the another corporation, it may be able to elect the majority of people to the Board of Directors. It has, however, elected them through the cooperation of the other shareholders. If those shareholders become dissatisfied with the way the Board of Directors manages the corporation, they could get together and outvote the 40% shareholder. For this reason, a corporation with a 40% interest in another corporation would likely not prepare consolidated financial statements, but a corporation that owned 51% probably would prepare them.

In a share acquisition, the investee remains a legal entity separate from the investor. The investor corporation is like any other owner in that it has limited liability with regard to the debts of the investee. The investor's liability is limited to the amount invested in the shares. The separation of the legal status of the two corporations is one reason this form of acquisition is appealing. The tax status of each corporation is also separate. Each corporation must file its own return. For accounting purposes, the separate legal status also means that the investor and the investee each keeps its own set of accounting records, even if the investor has acquired 100% of the investee's shares. This presents an accounting problem if the investor controls the investee because they are, in substance, one accounting entity.

◖◗ VALUATION ISSUES AT DATE OF ACQUISITION

In any type of acquisition, whether the purchase of a single asset or of an entire corporation, the fundamental accounting valuation method is historical cost. The new asset or the investment in the investee is recorded at its cost. If the asset is acquired with a payment of cash, the amount of cash serves as the proper measure of the cost. If debt is exchanged for the asset or corporation, the value of the debt should be used as the measure of cost. Under GAAP, debt is usually measured at its net present value. The net present value of the debt at the date of issuance is used to measure the cost of an acquisition in which debt is exchanged.

When shares are issued in the acquisition, their fair market value should be used as the measure of cost at the date of acquisition. A problem exists in valuing shares when the issue is large because the number of shares outstanding increases significantly and the value of the investment acquired is not exact. How the market will adjust the existing share price to reflect this acquisition is not known at the date of acquisition. In these situations, instead of using the value of the shares to measure the acquisition, accountants sometimes turn to the fair market value of the assets acquired to measure the value of the shares given up in these types of transactions. If the shares are used to swap for the shares of another corporation, the value of the shares of the other corporation may not be estimated easily. Stock swaps involving 100% of the shares of another corporation present the most difficulty in measuring the value of the transaction.

Share Acquisition

In a share acquisition, the investor records the cost of the acquisition in an investment account. There is no breakdown of this cost into individual assets and liabilities because the assets and liabilities do not technically belong to the investor; they remain the legal property or legal obligation of the investee. An investor that owns a large enough percentage of the investee's shares may control the assets economically through its voting rights, but it does not hold the title to the assets nor is it legally obligated to settle the liabilities. Under GAAP, two methods are currently used to account for an acquisition of a controlling interest: the **purchase method**, and the **pooling method**.

Purchase Method

The purchase method assumes that after the shares are purchased or exchanged, one corporation can be identified as an **acquirer**. This method is always used when the investor pays cash or issues debt in exchange for the shares of the investee. When shares are swapped for the shares of the investee, this method is used when the original shareholders of the investor corporation control more shares than the new shareholders from the investee corporation. For example, assume that Corporation A has 500,000 common shares currently issued. It is interested in purchasing all of the shares of Corporation B, which has 100,000 common shares currently issued.

The purpose of most share exchanges in Canada is to gain control of another corporation. When this is achieved, the acquiring corporation is called the **parent** and the acquired corporation is called the **subsidiary**. The subsidiary is an integral part of the total operations of the parent corporation and, therefore, users need to know how it is performing. Both parent and subsidiary are separate legal entities that keep separate books, prepare separate financial statements, and pay separate taxes. To provide users with information about the whole entity (parent and subsidiaries),

<table>
<tr><td>

CORPORATION A

500,000 shares issued

Corporation A issues 100,000
new shares and exchanges them
with the shareholders of
Corporation B on a 1 for 1 basis

After the exchange
600,000 shares issued
(500,000 shares held by original
shareholders of Corporation A;
100,000 held by the old
shareholders of Corporation B)

</td><td>

CORPORATION B

100,000 shares issued

100,000 shares issued now owned
by Corporation A

</td></tr>
</table>

Result: The original shareholders of Corporation A still hold most of the shares of Corporation A and therefore still control Corporation A, which now controls Corporation B.

accountants prepare consolidated financial statements, which add the components of the various financial statements of the parent and the subsidiaries together. Users see the total cash controlled by the entity, the total inventory owned by the entity, the total revenues earned by the entity, and so forth. Complications in this addition arise if there have been transactions between the parent and the subsidiaries. Because such transactions occur within the total accounting entity (parent and subsidiaries), they are deemed not to have occurred. They must be eliminated. More will be said about this later.

As well as providing information about the total entity, consolidated financial statements hide information about the individual corporations in the group. Because users are often not given information about individual corporations in the group, they have difficulty determining the risks and rewards contributed by the separate corporations. If a corporation through its activities is involved in various industries or geographic locations, it is required to disclose segmented information in the notes to its financial statements. The segmented information provides some breakdown of accounts in the different segments so that users can evaluate the potential future impact of the segments on the total entity.

As mentioned earlier, when the parent purchases a controlling number of shares in a subsidiary corporation, it has an investment on its books that it has recorded at the cost of the purchase. Because another corporation is being controlled and consolidated financial statements are going to be prepared, the transaction is viewed like a basket purchase. The cost to acquire the subsidiary needs to be allocated to the individual assets and liabilities of the subsidiary based on their relative fair market values at the date of acquisition, just as with any other basket purchase. This allocation is not recorded on the actual books of either the parent or the subsidiary, but rather is determined during the worksheet preparation of the financial statements. When the assets and liabilities of the subsidiary are added to the assets and liabilities of the parent so that consolidated financial statements can be prepared, it is the fair values of the subsidiary's assets and liabilities that are added to the historical cost assets and liabilities of the parent.

In the allocation of the purchase price, all the assets and liabilities in the subsidiary are first measured at their fair market values. Some assets that did not exist on the books of the subsidiary may be found and included in this measurement process. For example, if the subsidiary developed a patent or a trademark internally, the costs of such an item would have been expensed (see Chapter 8 for a discussion of whether to capitalize or expense the costs of these types of assets). The parent would need to identify all assets that the subsidiary owned or had the right to use, and establish values for those items using current items like them in the market as a guide, estimations of future benefits, or appraisals. By buying the shares, the parent is now controlling these assets as well, and part of the acquisition cost should be allocated to them if they have a measurable market value. All of these assets and liabilities, those on the books and those that have value but are not on the books, are known as the **identifiable net assets** of the subsidiary. In the year that a parent buys a subsidiary, the components of the assets and liabilities that were purchased will be disclosed in the notes to the consolidated financial statements. Exhibit 13-1 includes an example of this disclosure from the financial statements of SoftQuad International.

You should note from SoftQuad's description that values have been assigned to three asset groups and three liability groups. By far the most valuable asset acquired was "software products". This asset probably represents various software programs that Carolian Systems Corporation had developed prior to being acquired by SoftQuad, and was likely one of the main reasons why SoftQuad wanted to acquire it.

EXHIBIT 13-1

SOFTQUAD INTERNATIONAL
Excerpted from Notes to the Statements

3. Business Acquisition

Effective February 7, 1994, SoftQuad International Inc. acquired all of the issued and outstanding shares of Carolian Systems Corporation for 2,000,000 common shares of the company with an ascribed value of $3,200,000.

The transaction has been accounted for by the purchase method and includes the results of operations from the date of acquisition.

Details of the acquisition are as follows:

Net assets acquired, at assigned values

Current assets	$ 531,944
Fixed assets	67,628
Acquired software products	2,500,000
	3,099,572

Less:	
Bank indebtedness	86,810
Other current liabilities	727,802
Long-term debt	494,000
	1,790,960
Goodwill	1,409,040
Share consideration (Note 9)	$ 3,200,000

The fair value of the identifiable net assets was $1,790,960 ($3,099,572 − $1,308,612). Because SoftQuad paid $3,200,000 to acquire all the shares of Carolian Systems Corporation, it assigned the difference, $1,409,040, to something called goodwill.

If the purchase price is more than the fair market value of the identifiable net assets, another asset called **goodwill** must be reported (refer to Chapter 8). It represents all the intangible reasons that motivated the investor to pay more for the investee than the sum of the fair market values of its individual assets and liabilities. Perhaps the acquirer expects to earn extra future cash flows, or perhaps the business is located in a high traffic area and so has a greater chance at higher revenues than businesses located elsewhere. Perhaps the sales personnel in the business have created a loyal customer following which leads to consistent revenues, or previous advertising campaigns may have made this a well-known business. If, on the other hand, the purchase price is less than the fair value of the identifiable net assets, some amount of the fair value of the identifiable assets must be reduced. GAAP gives no specific guidelines regarding which assets should be reduced other than to specify that they should be nonmonetary in nature.

■ ■ Pooling of Interests Method

When shares are exchanged for all of the shares of another corporation, it may not be possible to identify the parent corporation. Referring to our previous example of Corporation A, and Corporation B, let us assume that Corporation A issues 500,000 shares and exchanges them with the shareholders of Corporation B for all of their 100,000 shares on a 5 for 1 basis.

CORPORATION A	CORPORATION B
500,000 shares issued	100,000 shares issued
Corporation A issues 500,000 new shares and exchanges them with the shareholders of Corporation B on a 5 for 1 basis	
After the exchange	
1,000,000 shares issued (500,000 shares held by original shareholders of Corporation A; 500,000 held by the old shareholders of Corporation B)	100,000 shares issued now owned by Corporation A

Result: The original shareholders of Corporation A hold half of the 1,000,000 shares of Corporation A, and the old shareholders of Corporation B hold the other half. Neither group of shareholders can exercise control; they must share it. As in the previous example, Corporation B is controlled by Corporation A, but this time there is joint control of Corporation A.

When no acquirer can be identified, we think of these two corporations as having pooled their resources to create a larger organization. Only very rarely are share exchanges arranged to accomplish a pooling. Because they happen so rarely, we are going to mention them only briefly here and concentrate for the rest of the chapter on acquisitions acquired under the purchase method. The guidelines with respect to pooling are quite different in the United States where, as a result, pooling is quite common.

In a share exchange in which an acquirer cannot be identified, no new shareholders are created; the previous owner groups are simply merged, as are the assets and liabilities. Because one company has not been purchased by the other, there is no reason to change the cost basis of the assets and liabilities. In the pooling of the two corporations, the assets and liabilities are, therefore, reported at their previous book values rather than at their fair market values. The concept used here is that the ownership interests in the net assets of the two corporations have been pooled; hence, the term **pooling of interest** is used for this type of transaction.

◼◼ Implications of Purchase versus Pooling Treatment

At the date of acquisition, the investor corporation will report a different set of values for the assets and liabilities using the purchase method than would be reported using the pooling method. If the fair market value of the net assets acquired is higher (as it is in many cases) than the old historical cost book value, the net assets with the purchase method will be higher, sometimes significantly so, than with pooling. The new asset, goodwill, will often be one of the assets that forms part of a purchase acquisition, but will not be part of a pooling.

Another difference between purchasing and pooling is that, in pooling, the combined corporations are assumed to have been combined (pooled) forever. This means that any income generated by the investee during the accounting period leading up to the merger should be shown on the income statement of the combined corporation, even if the investee was acquired (pooled) on the last day of the year. If the purchase method is used, no income can be recognized prior to the date of purchase because the transaction is viewed as a new purchase of assets. Therefore, if the merger was accomplished on the last day of the year, no income from the investee could be recorded by the combined corporation in the year of merger using the purchase method. The concept of being together forever (in the pooling method) also means that the retained earnings balances of the two corporations are pooled at the date of merger. With the purchase method, only the retained earnings of the investor corporation survives in the combined entity. The earnings history of the investee is not preserved with the purchase method because the assets and liabilities are viewed as having been acquired at the date of the merger.

INCOME RECOGNITION ISSUES SUBSEQUENT ◖◗ TO ACQUISITION

Income recognition issues subsequent to acquisition are a consequence of the valuation decisions made at the date of acquisition. In the following subsections, these issues are discussed for asset acquisitions and share acquisitions.

Asset Purchases

Subsequent to purchase, asset acquisitions are accounted for in the same way as any other acquisition of assets. If the asset acquired is property, plant or equipment, it is amortized like any other such asset. If the asset purchased is inventory, it ultimately affects cost of goods sold when it is sold.

Share Acquisitions

The accounting treatment of income subsequent to a share acquisition depends on the level of control the investor exerts over the investee. As examples of the conceptual differences, consider two extreme cases. The first case is one in which the investor owns only a few shares in the investee, and the second is one in which the investor buys 100% of the shares of the investee.

Case 1

If the investor buys only a few shares of the investee, it has virtually no control or influence over the investee. The investor may not dictate the dividend policy or any other operating policy to the investee. As indicated earlier, this is a passive investment. The shareholders of the investor corporation in such a situation are unlikely to be interested in the full details of the operating performance of the investee. They are probably more interested in the cash flows that have come in from their investment (dividends) and in the current market value of their investment. Therefore, income recognition should probably show dividend revenue.

Case 2

In this case, where the investor owns 100% of the shares of the investee, the shareholders of the investor are likely to want to know the operating details of the performance of the investee because they economically control all the assets and liabilities. For example, if the investee purchased was a competitor, the results of sales of the corporation's product are the combined results of the investor and the investee. To show only the details of the investor would be misleading in terms of the resources controlled by the shareholders. The investor's shareholders would probably find information about the combined assets and liabilities of the two corporations more useful than simply a listing of the investor's assets and liabilities. A set of statements that conveys this information is a set of **consolidated financial statements.** Consolidated financial statements are prepared **as if** the investor and investee were one legal corporation. Under GAAP the two corporations represent one economic accounting entity. In this situation, the investor is typically referred to as the **parent corporation** and the investee as the **subsidiary**.

GAAP

This section of the chapter will describe the guidelines that have been established under Canadian GAAP for the acquisition of various blocks of shares. It is important to understand these guidelines because corporations will describe their various acquisitions and tell you how they are accounting for them. You will need to know the various methods used so that you can understand the method's effects on the financial statements.

Under Canadian GAAP, control is determined by the investor's ability to determine the strategic, operating, investing and financing activities of the investee without seeking the permission of any others. It usually means that the investor owns more than 50% of the voting shares of the investee, but there are circumstances where the investor could own less than 50% of the voting shares and still be able to exercise control.

Because control is evidenced by the ability to determine certain activities in another corporation, GAAP provides guidelines for recommended cutoffs for the percentage ownership (in voting shares) that require different accounting treatment. Exhibit 13-2 outlines these cutoffs. For small investments (less than 20%), GAAP specifies the **cost method**. Small investments are also subdivided into those that are current, which we usually label temporary investments, and those that are noncurrent, which are generally labeled investments. Larger investments (greater than 50%) require **consolidation**; that is, consolidated financial statements must be prepared. For investments that fall between these two extremes, the acquirer is considered to have **significant influence** over activities in the investee. Significant influence is evidenced by being able to elect a person to the Board of Directors, having significant transactions between the two corporations, or having an exchange of technology or managerial personal. When significant influence exists, another method, called the **equity method**, is required. Each of these methods is discussed in detail in the following pages.

The percentage cutoffs identified in Exhibit 13-2 are only a guide. If a corporation can demonstrate that it possesses either more or less control than the percentage ownership indicates, the corporation can apply a different method. For example,

EXHIBIT 13-2

Accounting Methods for Investments

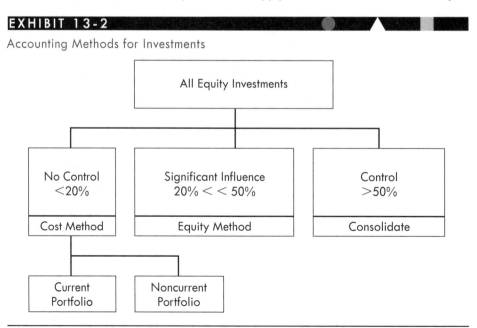

if a wholly owned subsidiary (100% ownership) goes into receivership, control often passes from the parent corporation to a trustee. The investment in the subsidiary should then be carried using the cost method. Also, an investor that owns less than 50% of an investee's voting shares but also owns convertible rights on other securities which, if converted, would increase its ownership beyond 50%, would be required to prepare consolidated financial statements. Each method carries its own set of implications for the corporation as discussed in the following subsections.

COST METHOD The cost method is discussed in Chapter 6. To refresh your memory, the investment is carried in the investment account at its cost. During the period in which the investment is held, dividend revenue is recognized. If the investment is in marketable securities (short-term), at the end of each period the portfolio of securities is valued at the lower of its cost and market value. The unrealized losses (or recoveries) are shown in the income statement. If the investment is long-term, the portfolio is compared to market, but written down only if the decline is a permanent one. Once a long-term investment is written down, it is not written back up. To review the details of these accounting procedures, see Chapter 6. Note that no recognition is made of the net income results of the investee during the period except to the extent that these results are captured by its willingness to pay dividends.

CONSOLIDATION METHOD Consolidation is required when an investor (parent corporation) controls the activities of an investee (subsidiary). For instructional purposes here, we will assume that the investor owns more than 50% of the outstanding shares of an investee. Because the subsidiary is still a legally separate corporation, the parent corporation records its investment in the subsidiary corporation in an investment account on its books. However, because the parent corporation economically controls the assets and liabilities of the subsidiary, it is probably more useful to the shareholders of the parent corporation to report the full details of the assets, liabilities, and income statement items rather than a single amount in the investment account and a single amount of income from the subsidiary on the income statement. The purpose of consolidating, therefore, is to replace the investment account with the individual assets and liabilities of the subsidiary. On the consolidated financial statements, it then looks as though the two corporations are legally one, that is **as if** they had merged. You must recognize, however, that this is simply an "as-if" representation of the combined corporation. The accounting systems are not merged. In fact, the consolidated statements are prepared "on paper;" there are no actual entries made to either corporation's accounting system.

Because a consolidation tries to make it look as though the two corporations were merged, the issues of purchase versus pooling also apply in a consolidation. If the acquisition transaction qualifies as a pooling, the consolidated statements are prepared by combining the book values of the two companies' assets and liabilities. If the purchase method is indicated, the consolidated statements are prepared using the fair market value of the assets and liabilities acquired, as well as any goodwill.

EQUITY METHOD Between the two extremes of no control and complete control lies the situation in which the investor can significantly influence the investee but not completely control its decisions. The accounting method used, the **equity**

method, tries to strike some middle ground between showing the results of all the assets, liabilities, and income items in the financial statements (consolidation) and showing only the dividend revenue from the investment (cost method). The equity method requires that the investor show the effects of its share of the financial results of the investee, that is, as if it consolidated its share of the assets, liabilities and income statement items. The difference is that its share of the net assets (assets minus liabilities) is reported as a single line item, "Investment in shares" on the balance sheet of the investor. Its share of the net income is also reported as a single revenue item, "Equity in earnings of investment" or simply "Income from investment" on the income statement. Because of the netting of assets and liabilities as well as revenues and expenses, this method is sometimes referred to as a **one-line consolidation**.

To illustrate the entries made in a simple case using the cost method and the equity method, let us assume the following facts. Assume that the investor bought 30% of the outstanding shares of an investee for $10,000. During the first year of the investment, the earnings of the investee were $3,000 and $1,500 of dividends were declared. We will assume that in Case A, the 30% does not give the investor significant influence (cost method required), and in Case B significant influence is present (equity method required). The entries the investor makes to account for the investment in the first year are as follows:

CASE A (COST METHOD)		CASE B (EQUITY METHOD)	
Investor's entry for acquisition:			
A – Investment in Shares 10,000		A – Investment in Shares 10,000	
A – Cash	10,000	A – Cash	10,000
Investor's entry to record earnings from investee:			
No entry		A – Investment in Shares 900	
		SE – Equity in Earnings	
		of Investment	900[a]
Investor's entry to record dividends from investee:			
A – Cash	450[b]	A – Cash	450
SE – Dividend Revenue	450	A – Investment in Shares	450

[a]Investor's percent ownership $\times$ Earnings of investee = 30% $\times$ $3,000
[b]Investor's percent ownership $\times$ Dividends of investee = 30% $\times$ $1,500

The entry to record the earnings shows that the investment account increases by the investor's share of the earnings of the investee. Under the equity method, the investment account represents the investor's investment in the investee and, as the investee earns income and increases its shareholders' equity section, the investor's investment increases in value as well. The credit part of this entry is to the income statement in a revenue line item called **Equity in Earnings of Investment**. We will subsequently abbreviate this as **EEI**.

The entry to record the dividends of the investee causes a decrease in the investor's investment account. This should make sense because, on the investee's books, the declaration of dividends causes a decrease in the shareholders' equity of the corporation. Because the investor's investment account measures its share of that equity, the investment account should decrease with the declaration of dividends. Another way to think about this is to imagine that the investment represents a deposit in a savings account. The interest on the savings account would be equivalent to the earnings of the subsidiary. Withdrawals from the savings account would be the equivalent of the dividends declared. Withdrawals decrease the balance in the savings account in the same way that dividends reduce the investment account.

■ ● ■ CONSOLIDATION PROCEDURES AND ISSUES

Numerous procedures and issues are important to understanding consolidated statements but they are complex enough that an advanced accounting course is usually necessary to thoroughly understand them. To give you a general idea of the procedures necessary for consolidation, we will show you the consolidation of a 100% owned subsidiary. This will be followed by a discussion of the issues surrounding the handling of intercompany transactions.

◢◣ Consolidation Procedures — 100% Acquisition

To illustrate the concepts behind the preparation of a consolidated set of financial statements, let's consider a share acquisition in which the parent acquires a 100% interest in the subsidiary. To make the example as concrete as possible, let's assume that the balance sheet of the parent (referred to as Parent Corporation) and the subsidiary (referred to as Sub Corporation) just prior to the acquisition are as shown in Exhibit 13-3.

Assume that, at acquisition, Parent Corporation pays $1,400, in cash, for all the outstanding shares of Sub Corporation. In a cash transaction, the acquisition would be considered a purchase and not a pooling because the shareholders of Parent Corporation have not changed. Because the book value of Sub Corporation's equity (net assets) is $1,000 at the date of acquisition, Parent Corporation has paid $400

EXHIBIT 13-3

Parent and Subsidiary Balance Sheets
Prior to Acquisition

Balance Sheet

	Parent Corporation	Sub Corporation
Assets other than PP&E	$2,200	$2,500
Property, plant and equipment	1,800	1,500
Total assets	$4,000	$4,000
Total liabilities	$2,000	$3,000
Shareholders' equity	2,000	1,000
Total liabilities and shareholders' equity	$4,000	$4,000

EXHIBIT 13-4

Representation of the Purchase Price Composition
Parent Corporation's 100% Acquisition of Sub Corporation

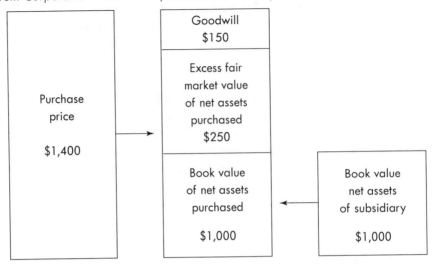

Note: Boxes are not scaled proportionately to dollar amounts.

more than the book value for the assets and liabilities of Sub Corporation. Assume further that $250 of this $400 relates to the additional fair market value of the property, plant and equipment of Sub. It will be assumed that the fair market value of the other assets and liabilities of Sub are equal to their book values. This means that the remainder of the $400, or $150, is due to goodwill. Exhibit 13-4 represents these assumptions.

The parent corporation records its investment in an account called Investment in Sub Corporation. Because Parent Corporation owns more than 50% of the shares of Sub Corporation, it controls Sub Corporation and will have to prepare consolidated financial statements. Because Sub Corporation remains a separate legal entity, it will continue to record its transactions on its own set of books. Parent Corporation will also continue to keep track of its own transactions on what are known as the **parent-only books**. At the end of each accounting period, the separate financial statements of the two entities will be combined on a worksheet to produce the consolidated financial statements, as if the two corporations were one legal entity. One question that arises is how Parent Corporation should account for its investment in Sub Corporation on its parent-only books. Because the investment in Sub Corporation account will be replaced in the consolidation process by the individual assets and liabilities of Sub Corporation, it does not really matter, from a consolidated point of view, how the parent accounts for its investment on the parent-only statements. It will make a difference in the parent-only financial statements. GAAP is somewhat silent on this issue, and there is some diversity in practice. Some corporations use the equity method to account for the investment; some use the cost method. It will be assumed that Parent Corporation uses the equity method. The investment entry would be:

> **INVESTMENT ENTRY:**
> A – Investment in Sub Corporation   1,400
>   A – Cash   1,400

The above entry would be the same if the corporation was intending to use the cost method. After recording the investment, the balance sheets of Parent Corporation and Sub Corporation will appear as in Exhibit 13-5.

To prepare a consolidated balance sheet for Parent Corporation at the date of acquisition, the Investment in Sub Corporation account must be replaced with the individual assets and liabilities of the Sub Corporation. This would normally be done on a set of **consolidating working papers**, and no entries would be made directly on either the parent corporation's books or the subsidiary corporation's books. The consolidating entries that are discussed next are made on the consolidating working papers. The accountant starts the working papers by placing the financial statements as prepared by the parent corporation and the subsidiary side by side as shown in

EXHIBIT 13-5

Parent and Subsidiary Balance Sheets at Date of Acquisition

Balance Sheet

	Parent Corporation	Sub Corporation
Assets other than PP&E	$ 800	$2,500
Property, plant and equipment	1,800	1,500
Investment in Sub Corporation	1,400	—
	$4,000	$4,000
Total liabilities	$2,000	$3,000
Shareholders' equity	2,000	1,000
Total liabilities and shareholders' equity	$4,000	$4,000

EXHIBIT 13-6

Consolidating Working Papers

Account	Parent Corporation Debit	Parent Corporation Credit	Sub Corporation Debit	Sub Corporation Credit	Consolidating Entries Debit	Consolidating Entries Credit	Consolidated Totals Debit	Consolidated Totals Credit
Assets other than PP&E	800		2,500					
Property, plant and equipment	1,800		1,500					
Investment in Sub Corporation	1,400							
Liabilities		2,000		3,000				
Shareholders' equity		2,000		1,000				
Totals	4,000	4,000	4,000	4,000				

Exhibit 13-6. The working papers will then have columns for the consolidating entries and for the consolidated totals. Note that the exhibit shows debit and credit columns for all four items.

On the consolidating working papers, each row will be added across to obtain the consolidated totals. Without making any adjustments to the balances as stated in Exhibit 13-6, several items will be double-counted. In the first place, the net assets of the subsidiary will be counted twice, one in the individual accounts of Sub and again as the net amount in the parent's investment account. One or the other of these two must be eliminated. Because the idea of consolidated statements is to show the individual assets and liabilities of the subsidiary in the consolidated totals, the best option is to eliminate the parent's investment account. The second item that will be counted twice is the shareholders' equity section. The only outside shareholders of the consolidated corporation are the shareholders of the parent corporation. The shareholders' equity represented by the subsidiary's balances is held by the parent corporation. The shareholders' equity section of the subsidiary must, therefore, be eliminated. Both of these are eliminated in a working paper entry called the **elimination entry**. The elimination entry in the example would be:

WORKING PAPER ELIMINATION ENTRY:		
SE – Shareholders' Equity (Sub Corporation)	1,000	
???	400	
A – Investment in Sub Corporation		1,400

In the preceding entry you can see that, in order to balance the entry, a debit of $400 has been made. What does this represent? It represents the excess amount that Parent Corporation paid for its interest in Sub Corporation over the book value of the net assets. Remember the assumption that this excess is broken down into $250 for **excess fair market value** of property, plant and equipment over its book value and $150 for goodwill. Therefore, the complete entry would be:

WORKING PAPER ELIMINATION ENTRY (ENTRY 1):		
SE – Shareholders' Equity (Sub Corporation)	1,000	
A – Property, plant and equipment	250	
A – Goodwill	150	
A – Investment in Sub Corporation		1,400

As a result of the elimination entry, the consolidating working papers would appear as in Exhibit 13-7. The working paper entries are numbered so that you can follow them from the journal entry form to the working paper form.

Note that shareholders' equity on a consolidated basis is the same as on the parent corporation's books. This is true because all the consolidation has really done is to replace the net assets represented in the investment account with the individual assets and liabilities that make up the net assets of the subsidiary. In this sense, the statements of the parent corporation (which are referred to as the **parent-only statements**) portray the same net results to the shareholders as a consolidation. However, the consolidated statements present somewhat different information to the shareholders in that ratios,

EXHIBIT 13-7

Consolidating Working Papers (Balance Sheet Only)

Account	Parent Corporation		Sub Corporation		Consolidating Entries		Consolidated Totals	
	Debit	Credit	Debit	Credit	Debit	Credit	Debit	Credit
Assets other than PP&E	800		2,500				3,300	
Property, plant and equipment	1,800		1,500		(1) 250		3,550	
Goodwill	—		—		(1) 150		150	
Investment in Sub Corporation	1,400					1,400 (1)	—	
Liabilities		2,000		3,000				5,000
Shareholders' equity		2,000		1,000	(1) 1,000			2,000
Totals	4,000	4,000	4,000	4,000	1,400	1,400	7,000	7,000

such as the debt/equity ratio, can be quite different from those found in parent-only statements. For example, from Exhibit 13-7 you can calculate the debt/equity ratio for the parent-only statements as 1.0 ($2,000/$2,000) whereas, in the consolidated statements, it is 2.5 ($5,000/$2,000). This occurs because the parent corporation has acquired a subsidiary that is more highly leveraged than it is (note that the debt/equity ratio for Sub Corporation is 3.0 [$3,000/$1,000]). The consolidation of the two corporations produces a leverage ratio that is a weighted average of the two ratios. Although the debt/equity ratio appears to be less favourable on the consolidated statements, users must remember that Sub Corporation is a separate legal entity and is responsible for its own debts. Parent Corporation has limited liability. For this reason, creditors like banks prefer to see parent-only financial statements when they assess a corporation's ability to repay debt.

Now, consider what the financial statements of Parent Corporation and Sub Corporation might look like one year after acquisition. The accounts of the two corporations are shown in Exhibit 13-8 (remember that EEI stands for equity in earnings of the investment).

Using the equity method, Parent Corporation would make the following entries during the year to account for its investment using the equity method:

ENTRIES USING THE EQUITY METHOD (ON PARENT CORPORATION'S BOOKS):

Parent's share of Sub's income:

A — Investment in Sub Corporation	300	
SE — EEI		300

Parent's share of Sub's dividends:

A — Cash	150	
A — Investment in Sub Corporation		150

After these entries, the ending balance in the investment account would be $1,550 ($1,400 + $300 − $150). You will note in the statements in Exhibit 13-8 that the investment account has a balance of $1,490. The difference in these amounts is due to the fact that Parent Corporation paid more than the book value for the net assets of

EXHIBIT 13-8

Parent and Subsidiary Balance Sheets & Income Statements
One Year Subsequent to Acquisition

Balance Sheet

	Parent Corporation	Sub Corporation
Assets other than PP&E	$1,440	$3,000
Property, plant and equipment	1,850	1,600
Investment in Sub Corporation	1,490	—
Total Assets	$4,780	$4,600
Total liabilities	$2,420	$3,450
Shareholders' equity	2,360	1,150
Total liabilities and shareholders' equity	$4,780	$4,600

Income Statement

	Parent Corporation	Sub Corporation
Revenues	$1,500	$2,000
Expenses	(1,010)	(1,474)
Amortization	(250)	(225)
EEI	240	—
Net income	$ 480	$ 300
Dividends declared	$ 120	$ 150

Sub Corporation. As we assumed earlier, Parent Corporation paid $400 more than the book value ($1,000). The $400 is due to the extra fair market value of property, plant, and equipment ($250) and goodwill ($150). Subsequent to acquisition, these amounts must be amortized, and the amortization is shown as part of the EEI. Corporations will establish amortization periods based on the expected useful life of the assets acquired. Assume that the property, plant and equipment has a remaining useful life of five years, has a residual value of zero, and is amortized straight-line. Therefore, parent Corporation must take an additional $50 ($250/5 years) in amortization expense over that shown on the books of Sub Corporation. The $150 of goodwill also has to be amortized. If it is assumed that the goodwill is amortized over 15 years (the maximum allowed is 40 years), the goodwill expense will be $10 per year ($150/15 years). Adding these two new expenses together means that Parent Corporation has to report an additional $60 in expenses during the year subsequent to acquisition. Using the equity method, Parent Corporation shows these additional expenses as a part of the EEI. The following entry is made (in addition to those shown earlier in the section):

AMORTIZATION ENTRY UNDER EQUITY METHOD (ON PARENT CORPORATION'S BOOKS):

SE – EEI	60	
A – Investment in Sub Corporation		60

With this additional entry, the balance in the investment in Sub Corporation account is $ 1,490, exactly the balance shown in Exhibit 13-8.

The consolidated working papers at the end of the first year are presented in Exhibit 13-9. You should note that they are shown in the **trial balance phase**. In the trial balance phase, the temporary income statement and dividends declared accounts still have balances that have not been closed to retained earnings (refer to Chapter 2 if you need to refresh your memory concerning the meaning of the trial balance phase). Note that shareholders' equity has the same balance as at the beginning of the year. This is how the accounts must be listed in order to prepare the consolidated financial statements properly.

In the year subsequent to acquisition, three basic consolidating working paper entries are made if the parent corporation is using the equity method to account for the investment on the parent-only financial statements. In addition to eliminating the investment account and the shareholders' equity accounts discussed earlier, the EEI must be eliminated, as well as the dividends declared account of the subsidiary. Otherwise, the income of the subsidiary would be counted twice, once as EEI and a second time as the individual revenue and expense items. Dividends declared by the subsidiary are really just inter-corporation transfers of cash from a consolidated point of view. They are not dividends to outside shareholders and, as such, they should be eliminated in the consolidations process. The entry to eliminate EEI and dividends will be called the *reversal of current year entries* because the entry is, in effect, removing income and dividends recognized during the period. Once these two entries have been

EXHIBIT 13-9

Consolidating Working Papers (Year Subsequent to Acquisition)

Account	Parent Corporation		Sub Corporation		Consolidating Entries		Consolidated Totals	
	Debit	Credit	Debit	Credit	Debit	Credit	Debit	Credit
Assets other than PP&E	1,140		3,000					
Property, plant and equipment	1,850		1,600					
Goodwill								
Investment in Sub Corporation	1,490							
Liabilities		2,420		3,450				
Shareholders' equity		2,000[a]		1,000[a]				
Revenues		1,500		2,000				
Expenses	1,010		1,475					
Amortization expense	250		225					
Amortization expense – goodwill								
EEI		240						
Dividends declared	120		150					
Totals	6,160	6,160	6,450	6,450				

[a]Beginning of period balances (trial balance phase).

made, the third set of entries recognizes the extra amortization expense and goodwill expense discussed earlier. The consolidating working paper entries are as follows:

CONSOLIDATING WORKING PAPER ENTRIES:

Reversal of current year entries (Entry 1):

SE – EEI	240	
SE – Dividends Declared		150
A – Investment in Sub Corporation		90

Investment Elimination Entry (Entry 2):

SE – Shareholders' Equity	1000	
A – Property, Plant and Equipment	250	
A – Goodwill	150	
A – Investment in Sub Corporation		1,400

Amortization of Assets and Goodwill (Entry 3):

SE – Amortization Expense	50	
A – Property, Plant and Equipment		50
(Accumulated Amortization)		
SE – Amortization Expense — Goodwill	10	
A – Goodwill		10

The preceding entries are added to the consolidating working papers as shown in Exhibit 13-10. Note that a separate accumulated amortization account has not been provided and that the amount of extra amortization has simply been credited to the property, plant and equipment account for the amortization for the period. You can think of property, plant and equipment as a net account, that is, net of accumulated amortization.

Income, on a consolidated basis, is as follows:

PARENT CORPORATION — CONSOLIDATED NET INCOME:

Revenues	$3,500
Expenses	(2,485)
Amortization expense	(525)
Amortization expense — goodwill	(10)
Net Income	$ 480

Note that this is exactly the same as the net income that was reported by Parent Corporation using the equity method as shown in Exhibit 13-8. This will always be the case. As mentioned earlier, the equity method is sometimes referred to as a *one-line consolidation*. It is a one-line consolidation because the balance sheet effects of consolidation are captured in the one-line item called the investment account. The income statement effects of consolidation are captured in the one-line item called EEI. The only difference, then, between the equity method and a full consolidation is that the one-line items are replaced with the full detail of the assets and liabilities of the subsidiary on the balance sheet and the full detail of the revenues and expenses of the subsidiary on the income statement.

EXHIBIT 13-10

Consolidating Working Papers (Year Subsequent to Acquisition)

Account	Parent Corporation		Sub Corporation		Consolidating Entries		Consolidated Totals	
	Debit	Credit	Debit	Credit	Debit	Credit	Debit	Credit
Assets other than PP&E	1,440		3,000				4,440	
Property, plant and equipment	1,850		1,600		(2) 250	50 (3)	3,650	
Goodwill					(2) 150	10 (3)	140	
Investment in Sub Corporation	1,490					90 (1)	—	
						1,400 (2)		
Liabilities		2,420		3,450				5,870
Shareholders' equity		2,000ᵃ		1,000ᵃ	(2) 1,000			2,000
Revenues		1,500		2,000				3,500
Expenses	1,010		1,475				2,485	
Amortization expense	250		225		(3) 50		525	
Amortization expense — goodwill					(3) 10		10	
EEI		240			(1) 240			—
Dividends declared	120		150			150 (1)	120	
Totals	6,160	6,160	6,450	6,450	1,700	1,700	11,370	11,370

ᵃBeginning of period balances (trial balance phase).

Consolidation Procedures — Less than 100% Acquisition

One complication that arises in many acquisitions is that the parent corporation does not always acquire 100% of the shares of the subsidiary. Suppose, for example, that Parent Corporation buys 80% of the shares of Sub Corporation for $1,120. The balance sheets of Parent Corporation and Sub Corporation immediately after acquisition are shown in Exhibit 13-11. A column that represents 80% of the balance sheet of Sub Corporation is also presented for future reference.

Assume that the same fair market values of the assets and liabilities apply to Sub Corporation as before. The only asset that had extra fair market value is the property, plant and equipment, with excess value of $250. Since Parent Corporation purchased only 80% of the subsidiary, it acquired only 80% of this extra fair market value, or $200. The calculation of goodwill would be made as follows:

PARENT CORPORATION — CONSOLIDATED NET INCOME:	
Purchase price	$1,120
Less 80% of book value acquired (80% of $1,000)	(800)
Less 80% of extra fair market value (80% of $250)	(200)
Goodwill	$ 120

EXHIBIT 13-11

Parent and Subsidiary Balance Sheets at Date of Acquisition (80% Acquisition)

Balance Sheet

	Parent Corporation	Sub Corporation	80% of Sub Corporation
Assets other than PP&E	$1,080	$2,500	$2,000
Plant, property and equipment	1,800	1,500	1,200
Investment in Sub Corporation	1,120	—	—
Total assets	$4,000	$4,000	$3,200
Total liabilities	$2,000	$3,000	$2,400
Shareholders' equity	2,000	1,000	800
Total liabilities and shareholders' equity	$4,000	$4,000	$3,200

If Parent Corporation owns 80% of Sub Corporation, who owns the other 20%? The answer is, other shareholders. Because Parent Corporation controls Sub Corporation, it must prepare consolidated financial statements. When consolidated financial statements are prepared, Parent Corporation adds 100% of Sub Corporation's assets, liabilities, revenues and expenses to its own accounts. But Parent Corporation does not own 100% of Sub Corporation. It must, therefore, show the 20% as being owned by the other shareholders. It does this by creating an account called **Non-controlling Interest** (NCI) or sometimes called **Minority Interest**. The NCI account on the balance sheet is located at the end of the long-term liabilities. It contains 20% of the book value of Sub Corporation, $200 (20% of $1,000). There is another NCI account on the income statement that holds 20% of Sub Corporation's net income. It appears like an expense and reduces the income by 20% so that consolidated net income represents only the 80% that belongs to Parent Corporation. These two NCI accounts allow the parent to consolidate 100% of its subsidiaries and then to back out the part that does not belong to it.

To illustrate the NCI (minority interest) disclosure, we have included the 1994 balance sheet and income statement of Cominco Ltd. in Exhibit 13-12. The minority interest in 1994 on the income statement is $2,424,000, and on the balance sheet is $39,441,000. Cominco Ltd. has several subsidiaries. On the inside back cover of the 1994 annual report, it lists its subsidiaries and tells the user how much of the subsidiary it owns (see Exhibit 13-13). The minority interest likely came from the consolidation of Cominco Resources International Limited (55.7%) and Sociedad Minera Refineria de Zinc Cajamarquilla S.A. (82%). It is not clear if Cominco Ltd. would have consolidated Highland Valley Copper because it owned exactly 50% and may or may not control this corporation. It would consolidate all of the 100% owned corporations, but not Compania Minera Quebrada Blanca S.A. because it owned only 38.25% of this corporation. It likely used the equity method for this investment.

When a parent owns less than 100% of a subsidiary, the accounting can become quite complex. The discussion of these aspects will be left to more advanced texts. It is enough that you understand what the NCI account represents.

EXHIBIT 13-12

COMINCO LTD.
Consolidated Statements of Operations
Years Ended December 31, 1994 and 1993

	1994	1993
		(thousands)
Revenue		
Sales of products and services	$1,097,931	$ 982,504
Gain on sale of exploration properties	25,610	20,997
Income from sale of investments and other	3,267	11,314
Equity in net earnings of associated companies	11,761	10,029
	1,138,569	1,024,844
Costs and Expenses		
Costs of products and distribution	772,016	949,725
Depreciation, depletion and amortization	115,774	127,271
General, administrative and selling	53,792	56,403
Interest (Note 11)	32,469	37,129
Mineral exploration	41,419	30,739
	1,015,470	1,201,267
Earnings (Loss) Before the Following	123,099	(176,423)
Gain on sale of power expansion rights (Note 15[f])	51,356	—
Gain on sale of associated companies (Note 12)	64,716	57,935
Earnings (Loss) Before Taxes and Minority Interest	239,171	(118,488)
Income and resource tax (expense) recovery (Note 13)	(109,519)	6,522
Minority interest	2,424	(1,244)
Net Earnings (Loss)	$ 132,076	$ (113,210)
Net Earnings (Loss) Per Common Share (Note 9[e])	$ 1.62	$ (1.46)

Consolidated Statements of Earnings
Reinvested in the Business
Years Ended December 31, 1994 and 1993

	1994	1993
		(thousands)
Amount at Beginning of Year	$ 393,002	$ 509,451
Net Earnings (Loss)	132,076	(113,210)
	525,078	396,241
Premium on redemption of preferred shares	54	158
Dividends paid		
Preferred – Series A $2.00 per share	276	287
– Series B $2.44 per share	2,715	2,794
	3,045	3,239
Amount at End of Year	$ 522,033	$ 393,002

Consolidations — Intercorporate Transactions

One final complication that deserves mentioning is the impact that intercorporate transactions have on the consolidated financial statements. When a parent corporation buys a controlling interest in a supplier or a customer, it is likely that there are many transactions between the two corporations. Prior to the acquisition, these transactions are viewed as taking place between two independent parties but, after the acquisition, they are viewed as intercorporate transactions. Sales of goods and

EXHIBIT 13-12 (continued)

COMINCO LTD.
Consolidated Balance Sheets
At December 31, 1994 and 1993

	1994	1993
	(thousands)	
Current Assets		
Cash and short-term investments	$ 46,112	$ 12,327
Accounts receivable	207,723	191,953
Inventories (Note 2)	366,921	293,307
Prepaid expenses	11,580	8,629
	632,336	506,216
Investments		
Associated companies (Note 12)	—	48,100
Other (Note 4)	40,770	33,878
	40,770	81,978
Fixed Assets (Note 5)		
Land, buildings and equipment	1,528,972	1,464,428
Mineral properties and development	191,525	170,521
	1,720,497	1,634,949
Other Assets (Note 6)	52,367	48,077
	$2,445,970	$ 2,271,220
Current Liabilities		
Bank loans and notes payable	$ 3,998	$ 11,669
Accounts payable and accrued liabilities	208,681	169,878
Income and resource taxes	38,513	11,687
Long-term debt due within one year	52,519	31,824
	303,711	225,058
Long-Term Debt (Note 7)	505,496	622,022
Deferred Liabilities (Note 8)	115,212	113,573
Income Tax Provided but not Currently Payable	305,270	240,107
Minority Interests	39,441	33,520
Shareholders' Equity		
Capital (Note 9)	609,017	609,123
Earnings reinvested in the business	522,033	393,002
Cumulative translation adjustment (Note 10)	45,790	34,815
	1,176,840	1,036,940
	$2,445,970	$ 2,271,220

Commitments and Contingencies (Note 15)

Approved by the Board:

N. B. Keevil   Director   D.A. Thompson   Director

EXHIBIT 13-13

COMINCO LTD.

PRINCIPAL SUBSIDIARIES AND ASSOCIATED COMPANIES

	Country of Operation	Ownership
Cominco American Incorporated	United States	100%
Cominco Alaska Incorporated	United States	100%
Cominco Engineering Services Ltd.	Canada	100%
Cominco (U.K.) Limited	England	100%
Cominco Resources International Limited	Canada	55.7%
Highland Valley Copper	Canada	50%
Sociedad Minera Refinería de Zinc Cajamarquilla S.A.	Peru	82%
Compañía Minera Quebrada Blanca S.A.	Chile	38.25%

---

services between a parent and a subsidiary cannot be viewed as completed transactions unless there has been a sale of the goods or services outside the consolidated entity. Therefore, any profits (revenues and expenses) from those transactions that are not completed by a sale outside the consolidated entity must be eliminated. If there are remaining balances in accounts receivable and accounts payable that relate to intercorporate transactions, these, too, must be removed.

To show you briefly this elimination process, let us consider the following example. Corporation A owns 100% of Corporation B. During 19x8, Corporation A sells a parcel of land to Corporation B for $60,000. This land had originally cost Corporation A $45,000. Corporation A records the transaction on its books in the following manner:

A – Cash	60,000	
A – Land		45,000
SE – Gain on Sale of Land		15,000

Corporation B records the acquisition of the land as follows:

A – Land	60,000	
A – Cash		60,000

Note that Cash went out of one entity into the other entity. The consolidated entity still has the same amount of Cash. Land went from $45,000 on one entity's books to $60,000 on the other entity's books. To the consolidated entity, this is the same parcel of land that was on last year's consolidated balance sheet at its historical cost of $45,000. If it is not reduced back to $45,000 on the consolidated balance sheet, it will be overstated. If we allowed the sale price of items sold intercompany to appear at the sale price on the consolidated financial statements, the two entities could sell items back and forth merely to increase asset value and to record revenue when, in reality, no external transactions with independent third parties took place. The last item, the Gain on the Sale of Land, must also be removed from the consolidated income statement. No gain can be recognized by the consolidated entity because the land has not been sold to an outside party. The journal entry to eliminate this unrealized gain on the consolidating working papers would be:

SE – Gain on Sale of Land	15,000	
A – Land		15,000

This entry on the consolidating working papers would have to be repeated each year when the consolidated financial statements are prepared. Entries similar to these are prepared for all the intercompany transactions that occur between the two entities.

◖◗ STATEMENT ANALYSIS CONSIDERATIONS

The consolidation of a subsidiary considerably changes the appearance of both the income statement and the balance sheet from the parent-only financial statements under equity. The income statement is different only in its detail; the net income for the period is the same regardless of whether or not the subsidiary is consolidated. Also, because the balances in the shareholders' equity accounts are the same with either method, ratios such as return on equity are unaffected by the consolidation policy.

Other ratios that involve other balance sheet figures can be dramatically affected. Earlier in the chapter, the effect that consolidation has on the debt/equity ratio was described using the information provided in Exhibit 13-7. The debt/equity for Parent Corporation was 1.0 whereas the debt/equity for the consolidated entity was 2.5. Users who need information about an entity's ability to repay debt should not rely on consolidated financial statements. These statements contain the liabilities of all the corporations in the consolidated entity, but each of those corporations is responsible for only its own debt. A parent and its subsidiaries may guarantee each other's debt. This would reduce the risk of nonpayment and could result in lending institutions charging lower rates or loaning larger amounts. When the debt is guaranteed, the debt/equity ratio of the consolidated entity is useful. All of the assets are available to service the debt.

Other ratios will also be affected. The ROA ratio, for example, divides the net income before interest by the average total assets. The numerator changes to the extent that the interest expense of the subsidiary is included on the consolidated income statement and is, therefore, added back to the net income. The denominator (average total assets) also changes because the investment account is replaced with the individual assets and liabilities of the subsidiary. In the example in Exhibit 13-8, the total assets of the parent prior to consolidation was $4,780. After consolidation the total assets were $8,230 (Exhibit 13-10). This dramatic increase would certainly affect the ROA. The ROA prior to consolidation would have been 10% ($480 / $4,780). After consolidation, the ROA was 5.8% ($480 / $8,230).

The current ratio will also be affected. The current assets and liabilities that are embedded in the investment account are shown in full detail when they are consolidated. The current assets and liabilities of the subsidiary would be added to the parent's when they are consolidated. Because our example in Exhibit 13-7 does not distinguish current liabilities from long-term liabilities, it is not possible to demonstrate the change that would occur. Obviously, the quick ratio will also be affected by consolidation for the same reason as the current ratio.

Shareholders, potential investors, and most other outside users may not be able to determine the impact that various subsidiaries have on the consolidated financial statements. If a parent owns 100% of a subsidiary, the subsidiary will often not publish financial statements for external users other than Revenue Canada. A lender would be able to request individual financial statements for any corporation that wanted to borrow funds, but most other external users would not have this luxury. This means that users should have some understanding of which ratios are affected by the consolidation process. If the parent owns less than 100% of the shares, the subsidiary, if it is traded on the stock market, must publish publicly available financial statements. Users then have the opportunity to get more information about the components of the consolidated entity. A 100% owned subsidiary does not trade on the stock exchange and does not need to make its financial statement public. Parent corporations often have many subsidiaries. Evaluating each subsidiary individually is usually not necessary. Rather users determine the ratios but keep in mind that each corporation is responsible for its own debt and taxes.

SUMMARY

The environment of corporate financial reporting is one of constant change and growing complexity. This book has introduced you to most of the fundamental concepts and principles that guide standard-setting bodies, such as the Accounting Standards Board, as they consider new business situations and issues. You should think of the completion of this book as the end of the beginning of your understanding of corporate financial reporting. As accounting standard-setting bodies and regulators adjust and change the methods and guidelines used to prepare financial statements, you must constantly educate yourself so that you understand the impacts of these changes on the financial statements of your corporation or of other corporations you need to understand.

AN INTERNATIONAL PERSPECTIVE
REPORTS FROM OTHER COUNTRIES

In 1991, the FASB in the United States issued a discussion memorandum entitled "International Accounting Research Project: Consolidations/Equity Accounting" that concerned consolidation issues. Conducted by Price Waterhouse, the study surveyed practices in Australia, Canada, France, Germany, Italy, Japan, The Netherlands, the United Kingdom and the United States as of November, 1990.

In its findings, Price Waterhouse concluded that, in virtually all the countries surveyed, consolidated financial statements were required for corporations that were publicly traded on securities exchanges. In some countries, however, the consolidated statements are not considered the primary financial statements. In Japan, for instance, consolidated statements are provided as supplementary information. In many of the countries surveyed, non-publicly traded corporations did not prepare consolidated financial statements.

The survey also found widespread use of a criterion of control rather than ownership in deciding whether to consolidate an entity. France, for instance, explicitly allows subsidiaries in which the parent owns greater than 40% to be consolidated if no other group of shareholders has a greater share. Finance subsidiaries were generally not consolidated in countries other than the United States, but within seven months after the survey had been completed, Canada, New Zealand, and the United Kingdom had revised their standards to require consolidation of these subsidiaries. The revised international standard, IAS 22, on business combinations requires the use of the purchase method with the criterion of control and the consolidation of all subsidiaries.

SUMMARY PROBLEM

The Pacter Corporation (parent) bought 100% of the shares of the Sweeney Corporation (subsidiary) on January 1, 19X6, for $600,000. On January 1, 19X6, the shareholders' equity section of the Sweeney Corporation was as follows:

Common shares	$125,000
Retained earnings	75,000
Total shareholders' equity	$200,000

The amount paid by Pacter for Sweeney was larger than the book value of the assets acquired. This excess amount was attributed partially to land ($50,000) and equipment ($250,000). The equipment had a remaining useful life of 10 years and an assumed residual value of zero. Pacter amortizes its assets straight-line and amoritzes any goodwill over five years.

The following represents the trial balance of Pacter and Sweeney as of December 31, 19X6 (the end of the fiscal year).

Trial Balance, December 31, 19X6

Account	Pacter Corp. Debit	Pacter Corp. Credit	Sweeney Corp. Debit	Sweeney Corp. Credit
Cash	$ 780,000		$ 240,000	
Account receivable	400,000		200,000	
Inventory	525,000		350,000	
Investment in Sweeney	675,000		—	
PP&E	800,000		600,000	
Accumulated amortization		$ 300,000		$ 200,000
Accounts payable		425,000		290,000
Long-term debt		900,000		580,000
Common shares		700,000		125,000
Retained earnings (1/1)		400,000		75,000
Revenues		5,000,000		2,000,000
Expenses (other than amort'n)	4,200,000		1,700,000	
Amortization	100,000		100,000	
Equity in Sweeney earnings		155,000		—
Dividends declared	400,000		80,000	
Totals	$7,880,000	$7,880,000	$3,270,00	$3,270,000

Required:

a. Reconstruct the entries that Pacter made during 19x6 to account for its investment in Sweeney using the equity method.

b. Prepare a set of consolidating working papers for Pacter and Sweeney for 19X6. Separately, show the consolidating entries in journal entry form.

c. Calculate the following ratios for Pacter Corporation using its parent-only financial statement information and the consolidated entity information:
  1. Debt/equity
  2. Return on equity
  3. Return on assets
  4. Current ratio

SUGGESTED SOLUTION TO SUMMARY PROBLEM

a. Using the equity method, the following entries would be made:

At Acquisition:

A – Investment in Sweeney	600,000	
A – Cash		600,000

At Year-end:

To recognize income: The net income of Sweeney is calculated as follows:

Revenues	$2,000,000
Expenses	1,700,000
Amortization	100,000
Net income	$ 200,000

Since Pacter's share of Sweeney's income is 100%, the following entry would be made:

A – Investment in Sweeney	200,000	
SE – Equity in Sweeney Earnings		200,000

To recognize dividends: Sweeney declared $80,000 in dividends and Pacter's share is 100%; therefore, the following entry would be made:

A – Cash	80,000	
A – Investment in Sweeney		80,000

To recognize amortization of goodwill and excess fair market value: At the date of acquisition, Pacter paid $400,000 more for the shares of Sweeney than the book value($200,000) of the net assets. This excess amount would be attributable to the following balance sheet items:

Land	$ 50,000
Equipment	250,000
Goodwill	100,000
Total	$400,000

The land is not amortized, but the excess amount due to the equipment must be amortized. Since Pacter uses straight-line amortization, the extra amortization expense would be $25,000 per year ($250,000/10 years). The goodwill would also have to be amortized and, since it is Pacter's policy to amortize goodwill over five years, extra amortization expense of $20,000 per year would have to be recognized ($100,000/5 years). Using the equity method, the sum of these two extra expenses would be recognized with the following entry:

SE – Equity in Sweeney Earnings	45,000	
A – Investment in Sweeney		45,000

Based on these entries, the investment account balance would be $675,000, and the equity in Sweeney earnings would be $155,000 as shown in the trial balance.

b. The consolidating working papers are shown in Exhibit 13-11.

The consolidating working paper entries are as follows:

1) To reverse current income and dividends:

SE – Equity in Sweeney Earnings	155,000	
SE – Dividends Declared		80,000
A – Investment in Sweeney		75,000

EXHIBIT 13-11

Consolidating Working Papers, Pacter Company and Sweeney Company, 19x6 — 100% Acquisition

	Pacter Corp.		Sweeney Corp.		Consolidating Entries		Consolidated Totals	
Account	Debit	Credit	Debit	Credit	Debit	Credit	Debit	Credit
Cash	780,000		240,000				1,020,000	
Accounts receivable	400,000		200,000				600,000	
Inventory	525,000		350,000				875,000	
Property, plant, & equipment	800,000		600,000		(2) 300,000		1,700,000	
Accumulated amortization		300,000		200,000		25,000 (3)		525,000
Goodwill					(2) 100,000	20,000 (3)	80,000	
Investment in Sweeney	675,000					75,000 (1)	—	
						600,000 (2)		
Accounts payable		425,000		290,000				715,000
Long-term debt		900,000		580,000				1,480,000
Common shares		700,000		125,000	(2) 125,000			700,000
Retained earnings		400,000ᵃ		75,000ᵃ	(2) 75,000			400,000
Revenues		5,000,000		2,000,000				7,000,000
Expenses	4,200,000		1,700,000				5,900,000	
Amortization expense	100,000		100,000		(3) 25,000		225,000	
Goodwill expense					(3) 20,000		20,000	
EEI		155,000			(1) 155,000		—	
Dividends declared	400,000		80,000			80,000 (1)	400,000	
Totals	7,880,000	7,880,000	3,270,000	3,270,000	800,000	800,000	10,820,000	10,820,000

ᵃBeginning of period balances (trial balance phase).

2) To eliminate the investment account and shareholders' equity and to create extra fair market value and goodwill:

SE – Common Shares	125,000	
SE – Retained Earnings	75,000	
A – Land (PP&E)	50,000	
A – Equipment (PP&E)	250,000	
A – Goodwill	100,000	
A – Investment in Sweeney		600,000

3) To amortize the extra fair market value and to amortize goodwill:

SE – Amortization Expense	25,000	
XA – Accumulated Amortization		25,000
SE – Goodwill Expense	20,000	
A – Goodwill		20,000

Solution:

c. Parent-only   Consolidated entity

1. $\$1,325,000/1,555,000^a = 0.85$ $\$2,195,000/1,555,000^b = 1.41$

---

[a] $\$700,000 + 400,000 + 5,000,000 - 4,200,000 - 100,000 + 155,000 - 400,000 = \$1,555,000$

[b] $\$700,000 + 400,000 + 7,000,000 - 5,900,000 - 225,000 - 20,000 - 400,000 = \$1,555,000$

2. $\$855,000^a/1,555,000 = 0.55$ $\$855,000^b/1,555,000 = 0.55$

---

[a] $\$5,000,000 - 4,200,000 - 100,000 + 155,000 = \$855,000$

[b] $\$7,000,000 - 5,900,000 - 225,000 - 20,000 = \$855,000$

3. $\$855,000/2,880,000^a = 0.30$ $\$855,000/3,750,000^b = 0.23$

---

[a] $\$780,000 + 400,000 + 525,000 + 800,000 - 300,000 + 675,000 = \$2,880,000$

[b] $\$1,020,000 + 600,000 + 875,000 + 1,700,000 - 525,000 + 80,000 = \$3,750,000$

4. $\$1,705,000^a/425,000 = 4.0$ $\$2,495,000^b/715,000 = 3.5$

---

[a] $\$780,000 + 400,000 + 525,000 = \$1,705,000$

[b] $\$1,020,000 + 600,000 + 875,000 = \$2,495,000$

ABBREVIATIONS USED

EEI   Equity in earnings of investment
NCI   Noncontrolling interest
PP&E Property, plant and equipment

GLOSSARY

Asset purchase An acquisition of assets from another corporation in which the acquiring corporation purchases the assets directly rather than buying a controlling interest in the shares of the other corporation. Title to the assets passes to the acquiring corporation.

Consolidated financial statements Financial statements that represent the total financial results of a parent corporation and its various subsidiaries as if they were one corporation, even though they are separate legal entities.

Consolidating working papers A worksheet that adjusts the financial statements of a parent and its subsidiaries so that the statements can be combined to show the consolidated financial statements.

Consolidation An accounting method that corporations are required to use to represent their ownership in other corporations when they have control over the activities in other corporations. The method requires the preparation of consolidated financial statements.

Controlling interest The amount of ownership of a subsidiary that a parent corporation must have in order to control the strategic, operating, financing and investing activities of the subsidiary. An ownership interest of greater than 50% usually meets this criterion.

Cyclical business A business that is subject to significant swings in the level of its activity, such as the greeting card business.

Debt for equity swap A transaction in which debt securities are exchanged for equity securities.

Diversification A reason for acquiring ownership in another corporation. Diversification typically implies that the new corporation acquired is in a business very different from the current business of the corporation. The idea is to find a business that is countercyclical to the corporation's current business.

Elimination entry A working paper consolidating entry that eliminates the balance in the investment in subsidiary account against the shareholders' equity accounts of the subsidiary. At the same time, if the price paid by the parent corporation exceeds the book value of the subsidiary's shareholders' equity section, excess fair market value of the net assets acquired and goodwill are recognized as part of the entry.

Equity in earnings of investment An account used in a parent corporation's books to record its share of the subsidiary's net income for the period using the equity method.

Equity method An accounting method that corporations use to represent their ownership in corporations in which they have significant influence. This is usually true when the percentage of ownership is between 20% and 50%. In addition, this method is often used in parent-only statements to account for the investment in a subsidiary. In this case, the account will be eliminated on the consolidating working papers at the end of the year when consolidated financial statements are prepared.

Excess fair market value The difference between the fair market value and book value of the assets of a subsidiary corporation whose shares are acquired by a parent corporation. The difference is measured at the date of acquisition.

Goodwill An intangible asset that arises when a parent corporation acquires ownership in a subsidiary corporation and pays more for the shares than the fair market value of the underlying net identifiable assets at the date of acquisition. The difference between the price paid and the fair market value of the identifiable net assets at the date of acquisition is the value of the goodwill. It can represent expected excess earnings that result from the accumulated reputation of the subsidiary, its exceptional sales staff or an advantageous location.

Horizontal integration A type of acquisition in which a parent corporation buys a competitor corporation in order to gain a larger market share or to expand the corporation's markets geographically.

Identifiable net assets The assets and liabilities that can be specifically identified at the date of a merger or acquisition. Some of the identifiable assets may not have been recorded on the subsidiary's book, such as patents and trademarks.

Investee A corporation whose shares are being acquired by another corporation (the investor).

Investor A corporation that acquires shares of another corporation as an investment.

Minority interest A synonym for noncontrolling interest.

Noncontrolling interest The portion of a less than 100% owned subsidiary that is owned by other shareholders.

One-line consolidation The equity method is referred to as a one-line consolidation method because it produces the same net results as the full consolidation method except that the results are shown in a single line on the balance sheet (the investment account) and a single line on the income statement (the equity in earnings of investment).

Parent corporation A corporation that acquires control (usually can elect a majority of the Board of Directors) of another corporation. The acquired corporation is referred to as a subsidiary.

Parent-only books The accounting records of a parent corporation that have not been combined with its subsidiary's records in consolidated financial statements. The parent typically records the investment in its subsidiary using the equity method on the parent-only books.

Passive investment An investment by one corporation in another corporation in which the acquiring corporation has no capability of controlling or influencing the decisions of the acquired corporation.

Pooling of interests method An accounting method used in acquisitions involving an exchange of shares that results in neither corporation being recognized as an acquirer of the other. The underlying concept of the method is that the ownership groups of the two corporations are pooled together and, therefore, there is no basis on which to revalue the assets and liabilities of the two corporations. In consolidation, the assets and liabilities are combined at their book values at the date of acquisition.

Purchase method An accounting method used to record the acquisition of another corporation. The acquisition is treated as a purchase, and the assets and liabilities acquired are measured at their cost. Because this is typically a basket purchase, the cost is allocated to the individual assets and liabilities on the basis of their relative fair market values.

Stock acquisition An acquisition of another corporation that is accomplished through the acquisition of shares of the acquired corporation. The acquired corporation continues as a separate legal entity.

Stock swap An acquisition in which an acquiring corporation swaps its shares for the shares of the acquired corporation.

Subsidiary A corporation controlled by another corporation (the parent) usually by the parent owning more than 50% of its outstanding shares and controlling its strategic, operating, financing and investing decisions.

Trial balance phase A phase in the preparation of financial statements in which the temporary accounts still contain income statement and dividend information from the period and have not been closed out to retained earnings.

Vertical integration A type of merger or acquisition in which a parent corporation buys a supplier or a customer corporation in order to assure a supply of raw materials or a market for its end product.

Widely held shares Shares of a corporation that are held by a larger number of individuals or institutions such that no one shareholder has significant influence on the decisions of the corporation.

ASSIGNMENT MATERIAL

◥◣ Assessing Your Recall

1. Identify and briefly explain the major reasons why a corporation might want to buy shares in another corporation.

2. Compare and contrast a share acquisition and an asset acquisition in terms of their effects on the financial statements.

3. Explain the conceptual differences between an acquisition treated as a purchase and one treated as a pooling.

4. Explain the financial statement implications of accounting for an acquisition using the purchase method versus the pooling method:
   a. At the date of acquisition
   b. Subsequent to the date of acquisition

5. Explain the nature of goodwill and how it arises in the context of an acquisition.

6. Briefly describe the GAAP guidelines for the accounting of long-term acquisitions in the shares of other corporations. In your description, identify the criteria used to distinguish the various accounting methods.

7. The equity method is sometimes referred to as a one-line consolidation. Explain.

8. Discuss what a consolidation is trying to accomplish.

9. The consolidated balances in the asset and liability accounts do not exist on either the parent corporation's or the subsidiary corporation's books. Explain why you agree or disagree with this statement.

10. The consolidating working paper entries are needed to eliminate double accounting for certain items on the parent's and subsidiary's books. Explain which items would be accounted for twice if the subsidiary corporation's books were added directly to the parent's books.

▶◤ Applying Your Knowledge

11. On April 1, the Royal Tin Corporation acquired some common shares of the Tungsten Steel Corporation. The book value of the Tungsten Steel Corporation's net assets on April 1 was $10 million, and the market value of the net assets was $12.5 million. During the year, the Tungsten Steel Corporation had net earnings of $1,000,000 and declared dividends of $600,000.

Required:
For each of he following assumptions, give the amount of income recognized by the Royal Tin Corporation from its investment in Tungsten Steel Corporation, and show the beginning and ending balances for the investment account on Royal Tin's books. Both corporations close their books annually on December 31. Goodwill is to be amortized over a period of 20 years. Assume that any excess fair market value is to be amortized straight-line over five years. Assume in each case that the market value of the shares on December 31 is the same as the acquisition price.
   a. The acquisition price is $1,250,000 for 10% of the common shares of Tungsten Steel.
   b. The acquisition price is $1,500,000 for 15% of the common shares of Tungsten Steel.
   c. The acquisition price is $3,125,000 for 25% of the common shares of Tungsten Steel.

d. The acquisition price is $6,000,000 for 45% of the common shares of Tungsten Steel.

e. The acquisition price is $13,000,000 for 100% of the common shares of Tungsten Steel.

12. On January 1, Prism Corporation acquired portions of the common shares of two companies, Quartz Corporation and Gem Corporation. The data relating to the acquisition and the first year of operations are as follows:

Corporation	Common Shares Acquired	Book Value of Net Assets as of 1/1	Market Value of Net Assets as of 1/1	Acquisition Price	Net Income for the year	Dividends Declared for the year
Quartz Corp.	18%	$3,500,000	$5,000,000	$900,000	$1,250,000	$800,000
Gem Corp.	40%	$8,000,000	$9,500,000	$4,800,000	$3,000,000	$2,000,000

All the corporations close their books annually on December 31. Goodwill, if any, is to be amortized over a period of 40 years. Property, plant and equipment acquired has a remaining useful life of six years, has a residual value of zero, and is amortized using the straight-line method. Any excess fair market value in the transaction relates to property, plant and equipment. The market value of the Quartz Corporation and the Gem Corporation shares held on December 31 was $850,000 and $4,500,000, respectively.

Required:
Show the journal entries to account for these two investments during the year.

13. On January 1, the Lynnen Corporation acquired 100% of the common shares of Antler Incorporated at a price of $1,500,000. The book value of the net assets of Antler Corporation on January 1 was $1,250,000. The book value of the net assets approximates the fair value at the date of acquisition. During the year, Antler earned $340,000 and declared dividends of $290,000. At the end of the year, the dividends receivable of Lynnen Corporation included an amount of $290,000 that was due from Antler Inc. [Hint: Lynnen's balance sheet would have a dividend receivable and Antler's would have a dividend payable. The consolidated entity cannot owe money to itself. Therefore, both of these accounts must be removed on the working papers before consolidated financial statements are prepared.] Goodwill, if any, is to be amortized over a period of 20 years.

Required:
a. Show the journal entries for the acquisition of the common shares and other entries during the year, assuming that Lynnen uses the equity method on its own books.
b. Prepare the consolidating working paper entries.

14. The following are the balance sheets and income statements for Gentel Corporate and Giant Corporation as of December 31, 19X7:

Balance Sheet as of December 31, 19x7

	Gentel Corp.	Giant Corp.
Assets		
Cash	$ 29,000	$ 15,000
Accounts Receivable	35,000	45,500
Investment in Giant Corp.	128,750	—
Other Assets	61,000	74,500
Total Assets	$253,750	$135,000
Liabilities & Shareholders' Equity		
Accounts Payable	$ 39,500	$ 20,000
Other Current Liabilities	10,500	10,000
Common Shares	150,000	80,000
Retained Earnings	53,750	25,000
Total Liabilities & Shareholders' Equity	$253,750	$135,000

Income Statement for the year ended December 31, 19X7

	Gentel Corp.	Giant Corp.
Sales Revenue	$100,000	$ 60,000
Cost of Goods Sold	(55,000)	(35,000)
Amortization	(25,000)	(5,000)
EEI	18,750	—
Net Income	$ 38,750	$ 20,000
Dividends Declared	$ 25,000	$ 15,000

On January 1, 19x7, Gentel had acquired 100% of the common shares of Giant Corporation. The acquisition price was $125,000. The shareholders' equity section of Giant on January 1 was as follows:

Giant Corp.	
Common Shares	$ 80,000
Retained Earnings	20,000
Total	$100,000

The fair market value of Giant's net assets equalled their book values at the date of acquisition. Goodwill, if any, is to be amortized over a period of 20 years.

Required:

a. Prepare the consolidating working papers, supported with the necessary working paper journal entries.

b. Prepare the consolidated balance sheet and income statement.

15. On January 1, 19x7, the Noble Corporation acquired 100% of the outstanding shares of Baxter Corporation. The acquisition price was $250,000, which included $20,000 related to the excess fair market value of the capital assets acquired. The shareholders' equity as of January 1, 19x7, was as follows:

	Noble Corp.	Baxter Corp.
Common shares	$500,000	$150,000
Retained earnings	10,000	50,000
Total	$510,000	$200,000

During the year, Noble Corporation lent $50,000 to Baxter Corporation, which was to be repaid by December 31, 19x7; however, $20,00 was still due from Baxter at the end of the year. The trial balance of Noble and Baxter on December 31, 19x7, was as follows:

Trial Balance, December 31, 19x7

	Noble Co.		Baxter Co.	
Account	Debit	Credit	Debit	Credit
Current assets	$ 150,000		$ 90,000	
Capital assets	350,000		200,000	
Investment in Baxter	249,800		—	
Cost of goods sold	200,000		75,000	
Other expenses	25,000		10,000	
Dividends declared	50,000		30,000	
Current liabilities		$ 85,000		$ 35,000
Noncurrent liabilities		100,000		50,000
Common shares		500,000		150,000
Retained earnings		10,000		50,000
Sales revenue		300,000		120,000
EEI		29,800		—
Totals	$1,024,800	$1,024,800	$405,000	$405,000

The entire fair market value of the capital assets is to be amortized using the straight-line method. The remaining useful life is five years, and the residual value is zero. Goodwill, if any, is to be amortized over a period of 25 years.

Required:
a. Prepare the consolidating working papers, supported by the necessary working paper journal entries.
b. Prepare the consolidated balance sheet.

16. On January 1, 19x6, Carter Incorporated acquired 100% of the outstanding common shares of Stein Corporation and Lloyd Corporation. The details of the acquisitions and the earnings of both corporations are as follows:

	Stein Corp.	Lloyd Corp.
Book value of net assets as of 1/1/x6	$140,000	$175,000
Acquisition price	150,000	200,000
Earnings (loss) for 19x6	(20,000)	15,000
Dividends declared for 19x6	—	10,000

Goodwill, if any, is to be amortized over a period of 40 years. Assume that the fair market value of the net assets on 1/1/x6 is adequately measured by the book values.

Required:

a. Construct the journal entries that Carter will make in 19x6 to account for these investments on its own books assuming it uses the equity method.
b. Prepare the consolidating working paper entries for the consolidation of these investments as of 12/31/x6 assuming the entries in part (a) have been recorded.

17. The following are the balance sheets for Triumph Inc. and Kaydee Corporation as of December 31, 19x7 (prior to any acquisition):

Balance Sheet as of December 31, 19x7

	Triumph Inc.	Kaydee Corp.
Assets		
Current Assets	$175,000	$ 65,000
Noncurrent Assets	500,000	130,000
Total Assets	$675,000	$195,000
Liabilities & Shareholders' Equity		
Current Liabilities	$ 85,000	$ 28,000
Noncurrent Liabilities	190,000	57,000
Common Shares	350,000	100,000
Retained Earnings	50,000	10,000
Total Liabilities & Shareholders' Equity	$675,000	$195,000

On December 31, 19x7, Triumph Inc. issued 5,000 shares having a market value of $300,000 in exchange for all 7,500 shares of Kaydee. Just prior to the new issuance of shares, Triumph Inc. had 25,000 shares outstanding. The value of the shares exchange over the book value of Kaydee includes $100,000 of excess fair market value of the noncurrent assets. All other assets and liabilities of Kaydee were properly valued on its books.

Required:

a. Explain whether this acquisition should be accounted for as a purchase or a pooling.
b. Construct the entry that Triumph would make on its books to account for its investment in Kaydee.
c. Prepare a consolidated balance sheet as of December 31, 19X7.

18. Refer to the data in Problem 17. For 19x7, the details of the net income and dividends reported by the two corporations were as follows:

	Triumph Inc.	Kaydee Corp.
Net Income for 19x7	$250,000	$75,000
Dividends declared for 19x7	$225,000	$65,000

What is the net income of Triumph, Inc. on a consolidated basis?

19. Refer to the data in Problem 17, and assume that the net income and dividends declared for 19X8 are as follows:

	Triumph Inc.	Kaydee Corp.
Revenues	$700,000	$280,000
Cost of goods sold	400,000	160,000
Other Expenses	95,000	30,000
Net Income	$205,000	$ 90,000
Dividends Declared	$150,000	$ 75,000

Triumph's net income excludes the income from its investment in Kaydee. Goodwill is to be amortized over a period of 30 years, and any excess fair market value of noncurrent assets is to be amortized using the straight-line method over a 10-year useful life with a zero residual value.
Prepare a consolidated income statement for 19X8.

▶◣ Reading and Interpreting Published Financial Statements

20. In its 1994 balance sheet, Tritech Precision has a long-term investment listed in the amount of $8,791,000. Details about this investment are described in the following note:

4. Long-term investment
   The Company's investment consists of 4,633,650 common shares of Haley Industries Limited which represents a 44.8% interest. The Company's cost of the investment exceeded the net book value of the underlying assets of Haley Industries Limited by approximately $2,335,000 (1993—$2,398,000), which is being amortized on a straight-line basis over 40 years.

Required:
a. What accounting method is Tritech using to account for this investment? What items in the note led you to that conclusion?
b. From the information provided in the note, determine the excess amount that the cost of the investment exceeded the book value at acquisition. Using that information, determine in what year Tritech acquired its investment in Haley.
c. Tritech Precision Inc. designs, manufactures and distributes precision castings for the automotive, commercial, mining and aerospace industries. Haley Industries manufactures precision magnesium and aluminum castings principally for the aerospace industry. Knowing these facts about the two corporations, explain whether this is horizontal integration, vertical integration or diversification.

21. In 1994, Cara Operations made two acquisitions described in Note 9 of its 1995 annual report. Note 9 is reproduced in Exhibit 13-14.

Required:
a. The two acquisitions, one in catering and the other in office products, were made through subsidiaries. If the acquisitions were made through subsidiaries of Cara Operations, would they still be considered as part of the consolidated entity of Cara Operations? Explain.

EXHIBIT 13-14

CARA OPERATIONS LIMITED
Excerpted from Notes to the Statements

Acquisitions (Previous fiscal year)

a) **Catering**
On January 26, 1994, the corporation, through its subsidiary Beaver Foods Limited, acquired substantially all of the contracts and related assets of Capital Foods in the Ottawa/Quebec area and Scott's Foodservice in Southern Ontario. The food service contracts include government, educational institutions, corporate cafeterias and sports facilities. The total purchase price including acquisition-related expenses amounted to $15.2 million and was paid for by cash from existing corporate resources and bank borrowings.

b) **Office products**
On July 22, 1993, the corporation, through its subsidiary Grand & Toy, acquired the majority of Willson Stationers' British Columbia-based operations including customer lists and capital assets for $2.1 million.

c) The above transactions were accounted for by the purchase method, and the results of their operations are included in these consolidated financial statements from their effective dates of acquisition. The transactions summary is:

(In thousands of dollars)	Catering	Office Products	Total
Current Assets	$ 2,580	$ 889	$ 3,469
Capital Assets	4,237	263	4,500
Goodwill, contracts and trademarks	9,633	962	10,595
Accrued expenses	(1,270)	–	(1,270)
	$ 15,180	$ 2,114	$ 17,294

b. Were these two acquisitions asset purchases or share acquisitions? How would the subsidiaries have accounted for the acquisitions?

c. Cara Operations describes its company as having two core businesses: Food Services, and Office Products. Explain how the two new acquisitions would fit into Cara's business strategy.

d. In that food services and office products do not seem to have much in common, why do you think Cara Operations decided to expand into these two areas?

22. In 1995, Western Star Trucks Holdings, Ltd. established two subsidiaries, Orion Industries Ltd. and a subsidiary of Orion Industries Ltd. named Orion Bus Industries, Inc. (a United States subsidiary). Note 2 from Western Star Trucks' 1995 annual report describes how the subsidiaries were established, and the purpose of the subsidiaries (Exhibit 13-15):

When a parent wants to establish a subsidiary, it will do the legal paperwork to incorporate a business and then it will have that new business issue shares. The parent buys all of those shares. This serves two purposes. First, the parent has a new subsidiary that is a separate legal entity that can buy assets and borrow, with limited risk to the parent. Second, the subsidiary has just received an infusion of cash that it can use to carry out the plans of the parent. In the case of the new subsidiaries of Western Star Trucks Holdings, they were established to acquire the assets of a specific corporation owned by a Crown corporation of the Province of Ontario.

Required:

a. From the information given in Exhibit 13-15, is Orion acquiring a subsidiary or purchasing assets? Explain.

EXHIBIT 13-15

WESTERN STAR TRUCKS HOLDINGS LTD.
Excerpted from the Notes to the Financial Statements

2. Orion Acquisition

In May 1995, the Company incorporated Orion Bus Industries Ltd. and its wholly owned United States subsidiary, Orion Bus Industries Inc., [collectively "Orion"] for the purpose of acquiring selected assets [the "Orion Assets"] of Ontario Bus Industries Ltd. and its subsidiaries, [collectively "OBI"] which manufactured Transit Buses for municipal and local transit authorities under the "Orion" trademark [the "Orion Acquisition"]. OBI is a wholly owned subsidiary of Urban Transit Development Corporation ["UTDC"], a Crown corporation of the Province of Ontario.

The acquisition of the Orion Assets was funded by a $36 million share subscription in Orion from the Company and a $15 million preferred share subscription from UTDC [note 10]. The Company used $15 million of its own funds for the common share subscription and received share purchase incentives from the Province of Ontario and Boreal P & C Insurance Company, aggregating $21 million, thus reducing the cost of its investment in Orion's common shares to $15 million.

In connection with the acquisition of the Orion Assets, Orion is entitled to receive financial assistance from UTDC to a maximum of $1.7 million to assist Orion with the costs of disassembling, transporting and reassembling the property, plant and equipment at a new location. These funds were placed in a trust fund on June 7, 1995 and are not reflected in the financial statements.

The acquisition cost for the Orion Assets was allocated by Western Star, on a consolidated basis, as follows:

[in thousands of dollars]	
Inventory	26,845
Capital assets	10,263
Intangibles and deferred costs	385
	37,493
Less: Liabilities assumed or adjusted	[33,149]
Cash consideration paid or payable	4,344

The liabilities assumed or adjusted include $15.5 million which reflect the costs associated with commencing Orion's operations over the estimated start up period and which will be included in Western Star's income on a diminishing basis over that period.

b. Western Star Trucks created a subsidiary and a subsidiary of its subsidiary. The second subsidiary is in the United States. With respect to this second subsidiary, identify some difficulties that Western Star Trucks will have to resolve when it prepares its consolidated financial statements.

c. Western Star Trucks is taking advantage of the Ontario government's plan to divest itself of assets in a Crown corporation. From the note, describe how the government is making it easy for a corporation like Western Star Trucks to buy its assets.

23. Mackenzie Financial Corporation described the changes that it had made in 1993 and 1994 to its long-term investments. Those changes are described in Note 5 of its 1995 annual report (Exhibit 13-16).

Required:

a. The sale of part of its investment in VMSL is describe in the note. VMSL (Versa Management Systems Limited) owns the computer software systems that Mackenzie uses to administer the many fund accounts that it manages. From the note and the above statement, provide reasons why selling part of this investment has advantages for Mackenzie. What does the fact that it will use the equity method to account for this investment tell you about its new relationship with VMSL?

EXHIBIT 13-16

MACKENZIE FINANCIAL CORPORATION
Excerpted from Notes to the Statements (000's of dollars)

5. Acquisitions and Diverstitures

(a) Effective June 30, 1994, the Corporation sold 50% of its investment in VMSL to employees of VMSL for $550. Commencing July 1, 1994, the Corporation accounted for its investment in VMSL using the equity method.

(b) Effective after the close of business on March 31, 1993, the Corporation purchased 90% of the issued and outstanding shares of MRSI and effective April 22, 1993 the Corporation purchased the remaining 10% of the issued and outstanding shares for an aggregate purchase price of $11,174. The purchase price was comprised of $10,063 in cash and 167,715 common shares of the Corporation.

The fair value of MRSI at the dates of acquisition was:

Assets	$6,000
Liabilities	4,786
Net assets acquired	1,214
Purchase price	11,174
Excess of purchase price over value of net assets acquired	$9,960

The excess of purchase price of MRSI over value of net assets acquired is included in goodwill and is being amortized over ten years.

b. The second part of the note describes a new investment. How much goodwill arose from the purchase?

c. MRSI (Multiple Retirement Services Inc.) administers independent dealer registered plans such as RRSPs. In that almost 90% of the purchase price was used to buy the goodwill, suggest reasons why Mackenzie would have been willing to pay so much more than the fair value of the net assets.

24. Petromet Resources Ltd. is a natural gas exploration, development and production company, concentrating its activities in Alberta. In 1993, it purchased two private oil and gas companies. The acquisition is described in the following note from its 1994 annual report:

2. Acquisitions of subsidiaries

During 1993 the company purchased all of the issued and outstanding shares of two private oil and gas companies. Both acquisitions were accounted for as purchases with results of the subsidiaries' operations included in the consolidated statement of income from the respective dates of acquisition. Total consideration for the purchases was $5,750,000 consisting of $500,000 and 1,570,588 common shares of the company. The total purchase price, including costs associated with the acquisitions, was attributed to property, plant and equipment.

Required:

a. What was the value of Petromet Resources' common shares at the date of acquisition of these two companies?

b. Explain why it is reasonable that there is no goodwill in these acquisitions.

c. What are the advantages to Petromet Resources to buying these companies as subsidiaries instead of just buying their assets?

25. Imperial Parking Limited made four acquisitions between 1993 and 1995. Those acquisitions are described in Note 3 in its 1995 annual report (see Exhibit 13-17).

Required:

a. Read through the four acquisitions and identify those that were accomplished through an asset purchase and those through a share acquisition. What factors led you to your conclusions?

b. Imperial Parking Limited manages parking lots and parkade facilities. In three of the four acquisitions, it purchased "Management and lease agreements." What are these items and why are they so important to Imperial Parking?

c. In many acquisitions, the acquirer pays more than the fair value of the net assets, with excess amounts being assigned to goodwill. Explain why you think that Imperial Parking did not buy any goodwill.

d. In three of the four acquisitions, shares were issued to the previous owners as part of the consideration paid for the acquisition. Assuming that the previous owners were not current shareholders of Imperial Parking, what effect will these new issuances of shares have on the original shareholders. Should those

EXHIBIT 13-17

IMPERIAL PARKING LIMITED
Excerpted from Notes to the Financial Statements

3. Acquisition of Businesses

(a) Citipark Inc.:

On February 8, 1995, the Company acquired a parking business from Citipark Inc. ("Citipark"). The acquisition was accounted for by the purchase method with the results of operations included in these consolidated financial statements from the date of acquisition. The values assigned to the assets acquired and liabilities assumed were as follows:

Current assets	$ 3,810
Other non-current assets	332
	4,142
Liabilities assumed	4,057
	85
Management and lease agreements	12,558
	$12,643
Consideration:	
Cash including costs	$11,143
Shares (note 10)	1,500
	$12,643

EXHIBIT 13-17 (continued)

IMPERIAL PARKING LIMITED
Excerpted from Notes to the Financial Statements

3. Acquisition of Businesses

(b) Inner-Tec Security Consultants Ltd.:

On January 31, 1995, the Company acquired 100% of the issued shares of Inner-Tec Security
Consultants Ltd. ("Inner-Tec") from its major shareholder. The acquisition has been accounted for
by the purchase method with the results of operations included in these consolidated financial
statements from the date of acquisition. The values assigned to the assets acquired and liabilities
assumed were as follows:

Current assets	$ 3,486
Other non-current assets	1,159
	4,645
Liabilities assumed	1,054
	$ 3,591
Consideration:	
Shares (note 10)	$ 3,451
Costs	140
	$ 3,591

(c) Park Rite Ltd.:

On May 31, 1994, the Company acquired the parking assets of Park Rite Ltd. for cash consideration of $1,079,424. The acquisition has been accounted for by the purchase method with
the results of operations included in these consolidated financial statements from the date of
acquisition. The values assigned to the assets acquired were as follows:

Current assets	$ 97
Management and lease agreements	982
	$ 1,079

(d) City Collection Company Ltd.:

On December 13, 1993 but with effect from October 5, 1993, the Company purchased City
Collections Company Ltd. ("City Collection"), a corporation privately controlled by certain
management of the Company. This purchase was accounted for by the purchase method with the
results of operations included in these consolidated financial statements from the date of
acquisition. The values assigned to the assets acquired and liabilities assumed were as follows:

Current assets	$ 50
Management and lease agreements	2,015
Other non-current assets	86
	2,151
Current liabilities	(401)
	$ 1,750
Consideration:	
Shares (note 10)	$ 875
Cash	875
	$ 1,750

EXHIBIT 13-18

CHC HELICOPTER CORP.

Excerpted from Notes to the Financial Statements

2. Acquisitions

a) Brintel Holdings Limited (Brintel)

On January 27, 1993 the Company acquired an equity investment in Brintel Holdings Limited, a company based in Aberdeen Scotland conducting helicopter operations in the U.K. sector of the North Sea. The investment consisted of 40% of the outstanding ordinary shares and 50% of the non-voting preference shares of Brintel. Consideration for the investment was $6,138,000 in cash and a helicopter with a value of $5,960,000.

Effective December 15, 1993 the Company acquired an additional 50% of the outstanding ordinary shares and the remaining preference shares of Brintel. The remaining 10% of the ordinary shares were acquired on February 18, 1994. As a result of these acquisitions the Company now owns 100% of the outstanding shares of Brintel.

The acquisition has been accounted for by the purchase method and the results of Brintel's operations are included in these consolidated financial statements from December 15, 1993. Prior to that date the Company's initial 40% interest in the ordinary shares of Brintel was accounted for on the equity accounting basis.

The following is a summary of the net assets acquired, at the fair value assigned thereto:

Working capital (excluding bank indebtedness of $1,346)	$ 11,503
Property and equipment	79,352
Other assets	1,083
Long term debt	(29,210)
Deferred income taxes	(4,318)
	58,410
Prior investment, accounted for by the equity method	(15,973)
Purchase consideration	$ 42,437
Comprised of:	
Cash	$ 41,258
Notes	1,179
	$ 42,437

a) Brintel Holdings Limited (Brintel)

The excess of the cost of the Company's investment over the net book value of Brintel's net assets was $27,429,000. This amount has been allocated to capital assets and is being amortized at the same rate which these assets are depreciated.

The following information summarizes, on a pro forma basis, the combined results of operations as though 100% of Brintel had been consolidated in 1994.

Revenue	$ 286,801
Net loss	$ (2,971)
Loss per share	$ (0.31)

shareholders be concerned? What other information would you need to know in order to adequately answer this question?

26. CHC Helicopter Corporation made three acquisitions in 1993 and 1994. The acquisition of Brintel Holdings Limited in Scotland is described in Exhibit 13-18.

Required:

a. Describe the process by which CHC Helicopter acquired 100% of Brintel Holdings.

b. What difficulties will CHC Helicopter encounter when it attempts to consolidate Brintel Holdings at the year end?

c. CHC Helicopter Corp. has two main lines of business: helicopter service, and helicopter and fixed wing aircraft repair and overhaul. What does Brintel Holdings do? Does the acquisition of Brintel Holdings represent horizontal integration, vertical integration or diversification for CHC Helicopter?

d. Did any goodwill arise from this acquisition? If so, how much? If not, what reasons could you suggest for there not being any?

◤◣ Critical Thinking Question

As explained at the beginning of this chapter, corporations buy all or parts of other corporations for many reasons. You might assume that this type of activity is undertaken only by large corporations, but that is not the case. Many owners of small businesses will establish or buy subsidiaries as they start to expand. Often these small subsidiaries will represent a specific niche in the business plan of the owner. This enables the owner to undertake various activities without exposing the whole organization to the risk of failure.

Assume that you are the owner of a small business. Your initial business is installing carpets. You have a crew of three people who do the installation for you. Your ultimate goal is to do finishing contract work on residential and commercial construction. You hope eventually to control a multimillion dollar operation. Think about the path that could be taken so that you can expand your business from carpet installation to your eventual goal. Draft a plan of expansion that would take you gradually from one to the other. Include in your plan the purchase or establishment of subsidiaries.

APPENDIX

Time Value of Money

E arlier in the book we discussed the concept of the time value of money with regard to the valuation of assets and long-term liabilities. In particular, the present value of the future cash flows of an asset was suggested as a possible valuation method for almost all asset categories. Except for long-term receivables, present-value methods are not typically used when accounting for assets under GAAP because of the difficulty in estimating the future cash flows that result from the use of those assets. The accounting for liabilities, on the other hand, relies primarily on present-value methods. The basic concepts of the time value of money are discussed in this appendix.

◖◗ BASIC CONCEPTS

To gain an appreciation for the time value of money, consider the following situation. Lee, a college student on a reasonably tight budget, would like to raise some cash. Lee has a compact disc player that could be sold. Carlos and Darcy have made Lee separate offers to buy the CD player. Carlos has offered $300 today. Darcy has made a higher offer, $330, but will not have the cash for another two months. Regardless of which offer Lee accepts, Lee has agreed to exchange the CD player today. Which offer should Lee accept? Before you read on, come to some decision about what you think Lee should do and why.

There are numerous reasons why Lee might accept either Carlos' or Darcy's offer. Carlos' offer is attractive because Lee gets the cash immediately. This may be important because Lee may need to eat. If Lee has run out of money, it may not be feasible to wait two months to collect from Darcy, even though Darcy is offering more money. Another reason why Carlos' offer is attractive is that collecting the cash presents no **risk**. Carlos will hand over the cash as Lee hands over the CD. With Darcy's offer, there is some possibility that Lee will never be paid the $330.

A third reason for accepting Carlos' offer is that if Lee does not need the money to live, Lee can invest the $300 today and have more than $300 two months from now. For this reason, it is inappropriate to compare the $300 offer directly with the $330 offer. It is more appropriate to compare what the $300 would be worth two months from now with the $330 offer. In the terminology of the time value of money, the $300 is a **present value** and the $330 is a **future value**. To compare them on a dollar-for-dollar basis, Lee would have to calculate either what the $300 will be worth in two months (its future value), or what the $330 is worth today (its present value).

Assume that Lee takes the approach of calculating what the $300 offer will be worth two months from now. How much the $300 will generate will depend on what investment opportunities are available to Lee. For example, suppose that the best Lee can do is invest the money at 10% annual interest. The $300 could earn $5 in two months ($300 × 10% × 2/12). Lee would, therefore, have $305 at the end of two months. This is clearly less than the $330 that Darcy is offering, which makes Darcy's offer more attractive. But, Lee might also want to consider the riskiness of the investment compared to the risk that Darcy won't pay. For example, if Lee invests in wildcat oil wells (a risky investment) and no oil is found, the $300 investment may be lost. In this case, it may be more risky to invest than to accept the risk that Darcy won't pay.

The advantage of Darcy's offer is clearly that it is for more money. Compared with the next best investment Lee can make (invest at 10%), it is clearly superior (assuming that accepting Darcy's offer and investing have similar risks). To make the offers equivalent on a dollar-for-dollar basis, Lee would have to be able to earn a 60% return on the $300 investment ($300 × 60% × 2/12 = $30).

A corporation faces many decisions similar to this example in which cash flows occur at different periods of time with various alternatives and risks. The only way to compare the dollar amounts properly is to use time value of money concepts and computations. One standard approach is to calculate the present value of all alternatives and then compare them. All other things being equal, the corporation would choose the option that produced the highest present value. Unfortunately, all other things are not usually equal. As our example points out, there may be differences in the risk associated with the alternatives. It may also be that the corporation has objectives other than maximizing the present value; that is, it may need to spend its money in other ways to survive, just as Lee may need to get the cash immediately in order to survive. A corporation, for example, may have a loan coming due and so may need cash immediately. It cannot wait to receive cash in the future.

Decisions comparing the present value of alternatives are not the subject of this book. The accountant generally is faced with recording the results of the decisions already made by management, or providing data for management to make those decisions. Time value of money considerations enter into the accountant's work when a present-value method is used to record the results of a particular transaction. There are at least two situations in which present-value methods are used under GAAP. The first situation is in the accounting for liabilities. Most liabilities are carried on the corporation's books at their net present value under GAAP. Interest on these liabilities is then recorded over time based on time value of money calculations. The second situation in which present values are used is in the accounting for long-term receivables. These receivables, on the books of a lender, are the mirror image of the long-term liabilities that appear on the books of a borrower.

FUTURE VALUE

In the example of Lee and the CD player, the future value of an amount was calculated by using the present value, an assumed interest rate, and the time period between the present and future dates. There are many contexts in which a corporation or an individual must make a future-value calculation of this type. For example, if you are saving money for a future purchase, such as a car or a house, you would like to know how long it will take to accumulate the appropriate amount (the future value) based on the amount deposited in a savings account and the rate of interest offered. In a corporate context, a corporation might like to know whether it will have sufficient funds available from its investments to pay a liability that comes due at some future date.

To illustrate the calculation of a future value, consider a simple example. Suppose that $100 is invested in a bank savings account that pays interest at a 10%

annual rate. (Interest rates are always stated as an annual rate unless otherwise indicated.) How much will be in the savings accounts at the end of the year? The answer is $110. The calculation of the interest is as follows:

$$\text{Interest} = \text{Principal} \times \text{Interest Rate} \times \text{Time} = P \times I \times T$$
$$= \$100 \times 10\%/\text{year} \times 1 \text{ year} = \$10$$

In addition to calculating the interest, we could also represent the ending balance in the account with an equation. The amount at the end of the period could be calculated using the following formula:

$$\text{Ending Balance} = \text{Beginning Balance} + \text{Interest}$$
$$= \text{Beginning Balance} + (\text{Principal} \times \text{Interest Rate} \times \text{Time})$$
$$= \$100 + (\$100 \times .10/\text{year} \times 1 \text{ year}) = \$110$$

Another way to express the relationship is to use the terminology of the time value of money. The **principal** is the **present value**, and the **interest rate** is sometimes referred to as the **discount rate**. The **beginning balance** is the same as the **present value**, and the **ending balance** is the **future value**. The formula to calculate the ending balance (future value) is:

Calculation of Ending Balance — First Year:
$$\text{Ending Balance} = \text{Beginning Balance} + (\text{Principal} \times \text{Interest Rate} \times \text{Time})$$
If we let:
$$PV = \text{Present Value}$$
$$FV = \text{Future Value}$$
$$r = \text{Discount rate per period}$$
then:
$$FV = PV + (PV \times r \times 1)$$
Simplifying this yields:
$$FV = PV \times (1 + r)$$
$$= \$100 \times (1 + .1) = \$110$$

How much will be in the account at the end of the second year? The answer depends on whether the interest that was earned in the first year is left in the account or withdrawn, and whether the bank then pays interest on the interest that is left in the account. If the bank does not add the interest to the principal before it calculates the interest in the following period, then the interest calculation is said to be one of **simple interest**. In the case of simple interest, the interest earned in the second period will be the same as the first period as long as the principal is not changed. In most situations involving more than one year, simple interest is not used. Most banks would calculate **compound interest**, which means that the interest earned in one period is added to the principal and then this amount earns interest in the next period. The standard assumptions used in the discussion that follows are that interest is not withdrawn at the end of the period, and that it is compounded. In our example, this means that the $110 that existed at the end of the first year then earns interest in the second year, producing $11 in interest ($110 × 10%) for an ending balance of $121. The formulation for the situation in the second year would be (the time variable is dropped at this point and is assumed to be one year):

Calculation of Ending Balance — Second Year:

Ending Balance = Beginning Balance + (Principal × Interest Rate)

If we let:

PV = Present Value

FV_i = Future Value

where i represents the year

r = Discount rate per year

then:

$$FV_2 = FV_1 \times (1 + r)$$

where FV_1 is the value at the end of the year 1. Substituting for FV_1 from the equation shown earlier, we get:

$$FV_2 = [PV \times (1 + r)] \times (1 + r)$$
$$= PV \times (1 + r)^2$$
$$= \$100 \times (1 + .1)^2 = \$121$$

This result can be generalized to N years into the future so that the relationship between present and future values is as follows:

Future-Value Formula:

$$FV_N = PV \times (1 + r)^N$$

This formula applies to what is known as **lump sum amounts**, that is, single cash flows (or single payments). The future value of a single amount, at the present value (PV), N years into the future, at an interest rate of r per year, can then be calculated by applying this formula.

Note that, in the future-value formula, the last term on the right is a function only of r and N. This last term is called a **future-value factor** and can be summarized in a two-way table with values of r on one dimension and values of N on the other. These factors, which are sometimes called **future value of $1 factors**, are provided in Table 1 at the end of the appendix. The term $FVF_{r,N}$ will be used to represent future value of $1 factors. The formula can then be expressed in terms of the factors as:

Future-Value Formula:

$$FV_N = PV \times FVF_{r,N}$$

Suppose that $1,000 is deposited in a savings account today at 12%. What amount will be available in the account by the end of five years, assuming interest is compounded at the end of each year? Using the preceding formula, the factor from the table for N = 5 and r = 12% is used and plugged into the formula:

Future-Value Formula:
$$FV_5 = \$1,000 \times FVF_{12\%,5}$$
$$= \$1,000 \times 1.76234 = \$1,762.34$$

◖◗ COMPOUNDING PERIODS

In the previous examples, an annual period for compounding interest was used in the computations. Interest can be compounded more often than annually; in fact, most banks compound interest more often than once a year. Some compound it quarterly, some monthly, some daily, and some even compound it on what is known as a continuous basis. How does changing the compound period affect the calculation?

To incorporate a different compounding period into the future-value formulas (and the present-value formulas discussed later), the number of periods N and the interest rate per period r are adjusted to reflect the appropriate compounding period. For example, in the example of the future-value calculation in which $1,000 was deposited at 12%, compounded annually for five years, suppose that the problem is changed so that interest is compounded semi-annually (twice a year). There would now be two compounding periods per year and, therefore, a total of 10 periods (of six months each) over the five years. The interest rate per period would then be adjusted to 6% per period (12%/2 periods per year). The calculation would then be:

Future-Value Formula:
$$FV_{10} = \$1,000 \times FVF_{6\%,10}$$
$$= \$1,000 \times 1.79085 = \$1,790.85$$

Note that the future value is larger when interest is compounded more often (it was $1,762.34, compounded annually). This makes sense because the interest has a greater chance to earn interest itself.

To provide a comparison of the effects of different compounding periods, consider the data in Exhibit A-1, which show the effects of changing the compounding period on a $1 investment for one year.

You can see from Exhibit A-1 that the future value increases as the compounding period increases in frequency. The continuous compounding formula will not be discussed because it is not used often for accounting purposes. It provides the maximum improvement in return that can be obtained based on changes in the compounding period. On a yearly basis, it is clear that the compounding period affects the return on the investment: yearly compounding yields a 12% return, and monthly compounding yields a 12.683% return. Both investments are based on a 12% interest rate, but different compounding periods. The 12% is generally referred to as the **nominal interest rate,** and the 12.683% as the **effective interest rate**. Because of differences in the compounding periods, banks in Canada are required to disclose effective interest rates (known as the annual percentage rate or APR) as well as nominal interest rates on the products they offer.

EXHIBIT A-1

Effects of Compounding Periods

Assumptions:

Investment (PV) = $1
Yearly interest rate = 12%
Investment period = 1 year

Compounding Period	r(%)	N	Factor	Future Value
Yearly	12	1	1.12000	$1.12
Semi-annually	6	2	1.12360	$1.1236
Quarterly	3	4	1.12551	$1.12551
Monthly	1	12	1.12683	$1.12683
Continuously	a	a	1.12750	$1.12750

[a] The continuous method calculates the ending value of e^r, where e is the base of the natural logarithms.

PRESENT VALUE

The calculation of a present value from a future value is simple once the future-value formula is known. Simply rearrange the future-value formula so that the present value appears on one side and the rest of the formula appears on the other. The present-value formula would then be:

Present-value formula:

$$PV = FV_N \times \frac{1}{(1 + r)^N}$$

Note again that the second term on the right side of the equation depends only on r and N. Table 2 at the end of the appendix provides a listing of these present value of $1 factors. The term $PVF_{r,N}$ is used to represent present value of $1 factors. The formula can then be written as:

Present-value formula:

$$PV = FV_N \times PVF_{r,N}$$

This formula can be used in situations in which the future value is known and the present-value information is needed. For example, if $1,000 is needed five years from now and you want to know how much should be deposited in the bank today at 8%, compounded annually, to have the $1,000 by then, the calculation would be:

Present-value formula:

$$PV = \$1,000 \times PVF_{8\%,5}$$
$$= \$1,000 \times 0.68058 = \$680.58$$

Note that the present-value factors are simply the reciprocals of the future-value factors. Two tables of these factors are not really needed as one can be easily derived from the other by taking the reciprocal.

MULTIPLE CASH FLOWS

The foregoing discussion dealt only with single present values and single future values. In many contexts, however, more than one cash amount is involved. For example, if the accountant needs to record the present value of a loan that is to be repaid with monthly payments over five years, there will be a total of 60 payments. Multiple cash flows can be handled using the formulas that have been derived here. In a present-value problem, the present-value formula derived could simply be applied to each of the cash flows separately, and then added together to get the total present value. Future values could be handled in a similar fashion.

ANNUITIES

A special and simplifying situation occurs if the multiple cash flows are all equal. This is a fairly common occurrence in business. For example, most loans are structured so that payments are the same. Many lease agreements also call for equal payments over an extended period of time.

A stream of cash flows in which the amounts are the same is called an **annuity**. Annuities are characterized in two ways. The first is by the number of payments required. The second is by the timing of those payments, especially the timing of the first in a series of payments. An annuity in which the first cash flow (payment) comes at the end of the first time period is known as an **ordinary annuity**. It is also sometimes referred to as an **annuity in arrears**. Most equal payment loans are structured as ordinary annuities. The first payment comes a month after the loan is made.

An annuity in which the first payment comes at the beginning of the first time period is called an **annuity due**, or sometimes an **annuity in advance**. Most rental agreements and leases are structured as annuities in advance.

Annuities in which the first payment is delayed beyond the end of the first period are referred to as **deferred annuities**. Some annuities are structured so that there is no terminal date; that is, the payments are theoretically paid forever. Such annuities are called **perpetuities**, and they can either be **in advance** or **in arrears**.

Annuities in Arrears (Ordinary Annuities)

The present or the future value of an annuity in arrears can be calculated by applying the formulas developed earlier to each of the payments separately, and then adding them together. A more efficient way is to take into consideration the simplifications that result when the payments are equal.

Consider the situation of an annuity in arrears for N periods. The following time line represents the pattern of payments (referred to as PMT):

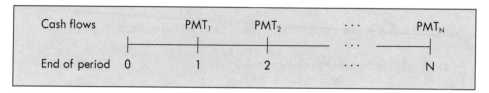

Cash flows		PMT_1	PMT_2	$\cdots$	PMT_N
End of period	0	1	2	$\cdots$	N

To develop an equation to calculate the present value of the annuity, start by creating a formula for the sum of the individual cash payments using the formula developed earlier. The equation would be as follows:

$$\text{Total present value} = PV_1 + PV_2 + \ldots + PV_N$$

where PV_i is the present value of payment i.

Substituting the formula for each PV_i:

$$\text{Total present value} = (PMT_1 \times PVF_{r,1}) + (PMT_2 \times PVF_{r,2}) + \ldots + (PMT_N \times PVF_{r,N})$$

Now, recognize that $PMT_1 = PMT_2 = \ldots = PMT_N = PMT$, and simplify the preceding equation:

$$\text{Total present value} = PMT \times (PVF_{r,1} + PVF_{r,2} + \ldots + PVF_{r,N})$$

Note that the last term (i.e., the sum of the present-value factors) is a function of only the interest rate and the number of periods. It is, therefore, **a present-value factor for an annuity in arrears**. It can be expressed in a simplified formula (which will not be derived) as:

Present value of an annuity in arrears factor:
$$PV_AF_{r,N} = (PVF_{r,1} + PVF_{r,2} + \ldots + PVF_{r,N})$$
$$= \frac{[1 - (1 + r)^{-N}]}{r}$$
where $PV_AF_{r,N}$ is the annuity in arrears factor for N periods at r% interest.

The formula for the present value of an annuity in arrears can then be expressed as:

Present value of an annuity in arrears formula:
$$PV = PMT \times PV_AF_{r,N}$$

The present value of an annuity in arrears factors appear in Table 3 at the end of the appendix. To illustrate the usage of this formula, assume that the payments on a loan are $300 a month for three years at an interest rate of 12%. Calculate the present value of these payments (i.e., the principal of the loan). Note that because the loan requires monthly payments, the compounding period is, implicitly, monthly. To calculate the present value, the following calculation would be made:

Present value of an annuity in arrears formula:
$$PV = \$300 \times PV_AF_{1\%,36}$$
$$= \$300 \times 30.10751 = \$9,032.25$$

The present value of an annuity in arrears formula can also be rearranged to calculate the payments required to pay off a loan, given the principal of the loan, the interest rate, and the number of payment periods. Suppose that you want to borrow $15,000 to buy a car. The bank will lend you money for three years at 12%, with monthly payments. The calculation to determine the monthly payments is:

Annuity in arrears payment formula:
$$PMT = PV/PV_AF_{1\%,36}$$
$$= \$15,000/30.10751 = \$498.21/month$$

The future value of an annuity can also be calculated using the formula derived for the lump sum amounts. Again, because of the unique nature of annuities, a simplified formula exists for calculating the future value of an annuity in arrears. The formula is as follows:

Future value of an annuity in arrears factor:
$$FV_AF_{r,N} = (FVF_{r,1} + FVF_{r,2} + \ldots + FVF_{r,N})$$
$$= \frac{[(1 + r)^{N-1}]}{r}$$

where $FV_AF_{r,N}$ is the future value of an annuity in arrears factor for N periods at r% interest.

The future value of an annuity in arrears formula then becomes:

Future value of an annuity in arrears formula:
$$FV_N = PMT \times FV_AF_{r,N}$$

The future value of an annuity in arrears factors appear in Table 4 at the end of this appendix.

To use this formula, suppose that you were able to save $100 each month out of your pay. You deposit this amount at the end of each month in a savings account that pays interest at 12%, compounded monthly. You want to know how much you will have accumulated in the savings account at the end of two years. This is a future-value question that can be solved as follows:

$$FV_N = PMT \times FV_AF_{r,N}$$
$$FV_{24} = \$100 \times FV_AF_{1\%,24}$$
$$FV_{24} = \$100 \times 26.97346 = \$2,697.35$$

In another situation, you might want to know how much you must save every month to accumulate a certain amount in the future. Suppose that you want to save $10,000 for a down payment on a house. You want to accumulate it over a five-year period, and you can invest your money at 8%, compounded quarterly. How much must you deposit at the end of each quarter to accumulate the $10,000? The solution can be found by rearranging the future value of an annuity in arrears formula to allow you to calculate the payment:

$$PMT = \frac{FV_N}{FV_A F_{r,N}}$$

$$PMT = \frac{FV_{20}}{FV_A F_{2\%,20}}$$

$$= \$10,000/24.29737 = \$411.57 \text{ per quarter}$$

▶◣ Annuities in Advance

An annuity in advance differs from an annuity in arrears only in that the first payment is made at the beginning of the first period rather than at the end. The same total number of payments are made. The following time line shows the pattern of payments for an N-period annuity in advance.

Cash flows	PMT$_1$	PMT$_2$	$\cdots$	PMT$_N$	
			$\cdots$		
End of period	0	1	$\cdots$	N − 1	N

Notice that the first payment comes at the beginning of period 1 and the last payment comes at the beginning of period N.

A present-value factor for an annuity in advance can be derived in the same way as the one developed for the annuity in arrears factor. However, knowledge of the annuity in arrears factors will be used to calculate the present value of the annuity in advance problem.

The trick to using the annuity in arrears factors in an annuity in advance problem is to make the annuity in advance problem look like an annuity in arrears problem. To do this, look at the N−period annuity in advance time line and cover up the first cash flow. This leaves N − 1 remaining cash flows, the first of which comes at the end of the first period. This is an annuity in arrears problem for N − 1 periods. You already know how to find this present value. The present value of the cash flow that was covered up is equal to the payment itself since it comes at time zero. Therefore, if this payment is added to the present value of the annuity in arrears for N − 1 periods, the present value of the annuity in advance is obtained. In a formula, this relationship can be shown as follows:

$$PV \text{ annuity} = PV \text{ of first cash flow} + PV \text{ of remaining } N - 1 \text{ cash flows in advance}$$
$$= PMT + (PMT \times PV_A F_{r,N-1})$$

This can then be simplified as follows:

$$\text{PV annuity in advance} = \text{PMT} \times (\text{PV}_A\text{F}_{r,N-1} + 1)$$

The last term in this expression (in parentheses) is the factor for an annuity in advance problem. Note that you multiply this factor by the payment to get the present value. Therefore, the conversion of present value of annuity in arrears factors to present value of annuity in advance factors is to take the present value of annuity in arrears factor for one less period $(N - 1)$ and add 1. In many annuity in arrears factor tables (including Table 3), this conversion is stated in a footnote to the table.

A similar conversion can be made for the future-value factors. The trick, in this case, for making the problem look like an annuity in arrears problem is to add one cash flow. This extra cash flow appears in the diagram below as PMT*.

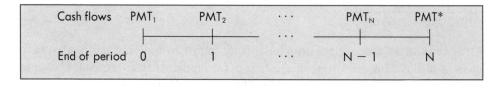

The diagram now shows $N + 1$ payments, which could be viewed as an annuity in arrears if you start at time period -1. You could then use the future value of an annuity in arrears factors to calculate the future value of this annuity at time N. Then, recognizing that the future value of PMT* is equal to PMT, you could subtract PMT from the future value of the annuity, which would leave the future value of the annuity in advance. In a formula, this is expressed as follows:

$$\text{FV annuity} = \text{FV of } N + 1 \text{ cash flows} - \text{FV of cash flow at time N in advance}$$
$$= (\text{PMT} \times \text{FV}_A\text{F}_{r,N+1}) - \text{PMT}$$

This can then be simplified to:

$$\text{FV annuity in advance} = \text{PMT} \times (\text{FV}_A\text{F}_{r,N+1} - 1)$$

The conversion is, therefore, to take the annuity in arrears factor for one more period $(N + 1)$ and subtract 1. Again, this conversion appears in the footnote to Table 4.

Consider a problem in which a company decides to rent a piece of equipment for five years. It will make yearly payments of $1,000 each, in advance. If the corporation can invest its money at 10%, how much would it have to put in the bank today to allow it to make the payments from the bank account? In other words, what is the present value of the payments the corporation has to make? This is an annuity in advance problem. It can be solved as follows:

$$\begin{aligned}
\text{PV annuity in advance} &= \text{PMT} \times (\text{PV}_A\text{F}_{r,N-1} + 1) \\
&= \$1,000 \times (\text{PV}_A\text{F}_{10\%,4} + 1) \\
&= \$1,000 \times (3.16987 + 1) = \$4,169.87
\end{aligned}$$

Perpetuities

A perpetuity is a special form of annuity since it has no ending date (the cash flows continue forever). In this case, the formula for the present value simplifies even more and becomes:

$$\begin{aligned}
\text{PV perpetuity in arrears} &= \text{PMT}/r \\
\text{PV perpetuity in advance} &= \text{PMT} + (\text{PMT}/r) = \text{PMT}(1 + 1/r)
\end{aligned}$$

As an example of the use of a perpetuity calculation, consider the problem of trying to establish the appropriate price to acquire another corporation. While there are several ways analysts may estimate the value of a corporation, one approach is to estimate the cash flows that would occur in the future and discount them using an appropriate discount rate. A rough estimate can be made if the analyst estimates the average amount of cash the corporation generates each year. Using this estimate and assuming that the corporation can continue to generate this level of cash flows forever, the present value can be calculated using the perpetuity formula. For example, if you estimate that the corporation can generate $100,000 a year in cash for the foreseeable future and you estimate that 10% is an appropriate discount rate for the riskiness of the corporation, then the market value of the corporation should be the present value of the perpetuity of cash flows. This would be $1 million ($100,000/10%).

INTERNAL RATES OF RETURN

In the formulas and problems discussed earlier, we were interested in calculating the present value, the future value, or the payments, given information about the number of periods and the interest rate. We treated the interest rate as having been given in these problems. In some situations, the interest rate is not explicitly given but is implicit in the structure of the cash flows. For example, a non-interest-bearing note would state the proceeds from the note (the original principal) and the amount due at maturity. No interest rate would be stated in the contract. The interest, of course, is the difference between the proceeds at issuance and the amount repaid at maturity. To calculate the implicit interest rate, consider the following example.

Suppose that a corporation issues a note (i.e., borrowed money) for $1,000 that requires repayment in two years at $1,210. The $1,000 is the present value of the loan, and the $1,210 is the future value. The interest paid over the life of the note is $210, but no explicit interest rate is stated. The interest rate could be calculated by making some assumptions about how interest is compounded and making use of the formulas derived earlier. Suppose it is assumed that interest is compounded annually. This means that there are two periods between the present value and the future value. The interest rate can then be found using the present-value formula for a lump sum:

Present-value formula:

$$PV = FV_N \times \frac{1}{(1 + r)^N}$$

$$\$1,000 = \$1,210 \times \frac{1}{(1 + r)^2}$$

To solve for r in the preceding equation, two strategies may be employed. The first is to solve the quadratic equation for r. This requires that you know how to solve a quadratic equation. While many readers may know how to solve this equation, imagine the situation where $N = 15$ rather than $N = 2$. The equation then becomes much more difficult. The second approach to solving this equation is to make a guess at the appropriate value for r and then compare the right side of the equation to the left side. If the right side is higher, then you know that the r you picked was too low. You then try a higher value of r and recalculate the right side. You continue to iterate this process until the right side equals the left side. When they are equal, you have found the interest rate that equates the future value with the present value. This rate is known as the internal rate of return.

If you have only the formula or the tables to work with, the calculation of the internal rate of return is probably best done using the iteration procedure. If, on the other hand, you have access to a sophisticated calculator or a computer with a spreadsheet package, the calculation of the internal rate of return is usually a built-in function. You simply have to plug in the cash flows and invoke the built-in function. This is a much more efficient way to solve for the internal rate of return than the iterative procedure.

To illustrate the iterative procedure, Exhibit A-2 presents the calculation of the internal rate of return for the problem just posed. The initial guess is 8%.

EXHIBIT A-2

Iterative Procedure of Calculation of Internal Rate of Return

$$PV = FV_N \times PVF_{r,N}$$
$$\$1,000 = \$1,210 \times PVF_{r,2}$$

Interest Rate, %	Value of Right-Hand Side	Decision
8	$1,210 × 0.85734 = $1,037	Rate too low
12	$1,210 × 0.79718 = $965	Rate too high
10	$1,210 × 0.82645 = $1,000	Correct Rate

SUMMARY PROBLEM

As a final example, consider a situation with multiple sets of cash flows. Suppose that a corporation wants to borrow money from a lender. The corporation wants to borrow the money for seven years. The corporation has determined that it can afford to make periodic payments of $75 at the end of each six months (a small dollar amount is used in the example, but you can add more zeros to make the amounts larger and more realistic). The corporation also agrees to make a large payment (sometimes called a **balloon payment**) of $1,000 (in addition to the last $75 payment) at the end of the seven years.

Under the conditions outlined earlier, what would the lender be willing to lend to the company? The lender would have to determine what the payments would be worth based on an appropriate interest rate. Suppose the lender wants to earn 12%. The lender would present-value the cash flows to be received from the corporation at the 12% discount rate. The present value will then tell the lender what amount can be lent in order to result in a return on the investment of 12%.

The loan is structured such that there are to be 14 payments (7 years × 2 payments per year) of $75 each and a final payment of $1,000 at the end of the 14 six-month periods. This is an annuity in arrears and a lump sum. The interest rate per period is 6%. The present value of the cash flows is calculated as follows:

$$
\begin{aligned}
PV &= PV \text{ (annuity in arrears)} + PV \text{ (lump-sum)} \\
&= PMT \times PV_A F_{r,N} + FV_N \times PVF_{r,N} \\
&= \$75 \times PV_A F_{6\%,14} + \$1,000 \times PVF_{6\%,14} \\
&= \$75 \times 9.29498 + \$1,000 \times 0.44230 \\
&= \$697.12 + 442.30 = \$1,139.42
\end{aligned}
$$

The $1,139.42 is the amount the lender should be willing to lend the corporation. If the lender lends this amount to the corporation and receives the $75 periodic payments and the $1,000 at the end, the lender will have earned 12% (compounded semi-annually).

The preceding calculation is exactly the same as the one used to calculate the price of a bond. Bonds are long-term borrowings of a corporation and are discussed in detail in Chapter 10.

TABLE 1

Future Value of $1

Periods	0.50%	0.75%	1.00%	1.50%	2.00%	3.00%	4.00%	5.00%	6.00%	7.00%	8.00%
1	1.00500	1.00750	1.01000	1.01500	1.02000	1.03000	1.04000	1.05000	1.06000	1.07000	1.08000
2	1.01003	1.01506	1.02010	1.03023	1.04040	1.06090	1.08160	1.10250	1.12360	1.14490	1.16640
3	1.01508	1.02267	1.03030	1.04568	1.06121	1.09273	1.12486	1.15763	1.19102	1.22504	1.25971
4	1.02015	1.03034	1.04060	1.06136	1.08243	1.12551	1.16986	1.21551	1.26248	1.31080	1.36049
5	1.02525	1.03807	1.05101	1.07728	1.10408	1.15927	1.21665	1.27628	1.33823	1.40255	1.46933
6	1.03038	1.04585	1.06152	1.09344	1.12616	1.19405	1.26532	1.34010	1.41852	1.50073	1.58687
7	1.03553	1.05370	1.07214	1.10984	1.14869	1.22987	1.31593	1.40710	1.50363	1.60578	1.71382
8	1.04071	1.06160	1.08286	1.12649	1.17166	1.26677	1.36857	1.47746	1.59385	1.71819	1.85093
9	1.04591	1.06956	1.09369	1.14339	1.19509	1.30477	1.42331	1.55133	1.68948	1.83846	1.99900
10	1.05114	1.07758	1.10462	1.16054	1.21899	1.34392	1.48024	1.62889	1.79085	1.96715	2.15892
11	1.05640	1.08566	1.11567	1.17795	1.24337	1.38423	1.53945	1.71034	1.89830	2.10485	2.33164
12	1.06168	1.09381	1.12683	1.19562	1.26824	1.42576	1.60103	1.79586	2.01220	2.25219	2.51817
13	1.06699	1.10201	1.13809	1.21355	1.29361	1.46853	1.66507	1.88565	2.13293	2.40985	2.71962
14	1.07232	1.11028	1.14947	1.23176	1.31948	1.51259	1.73168	1.97993	2.26090	2.57853	2.93719
15	1.07768	1.11860	1.16097	1.25023	1.34587	1.55797	1.80094	2.07893	2.39656	2.75903	3.17217
16	1.08307	1.12699	1.17258	1.26899	1.37279	1.60471	1.87298	2.18287	2.54035	2.95216	3.42594
17	1.08849	1.13544	1.18430	1.28802	1.40024	1.65285	1.94790	2.29202	2.69277	3.15882	3.70002
18	1.09393	1.14396	1.19615	1.30734	1.42825	1.70243	2.02582	2.40662	2.85434	3.37993	3.99602
19	1.09940	1.15254	1.20811	1.32695	1.45681	1.75351	2.10685	2.52695	3.02560	3.61653	4.31570
20	1.10490	1.16118	1.22019	1.34686	1.48595	1.80611	2.19112	2.65330	3.20714	3.86968	4.66096
24	1.12716	1.19641	1.26973	1.42950	1.60844	2.03279	2.56330	3.22510	4.04893	5.07237	6.34118
36	1.19668	1.30865	1.43077	1.70914	2.03989	2.89828	4.10393	5.79182	8.14725	11.42394	15.96817
48	1.27049	1.43141	1.61223	2.04348	2.58707	4.13225	6.57053	10.40127	16.39387	25.72891	40.21057
60	1.34885	1.56568	1.81670	2.44322	3.28103	5.89160	10.51963	18.67919	32.98769	57.94643	101.2571
120	1.81940	2.45136	3.30039	5.96932	10.76516	34.71099	110.6626	348.9120	1088.188	3357.788	10252.99
240	3.31020	6.00915	10.89255	35.63282	115.8887	1204.853	12246.20	1.22E+05	1.18E+06	1.13E+07	1.05E+08
360	6.02258	14.73058	35.94964	212.7038	1247.561	41821.62	1.36E+06	4.25E+07	1.29E+09	3.79+10	1.08E+12

(continued)

TABLE 1 (continued)

Future Value of $1

Periods	9.00%	10.00%	11.00%	12.00%	13.00%	14.00%	15.00%	16.00%	18.00%	20.00%	25.00%
1	1.09000	1.10000	1.11000	1.12000	1.13000	1.14000	1.15000	1.16000	1.18000	1.20000	1.25000
2	1.18810	1.21000	1.23210	1.25440	1.27690	1.29960	1.32250	1.34560	1.39240	1.44000	1.56250
3	1.29503	1.33100	1.36763	1.40493	1.44290	1.48154	1.52088	1.56090	1.64303	1.72800	1.95313
4	1.41158	1.46410	1.51807	1.57352	1.63047	1.68896	1.74901	1.81064	1.93878	2.07360	2.44141
5	1.53862	1.61051	1.68506	1.76234	1.84244	1.92541	2.01136	2.10034	2.28776	2.48832	3.05176
6	1.67710	1.77156	1.87041	1.97382	2.08195	2.19497	2.31306	2.43640	2.69955	2.98598	3.81470
7	1.82804	1.94872	2.07616	2.21068	2.35261	2.50227	2.66002	2.82622	3.18547	3.58318	4.76837
8	1.99256	2.14359	2.30454	2.47596	2.65844	2.85259	3.05902	3.27841	3.75886	4.29982	5.96046
9	2.17189	2.35795	2.55804	2.77308	3.00404	3.25195	3.51788	3.80296	4.43545	5.15978	7.45058
10	2.36736	2.59374	2.83942	3.10585	3.39457	3.70722	4.04556	4.41144	5.23384	6.19174	9.31323
11	2.58043	2.85312	3.15176	3.47855	3.83586	4.22623	4.65239	5.11726	6.17593	7.43008	11.64153
12	2.81266	3.13843	3.49845	3.89598	4.33452	4.81790	5.35025	5.93603	7.28759	8.91610	14.55192
13	3.06580	3.45227	3.88328	4.36349	4.89801	5.49241	6.15279	6.88579	8.59936	10.69932	18.18989
14	3.34173	3.79750	4.31044	4.88711	5.53475	6.26135	7.07571	7.98752	10.14724	12.83918	22.73737
15	3.64248	4.17725	4.78459	5.47357	6.25427	7.13794	8.13706	9.26552	11.97375	15.40702	28.42171
16	3.97031	4.59497	5.31089	6.13039	7.06733	8.13725	9.35762	10.74800	14.12902	18.48843	35.52714
17	4.32763	5.05447	5.89509	6.86604	7.98608	9.27646	10.76126	12.46768	16.67225	22.18611	44.40892
18	4.71712	5.55992	6.54355	7.68997	9.02427	10.57517	12.37545	14.46251	19.67325	26.62333	55.51115
19	5.14166	6.11591	7.26334	8.61276	10.19742	12.05569	14.23177	16.77652	23.21444	31.94800	69.38894
20	5.60441	6.72750	8.06231	9.64629	11.52309	13.74349	16.36654	19.46076	27.39303	38.33760	86.73617
24	7.91108	9.84973	12.23916	15.17863	18.78809	23.21221	28.62518	35.23642	53.10901	79.49685	211.7582
36	22.25123	30.91268	42.81808	59.13557	81.43741	111.8342	153.1519	209.1643	387.0368	708.8019	3081.488
48	62.58524	97.10723	149.7970	230.3908	352.9923	538.8065	819.4007	1241.605	2820.567	6319.749	44841.55
60	176.0313	304.4816	524.0572	897.5969	1530.053	2595.919	4383.999	7370.201	20555.14	56347.51	652530.4
120	30987.02	92709.07	274636.0	805680.3	2.34E+06	6.74E+06	1.92E+07	5.43+07	4.23E+08	3.18E+09	4.26E+11
240	9.60E+08	8.59E+09	7.54E+10	6.49E+11	5.48E+12	4.54E+13	3.69E+14	2.95E+15	1.79E+17	1.01E+19	1.81E+23
360	2.98E+13	7.97E+14	2.07E+16	5.23E+17	1.28E+19	3.06E+20	7.10E+21	1.60E+23	7.54E+25	3.20E+28	7.72E+34

TABLE 2

Present Value of $1

Periods	0.50%	0.75%	1.00%	1.50%	2.00%	3.00%	4.00%	5.00%	6.00%	7.00%	8.00%
1	0.99502	0.99256	0.99010	0.98522	0.98039	0.97087	0.96154	0.95238	0.94340	0.93458	0.92593
2	0.99007	0.98517	0.98030	0.97066	0.96117	0.94260	0.92456	0.90703	0.89000	0.87344	0.85734
3	0.98515	0.97783	0.97059	0.95632	0.94232	0.91514	0.88900	0.86384	0.83962	0.81630	0.79383
4	0.98025	0.97055	0.96098	0.94218	0.92385	0.88849	0.85480	0.82270	0.79209	0.76290	0.73503
5	0.97537	0.96333	0.95147	0.92826	0.90573	0.86261	0.82193	0.78353	0.74726	0.71299	0.68058
6	0.97052	0.95616	0.94205	0.91454	0.88797	0.83748	0.79031	0.74622	0.70496	0.66634	0.63107
7	0.96569	0.94904	0.93272	0.90103	0.87056	0.81309	0.75992	0.71068	0.66506	0.62275	0.58349
8	0.96089	0.94198	0.92348	0.88771	0.85349	0.78941	0.73069	0.67684	0.62741	0.58201	0.54027
9	0.95610	0.93496	0.91434	0.87459	0.83676	0.76642	0.70259	0.64461	0.59190	0.54393	0.50025
10	0.95135	0.92800	0.90529	0.86167	0.82035	0.74409	0.67556	0.61391	0.55839	0.50835	0.46319
11	0.94661	0.92109	0.89632	0.84893	0.80426	0.72242	0.64958	0.58468	0.52679	0.47509	0.42888
12	0.94191	0.91424	0.88745	0.83639	0.78849	0.70138	0.62460	0.55684	0.49697	0.44401	0.39711
13	0.93722	0.90743	0.87866	0.82403	0.77303	0.68095	0.60057	0.53032	0.46884	0.41496	0.36770
14	0.93256	0.90068	0.86996	0.81185	0.75788	0.66112	0.57748	0.50507	0.44230	0.38782	0.34046
15	0.92792	0.89397	0.86135	0.79985	0.74301	0.64186	0.55526	0.48102	0.41727	0.36245	0.31524
16	0.92330	0.88732	0.85282	0.78803	0.72845	0.62317	0.53391	0.45811	0.39365	0.33873	0.29189
17	0.91871	0.88071	0.84438	0.77639	0.71416	0.60502	0.51337	0.43630	0.37136	0.31657	0.27027
18	0.91414	0.87416	0.83602	0.76491	0.70016	0.58739	0.49363	0.41552	0.35034	0.29586	0.25025
19	0.90959	0.86765	0.82774	0.75361	0.68643	0.57029	0.47464	0.39573	0.33051	0.27651	0.23171
20	0.90506	0.86119	0.81954	0.74247	0.67297	0.55368	0.45639	0.37689	0.31180	0.25842	0.21455
24	0.88719	0.83583	0.78757	0.69954	0.62172	0.49193	0.39012	0.31007	0.24698	0.19715	0.15770
36	0.83564	0.76415	0.69892	0.58509	0.49022	0.34503	0.24367	0.17266	0.12274	0.08754	0.06262
48	0.78710	0.69861	0.62026	0.48936	0.38654	0.24200	0.15219	0.09614	0.06100	0.03887	0.02487
60	0.74137	0.63870	0.55045	0.40930	0.30478	0.16973	0.09506	0.05354	0.03031	0.01726	0.00988
120	0.54963	0.40794	0.30299	0.16752	0.09289	0.02881	0.00904	0.00287	0.00092	0.00030	0.00010
240	0.30210	0.16641	0.09181	0.02806	0.00863	0.00083	0.00008	0.00001	8.4E-07	8.9E-08	9.5E-09
360	0.16604	0.06789	0.02782	0.00470	0.00080	0.00002	7.4E-07	2.4E-08	7.8E-10	2.6E-11	9.3E-13

(continued)

TABLE 2 (continued)

Present Value of $1

Periods	9.00%	10.00%	11.00%	12.00%	13.00%	14.00%	15.00%	16.00%	18.00%	20.00%	25.00%
1	0.91743	0.90909	0.90090	0.89286	0.88496	0.87719	0.86957	0.86207	0.84746	0.83333	0.80000
2	0.84168	0.82645	0.81162	0.79719	0.78315	0.76947	0.75614	0.74316	0.71818	0.69444	0.64000
3	0.77218	0.75131	0.73119	0.71178	0.69305	0.67497	0.65752	0.64066	0.60863	0.57870	0.51200
4	0.70843	0.68301	0.65873	0.63552	0.61332	0.59208	0.57175	0.55229	0.51579	0.48225	0.40960
5	0.64993	0.62092	0.59345	0.56743	0.54276	0.51937	0.49718	0.47611	0.43711	0.40188	0.32768
6	0.59627	0.56447	0.53464	0.50663	0.48032	0.45559	0.43233	0.41044	0.37043	0.33490	0.26214
7	0.54703	0.51316	0.48166	0.45235	0.42506	0.39964	0.37594	0.35383	0.31393	0.27908	0.20972
8	0.50187	0.46651	0.43393	0.40388	0.37616	0.35056	0.32690	0.30503	0.26604	0.23257	0.16777
9	0.46043	0.42410	0.39092	0.36061	0.33288	0.30751	0.28426	0.26295	0.22546	0.19381	0.13422
10	0.42241	0.38554	0.35218	0.32197	0.29459	0.26974	0.24718	0.22668	0.19106	0.16151	0.10737
11	0.38753	0.35049	0.31728	0.28748	0.26070	0.23662	0.21494	0.19542	0.16192	0.13459	0.08590
12	0.35553	0.31863	0.28584	0.25668	0.23071	0.20756	0.18691	0.16846	0.13722	0.11216	0.06872
13	0.32618	0.28966	0.25751	0.22917	0.20416	0.18207	0.16253	0.14523	0.11629	0.09346	0.05498
14	0.29925	0.26333	0.23199	0.20462	0.18068	0.15971	0.14133	0.12520	0.09855	0.07789	0.04398
15	0.27454	0.23939	0.20900	0.18270	0.15989	0.14010	0.12289	0.10793	0.08352	0.06491	0.03518
16	0.25187	0.21763	0.18829	0.16312	0.14150	0.12289	0.10686	0.09304	0.07078	0.05409	0.02815
17	0.23107	0.19784	0.16963	0.14564	0.12522	0.10780	0.09293	0.08021	0.05998	0.04507	0.02252
18	0.21199	0.17986	0.15282	0.13004	0.11081	0.09456	0.08081	0.06914	0.05083	0.03756	0.01801
19	0.19449	0.16351	0.13768	0.11611	0.09806	0.08295	0.07027	0.05961	0.04308	0.03130	0.01441
20	0.17843	0.14864	0.12403	0.10367	0.08678	0.07276	0.06110	0.05139	0.03651	0.02608	0.01153
24	0.12640	0.10153	0.08170	0.06588	0.05323	0.04308	0.03493	0.02838	0.01883	0.01258	0.00472
36	0.04494	0.03235	0.02335	0.01691	0.01228	0.00894	0.00653	0.00478	0.00258	0.00141	0.00032
48	0.01598	0.01031	0.00668	0.00434	0.00283	0.00186	0.00122	0.00081	0.00035	0.00016	0.00002
60	0.00568	0.00328	0.00191	0.00111	0.00065	0.00039	0.00023	0.00014	0.00005	0.00002	1.5E-06
120	0.00003	0.00001	3.6E-06	1.2E-06	4.3E-07	1.5E-07	5.2E-08	1.8E-08	2.4E-09	3.1E-10	2.3E-12
240	1.0E-09	1.2E-10	1.3E-11	1.5E-12	1.8E-13	2.2E-14	2.7E-15	3.4E-16	5.6E-18	9.9E-20	5.5E-24
360	3.4E-14	1.3E-15	4.8E-17	1.9E-18	7.8E-13	3.3E-21	1.4E-22	6.2E-24	1.3E-26	3.1E-29	1.3E-35

TABLE 3

Present Value of an Annuity in Arrears

Periods	0.50%	0.75%	1.00%	1.50%	2.00%	3.00%	4.00%	5.00%	6.00%	7.00%	8.00%
1	0.99502	0.99256	0.99010	0.98522	0.98039	0.97087	0.96154	0.95238	0.94340	0.93458	0.92593
2	1.98510	1.97772	1.97040	1.95588	1.94156	1.91347	1.88609	1.85941	1.83339	1.80802	1.78326
3	2.97025	2.95556	2.94099	2.91220	2.88388	2.82861	2.77509	2.72325	2.67301	2.62432	2.57710
4	3.95050	3.92611	3.90197	3.85438	3.80773	3.71710	3.62990	3.54595	3.46511	3.38721	3.31213
5	4.92587	4.88944	4.85343	4.78264	4.71346	4.57971	4.45182	4.32948	4.21236	4.10020	3.99271
6	5.89638	5.84560	5.79548	5.69719	5.60143	5.41719	5.24214	5.07569	4.91732	4.76654	4.62288
7	6.86207	6.79464	6.72819	6.59821	6.47199	6.23028	6.00205	5.78637	5.58238	5.38929	5.20637
8	7.82296	7.73661	7.65168	7.48593	7.32548	7.01969	6.73274	6.46321	6.20979	5.97130	5.74664
9	8.77906	8.67158	8.56602	8.36052	8.16224	7.78611	7.43533	7.10782	6.80169	6.51523	6.24689
10	9.73041	9.59958	9.47130	9.22218	8.98259	8.53020	8.11090	7.72173	7.36009	7.02358	6.71008
11	10.67703	10.52067	10.36763	10.07112	9.78685	9.25262	8.76048	8.30641	7.88687	7.49867	7.13896
12	11.61893	11.43491	11.25508	10.90751	10.57534	9.95400	9.38507	8.86325	8.38384	7.94269	7.53608
13	12.55615	12.34235	12.13374	11.73153	11.34837	10.63496	9.98565	9.39357	8.85268	8.35765	7.90378
14	13.48871	13.24302	13.00370	12.54338	12.10625	11.29607	10.56312	9.89864	9.29498	8.74547	8.24424
15	14.41662	14.13699	13.86505	13.34323	12.84926	11.93794	11.11839	10.37966	9.71225	9.10791	8.55948
16	15.33993	15.02431	14.71787	14.13126	13.57771	12.56110	11.65230	10.83777	10.10590	9.44665	8.85137
17	16.25863	15.90502	15.56225	14.90765	14.29187	13.16612	12.16567	11.27407	10.47726	9.76322	9.12164
18	17.17277	16.77918	16.39827	15.67256	14.99203	13.75351	12.65930	11.68959	10.82760	10.05909	9.37189
19	18.08236	17.64683	17.22601	16.42617	15.67846	14.32380	13.13394	12.08532	11.15812	10.33560	9.60360
20	18.98742	18.50802	18.04555	17.16864	16.35143	14.87747	13.59033	12.46221	11.46992	10.59401	9.81815
24	22.56287	21.88915	21.24339	20.03041	18.91393	16.93554	15.24696	13.79864	12.55036	11.46933	10.52876
36	32.87102	31.44681	30.10751	27.66068	25.48884	21.83225	18.90828	16.54685	14.62099	13.03521	11.71719
48	42.58032	40.18478	37.97396	34.04255	30.67312	25.26671	21.19513	18.07716	15.65003	13.73047	12.18914
60	51.72556	48.17337	44.95504	39.38027	34.76089	27.67556	22.62349	18.92929	16.16143	14.03918	12.37655
120	90.07345	78.94169	69.70052	55.49845	45.35539	32.37302	24.77409	19.94268	16.65135	14.28146	12.49878
240	139.58077	111.14495	90.81942	64.79573	49.56855	33.30567	24.99796	19.99984	16.66665	14.28571	12.50000
360	166.79161	124.28187	97.21833	66.35324	49.95992	33.33254	24.99998	20.00000	16.66667	14.28571	12.50000

(continued)

TABLE 3 (continued)

Present Value of an Annuity in Arrears

Periods	9.00%	10.00%	11.00%	12.00%	13.00%	14.00%	15.00%	16.00%	18.00%	20.00%	25.00%
1	0.91743	0.90909	0.90090	0.89286	0.88496	0.87719	0.86957	0.86207	0.84746	0.83333	0.80000
2	1.75911	1.73554	1.71252	1.69005	1.66810	1.64666	1.62571	1.60523	1.56564	1.52778	1.44000
3	2.53129	2.48685	2.44371	2.40183	2.36115	2.32163	2.28323	2.24589	2.17427	2.10648	1.95200
4	3.23972	3.16987	3.10245	3.03735	2.97447	2.91371	2.85498	2.79818	2.69006	2.58873	2.36160
5	3.88965	3.79079	3.69590	3.60478	3.51723	3.43308	3.35216	3.27429	3.12717	2.99061	2.68928
6	4.48592	4.35526	4.23054	4.11141	3.99755	3.88867	3.78448	3.68474	3.49760	3.32551	2.95142
7	5.03295	4.86842	4.71220	4.56376	4.42261	4.28830	4.16042	4.03857	3.81153	3.60459	3.16114
8	5.53482	5.33493	5.14612	4.96764	4.79877	4.63886	4.48732	4.34359	4.07757	3.83716	3.32891
9	5.99525	5.75902	5.53705	5.32825	5.13166	4.94637	4.77158	4.60654	4.30302	4.03097	3.46313
10	6.41766	6.14457	5.88923	5.65022	5.42624	5.21612	5.01877	4.83323	4.49409	4.19247	3.57050
11	6.80519	6.49506	6.20652	5.93770	5.68694	5.45273	5.23371	5.02864	4.65601	4.32706	3.65640
12	7.16073	6.81369	6.49236	6.19437	5.91765	5.66029	5.42062	5.19711	4.79322	4.43922	3.72512
13	7.48690	7.10336	6.74987	6.42355	6.12181	5.84236	5.58315	5.34233	4.90951	4.53268	3.78010
14	7.78615	7.36669	6.98187	6.62817	6.30249	6.00207	5.72448	5.46753	5.00806	4.61057	3.82408
15	8.06069	7.60608	7.19087	6.81086	6.46238	6.14217	5.84737	5.57546	5.09158	4.67547	3.85926
16	8.31256	7.82371	7.37916	6.97399	6.60388	6.26506	5.95423	5.66850	5.16235	4.72956	3.88741
17	8.54363	8.02155	7.54879	7.11963	6.72909	6.37286	6.04716	5.74870	5.22233	4.77463	3.90993
18	8.75563	8.20141	7.70162	7.24967	6.83991	6.46742	6.12797	5.81785	5.27316	4.81219	3.92794
19	8.95011	8.36492	7.83929	7.36578	6.93797	6.55037	6.19823	5.87746	5.31624	4.84350	3.94235
20	9.12855	8.51356	7.96333	7.46944	7.02475	6.62313	6.25933	5.92884	5.35275	4.86958	3.95388
24	9.70661	8.98474	8.34814	7.78432	7.28288	6.83514	6.43377	6.07263	5.45095	4.93710	3.98111
36	10.61176	9.67651	8.87859	8.19241	7.59785	7.07899	6.62314	6.22012	5.54120	4.99295	3.99870
48	10.93358	9.89693	9.03022	8.29716	7.67052	7.12960	6.65853	6.24497	5.55359	4.99921	3.99991
60	11.04799	9.96716	9.07356	8.32405	7.68728	7.14011	6.66515	6.24915	5.55529	4.99991	3.99999
120	11.11075	9.99989	9.09088	8.33332	7.69230	7.14286	6.66667	6.25000	5.55556	5.00000	4.00000
240	11.11111	10.00000	9.09091	8.33333	7.69231	7.14286	6.66667	6.25000	5.55556	5.00000	4.00000
360	11.11111	10.00000	909091	8.33333	7.69231	7.14286	6.66667	6.25000	5.55556	5.00000	4.00000

*To compute the present value factor for an annuity in advance use the arrears factor for one less period and add 1.

TABLE 4

Future Value of an Annuity in Arrears

Periods	0.50%	0.75%	1.00%	1.50%	2.00%	3.00%	4.00%	5.00%	6.00%	7.00%	8.00%
1	1.00000	1.00000	1.00000	1.00000	1.00000	1.00000	1.00000	1.00000	1.00000	1.00000	1.00000
2	2.00500	2.00750	2.01000	2.01500	2.02000	2.03000	2.04000	2.05000	2.06000	2.07000	2.08000
3	3.01502	3.02256	3.03010	3.04522	3.06040	3.09090	3.12160	3.15250	3.18360	3.21490	3.24640
4	4.03010	4.04523	4.06040	4.09090	4.12161	4.18363	4.24646	4.31013	4.37462	4.43994	4.50611
5	5.05025	5.07556	5.10101	5.15227	5.20404	5.30914	5.41632	5.52563	5.63709	5.75074	5.86660
6	6.07550	6.11363	6.15202	6.22955	6.30812	6.46841	6.63298	6.80191	6.97532	7.15329	7.33593
7	7.10588	7.15948	7.21354	7.32299	7.43428	7.66246	7.89829	8.14201	8.39384	8.65402	8.92280
8	8.14141	8.21318	8.28567	8.43284	8.58297	8.89234	9.21423	9.54911	9.89747	10.25980	10.63663
9	9.18212	9.27478	9.36853	9.55933	9.75463	10.15911	10.58280	11.02656	11.49132	11.97799	12.48756
10	10.22803	10.34434	10.46221	10.70272	10.94972	11.46388	12.00611	12.57789	13.18079	13.81645	14.48656
11	11.27917	11.42192	11.56683	11.86326	12.16872	12.80780	13.48635	14.20679	14.97164	15.78360	16.64549
12	12.33556	12.50759	12.68250	13.04121	13.41209	14.19203	15.02581	15.91713	16.86994	17.88845	18.97713
13	13.39724	13.60139	13.80933	14.23683	14.68033	15.61779	16.62684	17.71298	18.88214	20.14064	21.49530
14	14.46423	14.70340	14.94742	15.45038	15.97394	17.08632	18.29191	19.59863	21.01507	22.55049	24.21492
15	15.53655	15.81368	16.09690	16.68214	17.29342	18.59891	20.02359	21.57856	23.27597	25.12902	27.15211
16	16.61423	16.93228	17.25786	17.93237	18.63929	20.15688	21.82453	23.65749	25.67253	27.88805	30.32428
17	17.69730	18.05927	18.43044	19.20136	20.01207	21.76159	23.69751	25.84037	28.21288	30.84022	33.75023
18	18.78579	19.19472	19.61475	20.48938	21.41231	23.41444	25.64541	28.13238	30.90565	33.99903	37.45024
19	19.87972	20.33868	20.81090	21.79672	22.84056	25.11687	27.67123	30.53900	33.75999	37.37896	41.44626
20	20.97912	21.49122	22.01900	23.12367	24.29737	26.87037	29.77808	33.06595	36.78559	40.99549	45.76196
24	25.43196	26.18847	26.97346	28.63352	30.42186	34.42647	39.08260	44.50200	50.81558	58.17667	66.76476
36	39.33610	41.15272	43.07688	47.27597	51.99437	63.27594	77.59831	95.83632	119.1209	148.9135	187.1021
48	54.09783	57.52071	61.22261	69.56522	79.35352	104.4084	139.2632	188.0254	256.5645	353.2701	490.1322
60	69.77003	75.42414	81.66967	96.21465	114.0515	163.0534	237.9907	353.5837	533.1282	813.5204	1253.213
120	163.8793	193.5143	230.0387	331.2882	488.2582	1123.700	2741.564	6958.240	18119.80	47954.12	128149.9
240	462.0409	667.8869	989.2554	2308.854	5744.437	40128.42	306130.1	2.43E+06	1.97E+07	1.61E+08	1.31E+09
360	1004.515	1830.743	3494.964	14113.59	62328.06	1.39E+06	3.39E+07	8.50E+08	2.15E+10	5.41E+11	1.35E+13

(continued)

TABLE 4 (continued)

Future Value of an Annuity in Arrears

Periods	9.00%	10.00%	11.00%	12.00%	13.00%	14.00%	15.00%	16.00%	18.00%	20.00%	25.00%
1	1.00000	1.00000	1.00000	1.00000	1.00000	1.00000	1.00000	1.00000	1.00000	1.00000	1.00000
2	2.09000	2.10000	2.11000	2.12000	2.13000	2.14000	2.15000	2.16000	2.18000	2.20000	2.25000
3	3.27810	3.31000	3.34210	3.37440	3.40690	3.43960	3.47250	3.50560	3.57240	3.64000	3.81250
4	4.57313	4.64100	4.70973	4.77933	4.84980	4.92114	4.99338	5.06650	5.21543	5.36800	5.76563
5	5.98471	6.10510	6.22780	6.35285	6.48027	6.61010	6.74238	6.87714	7.15421	7.44160	8.20703
6	7.52333	7.71561	7.91286	8.11519	8.32271	8.53552	8.75374	8.97748	9.44197	9.92992	11.25879
7	9.20043	9.48717	9.78327	10.08901	10.40466	10.73049	11.06680	11.41387	12.14152	12.91590	15.07349
8	11.02847	11.43589	11.85943	12.29969	12.75726	13.23276	13.72682	14.24009	15.32700	16.49908	19.84186
9	13.02104	13.57948	14.16397	14.77566	15.41571	16.08535	16.78584	17.51851	19.08585	20.79890	25.80232
10	15.19293	15.93742	16.72201	17.54874	18.41975	19.33730	20.30372	21.32147	23.52131	25.95868	33.25290
11	17.56029	18.53117	19.56143	20.65458	21.81432	23.04452	24.34928	25.73290	28.75514	32.15042	42.56613
12	20.14072	21.38428	22.71319	24.13313	25.65018	27.27075	29.00167	30.85017	34.93107	39.58050	54.20766
13	22.95338	24.52271	26.21164	28.02911	29.98470	32.08865	34.35192	36.78620	42.21866	48.49660	68.75958
14	26.01919	27.97498	30.09492	32.39260	34.88271	37.58107	40.50471	43.67199	50.81802	59.19592	86.94947
15	29.36092	31.77248	34.40536	37.27971	40.41746	43.84241	47.58041	51.65951	60.96527	72.03511	109.6868
16	33.00340	35.94973	39.18995	42.75328	46.67173	50.98035	55.71747	60.92503	72.93901	87.44213	138.1085
17	36.97370	40.54470	44.50084	48.88367	53.73906	59.11760	65.07509	71.67303	87.06804	105.9306	173.6357
18	41.30134	45.59917	50.39594	55.74971	61.72514	68.39407	75.83636	84.14072	103.7403	128.1167	218.0446
19	46.01846	51.15909	56.93949	63.43968	70.74941	78.96923	88.21181	98.60323	123.4135	154.7400	273.5558
20	51.16012	57.27500	64.20283	72.05244	80.94683	91.02493	102.4436	115.3797	146.6280	186.6880	342.9447
24	76.78981	88.49733	102.1742	118.1552	136.8315	158.6586	184.1678	213.9776	289.4945	392.4842	843.0329
36	236.1247	299.1268	380.1644	484.4631	618.7493	791.6729	1014.346	1301.027	2144.649	3539.009	12321.95
48	684.2804	960.1723	1352.700	1911.590	2707.633	3841.475	5456.005	7753.782	15664.26	31593.74	179362.2
60	1944.792	3034.816	4755.066	7471.641	11761.95	18535.13	29219.99	46057.51	114189.7	281732.6	2.61E+06
120	344289.1	927080.7	2.50E+06	6.71E+06	1.80E+07	4.81E+07	1.28E+08	3.39E+08	2.35E+09	1.59E+10	1.70E+12
240	1.07E+10	8.59E+10	6.86E+11	5.41E+12	4.22E+13	3.24E+14	2.46E+15	1.84E+16	9.92E+17	5.04E+19	7.25E+23
360	3.31E+14	7.97E+15	1.88E+17	4.36E+18	9.87E+19	2.19E+21	4.73E+22	1.00E+24	4.19E+26	1.60E+29	3.09E+35

*To compute the annuity in advance factor use the arrears factor for one more period and subtract 1.

ABBREVIATIONS USED

PV	Present value
FV	Future value
PMT	Payment (in an annuity)
r	Interest rate per period (discount rate)
N	Number of periods
$FVF_{r,N}$	Future value of $1 factor
$PVF_{r,N}$	Present value of $1 factor
$PV_AF_{r,N}$	Present value of an annuity in arrears factor
$FV_AF_{r,N}$	Future value of an annuity in arrears factor

SYNONYMS

Annuity in advance/Annuity due
Annuity in arrears/Ordinary annuity
Discount rate/Effective rate/Market rate

GLOSSARY

Annuity in advance A series of equal cash flows in which the amounts are received or paid at the beginning of each period.

Annuity in arrears A series of equal cash flows in which the amounts are received or paid at the end of each period.

Compound interest Interest calculated by multiplying the interest by the principal. Interest earned in one period is added to the principal to calculate the interest in the next period.

Compounding period The shortest period over which interest is earned and added to the balance of the principal.

Deferred annuity An annuity in which the first cash flow is deferred until a subsequent time period.

Discount rate The interest rate per period used to discount or present-value a set of cash flows.

Effective rate The interest rate per period (sometimes annualized) used to discount or present-value a set of cash flows.

Future value The value at some date in the future of a single amount of cash or a series of cash amounts.

Future-value factor A factor used to convert a present-value amount into a future-value amount.

Internal rate of return The interest rate that equates a current outflow of cash with a single future cash flow or a series of cash flows.

Nominal rate The annual interest rate used to present-value a set of cash flows. The nominal rate does not take into consideration the compounding of interest during the year.

Perpetuity An annuity in which there is no maturity date; i.e., the cash flows are assumed to continue forever.

Present value The value today of cash to be received at some date or multiple dates in the future.

Present-value factor A factor used to convert a future-value amount into a present-value amount.

Simple interest Interest calculated by multiplying the interest rate by the principal. Interest earned in one period is not added to the principal to calculate the interest in the next period; i.e., it is not compounded.

ASSIGNMENT MATERIAL

◤◣ Applying Your Knowledge

1. SBEG Inc. has excess cash that it wants to invest for five years. It can either deposit $25,000 in a money market bank account and earn 9%, compounded annually, or deposit at a bank that pays 8%, compounded quarterly. What should it do?

2. Nur and Sarita plan to buy a house in three years. They will need $15,000 for the down payment. How much must they deposit today if they can earn 8% interest, compounded in each of the following ways:
   a. Annually
   b. Semi-annually
   c. Quarterly

3. a. Ann Marie is saving to buy a car. She plans to deposit $50 at the end of each month into an account that pays 6%, compounded monthly. How much will she have for a down payment in two years?
   b. If she uses the amount arrived at in part (a) to put a down payment on a $15,000 car, how much will her monthly payments be? The loan is at 12% for four years, and the payments will come at the end of the month.

4. The law corporation of Chase & Soo is considering the acquisition of computers for its offices. It plans to lease (rent) a system. The lease (rent) payments of $2,000 are due on the first of each month. The corporation has signed an 18-month contract, and the first payment was due upon signing. If the corporation is able to invest at 9% annually, how much does it need today to ensure that the lease payments will be paid?

5. Today is your niece's fourteenth birthday. You anticipate that she will enter university on her eighteenth birthday. She will need $10,000 at the end of each of the four years, once school has begun. You plan to make a deposit one year from today into an account that pays 12% annually, and to make three more identical deposits, one each year until she starts university. To reach your goal, what must the annual deposits be?

6. Dani Inc. has issued bonds that pay $100 at the end of each year indefinitely. If you require a 12% rate of return (i.e., the discount rate is 12%), what is the value of such a bond?

7. Karen is the lucky winner of $1 million in a special lottery. In this lottery, she will receive 20 annual payments of $50,000 each, starting today. She can earn 8% on this money. Are her winnings actually worth $1 million?

8. Mr. Hunter wants to buy a house that costs $180,000. He is evaluating the possibilities of how to pay for the house and has come up with the following alternatives. Calculate the monthly payments that Mr. Hunter will have to make under each alternative.

    a. 20% down, monthly payments, maturity 30 years, rate 12%

    b. 10% down, monthly payments, maturity 20 years, rate 9%

    c. 0% down, monthly payments, maturity 10 years, rate 9%

9. Mr. Green takes out a three-year graduated-payment loan. The monthly payments under this loan are as follows:

Year 1: $100/month
Year 2: $125/month
Year 3: $150/month

If interest rates are currently 12%, how much did Mr. Green borrow, given the payments that are to be made?

10. Ms. Bedard wants to establish a scholarship that will pay out $4,800 a year indefinitely in monthly instalments. The first monthly instalment of the award is to be paid immediately. How much will she have to donate if the university can invest at 9% compounded monthly?

11. How does the answer to Question 10 change if the first monthly instalment is to be paid one month after the initial donation?

12. You want to go through university, for which you will need $9,000 per year for four years, starting next year. Your parents agree to support you in this endeavour and decide to deposit an amount of money today that is sufficient to provide the four payments. They can deposit the amount in an account that pays 8%, compounded annually.

    a. Calculate the amount that your parents should deposit.

    b. Calculate the amount that will be left in the account after the first withdrawal.

13. A finance company advertises that it will pay a lump sum of $8,115 at the end of six years to an investor who deposits $1,000 annually (at the end of the year) for six years. Calculate the interest rate that is implicit in this offer.

14. On your retirement, you deposit $100,000 in a bank that pays 10% annual interest. Calculate how much you will be able to withdraw at the end of each year to deplete the fund in exactly 10 years.

15. Mr. Scott is considering two investment alternatives:

    a. A bond that costs $1,000 today and makes annual interest payments of $75 at the end of each year for the next three years and a final payment of $1,075 at the end of year 4.

    b. A zero coupon bond that costs $735.03 today and pays back $1,000 at the end of year 4.

    Which alternative should Mr. Scott take and why?

16. A manufacturing corporation is considering an option to sell a machine via a lease. The machine cost the manufacturer $100,000. The lease agreement requires lease payments to be made at the beginning of the month for three years, with the title to the machine passing to the buyer at the end of the lease term. If the manufacturer wants to earn a return of 9%, what monthly payments must be set for the lease?

17. SBT Corporation wants to establish a fund that will be used to meet a $900,000 commitment at the end of 10 years. The corporation plans to deposit a fixed amount in the fund each year for 10 years beginning today. The corporation estimates that the assets in the fund will earn a return of 9%. Calculate the annual contribution that SBT should make to the fund.

18. You have just won $1 million in a special lottery. This amount will be paid to you in yearly instalments of $50,000 for 20 years. You are expecting to receive the first cheque today. If you can invest this money at 10%, how much are your winnings worth today?

19. Suppose that an investment corporation offers you a contract that will pay you and your heirs $750 a year for your lifetime and for that of your heirs. If your next best alternative is to invest at 8%, how much should you be willing to invest in this contract?